A Family Restoration Manual for a New Generation

BIRTHING GOD'S MIGHTY WARRIORS

RACHEL SCOTT

Commentary by Christopher Scott

Copyright 2004 Rachel Scott

First Printing 2004 Xulon Press

Second Printing 2024 Rachel Scott

ALL RIGHTS RESERVED. No part of this book or its associated ancillary materials may be reproduced or transmitted in any form or by any means, electronic or mechanical, including photocopying, recording, or any storage information or retrieval system, without permission from the author.

New International Version (NIV) Holy Bible, New International Version®, NIV® Copyright ©1973, 1978, 1984, 2011 by Biblica, Inc.® Used by permission. All rights reserved worldwide.

King James Version (KJV) Public Domain

Sources taken from the internet have been checked and verified, and all links were active and current at the time of printing. However, with the internet being what it is, links might change, or information removed. These changes are beyond the author's control and do not reflect the author's research or intent in giving sources.

~Rachel

CONTENTS

The Vision	1
A Special Thank You	5
Dedication	7
Generations	9
Preface	13
Introduction	17
A Note To Readers	37
A Thought From Rachel	39
CHAPTER 1: Mary, Can I Borrow Your Womb?	43
CHAPTER 2: The Real First Commandment	64
CHAPTER 3: When Did Concieving Children Become Our Choice?	99
CHAPTER 4: What Is Really Going On Here?	186
CHAPTER 5: Who Will You Leave Behind When You Die?	227
CHAPTER 6: The Destiny Of Your Seed	260
CHAPTER 7: A Barren Womb Is Never Satisfied!	285
CHAPTER 8: The Idol's Altar	337
CHAPTER 9: The Devil's Plan	371
CHAPTER 10: Truth Or Consequences	413
CHAPTER 11: Should You Seek A Supernatural Healing Of Your Family Planning Organs?	461
CHAPTER 12: God Is Calling Us, Back To Our Future!	495
APPENDIX: Conversations On Birth Control	501

BIRTHING GOD'S MIGHTY WARRIORS

God's powerful message that has been lost for generations; an ancient pathway to be discovered

THE VISION

I must begin this book by sharing with you a vision the Lord has given me about a special generation who will walk the earth before the Lord returns.

I believe that some of these people may already be here, but many have not even been born yet! *Let this be written for a future generation that a people not yet born may praise the Lord (Psalm 102:18)*. A large group in this generation will be children and young people whom God brings to earth in these final generations, *for such a time as this (Esther 4:14)*. The following is my vision of what this generation will be about.

There is a generation coming who will walk with God as intimately as Enoch walked with Him (Genesis 5:24). They will be so completely in love with the Lord that they will follow Him wherever He leads and will be consumed with His purposes. They will not be afraid to be martyred and will be a living testimony in all the earth. They will not love their lives so much that they shrink back from death (Revelation 12:11).

Their love for the Lord will cause great revivals to sweep the earth, bringing untold millions into the kingdom of God to join the ranks of worshippers awaiting the return of their beloved bridegroom Savior, Jesus Christ. This will be a spiritual generation that will consist of people of all ages, yet within this generation will be children unlike any the world has ever known. It is in the hope of these children that this book has been written. There is an anointed generation of children that must come to the earth to prepare the way for the Lord. *From the lips of children and infants, you have ordained praise because of your enemies to silence the foe and the avenger* (Psalm 8:2). The Bible says:

> *A little child will lead them (Isaiah 11:6).*

Jesus said that we cannot enter the Kingdom of God unless we come as a child (Matthew 18:3) and that the kingdom belongs to the children (Matthew 19:14).

THE VISION

Children play a significant role. They possess a unique innocence and tenderness, which softens human hearts and helps bring people closer to the love of God. This love will create a unified generation of people ready to meet the Lord.

Many of the anticipated children will be the Godly offspring of mothers and fathers who revere the name of Jesus and who also have a strong desire to follow Him. Some will be born to parents who do not know the Lord, yet God's grace will be upon their children. These children will find God and lead their families to Him. The salvation of these children will come as the result of prayers prayed by previous generations of believers, who faithfully prayed for the unbelievers in their country and in foreign lands. At this time in history, God will ripen those prayers and allow these children, destined to know Him, to be born and to come to salvation.

In families where God has been served for multiple generations, specific spiritual gifts will be released upon these children and will continue to be passed down from generation to generation. *His children will be mighty in the land; the generation of the upright will be blessed* (Psalm 112:2). These Godly parents will nurture, raise, and train up these children. *Fathers will tell their children about your faithfulness* (Isaiah 38:19). These young children will be like *arrows in the hand of a mighty warrior* (Psalm 127:4).

Parents today who walk with God, already see that their children have spiritual awareness and gifts that resemble those of adults. The Body of Christ as a group is seeing an increase of this blessing every day, and it will continue to increase to prepare for the seasons to come (Haggai 2:9).

As these *special warriors* are being created in God's secret place (the womb) they will be with God and will be ready to serve Him from birth (Luke 1:15). Like John the Baptist, they will be born *knowing* their destiny before them.

> *From birth I have relied on you, you brought me forth from my mother's womb. I will ever praise you* (Psalm 71:6).

Many of these children will possess characteristics that will remind us of the righteous people of old. As the generational bloodlines of history come to completion, these children will follow in the way of their ancestors. They will walk in the *faith* of Abraham and possess the *humility* of Moses, they will have Joshua's *conquering spirit*, and the *servant's heart* of Ruth, a *worshiper's heart* like David, and the *prophetic eye* of Jeremiah and Isaiah, they will *dwell in the miraculous* like Elijah and Elisha. They will possess the *boldness* of Paul and have the *knowledge* of Esther, simply knowing that they have come into the kingdom *for such a time as this* (Esther 4:14).

They will be lights in the darkness everywhere they go and will not possess the *fears* of previous generations because they will be firmly rooted and established in the living word of God. This will cause the Lord's hand to be upon them (Luke 1:66) as they march in unison and respond to the voice of the Holy Spirit. Their lives will not be about *themselves* or *fulfilling their own desires* but will instead be consumed with the things of the Lord.

On the other hand, the enemy is preparing his side for battle. Believers do not need to *fear* the other side, but we do need to be aware that they exist. I believe there are children being born right now who already desire to promote the enemy's agenda. Some are chosen in the womb through satanic rituals or other forms of evil. The only hope these children have is to find Christ. But until they do, they will be increasingly susceptible to the deeds and plans of the enemy.

As the world's people sink deeper into the dark deceptions that will eventually lead them to embrace the ways and lifestyles of the Antichrist, both the Lord's army and Satan's forces will continue to prepare. No matter when this time comes in history, the bottom line will be that a generation of people will be alive on earth awaiting their beloved Jesus to come for them. This generation is God's spiritual army, fighting the enemy's lies and being overcomers until that time comes (Revelation 2:7, 11, 17, 26; 3:5, 12, 21).

Biblical scholars believe we are now living in the last few generations before Christ returns. The children that we are birthing right now are the beginnings of this spiritual end-time army of worshippers who will prepare the way of the Lord.

> See I will send my messenger, who will prepare the way before me. Then suddenly the Lord you are seeking will come (Malachi 3:1).

But before any of this can come to pass, these anointed children *must be allowed to be born!* They each need parents who will be open to what

THE VISION

God wants to do and be visionaries of God's great purposes. For these children to be part of God's spiritual end-time army of believers, they must first be *conceived* and then be *allowed* to be born.

This is not to be taken lightly! The enemy has tried hard to limit the conceptions and births of entire generations of children. During these last several generations, he has convinced God's people that children are a *personal choice* and a hardship and has successfully fooled Christians into *greatly limiting their offspring*. The enemy would like to never see these prophesied generations come forth because their purpose is to become participants in God's triumphant climax of history.

Mom and Dad, NOW IS THE TIME to overcome all the lies you've been fed about birthing children and honor the Lord by grasping ahold of the task at hand. As parents, we have been given the privilege that no other generation has ever been given before: To CONCEIVE and BIRTH the END-TIME SPIRITUAL ARMY of the LIVING GOD!

MOM and DAD, it's time to be Birthing
God's Mighty Warriors!

A SPECIAL THANK YOU

I want to thank those who made this book possible. I thank my husband Christopher for obeying what the Lord showed him in his angelic dream, which started this journey. Christopher wanted to thank me for all the hours of writing about the things God showed us. Christopher, always incredible, gave immense wisdom and support to the *Birthing God's Mighty Warrior* Project. I want to thank our computer whiz son Shawn, who rescued me more than once from my computer inadequacies, and Ashley, Heather, and Courtney, who allowed me time on the computer. They also kept house and cared for Judah, Destiny, Haven, and Leviticus, who were all born during this writing process. I want to thank my dear friend SS, who spent hours correcting my manuscript while encouraging, uplifting, and pushing me to *get this book out!* I want to thank my fabulous proofreaders and Debbie for the prayers and all the other friends who read various parts of our manuscript and encouraged me to stay the course. A special thank you to Paula for her encouragement and for wanting to buy ten copies of our first edition, one for a baby who was not yet born!

We want to thank everyone who sent in testimonies; and a special thank you for the many fantastic reviews and support of God's message. To all, we are truly grateful. Thank you! Last but certainly not least, we both want to thank the Lord for showing us His great plan of restoration for the family and allowing us to take part. The Lord has given us the wisdom to understand His message of hope, and we are forever grateful for this privilege.

DEDICATION

This book is dedicated to **a new generation** who desires to discover God's best for their marriage. To those who seek to love the Lord with a love that says, "I am willing to do whatever it takes to follow all Your ways, no matter what it might cost me."

This is for those who realize that what God is doing on earth in this hour is not about themselves, but about the name of the Lord being glorified. These are those who are not afraid to be completely surrendered to follow the Lord wherever He may lead them.

> *A Blessing for the Righteous*
>
> Blessed are all who fear the LORD, who walk in His ways
>
> You will eat the fruit of your labor.
> Blessings and prosperity will be yours.
>
> Your wife will be like a fruitful vine within your house; your children will be olive shoots around your table.
>
> Yes, this will be the blessing for the [people] who fear the LORD.
>
> May the Lord bless you from Zion, all the days of your life.
>
> May you see the prosperity of God's people and may you live to see your grandchildren.
>
> Psalm 128

GENERATIONS THAT DEFINE US

SILENT GENERATIONS (1925-1943) Born and raised during the Great Depression, often into large families. For these families, life was simple, and divorce was rare (1-2%). Love of country and obedience to parents was essential. Silent Generation parents believed *hard work led to success*. This generation fought in World War II, which shaped their worldview. These cherish freedom.

BABY BOOMERS (1944-1961) Primarily raised by the Silent Generations, who after World War II, desired to work hard, get good jobs, and forget about tough times. Silent Generations birthed record numbers of children in one of the largest baby booms in American history. Baby Boomers were the first generation to have a TV. A not so Christian media shaped their worldview. TV brought new ideas from Dr. Spock to the idea that smaller families would bring more happiness, more material wealth and promote better parenting. TV families were often small and materialistically prosperous, which laid a foundation for needing birth control to control family size. As they aged into adulthood, they called themselves the ME Generation.

POST-BIRTH CONTROL PILL GENERATIONS

GENERATION X (1961-1984) Grandparents and parents of this generation did not plan their families, but when it was the Baby Boomer's chance, they rebelled against tradition. The birth control pill became legal in 1960, which popularized the idea that no one should have to birth or raise an *unwanted* child. Abortion became legal in 1973, and parents started killing Gen X babies. Children were X-ed out of homes; aborted and prevented. The pill and easy abortions brought a *sexual revolution* which caused infidelity & divorce. Gen X-first generation to live in blended families. Raised watching TV, while parents worked, secular ideals promoted a life without God. Boomer parents wanted self-fulfillment, the message to their Gen-X children: careers, power, sex, and material wealth are far more important than you are. Parents *worked and forced* children to endure long hours of daycare. The state raised Gen-X giving many a not so happy taste of family. Gen X felt dumped and abandoned, so to get their parent's attention, Gen X had higher rates of teen pregnancies, suicide, sexual abuse, and addictions than previous generations. As adults, Gen-X do not want to be parents; some opt-out of parenthood altogether.

MILLENNIALS (1984-2000) Millennials/Gen Y are children of Baby Boomers and older Gen X. Millennial parents agreed: children must be *wanted* to have value; otherwise, abort them or prevent them. This generation saw very few families with two or more children; a third only for a specific gender. Conceptions were *planned* and *wanted*. Choice, age, and economics caused parents to limit their family size to one or two *wanted* children. This gave highly educated, two-income parents extra money/time to spend on each child. Parents put off childbearing, and infertility rose, but Invitro-fertilization gave them a child. This generation was the first to see a few working parents leave corporate America, for home, but their millennial child became their next project. Parents became highly involved in pressuring children to perform, while hovering over their child's every move. This generation is over-scheduled, overindulged, often spoiled, and rarely told "No!" They have always been catered to and seriously over-parented, yet they are blessed to have been born at this time in history, a season of transitioning technology. This generation is a powerhouse, full of technological planners, community shapers, institution builders, and world leaders.

GENERATION Z (1999-2012) Gen Z literally grew up on the internet and surrounded by electronics even before birth! Gen Z conception and pregnancy was *planned* and *wanted* and maybe *cost thousands* if through Invitro. Gen Z is absorbed into media from birth, often living their life based on social media. They invented *selfies* and love online buy-sell. Gen Z suffers higher rates of sadness, depression, and suicide due to negatives of social media. Gen Z also suffer from higher rates of allergies, obesity, diseases than previous generations due to toxins in the environment/food and radiation exposure. Parents groomed Gen Z for success with nearly everyone thinking about their future job, career, and family. Due to positive media influences, some want at least two children, yet Gen Z's infertility rate is the highest ever. Unless big changes occur, Gen Z might not achieve all the elements of the American Dream.

GENERATION ALPHA (2012-2024) Gen Alpha will be the first generation to grow up completely in the 21st century. From birth they've been surrounded by smart phones, tablets and smart technology and before they enter school, they will interact with Ai, voice assistants and virtual reality. Rapid advances in technology will be part of their daily life. Personalized and interactive learning experiences will be how they learn and live. They will grow up in a world that is more culturally diverse and globally connected than previous generations and their tech savvy Millennial parents will raise them with differing parenting styles. It will be difficult for Gen Alpha to form relationships as most everyone will interact on screens. They face social isolation, cyber bullying and decreased privacy and will live in a world of surveillance. Ai will remove jobs; tech will be worshipped, and Gen Alpha will face instability and loss of interpersonal interactions. Life will move at rapid speed. It will be hard for Gen Alpha to keep up.

PREFACE

I believe the message of this book is like the *voice of one calling in the desert, sounding an alarm to God's people,* calling today's generations back to truth.

God is saying to you:

> ...Prepare the way for the Lord, make straight paths for Him (Mark 1:3).

> See, I will send you the prophet Elijah before the great and terrible day of the Lord comes. He will turn the hearts of the fathers back to the children and the hearts of the children back to their fathers lest I come and smite the land with a curse (Malachi 4:5, 6).

Birthing God's Mighty Warriors will begin a new adventure in God, embracing a lifelong quest to follow the Lord in a new way. As I take the *age-old theme of birthing children* and shed some new light, you will discover an ancient path. I pray your generation will follow this path and restore your family.

> The god of this age, (Satan), has blinded the minds of unbelievers, so that they cannot see the light of the glorious gospel of Christ, who is the image of God (2 Corinthians 4:4).

In *Birthing God's Mighty Warriors*, I will expose an area where recent generations of church going parents were told by their leaders: "The size of your family is up to you, but make sure you are responsible and do not bring more children into the world than you can socially, physically, emotionally and spiritually handle." As a result of doing all kinds of things to their bodies to prevent children, parents destroyed their health. Some got reproductive diseases and cancer. They also brought infertility upon future generations through permanent sterilization and some even sacrificed their children through abortion. All these sorrows are because somebody lied to them about *their choice*.

> *They exchanged the truth of God for a lie and worshipped and served the created things rather than the creator-who is forever praised (Romans 1:25).*

A slow decay since the early 1900s caused the hearts of both the fathers and the mothers to turn against their children and to *despise* their offspring. Because of this great sin, Malachi 4: 5-6 has been fulfilled, causing our lives and land to be *struck with a curse!* God wants to reveal this sin to all denominations of church goers encouraging people to repent. After our repentance, He promises in Malachi 4:5-6, He will remove the curse over our land and restore parent's hearts to their children and children's hearts back to their parents.

The Lord wants to forgive the past generations (2 Chronicles 7:14), prosper the present generations, and give the upcoming generations a future and a hope (Jeremiah 29:11).

The timing of this message is a clear call to wake up!

> *Wake up, O sleeper, rise from the dead, and Christ will shine on you (Ephesians 5:14).*

We are at a pivotal point in history, and we are living in the most significant time ever to be birthing children!

A new generation of couples is standing at a crossroads. Which choice will you make? Will you rediscover God's ancient path (Jeremiah 6:16), find the good way and walk in it, or will you do the same thing your parent's generation did and increase family sadness, separation, fractured health and marital unhappiness?

You may not know that the Lord wants you to consider having children (Genesis 1:28, Psalm 127:3-5). They are God's creation and a reflection of His glory. Even if you have all the children, you think you want, have not decided if you want more, or have not even started your family, the Lord wants to give you a new understanding of what it means to add children to your family. Did you know that creating your family is *an act of worship?*

Children play a vital role in God's plan and in your vision of understanding His desires for your life. **But please hear my heart. Do not let this message become a yoke of bondage!** After you read it, do not feel pressure. Do not feel shame. This would be the enemy. This message is about God's ideal. It is about the greatest treasures He has for your marriage and family. God wants you to hear these truths and think about and talk about what He is saying to you. Pray and ask God how He wants *you to follow and apply these revelations*. There is the potential here to see God restore families in one generation and to carve out a miraculous family plan to bless you now and far into the future.

When the Lord gave me this revelation about the importance of being open to birthing more children, I already was the mother of four children, yet I uncovered something in the Bible that I was not even looking for! The truth about family has always been in God's word, but my husband and I had never heard this before, and we had both been attending church since we were born!

I had read through the entire Bible many times. Additionally, I had read the book of Revelation several times and knew this would be a volatile time on Earth, but I never stopped to think, that I could personally have a part to play in bringing a family member to earth who could be the very people who will participate in the book of Revelation.

I had not grasped that my children, my grandchildren, or my great-grandchildren are now the people God was talking about!

It saddens me that many couples in the older generations missed what God wanted to do through them and now they suffer from the consequences of denying God's plan: their families in upheaval, disconnected, scattered. Some suffer from reproductive cancers, the pangs of divorce, loss of marital intimacy, sadness, sorrow, rejection of their role, loss of respect from their children and even committing death to their own flesh and blood through abortions.

They were not warned when they adopted the ways of a godless culture. When their clergy never discussed the subject and the parents never heard what was in God's word, how could anyone know there was any other plan? It was easy for the enemy to deceive everyone (John 8:44). It is time to *expose the lies* so the light of the *glorious gospel* can restore families back to God.

PREFACE

Birthing God's Mighty Warriors is a message of hope for all generations to read, think about and absorb. My prayer for those who read this book is that you will allow the Lord to open your heart and mind to discover His plan for your family and experience the wonder of **Birthing God's Mighty Warriors.**

INTRODUCTION

Why do you have all these children?

(Our Story)

"**H**ey lady, why do you have all those children?" If I had a dollar for every time someone said this to me, I would be a richer woman. When we had our large family in the 1990s' and 2000's, seeing a large family out in public had become so rare that seeing us naturally invoked curiosity. People loved asking  all sorts of questions. Fairly often I encountered a husband or a wife confessing to me how much they had wanted *just one more child* from their spouse and seeing our family inspired them! When they shared, they wanted another child, I would always tell them, *"If you feel a tug on your heart, that your family is not complete, please try to have another baby because you will never regret the children you decide to have but you will regret the children you don't have but feel you needed. In your heart, you will always miss those children."*

My husband and I were married in 1980, when the baby boom generation was "X-ing" children out of their lives. Even though we grew up in Bible-believing churches, our ministers did not teach us to love children the way God does. Instead, we were encouraged to limit children and use birth control and sterilization. In most evangelical denominations these are acceptable choices without protest and like *sheep led astray*, our ministers taught us to embrace the ideas of our ungodly culture. We were in spiritual darkness and didn't know the Bible had anything to say about the family except what we were told. As for family size, we were repeatedly told that the size of our family was strictly our choice and had nothing to do with God.

Our entire generation was surrounded by these spiritual lies, and if not for the grace of God, we would have continued to miss the blessings

INTRODUCTION

God wanted to bring us. In His mercy, the Lord reached out of Heaven and freed my husband and me! Now my prayer is that we can help free a new generation. I offer our story as a living testimony of what God can do in regular people's lives, and the reason why I wrote Birthing God's Mighty Warriors.

I have always been the type of person who asked theological questions that no one could answer. This often happened in my Sunday School classes and during the six years I attended Christian school. I would raise my hand and ask a valid and thoughtful question, but the teacher either could not answer my question, or, sometimes, did not want to answer it. Teachers often challenged me to find the answer myself and report back. This usually sent me on a journey to find the answers in scripture.

In 1995 I found myself asking questions for which no one seemed to have an answer. This time the subject was *family planning* and whether believers should consider sterilization.

But our wonderful story began in the late 1970s when my husband and I meet at our church youth group. We fell in love instantly as high school sweethearts. He always said *it was love at first sight*, and I agree. We were married almost 43 years. We had a wonderful marriage based on our love for Jesus, and a mutual trust in each other. We both accepted Jesus as our Savior when we were very young and we both grew up loving the Lord. It was only by His grace that we lived our lives faithfully serving Him.

When we married in 1980, it was at the height of the second wave of the feminist movement. We both agreed, "We *did not want a large family,*" in fact, we were positive we didn't want any children. I would tell people, *"I don't want anyone calling me mommy."* (Thankfully God overlooked those words!). Yet, periodically, we would discuss the *possibility* of children and then we would go back to pouring into our education and careers. We were sure that since I was from a family with three children and Christopher was from a family with five children, that if we did decide to have any children, one child and maybe a second would be more than sufficient for us. We both agreed that any more children would be expensive and too much work. We wanted the freedom to do other things with our lives instead of being burdened with the raising of children. Our attitudes were *in complete agreement* with everything we were being told in the media, in our culture, and at our church.

We saw no purpose in having a large family. Even though we were raised in Bible-believing homes and churches, we had never heard a sermon on family planning and were ignorant about what the Bible says. The only reference to the verse *"be fruitful and multiply"* was when it was applied to having a fruitful life. It was never used, not in a single sermon, to challenge us to have children. We formed our beliefs and attitudes from movies, from TV, from society, from Sunday school class comments, and from the other couples we met through our workplace, church or neighborhood.

At churches we attended; we knew multiple couples who had two children and then got sterilized. Most were older than us, but they often shared their stories. After we turned thirty-five, we noticed increasing numbers of couples in our age group sharing the joys of sterilization with us. Usually, the wife would comment on how the husband was not feeling well because he had just been *sterilized*. They would joke about him being home sitting on an ice pack and not feeling *quite up to snuff*, or the man would share how his wife had just had her tubes tied, after the delivery of their last baby, and how happy he was that he would never have to *worry* again about any more pregnancies.

Whenever I heard one of these couples make a comment, I asked Christopher if their choice bothered him. He would tell me, *"They have a right to do what they want, and besides, children cost money, and they don't want that burden."* I understood what Christopher told me, but whenever I heard a sterilization story, something inside me would *cringe* a little. In my spirit, I would let out a heartfelt cry. Yet I always dismissed it. I knew these people loved the Lord, and did what was right for them, but something *seemed uneasy inside my heart* about the idea of permanent infertility. My heart was aching for them, and I was mourning a loss, but I did not know why, nor could I understand why I cared. After all, it was not my business. This nagging feeling always occurred whenever the subject was discussed. I just knew something was not quite right, and that the spirit of God was trying to communicate something to me, but I had no idea what it was.

When I was growing up in the 1960s and 1970s, it was becoming increasingly popular for women to be on *the pill* and to have their tubes tied. I remember my mother was against both *the pill* and *against tubal ligation sterilization*. Not that my mother spent very much time discussing it with me, but she was a preacher's daughter, and I don't think her parents used birth control and even though my mother used birth control herself, she thought *the pill* was evil. I often heard her talking with her girlfriends. She believed the ease of the pill made the idea of having an affair look desirable. My mother had also become a health and vitamin advocate, and I might add, in the late 1960s-1970s *no one believed* in health or vitamins, so my mother was a health pioneer, and her beliefs were *way ahead of her time!*

My mother started to understand the concept of taking personal responsibility for our health and she felt it was terrible for a woman to alter her fertility with any operation that could affect her future long-term health. Many of her friends suffered complications after being on *the pill*, and my mom cautioned them and then cautioned me when I was getting married that using anything unnatural or with artificial hormones would definitely affect my health. She persuaded me to *not take the pill* when I was getting married, but my gynecologist prescribed it anyway. Being eighteen and in college, I did not want to get pregnant. So, I reluctantly went on it at the very beginning of our marriage. Thankfully it made me ill, and instead of adjusting the hormone levels, I stopped taking it three months later. *(Possibly my mother's wisdom was echoing in my ear)*. I also remember how my mother also opposed a woman getting her tubes tied. She thought this was also wrong because, *"You never know if you might want to have more children someday."* My mother often tried to talk her friends and relatives out of their decision to have their tubes tied, but most often, their mind was already made up, and her suggestion fell on deaf ears. Later, every woman admitted to her at some point, that they regretted their decisions and were struggling emotionally or physically to live with the consequences of their choices. My mother would share their stories with me and seeing these older women suffer caused me to develop my own opinion on this subject. Even though I never thought it out, my opinion was not a scriptural one, but a rational idea based on my mother's wisdom and on seeing these other women suffer. I knew I would never want my tubes tied, but Christopher felt differently about male sterilization.

Christopher says, *"I was raised in a churchgoing family with five children, and we did not have the luxuries many families enjoy today. Once we began to have our children, the financial lack that I had grown up with caused me to want a small family so that I could give my children the things I had never enjoyed. In 1983, after we had our first son,* **Shawn** *(when Rachel was only 21 years old and I was 24), I was content to never have any more children. Yet after a few years, our son kept asking for a sibling, and I think it wore Rachel down. She started yearning for a daughter to make our family complete. We did occasionally have discussions about having another child but then we changed the subject. After our son's fourth birthday, Rachel finally convinced me that she would be unfulfilled if we did not at least try to have a little girl. I finally agreed, but the cost of another child weighed heavily on my mind. I didn't want the burden of more children and to me, a family of two children was enough!"*

In 1988, when our son was five, God blessed us with a beautiful daughter, **Ashley**. We both felt our family was now complete. We were both under thirty years old, and neither of us wanted sterilization yet, but in our minds, we were finished having children. We would tell people, *"We're done!"*

Christopher and I always feared pregnancy, so we were extremely careful to use contraceptives every time we made love. We were never careless and were confident that we were in control of our situation.

INTRODUCTION

Two and half years after our daughter's birth, I got very sick with the flu, then Christopher got sick and as soon as he recovered, I got the flu again. At the doctor's office it turned out that I did not have the flu, *I was pregnant!* We were both in shock! We had both been so sick, neither one of us remembered being together. It was a *mystery*, and both of us were very upset, particularly Christopher. He kept saying, *"How did this happen? How did this happen?"* Neither of us wanted more children, and we felt God had let us down. As the pregnancy progressed, we began to accept the idea of having another child. I still didn't understand what God was doing or why. We were so entrapped with the mindset that children were to be *our choice* and *not God's* that we were blinded to the blessing of this third child. I finally concluded that God must know a perfect reason why we needed another child because I couldn't figure out why. Christopher could not figure it out either. Yet from the moment of her birth **Heather** was perfect. I realized how much in my heart I really wanted another baby. When I saw her, I repented for thinking, *"I knew what was best for my life."* Instantly, the shackles came off my eyes and I realized, *"I love her, I really love this child!"* Then I realized she is a miracle, a perfect little miracle!

God always knows what our heart needs far more than we do. Christopher was amazed at her birth; she was so small and beautiful. When he held her for the first time, I joked, *"You're sure that you don't want to send her back?"* and Christopher said, *"She's a keeper!"* At that moment, we both felt something was going on because God had given us a child we had not anticipated.

Christopher loved our new daughter the moment he first saw her, but he continued to be upset about the growing cost of our children's future needs. Christopher's feelings were mixed. He said, *"I was a builder and running my own business, the nature of which made our finances unpredictable. When we were experiencing our leaner months, I was afraid I would be raising children I could not afford. I did not want my children to miss the same things I had missed. The reality that this could happen to them upset me greatly. God was watching over us faithfully, but it was not easy. Looking back, we managed somehow, but Rachel and I both had to work, and occasionally it was tough making ends meet. There was a great fear that even though Rachel always had a part-time job, our finances would sink if something ever happened to me."*

Yet we began to enjoy parenting more than we thought possible. Our little family was so sweet, and our children were very loving. Yet Christopher continued to place financial pressures on himself, even though we paid all our bills on time. Christopher continued to worry. Three years later, we experienced a birth control failure, and I became pregnant again! We were both shocked and upset. Again, we were not thinking of the great joy another child would bring us. Instead, this time Christopher was quite distressed.  *"I could not understand why God was bringing added responsibility to me. I wanted my children to have so many things like private school, be able to join sports teams, take after-school lessons, and have opportunities to travel. With another child now on the way, I saw myself slipping deeper and deeper into a hole I thought I would never come out of."*

 During this pregnancy, we were attending a church with a dynamic young pastor, but this pastor thought every man should get a vasectomy when his family was complete. The couples in our church group all got theirs and since we were one of the younger couples the men started putting pressure on Christopher. They knew how concerned he was about finances, so they started asking when he was getting his vasectomy. Christopher would tell me, *"Rachel, four children is a huge family. I want an end to the possibility of any more children!"* It was not that Christopher did not love our children. He was a very caring and loving father. The

INTRODUCTION

pains from his upbringing *echoed in his ear* and his financial responsibilities had him trapped.

The more he talked about getting a vasectomy, during my pregnancy with my fourth child, the more upset I became. I did not believe in sterilization because of how I always felt when other people talked about it. I knew it was not the right thing to do. Yet Christopher wanted a vasectomy and pressured me, but I could not agree. I was pregnant, emotional, and unsure about everything. Every time we talked about it, if I said it was unhealthy, he would say he didn't care. If I said what if something happened to one of our children, he would say don't walk in fear. No matter what I said, eventually he would explode! We would have a huge fight. But deep down, I couldn't let go of my feelings against permanently doing something unhealthy. I didn't even understand my feelings, I simply knew they were there. Christopher worked harder than ever. Christopher recalls, *"As I felt the unbearable financial pressures closing in on me, it seemed like Rachel didn't care. I had to do something and take charge of our situation before it was too late. At the time, we lived in a huge southern city saturated with billboards advertising a 'no-scalpel vasectomy with quick results.' I called the clinic to price the surgery."*

At the birth of Courtney, our fourth child, Christopher was again delighted, but he was also anxiously waiting for my agreement to get his vasectomy. I was struggling with this decision; I could not find peace. Since we could not agree and had no scripture to guide us, Christopher sought counsel from our pastor.

Our pastor is a wonderful man but agrees with men having vasectomies. He often spoke of his plans to get one for his 40th birthday. Even though he did not see anything wrong with getting a vasectomy and felt it would end Christopher's financial concerns, he gave excellent counsel and told him that this kind of decision must be made from a point of marital agreement. He advised Christopher not to get a vasectomy until I agreed. After Christopher saw our pastor, he came home and told me what he said. Again, I had an infant and was emotional and had three little ones and was breastfeeding and lacking sleep, so *not the best timing* for a life-changing discussion. I still could not agree, so we had another big fight about it. I couldn't let go of something in my heart, and I did not like the idea of surgery to break something in the body that was working perfectly. Maybe it was because of all my mom had taught me about health and how the body works, and this part bothered me greatly. Even when vasectomies were advertised as completely safe and healthy, I wasn't convinced they were. Our disagreement left us at a serious stalemate, waiting for one of us to change our minds, and this was when God supernaturally stepped in.

(If you are from a mindset that does not believe that God can talk to people in dreams, I am sorry you feel that way. But this dream was of monumental importance, and it is real. It really did happen. I hope you can leave your theology at the door long enough to appreciate this testimony).

Unbeknownst to me, my husband decided to take matters into his own hands and *behind my back* he made an appointment for a consultation at a vasectomy clinic. The night before his appointment, this is what happened. He had a dream.

Christopher later told me, "In this dream, I saw a huge warrior angel. It was as big as the sky, and I was in both fear and awe of this enormous angel. But as I was observing this glorious angel, I noticed the angel held something in his hand. It looked like a huge sword! Suddenly... the angel raised this tremendous sword up to the sky and it was completely on fire; it was a flaming sword! Just like out of the Bible! He thrust the sword downward until its flaming tip pointed directly at my penis. The angel shouted, "Do NOT abort the plan of the Lord!" then I woke up!"

When Christopher awoke, he was hyperventilating. Hearing him gasping for breath, I woke up and turned on the light and looked at him. He looked horrible! His face had lost all its color, sort of how one looks if someone was strangled. I thought he was having a heart attack and started to call 911. This was when he grabbed the phone and tried to speak, but he couldn't talk because he was still gasping for breath. After a while, he started breathing better and then he told me his dream.

I was not happy. Instead, I was quite upset! He was going to go *behind my back* to see a vasectomy doctor! We were up the rest of the night, and let's just say, the next day he was a *"no-show"* for his appointment.

But the dream made no sense to either one of us! Why an angel? Why a flaming sword? Abort what plan of the Lord? We sought counsel at our church. We asked pastors, Bible study teachers, friends and relatives. We even tried looking in the Bible but could not find answers. We

INTRODUCTION

asked nearly everyone we knew, about *why* he would have this dream, and nobody, not one person offered us any answers. Some might think this is a no-brainer but seriously no one understood any of what God was communicating to us. Months passed, and about a year into our quandary over the dream, I finally felt a new nudge from the Holy Spirit to look again in the Bible. I had already looked before but did not know what to look up. It's not like the word vasectomy or the phrase "abort the plan of the Lord" is in there, and this was why I had been so perplexed about the meaning of the dream. But this time, by the spirit's leading God started showing me verses I had never seen before, or made a connection about, even though I had studied the scriptures hundreds, if not thousands of times before.

I asked God questions no man could answer, and the Lord graciously led me on a personal journey to search out these miraculous new truths. As I searched God's Word, what I found truly amazed me. I *discovered* God's beautiful plan for marriage and the family; a plan which no one had ever shared with me during the 35+ years I had faithfully attended church. I typed up my findings and handed out booklets to all the couples at my church. Most of the people tossed it aside but several read our story and commented that I should write more, maybe even write a book, to which I chuckled!

After the dream and our newfound information, we did not run out and have another baby. We were not sure about anything. I continued to do Bible research, and we continued using birth control, (condoms). As time passed, God was merciful to us. The Lord was working on Christopher's heart and mine. After that dream, Christopher would say *he would not mind having one more child if we at least had the time and money to raise another.* He became more open to God and believed there might be a plan for our family that we knew little about.

He switched jobs and gained more knowledge in his career field, and the Lord began to bless him. The more open he became to allowing God to show us His plan for our fertility, the more the Lord blessed him. Christopher would come home from work, and I would read Bible verses, I had found that day, but sometimes the word of God freaked Him out. He could not wrap his head around giving God our fertility. He would say, *"If we did that, as fertile as we are, we might have a baby every year!"* But over time, God's word softened our hearts, and God revealed His plan in scripture, and we grew in our faith. It took almost three years after the dream to clearly understand that children were a gift from God and that dream meant we were supposed to have at least one more child. We finally decided to have our 5th child. We went off birth control and I got pregnant immediately. By this time, I was 38 years old.

When I did get pregnant, Christopher was no longer upset at the thought of another child; instead, he was very excited. This was a testimony of how God used His truths and our circumstances to change our hearts. During this pregnancy, Christopher said, *"I liked telling people that my wife was pregnant with our fifth child, I wanted to see their reaction—especially at church, where I had already been persecuted for not getting a vasectomy. It did not bother me when the rudest remarks were made by believers, who always gave me a negative response. I no longer cared as much about what they thought. Somehow Rachel and I both knew that this child would be an extraordinary blessing, and that God had chosen to do something exceptional through us."*

During that pregnancy I came alive again. I realized I had discovered something real. This baby was a child I never thought I would have, and I got *super excited* about what this child's life would mean for our family and for the world. I wanted to shout from the rooftops that we had been lied to about everything!! If not for God's intervention we would never have had this new baby, plus our other four children were also very excited. We could not begin to fathom the love we would experience by adding this 5th child to our family.

My husband was such a jokester, when you look at him- think John Candy. Christopher was always making us laugh. At the birth of our other children, he would always tell me he was naming the child *Finale'* and I would laugh and tell him we cannot name a child *Finale!* On the way to the hospital, I remember, between my hard contractions, we were so excited about having another child. This time we both agreed that if this baby was a boy, his name would be Judah, which means *Praise*. We had become a family that loved to worship together, and we felt adding another worshipper to our little crew would be quite a blessing. Judah came into our life on Mother's Day 1999, of all days! And all the children were close by and several of my special girlfriends.

INTRODUCTION

When I got home from the hospital, I looked up the story of Rachel and Leah in Genesis and was amazed to read the scriptural account of these two women and their competition to bear children for Jacob. When Leah had Judah, she said, *"This time, I will praise the Lord!"* With tears in my eyes, I realized why we had named our baby Judah. *With this fifth child, this time, we praised the Lord*! God had changed both our hearts and our attitudes towards adding children. We began to grow in our faith to trust God more and began to highly value our ability to receive God's gift of life.

After Judah was born, the Lord began convicting our hearts about controlling our *family planning*. The Lord placed a deep desire in us to give Him this area of our lives and a peace that everything would be alright. But even with all the scriptural truths God had already revealed to us, we were both really scared. This was a new reality for us. We had never *trusted the Lord* with our family plan before. We were not sure we could trust the Lord with something as great as the size of our family. Maybe because we never completely figured out how we conceived Heather, our third child. It was always the joke between us: *"We are so fertile that we don't even have to make love to get pregnant. We can get pregnant by osmosis."*

Trusting God in this area of our lives could mean many more children. Yet the more we prayed about it and read the Word, we felt the Lord was trying to persuade us to at least be open to allowing Him to choose the size of our family. This was a massive step of faith because those around us were not following in the same footsteps. We were the only ones in our church group who had not gotten sterilized. Our actions to do the opposite and have more children *stuck out like a sore thumb*. We had to be very brave to trust God to move us forward. We had no one to follow, no book, no manual, no tape series, simply our agreement with God, our faith, the scriptures and the voice of the Holy Spirit. I can't lie, we both thought *we were crazy* and that this was the scariest thing we ever decided to do!

It had been spoken over our family that we would experience a time of significant breakthroughs after our fifth child's birth. A month before Judah was born, Christopher and I saw the beginning of one of God's miracles, this one was financial. He was recruited to a new project. We moved from Atlanta to Orlando, and he received a $25,000 raise! This was the first sign of God's hand miraculously moving upon our finances in several years! I believe it was because God kept us in a *holding pattern* to teach us this new thing. I guess we passed the test. The new salary pushed us over a financial barrier we had never surpassed. We learned the secret to prosperity, and it was being open to children. God never brings the increase until after the child is born. God's Word says, *I was young and now I am old, yet I have never seen the righteous forsaken or their children begging bread (Psalm 37:25)*. He will provide for His children but sometimes it is after our trusting Him to step out in faith. Then the increase comes after the baby is born.

Not long after Judah's birth, we stopped using birth control. We decided that God knew better than we did about what would make us happy. We then conceived our sixth child! We never had children this close together before! If we had tried to control things ourselves, we probably would have waited a little longer, but God knew it was time for these children to be born!

Destiny was born in 2001 and resulted from 100% trusting the Lord with our family planning. With this new daughter, we did not have a name picked out for her until we drove out of the hospital parking lot when the name Destiny came to me. I knew the Lord was giving me this name. We had received a valuable treasure in learning to trust God in this area. This trust has placed our *family's destiny* in the Lord's hands instead of our own. Shortly after her birth, Christopher finished his project and was assigned a new one, and his salary increased again! His salary was now double what his salary was when we started on this journey so many years ago. God was doing another financial miracle because Christopher's fears had been money-related, and God was putting the money where we could see it. In 2002, we were surprised again with another daughter we named Haven. Our home and family have become our haven of rest, happiness, laughter, and joy. In 2004 we were blessed again with our 8th child, Leviticus. We were so excited to have a third boy! Since the birth of Haven and Leviticus, Christopher's salary was triple what it was seven years before when we started on this journey to let God show us His best. Financial miracles continued from this point onward.

INTRODUCTION

We often wonder what we would do if the Lord had not blessed us with these additional children. If it had been left up to us, we would have only had the first two. Then we would probably both be working full-time jobs. Christopher says we might have taken a few more vacations or bought our children more luxuries. Surely there would have been more money to spoil our children with. Yet somehow, we don't seem to miss those things.

But we would have missed the commotion of the younger siblings opening presents on the holidays, the uproar from our entire family cheering for our oldest daughter as she graduated from high school, or the laughter around the dinner table each night. A few more material items would have been *as cheap trinkets compared* to the joy that my older children have received from their younger counterparts. Often their friends told them how blessed they were, even in the chaos of so many people living under one roof. Now that the older ones are grown, have graduated high school and college, and several have gotten married, I often wonder what life might be like had I not had the last four children. Dull! Not nearly as much fun and probably very boring and because I had four additional children, I've met so many more amazing people through the vast networks of new friends who have crossed our paths.

Fast forward twenty years, 2024. When I wrote the above testimony in 2004, I had no idea the road ahead. With complete confidence our decision to have 8 children was and is the greatest thing my husband and I ever did! Our family has met with significant challenges but now as a grandmother the story of our family brings me cause to reflect. I am now the proud grandmother of 14 grandchildren. All my children are now grown. My baby is 20 years old and a junior in college. Four of my children are now married and others are seriously dating. More weddings will be announced in the next few years.

What can I say of the goodness of God? How can I praise Him enough for our family story!

When I was having all these children and nearly 40 years old countless people made comments that I would be mothering children until my sixties, and why would I do that? I could have been an empty nester by 48 yrs. old so what was I thinking? Blah! blah! blah! *Don't listen to other people telling you how to live.* Instead, by having children after 40 years old, I was adding twenty more years to my parenting. But all those people were fools and had no idea what I needed. By starting my family over after a five-year gap between child number four and five, I became alive again. My motherhood was re-birthed. Nearing 40 years old, I saw the world differently and I parented differently. Everything shifted in a miraculous way, and besides, this is MY story, not anyone else's!

When we started to add the last four siblings. I had a 16-year-old son, an 11-year-old daughter, an 8-year-old daughter and a 5-year-old daughter. Over the next five and a half years we added their four siblings.

Our family completely re-birthed. The older children continued their own paths, but they loved their younger siblings! They took them places, played games with them, held them, fed them, helped dress them, and we enjoyed so much laughter as each new little sibling brought so much energy and excitement. My grown children were not seen as the "babysitters" as so many large families make this mistake. They still lived their lives, being involved in music lessons, sports teams, school plays, family boating, cheerleading, competition dance, youth group and other activities.

I loved watching the older children care for our little ones because *they wanted* to be with them. It was beautiful to watch. The older children formed specific bonds with their younger siblings. Some days my heart ached inside thinking the younger children had no idea how much they were missing out on learning how to love a younger sibling. Plus, the younger four *had no idea their siblings were growing up* and would someday leave us and move on and I knew they would miss those close relationships.

As each older child graduated and moved on to college, the family started shrinking and the younger children became more manageable and yes, they missed their siblings. Each time the older ones were home it was a celebration. Years passed and the older siblings got married and started to have their own children. My younger four grew up as well and started to drive and often flock over to their older siblings' homes. They are now forming bonds and relationships with my grandchildren! They take their older sibling's children to all sorts of places; to theme parks and the movies and the beach and they also buy them things, and occasionally babysit when their older siblings go out. Back when I was raising the younger four children, I did not see this blessing coming. I did not see that the love in our family would come full circle! I had no idea this is how God's way works. No one has missed out. Everyone has experienced the joy of children and family.

In 2014, our family suffered a significant tragedy. My dear sweet husband suffered a massive stroke at 54 years old. He was very young. This stroke left him completely paralyzed on his left side, blind in his left eye, bedbound and incontinent. He suffered significant brain damage and had limited language. He needed 24/7 care. *His stroke was such a tragedy that it felt like the enemy had shot one gigantic arrow at the Scott family, aiming to take all of us out in one hit!*

His stroke happened at a pivotal season in the life of our family. The younger five children were 19, 15, 13, 11 and 8 years old and most days our 6-year-old grandson was also hanging out at our house. When he first had his stroke, it was so severe my husband almost passed away.

When he was in ICU, *I went numb, and the children were in shock.* Overnight their funny, sweet and beloved daddy shifted to a bedbound invalid who could barely talk and when he did talk it didn't make a lot of sense. This was such a critical time in their lives, when a father can shape destiny and now, he could not think or do much speaking. *God, what are you doing?* My children still needed significant love and care from their father, but he was now severely limited in what he could give back. *It felt as if the enemy had shot us straight in the heart.*

At the time, I was working part time and home-schooling. *I was left with a broken husband, and he was left with a broken life, and I did not know what to do.* Friends and family rallied around us, but we were in a mess! My husband needed help, and this was when the beauty of having a large family, with a lot of family members kicked in.

The family rallied together, and we all took shifts caring for him. After some time doing this in our home, it became abundantly clear I needed additional help, and we had to make the sad decision to put my sweet husband into a care facility. I was devastated, and so was he. His social worker and case worker told us our state would not allow him to stay at home. That was what we wanted and so did he! But once he was in a senior care facility, very close to our house, he was visited every day by someone in the family, some days multiple family members visited, and I went there every day. It was a very long and very hard season for me and the children. It was nine years! Dad was now in a wheelchair which meant he could not walk his daughters down the aisle but instead he had to be pushed in his wheelchair. Christopher went to sports games, graduations, church, family outings and everything else in his wheelchair.

The children grew up and daddy was no longer present for all the events in their lives because getting dad to come was not the easiest thing to do. When we wanted to take him somewhere it took effort! Several of us would drive to his care facility and get him. We had to

INTRODUCTION

move him from his wheelchair to his van seat. At the event, we had to move him from his van seat back into his wheelchair. He was heavy and could not stand so it took two to three of us to maneuver him. After the event, we had to move him from his wheelchair back into his van seat and drive him back to his room, where we again moved him from the van's seat back into his wheelchair! He was a grown man and yes it was exhausting, but we did it because we loved him, and it took at least two of us to make it work! Finally, after three years of doing this, a charity bought us a beautiful wheelchair van which was a game changer. I was able to get him all by myself and I did it all the time. We took him everywhere. He hated being in the care home and I hated him being there. Multiple times I simply brought him home all day, on my days off, so he could be home with me and see the children. Also, he always came home every week for church and Sunday dinner. Finally, during covid, God opened an incredible door for private in-home care, and we brought him

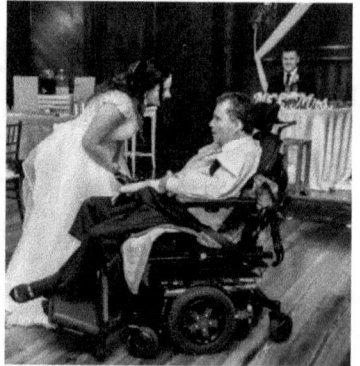

home permanently! He remained home with me and the children for several years until he passed October 2022.

Our story is a very sad story, yet it is a miraculous story. At his Celebration of Life ceremony, each child shared how their dad's tragedy had changed them. How they had grown deeper in the Lord and how they were now sensitive to people in wheelchairs. They shared how they had seen what *real marriage* looks like by watching me take care for their father. We laughed, we cried, we clapped, we reminisced about their dear sweet father and the impact he made on all our lives. After the funeral concluded, many people in the crowd were crying and speechless. They would come up to me or to my children and hug us, bawling and couldn't even talk. They didn't have words for what they had just experienced. I had never seen people so moved. So many had watched us from afar, amazed at our love for Christopher and our tenacity to serve him for nearly a decade. People have told us, *this story* is one of the most incredible stories, the entire world should hear the story of your family!

The Scott children are the people who my husband Christopher left behind. They are a picture of legacy; a reflection of the man and the life he lived for Jesus. We could not have asked for a better picture of what the message of Birthing God's Mighty Warriors is. We lived this book out in our own lives.

My family is a living testimony of God and His plan for you. God knows what to give you before you even know to ask for it. How could I have gotten through this tragedy without my 8 dear children and their spouses? My family lifted me up on days I thought I was going to collapse; they held my arms up, and others held up our family's arms as well. We were there for each other so many times along the journey! What if I had never had these 8 amazing children?

The SCOTT FAMILY is not sharing this story of our family to tell you that we are anything out of the ordinary. This book you are about to read is a labor of love. It took me over seven years to write, and for

INTRODUCTION

twenty years since I've been teaching its message. The topic of what God has to say about the family is so vast, one could spend a lifetime embracing the beauty of the message and of the plan the Lord has laid out before each marriage, if we would only take Him at His word...and say yes. As you read the pages of **Birthing God's Mighty Warriors,** I pray that the Lord will help you see that family planning is something that our loving Heavenly Father cares greatly about. I believe God will speak something unique to each person who reads this book!

These are exciting times to live as we participate with the Lord in bringing these mighty warrior children to earth, those whom He desires to give us. These children will partner with God, as participants in God's end-time plans, and be members of His great unseen spiritual army. We have an exciting and extraordinary privilege to be the parents who get to birth and raise the children of the last days.

A NOTE TO READERS

B*irthing God's Mighty Warriors* is a message to encourage couples to birth children and to lovingly point out some generational patterns. It aims to challenge the ideas and attitudes that caused the last two generations to dismiss the inherent value of God's gift of children. Through this message, I am seeking to help people desire to have a family.

There are increasing numbers of couples who struggle with infertility who would love to birth children if God would grant them this blessing. I wish I could give each couple the children they desire, but I realize this is not always what God wills, but we can always pray, ask and believe for miracles.

If you are struggling with infertility, you can still benefit from the message of ***Birthing God's Mighty Warriors.*** You will learn what scripture says about children and gain an understanding of the generational blessings that result from raising children. Nothing in this book is meant to dismiss the idea of adoption; all children need a parent's love, and sometimes this path brings even more blessings than traditional parenthood. Once one views children through the eyes of God, people desire to have children and to become parents. It's as simple as that!

> ABORTION will never leave our land until a new generation repents for the sins of their parents. The SIN of not just abortion but the root sin of not wanting children. A new generation must repent and turn from their parents' and grandparents' wicked ways and follow a new path.

A THOUGHT FROM RACHEL

Could what happened be a sign from God or a unique coincidence?

You are reading Birthing God's Mighty Warriors 2nd edition. An interesting scenario happened when the 1st edition of this book was released.

Birthing God's Mighty Warriors was released on August 5, 2004, when I was pregnant with baby #8. The very next week on Thursday August 12th I gave birth. The next day was Friday the 13th and, on that day, Orlando was hit with Hurricane Charlie. My family was safely at home when the eye of the hurricane came directly over my hospital room in downtown Orlando. I was alone with my new baby, and it was quite scary, but we came through and I did not name my new son *Charlie!*

Within the next twenty-three days, Florida was hit with three more hurricanes! The next hurricane was Hurricane Francis on September 5, 2004. Eleven days later, September 16th came Hurricane Ivan. Ten days after, but in the same month, Hurricane Jeane made landfall on September 26th! Yes, this was interesting to have a new baby during a series of hurricanes.

Maybe these hurricanes might not seem unusual to anyone other than to our family, but Christopher and I found it quite intriguing. We don't know anyone at the National Weather Service or at whatever agency names the storms, but what is the chance that Christopher's mother's name is Francis and my mother's name is Jeane? Was this some sort of strange coincidence? Maybe, but in the Bible when something strategic was happening, God often announced it in the Heavenlies.

But what was strategic about this book? Several things. It started when Christoper had a visit from an angel holding a *flaming sword*. There was only one flaming sword in the entire Bible and the sword was placed at the gate of the Garden of Eden. The flaming sword represents spiritual warfare, and God's divine judgement against sin but also a flaming sword represents God's divine protection and purification that leads to restoration. This one element is divine. Furthermore, this book took me seven years to write, and the Lord did inspire me and gave me a supernatural download of this message. *(I'm sorry if you don't believe in that sort of thing but it did happen!)* I believe this book is a word from the Lord.

Most importantly the goal of Birthing God's Mighty Warriors is to get us to look again at God's plan for the "FAMILY." We've missed what God intended and we have been living in the counterfeit. This message is also an inspiring look at motherhood and its sixty-five-year downgrade in our culture. Is it mere coincidence these hurricanes reflected the two most important women in our lives, our mothers? The mother is always the person who gives life to the next generation, and I had just given birth again, making these two mothers into grandmothers once more. At that moment in time, our family was a picture of the generations, and a picture of what Birthing God's Mighty Warriors is all about, an attempt to restore the multi-generational family!

Plus, not only were the two hurricanes named after both of our mothers, but both Hurricane Francis and Hurricane Jeane struck the Florida coast in the exact same place! Yes, what is the chance of that?! Both hurricanes hit Hutchison Island off the coast of Stuart, Florida. *Crazy, right?* Plus, both hurricanes hit in the middle of the night, one hour apart within the same hour of the night! *Crazy again!* Also, both hurricanes took a path across Florida that was virtually identical! *Crazy for the third time!* Both hurricanes hit many of the exact same locations, not once, but twice!

We speculated and tried to figure out what this all might mean. One thing we both knew was that we both agreed about the message of Birthing God's Mighty Warriors. We knew it was from God and is powerful. Here is what we came up with. Maybe Hurricane Francis's path across Florida represented Christopher and Hurricane Jeane's path represented me, or possibly since the two hurricanes basically followed the same path it indicated a double generational blessing on this message. We were not sure, but these two hurricane paths then intersected Hurricane Charlie's path right under Lakeland, Florida. What is the chance that at the time this book was published, my husband was the Senior Project Executive on a huge outdoor shopping mall project in South Lakeland, Fl, not far from where the three hurricane paths intersected! *(At the time, Christopher was super happy the hurricanes did not land directly over his building project. That would have been a mess! Intersecting South of his project was a good enough of a sign for us).*

If you believe in happenstance then maybe we are reading too much into this and it's all simply a coincidence, but if it is, then a lot of things aligned all at once, which rarely happens...so something was up for sure!

What are the chances that in the same month this book came out, and at the same time I gave birth, these two hurricanes were named after our mothers?

And the two hurricanes, both hit Florida in the exact same month,

And both entered Florida, at literally the exact same location,

And both hit Florida at the exact same time of the night,

And both followed a near identical path across Florida,

And both intersected with the first hurricane, exactly where Christopher was working?

And all this happened within the first fifty-three days the book was published.

Without reading too much into this, clearly God was demonstrating something. After the book was released, immediately we started seeing miracles. I only printed 250 copies, and they went around the world! This book got me on national TV countless times, (ABC Good Morning America, Fox News, CNN-The Joy Behar Show, clips from an interview were even seen on Comedy Central on the Jon Stuart Show! Where they opened the segment with *"Now we will hear from God"*). Documentaries were also made about our family and about this message. This book was mentioned in Newsweek Magazine, in books, in magazine articles and I spoke multiple times on radio and in podcast interviews. This book brought us an African pastor all the way from Zimbabwe, healed infertility for a pastor's wife in Kenya and people have been healed of infertility in Australia, Germany, Canada, the UK and across the USA. God has put His Hand on this message. I share all this because I am very excited to see what God will do this time with the re-release of Birthing God's Mighty Warriors!

A THOUGHT FROM RACHEL

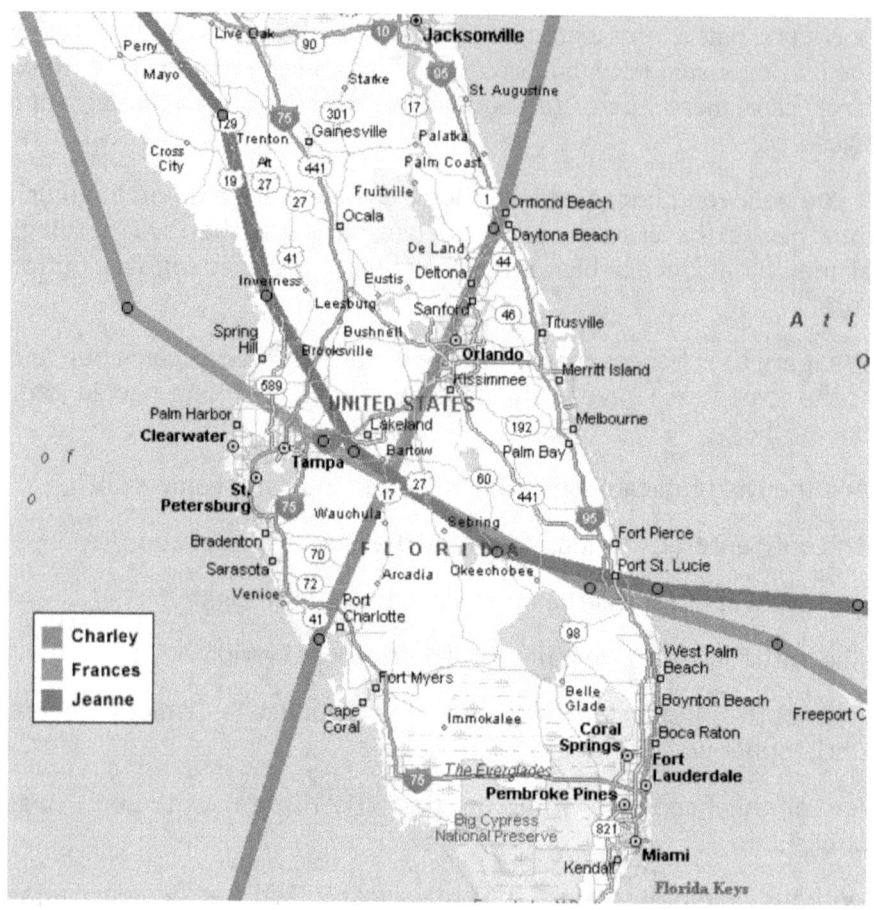

Chapter 1

MARY, CAN I BORROW YOUR WOMB?

The womb, which houses the unborn baby, is a special place of mystery where God perfects His creation. Every woman can allow God to use her womb. There are many obvious and hidden blessings for the woman who walks this road with God and is willing to be God's handmaiden.

As the mother of eight children, I had the amazing opportunity of giving birth eight times. On each occasion, as my Heavenly Father allowed a *beautiful little child* to come into my life, I became increasingly aware of *His great love* for me. Through the miracle of birth, I was given the privilege one more time of *bringing forth* a person who could become a *mighty warrior* for God and to train help each child find a personal relationship with the Lord. It is a thrill to be able to participate in this magnificent process called *motherhood*.

Each time I gave birth, it seemed as if God was giving me a deeper understanding of the incredible role He has reserved exclusively for females. As each woman gives of herself to God, she helps fulfill His desire to bring the generations of humankind to earth. Through the miracle of birth, He allows us to experience the power of God as new life passes through our bodies and comes to this planet! WOW!

YOUR WOMB AND YOUR CALLING, ARE THEY CONNECTED?

If we stood outside a Protestant or even a Catholic Church and polled the women coming out of the services, I bet we would find that few women could tell us that *they are certain* about what God has called them to do. Not many people clearly understand what God wants them to do with their lives. Knowing God's plan and *purpose* is perhaps one of the most significant sources of confusion among God's people today. People seem to be *dumbfounded* about why God put them on this earth. People flock to churches looking for their purpose. They take church courses and learn about their *faith*. Usually, they are told they need to share what they have learned with others, but this still does not satisfy their curiosity. Most people, even those who do not follow a religion, feel confident they have a specific purpose. The *enemy* has been very successful in confusing people. Men and women used to understand why the sexes were created to be different, but now society has successfully confused the sexes and clouded God's traditional roles. We have become *unisex*, and the roles of men and women have blended so much that today's people cannot see even the *most obvious course* for their lives; nor do they understand the purposes their hearts are crying for.

From the beginning of creation, God told ALL humans to *"be fruitful and multiply."* He gave people a calling to procreate and replenish the earth with more people. This was given to *humanity as a task*, it is one of our jobs. It is something for us to do. To succeed at this God-given assignment, God created males and females with specific differences in their physical anatomy. The female's body differs from the males, and vice versa. Both bodies were created for *procreation*. For the female to be successful, God created her with a bonus. She was a *man-creature* with a womb, a *womb-man*! Only her body could house, nurture, and feed another human being.

Interestingly, God gave Eve the womb *before* Adam and Eve sinned, not afterward. God's plan all along was to use the female's body to house new life. This role had not been given to Adam. *God planned* something else for Him. He would *donate* while she would *create*. Together the female egg and male sperm would grow a beautiful new person *(Isaiah 64:8)*. Each would participate, but God separated the female from the male. Her role in creation would be exceptional. The act of housing God's creation was unmistakably meant for the female.

Ladies, the fact that we get to participate in creation should excite you. Women get to touch and feel and take part in creating a new human being with God *(Psalm 100:3)*. The men do not get this privilege. All they can do is watch and wait, but we get to *experience God's power* as it happens inside our bodies! We get to meet *God's creation* before anyone else can. Mothers are *FIRST* in God's plan. Our pleasure is to experience God's creation (Genesis 18:12). This precious bonding time is God's way of saying *"Thank you"* to females for allowing Him to use our physical bodies.

Being able to *grow a new life* is an extraordinary event for a woman, yet it is not always something a woman wants to experience. The *thought* of pregnancy: the weight gain, the discomforts, the sleepless nights, and then dealing with a screaming baby all make some women afraid and unwilling to *surrender* themselves to this all-consuming sacrificial task. As a woman, I can *sympathize* with these women in their hesitation. Pregnancy can be very hard physically. Furthermore, raising children involves a lifetime of sacrifices! Yet God can and does honor woman's choices and sends supernatural grace *(2 Corinthians 9:8)*. Even with God's help, some women still perceive the whole *ordeal* as too overwhelming for them.

Can God understand a woman's struggles with the process of motherhood? I believe that He can, and He does! The Bible reveals the beautiful love of the *Father's heart* for women and their willingness to participate in the birthing process through the encounter of the angel Gabriel and the Virgin Mary. The Lord *cared* about Mary's thoughts and feelings, so He sent an angel to announce His plans and to get a response from this *exceptional* young woman.

For us to grasp the *depth* of this visitation, it is necessary to separate ourselves from the viewpoints of our Western culture and try to understand this event in the *cultural period* in which it occurred. In Biblical times, it was the custom for men to treat women with little respect outside of their role of mother. *Women* were often viewed as having menial value and some women were even denied their basic rights and could be *bought or sold* if their husband or master wished to do so.

God **did not** see Mary this way. The *honorable* way that God treated Mary revealed how He views females. He cared about Mary and valued her as a *person* and woman. His *desire* was for Mary to be happy. He did not want to impose His will on a young maiden who may not have wanted the responsibility of caring for the **Savior of the World**. God knew that this would be a big job for a mother. He cared enough about her to send an angel to announce His plans and to hear from *Mary's lips* that she was willing to surrender her life for this *purpose*.

MARY, CAN I BORROW YOUR WOMB?

In the gospel of Luke (1:28-38), we can read the account of the angel Gabriel's visit to the Virgin Mary. God sent Gabriel down from Heaven to tell Mary that she was *highly favored*, and that God was with her. He also said that soon she would be with child, and this child would be *special*, for He would be the *Savior of all humanity*.

In this passage, we must understand that God did not send Gabriel to tell Mary that she must give birth to Jesus. Gabriel came to *announce God's plan* and see if Mary was *willing* to agree and submit to God's plan. After giving Mary, the details of how this would come about, the angel waited for Mary's reply...

Mary had a choice to make.

Through the angel, God asked, *"Mary, can I borrow your womb? Mary, can I use you?"*

God sought her willingness to birth Jesus and her agreement with His plan. What Mary needed to decide was if she wanted to have this child and sacrifice her life for this purpose.

She could have given Gabriel a contemporary answer that a woman might give today," Hey *Gabe, please tell God No Thank You. I have other more important things to do with my life right now. Joseph and I want to spend time with each other before we have children, and Joseph just started his carpentry business. He needs to build up his clientele first before we bring children into this world, and we need to get a house and set up housekeeping, and we want to do some traveling and visit nearby Egypt and the Greek Isles, and I need to focus on what I am supposed to do. I've invested a lot of time into my education and now it is time for me to find my place in this world. Raising a child will take work and I don't want to waste my time doing that now. Tell God, Thanks for thinking of me."*

Of course, we know she did not say anything like this, but her response was an overwhelming *"Yes! Do unto me according to what you have spoken. I am God's servant, and He can use me (my womb and physical body to house and nurture the Savior of the world). I am a willing participant!"*

Mary made a wise choice. Her first love was God, and this love made her open to His plans and purposes more than her wishes and desires. Her willingness to cooperate caused her to be blessed above all women *(Luke 1:42)*. She said, *from now on all generations will call me blessed (Luke 1:48).*

Our wonderfully loving God valued the wishes of Mary enough to give her a choice. God knew Mary's heart and knew she would say *"Yes,"* but I believe if Mary had said *"No,"* then God would not have used her. God's way is never to force *servanthood* on anyone but to find people who are willing to be open to His plan *(Psalm 2:11; Isaiah 56:6; Revelation 7:15; 22:3).*

God did not want to *force* Mary to become the mother of Jesus, and He is not looking to force any woman to become a mother. God was seeking Mary's *willing heart* to participate with Him. The *God of the Universe* knows the stress pregnancy and birth can bring. He also knows the fears many women have concerning motherhood. God knows it is not easy to birth and raise children. It is a *role* that anyone could easily discount as being too much trouble.

Women *want* their time to have value but often view motherhood as a small contribution because it appears to be *basic*. We've allowed God's most *sacred role* to become devalued and *secular feminists* tell women *they must do more*. This is why women feel pressured to be *more than just mothers*. This attitude has contributed to the downfall of society. We place little value upon families and the future, and we act like the role of mothering is so easy that any woman should be able to have a family and be able to juggle a career as well. This is why many women do not want to say that they are *only mothers*, yet to God, bearing children is no ordinary role.

Bringing forth life is a powerful spiritual act, and when females give in to God's plan, they become *fulfilled* in their lifelong *purpose*. Being a mother is a significant part of the happiness God intended for women to experience.

To *nurture is an innate gift*. When a woman walks in her nurture gifting, it satisfies many of the deepest needs of her heart. Furthermore, the *blessing of motherhood* crosses all denominational lines, racial lines, and global separations and unites all females into one main objective that gives them great joy.

This was God's intention from the beginning to join the heart of the female to His heart. We carry His heart within our hearts. Women, more than men, know what it means to love another person the way God loves. He gives us His heart through the miracle of motherhood! Isn't that beautiful? We carry His heart!

Are you willing to be used? Motherhood is an amazing gift, but it needs to be embraced. A woman can say *"No"* to Father God. Today God is looking for women with willing hearts who will say *"Yes."* He is still looking for women who, *like Mary, will be willing to lay down their lives for the sake of the call*—women who will look past what society has said their *personal plans* and dreams should be and see that motherhood is their *highest calling!* God is looking for those handmaidens who will say to Him, *"Do unto me according to your word. I am a willing servant"*— women who will see their wombs as holy unto the Lord, who will lay their lives upon the altar, just like Mary did, and who will say,

"Lord, I lay down my life and personal agenda so that You can bless me. Please give me children. I want to see my children be mighty spiritual warriors and a blessing to others. I will allow You to keep my womb and heart open so that Your plans will come forth on the earth. Please use ME, Lord!"

THE WOMB: A PLACE OF HOLY SIGNIFICANCE

It is a fact that a woman is given a *womb*. How many women focus on this *physical marvel?* To most women, a womb is something women have but is a body part rarely discussed. Unlike breasts, which are visible to the outside world, *wombs are hidden.* Even though they are part of a female's physical makeup, women usually do not sit around discussing their wombs unless they are sharing a medical horror story. Wombs are *not bragged* about or compared from one woman to the next. Simply said, in our society wombs have not gained our attention.

Most Godly women do not realize the Bible talks about this *amazing organ*, placing a *high value* upon it *(See Judges 13:5, Psalm 139:13, Isaiah 49:1, Jeremiah 1:5, Luke 1:15).* God gave the womb to women for an important reason, and the Bible tells us some wonderful things about the *female womb.* One of the clearest truths is that Jesus came to earth through His mother's womb. This is an interesting *observation.*

Why did Jesus, the Savior of the World, have to come to earth through a womb?

God could have brought Jesus here through another passageway instead of a womb. One day *Jesus* could have just appeared on earth as a *grown man teaching* in the temple, or He could have made a grand entrance by flying in on a cloud, or the angel *Gabriel* could have visited Mary and handed her a *supernatural infant.*

God did not have to choose the womb of an *ordinary young woman* unless there was something about the womb, something so *magnificent*, so supernatural, so extraordinary, that even God Himself had to *enter earth through this doorway*. What was God communicating when He chose to submit to the womb?

THE WOMB: THE ONLY DOORWAY TO EARTH

God spoke, and the world came into existence *(Genesis 1:3)*. God took dust and formed man in His image *(Genesis 2:7)*. After He completed creation, God rested *(Genesis 2:2)*. God was finished. Since the female was now here, God's *plan* was for no other human to ever come to earth by God's direct hand. God had a new door: *the womb*. The womb had been created, and now every human must first be *conceived* by two humans, *grown inside* the female womb, and then *transition* from the womb to the world. God never chose any other door in the history of humankind to allow people to come to earth except the human womb! It is a *requirement* that every soul experience the womb, even if ever so brief. God has made the womb *the only passageway to Earth!*

This is significant! God allowed Enoch and Elijah to *leave Earth* without exiting through death's door (as both were taken directly to Heaven), but God will not allow a human soul to enter Earth *without* coming through the female womb. *It is not possible!* Nicodemus understood this physical passageway when he questioned Jesus about being born again.

...Nicodemus asked. "Surely I cannot enter a second time into my mother's womb to be born!" (John 3:4).

Since scripture so clearly establishes the womb as the *only doorway* to earth, God must be the keeper of the door! No *soul* comes to earth unless God allows them to come—*no one!*

By His choice, God *needs women*. As the doorkeeper, God must find an *available* female womb and open it to bring a new human to earth. Because He is omnipotent, He could have chosen not to use the woman or let her enjoy this pleasure. Instead, He has never ceased touching the female womb with *His life-giving power*. This is a fascinating fact about God.

In *Psalm 139*, King David describes the womb as being an experience with God, as if it is a special time of preparation:

...He who made you, formed you in the womb... (Isaiah 44:2).

This holy preparation was something that God made part of the human experience.

For you created my innermost being, you knit me together in my mother's womb. I praise you because I am fearfully and wonderfully made; your works are wonderful; I know that full well. My frame was not hidden from you when I was made in the secret place, when I was woven together in the depths of the earth. Your eyes saw my unformed body; all the days ordained for me were written in your book before one of them came to be (Psalm 139:13-16).

Inside the womb, *God* watches. He is the caretaker of our creation. David also calls the womb the *secret place.* It only exists inside a female's womb. This special place is where God knits together the soul and spirit of every new *human being.* God prepared *Himself* in this location, as well as David and the other prophets and saints of old. Everyone was prepared in God's *mysterious space.* This incredible place is a quiet sanctuary filled with God's sacred presence. Technology is not supposed to disturb God's holy work unless it is an absolute emergency because this place is where the human soul is in His presence while He knits together soul and spirit. This area is where *holiness abounds.* This undisclosed place is God's. It is not of this world; as David says, it is hidden in the depths of the earth, a spiritual pocket deep inside the realm of the Father. Man does not understand this spiritual dwelling place. *The womb is a mystery and very close to the eyes of the Father.*

The womb is where God prepared Himself and will prepare the next generation!

David's marvelous illustration in *Psalm 139* establishes the womb as a secret place of holiness where creation transpires in the presence of *our Heavenly Father.* We can surmise that something supernatural is happening inside the womb of every pregnant mother. Perhaps God speaks to the *child* being formed; maybe each soul experiences the reality of God's presence before birth or previews their lives. *Who knows but God alone?* The Bible does not describe the details of our womb experience. Still, we each had one, and David leads us to believe that something *extraordinary* and *significant* to God's plan and our purpose happens to each person when they are deep inside their mother's womb. There had to be a reason why the King of kings and Lord of lords voluntarily submitted to being inside a *woman's womb* and came to earth through this door. Can we even grasp that there must be something supernatural to gain from going through the conception-to-birth experience, something so vital that even *God wanted to put Himself* through this process?

The *fact* that God submitted to the womb tells us that participating in birth is a holy event, for everything God does is holy. The womb experience must be a significant part of what it means to be both holy and human, for God chose both. Just as scripture establishes that the womb is a doorway, it also describes it in another *incredible way*.

THE WOMB: WHERE LIFE ASSIGNMENTS ARE GIVEN

In his hand is the life of every creature and the breath of all mankind (Job 12:10).

The Bible also *describes* the womb as a place where people are chosen and given life's assignments. In the same way that Jesus was chosen before conception, the Bible tells of other chosen people who were set apart for *God's service* while still in the womb.

Samson was chosen in the womb to be a Nazarite and set apart for God (Judges 13:5).

Isaiah was chosen in the womb to be a prophet (Isaiah 49:1).

Jeremiah was called by God from the womb to be a prophet (Jeremiah 1:5).

John the Baptist was filled with the Holy Spirit from the womb (Luke 1:15).

The Apostle Paul was chosen in the womb to preach to the Gentiles (Galatians 1:15).

DOES GOD HAVE A WOMB?

Does God have a womb? **The Nation of Israel** was formed in God's spiritual womb to be set apart as a nation unto Him (Isaiah 44:2, 24; 49:1, 5).

The Bible speaks of the spiritual womb as being an origination point for God's creation, from which the sea bursts forth *(Job 38:8)*, where ice and frost are born *(Job 38:29)*, and where the dawn originates *(Psalm*

110:3). This womb of creation is hidden from man, as Job stated: *...things too wonderful for me to know (Job 42:3)*.

No place in scripture do we find a reference that humans come out of God's womb.

Does God have a physical womb? Apparently not. Scripture says that God has loins *(Ezekiel 1:27)*, but it does not tell us He has a physical womb. Instead, the Bible clearly illustrates that God borrows the female womb to bring forth the supernatural physical creation of each new human soul.

Therefore, a woman's womb must be God's! Wow!

Could God have created a physical womb for Himself? Of course, *He is God*. He can have whatever He wants. Yet as far as we can interpret scripture, God has not chosen to give Himself a physical womb. Instead, He has chosen to borrow the womb from the female and make her womb the place where *He knits soul and spirit together* within her physical body. The supernatural marries the natural inside the female's womb.

Most women have not even begun to grasp what an *incredible privilege* it is to have been created female. God gave us a WOMB! It is time we open our eyes to see that our womb is valuable. A womb is something that no man has, and no man can ever have!

"I am woman; hear me roar!" Women need to roar with great joy that we were created female and have been given a womb! It is a special place of new beginnings happening inside of us. It should never be taken for granted or complained about, for He accomplishes *His purposes through our physical bodies!* The female's part in creation is extraordinary.

The *men have no idea* what is happening inside a woman's heart as a new life is being created inside her body. Every little kick and movement are a reminder of a mother's *thoughts, plans, and dreams for the coming child*. This is a privilege that God chose to give exclusively to females. No male on earth will ever be able to experience the same anticipation that a female feels as she looks forward to the birth of her child. She *anticipates* while he watches. She *feels* while he waits. She *experiences* the depths of creation while he observes. Males will never understand her expectations of the first time she will hold her precious baby in her arms, comfort its cries, and cancel all its fears. *The female grasps creation!* Males cannot! The female, along with God, takes part in the miracle. She touches God while He touches her heart.

Ladies, do you grasp how much God loves women? He *prepares us* and gives us a special heart for our child! He knits our hearts together before our child is born. So, by the time our baby arrives, our child already has an advocate: a mother. God knows that because we took part in the *miracle of creating this new human*, we will love and defend our child forever because he is ours, and we are his mother. We knew our child before our child was here. *God did this.* He establishes mothers and blesses our role. Countless women throughout history expressed that the days when their bodies were creating a new life were the most cherished days of their lives!

Yet even with God placing great value upon the female role, many women in our culture, even churchgoing women, do not want to participate in this *holy act* of motherhood. For various reasons acceptable by society and those around them, women choose whether they want to be with child or not. The women want to *plan* this event *around their careers, personal lives,* or have other goals. They want convenience. They find other good things to be doing with their time and feel they have far too much to offer the rest of the world than to be wasting their prime years parenting a *group of children*.

I have been in *countless* Bible studies and have listened to the women who have a couple of children and now don't know what God wants them to do with their lives. They wonder what their primary purpose in life is supposed to be. They are struggling with the questions: *What am I here for? What is my purpose? What does God want from me? What will make me happiest?* When I tell them their purpose is motherhood, they look at me as if I am crazy. They tell me, *"This is too basic; God has to want me to do more than this with my life."* It's not that they can't do other things and shouldn't be adding fun to their lives, *but women don't get it!* Why do we want to make something complicated that is so easy? Women keep wrestling with where they fit in. Instead of enjoying their role, they continue to look for a greater purpose than *nurturing, loving, and expressing their femininity through motherhood.*

We can't help it—we are met with these lies everywhere we go, *even at church*. I believe that every time we go to church, mothers should be honored with an almost royal-like focus for our daily task of raising the next generation. We cannot *escape* the fact that many fathers travel and are not home in today's world, and many women are *single moms*. Often children are being raised nearly exclusively by their mothers. Instead of mothers being saluted for their exhaustive, never-ending 24-hour-a-day, 7-days-a-week role, women are *rarely honored except on Mother's Day*. It's not enough! Women should stand and be applauded weekly. If we did this, more moms would feel better about their role. Yet, except for Mother's Day, *the task of motherhood is overlooked*.

This is why women birth the number of children *they feel they can handle* and then move on. Birthing children is not seen as an *act of worship* but as something to do until God shows a woman what she is *really* here for. The very idea of giving God Lordship over this task has been nonexistent. This devalued attitude toward motherhood has contributed to the *downfall of society*.

The LIE of the enemy has deceived masses of women!

Paul knew that being a mother was vital to a woman's spiritual walk because it is a role that builds the future. This is why Paul told Timothy to encourage the young women to marry, have children, and manage their homes (1 Timothy 5:14). He also encouraged women to love their spouses and children and older women to train the younger women to be happy mothers (Titus 2:4). Paul knew, as God also knows, that the most fulfilling avenue on earth for the *female is motherhood*. Yet today, among God's people, some women do not understand the profound role of motherhood because it has not been *taught to them*! It does not appear as a *calling* on spiritual gift tests, so females dismiss it as an option of importance. Women have not been shown the powerful significance of their *role as mothers*.

To God, birthing or adopting children and then training them to be Godly children IS the fulfillment of a woman's greatest dream (Proverbs 31:26).

Thank goodness, the great women of the faith like Eve, Sarah, Rebekah, Rachel, Naomi, Ruth, Jochebed, Hannah, Bathsheba, Elizabeth, Mary, and Eunice saw that motherhood was their most valuable *lifelong contribution*, and they shaped history by the *fulfillment* of their role as a mother. I am praying the *next generation* will begin to see the deception that stole the fruit of several generations of women and that a new generation will *re-establish* the important role of motherhood God's way. One reason I wrote this book is to *attack the lie* that motherhood is simple, basic and meaningless, and to help women see that motherhood is a huge contribution! Motherhood not only blesses society but also honors and worships God.

Trusting God with your physical body and possibly giving up a self-focused lifestyle takes faith. It takes women of faith like the ones in *Hebrews 11*. These women counted the cost and decided that following God was worth their effort. Building a family is a role that lasts far past this lifetime (Psalm 127:3).

Oh, to be used by God! This is why Rebekah's brothers blessed her: And they blessed Rebekah and said to her, *"Our sister, may you increase to thousands upon thousands; may your offspring possess the cities of their enemies." (Genesis 24:60).*

This is what the scripture meant when it says that a woman will be *saved* through childbearing (1 Timothy 2:15). Her life is redeemed when *she gives birth*. She does not receive eternal salvation like she would when she receives the Lord Jesus as her personal Lord and Savior, but instead the word *saved* means for the woman, her life takes on its inherent value. As she gives of herself in motherhood, a woman finds herself. When she allows her body to be used by God and submits to her role of birthing God's mighty warriors, she participates in the most significant contribution of her *lifetime!*

Since time began, God has been using women and wombs to bring life to this planet.

Women are highly called by God to take part in this process with Him.

Ladies, the Lord values females and wants to celebrate our womanhood by blessing our lives with children. This great blessing was not something God only meant for the ancient women of the Bible. This is a message for women of today; women who are newly married and those who are not; moms who already have children, who home-school; who run businesses, who are doctors and dentists and CEO's and CFO's of their companies, and those who love going to the mall; who enjoy decorating their homes, and for those who love making crafts with their children. *This is a NOW message for today's females!*

I encourage you to dedicate your life to motherhood: *conceiving, birthing, and even adopting for some moms* and then raising these *mighty warriors* for God. It will take all your faith to accomplish this, but it will be worth it. You will be happy that you spent your days mothering God's children and giving your life to this task. God calls you to be the woman He made you to be. You could easily spend your life pursuing other personal fulfillments, but today if you hear His voice and harden not your heart *(Psalm 95:8)*, He will establish you *(Psalm 90:17)*. This is something beautiful that needs to be embraced. Today God is asking you to consider serving Him by allowing Him to fill your womb with the children He has specially planned for your womb to carry.

Woman of God, power is being released here, and it starts inside your womb. The calling of motherhood is the highest calling for women! Few women realize how powerful their motherhood calling is.

Females are the *stars* on this stage of life. They are the ones who get to present God's *newest* gift to the world—a human child—and that child can only come through a female womb that has been lent to God.

God is calling ALL females. Are you a handmaiden of the Lord willing to let God give you the joy of children? Will you allow Him to let you experience motherhood as you lay down your desires for His? You will never be happier than when you allow God to give you the children in His plan.

Do not be afraid. I know that for many of you, your heart agrees with this message, but you are scared. This is an understandable fear. Most women do not want to be pregnant nonstop, and the enemy will tell you that this will happen if you allow yourself to believe God in this area of your life. The enemy is so afraid that you might heed this message of the Lord and create mighty warriors who will spiritually defeat him that he will try to use your fears to make you think that:

- You will not have a life outside of diapers and bottles.
- You will not have any money.
- Your health will go to pot.
- You are crazy to obey God.

This is what the Lord says to you:

- Do not fear, for I am with you.
- Do not be dismayed, for I am your God.
- I will strengthen you and help you.
- I will rescue you with my righteous right hand (Isaiah 41:10).

The Lord knows your fears and the lies that the enemy tells you. He also knows the plan that He must bring a blessing to you and to make you happy. As the lover of your soul, God wants you to submit your will to Him, to trust Him with your physical body and your life and because *you love* Him, don't you want to obey Him and be open to what He might do through your willing *submission?*

"For I know the plans I have for you," declares the Lord, "Plans to prosper you and not to harm you, plans to give you hope and a future!" (Jeremiah 29:11). Put aside the enemy's lies and say, *"Yes, I will trust You God! Give me the children that you have planned for my life. I am your willing servant!"*

Wife's Prayer

Heavenly Father, I thank You that You made me *special* by giving me a *womb*. I thank You that *my womb* is a place of holiness to You. Wow. Like Mary, I want my *womb* to be available so that You can bring wonderful blessings to me, but I am scared. This is a new idea for me and something I must think about. If this really is Your plan to possibly have more children than I had planned, I need time to let this sink in. Please see my heart, my physical capabilities, my finances, and my willingness to participate and help me set aside my fears. I've never trusted You this way before and I am not sure I can. But if I am willing, it will be because by saying yes, my husband (future husband) and I will see many blessings.

Amen

Husband's Prayer

Heavenly Father, I thank You that my wife (future wife) has a *womb* and that it is a place of *special beginnings*. Please help me be sensitive to her needs and understand that any time she is willing to have our children, that this is a *sacrifice* for her. Since I am so grateful that I am not the one who must go through a pregnancy, please help me honor *her role* as a mother, and help me always remember, that without her participation we would not have a family. Thank You for this opportunity to be a blessed man. Please help me always love her.

Amen

Christopher's Commentary

Borrow my womb? Since men do not have one, it's hard for me to relate to this. I guess it's like sharing your soul with God; now, that would be powerful. If God asked me to share something this intimate, I hope I would say, "Yes!" and consider the details later. The Bible says that after the angel visited Mary, she pondered all these things in her heart. I guess this is what happened to me as well. After my dream, I pondered what had happened and considered what God meant. I said "Yes" to God but then pondered why I had just said what I said. Is this pondering? I am not sure exactly, but I know that afterward, I tried to keep this close to my heart instead of thinking too hard about it. I know I would have backed out if I had thought about it.

In my dream, the angel told me that God required something of me. I had to take some action and make a sacrifice on my part. God graciously allowed me time to consider what He was saying as he did with Mary. I still had the choice to tell God, "No way," and then God would have said, "Okay, that is your choice." He had already been doing this with me for years anyways. I had justified my reasons to use birth control, and the Lord had let me go right on using our condoms and blocking the conception of our seed, never thinking another thought about it. This dream was my wake-up call. God asked me if I would change my mind and the course of my life and agree to His plan instead of my own. Just as Mary said, "Yes to God," I was given the same opportunity. Would Christopher Scott say," Yes" too? I guess I did without considering where it was going to lead.

This decision was unknown territory, and at first, it was not awesome, it was scary! This was not the part I liked, but looking back, I now understand why God did what He did. God wanted me out of my comfort zone, and the process was not fun, but it was the best thing to ever happen to my family and me!

I guess this is how God works in much of our lives. He makes these things a *God-thing* because people would mess them up. I know I always do a pretty good job of messing things up myself, so for God to choose me specifically was cool. I guess God knew He had to dramatically set the situation up to get my attention, or else I might not have thought it was God. For a massive warring angel with a sword on fire to show up in a dream shook my world and got my attention. I don't know why God does what He does. I guess it's because He is God, and He can do what He wants, and if we let Him include us, He will.

If you are intelligent, you will allow God to do His thing in your family and forget about trying to figure it out. Simply tell God, "Yes!" and agree to let Him do something powerful with you and your seed. If your wife is intelligent, she will see what a gift God wants to give her. She will carry within her body a child of the last days. She needs to go ahead and allow God to do this for her because she will live the reward. You will agree with God's best if you are an intelligent couple. Tell Him, "Please choose us, Lord. Please choose us now. Oh God, please use us!"

Christopher Scott

Investigate and Questions

- Do you think women today are hesitant about motherhood? If yes, why are they hesitant? How did your mother view birthing children?
- Do you have any personal fears about motherhood? List what excites you about pregnancy and what parts do not appeal to you.
- Read Isaiah 64:8; then express what this statement means to you: *As each woman gives of herself to God, she helps to fulfill His desire to bring to earth the generations of mankind. The wonder of birth allows women to participate with God in fulfilling His vision for mankind. Through the miracle of birth, women can experience His creative power as new life passes through their bodies!*
- Read Luke 1:28-38. The life of Mary presents a beautiful picture of God's calling on women to be the creators of new life. This encounter illustrates a perfect example of how Mary had to receive God's vision for her life and submit to her calling on earth. Have you received God's vision for your life as a woman and have you submitted, or will you submit to this incredible calling of motherhood? Why or why not? What part are you struggling with?
- Historically we say that a woman *gives birth*. The gospel of Luke says, "*and she gave birth to her firstborn, a son*" (Luke 2:7). How does a woman *give* in the birthing process, and why could this giving be viewed as *holy*?
- The Bible talks about wombs. Read Judges 13:5, Psalm 139:13, Isaiah 49:1, Jeremiah 1:5, Luke 1:15, and John 3:4. Jesus (God in human flesh) came to earth through a woman's womb. Why do you think God chose the women's womb as the only doorway to Earth?
- God has chosen not to have a womb unless He uses a woman's womb. If you are female, what do you think of this privilege? Does it change your view about God? Is He pro-woman?
- After gaining a new understanding of the female purpose and calling, what does it mean for a female to surrender herself to this process of Birthing God's Mighty Warriors? If you are female, are

you feeling called to surrender yourself? If you are male, how could surrendering *her body* possibly affect your wife's attitude toward pregnancy and birth?

- As God forms new life in her womb (Psalm 100:3), the Lord gives the woman the pleasure of meeting His creation before anyone else can. Her pleasure is to experience God's creation while it is happening inside her body (Genesis 18:12). This pleasurable bonding time is God's way of saying "Thank you" to the female for allowing Him to use her physical body. How does that make you feel to be born female?

- Read Psalm 139. What do the Scriptures mean when they say,

    My frame was not hidden from you when I was made in the secret place, when I was woven together in the depths of the earth. Your eyes saw my unformed body... Psalm 139:15-16. From this verse, there appears to be a precious and holy secret place for God and babe. A place of mystery. What is your impression of the secret place, where is it, and what happens there?

- The last several generations missed out on this ancient path by controlling their fertility. Do you believe Generation Y has any greater desire for family than previous generations? Describe how your generation handled the choice to include children in their lives and discuss the attitudes your peers have expressed both pro or con about having children in general.

Impacting Others

Rachel, after reading your book I must share that I believe trusting God with our family size is God's way of molding our lives into something beautiful. Selfishness has no rightful place; wherever we are selfish, it will be revealed. There is no way for anyone to be pregnant multiple times and not bear the fruit of love. The giving that it takes to be pregnant even one time bears fruit. This walk of trusting Him is God's way of teaching us how to know the fellowship of His sufferings. I have been married for 27 years and have been pregnant or nursing for most of my marriage. Out of 320 months of marriage, I have NOT been pregnant for only 57 months. I loved seeing the doctor and telling him my last period was in March 1985! —as often I do not have a regular period between births. Sure, there have been rough times when I questioned God and wondered if I was doing the right thing with my life. Then I would go on a walk with my children, and the things they would say as we spent time together and the laughter we experienced, would renew my strength once again, and I would remind myself, "I am the most blessed woman in the world!" **Sarah Emily, Mom to 11, Married 27 years.**

Rachel, I loved your book, and I read it so fast-I couldn't put it down! I even called my sister and read parts of it to her. But it got me thinking because I am surrounded at my church and in my neighborhood by many working parents who all seem to complain about their children. They think I am nuts to have the four I do, and I must listen to negative comments about children. I think those who complain don't understand what life is truly about. Often, people do not look at children for the love they will bring or the joy they will get. Instead, they look at children like they are objects. They only think about how busy they are and how much children cost, and they don't look at them through the eyes of the Lord. I think they miss the richness of what life is all about. I can't imagine life without my four children. I was married before, have a teenage daughter, and enjoy her friends so much. We laugh and share, and I love taking her shopping and hearing about which boy she thinks is cute. My life would be boring without her, and my three little ones are precious. She loves them, even though she has her own life outside our home. Her friends tell her how lucky she is to have little siblings. When I am 80 and looking back on my life, I hope and pray that one of my most significant accomplishments will be that I was a good mother. Some days I am not as sweet as others, but I try to be, and I know my children love me. Children are my contribution to society; hopefully, they will grow up to be good leaders and teachers. I know my life is counting for something good; someone had to be Edison's mother, George Washington's mother, and Martin Luther King's mother. Can you imagine life without the contributions of these men? Someone had to conceive them, birth them, wipe their bottoms, rock them to sleep, care for them when they were sick, and love them so they could grow up to become who they were. The saying, "Behind every great man is a woman," is true, and the woman is their mother! That's my two cents. Thanks for writing a great book! Can you give me a discount if I buy a case of them? **Sarah H. Mom to 4 and hoping for more, Hampton, Virginia**

Chapter 2

THE REAL FIRST COMMANDMENT

Be Fruitful and Multiply

God blessed them and said to them, "Be fruitful and increase in number; fill the earth and subdue it. Rule over the fish in the sea and the birds in the sky and over every living creature that moves on the ground" (Genesis 1:28).

Have you ever heard the statement, "You'll never understand the end unless you first understand the beginning?" If we can grasp why God set things up the way He did at the beginning of time, it will more readily prepare us to walk through and understand His goals for these last days.

Anyone who has raised small children knows that parents spend a great deal of time helping their children get acquainted with learning the proper way to behave in the world. Parents are constantly praising their children's good behavior or guiding them to behave more appropriately. When parents are helping their children make better choices, parents will say, *No!"* or *"Don't touch that, because it can hurt you!"* or *"Don't do that, it isn't nice!"* They are cautioning their little ones to stay away from trouble. One of our greatest desires, as parents is that our children *will listen* to us because we believe we know what is best for them. By helping them learn the rules of this world, we are pointing in the proper direction so they can grow up to be successful and productive members of society. We also hope that our constant care will promote trust and loyalty in them, so that as they grow, our wisdom and advice will help them avoid the pitfalls of life.

I believe our Heavenly Daddy, the Almighty Father God, believes the same things for humanity. He created humans to be His children, and He knows what is best for us. He gave us His word and He put information in our Bibles that would help us make proper choices for our lives. In the same way that we want our children to listen to us, I believe God desires that we listen and obey His guidelines for life. If He asks us to do something, then we should do our best to do it! If He tells us in His word that a particular thing is bad for us, we do not need to pooh-pooh what God says and decide whether it applies to us just because we have a good reason. How would you feel if every time you tried to keep your children from stepping in doo-doo they simply refused to listen, and then they step in the doo-doo and are shocked because it is nasty and smells and then they want you to wipe it off their foot! Isn't this what we do sometimes? God warns us but we do not listen. He tells us what we need to do to be happy and we refuse because we think our way is better. Then when we are covered with pooh, we look to Him and ask, "why did this happen?" But it's not His fault, we didn't listen. Let's just do what God says, so we can be happy!

OBEYING GOD'S FIRST COMMAND

Modern-day theologians have spent years analyzing the scriptures and pointing out pertinent information about God's Word. We have bookstores filled with their commentaries, and churches regularly conduct Bible studies based on their findings. For years believers have benefited from the opinions of theologians. Clergy often rely on theologian's information for doctrinal talks, homilies and sermons.

What I do not understand as I have been studying the subject of *family planning* in the Scriptures, is why modern-day evangelical theologians, unlike past Church fathers, have overlooked a very important foundation stone in God's plan for humanity.

In past centuries, church leaders, theologians, and church writers believed God's Word was clear. God's first commandment was *be fruitful and multiply*. In their writings and statements, church leaders clarified their belief. Scripture was quite clear, *be fruitful and multiply* was not simply a pleasant thought, but indeed a spoken blessing by God, commissioning humankind toward fruitful multiplication to propagate human existence. This would maintain order and the balance of creation on the earth. Throughout the ages, Godly men and women, traditionalists, famous church writers and founders of the Judeo-Christian denominations voiced strong, biblically sound convictions about this. Yet today in Protestant churches and often even in many Catholic churches, there seems to be little emphasis from leaders on the subject. Even though Catholics have these truths in their catechism, I'm finding that few know why. Overall due to lack on teaching nearly everywhere, most all Christians are uneducated about why God wants people to have children. Yet, the commandment to be fruitful and multiply is still very important to God. The opposition has found a clever way to bury this truth and has made it seem *old-fashioned* to generations born in a modern era.

I have followed God since I was small, and I've never heard a sermon specifically about the very first thing God said to humans. If we go back to Genesis Chapter One, we read God's first words to creation were, "Be fruitful and multiply!" (Genesis 1:26-28).

God STARTED human history by telling people the most important thing they were to do. Men and women, plants and animals and all of creation were to be fruitful and multiply. This was His plan right from the start and will still be His plan all the way until the final moments of life on earth.

In Genesis, God begins His book with this theme, and if we look for confirmations, we will find them throughout the Word of God. The scriptures are clear. Here are a few examples of God's emphasis on human reproduction and creating a family:

- Be fruitful and multiply (Genesis 1:28; 9:1; 9:7; 17:6).
- Generations will come from your loins (Genesis 35:11).
- There was a man with 70 sons (Judges 8:30).
- The son of _____ and he begat _____. He was the father of _____ (Luke 3:23-38).
- All nations will come to your throne (Revelation 15:4).
- Many peoples, multitudes, languages, and nations (Revelation 17:15).
- The scriptures make it clear that on the day Jesus Christ steps down upon the Mount of Olives, new people (babies) will still be coming into the world! (Matthew 24:38).

Reproduction was not merely a casual request; God was *serious* about this commandment. To make sure that people DID NOT MISS IT, God cleverly placed this command at the very front of the Bible! On the very first page!

The Lord commands that people reproduce within the first twenty-eight verses of the Scriptures! (Genesis 1:28). Human reproduction would guarantee the blessings of replenishment to the earth and ensure that God's blessing of new life would continue throughout the generations.

GOD'S STORY IS A STORY OF FAMILIES

After God introduced His plan in Genesis 1:26-28, He continually emphasized His theme of human reproduction as families take dominion. The first book of the Bible is a book all about families reproducing by recording and listing family lineages! As people reproduced, Genesis detailed the lives of their families. In Genesis 9, God REPEATS the commandment to be fruitful and multiply again! Then seven chapters later, God describes the plight of the patriarch Abraham and establishes the lineage of God's people from Adam to Noah, and then through the sperm of Abraham. In Genesis 16, Abraham and his barren wife, Sarai, are given God's promise of forthcoming reproduction! God blessed and gave offspring and kept Abraham fertile when he should have been far beyond his reproductive years. He gives life to Ishmael at seventy-five years old and then Isaac at ninety-nine years old! Years later after Sarah dies, Abraham is 136 years old, and he remarries and fathers six more sons! (Genesis 25:1, 2) This man was a virility hero!

The Lord desired all families to have dominion on the earth. Yet, for individuals to be included in God's plan to create a people to love Him, every person must first be conceived by their parents.

We see details in Genesis 38 of a man who refused to allow conception. His name was Onan, and in rebellion of God's plan, he refused. Each time he had intercourse, he practiced birth control by withdrawing himself (coitus interruptus)[2], spilling his seed on the ground (Genesis 38:9). This was not a one-time occurrence. He did this every time he had intercourse with his sister-in-law.

Some say Onan's refusal to carry on the custom of family lineage through his dead brother's wife has nothing to do with birth control. However, the Lord could have given us many other details about Onan's life, but He chose to leave them all out. Instead, God tells us Onan was a wicked man. The only information we learn of his wicked actions is his seed spilling during intercourse; a clear refusal to procreate. God tells us He struck Onan dead due to his *wicked action*. Why would God include only one detail if other things Onan did were wicked? Wouldn't God have told us those things as well? Clearly, God is showing us that God considered this action to be very evil because God is not playing around with procreation. God considered Onan's breech worth mentioning. This story is very specific and to the point. This act of birth control proved to be deadly!

A human's procreative seed and egg is precious to God, and He is not messing around with a casual approach to sex. New humans will always be needed to sustain the earth. Individuals who allow God to bless them with children will be blessed, and those who don't should consider Onan's demise!

As the Old Testament unfolds, the second book of Exodus further confirms family reproduction. The book shows what will happen when God's people are obedient and multiply; they will be prosperous in number (Exodus 1:12). God's people gave birth to so many children that they became one gigantic family whose size alone intimidated the pharaohs of Egypt! The miracle of reproduction is quite evident in this story. Some people believe that the Bible is silent about birth control. The Bible is obvious about the blessings of reproduction, especially in this story! If God's people were using some form of birth control, they wouldn't have been *busting at the seams* in Egypt nor become the large people group God desired.

As the scriptures progress, God's theme of birthing children continues. God names His fourth book in the Bible: Numbers! (Numbers sounds like an obvious clue, doesn't it?) The book of Numbers is a historical book recording, among other things, the reproductive numbers of God's people. It contains census records listing the family tribes and the territories they gained dominion over. People in these families wouldn't have been on earth if their parents had not conceived them; God's people were obedient by not using birth control.

Countless times in the Old Testament, God verified that His people were reproducing by giving us birth records. Even under pressure, God's people obeyed this reproductive commandment. Throughout the Old Testament, God emphasized over and over how happy He was that people all over the earth continued to bring forth children. Large family clans flourished, and families ruled over whole territories. We also see the main characters of the Old Testament with vast wealth. God's word carefully records their ancestral lineage. We easily see the benefits of completely following God's plan. Several times God cautions His people to ensure they *do not decrease* their numbers!

When people try to say the Scriptures are silent about birth control, they do not know their Bible! If we were serving a pro-birth control God, whose word is silent about human reproduction, why did He tell His people to increase their numbers in these 30 additional verses? It's as if God is saying to us...*In case you think I am not serious about procreation, here are 30 more times I instruct humans to create children!* (Genesis 1:28, 9:1, 9:7, 16:10, 17:2, 17:20, 24:60, 26:24, 28:3, 35:11, 47:27, 48:4; Exodus 1:20, 23:20; Leviticus 26:9; Deuteronomy 1:10, 6:3, 7:13, 13:17, 30:16; Jeremiah 3:16, 23:3, 29:6, 30:19; Ezekiel 36:11, 37:26; Psalm 107:38, 41; 115:14; Acts 7:17.)

God loves people and wants to see us happy. This is why He blesses people with children! He knows that children bring great joy. To show how important the family is in His plan for humankind, God both starts and ends the Old Testament emphasizing the family. In Malachi, the final book of the Old Testament, God says He put people together to produce Godly offspring (Malachi 2:15).

Furthermore, the book of Malachi recognizes the importance of fathers. In Malachi 4:6, Malachi cautions the fathers not to let their hearts grow cold toward their children, or else their land, homes, and lives would be cursed. When the fathers no longer want their children or want to conceive them, society will decline. Quite often in today's world, fathers do not want more children and decide to get a vasectomy or make their wife go on the pill or get a tubal ligation. Many families are fatherless. Children are estranged from their parents. Where are the fathers? Our society is under a curse. We need God to help us. It was no mistake that God chose to open and close the Old Testament around the family theme.

AS THE STORY PROGRESSES...

God's story of families continues into the New Testament as God stays true to His family and the human reproduction theme. The Scriptures are not silent again about this but continue to prove God's theme of the family. At the very beginning of the Old Testament in Genesis, we are introduced to the family as a Biblical theme and then at the end of the Old Testament in the book of Malachi, God closes the Old Testament focusing on the family. Then we see the family again at the very beginning of the New Testament when God brilliantly opens the New Testament with a carefully recorded family genealogy! God clearly expressing Himself through the establishment of the family, sharing with the readers what comes from marrying and multiplying!

In the first words of the New Testament, in the very first verse of the New Testament, Matthew 1:1, God gives us the lineage of Christ. God uses Jesus's generational birth record to show us the power of and accuracy of human multiplication!

Historical, genealogical records recorded family kin to prove ownership. These ancient records were carefully passed from father to child, generation after generation, to prove ancestral heritage and to establish identity. Every society was organized around individual families. By using the example of the Messiah's genealogy, God's word honors the fathers who contributed their sperm, and the mothers who contributed their egg to establish each family. This gift of life passed to each new generation and eventually led to the conception of Jesus birthed through the virgin Mary (Luke 3:23-38), be fruitful and multiply was verbally repeated by God in Gen. 1:28, 9:1, 9:7.

God is not subtle! He wanted us to see these fathers and mothers of the Old Testament had been obedient as they gave their precious seed. What a beautiful example of the importance of multiplication! It indicates that God is not silent about controlling birth. He proves His point in every way He can so that people would understand this blessing.

*If just one of the fathers or mothers had been using birth control or mutilated, altered, or blocked their reproductive organs, then the person God chose would not have been born at the exact time in history. The genealogy of Christ would have been altered!

Think of the impact of this! God's plan was exact. It was perfect and pure. If one person had used contraceptives, what might have happened? It makes you wonder about the times we live in. By casually using birth control or getting a vasectomy or tubal ligation, have contemporary parents caused their children to miss their chance of conception?

If someone read only the Old Testament, they would see the theme of the family on the very first page! Equally, if someone read only the New Testament, they would see the theme of the family on the very first page! And even more profound, God closes the Old Testament talking about the fathers and the children and then God closes the New Testament and the entire Bible with the words of blessing coming from the completed Family of God, who were created through earthly mothers and fathers! Talk about mind blowing! God was extremely clear when He connected the Old and New Testaments with the same theme: conception, birth, lineage, family, children, love, and marriage. Family creates history!

It's sad when people try to say the Bible is silent or unclear about the birth control issue. How much clearer does God need to be? The Bible starts and ends with the story of the family.

THE FAMILY IS ALL OVER THE NEW TESTAMENT

In the four gospels, we see why God wants us to multiply. The Messiah came to save the people. If many people are created, many more will be able to know Him. Reproduction honors Christ's work on the cross and helps us agree with our Savior's agenda. As the New Testament progresses, God continues by giving us another example consistent with His theme: *The Messiah was born in the middle of a census ordered to count the reproduction of the people!*

Think about this: If God doesn't care about birth control and procreation doesn't count, then why would the Bible mention a family genealogy, a census that counts births, and start the most incredible story ever told with the conception of a baby? The Bible, including the story of God coming to earth, points to the command to *be fruitful and multiply!*

The natural progression of marriage is to have children. The theme of the family as an institution continues into the New Testament. Many of the disciples came from a family, as several were brothers. As we read about the Lord's ministry, we see Him helping and supporting countless families by healing them and delivering their children from sickness, demons, and disease. We see the Messiah enjoying the hospitality of families, and in His teachings, He never condemns marriage nor discounts the choice to become married and Jesus Himself also came from his own loving family.

In the book of Acts, Peter has a vision, and the next day Cornelius, an Italian Centurion, becomes the first Gentile believer (Acts 10) and salvation comes to his entire *family*. Later in the New Testament, the Apostle Paul further emphasizes to the early church God's guidelines and conduct for men and women in marriage (Titus 2:3-5). We also see guidelines for children within the *family* (Colossians 3:20; Ephesians 6:1). Paul teaches that to be married is better than falling into sexual sin. He also speaks about supporting the procreation of children by giving guidelines for the only time when it is acceptable for married partners to abstain from sex (1 Corinthians 7:1-7).

Additionally, he gives guidelines for church leaders, indicating that to serve in leadership, a man should be faithful to his *family* and be the man of one Godly wife (1 Timothy 3:2, 12). The New Testament continues in story after story showing the importance of *families* and reemphasizing that God's plan is for the redemption of the *families*. Furthermore, we see no support for a birth control mindset or support anywhere in God's word for limiting our reproduction.

AT THE BEGINNING OF THE VERY FIRST BOOK

If God didn't care about passing the blessing of life onto the next generation and if this was not very important to God, then wouldn't He have placed this commandment to *be fruitful and multiply* elsewhere in scripture, possibly at the end of a verse in some less-read book?

For several generations leaders and theologians have treated the commandment *to be fruitful and multiply* as if it was placed elsewhere in our Bibles. The Lord certainly could have tucked this commandment into a less read part of the Scriptures and maybe He would have done this if *be fruitful and multiply* was not very important. Yet God didn't treat His life-giving commandment lightly! Instead, He placed this instruction on the *very first page* of the *very first book* in the Scriptures. Isn't this an *obvious clue* that we should not miss its importance? One can only surmise that God intended people to be open to reproduction. The blessing of marriage, children, and family is the foundation for love, and love is the foundation for knowing GOD.

In the Beginning God said...

Let us make man in our image, in our likeness, and let them rule ... so God created man in His own image, in the image of God, He created him, male and female He created them (Genesis 1:26-27).

God then blessed them and said to them, **be fruitful** *and* **increase in number**, *fill the earth and subdue it. Rule over the fish of the sea, the birds of the air, and over every living creature that moves on the ground (Genesis 1:28).*

Please take a moment and think about this: **God could have said something entirely different to His new creation. HE is God. HE is the Creator. He didn't have to instruct humans to make babies. He could have said ANYTHING ELSE besides this, but HE didn't!**

God could have started creation by telling people always to *love* their neighbor, be thankful, or give instructions on *evangelizing* the earth. These are the things believers today think are **far more critical than birthing babies.** Volumes of books have been written on these other subjects; entire ministries have been created to emphasize these other themes. Yet God did NOT START with these other things! God knew that people could not grasp anything else until they got the first part correct. Creation lays the foundation, and it had to be laid first. Therefore, God started with this first foundational truth, which would be simple for humanity to grasp: *the creation of the family.* To accomplish this, God commanded people to:

BE FRUITFUL - Enjoy the act of making babies!

MULTIPLY - Create many offspring, don't stop!

FILL THE EARTH WITH PEOPLE - From the beginning to the end of time.

TAKE DOMINION - Families of humans will rule the earth.

It was very simple. God had a plan, and humanity was given a task that would result in human happiness. God knew what people needed! His plan would introduce humans to the meaning of *love*, how it feels to be *loved*, and how it feels to give *love*.

Every generation must learn about *love*, or else *love* will leave the earth. *Love* is God because God is *love*. (*Hmm, maybe this is a clue for us today.*) As people replenished the earth, humanity would continue, and humans would find the hidden pleasures of marriage and family *love*. *Soon-to-be pregnant* Sarai remarked about this in Genesis, "...*After I am* worn out and my master is old, will I now have this pleasure?" (Genesis 18:12).

However, as the first people began multiplying on the earth, Genesis 6:1-7 tells us darkness invaded procreation. Demonic forces caused human hearts to leave *love* and grow evil, which deeply saddened God. He wished He had never made people! After 120 years of warning, God sent a flood and started over with the eight righteous people whom God chose to survive. When the flood waters receded, God again decided to say a few words to these survivors.

Think of the significance of this event. God has His moment; God wants to speak to humanity. This was His big chance to bring forth a new amazing truth, promote a new belief, and give humans new instructions or more wisdom. After all, He is God and in charge of the earth. Therefore, hearing from Him mattered. Yet what does God choose to say? Again, He says the exact same thing He said at the beginning, "Be fruitful and multiply!" (Genesis 9:1, 9:7).

Are you catching this? GOD REPEATS HIS FIRST WORDS! He gives humanity the same instructions again!

This is very powerful! God could have told these flood-worn survivors what season it was on earth and instructed them how to care for the animals from the ark. Or He could have talked about the changing atmosphere and the new farming principles that would be best in the newly formed soil. He could have given plans for all kinds of things, which to us seem more appropriate for these lone survivors, yet God did not start with any other information. Instead, God spoke the truth about how they would rebuild human society. God repeated the plan for humankind by giving His first instructions again! It was as if God was saying, "Get this part right, procreation is the plan now and always will be, so be fruitful and multiply!"

Dear Brothers and Sisters, let's get this part straight here: If God said this commandment not only once but twice and then repeated the theme of reproduction throughout the Scriptures, why haven't we cared about its relevance to today's generations? If God says *be fruitful and multiply our seed*, surely it is clear that He is not being silent about human reproduction. He is all for it and He is not for stopping it! Why have we let modern ideals dismiss the value of birthing children?

THE FAMILY CAME BEFORE THE TEN COMMANDMENTS

Modern believers hold the Ten Commandments in deep reverence, as they should. They are often quoted, debated, and committed to memory. Monuments are erected to them, and in our history, they've been displayed in every courthouse in our land. Yet, in our focus on the importance of these commands, almost everyone misses that God did not start with them; they came quite a while later. In the beginning, God spoke, "Be fruitful and multiply" (Genesis 1:28, 9:1, 9:7) and then thousands of years passed until God talked formally to humankind again. During this time, God left people to master His first commandment of fruitful multiplication. Families could gain dominion in the earth and discover His blessings of the family. Those who embraced God's command and multiplied prospered in the earth; those who did not eventually faded from existence.

In Exodus 1, God gives us the story of the children of Israel enslaved in ancient Egypt. Seventy people came to Egypt from the loins of Jacob, and because Israel obeyed God, He multiplied their seed! In 430 years, God multiplied seventy people into more than 600,000 men, and this group would have easily numbered into several million people including the families (Exodus 1:5, Exodus 12:37). The only way they could have grown into a nation of this size, would have been because of their obedience to God's first commandment to be fruitful and multiply.

(70 people) X (fruitful sex) = 2 million people and a deliverance to their destiny!

This is not addition here. The only way Israel could have grown into a nation was not to use birth control and to allow God to bless their seed. There is no other way to look at this. The children of Israel's story is proof that God's blessing is multiplication of real human beings. Their obedience to the first commandment forced open a door that led to their release.

Historical documents from 1500 B.C.[3] prove that the ancient Egyptians were limiting Egyptian offspring by practicing infanticide, birth control, and primitive forms of abortion. The Hebrews did not willingly take part. If the Hebrews had used birth control, we would not have evidence of their population explosion.

THE REAL FIRST COMMANDMENT

In this account, we must remember the Hebrews were lowly slaves, treated as scum, and looked down upon by the Egyptian sophisticates. The upper echelon of Egyptian society practiced primitive forms of birth control, but their birth control was complicated and made from very expensive materials. It was time-consuming for the Egyptians to harvest crocodile dung, dry out papyrus leaves and mold them into sheaths to mix with precious herbs. It would not have been cost-effective to waste precious birth control on slaves! There is no way the Egyptians would have invested the time and expense it would have taken back then to provide birth control for several hundred thousand Hebrews. It was far easier for Pharaoh to kill their infants once born than to invest in population control. Scripture says the Hebrews were multiplying like rabbits, as evidenced by their population numbers. Hebrew women continued to birth children, often at great risk, as we see this in the story of Moses when Pharaoh was slaughtering Hebrew infants (Exodus 1:15-22).

Even through great trauma, God had a plan. The Hebrews were creating a nation of people; a family of people to be used for the purposes of God. When their time of fulfillment had come (Genesis 46:3), God came and rescued His people, and they emerged as a mighty nation; a large people group of many families who were ready to dwell in community. It was because of their obedience to God's promised blessing of reproduction; the Hebrew people had birthed their future!

By their reproductive numbers alone, we can see that they must have had sex and reproduced quite often because they were blessed with numerous offspring. Even in hardship, they had obeyed this commandment thoroughly. They allowed God to multiply their seed and by obedience, were now a reflection of the God of life.

The Hebrews were being led out of Egypt by an unseen God, one quite unlike the idols of Egypt. After their experience in Egypt, with its cruelty and disregard for human life, they saw more clearly why their God despised the worship of death. By creating their own families, these Hebrew parents had grown to understand this unseen God as their Creator. They had grasped the requirements of being servants to their masters. The foundation was laid for a Heavenly Father to communicate with His earthly children because now they could see that the gift of love expressed through marital sex brought God's blessing. As parents, each *family* was now ready for God to speak and give additional instructions.

God led them to the desert of Sinai. Through Moses God instructed every person to wash their clothes and to abstain from sex *(quite interesting; God used this very act to get them there)*. For three days, they abstained from sexual intercourse to purify themselves and focus completely on the Lord (Exodus 19:13, 1 Corinthians 7).

For the first time in thousands of years, humanity was positioned to hear a new word from God and God was ready to speak His ten additional instructions. These ten new commandments would bring *order* to and undergird the first command *to be fruitful and multiply*. God was building the foundation for how people should govern their lives.

God said **OBEY FIRST:** Be fruitful and multiply (Genesis).

Then God said **OBEY SECOND**: The Ten Commandments (Exodus).

Later God said **OBEY THIRD:** The Levitical Laws (Leviticus).

Further on, God said **OBEY FOURTH**: Come to my Cross (New Testament) which completes your lives.

Did you catch this? **God laid SALVATION on the foundation of be fruitful and multiply!**

Are you grasping the significance of this? *Be fruitful and multiply* started the family of God on earth, and the family IS *the foundational institution* necessary for everything else God is building on earth! This is why God started with asking two people to create new people.

The *family* is God's order.

Contemporary theologians have taught us The Ten Commandments were the first and only commandments and that nothing else matters. We've been told that using birth control is not an issue because it is not one of the Ten Commandments. Yet do you see that God gave the Ten Commandments to a non-birth control-using crowd who were already obeying God's first commandment to be fruitful and multiply? This was God's order.

God started THE FAMILY, and THE FAMILY started CIVILIZATION

Once individuals are born, they become part of their own family, and then individual families make up society. This is God's order. The Ten Commandments then show people how to live "in community" with one another within their own families, and within a society that historically has been made up of individual families. The Ten Commandments make no sense without understanding the family! It would have been impossible for people to have grasped the idea of additional commandments if they didn't first have a family, observe a family or come from a family!

The family is where it all begins! God clearly established this order.

Being in a family creates a sense of community where people live, grow together, and exist communally. Without a family, people wander aimlessly, looking for reasons to exist. What would it mean to a person to honor a father or a mother if that person had never had a father or a mother? The Ten Commandments are God's laws for relationships, laws to govern families, and laws that establish the boundaries of love. If the love in a family is good, people thrive and learn about healthy love between God and others. If the love in a family is tainted, all their relationships will falter. Yet when love is in its proper perspective, everyone is happy. God knew what He was doing. Once people understood how to govern their own family, they more easily could understand how to set up laws to govern society.

There is a richness in the family that transcends culture, time, and civilization. It is a thread that runs throughout God's word and is instrumental in our understanding of who God is and of the family of God which is being created while we all live on earth.

TO SHOW YOU THAT I LOVE YOU!

God's first statement to be fruitful and multiply was a commandment about LOVE. God wanted people to fall in love, make love, create from their love, and dwell in the love of a family. Isn't that beautiful? This commandment was to bring forth man's love for his bride and desire to create with her. It was intended for the man to prove his love for the woman and to cherish her as a precious female. Every time the couple lovingly created together it was meant to be an act of love setting forth a precedent of love on the earth. It was God establishing that children were to be the result of His love gift of sex.

To *be fruitful and multiply* was the first thing God said to the first couple, and He is still saying it to every married couple today. It was God's open invitation for everyone who would ever join in holy matrimony on this planet; to love, to marry, and through love, participate in the ultimate act of love, which is to create a child.

I do not understand why we do not see that this commandment was all about love or why we do not emphasize the importance of God's first commandment. Why aren't there seminary courses, commentaries, and theological books on the first thing God ever said to man? Why aren't our religious bookstores filled with books about one of God's most important statements?

I could not find a single reference where this commandment in Genesis 1:26-28 had ever been withdrawn or canceled by God. I could not find a single story where God said it was OK to stop having sex or to limit the number of children. Nor could I find a reference in scripture where God modified or did away with His command. I also could not find a reference where God said to quit reproducing once a couple felt they were finished, or once the global population reached a certain number, or once a specific denomination reached its membership goals. The Old Testament gives story after story of families, and the New Testament's covenant of grace speaks of the blessing of children and the duty of both the husband and the wife and the fathers and the mothers. The Apostle Paul did not ignore sex but spoke out against abstaining from it! Paul did not speak negatively about this, ignore families, or condemn people for being in a family. Instead, he encouraged Timothy to strengthen the mothers and fathers by supporting families in their efforts.

It is still as vital today to obey God's instructions to be fruitful and multiply as it was at the beginning. God never withdrew, canceled, or nullified His first commandment. We need to be teaching this topic! Couples today can think up some excellent reasons why they justify using birth control or getting sterilized. However, I searched long and hard and could not find even one reference anywhere in the Scriptures to support good reasons! The Old Testament supports complete abstinence after the birth of a baby (Leviticus 12:1-5) for the wife's body to heal, but it does not go along with using birth control after she is healed.

The New Testament provides an abundance of grace in every area; still, I could not find a single reference or story permitting us to use birth control! There is only one place: Paul is instructing on prayer, and he states that it is acceptable to abstain from sex for a season of prayer (1 Corinthians 7:3-5). Again, we see abstinence and not the use of contraceptives. There are no verifiable justifications for using birth control. Trying to say that God was silent can be disproven, as I have just done. The Bible is not silent about love, marriage, sex, and children. It simply isn't!

People think God did not care about this issue because it is not mentioned repeatedly, but maybe it was and is because the family theme is obvious in Scripture. He gave us countless Biblical stories that show the blessing of children and no stories supporting the use of any form of birth control. The issues surrounding conceiving, birthing, and raising the generations are woven into Biblical understanding.

God's commandment to be fruitful and multiply was more than a simple statement. The creation of the family establishes life. It is and always will be one of the absolute truths of Scripture!

When we look at the Ten Commandments and the reason why God gave them, we see it was primarily so that His people could continue to be holy and set apart from the heathen societies that surrounded them. He told the Israelites, *"I have called you to be a holy nation." (Exodus 22:31, Deuteronomy 7:6, 14:2)*. He wanted His people to be different from the unholy nations around them, and He also wanted His blessings evident on His people. God wanted the other nations to see His people and *to be jealous* of how the people of the one true God were living. We see a good example of this with the Egyptians. They certainly saw God's blessing of reproduction upon the children of Israel, because their birth number threatened the entire Egyptian civilization.

10 COMMANDMENTS: TRUSTING GOD'S PLAN

Certain believers today think that since the Ten Commandments appeared only in the Old Testament that they are not relevant to our walk with God today, but this simply is not true. Do not kill, do not lie, do not cheat, do not steal, do not commit adultery, etc. still apply! We are told multiple times in God's word that to be completely blessed we are to follow the wisdom of both the Old and New Testaments. Jesus, the apostles, the New Testament church all followed all these commandments. Jesus said, *I did not come to abolish the law I came to fulfill it"* (Matthew 5:17). Meaning I was there when it was written, I believe in every word of the law, and I am the living example of the law fulfilled. If Jesus thought the Ten Commandments were not important, He would not have followed them Himself, nor questioned the rich, young ruler about following them (Luke 18:18-23). Obeying the Ten Commandments is the basic moral code for a believer.

Couples who have not heard and who have not been shown God's word believe that it is *their right* to plan their family, leaving out the voice of God. But could this choice be the reason why so many believers look down upon and have trouble understanding and obeying these 10 simple, basic commands? Following the Ten Commandments involves trust. Lack of trust in God may be the very reason why so many of God's people have struggled in this century with simply following His commands. In fact, we have seen the greatest moral decline since *the pill* was introduced in 1960. After this massive departure from surrendering our lives to God's plan of creating our families, the moral code of our world changed forever! Once we *do not care about the children*, and no longer see our family as *sacred*, then it's far easier to stop caring about everyone else. Couples used to stay together *for the sake of the children*, but not anymore. The children are often not the most important consideration; personal happiness is. Plus, the lack of children to protect may be one reason why it is easier for marriages to dissolve. Our society's moral decline happened rapidly once people adopted *the right to choose*.

To whatever degree a person can trust God with their family planning, they may find the same degree of ease or difficulty in following the Ten Commandments.

Obedience to commandments is based on *trust*. Once we become ready to give God Lordship over our family plan, then we will be able to come even closer to understanding his Ten additional Commandments the way He intended. When we can trust God with our fertility, this means we are trusting Him with our money, our family plan, and our future. Once we give Him this, we literally could trust Him with most everything else. When we want to control our fertility then we will live through the *"lens of control"* putting trust behind ourselves. Let's look at each commandment to see how the way we handle our family planning could affect our obedience and outlook on every other command.

1. God says have no other gods before me.

The trust required to allow God to have His way in our family planning, helps us to be able to easily trust Him with other areas. Surrendering that trust will help to keep a person's heart free. Once people can trust God with their physical bodies, their paychecks, and their own plans, that is a great step towards being free from other temptations. When people use birth control, sterilization and abortion they are not placing their trust in God but instead are trusting in their own ability to control their situation. By doing this they become more susceptible to idolatry and false gods because they do not understand *basic trust, therefore putting other gods before God.*

2. Do not make an idol.

God does not want us to place our trust in anything except Him. God wants to be first in our lives because by putting Him first, we will not be consumed by idolatry. When we put false gods of greed (money), ambition (career), self-love (our desires), etc. before God, we find our time, our resources and our love wrapped up in the pursuit of what does not satisfy, and *these become our idols.*

3. Do not take the name of the Lord your God in vain.

God wants us to honor His name because His name is holy. We can honor His name by honoring how He loves. Reproduction honors His name because we honor His creation, and this obedience reflects God's ways.

4. Remember the Sabbath day and keep it holy.

The Sabbath, besides being a day of rest, also represents God's transference of His gift of creation to man. When we obey by giving Him our family planning, we enter His rest.

5. Honor your Father and Mother.

Our parents are important because they are the representation of God's love on earth. This is very special to God. Every time we create new life, we honor God. This also honors our parents. Therefore, by creating new family members we honor our previous generations by giving them grandchildren, great-grandchildren etc. thus continuing with the lifeline of our families.

6. Thou shalt not commit murder.

The value of life is precious to God. This is why he wants us to value life and not take the wasting of life casually. Murder steals God's precious gift of life. God does not want us to destroy the precious life that He has created by utilizing contraceptives, sterilization, or abortion. If we clearly submit to God overseeing our family planning, we will be allowing life to come, and this agrees with why God does not want us to murder. This trust gives us a strong sense of God's value of life.

7. Thou shalt not commit adultery.

The *sanctity of marriage* and *creating family* is precious to God. When a couple's family planning is submitted to God, then their goal for *family* will agree with God's goals. This agreement is very strong because it is foundational for learning how to trust God with everything else in their lives. If a couple is not submitted here, then Satan can more easily tempt them towards other sins like pornography, sexual perversion, or adultery because they disagree with the sanctity of the marriage vow.

8. Thou shalt not steal.

God wants us to *wait until He brings us the things that He has for us*. He does not want us to take what does not belong to us or is not intended for us. If we use contraceptives, sterilization or abortion we are not waiting on His timing. His right to provide for us and to bless us is taken away from Him. This makes God sad because He wants to provide and bless us so that we can experience His love.

9. Thou shalt not lie.

Using contraceptives, sterilization and abortion is largely about lying to the outside world. No one really knows what people are doing behind closed doors. A person may look one way to the outside world but may be living a lie. Being phony eats away at the person, eventually the lie becomes visible, and they can no longer hide the truth. Many times, this causes people to admit to others, they had an abortion or have been sterilized. Based on what they choose to believe about God's Word their admission may be casual or be because of conviction from the Holy Spirit.

10. Thou shalt not covet any of your neighbor's possessions.

God want us to be happy with what He has given us and trust Him for what He will give us. Coveting is about *being unhappy with what we have and wanting what others possess instead*. Using contraceptives, sterilization and abortion can cause us to covet unconsciously because we see the children that others have, and we may not be able to have them ourselves. This causes sadness and leads us to jealousy and envy. We experience the loss of what we could have had and now we do not have.

See how giving God our family planning and really trusting Him will increase our level of trusting God in other areas? It is amazing how trusting God with our family plan will allow us to view these commandments in a different light.

WHY DIDN'T JESUS REPEAT THE COMMANDMENT TO "BE FRUITFUL AND MULTIPLY?"

In Matthew 22:36-40, we see an interesting situation. The Pharisees, who strictly followed the Scripture's rules, regulations, and commandments wanted to know which commandments were most important and which were not. So, they asked Jesus which commandment is most important?

When the Lord was asked what the greatest commandment is, He had a very interesting response. He did not mention *be fruitful and multiply* even though it was God's first commandment, and the only instruction God repeated after the flood. It was also a repeated blessing among patriarchs and thirty other times it had been mentioned in the word of God, not counting all the other references to families, marriage, and children. Yet thousands of years later, when the Lord was asked what is most important, He didn't even mention birthing children or the family! His lack of reinforcement of be fruitful and multiply has led contemporary theologians to surmise that if, *"The Lord didn't say anything about being fruitful and multiplying, then He doesn't care what we do, therefore my choice to use birth control must be a grey area.* "Yet is using birth control a grey area? Or is it reasoned away because contemporary believers don't want to give birth to children they do not want to have?

If we consider the crowd the Lord was addressing, they would have been made up exclusively of Hebrew families that we would today call *Orthodox Jews*. The Orthodox carefully kept Torah. Torah teaching instructed that a couple should strictly obey Genesis 1:28, *be fruitful, and multiply*. When Jesus began to speak about what it meant to love or what it meant to bear *fruit that would last*, His audience would have already understood that children were the fruit of their marriage. According to God's law, this generational pattern of bearing children had already been firmly established and this truth was foundational.

We must be careful when we study scripture. We must look at the events of the culture and consider everything. Countless believers have isolated the Lord's response and interpreted it to mean that the Lord dismissed everything else; every foundation, every principle, every law, etc., but we cannot make that assumption here, that would make us irresponsible believers.

The Lord's response in Matthew 22 *was not an attempt to override the rest of the Scriptures.* God never tears down what He has previously built up! God is balanced. In Exodus 20, the Ten Commandments were given to the families of Israel in the desert of Sinai. In Matthew 22, Jesus was almost exclusively addressing families again. God had already established the family, the history, the Psalms, the prophets, the wisdom, and other laws and commands. So, when Jesus made His statement here, He was still in full support of everything previously said in the Old Testament, especially the Ten Commandments and the commandment to *be fruitful and multiply*. He was not attempting to start a new doctrine or override an old one. Instead, the Lord was reemphasizing LOVE.

Jesus did not condemn families or condemn reproducing or tell people to follow Him and forget about their family commitments, nor stop being in families! *Family life* was obvious. It is foundational to His plan! When Jesus spoke, He knew what He was talking about and to whom He was speaking, so why repeat something already being obeyed? *Family* life was already in proper order. *Our generations are the ones who have messed up the family order.* But back then, family order did not need to be taught again. Instead, the Lord reminded the people that while raising their families, to never forgot how important it was *to love God with all their hearts* and then to *love* others. Jesus perfectly tied everything together.

JESUS MERELY SUMMARIZED THE TEN COMMANDMENTS

Assuming the family was intact, Jesus's answer consolidated the Ten Commandments. He combined the first four by talking about *loving* God with all our hearts and honoring what is important to Him. He also consolidated the last six by talking about how we are to *love* others, parents, siblings, family members, and neighbors.

#1: Loving God: How God wants people to love Him with all our hearts.

#2: Loving People: How to love others more than ourselves; selfless love.

To put this into proper perspective, we show our Heavenly Father that we *love* Him with all our heart when we desire to obey His plan. *"Heavenly Father, Your first instruction is to be fruitful and multiply. We will do this because we love You."* Our obedience expresses our *love of God with all our heart.* The other way we agree with God would be to *love* our neighbor. We can *love* our neighbor or another human being by creating them and *not blocking their conception,* or allowing them to be born, *not killing them by abortion.* Whoa! Once born, we show our neighbor we *love* them by teaching them about the *love* of God so that they, too, can become one of God's friends. This was what Jesus was talking about when He answered this question.

He was not saying to love God with all your heart means not to have a family or to go into all the earth evangelizing and forget your family. These are man's interpretations. If He had wanted people not to have families, He would have told them this or told them to leave their children and evangelize. He never said this! He never threw away the family in lieu of any other form of obedience!! Catch this here. You need to see that God never gives up on *the family!*

He continued to build upon the foundation of *the family.* God is His Father. Jesus is the groom. The church is His bride. Human beings are His children. The foundation for Jesus's teaching was laid first at the beginning of the world when the Father, the Son, and the Holy Spirit all said together: *Be fruitful and multiply!*

We know from scripture that God the Father established the family and that Jesus and His Father are one! (John 10:30).

In the beginning was the Word and the Word was with God and the Word was God. He was with God at the beginning. Through Him all things were made; without Him nothing was made that has been made (John 1:1). [This would include people].

The Word became flesh and made His dwelling among us (John 1: 14).

Jesus was there at the beginning and invented *be fruitful and multiply* because HE was there! There is no question about where Jesus would stand on the principle of the birth control issue, He wouldn't like it! Artificial contraceptive use prevents the family from coming forth. According to John 1:1, 2, 3,14, the Father, the Son, and the Holy Spirit are one. Therefore, if the Father said it, Jesus agrees with it and found no need to repeat the same commandment to a crowd of families who were already following this first command.

Instead, Jesus summed up the mystery when He said the greatest commandments are about *love and* where does God first teach humans about love? In momma's womb, then at momma's breast, then in daddy's arms, or on grandma's lap, or when holding grandpa's hand, or when receiving a loving hug from a sister or brother.

Love is family, and family is love.

This incredible love mimics the love from our Heavenly Father. Isn't that amazing? Family love brings understanding. Why would we ever want to use an artificial substance to control and limit this beautiful expression of love?

BE FRUITFUL AND MULTIPLY IS GOD'S FOUNDATION FOR THE CROSS

At creation's birth, only God had experienced the *thrill* of creation, of new life coming forth. Yet, in His infinite wisdom, the Lord passes this experience over to humans! God wanted mere mortals to experience the same *thrill* of new life coming forth. This is such an amazing gift to humanity that it is almost too much to comprehend. God has allowed *men and women* to touch and participate in the supernatural side of creation with Him! Genesis 2:7 tells us that God breathed His life into Adam, and Adam came alive.

Women can feel the essence of life as her child passes through her birth canal and bursts forth into this world at its birth. Men too can experience the miraculous as they witness their child taking its first breath. In the treasure of these moments, humanity touches the living God! We witness new life and the miraculous of God. Then reality strikes as the couple usually through tears of joy realizes that TOGETHER, we MADE this new little person!

The significance of this moment cannot be duplicated in any other human experience. It is a moment outside of time and outside of this world's language. In these treasured moments, humans are in the supernatural. We touch God and His power, His dignity, His love, His miracles, and His glory! No matter what our religion is, even for an atheist, at the birth of their child they will tell you, they cannot describe what they just witnessed. By watching their child come alive they do not have words. No matter who we are on earth, or when we live on earth, or in what period of history, the miracle of giving life and watching a new person come alive causes us to *stand in awe of something miraculous we cannot describe* as we view birth and give birth.

God intended that throughout our marriages, couples were to continually partake in the bedroom of this supernatural realm. The beauty of who He is becomes evident at birth as we witness His love multiplied through us!

IN LOVE, GOD GAVE HIS GIFT TWICE

The only way a person, created from the dust of the earth, could give life would be if God made it possible. So, to make it possible, God transferred His supernatural power to people. This was the first gift God gave to us.

Are we catching this? In and of ourselves, we don't have any power. We are not of the supernatural. We are of the dirt of the earth. We can't create anything! Yet, the God of this Universe had compassion on humans and wanted to give the essence of life to us as His gift. He breathed His life force into Adam and placed eternity in His soul. Because of God's compassionate love, all of humanity received life and could now create new life. Wow!

The Bible tells us in Genesis that, *God saw all that He had made, and it was very good....* (*Genesis 1:31*), and God was happy!

By the seventh day God had finished the work He had been doing; so, on the seventh day He rested from all His work (Genesis 2:2).

He made man and woman. He gave them the gift of life and commanded them to carry on with His work of creation (Genesis 1:28). Now God could rest! He had FINISHED His part.

In scripture, we stand at a significant moment in Genesis 2:2. God is finished with the task He set out to do and is happy with how it turned out. His job was finished. This was a great moment. CREATION was now complete!

The significance of this moment cannot be grasped by human understanding but offers a clue about who God is. At another place in scripture, we have another moment just as significant. This is another time in scripture where God's part is complete.

On the cross, in John 19:30, our Savior says, "... It is finished!"

SALVATION is complete!

Are you catching this? Two great moments, two great things accomplished: **Creation** and **Salvation**. Two times His plan is complete. Two times He transfers supernatural power. Two offers to partake in His glory, both at our option and both offered in LOVE.

Each time God finishes His part so humans can embrace a greater part. Even before sin entered the world, God had a plan.

At CREATION, the family was born.

At THE CROSS, the family was restored!

CREATION and the CROSS are connected!

Isn't that just the most beautiful thing imaginable? Through the family of humankind would come a Savior, and from the Savior would come the family of God! Think of the significance of the family unit as a foundational institution.

A PARENT'S SACRIFICE IS A PICTURE OF THE CROSS

The beauty of God's heart is revealed through creation and the cross because both required sacrifices. Both demonstrated love and both show that NEW LIFE does not come without someone making a sacrifice. New life always costs someone something.

Creating NEW LIFE was hard work for God (Genesis 2:2).

Laying down HIS LIFE was hard work for Jesus (Mark 15:34).

Bringing NEW LIFE is hard work for women (John 16:21).

The woman must lay down her body and give herself to growing a baby. It is tiring, uncomfortable, and a long process. It is a sacrifice! She then must endure great pain to bring new life into this world. Once the child is here, the sacrifice continues. The baby is helpless and needs a constant caregiver; the sleepless nights, sore breasts, and the body that will not go back into shape. The mother is still giving. The child grows but requires constant supervision. Parenthood demands a life of sacrifice! Every time a couple lays down their lives and allows conception, it is a picture of God giving life at creation and it is a picture of the Savior giving eternal life on the cross. Both creation and the cross are a beautiful picture of the sacrifice of love!

A COMMAND, A BLESSING OR WHAT?

Was *be fruitful and multiply* meant to be a blessing instead of an actual commandment? This is one of the biggest questions asked when I discuss the commandment *to be fruitful and multiply*. Contemporaries question whether it was supposed to be taken literally or not. Protestant Bible teachers hold the opinion that God only meant it as a blessing. Others say it was just a simple mandate and no longer applies and that strict adherence without contraceptive use is unnecessary. Ever since Protestants and Catholics went their separate ways on this issue there has been non-stop confusion over the first thing God told people to do!

Yet God's word shows us that procreative sex was meant to establish a blessing! Webster's dictionary defines a blessing as *something that promotes or contributes to happiness, well-being, or prosperity*. This is how the commandment to *be fruitful and multiply* could be interpreted. It does bring happiness, prosperity, and well-being for generations.

Yet was it an actual command? The definition of a command is *to instruct, guide, and give an order*. When you read the verse, *be fruitful and multiply*, God is *instructing, guiding and giving an order*. God's word requires action on our part to get the blessing. In Genesis 1:27, 28, God said to the people of the earth: *creation* is now yours! The words *fruitful* and *multiply* are verbs meaning *take action*. In God's plan, God gave humans the physical equipment to do the action, and by doing our part, He promised He would multiply our efforts.

In the beginning, God established His order. If people didn't follow through, humankind would suffer, and since the last several generations stopped following this commandment as strictly, their actions tore the family apart. They affected ecology, the balance of society, the future of human reproduction, religion, health, marital stability, and placed the future of the family in jeopardy. God knew what He was doing when He commanded that we *be fruitful and multiply*!

REPRODUCTION IS THE BLESSING

When we look at scripture, we see God uses the word *blessed* more than once when referring to His creation of man. By using this specific word, He is trying to show us something. He seems to be giving us a clue to the mystery of His foundation of the family. What does He want us to uncover about this wonderful truth?

The first time the word *blessed* appears in the Bible is in Genesis 1:22. The Lord blessed the animals and declared that they should: Be fruitful and multiply and fill the earth with male and female animals.

The second time the word *blessed* is used is in Genesis 1:28, where God again blessed man and woman and told them what to do: Be fruitful and multiply and fill the earth with male and female people.

The third time the Lord uses the word *blessed* in the Bible is in Genesis 2:3 when God blessed the seventh day and made it holy, because on this day He rested from all the work of creating that He had done.

The fourth time the Lord uses the word *blessed* is in Genesis 5:2 when He blessed both male and female as His creation and named them man.

The fifth time the word *blessed* is used was in Genesis 9:1 when God told Noah and his sons after the flood to: Be fruitful and multiply and fill the earth.

The sixth time that the word *blessed* is used in the Bible is in Genesis 12:23, where God tells Abraham that: He will be *blessed*, and God will make him into a great nation.

God continues to use the word *blessed* and *blessing* throughout the Bible when referring to the increase of descendants and children. The scriptural references are too numerous to list. This is simply one more reason why this message of birthing children is HIS foundation.

One of the most amazing things about this fact is **the first time** God ever used the word blessed in the Bible was when He referred to the blessing of reproduction He gave to the animals! *He blesses* their existence on Earth.

The second, fifth, and sixth times He uses the word *blessed*, He refers to the gift of humankind's reproduction! This is very interesting and not something we should skim over. It has far more importance!

THE REAL FIRST COMMANDMENT

The third and fourth time He uses the word *blessed*, He refers to His own work being blessed and finished so He could now rest (Genesis 2:2,3). *"His work has been finished since the creation of the world"* (Hebrews 4:3). Since God was resting from His work of creation, humanity and animals were given the divine job of continuing with His creation! Since His work was finished by our continuing with it, we come under the same rest (Hebrews 4:9-11). Are we catching this incredible message God is communicating?

God begins the Old Testament with the *family* (Genesis 1:28). God ends the Old Testament with the *family* (Malachi 4:6). God begins the New Testament with the *family* (Matthew 1:1). God ends the New Testament and the Bible with the *family* (Revelation 22:17, 21).

God invites all persons created to become a part of **His new family.**

The Spirit and the *bride* say, "Come! ..." (Revelation 22:17). The *Bride* IS God's new family!

In the end, **the family of God** will consist of people conceived on earth. These are physical people, made of real flesh and blood, conceived by two parents, which leads to the opportunity to become spiritual sons and daughters of the most-high God.

In the first twenty-eight verses of Genesis, God starts His *family*. At the last word of the Scriptures, it says God dwells with His new *family*. *The grace of the Lord Jesus be with God's people, Amen (Revelation 22:21).*

Dear brothers and sisters, please let me ask you, if God did not care about our decisions regarding our childbearing capabilities, why does His word continuously emphasize marriage, sex, children, and the family?

After giving us His incredible gift of life. He tells us, *now go use this supernational ability to create more life. Along your way you are going to need a few rules to help you understand that you cannot live any old way or treat each other carelessly, so I'm giving you Ten Commands. These 10 guidelines are not only for your family, but once you put these into practice, you can use these same ten rules to help society govern itself properly. Because of the sins of Adam and Eve, I will come back to you and rescue you by dying for you. As each person you've created chooses to either love Me for this, or rejects Me, I will eventually form all those people who love Me into one gigantic family. One day I will come back for My family, and we will marry, and because from the beginning until the end you continued to bring forth new life, you now understand that you and I will someday create something new together.*

Isn't this INCREDIBLE?

As we sum up this chapter, we see that God laid the foundation for everything He was doing on THE FAMILY. From the first *family of Adam and Eve* to the conception and birth of the Messiah to the completed *Family of God*, we see God's purposes for BE FRUITFUL AND MULTIPLY are clear. The Bible is God's story of His love for people and revolves around the creation of the family.

Wife's Prayer

Heavenly Father, I want to enter your rest! Even though having children does not sound restful, I know that You are trying to bless me with a family to love. Please help me to enjoy motherhood to its fullest. Thank you for showing me that family is in the Bible and that my children now and those I might have in the future are the source of my happiness. I want the family You have for me.

Amen

Husband's Prayer

Heavenly Father, Your word is filled with scriptures I've never seen before! Please forgive me for misunderstanding the blessing of children. I didn't realize You might have more children for me than what I thought. I also did not realize that my actions could go against Your plan for my life. Help me work together with my wife, so we can have the family members that will bring us happiness.

Amen

Christopher's Commentary

As an executive on a construction site, I always hear men talking trash. They've been conditioned by society to think a certain way: no children at first, then after a while, she'd better pop out a couple of *kids* to get them out of the way, and then you're done. She can return to work, and you can get a vasectomy to retire on time. I have non-believing buddies who think this way, and I could name Christian men who also think the same way. It's almost like a manual we all follow, and we must do it the same way. If not, then a guy is breaking the unwritten rules, and that's when people comment about why you shouldn't have more children.

I came into marriage with a plan. Rachel and I didn't want children at all. I was convinced they were expensive, and I didn't marry my wife for children. I married her for sex, so children were not a desired goal. As I listened to other men talk, I think that, for the most part, men want a woman to look like a Barbie doll but who willingly and regularly seduce them and fulfill whatever fantasies he might have. However, they also want her to have a few brains so she can hold down a job and yet be nice enough to him to be mutually compatible. A man figures that if she looks nice enough, their children will also look nice. But he is not marrying her for her genes! Women seem to care much more about these details; how the children will look and if they look good together. That is how the women see it. To the men, none of this matters. Men don't care.

When I was growing up, my brothers and I watched many TV shows with one or two children in the households, and the parents gave their children all their time and attention. I thought this was how it was in smaller families because in our home of five children, my dad worked all the time, and my mom was always cooking or doing the laundry. Our only family outing was to church several times a week, and even there, my parents did not spend time with us. We all went to our various classes. They didn't use their time with us, but we took up all their time.

This was why I was not planning to be bothered with children. I worked, she worked, and after we had a child, she wanted to stay home, and I let her do all the rest. I think I did help Rachel a lot more than most men help because she tells me that I do more than most of her girlfriend's husbands, but overall, my life was a work pattern. The family was not my top priority all the time.

How could I know any different? My church never told me anything about this. I was there twice on Sunday and Wednesday, and Thursday nights. Yet, in all my Bible studying (my church studied the Bible intensely), no one ever talked to me about the value of children. We followed the worldly recipe, which was supposed to end after two children. This is why I was shocked when after having four, God interrupted my life with the dream, which led me to have four more children! After that, God gave me new eyes to see, and I became a completely different man and parent. Now I see my children as my heritage and the worldly plan as empty. I've sought the Lord with regrets and wondered why in all my Bible study, one of the essential Biblical messages was hidden from my generation. I never understood why I was so blinded. My last four children have been such a blessing. Without them, I would have seriously missed out. Had I known God's truth sooner, we might have added another eight to the eight we did get!

Christopher Scott

Investigate and Questions

- How does a *man touch God* when he creates a child, and how does a *woman touch God* when she gives birth?
- Read Genesis 1:26-28. What do you think of the statement if, *be fruitful and multiply* was not very important to God, wouldn't He have placed it elsewhere in scripture? Does the fact that we see it first in scripture and it was the very first thing God ever said to humankind, does this matter to its importance?
- Read Genesis 9:1 and 9:7. If God said the commandment not only once but twice, why have we let modern ideals dismiss its value to us? How does it hold relevance to your generation? How is the modern church responding to the practical application of this command? How does the church you attend handle this subject?
- Read Genesis 1:27-31. God transferred His supernatural creative power to humanity. Have you ever considered what it means to possess the same creative power God used to create the world? What responsibilities does possessing this power give us?
- Read Romans 1:22. What does this statement mean to you? Who are we to think that during the twentieth century and now at the turn of the twenty-first century, we have suddenly gained independence from the roles set down at the beginning of time? If only one person was not obedient, the entire lineage would have changed. It makes you wonder about modern times. By casually using birth control or the pill or by getting a vasectomy or tubal ligation, did some children miss their chance of conception? Did some parents miss parenting?
- What do you think of this statement? In today's world, what most couples struggle with in family planning is surrendering control of their money, the wife's body, and their plans. Why is surrendering to become God's servant in this area so foreign and so hard for couples?

- Read Matthew 22:37-40. How does obeying the command, *be fruitful and multiply*, fit into the two greatest commandments?
- Read Genesis 2:1-3. The last thing God did before He rested was give humanity this gift of procreation. Why was it then time for Him to rest? What are your thoughts about how humans have obeyed or disobeyed this command through the ages?
- Read Matthew 19:5-6; Ephesians 2:20; 1 Peter 2:5-9; Ephesians 5:30, 31. Is *be fruitful and multiply* the cornerstone of marriage? If not, what is?
- Since the 1960s society fell away from the Ten Commandments and became immoral. Churchgoers began to freely use contraceptives. Do you believe there is any correlation? What are your thoughts?
- Read Hebrews 4:1, 9-11. Obedience brings blessings- disobedience brings turmoil. Do you see parallels between societal unrest and families in distress? How could obedience or disobedience in family planning make a difference?
- Think about your lineage: If just one of the people hadn't been born at the appropriate time your genealogy would have been different. What are your thoughts on this?

Impacting Others

Rachel, I enjoyed your book so much and agreed with it all! I have six children and want to share what I met with on my journey. I live in Northern Michigan, and I have found that many people around me believe that birth control is OK and even the responsible thing to do because they don't believe that God creates everyone. They believe that God was the original Creator because He put the reproduction process into motion, but it is up to humans to rule over the process. Once they hold on to this false belief (that they can't prove in scripture), I can't get them to look at the verses that support children, birthing or the obvious fact that no one in the Bible used birth control. I feel that I am casting pearls before swine when I try to share with someone who refuses to believe that God is ultimately in charge. It's frustrating and it's so nice when someone, like yourself, agrees with me. Then I know I'm on the right track. **Jenna, Mom to six children, Northern Michigan.**

Rachel, I saw you on Fox News today, and I was amazed. Two years ago, the Lord had placed this very thing you have written a book about on my heart. Our society views children as a burden. Even in our churches, the mentality is that they are expensive, take up time, and are intrusive. Intrusive in such a way as to interfere with mom and dad's lives; this is shameful. We, as Christians, are as guilty of the it's all about me mentality as the secular world. You are right on target, too, regarding Satan's attack. I am convinced that abortion was round one in his attack plan to kill the children, and preventing conception is round two. This second strategy is more easily inserted into Christian thinking because it doesn't kill and is more palatable and, therefore, more dangerous. I applaud you for tackling this difficult and often ridiculed subject. It has been a confirmation to me that this burden for our families is truly a God-placed burden, and I need to continue to pray and encourage others to receive God's blessings. I think it is essential for you to continue to stress that much of what you are trying to bring attention to is our mindset toward children because I believe that once the mind and heart are changed, God will take care of the numbers and provision. God bless you, and I pray He gives you the strength to endure criticism. **Colleen, Mother of Five, Voorhees, New Jersey.**

Chapter 3

WHEN DID CONCEIVING CHILDREN BECOME OUR CHOICE?

The History of How We Got to Where We Are Today

> *This is what the LORD says: "When **seventy years** are completed for Babylon, I will come to you and fulfill my good promise to bring you back to this place. For I know the plans I have for you," declares the LORD, "plans to prosper you and not to harm you, plans to give you a hope and a future (Jeremiah 29:10-11).*
>
> *For **forty years** I was angry with that generation; I said, 'They are a people whose hearts go astray, and they have not known my ways.' So, I declared on oath in my anger, "They shall never enter my rest." (Psalm 95:10-11).*

I had this bumper sticker on my fifteen-passenger van for years; *"Motherhood, changing society one diaper at a time."* I loved it because it was true of my conviction. I was and am trying to change society. Whenever our large family of ten were out in public we naturally drew attention from onlookers who were staring, gawking and commenting. Routinely we listened to some ridiculous remarks and because my husband possessed a quick wit he came up with some very clever responses. When people asked, *"How do you do it all?"* he would say, *"The same way you do. How do you handle yours?"* Multiple times people admitted they were not handling theirs very well. Then my husband would say *"It gets easier the more you have! Maybe you need a few more."* Most people laughed and shook their heads. Others would comment, *"You've really got your hands full!"* which is a comment I despised because this remark insinuated that we were not doing an adequate job. This comment was especially silly when we were all nicely walking into a store together, holding hands and pushing a baby carriage or something. My husband usually responded by saying, *"Our hands are not full yet! We plan to have a few more than this,"* which caused most people to gasp—as if we must be crazy to want another child. With the Green Movement and climate change gaining in popularity we got sick of hearing, *"Think of the earth and overpopulation,"* to which we would say, *"As the earth needs replenishment to survive, so does the human race."* Yet my favorite was when people would ask, *"Do you have all those kids because you're Catholic?"* My husband would say, *"Obviously, I am in my sex life!"* and people always laughed as one of my younger children would quietly comment, *"What is a sex life?"* Over time we realized that people made these comments primarily because they were shocked at seeing a large family in action and not because they were trying to be rude. But to people who did not understand, we appeared to be a bit off the wall.

I can recount more than one occasion when our family walked into a non-denominational Protestant church for the first time, and we were immediately *shunned* and *judged as a threat* to the minister and his congregants. This prejudice was based on our family size. We could tell we were not welcomed when the pastor's first comment was, *"We don't really have large families here."* (Who says this to a visiting family?)

Since my husband and I have always attended church somewhere we knew the difference between acceptance and rejection. We came to believe our large family made people *uncomfortable* because we represented a couple who trusted God with our fertility, and this was considered *too radical* or *a Catholic thing* and something that should stay at the *Catholic church!* When large families invade the Protestant church world it often presents problems and persecution. People might not think this is true, but a large family often threatens their beliefs, and the craziest part is we did not even have to open our mouths. Our very presence caused pastors and congregants to feel *uncomfortable* and question their family size and ministers did not like us for that.

What I came to believe, and I stand by this statement, is that the Protestant position on family size (from nearly all the Protestant denominations I've

visited and have researched their theological views on this subject), would be that Protestants want couples to get married and to have children, but they really don't want couples to have a lot of them. The religious climate toward large families at any church will depend upon how a particular minister feels about the subject and this will vary from church to church. There is no across the board agreement about what the Bible says about family size when it comes to the Protestants. Couples in Protestant churches generally have families with 1-3 children. Historically Catholic churches have heavily promoted a pro-family environment with the trend towards parenting larger families, but this is more a reflection of the past. Catholics do believe in "being open to life" as this doctrine is part of their catechism but it is not being taught as often as it could be from the priests in the pulpit, even though the doctrine of life is a main teaching in Catholicism. Based on the statistics, many American Catholics do not follow their Church's teachings in this area. However, every time we visited a Catholic church, our large family was welcomed with open arms. We always received positive comments from parishioners and the priests, and especially the older women saying to me, "God bless you!" Which was a contrast from the Protestant women asking me, "Did you really want all these children?" Such a difference in the reaction between each group of Christians!

Most people today cannot figure out why anyone in their right mind would want to be raising a large family with the cost of living and the expense of weddings and college tuition. Larger families don't make sense to the way contemporary generations think.

This is very sad that we have gravitated away from the blessings large families can bring. Until the 1930s and 1940s, the average person would not have questioned a family with eight children, as many families had at least eight children, and quite a few families had more. America was built upon the backs of large families. They owned farms and businesses, and entire towns were started by large families and eventually their offspring governed across the entire country. Large families have been the norm for thousands of years. Every Judeo-Christian denomination understood and taught that God's word was clear; *it was a sin to use birth control* and *a sin to harm your gift of fertility!*

Believers did not use birth control!

Clearly, only those who did not *"know God"* tried to control this area. Let me repeat, *only those who did not know God* sought to control their fertility. Those who have experienced the ways of a loving and holy

God would never consider such sinful behavior. Throughout Christendom, using birth control has always been a sin.

Since Adam and Eve, God's people were ALWAYS *obedient* with their gift of fertility. The size of one's family was a badge of honor! People accepted this blessing in their marriage and lived their spiritual lives accordingly.

Children were a blessing. This was not challenged.

A rich man and rich woman were a person who had many children.

A blessed man and blessed woman were persons who had many children.

These views were not challenged until the beginning of the twentieth century when for the first time, birth control methods became safe enough for users to prevent conception and not suffer death. Before this time, when someone used birth control, tried to abort, or tried to be sterilized, they ran the risk of serious health complications. Most methods led to infection or death and *complications* were hard to keep secret.

WHEN BELIEVERS DRIFTED AWAY

(I find this very difficult to speak out here because God knows my heart has no ill intent. I do not want to do anything other than bring glory to God with the message in this book, but I must point out where God's people stopped agreeing with each other).

Personally, I believe the Protestant pastors have really dropped the ball. The Lord called them to follow and teach the Bible, but in the roaring twenties when birth control propaganda first came on the scene, I'm not sure where they were. I do believe there had to be some evangelical pastors who were fighting against this change and at least some orthodox Jewish rabbis, but not as many as were needed. Prior to 1930 all believers *(Jewish, Catholic, Protestant)* agreed birth control use was a SIN, but in 1930 the Church of England *(Anglican-Episcopalians)* embraced the new culture of birth control being promoted under the disguise of the eugenics movement and heavily influenced by Margaret Sanger-the woman who later started Planned Parenthood. This 1930 change, in thousands of years of doctrinal agreement, did occur in Europe, but the ramifications were heard around the world. Immediately the Orthodox Jews did not agree and did not comply, but

Reformed and Conservative Jews were supportive of the decision. Nearly all Protestant denominations made doctrinal changes, some were slower than others but by the 1960's nearly all Protestant churches supported the use of birth control, especially to decrease family size.

In my research I could not find a huge number of writings or speeches by Protestants speaking out against this 1930s change in doctrine, but I did find sermons and books by a few evangelical pastors. Pastor John R. Rice was a voice in the 1940s-1970s. He was well known for his publication, *The Sword of the Lord*. In these booklets he spoke out against birth control and said using it would lead to the breakdown of the family. Dr. Bob Jones Sr, founder of Bob Jones University, also spoke out against the use of artificial contraceptives, yet married students at his university have not historically been noted for large families. Christian Philosopher Francis Shaeffer also opposed birth control and supported the traditional family. Robert D. Hales, an LDS-Mormon, told his followers to trust in God's design for the family. (Mormons have been a sect who historically also tended toward having larger families). Orthodox Jewish Rabbi Moshe Feinstein also spoke out in his *Letters to Moshe writings*. He spoke against using birth control in favor of God's plan for marriage and family. These men did try! They did oppose the cultural shift towards using birth control and were outspoken, but due to shifting ideas and societal changes, these few opposing voices were either largely ignored or were later ignored. The global church world moved forward and embraced the shifting culture. Yet this rebellion against God's design has not always been the norm for God's people.

One of the most famous Christian leaders in Protestant church history, **Martin Luther**,[i] considered birth control and contraceptive use to *"be sins worse than adultery or incest."* He called birth control *"an inherent evil."*

Other Protestants, such as **John Calvin**[ii] spoke of the wickedness of Onan, *"deliberately avoiding the intercourse so that the seed drops on the ground is undoubtedly horrible, by this means one quenches the hope of his family."* Wesley, Spurgeon, and the Pilgrims condemned using all forms of birth control and considered using it worse than adultery.

Many Catholic popes and Catholic church writers condemned birth control and spoke out against its use.

Clement of Rome[iii] **(A.D. 35)** *"The kind of chastity that is to be observed: that sexual intercourse must not take place heedlessly and for the sake of mere pleasure but for the sake of begetting children."*

Clement of Alexandria[iv] **(A.D. 150)** *Because of its divine institution for the propagation of man, the seed is not to be vainly ejaculated, nor is it to be damaged, nor is it to be wasted."*

Epiphanius of Salamis[4] **(A.D. 310)** *"The body as a whole is pervaded by the things which God has rightly placed in it.... Thus, the sexual desire was given to the human race to fulfill the commandment, increase and multiply and fill the earth"* (Genesis 1:28).

Rabbi Eliezer Ben Hyrcanus[5] **(A.D. 50-130)** *Emphasized that procreation was essential in marriage as it fulfills the mitzvah of peru ur/vu (be fruitful and multiply). He was against Onanism-the spilling of the seed.*

Catholic, Protestant and orthodox Jewish church leaders believed the Scriptures were clear that procreation was necessary to replenish the earth and that children should be received from God with great joy, and there was complete agreement about this issue. But then in 1930, **to push an agenda, the wisdom of the past was buried.**

THE SHIFT IN BELIEF BEGINS [1930-1960]

At the start of the Great Depression in America, in 1930 a lot of people suffered financially, and this caused priorities to change. People were being tested. Hard times caused parishioners to question their faith. Was God still a good God? Some people turned from their convictions as times grew tougher. Food was scarce, and for some families, there were too many mouths to feed. Children ended up in orphanages and crimes against families were committed.

At this point, God's people had been preaching and obeying God's plan for the family for approximately 5,000-6,000 years! Families throughout history had endured many hardships yet children were still born. Yet by the 1920's something was different. There was a strong desire to reach for a better life and the *size of one's family* and *the hardship for women to birth a lot of children* was seen as the thing preventing a better life. In some family situations this might have been true but this longing for something else created the perfect timing for the evil one to use circumstances to get rid of and or prevent the offspring of a whole lot of Christians and Jews. Protestant and Jewish church authorities were sympathetic toward these ungodly atheist advisors who were pressuring Catholics, Protestants and Jews to usher in the *"permission to change church doctrine."*

1930, the Anglican Protestant church leaders "caved in" on their doctrine at their Lambeth Conference in England.

The Anglican-Episcopalians were the first Protestant denomination to change their doctrinal position on family planning. At about the same time, the Jews were also being pressured. The Central Council of American Rabbis[6] also voted to change their doctrinal stance on family planning, and in 1931 The Federal Council of Churches adopted a policy of accepting artificial birth control.

In 1930, the Anglican Church[7] ruled that birth control is acceptable in rare cases when the mother's life is at risk. This seemed a logical decision amidst the family struggles that were occurring. *(This is how humans view inconvenient truths; we try to weasel out of obedience because we have a good reason).*

Yet this initial ruling gave *permission* to change centuries of religious teaching that welcomed each *child as a gift* without parental control. Protestants crossed out scripture and headed down the destructive path toward viewing children as nothing more than *a parent's choice.*

If Protestants had stuck with the original narrow ruling and applied it only to extreme life-threatening situations (which is 1-2% of cases), the last several generations of believers would not have reaped the sorrows of abortion, infertility, reproductive cancers, 50% divorce rate, marital affairs and failed marriages that have resulted from the *mindset of choice.* (Families in the 1920's/1930's did not suffer these complications, instead nearly every family suffered financial problems due to hard economic times, but marriages and families stayed together).

> ****Note that permission to make a change was not given to God's people by God but by religious leaders who were heavily influenced and pressured by secular atheist ideals invading the church culture. These outsiders were people who did not know God, but evangelical church leaders listened to them and followed their advice!**

WHEN DID CONCEIVING CHILDREN BECOME OUR CHOICE?

Even before the Great Depression, a force was at work in society to alter Godly ideals. Researchers, scientists, doctors, and population control experts were beginning to support the revolution of contraceptive and sterilization methods to stop the growth of the global population and promote their own eugenic objectives.

These eugenic ideas originated somewhere. At the turn of the previous century, an English economist in the early 1800's, named Thomas Malthus wrote papers about overpopulation and the social economy. He was quite outspoken giving speeches about how abundance leads to overpopulation and overpopulation leads to not enough food sources. This vicious cycle does not solve problems. During those years England was overrun with itinerant poor, too many orphans, disease, crime, virtually a horrible existence for the lower classes and Malthus did not see how England could solve the problem of overpopulation unless they decreased it. Malthus theology created a foundation for debate on many ideas surrounding overpopulation and deficient food systems. Later his theories were debunked as soon as farmers found greater ways to grow food for the masses. Yet his ideas crossed the ocean to America and influenced Margaret Sanger who supported his theories and believed that sustainability cannot be achieved unless the world prevents overpopulation. Today much of what billionaire Bill Gates, owner of the Bill Gates Foundation, believes about overpopulation. His ideas to depopulate the earth stem from flawed Malthusian theories.

As early as 1893, the stage was set to change Christian doctrines in America. A secular paper called *The Nonconformist Weekly Journal*[8] in 1893 stated, *"There was a time when any idea of intervention was interfering with providence, but we are beyond that now and have become capable of recognizing that providence works through the commonsense of individual brains."* Articles such as this concluded that highly educated people understood the changes the world was going through and would use common sense. Couples should limit their offspring because more significant opportunities for advancement were on the horizon.

After the Anglican Episcopalians chose to allow for birth control, these same ideals of decreasing population size through eugenics and other Malthusian theories influenced other Protestant denominations to make similar changes in their theological interpretations of scripture. The word of God had not changed but as the culture slowly shifted from *a pro-child agenda* toward a *pro-choice agenda*, couples in all denominations were influenced. Couples everywhere began to make choices based on their increased desire for more time to pursue personal interests and more money to spend.

Over the next thirty years, 1930-1960, birth control use became *quietly acceptable* especially amongst the Protestants. People wanted it and used it. People wanted *choice in their bedrooms*, and this caused Jewish, Protestant and Catholic church goers to lose their *once unified agreement* on holiness in the bedroom. God's word had not changed but it was no longer being taught in the same way it once was. Not knowing what the Bible says about babies caused couples to walk away from the beauty, joy and blessing of the family clearly laid out in the Scriptures.

Although they claimed to be wise, they became fools (Romans 1:22).

Children were prevented through primitive contraceptives or were killed through primitive abortions. Birth numbers in families decreased, and the separation between Protestant, Jew, and Catholic became more apparent. Jewish and Protestant denominations sided with atheistic ideas in *society* and had smaller families, while a vast group of Roman Catholic Christians still obeyed the papal teachings and had larger families. These were the ones who *stood out* and by the time TV was invented, these families were often the brunt of late-night TV comedians joking about the Catholics.

The un-churched members of society did not know God, nor care what the Bible taught. Even though this was a very small percentage of the American people, this group used the influence of science, eugenics and the emerging media to influence those practicing religion. As the years passed and nearly ever Protestant denomination accepted the use of artificial contraceptives, society was ripe to enshrine the idea that *children are a personal choice* and not *a gift from God*. This was the continuous work of the enemy to get Godly people to stop reproducing children and the tug of war over *female rights vs. family size* became even more confusing than ever.

THE MAGICAL PILL

In 1960, nearly **65 years ago,** the FDA[9] (Food and Drug Administration) introduced *the birth control pill,* which is an artificial contraceptive, and they released it in 1960 on Mother's Day weekend, of all weekends as the pill's very existence was to curtail a female's ability to become a mother.

Having no idea how this pill might harm them, women greeted the idea with enthusiasm and surmised, *"Has this magical pill come down from Heaven just for ME?"*

After women began using *the pill,* things rapidly fell out of balance. Since the word of God was no longer anyone's authority on family size, the Protestant churches unquestionably accepted the *birth control pill. The secular world and the Protestant church world joined together* and embraced this miraculous new form of birth control, while completely ignoring 2 Corinthians 6:17 which says, *"Be ye separate!"*

Doctors told women *the new pill* was 99.99% effective in preventing pregnancy and could not *harm* a female's physical body. The birth control pill guaranteed to be easy, safe, and effective so women figured, *"Why not take it?"*

It was accepted *carte blanche'* by nearly everyone. No one questioned it. In my research, it sadly appears that few Protestant preachers or Protestant denominations spoke out against its use. It was as if God's people forgot whose people they were. Once the pill came on the scene, birth control use was completely separated out from everything else that was considered part of a Christian's Walk with God. It was quietly accepted amongst churchgoers, including Protestant pastors and their wives and many Catholic women. Everyone wanted it.

We all like sheep have gone astray, each of us has turned to our own way; and the LORD *has laid on Him the iniquity of us all (Isaiah 53:6).*

In 1960, when the birth control pill came out, believers accepted it so readily that couples acted as if GOD Himself invented it just for them!

Initially, women were not told any negatives; most doctors who prescribed it focused *only* on the benefits. However, as time went by, the negatives started to emerge. The pill had far too much estrogen and it could potentially damage a woman's reproductive health. But these negatives were not revealed at first. It took time for women to see how it harmed them and for doctors to admit what the pill really did in a females' body.

Yet in 1960, when the pill first came out:

A woman who didn't want more children could secretly take it and not tell her husband.

A man could have an affair, and if the other woman was on the pill, their chances of conceiving a child virtually disappeared.

A married couple could easily prevent the birth of more children, and outsiders would not question why.

People loved this! With this *new pill*, sex partners could have sex whenever they wanted but would not have to reap a child as the fruit of their sexual union. Couples rejoiced, *"How could anyone not want this wonderful new pill!"* Yet few realized the pain they might later suffer.

THERE IS A WAY THAT SEEMS RIGHT..FOR A SEASON

In the story of Jack and the Beanstalk, Jack was given some *magical beans*, and when planted, they grew into a giant beanstalk. Jack climbed the beanstalk and found a giant waiting at the top to destroy him. If Jack had known this, he probably would never have planted the beans.

This story seems to parallel the circumstances surrounding *the birth control pill*. People never seem to look at their choices long-term. Waiting for those who chose this *pill* was a huge giant. The consequences of waking the sleeping giant continued to be revealed. When *the pill* was released, people focused on having sex without the commitments and worries of pregnancy! No one focused on where its use might lead. However, this new attitude of sexual freedom affected every segment of society in some way and the media propaganda supporting it was intense.

The release of the *birth control pill* in 1960 opened *Pandora's box* and jump started the Sexual Revolution. The pill welcomed one-night stands, multiple sex partners, acceptance of a *free sex - free love* mentality while undergirding the newly launched pornographic empire of Playboy magazine.

WHEN DID CONCEIVING CHILDREN BECOME OUR CHOICE?

Hugh Heffner's Playboy[10] empire was launched in 1953, so the timing of the *birth control pill* was perfect and just what he needed to promote his idea of the playboy lifestyle: *leave your wife and have a new partner every night*. The pill seemed perfect!

It was also the primary component that *fueled 1969's Woodstock* and the *hippie lifestyle*, making it possible for the popularity of the phrase *make love-not war*, with the idea of *free love-free sex* and *no-commitments*. Yet choices do have consequences. The late 1960s saw a relentless rise in venereal[11] diseases, especially in the youth. This rise in venereal diseases had been slowly increasing since the 1950s but not at these high rates, yet people ignored the obvious connections. The agreements in the media and with education was just what the enemy needed to promote the idea that **sex was strictly for pleasure;** therefore, creating children could be dismissed from the act.

From the pulpits of America, Protestant church leaders should have fought back, rejecting the birth control pill and upholding God's plan for sex, as both pleasurable and procreative.

It *grieves me* to report that a lot of the church leaders accepted all forms of birth control and used it in their own marriages! By fully supporting the new pill, couples reinforced the idea that sex was no longer about *love, commitment* and *creating a new family member* together but was instead an act outside of this commitment and reserved strictly for personal pleasure. This is sad to report, but by their example, church leaders led parishioners into sin by supporting the cultural shift away from God's Plan.

They exchanged the truth about God for a lie and worshiped and served created things rather than the Creator, who is forever praised. (Romans 1:25).

They worshipped and served this new little pill and embraced the lie that the pill made it so that no one could ever get caught cheating in their marriage. What followed was God's judgement on church clergy. Over the next 65 plus years, numerous sex scandals emerged which severely impacted the church world. In the 1960s, 1970s, 1980s, 1990s and even into these first few decades of the new millennium, we've seen nothing but *sex scandals*[12] involving church clergy. Not all leaders compromised, but even one man falling into sexual sin is one too many. These situations have been devastating and sad for the victims, for the marriages that failed, and sad for the congregations involved. Deep sorrow has fallen on many a congregation whose minister fell into sexual sin.

At this point Americans have heard about nearly every kind of scenario; ministers who fell into sex scandals by leaving their spouse for their church secretary, pastors having affairs with women in their congregations, ministers involving themselves in pornography, youth ministers getting their teens pregnant and sometimes leaving their spouse for the young teen, clergy who were child molesters, male clergy who had affairs with other males and every other sort of sexual scandal. By not remaining holy in their bedrooms, the acceptance of birth control and a lifestyle of "sex is strictly for my pleasure" allowed God's hand of judgment to fall on church leadership and we have seen these unfortunate situations in both our Protestant and our Catholic churches.

Furthermore, just as they did not think it worthwhile to retain the knowledge of God, so God gave them over to a depraved mind, so that they do what ought not to be done (Romans 1:28).

All of us also lived among them at one time, gratifying the cravings of our flesh and following its desires and thoughts. Like the rest, we were by nature deserving of wrath (Ephesians 2:3).

> I believe the sins of sexual perversion will never leave Protestant church leadership *specifically* until there is repentance for the root sin of *not wanting children* which causes us to justify birth control and abortion, followed by repentance by Protestants for saying the Bible is silent on birth control *(therefore ignoring all the places where the Bible talks about God's desire for procreation)* and repentance for supporting and accepting artificial contraceptives.

I already stated it grieves me deeply that the above statement is true, but I could not find anywhere in my research where Protestant pastors *as a group* objected to the idea of the *new birth control pill or nearly every other kind of contraceptive*. As I've mentioned, a small minority of ministers spoke out against its use, but a handful of voices was not enough to collectively speak loud enough against the *hypnotic enticement* of the birth control pill. Even the most famous Protestant preacher of this era, Billy Graham, who was the father of five children himself, stayed away from the subject. Not one of his amazing sermons ever mentioned that using birth control was a form of sin. It was as if these followers eliminated this subject from Christendom.

WHEN DID CONCEIVING CHILDREN BECOME OUR CHOICE?

This 2022 article supports what I am sharing. *Protestants and the Pill: How US Christians helped make birth control mainstream.*[13] This article talks about how the Protestants compromised their theology by bringing in a doctrine of *responsible parenthood*. In the 1960s, clergy reframed the idea about family size, by encouraging couples to limit themselves to adding children they were positive they could *responsibly parent* and to avoid adding children they could not afford, nurture or educate. From this point forward Protestant couples in all denominations were taught *to be "responsible* Christians" with their family size. People argue that this is a good idea for parents to only birth children they can responsibly care for, but this is not the issue, it is a side note, life has no guarantees. A parent could parent one child poorly or ten children perfectly, family size became the victim of the secular push to depopulate the seed of Christians and Protestant clergy went along with this new idea and did not push back.

*My parents got married in 1960, and I asked my father why they only had three children since he was from a large Italian immigrant family with six children. My father said the Southern Baptist Sunday School material from the 1960s and 1970s pushed that parents must be responsible and not have more children than they could afford. My father also said couples were praised at church when they replaced themselves with a boy and a girl. This was supposedly a picture of being a responsible couple in the Southern Baptist world and lots of Baptist pastors and their wives had only two children. This was **serious propaganda** coming from this denomination! My parents had me, then my sister and they were done. My brother was their surprise child nine years later. My father told me at his church countless people questioned why my parents needed a third child, but since my brother was a boy that sort of got my dad off the hook from the criticism. Criticism? Congregants routinely kept each other in check in these areas even when it was none of their business how many children my parents had! Yet this is how it was and still is inside many of the Protestant churches even to this day!*

In 1961 the National Council of Churches[14] declared a *liberal birth control policy* based on a partners' mutual consent. There is no recorded disagreement from any mainline Protestant denomination. Catholic Popes fought back and stood against artificial contraceptives multiple times, but after the National Council of Churches gave permission to use it, Protestant couples used birth control however they wanted and by ignoring their church's doctrine, so did many Catholics.

Because of this, God gave them over to shameful lusts. Even their women exchanged natural sexual relations for unnatural ones (Romans 1:26).

Not only did women exchange their natural functions of giving birth and nurturing their young, but they exchanged their balanced body for a bunch of wacky hormones, PMS, harder menopause, unnecessary bleeding, weight gain, migraine headaches and other discomforts caused by artificial contraceptives, but they also opened the door to support sexual perversion!

Having lost all sensitivity, they have given themselves over to sensuality to indulge in every kind of impurity, and they are full of greed (Ephesians 4:19).

Lesbianism and homosexuality were practically nonexistent before 1960 and were later brought *out of the closet*. As the females began to embrace what was *unnatural*, the males also embraced each other. Then when the clergy *looked the other way*, it released sexual impurity on women and on our children! Look at the amount of sexual filth that is out there today. Compromise opened the door, just like in Biblical times when *everyone was doing what they thought was best in their own eyes* (Judges 17:6). People think they are pure. But it is only in their own eyes because they are not yet cleansed of their filth (Proverbs 30:12).

Within ten years of its release, the birth control pill was everywhere, and most every woman was using it, and many were paying the consequences by getting diseases in their reproductive organs. Countless women started to die of reproductive cancer and venereal disease complications!

Once evangelical couples accepted that a child is a choice and not a gift (1960), in the event of a birth control failure, one might assume an abortion might be necessary. The how, why, and when of birth control methods could be debated, but for the birth control user, abortion is simply a more violent form of preventing the unwanted child.

What began in 1930 with one Protestant denomination allowing for the use of contraceptives in extreme cases, eventually led to every mainline Protestant denomination supporting birth control in all its forms including artificial contraceptives and eventually the acceptance of abortion.

There is a way that appears to be right, but in the end, it leads to death (Proverbs 14:12).

WHEN DID CONCEIVING CHILDREN BECOME OUR CHOICE?

Silence led to abortion becoming legal in 1973 without a fight from the Protestants! A lot of Protestants were on the side of a woman's right to choose abortion!

Therefore, God gave them over in the sinful desires of their hearts to sexual impurity for the degrading of their bodies with one another (Romans 1:24).

Why should Protestants fight against it? **Abortion is needed when birth control fails!**

Theologians and ministers who did support birth control fell down a very slippery slope. If a couple uses a good contraceptive, they will not need an abortion because their contraceptive method will either prevent fertilization of their seed or disturb the implantation of their newly conceived child. But what would they do if their method failed?

THE COMPLETE BREAKDOWN OF THE FAMILY

Starting in 1961, an entire generation embraced an attitude against abundantly birthing children...as in the days of Noah ***...every man did what was right in his own eyes...*** (Judges 17:6). By the mid-1970s, the only denominations who were still teaching any scripturally accurate view about family planning were the Amish, Reformed Presbyterians, Orthodox Jews, Roman Catholics, the Mormons and a handful of various Protestant congregations where the pastor held to his own personal conviction. That's it!

ALL mainline Protestant denominations stood against the command to *be fruitful and multiply* and said *children as a gift* does not apply to contemporary generations. Instead, *children are a "choice"* which should be limited. Accepting *the birth control pill and artificial contraceptives as their 'god"* the Protestants led the people of God into generations of physical and emotional suffering, into agreement with abortion and eventually embraced the mutualization of their sex organs through sterilization.

After 1961 we saw the total breakdown of the family:

Mothers and fathers divorced and fought over children. The divorce rate[15] doubled! In 1960 it was 9% but by 1980 the divorce rate soared to 50%!

Children were forced to blend into families where they didn't want to be while at the same time losing meaningful sibling relationships.

Incest began when stepfathers and stepbrothers came after young stepfemales in their newly blended families.

100% increase in pornography meant sex was strictly for pleasure and not for making babies together.

Venereal disease rates escalated from casual sex with multiple partners.

Previously unheard-of **reproductive cancers** climbed to epidemic proportions.

Women suffered physically from the effects of the pill's hormones: infertility, miscarriages, breast cancer, hysterectomies and tubal ligations emerged.

Men suffered after vasectomies with prostate cancer, impotence, painful erections and autoimmune diseases.

Some even lost their lives due to their choices in the bedroom.

Do you think people were happier with this newfound freedom? NO!!

When the people of God embraced the *birth control pill* lifestyle, they all suffered. **Even wedding vows changed.** Up until this time couples vowed to *live together in holy matrimony, to love, honor and cherish and to be fruitful and multiply according to God's holy command.* Couples in mainline Protestant denominations used to promise this in their wedding vows! They promised God they would create a family together, but that part became *optional* after the pill and the sexual revolution. The mention of creating one's family has now been removed from most all traditional Protestant wedding vows and instead couples promise to love, honor and cherish each other until death they do part, but often unless their minister advises adding into their vows something about creating a family together, millions of Protestant couples no longer pledge in their wedding vows to create a family together. *Seriously?* The acceptance of birth control broke the family unit completely apart and this is one more example where the Protestant ministers assisted the enemy in his plan to greatly limiting the offspring of God's people.

In the 1960s the *birth control pill* was supposed to make having sex *easy and carefree*, but instead because the pill was too high in hormones, lots of females hemorrhaged and often bled for long periods of time. *This was no fun for the marriage when sex was neither easy nor carefree because your wife feels horrible and has a period for months that never stops!* Marriages were destroyed. The pill also caused and still causes emotional tension and emotional separations. Couples did not understand what was happening to their relationships, instead one day, they no longer felt *in love* with their spouse the way they once did. Couples were not told to *get off the pill* because its hormones made the female lose *her spark and sexual desire* due to how its hormones affected her physical, mental, and emotional health. Couples were not being told and are still not told the pill is what is ruining their sex life.

The wise woman builds her house, but with her own hands the foolish one tears hers down (Proverbs 14:1).

I remember the late 1960s and the things that were happening to families! When I was small, the moms and dads of all my friends seemed to be happy, but in 1968 when I was in first grade, I noticed some things were changing. From this point on, I saw sadness. I would be at school and a student in my class would disappear and the teacher would tell us the student would no longer be in our class. Then we would hear their parents got a divorce and the family had to move. I can remember this happening repeatedly to multiple classmates.

Then in third grade my favorite classmate was in her bedroom when she heard her parents shouting. Her dad came home and told her mom he did not love her anymore and was leaving her mom for a close family friend. This other woman was also leaving her husband for my friend's father! She had two children herself. (It was a mess!) My classmate's father packed his bags that night and walked out. Her mom was devastated. She was left with a family to support, no job, and no money in her name. It was so sad. My friend's family had one of the nicest houses in our neighborhood, and she had the prettiest bedroom. Her mother tried to reconcile but her dad refused. Eventually her father stopped paying the mortgage, and soon her mom had to move to an apartment. We visited. All her mom could afford was a dreary one-bedroom apartment in a not very nice area. She and her two siblings were crammed into one small room and her mom was sleeping in the living room on the couch. Their grandma helped watch her and her siblings after school, but this small apartment was all her mom could afford. She barely made enough money for them to live. I was only in third grade at the time, so it all did not make sense to me until I got older and realized why the situation was what it was. Years after my mom told me our church helped her mother get back on her feet again, but as a third grader trying to understand, I remember I lost my friend. It was indeed a horrible situation and one that was repeated across the country for many other women and children.

Seemingly overnight the culture shifted from *sex is for marriage so we can have children*, to *sex is for pleasure so let's have an affair*. Once it grabbed a hold of people's minds, scenes like I am describing were repeated in families across the USA! These situations were not the exceptions but were the "norm" for quite a few families. When a man *walked out on his family*-he literally left his wife with nothing! Most women in the 1960s were stay-at-home wives and had never been in the workforce. Families walked through unheard-of-situations and Family Laws in the court system were not yet in effect to help these females whose husbands left them for other women. Until laws were passed against *abandonment*, mothers and children suffered tremendous emotional and financial stress. Yet no one talks about how the emergence of the birth control pill ruined the family forever. But I am old enough to remember the way things were before; when mothers, fathers and families were happy, and the divorce rate was practically zero!

The birth control pill insanity grabbed a hold of society so rapidly that churches had to adjust to keep up. *In 1968, in the Baptist Church I grew up in, which was one of the most well-known and largest Baptist churches in the entire D.C. area. An unmarried woman came to our church who wanted to join the choir. She was recently divorced and was the mother of three small boys. My father was one of the deacons. The deacons had to call an emergency meeting to discuss this mother's situation because they didn't know what to do. This woman's husband had an affair and divorced her. Our church had never had a divorced person ask to be in the choir before! Divorces were extremely rare. The men searched the scriptures to try and figure out what to do. You might be laughing but this is a true story! Divorce was so far removed from the church world that people were not divorced, ever! After searching scripture and interviewing the mother, they did eventually let her join the choir even though she was divorced but only because her husband left her and not the other way around.* I know this sounds silly by today's standards, but things were very different sixty-five years ago. I must say it was great for children when no one's parents divorced.

Don't let anyone deceive you about history! Before the birth control pill came on the scene nearly every couple got married and stayed married including people in other cultures, countries and ethnicities. People stayed together for life. Couples rarely divorced and people only remarried if their spouse had died. Also, there was a very small amount of illicit sex, that was reserved for immoral people. Up until the late 1960s and early 1970s most American families attended church somewhere. In America, most everyone believed in God. On the street where I grew up in suburban Maryland, every single family went to church, and they went every Sunday. The two Jewish families on our street attended synagogue every Saturday. All the stores were closed on Sundays and families spent time together. This was how it was before sexual freedom contributed to tearing apart the family.

GOD HAS A REASON FOR YOUR OFFSPRING

The scriptures tell us that Lucifer took one-third of the angels (33%) with him when he was cast down from Heaven. Later, when Adam and Eve were created, Satan defeated them in the Garden when he tricked them, and they fell into sin. God was sad humans chose a life of sin, but in their downfall, God had a plan in place that would help humans *fight back* against this evil enemy. In Genesis 3:15, God told Satan, *"A human seed will crush you!* meaning through the birth of one, Jesus Christ, man would be redeemed but God also said there would be enmity between Eve's offspring and Satan. God warned Satan he would eventually be doomed. God knew this because he had already given humanity a very powerful gift. *(Satan probably did not understand what God had planned because Adam and Eve had never been together sexually, Genesis 4:1).*

When God created Adam from the dust of the earth, the Scriptures say *He breathed life* into Adam, and he became a living thing. Later he created Eve from Adam's rib. From that point onward God did something so incredible, He gave His gift of life to Adam who was merely a created being! **Think how powerful this is!** Think what incredible love this is! A created being, from the dust of the ground, was now being able to give to another created being the same gift of life that God alone could give! Dwell on this point a second, the gift of life stands outside of humans. It is supernatural and we have this ability to give life to another each time we make love on a fertile day.
With this supernatural gift, humans have been given a **super-power!**
We can now do something Satan cannot do!
We can REPRODUCE ourselves!

Plus, we can also pass this gift of life onto our offspring so they can also duplicate themselves! **Satan was not planning for humans to be able to defeat him this way.**

Our supernatural gift is *very important* because Satan cannot reproduce himself.

God limited Satan's power.
Satan cannot make more demons.
He cannot make more of anything.

He can get men and women to follow him, but he cannot procreate. Only humans possess *the gift of life* and the incredible *gift of creation!*

Humans giving life to one another is supernatural. Homosexual people cannot do this! They cannot produce anything supernatural from their union. God reserved this gift of supernatural creation only for heterosexual couples. This is why marriage is the state of "holy" matrimony. God is "holy" and unprotected sex between a man and his wife is also "holy." When their intercourse forms a new life, it is a supernatural act declaring the holiness of the union between God and man.

Do you understand now why the enemy hates procreative sex so much?

Only humans bring life to this earth, and it is to make more people who can love God and love others. Love is pure and beautiful and an extremely valuable power to have. The Bible states that *the weapons of our warfare are not carnal but are powerful in pulling down spiritual strongholds! (2 Corinthians 10:4)*. God gave men, women, their children and their future heirs the gift of reproduction. This way, Godly people and their heirs can stop the mean things the enemy does to harm people on the earth. However, bad people could use their families to harm others but in the end good always overcomes evil. This is how God set things up.

Good people can bless and replenish the earth through duplicating their family seed of goodness!

Each one of our heirs is eternal and can shake eternity with our family seed! The reason God gave us this gift is echoed in Malachi 2:15, *"Didn't the Lord make you one with your wife? In body and spirit, you are His. And what does God want? Godly children from your union, so guard your heart; remain loyal to the wife of your youth."*

Throughout history, the enemy's goal has been to *eliminate people.*

Catch this! He has successfully killed people through wars, murder, disease, and in the twentieth and twenty first centuries his most important strategy is **preventing people** from reproducing families! The last several generations of parents have used birth control and prevented the conception of billions of their offspring. At the same time these generations also aborted 60,000,000 million[16] of their own flesh and blood!

The Baby Boom generation ushered in this sin! *"The number of children I have are my personal choice and it is none of God's business!"* On a mass scale they prevented their children from conception but if accidentally conceived, they eliminated their unwanted children through abortion. It was the mother's *choice*. Now the Baby Boomer's fertile years are over, but these issues are not settled!

God calls *a new generation* to repent for their parents' sins and return to the Lord's plan. This is the reason for this book, global Holy Spirit led repentance.

Yet before a new generation can correct their parents and grandparent's mistakes, you need to know the history. Most people only know the lies they have been told about family planning and don't even know there is a history. I didn't know about it. I thought birth control was a modern phenomenon. My research found that birth control is as old as the first peoples and both birth control and abortion have been practiced throughout the ages, yet more often than not, people of faith resisted the cultural influences around them, and we have plenty of examples from the Scriptures to prove this.

This brief history will help you understand how God's people became entangled with this huge idol of birth control.

Have you ever heard a Sunday sermon on birth control at a Protestant church? I know in the 60+ years I've attended church I never heard one. In recent years a few Protestant pastors have posted pro-birth control using videos on You-tube where the subject is discussed but overall, contraceptive use is not Sunday morning sermon material. I do know there are a few Catholic priests who will preach Sunday morning sermons against artificial contraceptives because I have had girlfriends share with me what they heard at church, but these same ladies have told me it is a rare sermon. I do know a handful of Presbyterians who have told me their pastor has at least once spoken against birth control and I do believe across America there are a few Baptists, Amish, Reformed Presbyterian and possibly other denominal or non-denominational pastors who might preach the truth, but hearing a Sunday sermon on this topic is still extremely rare. Overall, even though the vast majority of people sitting in the pews are families raising children, most Catholics and Protestants and other sects of non-denominational members *are not being educated* by their clergy about this topic.

I believe once we know the history, we can understand where people of faith went wrong and can understand how Christians arrived at where they are today. We also need to look at how God's people have responded throughout history when the family planning practices of those surrounding them differed from what is taught in the Scriptures.

FROM THE BEGINNING, HUMANS WANTED BIRTH CONTROL

The first commandment was, *be fruitful and multiply.*

The first sin was eating a forbidden fruit.

The first disease was not being able to have a baby!

Isn't this interesting? The first plague that disturbed humanity was the *sorrow* of not being able to create a new human. I don't think this is a coincidence. *Barrenness* was considered the greatest curse and worst thing that could ever happen to a female and is still quite sad even to this day.

Genesis 16:1 The **first disease** mentioned in the Bible **is barrenness** *(the state of being unfruitful). (Have you ever heard this in a Sunday Sermon?)*

Within the first 22 chapters of the Bible, God examines the sin of not desiring to pro-create. Death resulted.

Genesis 38 The story of Onan and the withdrawal method. As previously stated, scripture proves that man attempted to use birth control in ancient times. Genesis 38 tells the story of Onan. We know nothing about Onan except one thing. His brother died and he was supposed to impregnate his brother's wife. This was the custom to help continue a family's seed on earth. But Onan did not want his brother to have heirs so when he had sex with the wife of his deceased brother, he practiced *coitus interruptus (known as the withdrawal method)*, and he pulled out of her and ejaculated his seed on the ground. The Lord was not pleased with Onan's actions, and God killed him! *Coitus Interruptus* has been practiced since ancient times and is still practiced to this day. There is evidence that this method has been and is the most common pre-medical form of birth control. Throughout history, it was practiced in Africa, Australia, Asia, the Middle East, and Medieval Europe where the Catholic Church spoke against it. In modern times, Pope Paul VI in his 1968 papal encyclical *Human Vitae* spoke against the sin of wasting a man's seed. This sin is often called Onanism and is still considered a sin by the Catholic church to this day.

Protestants who want to use birth control and are looking for a Biblical excuse say this story has nothing to do with the sin of spilling one's seed. I beg to differ. In the Scriptures, God calls Onan's actions wicked (Genesis 38:10). The only thing we know about Onan is that he spilled his seed to avoid pregnancy. God killed Onan for the only wicked act we know about. How much more obvious can a Bible story be?

Deuteronomy 23:1 Ancient Sterilization/Castration. Castration is the earliest form of sterilization, dating back to Ancient Samaria. Since primitive times men have suffered from the torture of male castration, which is the violent removal of the male testes. Once the man's testicles were removed, he would be sterile and could not impregnate a woman. On occasion, extreme castration was performed, including removing a male's entire reproductive organs, including most of his penis. This was usually extremely life-threatening, and often the man died from blood loss or infection. Castration was often used as a vicious form of humiliation toward defeated foes so that the victors could sexually rule over their women. According to the Old Testament, when a man's testicles had been mutilated or castrated, he could not become a priest or even enter the temple! Eunuchs were mentioned in both the Old and New Testaments. In the book of Esther, the king's eunuch helped Esther find favor with the king and in Acts 8, Philip baptized an Ethiopian eunuch.

> ** Birth control was attempted throughout history. Women have been advised to try various techniques, oral potions, and vaginal substances. They've been told that to prevent pregnancy, they should sneeze to expel sperm, drink cold water, and avoid orgasm.

Ancient Egyptian[17] evidence found by archaeologists indicates that primitive man tried to stop the process of procreation. Papyrus texts from ancient Egypt dating back to 1850 B.C. indicate that upper-class women put various substances into their vaginas to block or kill sperm. These included crocodile dung pessaries, plant gums mixed with sodium bicarbonate; and a mixture of ground dates, honey, and acacia tree bark ground into a paste and dipped in a lint tampon made from seed wool. These unusual mixtures had scientific properties. When fermented, acacia becomes lactic acid, a well-known ingredient in spermicide. Crocodile dung-poop *(later elephant dung was used)* is slightly acidic, like modern-day spermicides. Egyptians also discovered the herb vitex *(chasteberry root)*.[18] Small doses helped strengthen a female's menstrual cycle to promote pregnancy. Yet once pregnant, if the female did not wean herself properly off the herb she could suffer a spontaneous abortion. Throughout the ancient world, those seeking abortions often experimented with higher doses of this herb. To this day, chasteberry is used to help females become pregnant and rarely used to bring on an abortion.

Exodus 1:12, the Bible is clear the Israelites were not engaging in these practices. Exodus 1:12 tells us that God was increasing their numbers. The more the Egyptians oppressed them with slavery, the more their number of children increased! Some might say, *but this is still not proof they were not using birth control*. Okay, let's consider the facts. They were slaves. Birth control could not be purchased down at the corner market so how would a slave get it? Creating a papyrus sheath to place over the penis would be tedious and time consuming and costly. A random slave might have had the job of helping an Egyptian with this process but then being able to get their hands on one of these ancient condoms might have presented consequences. I am sure they were in hot demand for the Egyptians over giving one to a slave. The other method of harvesting crocodile feces to then insert into one's vagina had to also be risky, so how would a mass number of slaves get their hands on this substance? The Israelite's were birthing children into the millions, their high birth numbers clearly indicate they were not using birth control, but the birth rate of the Egyptians was slower than the Hebrews. It is obvious to see who was using birth control in ancient Egypt and who wasn't. *(Have you ever heard a Sunday sermon at your Protestant church on this obvious example?)*

Infanticide has been practiced since ancient times to deal with children no one wanted. It is the method the Ancient Egyptians used against the Hebrews during the time of Moses. Pharaoh feared a military uprising and feared a rumored deliverer had been born. Pharaoh didn't order all the slaves to be put on birth control, instead he ordered the midwives to kill every male newborn baby. He also sent soldiers to kill every child three years old and under. Later during the time of Jesus, King Herod feared a Hebrew savior had been born, and the king ordered male infants to be killed. Herod and Pharaoh ordered infanticide to kill the male babies.

In ancient times, sacrificing babies to idols, such as Baal and Molech, took the lives of countless infants. *You took your sons and daughters whom you had borne to Me and sacrificed them to idols to be devoured (Ezekial 16:20).*

Throughout the ages church leaders spoke out against such practices!

Tertullian,[19] a famous second-century Catholic, said, *"It does not matter whether you take away a life that is born or destroy one that is coming to the birth. In both instances, the destruction is murder."*

Sixteenth-century Protestant reformer John Calvin[20] said, *"The fetus, though enclosed in the womb of its mother, is already a human being, and it is a monstrous crime to rob it of its life, which it has not yet begun to enjoy."*

Infanticide is still practiced today in third-world countries and now in America with post-abortive death to babies who survive abortions. Abortion through the ninth month is also considered a form of infanticide. I am sad to report this is now practiced in America. Infants who survive an abortion are left to die in nineteen U.S. states who practice this form of infanticide:[21] Alaska, Oregon, Idaho, Hawaii, Ohio, Vermont, Colorado, New Mexico, New York, New Hampshire, North Carolina, Nevada, Utah, West Virginia, Kentucky, Minnesota, Michigan, Maryland, Connecticut. These states allow a perfectly healthy baby to die after a failed abortion. During the 1970s, 1980s, China killed an entire generation of females so they could build up their male army only to find by the 2000's, a severe shortage of females.[22] China's population is now decreasing due to this practice.

Breastfeeding: a natural method of birth control (Exodus 2:7). Full-time breastfeeding causes the woman's body to put off regular ovulation for a season to delay a repeat pregnancy soon after the delivery of a baby. This is called *natural spacing*. Breastfeeding was more common amongst the lower classes but for the upper-class women, depending on the time of history and the specific culture, it was not uncommon for an upper-class woman to give her baby over to a *wet nurse* to breastfeed the baby. We see this happening in the story of Moses in Exodus

2:7, where Pharaoh's daughter hires Moses's mother to nurse him. Since upper-class women in history tended to breastfeed less often, this may be one reason upper-class women resorted to risky, life-threatening methods of birth control. God provided *breastfeeding to be a natural form of birth control* and has been used in multiple cultures to help with natural spacing, but when rejected, women put themselves in the position where birth control might be desired.

Ancient Greeks experimented with birth control, as did the Egyptians. They used juniper berries on the penis, which was said to provide temporary sterility. They also placed cedar oil on the cervix's tip and ointments of lead or frankincense mixed with olive oil into the vagina to prevent sperm from surviving. Hippocratic texts advised women to drink copper in various forms to avoid pregnancy. Upper-class Greek women even used rolls of wool as a type of diaphragm.

Greek Philosopher Aristotle[23] held a 20th century eugenics mindset that abortion and infanticide were acceptable and necessary when a child was born deformed and would become a burden upon the welfare of the state. He also believed abortion was advisable when a family exceeded the number of children desired. *(Plato held similar views).*

630 B.C. Silphium Birth Control Plant,[24] also known as laser wort, was grown in Cyrene and was highly traded in Europe, Africa, and Asia. It was a natural abortifacient. Monthly, women drank this herbal juice to prevent pregnancy and to abort any newly conceived baby. The plant refused to grow outside of the Mediterranean climate and eventually was over-harvested and became extinct.

Ancient Romans[25] during the time of Christ, actively practiced birth control. Roman women used sea sponges soaked in lemon juice or vinegar. The acid acted as an effective spermicidal but did sting a bit, *"Ouch!"* Roman women also used barrier methods like traditional beeswax and positioned it in the vagina. These methods proved very effective and caused even Caesar Augustus to be worried about Rome's declining birthrate. He passed laws banning contraceptives and offered incentives for parents of three or more children. *(Sounds a bit familiar- the exact thing is happening in modern-day Italy!)*

God's people were obviously not engaging in modern birth control customs. Paul and Timothy advised women to stay home and be the caretakers of their homes, raising Godly children (Titus 2:4, 5; 1 Timothy 5:14). Paul further advised couples to not deprive each other of sexual relations except for a time of rest for prayer and fasting (1 Corinthians 7:5). Their advice coincides with the Old Testament principle *to be fruitful and multiply* and in Malachi 2:15 *to produce Godly offspring*. We have no evidence of God's people as a global group engaging in the use of birth control anywhere throughout history until the early twentieth century when teaching on the subject ceased.

After Rome fell, attempts to control birth continued. Ancient texts from India[26] recommended salt-water douches and eating carrot seeds. Islamic doctors of the fourteenth century advised using rock salt, tar, onion juice, and balsam oil on the penis; or tampons mixed with pomegranate pulp for women. Lemon juice has also been widely used in many cultures because of its acidic properties. Women also used elephant excrement for a pessary and neem oil. Four thousand years ago, Chinese women were encouraged to drink mercury. *(A bit deadly, don't you think?).*

Canadian women in New Brunswick, Canada,[27] were said to have drunk a brew of beaver testicles. These methods were unsafe, and women often suffered severe illness or death. Coastal women have been said to dip sea sponges in lemon juice at various times and place them inside the vagina as a sort of contraceptive sponge. African women used plugs of chopped grass or cloth. Balls of bamboo tissue paper were used by Japanese prostitutes, wool by Islamic and Greek women, and linen rags by Slavic women. A sea silk sponge wrapped in silk with a string attached was the most effective contraceptive until the modern diaphragm was developed.

1700's—Native Americans[28] used various herbs to prevent pregnancy, black cohosh, blue cohosh, thistles, stone seed, false hellebore, Indian paintbrush. Some worked, some made the woman very sick, and some caused death.

1776–1900s—America was founded on Godly principles and a firm commitment to follow God's ways. The pilgrims and other religious founders were trying to ensure that any form of birth control did not invade American culture, influenced by the unreligious who wanted to bring in apparatus and engage in unscriptural family planning practices. Eventually laws were passed to prevent the importing of birth control devices from other countries and cultures.

Throughout the ages, people have used various forms of condoms

CONDOMS: evidence from Ancient Egypt[29] has shown that condoms were used as male sheaths and were made of animal intestines and papyrus reeds, even Pharaoh Tutankhamun *(King Tut)* wore various sheaths. Archaeological excavations show many drawings and documented findings of males wearing sheaths. Even the Egyptian god Bes has been depicted wearing the birth control sheath in statuettes. Upper-class women in first-century Rome are believed to have used a goat's bladder as a condom or diaphragm.

Egypt 1550 B.C. —Egyptian manuscript directed women how to mix dates, acacia and honey into a paste, smear it over a man's wool sheath to use it as a spermicide to prevent conception.

In 1504—the invention of the linen condom by Italian inventor Fallopius[30]—to prevent the spread of syphilis—came about. He sewed strips of linen together to fit over the tip of the penis and held it in place with the foreskin and tied it with a pink string. These early condoms were often nicknamed *overcoats*.

1734—Giacomo Casanova[31] first invented condoms made of lamb intestine, and half a lemon inserted into the vagina as a makeshift cervical cap. Referring to a man as being a *"Casanova"* or a man who *"had a way with women"* were phrases originating from this man's inventions which increased sexual pleasure and prevented conceptions.

1840—*Condoms* didn't come to America until 1840, when Charles Goodyear[32] patented the vulcanization of rubber. He also invented condoms known as *rubbers*. Rubber condoms were mass-produced but were not quickly thrown away. They were washed, covered in petroleum jelly, and stored for later reuse. Early condoms became available in 1880 but were not used widely in America until the mid-1930s after the Protestant church began to allow the use of contraceptives.

1870s—Japanese men[33] wore a hard condom made from tortoise shells, horns, and leather. Japanese women used balls of bamboo tissue paper as diaphragms. Tribal women in Africa used seed pods as a female condom and plugs of chopped seed or grass as diaphragms.

ABORTION is an ancient practice.

Women have attempted to abort their children since ancient times. Women were told to drink potions made of herbs.[34] The Germans used marjoram, thyme, parsley, and lavender teas. During the time of Nero, a

Greek physician used the root of a worm fern. In France, the worm fern became known as the *prostitute root*. To kill their children, primitive women have tried using pastes of mashed ants, foam from camels' mouths, and the tail hairs of blacktail deer dissolved in bear fat. Eighth-century women tried sitting over a pot of hot steamed onions, hoping the aroma would somehow have an abortive effect. As people progressed, modern women have also tried elaborate concoctions such as turpentine, castor oil, tansy tea, horseradish, ginger, Epsom salts, ammonia, mustard, gin with iron filings, rosemary, lavender, opium, and quinine water in which a rusty nail has been soaked and even drinking Lysol disinfectant or douching with it at an attempt to kill the developing baby.

Throughout history abortions were subject to the theory of *quickening*.[35]

1755-1750 BC Hammurabi's Code[36] **(early law), people refused to believe that a child was viable at conception.** People lacked modern technology to prove that life begins at conception. The theory of *quickening* became the rule for whether a baby was murdered during an abortion. Before the moment when a woman felt her baby's first kick, this became the acceptable timeframe for the beginning of life. If a woman suspected pregnancy and tried to cause a miscarriage before quickening, she was not seen as murdering her baby. Even though God's word spoke out about life beginning at conception (Psalm 139:13-15; Jeremiah 1:5; Luke 1:39), without technology to prove that life begins at conception, abortions occurred and were justified. Isn't it interesting how people can always justify a reason for sin? Different gestational time frames were debated. Most women feel their babies first movement at or around 16-18 weeks (about 4-4.5 months gestation).

100-150 A.D. The Didache[37] **or the Teaching of the Twelve Apostles** forbade all abortions from conception. *"You shall not kill by abortion the fruit of the womb and you shall not murder the infant already born."*

175 A.D. Tertullian of Carthage [37a] The fetus in the womb is already a human being, and abortion is akin to homicide.

380 A.D. St. Augustine of Hippo[38] accepted the Greek Aristotelian theory that a human soul could not live in an unformed body. This theory was called *delayed ensoulment,* meaning that life began when the baby's soul joined its body at quickening (4.5 months gestation). He forbade abortion, *"those who marry out to align their desires and passions with God's intent for marriage"* the propagation of children. He believed killing the child in the womb or infanticide is sin.

1190 Rabbi Moses ben Maimonides[38a], a Jewish Philosopher living in Egypt, put together a compilation of Jewish Law called *Mishnah Torah*. He upheld the concept of *quickening* and believed abortion after quickening was *morally problematic*.

1116-1216 Pope Innocent[39] stated that the soul enters the baby at the time of quickening when the woman can feel the baby moving. He also stated that before quickening, abortions were acceptable.

1591 Pope Gregory XIV[40] revoked a previous Papal bull and reinstated that quickening was 116 days into pregnancy or about 16 weeks.

1600s-1900s Abortion was occurring in America, as verified by correspondence in women's diaries. It was unregulated and was not considered a sin when a woman could relieve herself of the pregnancy before quickening *(16 weeks)*. Abortion was not considered manslaughter in America until Congress enacted laws.

1798-Thomas Malthus 18th century scholar, wrote "Essay on The Principle of Population"[40a] in which he argued the world would run out of resources and that global population must be curtailed, starting with Europe by integrating birth control, delayed marriage, celibacy and advocating for smaller families. He was an early proponent of abortion at any stage.

1869 Pope Pius IX[41] stated that the soul entered the pre-embryo at conception.

1884 Pope Leo XIII[42] issued a decree against craniotomies, which is what we now call *partial-birth* abortion. **1886 Pope Leo XIII**[43] issued another decree against any abortion procedures that would directly kill the baby, even to save the life of the mother. He excommunicated people for abortion.

1800-1830, 1850-1880 Abortion and the Great Spiritual Awakening[44] **in America.** Citizens continuously re-evaluated moral issues as people again desired to uphold God's laws of scripture. They wanted to stop allowing degrading behaviors to deteriorate society. Murdering infants was one of those behaviors. The ungodly and non-religious minority wanted to popularize the idea of birth control and abortion. Congress was called upon to debate the issues and pass legislation banning abortion.

1857 The American Medical Association[45] produced a report attacking the quickening distinction and urging that abortion be a crime at all stages of pregnancy.

1860-1899 Most states adopted abortion statutes that made inducing an abortion any time after conception a crime.

In 1873, Anthony Comstock[46] successfully passed a law through the American Congress that defined contraceptive information as obscene. Congress and the entire country were unwilling to compromise God's principles. (*Look how far we have come: 2020's - Protestant pastors give birth control and sterilization information out to their parishioners!*) After 1873, advertising birth control devices in the newspaper or passing out literature discussing birth control choices became a criminal offense. The new legislation stated that *"the moment of conception was the beginning of life, and therefore the baby's life began at conception, and nothing should interfere with that purpose."* These new abortion laws and the Comstock Laws supported morality in America. My research indicates that pro-abortion advocate groups today claim that Congress passed pro-life laws like the Comstock Laws because the government encouraged population growth. America was booming economically and financially, they needed workers for farms and factories, but to get the workers, they were importing Western European immigrants by the millions. The pro-choice movement dismisses the fact that a God-fearing Congress cared about social morality and the killing of innocent life through abortion and viewed abortion as an indication of the moral degradation of American society.

In the background of these new reforms against the use of birth control and abortion, the *powers that be* in society were moving forward to redefine and reshape the views of the very conservative and religious *general* public. Overseas inventors wasted no time continuing to try and correct the "fertility problem" that God gave to humankind.

1879 Margaret Sanger[47] **was born in New York.** Margaret became the largest proponent of birth control in the twentieth century. She was a friend of Adolph Hitler and influenced religious leaders in Europe and later in the United States. She was heavily involved in politics to get laws passed so that birth control could be allowed. She was a proponent of abortion as a mother's ultimate control of her womb. Maragret started Planned Parenthood which became the largest provider of abortion in America. Margaret has the blood of millions of aborted babies on her hands.

1883 British scientist, Francis Galton,[48] created the science of eugenics which proposed that human perfection could be achieved through selective breeding. This would be accomplished in two ways. First to encourage birthing children to the *fit classes (rich and white, Germanic, English, Austrian, Swiss)* which were those in *the upper echelons of society*. At this time, the people groups that were considered *undesirable* and *unfit* were from Western Europe *(Italians, Greeks, Jews)* and later the brown and black races, virtually any race that was not white and of superior intellect. Eugenics advocates were to encourage white people to birth more children and to discourage black and brown people from bearing more of their kind, thus the foundation for Hitler's all white Germanic society. Eugenic science is evil.

1844-1873—A growing unregulated contraceptive industry flourished in the United States. Not only were rubber condoms being used, but various other devices were invented and used for experimentation. A form of the *cervical cap* was invented and called a womb veil. A cap used for only the tip of the penis was invented, known as a male cap. Douching and vaginal syringes were also invented, which were supposed to kill sperm on contact and prevent pregnancies, but few people knew about these inventions.

In the early 1880s, a poor New York City man named Julius Schmid[49] took extra sausage casings from butcher shops and made them into thick condoms. By 1890 it became a big business, so by the 1930s, his condom empire made him millions of dollars. Two of his brands, Ramses and Sheik, are still popular.

1880s-1900s—The Victorians[50] were said to have invented a wooden block with a carved-out dome on one edge which women would insert into the vagina as a diaphragm; it was later outlawed because it was said to be an instrument of torture.

1898 British playwright George Bernard Shaw[51] called the rubber condom the *"greatest invention of the nineteenth century."*

1898 Margaret Sanger's mother, Anna Higgens[52] died. Margaret Sanger's mother was a devout Roman Catholic who died at age 50 after 18 pregnancies and 11 live births. Her daughter Margaret was angry about her mother dying before her time and believed multiple pregnancies were the reason for her mother's ill health. She vowed to save women from the same *demise*. Margaret became a nurse to influence the medical establishment to adopt her beliefs and eventually Margaret was responsible for the deaths of more babies than any other woman in history, as the killings of babies in the womb come from her Planned Parenthood organization and continues to this day. If Margaret's mother were alive today, she probably would not have had 11 births and 18 pregnancies because Planned Parenthood could have stopped her. Then she might not have had Margaret. Margaret Sanger was her mother's sixth live birth. If her mother did what Sanger convinced millions of other moms to do, then Margaret Sanger *(live child #6)* would have never been conceived or born! Her mother would have either used birth control to prevent Margaret's conception or her mother might have killed Margaret by abortion.

In the early 1900s, before Margaret set up shop in New York City, President Teddy Roosevelt[53] *(the father of six children)* attacked birth control use and saw the trend toward smaller families as a *moral disease* and a breakdown of the institution of the family.

1906 President Roosevelt wrote a response letter to a Nebraska minister advocating for America to look to the French people who were limiting family size and decreasing the French population. President Roosevelt wrote the minister back and stated, *"to advocate for artificially keeping families small, with its inevitable attendants of prenatal infanticide (abortion), with its pandering to self-indulgence, its shirking of duties, and its innervation of character, is quite as immoral as to advocate theft or prostitution, and is even more hurtful in its folly, from the standpoint of the ultimate welfare of the race and the nation."* Roosevelt viewed the choice of a parent to limit family size as being equal to being a thief or a prostitute.

Roosevelt went on to say, *"the average child from a large family, in his experience was much better equipped than a child from a family of only one or two children where the cold self-indulgence, the selfishness and folly of wickedness of the parents was responsible for the fact that there are but one or two children."* These parents would be no better at parenting when selfish reasons were why they choose a smaller family size *(so true of people today)*. Roosevelt also added this theory of conduct, if adopted, would speedily collapse the Republic and Western Civilization. *He knew what he was talking about!*

At the same time, the *Women's Suffrage Movement* was gaining ground, and feminists proclaimed they wanted freedom. The vast majority of suffragists were mothers who wanted to vote. At about the same time, we saw breakthroughs in contraceptive technology. Scientists and medical doctors in the pro-choice movement were trying to find new ways to help men and women to have sex without the repercussions of reproduction. *(To gain their information they experimented on prisoners who were forced into these experiments!)*.

1907 to 1937 Forced sterilization in America on the unfit.[54] Most Americans do not realize there was a time, even in America, *the land of the free*, when the American government forced sterilization on its people. This happened when scientists were trying to gain medical knowledge about sterilization. These *forced* medical experiments were performed by doctors and fully supported by Margaret Sanger and her pro-choice eugenics mentality. Between 1907 and 1917, sixteen states adopted laws advocating the forced sterilization of socially dependent poor, criminals, mentally ill people, and others the government saw as allegedly *unfit to bear children*. (Today, this would be anyone on welfare, WIC, food stamps, or who was in jail for a crime or who had a mental illness, Down Syndrome, autism or other mental disorder that the government deemed unfit for procreation). The U.S. Government would sterilize you! Can you imagine?

1911-1914 Margaret Sanger writes about sex education. Margaret wrote a series of articles that eventually were published into a book called "What every GIRL should know". These were written for the socialist paper, New York Call.[56] Ministers, women and men were outraged at her assault on families. During these years Margaret traveled to Europe where she joined an organization started by Thomas Malthus who argued against family size and overpopulation. Margaret also visited the Netherlands, the first country to have birth control clinics. Margaret determined this would be her vision to start clinics where females could hear the truth about how to prevent pregnancy from physicians.

1916 Margaret Sanger opens the first birth control clinic in Brooklyn, New York.[57] Margaret and her workers passed out booklets to women in the neighborhood which said, *"Can you afford to have a large family?" Do you want any more children? If not, why do you have them?" "Do not kill, do not take life, but prevent."* Margaret claimed hundreds of women

133

came, but her clinic only stayed open nine days. Authorities shut it down and arrested Margaret and charged her as a public nuisance.

1916 to 1937—The First Birth Control Clinics violated Federal Comstock Laws. From 1921 to 1930, Sanger worked vigorously to repeal the Comstock Laws, but her efforts were denied.

1918—Condoms returned with the troops as America went to war[58]—the U.S. troops fought in World War One. While overseas, some men ignored the U.S. Army's warning to abstain from sex. Men used condoms overseas and brought them back to America.

1920 Margaret Sanger writes a controversial book "Women and the New Race,[59] Margaret shows her true intentions to eventually go as far as killing the unwanted children. This quote is from the chapter *"The Wickedness of Creating Large Families"*. In this chapter Margaret says, "The most merciful thing a large family does to one of its infant members is to kill it." Unbelievable! Margaret was a very deceived individual.

1921--Margaret Sanger founded The Birth Control League,[60] which later becomes Planned Parenthood Federation of America.

1920s—*Roaring Twenties*. A moral decline[61] is what President Teddy Roosevelt foresaw at the turn of the century. The country continued its moral freefall. Free expression and the benefits of a prosperous nation caused some Americans to stop appreciating God. Small segments of people began to turn from His ways, and started to combine condoms with withdrawal, the rhythm method, diaphragms, IUDs, and women started having more abortions and the U.S. birth rate dropped.

What were God's people doing during the early 1900s to 1920s? Churches were still teaching their people to choose what the Bible says and to *be fruitful and multiply*. The pastors spoke out against changing attitudes and against the flapper women who bobbed their hair and showed their legs in modern bathing suits. In the south especially, they spoke against *mixed bathing* which is men and women together at the waterfront (*the only reason people used to go to the beach, or a river was for taking a bath with soap and possibly stripped down to their underwear to do so, therefore watching the opposite sex do this was considered a sin). As the morality of society started to decline, pastors preached the word of God and what it said. Large families were still the norm in church and society, and it was not unusual for the minister to have a large family himself. Unfortunately, as society started to become more secular in the 1920s and beyond, church goers were pressured to come closer to adopting secular ideas.

1920's Catholics vigorously fought Margaret Sanger.[62] In 1921, Catholic Archbishop Patrick Hayes asked police to raid the first American Birth Control Conference. Margaret Sanger and other activists were arrested for giving public lectures on birth control, and Hayes told Catholics, *"Stop your ears to that pagan philosophy!"* Margaret got nationwide attention and then encouraged the Protestants to tell the Catholic Church you cannot force your Catholic opinions on others. Then in 1924 Catholics pressured the Syracuse New York City Council to ban Margaret Sanger from making a speech on birth control. Also, at one point the *Knights of Columbus* refused to do any business with hotels that hosted birth control events, and *The Catholic Welfare Conference* lobbied against birth control. In Boston, the Catholic Mayor would not allow Margaret Sanger to make any speeches, even the newsreel companies were pressured by Catholics to not cover any of Margaret Sanger's birth control related activities. In 1929 Catholics pressured police to raid Margaret Sanger's New York clinic and arrest doctors and nurses. Margaret fought back stating this was an assault on medical privacy. Catholic senators fought back. Father Charles Coughlin, a priest and popular radio host, reminded a House judiciary committee that God's command to increase and multiply was still important. Margret fought back and said a celibate Catholic priest was not the best source for procreation and parenthood. Even still, Catholics continued to lobby Congress and paid close attention to any legislation that was trying to emerge to overthrow the birth control laws in place.

Margaret Sanger was devoted to eugenics. Margaret became a diehard eugenicist. Once she set up her headquarters in New York City she focused much of her efforts on seeing the elimination of the children of the *poor immigrants* who lived in the ghettos of New York City. She believed certain people groups should not have the same rights to reproduce as others because they are *undereducated, poor, mentally* or *physically challenged*, or of a certain *race*. Sanger felt these groups should control their reproduction because all they were doing was reproducing more inferior and impoverished people. The people groups in the early 1900's that were invading New York were the *Jews, Italians, Greeks, Polish, Irish, Slovak, and Russians*. In her opinion these were the *lower* classes of *inferior intellect* and were *unfit to bear children!* She did her best to try and discourage these *races* and *classes* of people from reproducing. Later the people groups Margaret deemed *unfit*, and *inferior* were those from the brown and black races. She supported putting clinics in areas where the poor and unfit lived so they would have easy access to eliminate their children in the name of female progress.

Historians try to cover up Margaret Sanger's eugenic intentions, but Margaret made many speeches about why the *unfit people groups* should be stopped from reproducing and why they were causing the downfall of society. Her ideals were scary back then, but much of what she believed in is acceptable by many contemporary standards, even though some of the greatest leaders in U.S. history came from these people groups and these New York City ghettos.

By forcing medical experiments on prisoners and the poor, researchers used this information to make new birth control choices available and Margaret fully supported these male and female sterilization experiments. The goal was for people to become sterile yet remain sexually active. Before this point in history, people either died or could not successfully have sex due to the complications caused by crude hysterectomy, castration, and sterilization experiments.

1930—Protestants compromised, and the Anglicans (Episcopalians) held the Lambeth Conference and allowed birth control. At the same time latex technology brought better condoms. Europe introduced the modern-day IUD, first made in Germany. The Comstock Laws made these items illegal in America, but people could still get them because they were routinely smuggled in and sold on the black market. Objects used as IUDs had probably been placed in the uterus for years, but these modern inventions made this choice somewhat safer. In 1929, the beginning of the Great Depression brought poverty, then between 1930–1931, due to this poverty, the Anglicans (Episcopal) and the Jewish leaders began making doctrinal compromises on family planning. When times are tough, humans look for relief. Church leaders looked at a global economic collapse and surmised that things would be better if families had fewer mouths to feed, even if the situation might be temporary. It is often easier to find reasons to usurp the wisdom of God's plan than it is to follow it. To follow, takes a relationship with God and faithfulness which history is indicating was lacking amongst those who made these decisions.

1930 Pope Pius XI wrote Casti Connubii[63] in response to the Anglican Protestant Lambeth Conference. This document for Catholics stressed the sanctity of marriage, prohibited Catholics from using any forms of natural or artificial birth control and spoke against trying to abort a baby.

1930 Dr. Knaus[64] in Austria first came up with a theory for calculating a woman's ovulation cycle. His information was later used to help create the Rhythm Method of ovulation prediction.

1931 Time Magazine Article: "Religion: Protestant Birth Control."[65] The article quotes the Federal Council of Churches in America. *"Birth control is nearing the status of a recognized procedure in preventative and curative medicine. Knowledge of contraceptives is widely disseminated, and the question of their use has become one of great social importance."* Articles from notable publications appeared across the country, showing a continued support from the Protestants to side with the eugenics community, the medical community, the scientific community against all other religious voices, to usher in advances in the contraceptive industry. Each device meant big business for the manufacturers and eventually women paid the price when this industry introduced gadgets that harmed their health.

In 1933-1936, Margaret Sanger changed the law. Using the turn of the social landscape, Margaret Sanger convinced a few medical doctors to help her. In 1933, the medical community began to support her cause. **In 1936, she got a bill passed in the U.S. Court of Appeals for the 2nd district** and made it legal for a doctor to prescribe birth control. The Senate approved this even though they had blocked all previous legislation.

1932 *The Rhythm of Sterility and Fertility*[66] book by Dr. Leo. J. Latz, a Chicago doctor and devout Roman Catholic. He did more research on Dr. Knaus' approach and told ladies to avoid sex for 8 days a month when their bodies were most fertile. By 1942, the book sold 200,000 copies and Catholics everywhere were reading it.

By 1937 Sterilization was the law in 27 states.[66a] Each state adopted such laws against the feeble and mentally ill, but after 12,000 people were sterilized because of these laws, Congress finally stopped this heinous practice. Even still, 12,000 people had been sterilized! Maybe this does not have much of an impact on you, but it should. These people could never bear children again even if they suddenly came into a significant sum of money or if they became productive citizens after being released from prison. The U.S. Government had ordered that they be sterilized and had taken away their rights to bear children forever! It could happen again.

1938—Federal Judge lifts the federal obscenity ban on birth control[67] but artificial contraception remains illegal in most states, yet over 400 contraceptive manufacturers had revenues that exceeded $250 million that year. By the end of the 1930's the diaphragm with spermicidal jelly was the number one form of birth control that Margaret Sanger of Planned Parenthood recommended. During the 1940s and 1950s sizable fortunes were given to Sanger to encourage scientists to invent pills to prevent conceptions.

1939 Mahatma Ghandi in India spoke out against birth control.[68] Ghandi believed birth control was a sin and a corrupt western influence on the women of India. He said *women should not receive seed with the intention of letting it run to waste.*

1930-1960—Lysol disinfectant[69] became one of the most popular female contraceptives. Ads in various newspapers claimed that prominent European doctors supported using Lysol as a feminine hygiene product because of its effectiveness in preventing pregnancy. Years later, the American Medical Association investigated and found that the European medical experts never existed! Lysol does not work as a quality contraceptive; it caused poisonings and internal burns even though its use was popular for many years.

1940s—Margaret Sanger effectively renames her American Birth Control League to Planned Parenthood Federation of America.[70] She took advantage of the global crisis of World War II when men were at war, the women were afraid, and this caused family circumstances to become strained. Sanger saw this social outcome as an *opportunity*. She made speeches supporting Hitler's idea of eliminating degenerate people in society and *extinguishing* the sick and mentally ill and those with mental insufficiencies. She was an evil woman! The idea that some people are more valuable to society than others began to be instilled in people's minds. Feminists, world population organizations, and Protestants adopted Margaret's modern family beliefs. As people jumped on the bandwagon, these two ideas became accepted: *fewer people to support gives greater benefits to other family members* and *parents who choose to have more children than they should are selfish.*

When regular people started to adopt Margaret Sanger's beliefs, it indicated she was gaining success. Margaret said, "Birth control is the first *important step women must take toward the goal of her freedom. It is the first step she must take to be man's equal. It is the first step they must both take toward human emancipation."*[71]

Today, Planned Parenthood is the number one organization that supports and benefits financially from abortion-on-demand in our country. It is responsible for the largest number of abortions being performed daily in many parts of the world and has made millions upon millions of dollars off the deaths of these children.

1950s—Family Values continued to erode as birth control pill research advanced. After nearly five decades of pushing her rhetoric on American culture, Margaret Sanger's greatest dreams came to fruition during the 1950s, when scientists successfully developed synthetic hormones which could dislodge a newly formed embryo from the walls of a mother's uterus. It was first discovered during the 1930s that hormones prevent ovulation in rabbits, but it was not until the 1950s that researchers could use this information on humans.

1951 Pope Pius the XII allowed the Calendar or Rhythm Method[71a] of birth control for Catholics. After twenty years of Catholics complaining to Rome, the Pope allowed for what lots of people called *Catholic Birth Control*. The Pope said it is morally acceptable but spoke vehemently against artificial forms of birth control. An engineer created a "Rythmeter" device for Catholic women to be able to calculate their proper timing of monthly ovulation so they could avoid intercourse with their husbands, but were cautioned they would need nine months of information before this Rythmeter could properly access ovulation dates based on their past menstrual cycles. It sold for 10 cents. By 1955 65% of *Catholic women* were following this method. Eventually this approach proved inconsistent in preventing babies so a lot of Catholic women secretly rebelled and went on the pill when it came on the market.

1952 India[72] **became the first country to launch a nationwide family planning program.** *(I guess they threw out what Gandi stood against).*

Early 1950's Feminist Katherine McCormick[73] **used her fortune to fund Gregory Pincus's research into developing an oral contraceptive.** While in her eighties, Margaret Sanger, the founder of Planned Parenthood, raised $150,000 toward the research necessary to produce a human *birth control pill*. This was her lifelong dream, funded by globalists who wanted to see decreased human populations. The creation of the world's first *birth control pill* would mean that ALL women could have absolute control over their reproduction. This was what she had envisioned. The National Inventors Hall of Fame gives two researchers credit for their contributions to modern birth control pills: Frank Colton, who invented Enovid, the first oral contraceptive, and Carl Djerassi invented *the pill*. Two drug companies also funded the research: Syntax and Searle. Each company developed a form of synthetic progestin to mimic how natural estrogen and progesterone work in a woman's body. *The pill* was supposed to prevent ovulation so that no new eggs would be released. A female's body would be tricked into believing that she is already pregnant. It worked, but very little was known about its side effects. In a rush to get the *first human birth control pill* approved, it was released before it could be adequately tested on women, so doctors and researchers didn't know much about how it might harm females. Scientists and researchers were unaware of the side effects or the increased cancer risks. For the sake of advancement, women unknowingly became the female guinea pigs.

1953 Billings Ovulation Method[73a] was Dr. John and Evelyn Billings in Australia founded a monthly abstinence method based on observing cervical mucus during a woman's monthly menstrual cycle.

1954 John D Rockefeller III founded the Population Council.[74] Fear of overpopulation started to become a serious issue. The Population Council researches and develops contraceptives that prevent population increases. In the 1960s the Population Council researched the countries where women did not have access to contraceptives. They brought contraceptive programs to these counties and forced mass participation even when women did not want their contraceptives. Many forms of contraceptives were funded by the Population Council including the copper T IUD, Norplant, Jadelle (Norplant 2), Mirena. Some of these birth control devices have made women permanently sterile and in countries where the Catholic Church was in a majority, the Catholics often fought the government bringing in these devices and pills.

1960s—The Birth Control Pill was released, and the great *experiment on women* began. *The pill* was marketed as *the answer* to freeing all women of the drudgery of bearing unwanted children. Women shouted freedom from having kids we don't want! Yet God's word says for *the wages of sin is death (Romans 6:23)*. The new birth control pill caused life-threatening blood clots causing women to lose their lives. Others suffered heart attacks, strokes, brain embolisms, muscle spasms, irregular menstrual cycles, miscarriages, infertility, and other complications because there weren't any studies on the ill effects. After a slew of *deaths from the pill*, a few studies were conducted, and some cases where death and disease had occurred were observed, but these were not enough proof for the U.S. Food and Drug Administration (FDA) to stop production.

Even though deaths were occurring, the Food and Drug Administration refused to take the pill off the market because they said it needed only to make a few adjustments. Margaret Sanger and feminists' organizations put a lot of pressure on the doctors, researchers, and drug companies. They claimed to be on the side of women, but women paid a high price. Mothers died, children were left alone, husbands lost their wives, many families were in upheaval as the result of the lies about the pill, but do you think Margaret and feminists cared? Nothing was beneath their cause!

1961 National Council of Churches[75] granted a liberal birth control policy.

1965—Comstock Laws ended in Griswold vs. Connecticut.[76] In the early 1960s, most of America's families were still churchgoers. Once Protestants, Catholics and Jews were now using all kinds of birth control, the U.S. Supreme Court ended the Comstock Laws with the case Griswold vs. Connecticut. Comstock laws banned contraceptives and made it illegal to distribute birth control devices such as the diaphragm, cervical cap, condoms, and other birth control paraphernalia. This case reflected the moral instability of a society in decline. The Comstock law had stood for 92 years since 1873. The new law established the right of married couples to use birth control, allowing drug companies, Planned Parenthood, and the like to widely distribute contraceptives.

1965 26 states prohibited birth control for unmarried women.[77] Our country still had a few morals because only *married* couples were able to purchase birth control, *unmarried* college-age girls could not.

1966 Margaret Sanger died[78] **with the blood of millions of babies on her hands.** To some Margaret Sanger was the greatest heroine of women for she set women free from birthing babies to enjoy their lives or careers, but to achieve this her organization killed over sixty million children.

1967 Boston University students challenged Massachusetts *Crimes against Chastity, Decency, Morality and Good order law*.[79] Students asked Bill Baird to give a speech about birth control and then handed out condoms and contraceptive foam to unmarried female students. This act was considered indecent, Baird was arrested and sent to jail. His case was later overturned in 1972, and that case became the foundation for Roe vs. Wade.

The late 1960s—Lawsuits over the unsafe pill![80] Within the first decade the pill was released multiple women died from blood clots and other serious complications associated with *the pill*. Many more females saw their health decline, yet the drug companies continued to make a lot of money on the new pill. **It was the feminists of the late 1960s, who finally demanded answers.** Women were getting breast cancer; many were young women, but no one knew why. Several more studies were conducted, and researchers realized the original pill's dose of hormones was ten times higher than it needed to be and this hormone surge was causing death and near epidemic rates of breast, ovarian, endometrial cancers and leading to increased numbers of hysterectomies. *The birth control pill* was then adjusted for dosage and composition, but this was not until many women suffered ill effects and fatalities. *Who cared about the women?* Certainly not Margaret Sanger, or else she would have never wanted such a dangerous pill given to females before it was properly tested. Yet when someone has Margaret's drive, women and their lives are put on the back burner. *These casualties were necessary for the sake of the cause.* Thankfully some feminists woke up and challenged drug companies about the safety of oral contraceptives and the severe health risks associated with them. Feminist groups and consumer activists voiced opposition until the United States Congress held congressional hearings! These hearings led to modifications of *the pill*, but this took years, while thousands of mothers continued to suffer and die! It was not until the 1980s that the modern, low-dose, two and three-phase *birth control pills* became available. By this time, reproductive cancer was everywhere, as were female heart attacks and blood clots. As a result of promiscuous behavior, venereal disease had also increased to epidemic proportions.

And where was the outcry from the Protestant church pastors and female leaders? Didn't they care about the women in their congregations who were being harmed? Not sure. This fight was won by the **feminists** *in society as nearly all the ministers and denominational voices were silent!*

1968 Majority of Protestant denominations remained silent about artificial contraceptives, even when females in their congregations suffered ill effects. *During this time in America, it would have been unusual for a minister to cross over into the political arena, but even if a pastor did not want* to be active outside of the comforts of the four walls of his church, he could have dealt with these problems if they arose inside his church. I am sure there were probably a few pastors who did try, but we do not have evidence that denominational Christians as a group were fighting for female rights in this area.

1968 Birth Control: A Biblical View[80a] **book by Dr. John R. Rice.** He was an "Independent Baptist" pastor. He also had his own radio show where he preached on a variety of subjects. He produced a publication called *The Sword of the Lord* Newsletter and was quite outspoken about Protestants using contraceptives. He was one preacher who fought back against the culture. Thank God!

1968 Pope Paul VI releases Humanae Vitae[81] *(of human life)*, **one of the most significant religious documents of the twentieth century.** *The pope outlined the clear responsibility for Christians to birth children as mandated by God. This was a bold move for a Catholic pope to encourage Catholics to continue to birth children especially when the world and science were shouting overpopulation concerns. When released, not all Catholics were happy with Humanae Vitae. 500 Catholic scholars signed on, but liberal scholar Father Charles Curran of Catholic University released this statement, "172 U.S theologians and other Catholics, including all six American lay ministers of the pontifical birth control commission, rejected the encyclical as outdated, inadequate and not binding of conscience."*

1968 *The God Who Is There*[81a] **book by Francis Schaffer.** *"The birth of a child is not a random event or simply a biological function. It is a gift of God and to treat it as something to be controlled or avoided at will is to deny the Creators plan. He argues for support of a pro-family approach and against a shifting society.*

1969 The *Home: A Godly Christian Home*[81b] **book by Dr. John R Rice.** This was a second attempt by this independent Baptist preacher, to instill Biblical values in an ever-changing culture. He instructs couples on marriage, the family and their responsibilities to have children.

1969 The United Nations General Assembly announced, *"parents have the exclusive right to determine freely and responsively the number and spacing of their children."*[82]

1969 The United Nations Fund for Population activities was formed.[83] In 1987 they changed the name to the United Nations Population Fund. This agency is the sexual and reproductive health agency of the United Nations. During the last fifty-six years, they've masqueraded themselves as supporting female reproductive rights yet forced sterilizations and abortions on a large portion of women in third world countries. In the late 1960s and beyond, Protestant denominations have *worked alongside the United Nations Population Fund.* They've encouraged their parishioners to help decrease the global population and to practice, "responsible parenting", by not producing any children a parent could not socially, physically, spiritually or economically care for.

1969 Canada lifted an 1892 law that would not allow information on birth control.[84] Canada allowed for unmarried female students to hear about the birth control pill. Previously birth control discussions were considered indecent.

1960s-1972 Catholic Church adopts Natural Family Planning (NFP)[85] using the Billings method, the Creighton Method and the Sympto-thermal Methods. These methods teach a woman how to understand her body's natural fertility cycle. NFP is the only method the Catholic Church currently approves of globally. NFP classes are taught at most Catholic Churches.

1960s-1970s Native Americans[85a] were also subject of forced sterilization. The only reason these ideas are not being forced on citizens is because a large segment of the Baby Boom generation willingly agreed to be sterilized and stopped reproducing. Hence, sterilization is still a *free choice* instead of being forced upon us. Also, the United States needs birth numbers to increase its economy, but if we reach a surplus in the future, our reproductive rights could be in jeopardy again. There are already states that have suggested laws that would limit the number of children a couple can have, but thankfully, these laws have not been able to pass. In Louisiana in 2008, Representative John Labruzzo[85b] suggested that poor African American women be paid $1,000 to get sterilized if they wanted to continue to get government assistance. The ACLU immediately struck down his idea as promoting eugenics and racial discrimination. It is still happening in America, a 2020 case alleged that the Spanish speaking women in a Georgia prison were forced to have hysterectomies by the uterus doctor, often without anesthesia and if they complained they were sent to solitary confinement. This was because their future children might cost taxpayers money.

1971-1977 Population Research Act of 1970[86] forced sterilization on 25% of native American women through medical clinics placed on reservations. Northern Cheyenne Reservation Chief accused America of attempted genocide. Most sterilizations were forced, without consent and some women had no idea they were being sterilized. This is so evil. Later laws were passed for informed-consent and by 1977, the practice was outlawed.

1972—Supreme Court ruled in Eisenstadt vs. Baird[87] that birth control could be used by all people including unmarried women *(Baird was the one in 1967 who first gave a lecture on birth control to college aged females)*

1973—Abortion became the legal law of the land.[88] In 1873, a righteous congress passed the Comstock Laws to ban contraceptives and to outlaw birth control propaganda. Exactly 100 years later, an unrighteous Congress and unrighteous Supreme Court legalized the killing of the child that comes as the result of not using birth control. *A few Protestants protested but not enough. Most Protestant denominations were on the side of Jane Roe who wanted the right to an abortion. Oh, how the mighty have fallen (2 Samuel 1:25).*

1976 *The Act of Marriage* book by Tim and Beverly LaHaye[89] was the Protestant attempt to bring sex *out-of-the-shameful-closet* and to redeem sex as an act of love and pleasure. This book was given to millions of Protestant couples in their marriage preparation classes and encouraged the use of artificial contraceptives to help the woman relax. The book also encouraged sex play and sexual acts that were considered controversial at the time. The underlying theme of the book was pleasurable sex in a responsible way by using artificial contraceptives to assure no more children than the couple wants. This was the Protestant way. The book was released on the heels of the legalization of abortion and my husband, and I were given a free copy at our church.

1979 *Whatever Happened to the Human Race*[89a] book by Francis Schaffer and C. Everett Koop. This book argues against birth control and abortion. *"The practice of birth control is not neutral; it is part of a large shift that separates the act of procreation from the sanctity of life. What begins with the idea that life can be controlled and manipulated for convenience inevitably leads to the destruction of life itself."*

By the 1980s and 1990s, birth control use and devices flourished. Jews, Protestants, and Catholic couples everywhere were *following the herd*. Protestant denominations continued their agreement that it is up to each couple about what happens in their bedroom. The pulpits were silent giving no other options and not teaching that the Bible says *anything* about family size. This was when my husband and I were first married, birth control and pro-choice was *in*, and no one mentioned anything to the contrary.

1983-1995 FDA approves the Birth Control Sponge, called the *Today sponge,* [90] a round piece of donut shaped foam filled with spermicides. Women put it deep into their vagina to cover their cervix. It became the most popular over the counter method of birth control due to its non-hormonal capabilities. It was successfully used by over 6.3 million women.

1984 FDA approved the copper IUD.[91] It was supposed to be effective until a person was ready to have a child, but the negative was that it had to be surgically inserted and removed. The copper IUD was not as effective as they wanted it to be. There was a popular rumor that the IUD didn't work, and that babies were being born holding in their hand their mothers *IUD!* I am not sure this were true, but the IUD did get a bad rap when it was first released. It also caused heavy bleeding in many women and did not have any hormones. In 2000 the Mirena IUD was a new and improved IUD because hormones were added. It was later proven the IUD was an abortifacient because it causes a newly formed embryo, which is already attached to the uterine wall and is growing, to then become dislodged and die, basically causing a spontaneous abortion of the baby.

1990 FDA approves Norplant[92] **insert into the arm.** Birth control that lasts up to five years and was said to be 99% effective and can be removed by a minor surgery. Complications included unusual bleeding, weight gain, headaches and body aches which prompted early removal.

1992 the FDA approved Depo-Provera,[93] the first contraceptive hormone shot that could prevent pregnancy for several months. Complications include loss of appetite, nausea, menstrual changes, pain in extremities, swelling of face or limbs, sudden headache and an increased risk of stroke or breast cancer.

1998 the FDA approved The Morning After Pill,[94] the first emergency contraceptive. Women take the Preven pills up to 72 hours after sex and it causes a simultaneous abortion. After using the pill just one time some women become infertile forever. *(Population planners hid this fact from women and said there was no way it could happen, but thousands of* women have chatted on internet forums- complaining about not being able to get pregnant after using the morning after pill only one time! To this day, authorities claim it is a myth-but one can easily google and find women complaining on these forums).

2000—By the turn of the millennium, America no longer looked like the same country it was one hundred years before! Religious people slid farther and farther down this slippery slope, accepting just about anything and everything the medical community invented to mess with their fertility. Large families were gone and considered a novelty of the past, the norm was one or two children, and two-parent households were a premium. Population control experts continued bringing more birth control products to the market.

2001 NuvaRing FDA approves the NuvaRing[95] which is a small flexible ring as big as a silver dollar and is embedded with spermicidal drugs. The ring is inserted into the vagina and releases hormones for three weeks. The NuvaRing has a 3% failure rate. The risk was a small chance of strokes, blood clots and heart attacks especially in women over 35 yr. old who smoke.

2001 Ortho-Evra[96] **Birth Control Patch.** The FDA approved the birth control patch, slowly releasing hormones through the skin, freeing women from a daily pill.

2000 FDA approved Lunelle[97] **which is a monthly hormone injection.** Within three years it was no longer available in the United States.

September 11-2001—The World Trade Center collapsed, devastating America. After the nation's loss, a baby boom began and the subject of having larger families heated up.

2001 No menstrual cycle birth control pills were released.[98] Can you imagine? Drug companies released the first continuous *birth control pill*, and women wanted them. Women take a pill daily to suppress their periods and provide continuous birth control. The seasonal pill schedules four menstrual periods a year. Researchers are working on other pills that would schedule only one menstruation cycle a year. *(This seems crazy to me. Do drug companies think they can mess with nature like this without the female body paying the price? In my opinion, women who want to use these pills must demand long-term research).*

2006—HPV shot Gardasil[99] introduced to prevent Cervical Cancer yet for some females' adverse reactions were reported from the start. According to an FDA report released in July 2008, the shot is responsible for 18 deaths, and as many as 9,000 adverse reactions have been reported. These reports came from women and young girls in perfect health before they took the shot. Reactions such as paralysis, dizzy spells, seizures, Bell's Palsy, Guillain-Barre' Syndrome, blood clots, heart problems, miscarriages, and abnormal babies have been reported, some of these complications are rare but what if you were that person? People want to be informed first instead of thinking something is safe when it is not.

2006 Yaz[100] and Yasmin Birth Control introduced.

2008 *The Business of Being Born* Movie[101] by Ricky Lake about the million-dollar industry which largely controls how women birth their babies in America. The documentary features how the "system" advocates for one form of birth over another. The norm is a medicated birth which limits choice and abuses women. The medical community takes a woman's rights away and her voice and then limits her birthing options. Ricky Lake is an advocate for birthing centers, home births and midwifery and informs ladies in this movie that there are other options and healthier options available.

2010 Phexxi[102] nonhormonal birth control gel made of lactic acid, citric acid and potassium bitartrate is approved by the FDA for the prevention of pregnancy. Side effects include urinary tract infections, burning, stinging, and infection in the vagina. More serious complications are rare, but these are allergic reactions to the gel, and bladder, kidney and fungal infections. One more time, females are the human guinea pigs.

2012 Yaz and Yasmin Birth Control Pill $ 2.1 billion dollar settlement.[103] More that 100 women died from the Yaz pill and suffered heart attacks, blood clots and strokes. Yaz and Yasmin, both made by Bayer, settled more than 19,000 lawsuits and Yaz and Yasmin have both been removed from the market.

2017-2025 The Handmaid's Tale Series produced by Hulu is based on a 1985 book[103a] with the same name. This critically acclaimed series is about a futuristic dystopian totalitarian society in which *fertile* women are forced to be breeders for infertile couples. The underlying theme of the Handmaid's Tale is to warn women of the dangers of losing control over their bodies and their reproductive health due to the consequences of an unbalanced patriarchal society. From the viewpoint of a world-gone-mad, this series is supposed to influence women to make sure they fight for the strides feminism has made for them. I doubt we would ever get to a real-world scenario portrayed in this series but in 2025, many parts of our globe are spiraling toward a future without sustainable populations to uphold their countries' economies. I can see how a series, such as this, could provide some real-world warnings for women. My only problem with *finding fear* in this dystopian version, as it relates to what I am sharing in this book, is that in all the strides feminism has made for women, their biggest mistake was their attempt to dismiss motherhood as a viable and very important option. If any message in the Handmaid's Tale proves true, the fact that even in a futuristic dystopian world, having children and creating a family will remain a core human desire. Parenthood and family are fundamental aspects of human identity and culture even in a futuristic world.

2000-2025 Youth and women are becoming outspoken against abortion and how their abortions hurt women plus the connections between abortion and breast cancer are starting to be proven. Ministries like Rachel's Vineyard[103b] help women heal from abortion trauma.

2015-2025 influencers on YouTube and now Tik-Tok, speak out against the pill[103c] and how it has hurt their health, relationships and fertility.

2022 *The Business of Birth Control*[104] by Ricky Lake and Epstein. The most powerful film ever about exposing the lies and cover up surrounding the birth control pill and the money behind keeping this information from the public. After watching this documentary, one cannot deny that the pill is extremely harmful for women, ruins sex and contributes to the downfall of female health. Over sixty plus years women have died from this little pill. How many more will die before women wake up to its dangers?

2022 Roe vs. Wade federal law overturned by Supreme Court in Dobbs vs. Jackson.[105] This decision sent abortion rights back to the states. This long-awaited decision took sixty years to overturn. Each state must now decide to either be pro-life or pro-choice. Interestingly the Sunday after this decision was made, pulpits across America were tested. Some Catholic priests and Protestant pastors did express their gratitude, but others said nothing. Some people left their churches due to the pastor's silence, and I was one of them.

2023 The Global Fertility Business is booming.[106] 1 in 60 children are now born by IVF fertility treatments. IVF is a $25 billion-dollar global industry and projections expect this industry to reach $41 billion in sales by 2026.

2024 Rights to Contraceptive Act[107] **to enshrine the right for all to use artificial contraceptives.** The vote was 51-39 and lost on the Senate floor this time but the Democrats said they will try again in the new congress.

> That is the history of birth control and the creation of the pills, foams, cremes, gadgets, laws and trends. But since we are exploring this history, to establish how we got so far off course, we must look at World Religions to find clues about how each religion cares about what God said in the Scriptures.

WORLD RELIGIONS AND BIRTH CONTROL

Scripture describes sex as a beautiful act between a man and a woman. Adam knew Eve, and she conceived (Genesis 4:1). The two were naked and not ashamed (Genesis 2:25). They had children and created a family. Speaking of the family, God compares our relationship to Christ as being that of a bridegroom and His beloved bride (Revelation 21:2). Proverbs tells a man to *rejoice* with the *wife of his youth*...may her *breasts always satisfy him* (Proverbs 5:18-19). The Scriptures speak of *sex as being for creation* (Genesis) and as an *expression of love* (Song of Solomon).

We've already shown that Adam and Eve and their descendants, Noah and his sons and wives, Abraham and Sarah and her concubine, Isaac and Rebekah, Jacob and his two wives and two concubines, and the ancient Hebrews in Egypt, all of these did not use birth control. Nor did Job with his twenty children or David with Bathsheba, nor was it used in David's haram, nor did Solomon use it with his 700 wives and 300 concubines nor was it used anywhere else in the Old Testament world. Furthermore, we can assume that when Christ gave The Great Commission (Matthew 28:18-20) to the early church, which was made up of Hebraic converts, none were using birth control either. We can also assume that these early believers continued to obey this first mandate to create their families – which is commanded on the very first page of the Scriptures.

Yet as time passed, various religious leaders and church writers began to attach wrongful stigmas to sex. Various popes of the **Roman Catholic Church** brought forth rulings about sex that were often confusing. These rulings caused the followers of Catholic teachings to misunderstand the joys and pleasures of sex. Here are a few examples that were eventually abandoned and overruled by later church authorities. Early Catholic doctrine considered complete sexual abstinence to be the holiest state for humans, with marriage being a holy state for those without the fortitude required for a life of sexual abstinence. Celibate clergy considered sexual pleasure to be *sinful*. They warned that couples should not enjoy sexual pleasure and indicated that somehow when it was both enjoyable as well as procreative, the couple was in sin. This could not be further from how God intended for sex to be but when certain clergy re-enforced this upon their parishioners, the sex act became mechanical and strictly for procreation.

In A.D. 600 Pope Gregory[108] said all sexual desire was sinful.

In 1230 Pope Gregory IX, [109] in the Decretals, treated contraception and abortion as *homicide*. Some Christian Penitential of the early Middle Ages prescribed seven years of fasting on bread and water for a lay person who committed homicide, one year for performing an abortion, but seven years for sterilization *(castration)*. Sterilization was considered *more severe than abortion* because the issue was an attack against the *man's seed*. Onan spilled his seed on the ground, and the seed must come forth. Castrated men were never allowed to enter the ancient Jewish temples (Deuteronomy 23:1) and were banned from entering certain cathedrals.

1545-1563 The Council of Trent[110] said celibacy and virginity were superior to marriage.

1853—Pope Pius IX[111] allowed periodic abstinence to avoid pregnancy, which became the modern acceptance of the Rhythm Method.

1930 Pope Pius XI wrote *Casti Connubii* [112], an attempt to push-back against the changing religious landscape. The Pope's Catholic response warned against the outcome of the Anglican's Lambeth Conference in which using artificial birth control was deemed acceptable. Pope Pius

XI explicitly said that married people should have sex with the full expectation that children could result. To deliberately prevent children in marriage was a *grave sin* and using contraceptives was morally unacceptable.

1950 Pope Pius XII[113] **formally declared The Rhythm method** a church-approved form of birth control by upholding an 1853 encyclical which first considered it.

1960 Pope Paul VI provided theological backing for discussions of themes relating to marital unity which eventually became solidified in his famed 1968 encyclical.

1968 Pope Paul VI writes Humanae Vitae[114] reconfirmed the Catholic stance on married love, responsible parenthood and the stance against the use of artificial contraceptives. Humanae Vitae is considered one of the most thorough Catholic documents on the family. It established the present-day contraceptive policy of the Roman Catholic Church.

1979-1984 Pope John Paul II wrote Theology of the Body.[115] The Pope states that God cares what we do with our physical bodies and he wrote 129 lectures centering around the body; both visible and invisible and how this connection to our body relates to marriage, virginity and celibacy. Pope John Paul touches on relationships within marital love, sexuality and family life. Theologians, students and even lay parishioners agree *Theology of the Body* is one of Pope John Paul's greatest theological gifts to the Catholic church. In these writings Pope John Paul does make it clear, *"Using Natural Family Planning with a closed heart to life turns the method into a hidden form of contraception"* and that being open to life is a spiritual attitude and not simply a technical response. The beauty is in the willingness of the couple to seek God's will, to be open to life by being prayerful and discerning.

In 1997, the Vatican's Pontifical Council for the Family stated: *"The Catholic position on contraception is highly influenced by the natural law theory of Aristotle, Augustine, and Aquinas, which deems that sexuality has as its end purpose and procreation; to interfere in this end would be a violation of the natural law, and thus, a sin."* The Catholic Church sanctions only abstinence and the Natural Family Planning method (NFP) as suitable methods of birth control and they encourage the birth of children in marriage.

Today, the Roman Catholic Church, the largest global religious institution with over one billion converts worldwide, universally supports the sanctity of life. They believe all life is sacred and should not be taken by abortion or blocked by artificial contraceptives. They have upheld this stance amidst global criticism. Pope John Paul II was outspoken on the issue of birth control and family and held a very pro-family stance amidst international criticism. Pope Benedict upheld Pope John Paul II's position in 2012[116] that Catholics should be birthing more children as did Pope Francis. Even the newest Pope, Leo XIV[116a] in one of his first statements upheld the church's *definition of family* is founded upon the *stable union between a man and a woman.*

2007 Christopher West releases Theology of the Body Explained.[117] This book breaks down Pope John Paul's *Theology of the Body* papal teachings into bite size chunks so that everyone can more easily understand the depth of the Pope's wisdom. God cares what we do with our body which is a main emphasis of these teachings and Christopher West does an excellent job explaining these teachings. He is also a founder of the Theology of the Body Institute which offers advanced studies, further solidifying the depth of what it means to be human and to experience human love, sexuality, family life and one's outward reactions to our divine nature.

In **Feb 2015, Pope Francis**[118] said that couples who refuse to have children are *being selfish* and of a *greedy generation* if they chose to not procreate. In **May 2023** Pope Francis again addressed the issue, along with the Prime Minister of Italy, Giorgia Meloni[119] and both urged Italians to have human families instead of pet families, as the birth rate in Italy has fallen to an all-time low.

In **May 2024 Pope Francis**[120] urged young couples to go against the current trends and have children and resist climate change propaganda, because children *give hope to the future.* He encouraged national leaders to help women balance career and motherhood. This all sounds great, yet do most Catholics agree?

Statistics show that Catholic women disagree with the church's teaching. According to a Guttmacher[121] survey up to 98% of all sexually active Catholic women have used some form of birth control other than the Rhythm method or natural family planning. One Poll shows that 88% of Catholics (male and female) feel the official doctrine should allow for the use of the pill and condoms. Another poll had a result of 90%. A third poll showed 82% of Catholics felt that a Catholic couple could use contraceptives and still be a *good Catholic*. The church only sanctions Natural Family Planning and state's that it is supposed to be used only temporarily until stressful marital situations subside. Faithful Catholics use the NFP method, and the unfaithful Catholics ignore all the teachings and do what they want.

The Eastern Orthodox Church[122] does not discern a moral difference between artificial or natural birth control methods. They note that many Church Fathers and the Pauline texts in the New Testament do not strictly limit sexual intercourse to procreation; the Orthodox position is that sexual intercourse also constitutes an expression of love within the marriage contract. No official statement has been made on prohibiting artificial contraceptives, while abortion, infanticide, and permanent sterilization have been condemned, new writers in the church are starting to change their position and become more liberal. The Orthodox Church allows a married couple to decide on contraceptive use.

LDS[123] (Church of Jesus Christ of Latter-day Saints), formerly called Mormons. They believe that the command given to Adam and Eve to be fruitful took precedence over Adam and Eve eating the forbidden fruit because God said it first. That is why they oppose abortions and strongly discourage birth control. Therefore, large families are seen as creating *spirit children* occupying human bodies. Mormons believe that Adam acted in unity with Eve when eating the fruit because his unity kept the commandment of procreation. It was not until 1998 that the LDS church shifted its position on birth control. *"The decision of how many children to have and when to have them is intimate and private and should be left between the couple and the Lord. Church members should not judge one another in this matter. Married couples also should understand that sexual relations within marriage are divinely approved not only for procreation but also as a means of expressing love and strengthening emotional and spiritual bonds between a husband and wife."* Mormons still tend to have larger families than couples in other Christian denominations.

Moslems[124] believe that birth control is permissible, and they welcome sexual pleasure. Even ultraconservatives say that Mohammed allowed birth control. However, some sects choose not to use birth control and have large families for Allah, increasing the Muslim population. *"To Allah be the glory"* was written on a website by Muslim women involved in their current birthing movement expansion. Despite varying viewpoints, the emphasis remains on procreation within the family as a religious duty. There is unanimous rejection of sterilization and abortion.

There is a wide variation in attitudes concerning contraceptives in the Islamic faith. The Quran states: *"You should not kill your children for fear of want"* (17:31; and 6:151). Critics of birth control argue that this can be extended to include a ban on all family planning methods. In contrast, birth control advocates indicate that this passage explicitly refers to infanticide and note that there is no prohibition against birth control in the Quran. However, currently, the Muslims as a people group are out-birthing other world religions 8 to 1! It appears that they are following God's commandment *to be fruitful and multiply* because they are multiplying so rapidly that they are taking over Europe and other regions simply by birth numbers.

Hinduism[125] actively encourages prolific procreation within marriage, but there is no prohibition against birth control in the Hindu religion, while abortion is condemned. There is a wide variance of views on contraceptives by Hindu scholars: Gandhi advocated birth control based on abstinence and not through artificial means, while Radhakrishnan and Tagore, on the other hand, promoted the use of artificial methods. India was the first nation to establish a governmental population strategy based on birth control measures.

Buddhist[126] monks are celibate. Lay Buddhists are encouraged to live the *middle way* between the extremes of sensuality and the denial of pleasure. Sex is not limited to procreation but can bring pleasure too. Birth control is practiced.

Presbyterians support birth control and abortion. They believe that sex is God's gift to be enjoyed but not abused. Congregations of **Reformed Presbyterians**[127] are increasingly being made aware that all forms of birth control, sterilization, and abortion are wrong, and the Biblical stance on this issue is being preached. This does not mean all Reformed Presbyterians are not using some form of birth control, it simply means they are hearing some sermons against using artificial contraceptives.

Judaism[128] in most forms of Conservative and Reform **Judaism** believe in using birth control. **Orthodox Jews** believe that Torah is clear that children are a gift from God, and they do not use birth control. Some Orthodox couples practice the Laws of Niddah which means the woman abstains for seven days of her cycle and then an additional seven days. Unprotected intercourse is at or about her 14th day after the wife participates in a Mikvah bathing ritual.

WHEN DID CONCEIVING CHILDREN BECOME OUR CHOICE?

Seventh-day Adventists[129] **in 1999** reaffirmed their views at their annual conference. They believe it is vital for a couple to be responsible with their time and talents and to not have more children than they can physically and emotionally handle. They believe sex is for procreation and unity in marriage, and God gives each couple the responsibility to exercise wisdom when making decisions about using birth control. Both partners need to consider each other's needs and life's goals. Parents should first consider their finances, the mother's physical, spiritual, and mental needs, and the social and political circumstances globally at the time. As stewards of God's creation, couples need to look past their *selfish desires* for children and consider the needs of others and the effect that an additional child might have on themselves and the world. Seventh-day Adventists accept *the pill* and *IUD* as practical because most fertilized ova fail to implant or are lost after implantation. For the IUD, morning-after pill, injections, and implants, they advise letting a doctor help with the decision. They do not believe in abortion or promoting sex outside of marriage. Seventh Day Adventists have seen their numbers decrease as members age, and because couples have not been encouraged to birth large families.

After the World Council of Churches in 1961, supported the *birth control pill*, the enemy gained ground against God's plan for families. How could a Protestant pastor speak out against birth control or abortion if they were using birth control in their own marriage? Once mainline denominations supported birth control: *They exchanged the truth about God and His plan for a lie and worshiped and served created things rather than the Creator—who is forever praised. Amen. Because of this, God gave them over to shameful lusts. Even their women exchanged natural sexual relations for unnatural ones (Romans 1:25-26).*

The Book of Romans goes on to talk about homosexual sin. In Romans 1:28, once people's hearts and minds were numbed by the acceptance of the created thing (the pill and contraceptives), it allowed them to desire abortion as the thing that was needed whenever birth control had failed them. This fulfills this scripture: *Whose consciences have been seared as with a hot iron (1 Timothy 4:2).*

Christians think that using contraceptives is no big deal, but what I am pointing out here is vital to see; the key to destroying abortion is to repent for using contraceptives to prevent conceptions!

The Baptists, both evangelical and Southern Baptists, had been relatively silent on birth control use specifically since the 1960s and have left this decision up to individuals. I've already stated one of the boldest pastors who spoke out was Dr. John R. Rice author of The Sword of the Lord publication. He wrote two books arguing against the use of birth control and uplifting the same position I hold in this book. His two books: *Birth Control: A Biblical View* (1968) and *The Home: A Godly Christian Home* (1969). Being an "Independent" Baptist, I am not sure how many other Independent Baptist pastors agreed with his position. I was raised at a Southern Baptist church but later met my husband at a rather well known and quite large "Independent" Baptist church in the mid 1970s, and we knew nothing of Rice's ideas or teachings. When we planned to be married, our Baptist pastor discussed birth control choices at length with us in our premarital counseling sessions. Our pastor was a pro-contraceptive pastor who used contraceptives in his own marriage. He never mentioned to us that any other choice existed!

I believe very few Independent Baptist ministers agreed with Dr. John R. Rice, and I also believe the Southern Baptists drowned out Rice's influence. The famous Southern Baptist pastor of First Baptist Dallas, W.A. Criswell[130] believed that abortion was a solution to protecting the life of the mother. *In 1970, a Baptist Sunday School Board poll found that* **70% of Southern Baptist pastors supported abortion** *to protect the physical or mental health of the mother, 64% supported abortion in cases of fetal abnormality and 71% in cases of rape.* A prominent Southern Baptist Theological professor, Paul Simmons, in the 1980s even argued that God is *pro-choice!*

One reason why Baptists may have been silent on birth control might be because, in my research, I am very sad to report that Southern Baptists did not fight against Roe vs. Wade. In fact, one of the plaintiff's attorneys was a Southern Baptist! This landmark decision legalized abortion, yet the very liberal Southern Baptists, who were leading the denomination at that time were some of the major supporters of abortion legislation! As a Baptist, this may be a shock to hear. Being raised Baptist myself, it was a bit shocking to me, but support for a woman's health through abortion is written in the 1971 Southern Baptist Convention Documents.

In the **June 1971 Southern Baptist Convention,**[131] the liberal Southern Baptist leaders stated, *"We call upon Southern Baptists to work for legislation that will allow the possibility of abortion under conditions of rape, incest, clear evidence of severe fetal deformity, and carefully ascertained evidence of the likelihood of damage to the emotional, mental, and physical health of the mother."*

After Roe vs. Wade was passed in 1973, at the **June 1974 Southern Baptist Convention**[132] resolution stated women should not be discriminated against for having an abortion. At the **June 1977 Southern Baptist Convention,**[133] they again supported medical services for women who wanted abortions, meaning Baptists were jumping into and making money from this heinous crime at their Baptist Hospitals and other health facilities!

The Southern Baptists continued this pro-abortion tone until the **June 1979 Southern Baptist Convention,**[134] for the first time since Roe versus Wade, the conservatives overthrew the liberals and pastors such as W.C. Criswell of First Baptist Dallas began to change their previous *pro-choice* positions on abortion, to pro-life. In the 1979 SBC resolution,[135] the Baptists stated a reversal of their stance when they said, *"The practice of abortion for selfish non-therapeutic reasons destroys fetal life, dulls our society's moral sensitivity, and leads to a cheapening of all human life."*

June 1980 we finally see the **Southern Baptist Convention**[136] resolution calls abortion selfish, they take a stand against taxpayer money supporting abortion, they commit to supporting constitutional legislation against abortion, they call abortion a national sin, and they support alternatives to adoption. [137]**June 1987,** the SBC began supporting crisis pregnancy centers and created a staff position to support abortion alternatives, and **June 1988 committed to Sanctity of Life Sunday.** I don't know if the Southern Baptists ever made formal repentance for agreeing with abortion and working toward the legislation that made Roe vs. Wade into law, but from June 1979 on, their actions voiced repentance.

Baptist Health Care[138] still has information on its website about birth control pills, which they prescribe as part of its health care plan and administer in its health care system. They also still perform many sterilizations (tubal ligations and vasectomies) each year. Furthermore, they also administered abortions in their hospitals throughout the 1970s and even into the 1990s until the conservative voice rose and overturned the Baptist Health Abortion policy.

It was not until the **May 1993 Southern Baptist Convention**[139] that Baptist Health Care was mentioned, *"...We abhor the use of federal, state or local tax money; public, tax-supported medical facilities; or Southern Baptist supported medical facilities for the practice of selfish, medically unnecessary abortions and or the practice of withholding treatment from unwanted or defective newly born infants. We support and will work for appropriate legislation and or constitutional amendment which will prohibit abortions except to save the physical life of the mother and that we also support and will work for legislation which will prohibit the practice of infanticide."*

In 2005 **Dr. Albert Mohler,**[140] President of the Southern Baptist Theological Seminary, began raising concerns about whether Southern Baptists should continue their silence on contraceptives or begin to speak out about some forms of birth control, mainly the birth control pill. He states,

"Most evangelical Protestants greeted the arrival of modern birth control technologies with applause and relief. Lacking any substantial theology of marriage, sex, or the family, ***evangelicals welcomed the development of the pill much as the world celebrated the discovery of penicillin,*** *as one more milestone in the inevitable march of human progress and the conquest of nature. At the same time, evangelicals overcame their traditional reticence in matters of sexuality. They produced a growth industry in books, seminars, and even sermon series celebrating sexual ecstasy as one of God's blessings to married Christians."*

He reminded Baptists that sex was not simply for pleasure, but it was also intended for procreation (something that has been forgotten in the Baptist world for over 65 years, ever since the birth control pill first came out). In his 2005 and 2006 articles and radio statements, he encouraged Baptists to read Pope Paul VI's 1968 Human Vitae encyclical upholding the sanctity of human life. This development briefly brought some hope to evangelicals, and it helped but it did not start a war in the Protestant church and in my opinion, this is what we need! The Protestants remain very quiet on this subject even when Dr. Mohler called it a firestorm of controversy.

WHEN DID CONCEIVING CHILDREN BECOME OUR CHOICE?

I wish this had not happened to the Southern Baptists, and I believe that God has used the repentance for abortion from the ministers of the Southern Baptist Convention to bring forth life. Leaders like Dr. Mohler are being used by God today to preach the Biblical basis for restoring the family.

1970s-2000s IBLP- Basic Youth Conflicts Institute.[140a] Bill Gothard started out teaching seminars he wrote himself and he gave them to Christian high school and college aged students in the 1970s and 1980s. Bill Gothard never married but by the 1990s his student seminars advanced to family seminars where, he became a voice for homeschooling and a voice against Christians using birth control. He **pushed for large Protestant families** and his anti-birth control teaching was considered controversial and outside of mainline Protestant denominational interpretations of scripture. Yet there are people who love his teachings because he uses scripture for nearly everything he is saying. Much of what the *Duggar Family of 19 Kids and Counting* on TLC Network stand for; their lifestyle and belief come from his teachings. In the mid 2010s, Bill Gothard's ministry went through reorganization due to complaints about Gothard's actions around young women. Bill was removed from the organization he founded and is no longer leading or speaking.

1977 Above Rubies Magazine[141] is published by Nancy and Colin Campbell, parents of 10 children. Nancy's ministry is to encourage women in their highest calling of wives, mothers and homemakers and speaking against changing attitudes. Nancy is a faithful woman of God whose one lone voice has gone around the world! Her Above Rubies publication has reached 160,000 mothers across the globe.

1989 All the Way Home book by Mary Pride[141a] and **1989 Full Quiver: Family Planning and the Lordship of Christ**[142] **book by Rick and Jan Hess.** These two books were passed around at early homeschool conventions and promoted to Protestants the idea of viewing *children as a gift* and not *a parent's choice*. Families who read these books became known as Quiverfull because the Bible says, *blessed is the man whose quiver is full of children*. Later these couples formed an online community called the Quiver-full Digest which supported families in their discussion of family size and to exchange ideas about large family living.

1989 The Bible and Birth Control[143] **Book** by Charles Provan was a small little book giving scripture about what the Bible says about using birth control and has remained popular even to this day.

1990s Protestant Quiver-full Movement was the first awakening of Protestants that maybe they had been lied to by their denominations and that having a large family might not be simply *a Catholic thing* or something practiced by the *Amish* or the *Mormons*. Couples realized God's word might actually mean that people should have children. This movement was **the first sign** that those from mainline Protestant denominations and some non-denomination folks might someday turn back to scripture and turn away from using birth control.

1995 Baptist David C. Cloud[144] **was one of the first Baptists to speak out about this topic.** He updated a previous guide to birth control for Baptists concerning artificial contraceptives. This booklet, "*Family Planning and the Christian*", was widely distributed and clearly stated the Baptists' position. This booklet stated that in 1 Corinthians 7, the Apostle Paul said that one purpose of marriage is to protect men and women from fornication. In marriage, couples are entirely free to satisfy themselves and not defraud one another sexually. Abstinence is never a proper form of birth control, and abstinence within marriage is not good because it is disobedience to God's Word. This booklet also states that abortion and the pill are improper birth control methods because the pill might cause a silent abortion. *(This fact about the birth control pill has not been a widespread belief or teaching among Baptists.)* The booklet goes on to approve birth control methods that do not destroy a new life: condoms, diaphragm, foams, crèmes, Natural Family Planning and sterilization. The booklet does not indicate that sterilization is in any way a great sin, even though we know that it is the ultimate form of birth control, severing God's gift. The Bible speaks of abstinence from relations only during a female menstrual cycle (Leviticus 20:18).

1996 Book supporting Large Families: Yes, They're All Ours![145] **by Rick Boyer.** Another popular book which promoted the idea that large families are unique and Biblical.

1990s: IUD as a proven abortifacient created a problem for evangelicals. Women had been inserting IUD devices into their vaginas for years, when an increasing amount of literature came out showing the IUD was indeed an abortifacient. In 1974 a T-shaped IUD approved by the FDA was inserted by doctors providing birth control for up to 10 years. The Dalkon Shield[v] was one such device, but it fell out of favor when it was found to cause pelvic inflammatory disease in some women. Although other IUD designs were not implicated, all IUDs were taken off the market for fear of litigation until adjustments could be made. In recent years new evidence has proved that all IUD's act as abortifacients. This issue became increasingly problematic for the mainline evangelical denominations because ministers and their spouses were either using one or had used the IUD as their chosen contraceptive. Once the facts came out, **pulpits were silent.** Many Protestant women denied the facts and continued to use IUD's.

A few years ago, I met such a woman. She was at my church and seemed quite committed to the Lord. We talked about her family. She shared that her doctor had to insert an IUD to stop her uterine bleeding problem. I shared the facts I knew about IUDs, and her response was, *"Well, I don't care about those facts, my doctor knows what's best, and we don't want any more children, so it's a non-issue with us."* I heard her reasoning. She literally brushed it off as a medical issue without any spiritual consequences. On the flip side, I feel for her condition. Any time a woman is bleeding, she will want relief, and the medical community's only cure is an abortifacient. As people of faith, when do we accept the world's solution, and when do we resist and seek God's? An alternative method might have also worked and not acted as an abortifacient.

Dr. James Dobson and Focus on the Family's position on family planning.[146] The radio ministry of well-known psychologist Dr. James Dobson was started in 1977 and has been a cornerstone ministry promoting family values to Protestant and Catholic families. The ministry has been very careful about its stance on the issue of children and birth control. On the Focus on the Family website Dr. Dobson (born in 1936) says, *"The entire ministry of Focus on the Family was built around the belief that children are a blessing from God and that life begins with fertilization."* Yet based on Dr. Dobson's interpretation of scripture, preventing the fertilization of these blessings from God is not morally wrong. By not speaking out as pro or con, Dr. Dobson's position leaves believers to decide. Couples must weigh the evidence independently while attempting to sort out the facts. Dr. Dobson's ministry has been pivotal in promoting pro-life ideals. His ministry initially agreed for 20 years that the IUD was a safe birth control device and then in the late 1990s he helped convince Christian women that IUDs were abortifacients and that it was not a good idea to use one as their form of birth control.

On his website, Dr. Dobson has given insights from the medical community about the ongoing debate about whether birth control pills are abortifacients and does not agree with all forms of the pill.

I must add that I have had a healthy respect for the goodwill of Dr. Dobson's organization, but as more Christian people demanded answers, the Focus on the Family ministry continued to stand by the Protestant position of supporting birth control and artificial contraceptives. This position sees a child as *a parent's choice* more than a *child as a gift* from God. Focus on the Family says they love children and want people to have them but out of the other side of their mouth Focus does not seem to love children enough to encourage parents to have as many children as God might give them. Their *pro-parent's choice*, not *pro-God's gift* position has continually supported the use of artificial birth control and sterilization. If they ever wanted to debate their position, I would not hesitate to go to Focus on the Family to debate this issue.

Pro-life movement is gaining momentum. In the last sixty years fighting against abortion, hundreds of pro-life groups have formed and are organized and making a difference to the victims of abortion: National Right to Life, Bound4life, Stop Planned Parenthood, American Life League, Blackgenocide.org, Operation Rescue, Priests for Life, One More Soul, Silent No More.[147] More people have become vocal against abortion and thousands of Protestant pastors would tell you they are against abortion, yet they never talk about it from their pulpits, have never marched against it, have never given church money to an unwed mothers home or a crisis pregnancy center, will not even warn their parishioners when abortion legislation is pending in their state and have no connection that they are against abortion except when they are asked, they would say they are pro-life. At the same time, they remain pro-birth control and pro-sterilization. Somehow the Protestants can't make the connection that all these attacks on children from before conception till birth are all connected.

2003 Be Fruitful and Multiply Book[148] by Nancy Campbell. In her book, Nancy supports large families by using scripture. Nancy is amazing and has been a pioneer in encouraging women to have more babies and has traveled the world teaching against the use of birth control.

2004—Birthing God's Mighty Warriors[149] Book was released by me- Rachel Scott. The book contains a revelatory message calling a new generation to return to the ancient paths, to leave the sin of birth control behind, to correct their parent's and grandparent's generational mistake of preventing children, and believes for supernatural healing for the infertile, to move forward with passion to restore the family to its former glory, so that when the Lord returns the Family of God will be complete and His Bride will be ready to procreate with her Bridegroom Jesus! God's plan will be continued.

2004 You've Got to be Kidding[150] **Book** (family raising 19 kids!) by Pat and Ruth Williams. Pat Williams was the owner of the Orlando Magic. Through adoption he and his wife raised nineteen children, and they share their experience.

2005 Rachel Scott is interviewed on Good Morning America. I was interviewed by Deborah Roberts (one of 9 children) where I shared my views on large families.

2006 Family Unplanning book[151] by Craig Houghton. This was quite popular in the Protestant world and got a lot of Millennials to think about and question artificial birth control.

2006 Making Babies the Quiver-full Way article in Newsweek[152] and documentary.

2006 Blessings by the Dozen,[152a] article in American Life League Magazine features a Catholic family with twelve children. The mother read the Protestant book, "A Full Quiver" which gave her the Bible verses that led her to a deeper understanding of why the Catholic Church preaches against contraceptives. The couple eventually allows God to give them a beautiful family. One more testimony of God's goodness.

2007 Rachel Scott interviewed by Fox News[153] discussing the issue of large families with Martha McCallum.[154] Rachel shares reasons why Christians should see children as a gift and not as a choice.

2007 Does the Birth Control Pill Cause Abortions?[155] In this book Randy Alcorn tackles the elephant in the room which is why are Protestants still using the birth control pill? Fiery debates erupted after this book came out and finally Focus on the Family started admitting there is indeed evidence that the pill is an abortifacient, however there are still a few doctors who refuse to accept this for every form of the birth control pill.

2007 Kids by the Dozen[156] **reality-TV series** featured eight different large families who have had a total of 114 kids between the eight couples.

2007 Love is in the House Book[157] by Chris and Wendy Jeub. Chris, a former Focus on the Family staff writer, wrote about his large family. I am not sure Focus on the Family ever endorsed his book as Focus can't seem to ever take a position on large families.

2008-2015 19 Kids and Counting[158] **TV series featuring the Duggar Family.** Produced by the TLC network, this series followed the lives of one of the most famous American large families, the Jim-Bob and Michelle Duggar family, who lived an *unusual life* with their children. Their girls were always wearing long dresses, and never cut their long hair, their children were only allowed a courtship style of dating, no child could attend formal school and were only allowed to be homeschooled, and other controversial ideals were broadcast on this show. Every show was very sweet, and the Duggar children were amazingly disciplined and seemed happy. Years later several Duggar daughters released a series of books exposing the problems in their family. In my opinion it was an attempt to sell books after TLC ended the Duggar Reality Tv series. Even though there was truth to some of the things the girls claimed, raising a boatload of children is challenging for any parent. The Duggar parents were not the exception. They made mistakes, and I am not defending the Duggar parents because I do not know them, but as the mother of 8 children myself, to expect perfection from one's parents is quite unrealistic. Along with their spouses, the Duggar girls sold a bunch of books, got lots of media interviews and made money off their parent's blunders. Again, not a very nice thing to do to any parent.

2009 Duggars 20 and Counting Book.[159] The Duggars share their family philosophy and history of why they have a large family and give parenting tips.

2009 Quiver-full: Inside the Christian Patriarchy Movement Book[160] by Kathryn Joyce. I met Kathryn and she interviewed me for this book. She was a nice lady to talk to, but Kathryn is an atheist and yet a religion reporter, which is senseless. *[How can an atheist qualify to be a religion reporter? She does not follow a religion, is already biased against religious people, and really doesn't understand religion or else she would have a religion, not sure she can be impartial in her reporting].* In her book-critically acclaimed by progressives and feminists, Kathryn expresses an outsider's view of the phenomenon of the large family movement. She noted the similarities. All the families she observed were Protestants, most of them homeschooled, several lived all over the country, but a concentrated amount of these families lived in midwestern rural towns or on family homesteads. These couples were not friends and did not know each other but Katherine tried to imply it was an organized conspiracy to take over for the Republican party! What Kathryn failed to understand was that this was hardly an organized movement. God speaking to couples one by one about birth control, is sort of a *God-movement*, but not a political movement. Couples read what the Bible said about families and fell under conviction and started to obey God's voice and had more babies than they originally planned to have. Kathryn, tried to say that all these large Protestant families were following some sort of playbook, acting and dressing and discipling in the same way. But since the 1990s, the Protestants who did decide to have large families had never even heard the word quiver full much less dressed like the Duggar girls or made their children date through courtship. The majority had simply awakened to the call of God to add more children to their families and do what scripture teaches.

2009 Newsweek Magazine: Inside the Duggar's Conservative Ideology[161] article explains more about the phenomena of the large family movement amongst Protestants. *Birthing God's Mighty Warriors* was quoted in this article!

2009 WE-TV Secret Lives of Women documentary; Born to Breed[162] Produced by CBS/We-Tv. The documentary features three families who each share their large family story. Kathryn Joyce was featured as the expert critic and my family and I were featured and so was my book, Birthing God's Mighty Warriors.

2010 CNN The Joy Behar Show:[163] Joy interviews Rachel Scott[164] (author of Birthing God's Mighty Warriors) Kathryn Joyce (author of Quiver-full inside Christian Patriarchy Movement) and a very wounded Christian mother, turned atheist, Vicky Garrison - owner of the website: www. No longer quivering.

2012 Duggar Book: A Love that Multiplies.[165] More info from Michele and Jim Bob Duggar about their large family.

2013 Birth Control Movie: How did we get here?[166] George Grant, R.C. Sproul Jr. examines the history of birth control.

2016 Birth Control: Is it up to us?[167] George Grant, R.C. Sproul Jr. This movie shows how the Protestant world does not talk about birth control, gives no sermons on birth control and how Protestants simply ignore the subject.

2018 Quiverfulldocumentary.com,[168] another large family tackles the subject of what the Bible says about bearing children.

2021 Southern Baptists[171] **finally decided that abortion is wrong across the board.**

2004-2025 Catholic Prayer Movement called 40 Days for Life[172] began offering prayers to end abortion. Catholics have offered consistent prayer for the unborn ever since Roe vs. Wade was passed, but 40 days for life is an organized prayer movement for the ending of abortion. Catholics have had a much more consistent stance against abortion than other Christian denominations.

1991-2025- Priests for Life[173] was established in 1991 by Father Frank Pavone to provide pro-life encouragement to priests, deacons and other religious leaders to empower them to engage in pro-life efforts. Priests for Life is an ecumenical organization. Father Frank is one of the most dedicated people I have ever met in the pro-life arena. He is widely regarded as one of the most influential voices in America advocating against abortion and speaks with incredible passion and conviction. He captures hearts and gain's people's respect. Priests for Life organized the *National Day of Prayer for Life*, supports the *Silent No More* awareness campaign, and participates annually in the *March for Life*. They also support legislation to end abortion. Martin Luther King's daughter, Alveda King, is on the Priests for Life Board of Directors and is also a sought-after speaker against the evils of abortion.

2004-2025 Bound 4 Life Prayer Movement[174] **to end abortion** was launched by Protestant Lou Engle and gained national attention when representatives from his movement were featured on the cover of **Time Magazine**[174a] **2007**. The cover image showed teens and young people standing in front of the U. S. Supreme Court, with red tape over their mouths that said "LIFE." Students prayed silently to end abortion, raising awareness to protect the lives of future generations from being killed by abortion. Media outlets across the country covered this story. Lou Engle launched other initiatives called The Call, The Send with prayer campaigns to help Protestant Christians take a stand against the sin of abortion.

1974-2025 Annual March for Life[175] **in Washington DC.** This yearly pro-life event is held in January each year marking the 1973 date when the U.S. Supreme Court passed Roe vs. Wade to legalize abortion in America. Even though abortion has now returned to each state, this annual march signifies the continued killing of innocent babies in America. This march is ecumenical and unifying in nature and Christians from all over America participate. I have marched numerous times and every time this march for life is inspiring and how can it not be? You are marching to save lives! If you have never marched, I beg you to make the effort. It is life changing.

2024 The 1916 Project movie.[176] Produced by **Seth Gruber,** this movie exposes the truth about *eugenicist* Margaret Sanger, founder of Planned Parenthood. It covers her eugenic beliefs to wipe out Western Europeans and Jews. Later she moved her efforts towards diminishing the black and brown races and any other group her eugenic colleagues deemed unworthy of life. Margaret's belief and strategy for Planned Parenthood was to put her clinics specifically in the poorest neighborhoods so she could essentially murder all ethnic populations. Her associations with Darwinian theorists and Adolf Hitler propagate her practice of erasing entire people groups.

2025 Birthing Gods Mighty Warriors re-released 20 years later, for a new generation to read. Couples seem more ready than ever to understand that God's word speaks about people having children as a form of worshipping God.

> **Wow! After this section, do you have a better understanding of how World Religions approach the subject of birth control? I hope this history, along with the exhaustive history of contraceptive use, helps you understand how WE got to where we are today.

WHERE IS SOCIETY NOW?

Presently 99% of all adults, including 99% of Catholics, Jews and Protestants and 96% of other religious groups admit to using some form of birth control at one time or another.[177]

Doctrinally, Christians remain divided.

Catholic doctrine says a *child is a gift* and their doctrine allows for the responsible spacing of children utilizing natural forms of birth control. Liberal Catholic women tend to use every form of birth control including abortion and sterilization. This response is largely because these women have not studied or heard the Church's teachings. Conservative Catholic women, who have studied the subject, tend to practice what the church teaches.

Protestants still claim a *child is a parent's choice* and anything goes within the realms of artificial contraceptives except a few forms of birth control that could have abortifacient properties. Even this fact is hotly debated due to lack of agreement amongst doctors. Protestants leaders continually say the Bible does not address the subject and or say it is legalistic to follow God in this area.

Some Catholic ladies carry guilt when they use artificial contraceptives because it goes against church teaching, yet Protestant women have no reason to feel guilty because the majority have no idea the Bible even talks about birth control.

Are we better off since the birth control pill was introduced in 1960 and after The National Council of Churches accepted the birth control pill for all believers in 1961?[178]

Is the church world better? No, the decline in church attendance is severe.

- **Is life better for women?** Maybe in a few small ways, yet women admit to being more unhappy than ever.

- **Is life better for marriages?** No, birth control destroyed many a marriage and ruined sexual response.

- **Is life better for families?** No, families are more alienated than ever, parents are more selfish than ever.

- **Is life better for children?** Absolutely not! Children's lives, safety and happiness are at an all-time low.

- **Is life better in the area of sex?** No! casual sex and pornography led to promiscuity and sex trafficking. Pornography is now at epidemic rates and continues to escalate.

THIS IS WHERE WE ARE:

Did the birth control pill fulfill ALL its promises? Not any!

The birth control pill ruined sex and it ruined families.

The pill was advertised in 1960 as being *the answer for society*.

It was supposed to relieve society of overpopulation, large families, and the poverty of having too many children, and do away with unwanted children, child abuse, and marital stress. It was also supposed to eliminate the need for abortion by preventing a baby from ever being conceived. *(They lied!)*

The Stanton Times News[179] in Pennsylvania stated in 2000: *"Since the birth control pill began to be sold in 1960, divorces tripled, out-of-wedlock births jumped from 223,000 to 1.2 million, abortions doubled, and cohabitation soared tenfold from 430,000 to 4.2 million. Today there is more teen promiscuity, adultery, sexually transmitted disease, and infertility than ever before in our culture."*

A 1964 interview with Dr. John Rock,[180] one of the developers of the pill, who I might add was a Roman Catholic, stated that the pill revolution was *unstoppable*. Legal or not there was no turning back once it was released. The pill caused everyone to suffer loss; the men, the women, and the children but women truly were the biggest losers because the pill so dramatically deteriorates the health of their physical bodies.

In the 21st century, society and the church world are living in *the fall-out* from the pill.

The pill ruined sex.[181] Raw passionate sex is what God intended. The sex God created is two lovers, naked with all their emotional and physical walls down, coming into agreement with this beautiful act of love. This act allows the couple to *fully feel* each other! This is God's picture of the two becoming one flesh. This is sex God's way. But when artificial chemicals invade this space, sex changes. The hormones in the pill can wreak havoc on a female's sex life in more ways than she might realize. The chemicals in the pill introduce physiological factors that work against a woman. Once on these artificial hormones she cannot help that she is not as responsive sexually as she could be. With artificial chemicals running throughout her body, suppressing her libido and with chemicals altering her brain chemistry, her sexual receptors are completely disrupted. She might experience mood swings and dampened emotional responses to her spouse. She might experience decreased moisture and reduced blood flow to her vaginal area which means her sensations might not feel as great as they could. These chemicals often cause a decrease in her libido and alter her sensitivity to sexual stimuli. While operating under an artificially induced hormonal environment, the reality is that many women never realize how much sensitivity, connection and desire they've lost until they stop using hormonal contraceptives! Once they quit and go back to a natural state void of artificial chemicals, these same ladies have reported that sex is better than ever! *Wonder why?*

The pill caused female depression.[182] Depression rates increased dramatically at the same time millions of women were placed on *the pill*. Before the masses used *the birth control pill*, complaints of depression were considerably lower. Women say they were happy. Men were also happy. Overall, the rate of happiness was higher amongst both groups. Is it merely a *coincidence* the literature given with *the pill* warns that *depression* might occur? Is it a *coincidence* that female depression rates remained low until the 1960s when the birth control pill became popular among the masses and also when the rates of female unhappiness jumped dramatically.

The pill increased infertility.[183] The birth control pill propagandists try hard to convince a female that the pill won't affect her future fertility, but how can it not affect it in some way? The pill is artificial. It shuts down perfectly working bodily functions and causes the body to work artificially. It is not unusual for a female coming off the pill to have trouble conceiving, the literature with the pill states this. A female's body will take time to get back to normal. When this does not happen, women who can afford it, resort to in-vitro fertilization. Some women never conceive. American females before the 1960s had a high rate of fertility. *I can personally attest to this. When I was growing up women were pregnant everywhere. My mom's friends would joke, they could get pregnant at the drop of a hat.* Before artificial hormones females were fertile well into menopause! Occasionally, one would encounter a couple who couldn't have a baby, but it was not the norm. Lots of women had unexpected *"surprise"* pregnancies because women could get pregnant very easily. Plus, when a woman was ready to give birth, nobody had trouble going into labor! Women's bodies everywhere did what they needed to do. No one used Pitocin-no one ever even heard of using it before! Once all these artificial hormones flooded female's systems, all these problems began.

The pill caused fertile women to delay motherhood,[184] **often until their biological fertility clocks ticked out.** The *birth control pill was easy to use and advertised as giving a woman the freedom to control her life*. The pill created a *new form of womanhood* with the intent of doing away with

God's order. Feminist magazines approached the subject from the angle of establishing a career first before starting one's family. Modern feminists used the pill to sell women *a bill of goods* for the sake of a cause. All the movies, books, magazine articles and all of society pushed the idea of getting a career first. While women were busy establishing their careers, few realized their nurturing opportunities were passing them by. The hypocritical feminist movement of the 1960s, 1970s and beyond misled an entire generation of women who later went on the Oprah Winfrey Show in the 1980s and 1990s crying their eyes out and complaining they didn't realize they were trading motherhood for their career and were never told their biological clocks could tick out. Did they think promoters of the feminist movement cared? The movement was all about advancing females in the workplace and these ladies' lives were the unfortunate fall-out. Sadly, none of the feminists' leaders ever offered apologies or seemed to care that their movement caused so many women to end up with broken lives. There has never been any formal apologies, acknowledgement or care toward these women who believed the lies. *Nobody cares!*

The pill devalued women and made them objects of sex which led to human trafficking.[185] Once upon a time in the world and then in America, women were cherished and treated with dignity. Lovesick men worshipped the ground women walked on. *Love* songs told of men's desire and great love for their women. Men in folklore *slew dragons, won wars, climbed mountains,* and *even killed* others for their woman. The women and children were first in the lifeboats, first to have a seat on a bus, first to have their door opened, first for a seat at the table. Today's men do not even offer a pregnant woman, holding heavy groceries a seat on a bus or open a door for a mother with a toddler in tow, much less care about cherishing her as a female or worshipping the ground she walks on. In 1981, Pope John Paul II gave a speech before 15,000 Catholics where he quoted from Pope Paul VI encyclical Humanae Vitae. The Pope said, "*It is to be feared that man by using artificial birth control means, would end up **losing respect** for the woman and would come to consider her as a simple instrument of selfish pleasure and no longer as his respected lover and beloved companion.*" What was predicted by Pope Paul VI is exactly what the pill did.[186] It used women! It turned women into sex objects and sex industries flourished as a result. Pornography increased (*the female as the object*) and so did sex trafficking (*enslave the women to make money off her*).

The birth control pill caused sex crimes to increase.[187] In 1960 the rate of rape per thousand women was 9.6% but in 2018 it was 44%! This means nearly one third of women could experience rape in their lifetimes. There is more internet porn, more sexual abuse of children, a growing number of both men and women who are sex slaves, and more rapes and molestations occurring than ever before. *"Thirty-eight states have now enacted revenge porn laws and have criminalized the distribution of sexually explicit images without the owner's consent."*

Feminists argue the *birth control pill* helped women gain sexual freedom, but it also stole respect, previously given to women, and respect for the esteemed role of *mother*.

The pill encouraged casual divorce.[188] Marriages used to stay together *for the sake of the children*. When six or eight children were still home to raise, society looked down upon a man who would abandon his family for another woman and judged these men as *rascals* or *scoundrels*. Yet once women held down jobs, society no longer viewed the situation as abandonment. The *birth control pill* enabled this behavior. It promised women freedom, but the men were the ones who took advantage. They freed themselves, leaving their first wives for a younger, prettier woman! *Oh, the tears that have been shed due to the pill!* Since 1960, everywhere you see the breakdown of the family, *the pill* is the reason. In 1960, the rate of divorce was 2.2 divorce for every 1000 Americans but by 1969 the rate jumped to 3.3 divorces for every 1000 people. By the end of the 1970s the rate grew to 5.1, *(50% from 1960s)* then in 2018 the rate settled back down to 2.9 which is where it was in 1969. These rates may make one think everyone is getting married and not divorcing, but the opposite is occurring. In 1972 the marriage rate was 10.9 people per one thousand getting married in 2018 it is 6.5 people per one thousand getting married. This is the lowest rate since the 1900s.[189] People are no longer marrying at high rates and are co-habituating instead.

The pill caused family poverty.[190] In 1996 Lionel Tiger wrote in U.S. News and World Report, *"Since the early 1960s, we've seen a whole new class of **poverty** caused by the widespread use of the birth control pill: broken homes, male irresponsibility, legalized abortions, single moms, and deep resentment and alienation between men and women."* Yet instead of eliminating the need for abortion, the widespread use of the *birth control pill* set a moral tone for our world that opened the door for legalized abortion.

The pill put all the burdens on the female.[191] Once the pill came out men got all the joys of sex while the woman's body deteriorated from the hormone imbalances, bleeding, bloating, weight gain, mood swings, low libido, higher rates of blood clots, heart disease and even increased reproductive cancers. Her health problems increased while the male carried zero responsibility. *No wonder a man created this pill!*

The pill failed families. Women were forced to go out into the workforce due to the rise of the cost of living making it harder for families to exist on one income.[192] Starting in the late 1960s, stay-at-home neighborhoods started to empty. Now that mothers were on *the pill* and there would not be any further children, and or if their husband's had already left them for a younger woman, the mothers who had to get jobs, left their children and they kids were stuck in the middle. At first, there were no daycare centers[193] or few, if any, after-school programs anywhere! *(They had not been created or funded).* Mothers that had to work juggled their children between stay-at-home grandparents or stay-at-home neighbors.

When I was a child, every mother on our street stayed home. (20+ houses in suburban Md). Every mom at my school and every mom at my church, and every mom at my music lessons, and every one of my aunts and relatives, everywhere most everyone's mom stayed home. That was life in the 1960s in America. Moms were home! I know now this was not the case for every family, especially for minorities, but I am so thankful that it was my reality, because it felt safe. Everyone's mom was around, and their children felt cared for. Parents knew what was going on with their children. If their children ever caused mischief, parents felt responsible and punished their children accordingly. It was not until all the moms left home, that these bad things started to happen inside homes and outside in our communities. In the early 1970s, we would go places, and my friends would be there without their moms. We would walk past a house in our neighborhood, and no one would be home because my playmate's mom was at work all day. I had to stop seeing some playmates because no one was around except on weekends and the family had to spend Saturday running errands and doing chores. I remember it was sad.

Society had to make accommodations so that by the mid-1970s children went to daycare before 7 am and were left all day and or were taken by the daycare bus to the local school. After school, children went back to daycare and or were sent home with their house key around their neck. These older children became known as *latchkey* kids;[194] left to themselves until either mom or dad got home. This was how it was, starting in the late 1960s, 1970s, 1980s, and 1990s, and beyond. In every commercial, magazine, movie and book, young women and young mothers were exposed to feminists' ideas. The propagandists were trying hard to erase the society of yesteryear with stay-at-home moms and instead push the modern ideal for females to *want something for themselves!* With monthly magazines titled *ME and SELF!* this idea of (Its All about **ME** and do it for MY**SELF**) was continuously reenforced. After four decades, mothers started to react. In the 1980s, I would go to events with other couples and be afraid to admit that I stayed home and worked part-time, but by the mid-1990s, when I would tell women I worked part time and stayed home, the other mothers would say, '*Lucky you, now that the kids are in school my husband makes me work*'" Makes me work! Where's the feminist's freedom in that statement?

The pill did not make people happier with fewer children to raise.[195] Increasing our standard of living is one thing the *birth control pill* did for American society. After the birth control pill was introduced in 1960, the trend toward smaller families began. Couples voluntarily limited their family size to gain more material goods and dollars to spend. In "The Green Revolution," P. Scott discusses where there is an increase in the standard of living of residents, populations decrease but residents *do not express greater happiness* with more material items and smaller families.[196]

The Pill decreased family size and halted population growth in the U.S. In 1860, the average number of children in a family was 6. In 1970, the average number of children was 2.4. Then during the next thirty years, the birth rate declined to fewer than 2.0 children/couple, a rate insufficient to replace the population. In 2020, the birth rate dropped to 1.6 children/female, the lowest rate ever in America. In 2021 it rose slightly to 1.7 but the U.S. birth rate has been slowly declining for years.[197] This is largely due to artificial hormones seeping into our food and water and destroying fertility.

The pill is leading us toward a society void of children.[198] In the 1968 movie *Chitty-Chitty Bang-Bang*, the main characters visit a land where children were banned. The nasty king and queen did not like children. The monarchs hired a gruesome little man to *catch the children* and take them away! Although the story was fictional, the thought of being captured, taken away and eliminated was scary. Forty years later, our society mimics this movie with a new breed of working professionals who cannot be bothered with child-rearing. Society labels these couples *DINK: Double Income- No Kids*. They tend to migrate to cities and live lifestyles void of children. Sometimes because of increasing infertility, the lack of children is not by choice, yet far more often, most DINKs choose other things to do with their time than raise children. With two incomes and expendable cash, these people shop, travel, and enjoy a plush, materialistic lifestyle of constant indulgence. It may seem like fun now, but those who are *childless by choice* may be bound for a lonely future with no one around who cares for them; no one left to leave a legacy too, and no one left to prove they were ever here.

The pill did not even solve the problem of abortion! *"In the 1960s, it was promoted that the pill would prevent abortions! Abortion, both legal and illegal, has become the most widespread birth control method in the world today."* Not only did the birth control revolution led to the deaths of sixty million babies, but abortion is now a billion-dollar industry and has now led to another billion-dollar industry. This new industry's sole purpose is the *harvesting* and *selling of* aborted babies' body parts for foods, medicines and vaccines. Most abortive mothers are unaware their baby's body parts will be used in research, perfumes, hair products, food additives, vaccines and so much more! Using a baby's body parts in this way is a well-known fact throughout the baby harvesting industry. In 2024, the U.S. Republican House[199] allowed testimony from anti-abortion groups stating how Planned Parenthood and other abortion clinics routinely harvest baby organs and sell human body parts on the black market. There were even tapes shown of a Planned Parenthood executive bragging how Planned Parenthood would make $250,000 on a specific amount of body parts. Members of the House committee called the information horrific.

The pill took people down the slippery moral slope toward acceptance of human cloning.[200] Human cloning burst on the international scene in 1997 when *Dolly the sheep* was cloned. Ever since, the United States Congress and the United Nations are constantly being challenged on the morality of human cloning. Most people are not convinced it is a good idea to produce children who have been genetically altered to be identical to another person. Many nations have already outlawed cloning but not the USA. Pro-life organizations are against human cloning because it is one more way embryos and children are treated *as products* and not *as gifts.* Since 1997, when cloning was first presented, pro-life groups predicted human tissue farms emerging if cloning ever became legalized. In January 2024, New Jersey[201] passed a law on human cloning that clears a future path for human cloning farms in that state. *[The idea would be to use leftover embryos from in-vitro fertilization to clone and harvest for stem cells and or one day to grow until a specific developmental stage when the usable tissue would be cultivated and harvested].* They have not created these human tissue farms yet, but we are close with 24 states already passing some form of pro-tissue form of legislation. Unless pro-life groups fight back, legislation is inching closer to this sci-fi nightmare becoming a reality.

January 2024, The National Council of Catholic Bishops[202] spoke against these experiments as the possibilities are endless: farming potential babies for body parts, putting human babies inside animals to create a hybrid person/animal, buying and selling human embryos, patenting human beings. The Catholics are against a woman and her womb being used, as a piece of lab equipment or as a human incubator for growing research materials. *Where are the Protestant organizations and churches opposing this research?* One more time the Protestants are not making an impact in these areas of morality!

These are simply a few things the pill did, there are far more things the pill did to destroy people and society, but I will close with this final thought.

The pill is BIG BUSINESS![203] The pill created a billion-dollar contraceptive industry for drug manufacturers. Companies have made a whole lot of money off women causing the downfall and destruction of female health. Tested on only 130 women before it was rolled out, millions of women later and billions of dollars later the U.S. contraceptive market is valued at $8.3 billion dollars and the birth control pill is a $4.9 billion-dollar-per-year industry with a 75% profit margin!

WHERE DO WE GO FROM HERE?

I've covered where society has been by giving you an exhaustive history of birth control down through the ages and covered the brave men and women who have spoken out. I've also shown you the cowards who side with the enemy's agenda. I've also covered how world religions tackle the subject of birth control, abortion and sterilization. Then I brought us forward to show you why God's people and society are living in the fall-out from the birth control pill and other contraceptive paraphernalia: shots, patches, pellets, creams, foams, gadgets and devices. All of which ruin the purity of sex God's way and instead have devastated countless people's emotional and physical wellbeing. *My people are destroyed for lack of knowledge (Hosea 4:6).*

When God's people followed society *right off a cliff*, **it entangled all of us!** Now we've had nearly seventy years of pain and suffering from the pill alone! We've also had more than fifty years of babies dying from abortions and nearly one hundred years of doctrinal disagreements over birth control, abortion and sterilization amongst Protestants, Catholics and Jews. We now have epidemic infertility amongst our young people which causes incredible sadness because they cannot have the babies they desire. The world is now depopulating at a rapid rate with certain countries now experiencing near population collapse and the porn industry is flourishing at the highest rate ever while destroying the sex lives of our sons and daughters!

When will this madness end? God is reaching out to His people, calling us from the Scriptures to come back to His ways. We have taken something *holy* into our own hands that was *never* ours to control.

We would be the biggest fools ever to stay on this same path!

God wants us to REPENT and RETURN this area back over to Him.

You say I am rich; I have acquired wealth and do not need a thing. But you do not realize you are wretched, pitiful, poor, blind and naked. I counsel you to buy from me gold refined in the fire so you can become rich; and white clothes to wear so you can cover your shameful nakedness; and salve to put on your eyes so you can see (Revelation 3:17-18).

The verse I started off this chapter with reminds us that God can restore us: *When seventy years are completed for Babylon, I will come to you and fulfill my gracious promise to bring you back to this place. For I know the plans I have for you, declares the Lord, plans to prosper you and not to harm you, plans to give you a future and a hope" (Jeremiah 29:10-11).*

Wife's Prayer

Heavenly Father, You are opening my eyes. I had no idea there was so much controversy surrounding contraceptives. I also had no idea that the various denominations once agreed about not using birth control, and now they disagree. I've always assumed it was a bunch of religious men just trying to control women and that birth control was our answer to fight back. But with all this new information, I don't know what to think. I need more time to absorb what I am learning. It is all so new. But one thing I do know; I love children, and I do want what You have for me, I just don't know how it is all going to fit together, but I am willing. Please help me, Lord.

Amen

Husband's Prayer

Heavenly Father, there is so much I did not know. I had no idea there was any sort of history with birth control and I did not realize that at one point all faith groups agreed that scripture was clear. This is new news for me. I desire to learn more and be open. This is something that I have not spent time examining, but I believe that You want to show me a new way. I receive that, Lord. Please show me how You will provide if I trust You here. I need to have faith to believe. Please help me to submit my fears, as a man, and help me be open to what You want to say to me.

Amen

Christopher's Commentary

Growing up in a Baptist family, I was unaware of any doctrines being taught in the Catholic church. For that matter, I never visited a Catholic Church, and I was never invited to one, so I didn't know anything about what they believed or why they believed it. I did have some Catholic families in my neighborhood, and they did have a lot of children, and I did notice that often their families had more children than we had in our family, but being a child myself, I thought nothing of it. All I knew was that my family had five children, and we were considered a large family at the Baptist church we grew up in. With seven in our family, people always commented when we were out in public or at church that there were so many of us. I never quite understood what the problem was. This was the mid-1960s. I noticed that the other families at our church were much smaller. Most had only two children, a boy and a girl, including our pastor and his wife. Two children seemed to be the norm for most Bible-believing Baptist families. As the 1970s progressed and abortion was legalized, birth control use dominated American society.

Growing up in the Baptist Church, I was taught that "Baptists follow the Bible wholeheartedly." Yet we were told to follow the culture in this area, but we didn't realize this. All we knew was that our doctrine told us we must be *responsible and careful* with what we had been given. Since we never talked about the Catholics or any other religion producing large families, we didn't know any better. It was not like the truth was presented to us, and we walked away from it. We never learned the truth! The Scriptures about the family were interpreted as *meaning something else* and we never studied the family and what God was saying about the family in scripture, so we had no reason not to agree with the doctrine of *responsibility* because it made common sense. Then the ideals that supported it were subtly woven into our sermons in various non-intrusive ways. Like the pastor would read

Genesis 1:28, *Be fruitful and multiply* and then tell us, it only applied to our spiritual life or to gaining spiritual fruit. Sometimes the pastor might comment about how glad he was that it no longer meant physical children, and everyone would laugh.

If only we had asked our Catholic neighbors, but they probably wouldn't have told us either because pre-Vatican II the mass was in Latin and sadly most Catholics didn't understand it and would tell us they didn't understand it. The Catholics relied on the pope for wisdom and often, if you asked a Catholic about their faith, they could not tell you. Most just said they believed because their parents were Catholic.

Having a large family was what Catholics who loved God did, so they obeyed and had large families whether they understood why or not. Things were simply different back then. Catholics stayed in their churches; we stayed in ours and we never discussed these subjects. I never knew to ask because, as a young person growing up, I did not notice these kinds of things until later. I knew our family was larger than others at our church, but I still never made any connection between the Catholics and the Biblical truth that was being lived out right in front of me.

Christopher Scott

Investigate and Questions

- The exhaustive history in this chapter proves birth control has been around since the first peoples. Were you surprised at the history of birth control? From what you read, what information "jumped out at you?"
- In Genesis 38:8-10 we read about Onan. What do you think about this story? Have you ever heard of it before? What does it say about trying to control conception?
- Were you aware there was once agreement between Catholics, Jews and Protestants in the area of birth control? Upon learning there was a separation of doctrines, what are your thoughts about what happened in 1930, when years of Scripture was tossed out and church leaders separated themselves from Scripture in favor of societal changes? How do you think this decision affected your family in particular; the decisions your mom and dad made, or your grandparents made regarding their fertility?
- When God created Adam from the dust of the earth, the Scriptures say *He breathed life* into Adam, and he became a living thing. Later he created Eve from Adam's rib. From that point onward God did something so incredible, He gave His gift of life to Adam who was merely a created being! **Think how powerful this is!** Think what incredible love this is! A created being, from the dust of the ground, was now being able to give to another created being the same gift of life that God alone could give! Dwell on this point a second, the gift of life stands outside of humans. What does this one truth do to you? God gave us the gift of the supernatural, does this blow you away that great love God has for you and me. Does this help you understand more clearly why Satan wants to control, steal, stop and eliminate your gift to pro-create?
- Read Deuteronomy 30:19. After reading this chapter, are you pro-life or pro-parent's choice?

- Everyone used to be pro-life, the evil eugenics founder of Planned Parenthood, wanted all women to have the right to choose their method of contraception, sterilization and abortion. How have pro-choice ideals in the media and or at your place of worship influenced what you decided to do with your fertility?
- Read Exodus 20:13. How does the pill's idea of birth control freedom without consequence - the freedom of getting sterilized - and the freedom of abortion, each relate to each other?
- Read Proverbs 14:12 What do you think of this statement? "The birth control pill was so readily accepted by society, and unquestionably by believers that people acted as if GOD Himself had created the pill just for them. It seemed to be the answer that everyone was waiting for, to enjoy sex without the dilemma of procreating."
- Read Psalm 95:9-11. In 1961 the World Council of Churches announced a liberal policy of birth control use for all religions. How do you think this birth control mentality has affected society from 1960-present?
- Read Psalm 127:4, Proverbs 5:18, Malachi 2:14, Joel 1:8, Isaiah 54:6, Genesis 18:12, and Psalm 92:14. God's plan is for people to be surrounded by children. How does this relate to our ideas today?
- Read Revelation 3:17-19 and Hosea 4:6. How do these verses relate to you as an individual, the global church at large, and society?
- Were you aware that America had ever forced sterilization on individuals? What are your thoughts about yourself, or your children being sterilized against their will someday?

Impacting Others

Rachel, after reading your book, I wanted to share a few thoughts with you. I was raised with the belief that the girls should get married and get on the pill because it was up to us to space our children properly and be responsible. WOW! What an eye-opener your book was. It is difficult not to use birth control when most churches do not say a word about it. I think it is time for the truth to come out before we all lose sight of it. People need to know where the lies about birth control came from and how we are simply robbing ourselves. Thanks, Rachel, for opening my eyes. **Mom from Canada**

Rachel, I wasted time...Ten years ago, when I was first married, a friend gave me the book Full Quiver, and I must admit I never read it. I gave it away to a friend who did read it, and she started to have additional babies. I decided that it was a dangerous book. I only wanted two children and didn't want anything to change my viewpoint. When your book came out, a girlfriend from my homeschool co-op read your book and started telling me about it. Something about the title Birthing God's Mighty Warriors intrigued me, so when she was through, I borrowed her copy and began to read it. I cannot believe I missed out on these truths for so long! I am so mad at myself! I have been married for over ten years and only have two children. I mourn for the lost time when I was trying to control everything. I read your book out loud to my husband, quoting your words and sharing your stories. Your book has good examples! Anyway, he came under deep conviction from the scripture, and it was more me; he wanted another baby, and I didn't. Well, now we both have caught the baby bug. We were joking that we want at least 12 children, and we want them to live all over the country, and when we retire, we want to buy an RV and spend a month with each one of them! That's our fantasy; we'll see if God gives us this, but we are into birthing children, and I usually have good pregnancies. I am pregnant with my third child right now and so excited! Since I'm only 32, we have plenty of time to receive

God's blessings. Please pray that He wants us to have a bunch! I want them now! BTW, I love your book! Thanks for writing it. **Marsha Cincinnati, Ohio, pregnant with baby number three and desiring the fullest quiver possible**!

Chapter 4

WHAT IS REALLY GOING ON HERE?

Exposing *Politically Correct* Thinking

When the Lord started revealing His truths to me concerning what scripture teaches about children, it was a painful message for me to grasp because I had been raised in the humanistic culture of the United States. I had much resistance to even consider what He was showing me. It was foreign to my thinking. I had been subtly brainwashed to believe that I should look out for myself first and be concerned with how this revelation could affect me long term and my plans for my future. God had to open my eyes to show me how society had changed right to wrong and replaced it with my personal preference. This was when God opened my eyes that He had other plans for our family.

My high school biology teacher told my class that the easiest way to kill a frog is to boil him to death slowly. This could be accomplished by putting the frog into a pot of room-temperature water as it slowly heated up on the stove. The frog would not realize the temperature was increasing until it was too late.

Many of us do not realize how much we are like this frog. Our thought processes have been slowly boiled to death by media spin, cultural norms, and the opinions of the individuals surrounding us. Our culture has subtly brainwashed all of us. From a young age, we are taught to believe that it is essential for our self-esteem to care about *ourselves first* and not to be concerned with the *needs* of others, except perhaps during the holidays or other special occasions when it is socially acceptable to help. The rest of the time, society tells us we should concentrate our efforts on our *own* lives, goals, and personal dreams for the future.

We become perfectly comfortable knowing God wants us to live our lives for others, yet we live our lives to please ourselves. This often happens in family planning. We do what we want. Because of our lack of teaching and silence from our churches about birth control, we've accepted the cultural norms and adopted a world belief that we should *choose* the size of our family based on what will best suit *our* needs and goals for *our* future. We never ask God. It is our choice.

In my marriage, this was true; we had completely accepted the non-churchgoers' ideas about birth control. We didn't realize God had something better in mind. We were misled because we listened to the many voices speaking through our culture. We accepted the *politically correct* idea that parents should *never* have to raise children they do not want!

For decades advertising ads from toothpaste to cereal to Walt Disney World to movies and on TV Shows, the ideal family was portrayed as two parents: one boy and one girl. Rarely, if ever, an ad might show a third child and possibly only in an ad for a minivan or some other reason to sell something to a family with a third child. These advertisements consistently reflected United States census figures. The average American family (churchgoers and nonbelievers) had consisted of 2.1 children for more than sixty years in the USA but then fell below the replacement rate in 2010 and has not recovered.[1] The plan for a large family was diminished during the baby boomer's childbearing years. For these, raising children became viewed as a chore of *drudgery* and *bondage*, with the goal of quickly *getting it over with*.

The acceptance of society's ideas, unfortunately, caused my husband and I to not be able to combat the lies we heard from the culture. Instead, we accepted them and participated. Church going people cannot fight against the enemy's lies until they understand who and what they are fighting against.

Every generation is called to *submit* to God's ways, yet when *worldly* ideals infiltrate, believers can get confused. They forget God's plan, stumble and fall into sin because the world's standards lead them into lifestyles that do not agree with scripture.

WHAT IS REALLY GOING ON HERE?

The person without the Spirit does not accept the things that come from the Spirit of God but considers them foolishness and cannot understand them because they are discerned only through the Spirit (1 Corinthians 2:14).

Due to the deception we've all been led into, there are three terms I feel we need to understand to help us uncover the deception in our culture: humanism, hedonism, and self-worship.

Humanism[2] — any system of thought or action concerned with merely human interests or those with humanity. (In this belief system, man is first, instead of God or other humans)

Hedonism[3] — the doctrine that pleasure is the principal good and should be the aim of all actions. (In this belief system, seeking pleasure is a way of life).

Self-worship[4] — the state of caring only for oneself, regarding one's needs and interests, and viewing all decisions for personal advantage or gain. (This belief system promotes a self-centered lifestyle).

The religion of secular humanism — Humanism is a religious thought process. In humanism, man's glory is elevated above God's glory. (In this religious belief system, man accomplishes great things without the aid of a Higher Power.

Some national organizations promote secular humanism such as the National Humanist Foundation.[5] Groups such as this and others influence the public's thinking and push a cultural objective through the books we read, the films we see, and the talk shows we hear. They reflect one major attitude: God is unnecessary, and humanity is supreme.

Humanism's influences can especially be noticeable in Hollywood movies about catastrophic disasters but with the underlying message that God does not exist! *Apollo 13* (1995) about a group of astronauts who almost die, *Twister* (1996) about a killer tornado, *Dante's Peak* (1997) about a deadly volcanic eruption, *A Perfect Storm* (2000) about a group of fishermen trying to survive a killer storm, *Poseidon* (2006) about a cruise ship hit by a tsunami wave, *2012* (2009) about the disastrous end of the Mayan calendar, *San Andreas* (2015) about a killer earthquake hitting California, and *Greenland* (2020) about a comet hitting earth. In each of these movies, relatable characters face life-

and-death situations. Yet, in the terror of the moment, they never once *refer to God*. They do not call out to Him or lean on Him in prayer.

As we watch these films, we are subtly convinced that *people are superior to God* and that humans should not rely on a supreme being for their health and safety. When we are inundated with these subtle messages they tell us, *"God? who needs Him?"* it's easy to think we have what we have because of our greatness, and we forget that a gracious Heavenly Father has allowed our health and blessings.

However, in real life when people are faced with crisis situations, people often *cry out to God*. Even unbelievers pray, hoping supernatural help exists somewhere. In two real life stories about 9/11 people did pray. In the movie *United 93* (2006) there is a scene where two passengers say the Lord's prayer and in the movie *World Trade Center* (2006) the trapped fireman all recites the Lord's prayer together. In real life, people pray, but when a secular humanist has influenced the film, they portray that people do not cry out, because there is no God.

IF THE SITUATION ARISES...

One element of secular humanism is the belief that everything humans need to do to accomplish their personal goals can be justified if they have a good reason for their decision. We call these *situational ethics*.[6] In situational ethics, a person faces a choice that challenges a moral absolute. For example, scripture says, *you shall not murder* (Exodus 20:13). Yet in situational ethics, a person must decide whether it is justified to murder based on a particular set of circumstances. I remember when I was in college I took a woman's health class, and the teacher broke us into groups and told us we had to solve a dilemma. *"Suppose there was only one abortion left in the entire world and you have to decide which woman is worthy of this abortion."* The teacher went on to tell us the first woman is a 13 yr. old girl and the father is her 26 yr. old stepbrother, another is a 22 yr. old girl who was date-raped, another is a straight-A college student who just got accepted into Med-school and a baby would ruin her plans, another is a mother of three children-pregnant with her 4th child and her husband was just diagnosed with terminal cancer, and a 44 yr. old peri-menopausal woman whose only child just graduated high school.

The students in the room started discussing in groups and then each group voted. I remember I was disgusted but the other students felt that every single woman deserved the abortion! The teacher was so proud of the class and then went on to talk about the importance of abortion rights.

The reason situational ethics confuses people is because it dismisses that God's Word is the moral absolute. The truth is none of these women should abort her baby. Murder is morally wrong every time! But we reason out why murder might be OK because the situation justifies our reasoning. We don't know what to choose, so our only solution is to go against the moral absolute and justify our response. When we insert our very good reason, we are tempted to say, *"Well, I guess in that particular situation, it was correct to murder because there was no other choice."* Yet is it correct? God did not tell us to follow His commandments based on a specific situation. Unfortunately, once *situational ethics* took hold in our society, *situational Christianity* also affected our moral code.

WHATEVER I WANT TO DO IS *OK WITH GOD*

After being influenced by situational ethics in our media, culture, and classrooms, Christian teachers began to apply the same thinking to God's word, questioning whether God meant for His scripture to be taken literally all the time. *(Satan tricked Eve in the garden with the exact same thinking).* In **situational Christianity**, a person's walk is no longer based on God's written Word, instead, it is based upon however a person thinks or feels about their circumstances. This flexible form of Christianity was birthed from the *grace* message that infiltrated church theology in the 1990s. In the grace movement, God's grace permits people to look at their situation and not feel condemned when they choose to be disobedient.

Situational Christianity says, *"Whatever I do is OK with God if it is the best decision for my life and circumstances. In other words, God's word does not say, be fruitful and multiply all the time, after all, God knows that if we had too many children, we couldn't do the other things we want to do for God."*

Situational Christianity dismisses the purity of obedience in one area, and if we can come up with a good enough reason, we can justify our actions, in the other area. According to God's word, viewing God's grace as *permission* to reinterpret God's commands is sin! Yet in situational Christianity it does not acknowledge that introducing reasoning into God's Word brings consequences. Believers who interpret obedience to scripture as literal are seen by situational Christians as intolerant religious folks trying to enslave modern believers by demanding obedience to commandments that God's grace did away with. *(They try to put the message of this book in that category and then call this message legalistic!).*

Family planning is one of those areas where contemporary church goers completely missed the message. People do whatever they want and don't give a second thought that God might care.

If anyone builds on this foundation using gold, silver, costly stones, wood, hay or straw, their work will be shown for what it is If what has been built survives, the builder will receive a reward. If it is burned up, the builder will suffer loss (1 Corinthians 3:12-15).

Revelation 21:4 says, He will wipe away every tear from their eyes, but why are we crying? To be successful, we must follow God's order, and the family is God's order in society. After Protestant churches embraced birth control, society rapidly fell away from God's order. Family life deteriorated inside churches. Ministers started having affairs, getting vasectomies, recommending the pill and IUD for their wives and congregants, ministers fell into porn, families split up. Divorce was everywhere. The acceptance of sex without the need to reproduce a child created a culture of choice.

Do not deceive yourselves. If any of you think you are wise by the standards of this age, you should become "fools" so that you may become wise. For the wisdom of this world is foolishness in God's sight. As it is written: "He catches the wise in their craftiness" (1 Corinthians 3:18-19).

As the seculars started encroaching upon society with humanism and situational ethics and then once Christianity became situational, it was easy to *accept the feminist's ideals of women working outside-the-home* while also doing away with stay-at-home motherhood. The feminists' told women to start making demands. Gender roles became confused because the women confused them. This caused all kinds of other problems. The late 1960s-early 1970s fashion industry handled the confusion by blurring the lines and made a buck by introducing *his and her* blue jeans and *unisex* haircuts.

Once the lines between men and women began to erase, resentment and disregard for one another's roles contributed to increased unhappiness. Gender confusion caused women to act like men and men to become like women. Men no longer knew what it meant to be a man, and women no longer wanted to fall into the traditional roles for a female. Women gained a few wins. The movement brought equal pay for equal work and opened the door for greater education for women, this part was needed and very good for women but once women invaded the workforce, they lost the respect of the men. Men and women had no idea what was expected, and the confusion has continued to this day. Men despised and disregarded women for entering their world.

GIRLS RULE, BOYS DROOL

Once feminism was embraced by society, men and women were no longer considered unique in their gender roles but were instead regarded as complete equals. Roles reversed and changed. Men were no longer expected to *open doors* for women or *give up their seat on a bus*, not even for a pregnant or elderly woman. Women have also become confused about what they should be trying to accomplish. Our culture shouted *career* at young women and dismissed the role of wife and mother by never mentioning it in ads, magazine articles, or films. During the seventies, eighties, and nineties and into the new Millennia heroines are not mothers and rarely wives. The role of a young, happy twenty- something mother raising her young family nearly disappeared off the silver screen. Instead, young women were portrayed as either *career minded* women, students or tough women without an ounce of nurturing ability.

Furthermore, feminists made motherhood a *taboo* to consider. I know this because I was a twenty-something during those years. I didn't want to leave my baby screaming in daycare, so I decided to buck the trends, and became a stay-at-home mom when no one else was home in my neighborhood! I must admit it was hard. Few women my age were around and it was lonely, yet being with my children was well worth the sacrifice.

Who am I? This became a question many young women in my generation asked themselves and is also a question young women ask today. Giving in to society's pressures, all women head off to college and out into the career world, looking for the fulfillment we are promised is there for us, while motherhood is a distant goal. In the workforce, there is satisfaction, but at what cost? Who must suffer so that a woman can find her fulfillment? It's the innocent children or her husband.

In the late 1970s, 1980s and 1990s countless little ones were awakened before dawn to be dressed in their Oshkosh B'gosh overalls and Izod Lacoste shirts. Yawning and dragging their Smurf blankets and Barney lunch boxes behind them, while their moms were dressed in suits, heels and touting designer briefcases, these little ones were thrown into family minivans to spend their day at the local daycare. Most children were left by 6 am and not picked up till after the sun went down. Several decades of little children bore this burden of spending their days in an institution, instead of at home with a loving parent. All because *their mothers* were trying to *find themselves.*

Fulfillment in the world's workplace was likely not the primary place where God intended for a woman to find most of her happiness—at least not during the same years as she is capable of childbearing. Women have become increasingly more unhappy. New expectations for women brought pressure not experienced by previous generations, causing many women to suffer depression.

According to the 2008 CDC statistics, upwards of 30%[7] of females will suffer some form of depression in their lifetime. Much more is expected from women who must go out into the workforce and *bring home the bacon* and be able to also care for her children. Currently, the trend for working women is to resent the men for not helping more.

According to a Gallop Poll the female lifetime rate of depression was 26.2% in 2017 but in 2023 a new poll increased that rate to 36.9%[8] and according to the CDC 2023 nearly three in five teen girls say they feel sad and persistently hopeless.[9]

Men suffer from depression and loneliness because their role has changed.[10] Men used to come home to an adoring wife who cooked, cleaned, ironed, sewed and raised sweet children all day. Yes, this was really the way it was, and most women were very happy being able to be home taking care of their families. But then the woman's revolution changed all that thinking and brought in new ideas. At first, feminists tried to show they could work fulltime while still keeping up with all their other commitments.

A 1970's Calgon commercial touted the new woman. She could *bring home the bacon, fry it up in a pan and never let her hubby forget he was a man*. But that was sheer fantasy! Working women quickly learned the opposite. Women came home tired, weary from working all day, and his needs were the last thing on her list. Men revolted and divorce was everywhere.

Men had a hard time adapting to this new woman who was not interested much in her home life as her job. Her new identity was trying to find fulfillment elsewhere. Women started making increasing demands on the men. Seventy years after women went out into the workforce men must now come home to help with children, possibly fix dinner and do housework while all the time being extremely caring and sensitive to the needs of his wife and family. Sounds great, right? Yes, it is way better when men help around the house, but it is hard for men to make themselves fit into new roles that society constantly redefines and changes, and the women are still not happy!

WORKING MOMS: LIFE IS HARD

I've already talked about how the pill and feminists' propaganda convinced the women in my generation to delay motherhood. Many rose up the corporate ladder, but it cost them dearly, for when they finally awoke from their fog sometime in their late thirties or early forties, they found their biological clocks had ticked out, and for what? A job. Where was the fulfillment they were seeking?

In 1987 Hollywood produced an excellent movie that addressed this controversial subject. In *Baby Boom*, Diane Keaton played a cold-hearted Harvard-educated career woman. After the death of a relative, she was given a young child to care for. At first, she chose to give the child away but soon realized that in her heart, she could not let the little girl leave. Seemingly overnight, she was transformed into a caring mother. It is a beautiful story of one woman's transformation from what the world says *having it all should look like* to the realization that having it all by the feminists' standards leaves a void. She realizes that true happiness is not what she originally envisioned. Being a mother was what made her truly happy. This movie's underlying theme reflected the pain that baby boomer women were experiencing within the feminist movement. Their hearts told them there was more, but many did not realize their children were the answer. The movie was a breakthrough and reinforced the message that there is beauty inside of women's hearts that only children can bring out. It is a beautiful picture of how God's way IS the way!

Hollywood and TV have made a few positive strides at the beginning of the new Mellinia and portayed families in a much better light. However, the emphasis in pop culture has remained that people should not get themselves into unnecessary hardships. No wonder couples are now not wanting to even have children! This is what the Childfree by Choice movement is all about. Fertile people who don't want any hardships. They are completely against the idea of creating a family to the point of radical hatred for their own children. They feel justified by pop culture that continuously tells them that if something does not give them great pleasure, they should not have to put up with it!

POP CULTURE INFLUENCES US MORE THAN WE REALIZE

I believe that today, many church going people base their value of a human on secular ides. If we consider the effect that television and movies have had on our beliefs, we may find the reasons why God's people have seen children as a choice. The emphasis in pop culture has remained that people should not get themselves into unnecessary hardships by having more children than they can afford. When slogans such as, *"Be all that you can be,"* and *"Have it your way"* fill our minds, there is no reason to put ourselves into a hardship. When our magazines have titles such as SELF and ME and when we are inundated with the subtle messages that *everything should bring pleasure and not bring us grief, it is easy to quit everything!* If something does not bring comfort, we should not have to do it: e.g., not have to work a job (quit it), put up with a spouse we no longer have feelings for (get a divorce); endure hours of pregnancy labor (get an epidural or c section), not carry a baby (hire a surrogate) etc. Everything must be for our pleasure!

Sex is for pleasure and not for childbearing became the attitude in society and specifically in the Protestant church after the onslaught of the birth control pill in 1960.

When the Protestant church world embraced secular society's idea that sex is for pleasure and not for procreation, Bible-believing clergy encouraged couples to use birth control to relieve the marriage of messing with unwanted children. Couples were told that this would aid in a more sexually fulfilling marriage. Beginning in the 1970s, an onslaught of books, tapes, marriage seminars, and teachings about the joys of sex without the trials of parenthood invaded the Protestant church world. It grieves me that God's people wrote all these resources, deceived countless couples and blended with an idolatrous culture, each leading the other astray, and all for the pursuit of sexual *pleasure*.

Don't get me wrong; God intended sex to be very pleasurable, and enjoying that pleasure is scriptural. An entire book of the Bible, Song of Solomon, is dedicated to expressing the pleasures of the marital bed. Surely God's clear intention was that sex be filled with physical pleasure. But God also intended for the act to be open to creating new life. Sexual pleasure is purposeful. God created sex for our immediate pleasure, but the true joy of sex is the children that result from it.

We exchanged God's ways for the ways of our culture

Where in God's word does it ever say that cultural society and churchgoers should agree? Scripture clearly shows believers are never to blend with culture but to live separate lives. Yet the opposite happened in the 1960s when both believers and unbelievers unified on the birth control issue.

Unless a child is planned, the child has no value (the reason to use birth control).

Unless a child is planned that child should not be allowed to be born (the reason for abortion).

With this attitude in both society and amongst churchgoers, the underlying idea that no one should ever have to suffer a mistaken pregnancy and the attitude was, "*We should want children when we want them, and see no reason to create them if we don't want them!*" Today we at least hope that if a contraceptive failure does occur that churchgoers would at least go ahead and have their *surprise* child, rather than seek an abortion, yet as time went by, 43%[11] of women were attending church when they chose to have their abortions.

"WANTED" CHILDREN VS. "NOT WANTED"

Where did we get the idea that children must be *wanted* before we allow them to be born? The American people are constantly bombarded with stories of *unwanted children* in the news and on TV shows such as ABC 20/20, NBC 48 Hours, and CBS 60 Minutes. Media spin is used to create stories that push the mindset of our self-absorbed world. They tell us the tragic tales of *unwanted children* who are victims of poverty and broken homes. Of course, these stories are true for a tiny percentage of the population, but that point is not stressed. They tell us the worst thing that could happen to a woman is to be made to give birth and raise an unwanted child. When we see images of children being beaten and crack babies shaking, we wonder, *"Why should these children be allowed to be born if their parent does not want them?"*

These sad depictions of poverty and broken homes subtly cause us to reason out about who has value and who doesn't. We wonder why these parents would have a child if they did not want him. We are slowly being brainwashed to agree with child-prevention (birth control and abortion). After viewing all these messages about unwanted children and after hearing the word "unwanted" repeated over and over, we think that *"A child should always be carefully planned by their parents and unwanted children are not welcome."*

Even though this viewpoint opposes God, we can't help but get *sucked into an agreement* with this politically correct viewpoint. We get trapped into believing that people should not have to conceive, birth, or raise a child that was not planned because that child will always be unwanted. Slowly we take up the side of the godless culture who does not value every life. In less than one generation, we completely leave our standard. This brainwashing is so subtle that we do not even realize we have turned from the ideals preached in the Scriptures and we now agree with the ideas of our godless culture.

Yet in God's eyes, there is no such thing as an *unwanted child* because, to God, each child is sent to be a blessing (Psalm 127:5). The Lord says *every child is a gift* (James 1:17). Every person has value, and God has a wonderful plan for their life.

Because of their godless agenda, the media always fails to show us the other side of the *unwanted-child* scenario. They never explain about women who were initially shocked or displeased about being pregnant but once they got over the initial shock, they finally accepted it. Some of history's most remarkable people were born at inopportune times and into less than satisfactory family conditions. This side is rarely, if ever shown, even though it is a fact of history. Instead, we seek perfection and perfect life circumstances and are led to believe that once a person is conceived in an unwanted circumstance, he will be unwanted for the rest of his life, and his parents will never love him. This is not true! Unfortunately, these portrayals convince people—even God's people—that they should hesitate before conceiving a child. If we continually see only one side portrayed, our minds will not be programmed to consider alternatives. For almost fifty years, the media ignored the possibility of a positive side to an *"surprise pregnancy"* situation!

It was not until 2007, in the movie *Juno,* that the media dealt with teen pregnancy and brought a positive message about a high school girl who decided not to abort her baby. We saw a similar theme in the 2006 movie *Bella,* and in 2017 we saw the true story of Abby Johnson in the movie *Unplanned.* Abby's movie showed life in a Planned Parenthood clinic and the business of killing babies; the quotas, the money exchanged, the lies about chemical abortions and the push to kill babies for profit.

OUR LIVES—OUR BODIES—OUR CHOICES!

Many of the choices God's people make today in family planning are the same as those of the founder of Planned Parenthood: Margaret Sanger. During the last seventy years, her success can be measured by how much God's people have changed their opinion on birth control. Many believers use birth control, get sterilized, and think nothing about using all these options. This is because Margaret Sanger's ideas influenced our culture.

One of the pro-choice movement's most famous slogans is, "My Body, My Choice,"[12] meaning no one has the right to tell a woman what she can do with her body! By age forty-five, two in five women are sterilized (39.1%)[13] and one in ten men (10%).[14] Many of these sterilized folks are God's people! Think of this: almost half of the people over forty-five years old have willingly submitted to a medical procedure that has stolen their ability to create life!

Unfortunately, far too many of God's people have demonstrated and still agree in their bedrooms with this slogan. When we use birth control, abortion, or get sterilized, our actions are communicating to God: **It is MY LIFE, it is MY BODY, and it is MY CHOICE!**

Talk about churchgoers adopting secular humanism! When we insert *me,* use *grace incorrectly,* and throw out a life of sacrifice and obedience, we will not see our lives or bodies as belonging to God. Instead, we will rationalize that *because God loves me, He would never want to bring anything into my life that might bring me inconvenience or displeasure.*

Therefore, I can do whatever I want with my life and body, and God will be completely O.K. with my choice. Whatever happened to laying down our lives for a higher cause of servitude to the Lord?

I WANT WHAT I WANT!

"I don't want to spend too much of my life raising children. I need my freedom!" Both churchgoers and non-churchgoing women seem to resonate with the same thought. The men are no different. How many churchgoing men would say, *"I do not want to be raising children when I am old. I want to enjoy a few luxuries for myself."* When society cannot look to churchgoers to see a distinct difference, they will not want what we offer. We look the same as the non-church attendees, so why follow us?

One hundred years ago, families were larger. Parents did not use birth control or become sterilized. Cancers of the reproductive organs (breast, ovarian, cervical, prostate) were nonexistent. Miscarriages, autoimmune diseases, divorce, impotence, female problems, and infertility were extremely rare. These are the complications we see in people's lives today, where almost everyone uses some form of birth control. Most people had never even heard of these ailments one hundred twenty years ago.

Shortly after we moved to Florida, we visited a new church, and the pastor and his wife were just having their first baby. The pastor's wife said she only wanted one child and after this baby, *"I want them to burn, cut, tie, and seal my tubes off so I do not ever have to go through this again!"* I could see this woman was not having a happy experience. I don't know what happened to her, but I knew she had been wounded, and even though she loved God, in this area, she was rejecting any sort of future plan Jesus could have had for her life.

HELP, I HAVE BEEN BRAINWASHED!

Did the word of God suddenly change when society changed? For many churchgoers, it did! Once we became thoroughly indoctrinated into a politically correct mindset in family planning, we have had trouble discerning truth from lies.

One way we stay deceived is when society uses *politically correct words* to describe medical procedures that alter God's plan. Word specialists agree that word choices can make people feel more *comfortable*. Word choices can *soften* the effects of surgical procedures, which steal the inheritance of God's people. We should be outraged; instead, we accept and use politically correct terminology.

Test yourself by looking at these word exchanges. Think about how each word choice makes you feel:

> **Vasectomy** instead of STERILIZED
> **Tubes tied** instead of STERILIZED
> **Infertile** instead of BARREN
> **Fetus** instead of BABY
> **Pro-choice** instead of sucking the brains out and crushing the skull of a live baby to then sell and make money off its body parts
> **Anti-abortion** foes instead of PRO-LIFERS who stand in the gap and pray

How did you do? Did you pick up on the subtle word exchanges? Political correctness softens the impact and makes it easier for a culture that does not want to hear the truth.

Words such as *abortion* or *sterilized* bring a sad picture to our minds.

When we hear sterilized, we think of Hitler's regimes or China's one-child policy[15], and we'd rather not think about that. For comfort's sake, we use the word *vasectomy*.

When we hear *abortion* instead of *pro-choice*, we think of the abortive medical procedure with blood and dead babies. This ugly reminder might evoke strong emotions and cause people to act, so for comfort's sake and *to keep us numb*, our culture brainwashes us by using *politically correct* phrases. These dull our senses and appease our conscience. It is so effective that our clergy use the same terms from the pulpit!

If we were fed a diet of TRUTH about what God's word says about family planning, we might make different choices. What would happen if we heard pro-death or pro-murder instead of pro-choice? How about *destroying your God-given right to bear children* instead of *getting your tubes tied* or *blocking God's plan* instead of *being on the pill*?

If pastors were only brave enough to say something couples might make other choices, but how can they say something when they have had a vasectomy themselves?

To help people *wake up* from their hypnotic dream state, my husband created his own website dealing with the touchy subject of the vasectomy. For over seventy years, men have submitted to an operation that goes entirely against what the male's body was set up to do. Often men submit without a fight. This operation has not been studied to see the adverse side effects. Men simply surrender to the knife or laser, without questioning what the vasectomy operation is about. Will the real men out there please wake up?

My husband created a website called realmendontgetfixed.org[16] (*.org for sex organ! He was such a jokester!*) And he had one goal: to make men laugh but to also jar their minds about what they are doing when they submit to a vasectomy. With his dry sense of humor, his website was meant to be a comical way to communicate a touchy subject, but at the same time, he wanted men to realize that a vasectomy is the same operation we do on our pets. It's like being spayed or neutered. When men allow themselves to get sterilized, the dignity of the male species is lowered to the animal level, which is why REAL MEN DON'T GET FIXED ... like a dog! (Arf-arf)

TV AND MOVIES: TAKE US AWAY FROM GOD'S WAY

Today, many churchgoing people base their value of human beings on what they see in the media and in popular culture and not on the truths in the Word of God. It is rare to find a person of faith who knows what the Scriptures say about birth control and what it might mean to trust God with this area of their lives.

Considering the effect television and movies have had on our cultural beliefs; we may find some reasons why God's people and society do not want children. I noticed that from the time I was leaving high school in the late 1970s, TV shows like *The Brady Bunch* with their six children were long gone, and the new mindset was that **Fewer children is best.** Hollywood followed suit and started portraying smaller families with only one or two children.

In 1980 the Academy Award-winning movie *Kramer vs. Kramer* introduced a new idea not seen in previous cinema. The couple had one child and divorced. The movie introduced the concept that the father was the better parent than the mother. Before this film, it was assumed the mother was always the better parent, and that the best place for

WHAT IS REALLY GOING ON HERE?

children was always with their mother. Most states had laws supporting this idea. Kramer vs. Kramer did a lot to change popular views of the nuclear family and the role of motherhood. This movie was critically acclaimed, and afterwards fathers began to get custody of their children more often.

From 1980-2000 Hollywood followed with a series of movies during the next twenty years where the ideals of marriage changed, and family size was small. One child per family in *The Champ, Fatal Attraction, Pay-it-Forward, Sleepless in Seattle, Jingle All the Way, Richie Rich,* and *The Princess Diaries*. Two children (one boy and one girl) in *What about Bob? Father of the Bride,* and *Spy Kids*.

These ideas were nothing new Hollywood has been influencing us all along. This is a brief history.

The 1930s–1940s: Beginning in the 1930s, when many families were still quite large most Shirley Temple movies portrayed Shirley in a family without siblings. In nearly every movie, Shirley was alone as an orphan or living with a single parent. In her 1935 movie, *Our Little Girl*, Hollywood even tackled the idea of divorce, which was almost unheard of in those days. The divorce rate in 1936 was 1%. During the 1940s, films featured large families, but often the stories portrayed were stories of hardship and loss and The Great Depression, such as the family portrayed in *The Grapes of Wrath*. Whereas in the 1946 movie, *It's a Wonderful Life*, Hollywood portrayed a small family theme.

The 1950s: When the war was over, and our soldiers came home and started producing their own families, television was also pioneered. The great post-war baby boom was in full bloom, yet TV families were very small, with only one or two children per household, even though many children in the 1950s were being raised in families with three or more children! Shows such as *Ozzie and Harriet, The Donna Reed Show,* and *Leave It to Beaver* were popular and had two children, whereas *I Love Lucy, The Andy Griffith Show,* and *Dennis the Menace* had families with only one child. None of these shows ever portrayed the friends of any of the main characters as being from large families either. All these shows became very popular, but the studios did also still produce a few films that featured large families, such as *Cheaper by the Dozen* (a true story of a family with twelve children), *Spencer's Mountain* (nine children), *The Seven Little Foys* (seven children), and *Seven Brides for Seven Brothers* (seven boys). But society was drifting away from the large family thing, and more films were being made that featured working women.

By the 1960s, and after introducing *the birth control pill* into American society, Hollywood began to make a big switch. (Remember, millions of couples were now using the birth control pill, and with many women working outside the home, the idea of a large nuclear family was disappearing.) A small number of films featuring large families were still produced, but it was clear that these families were Roman Catholic. Since the Roman Catholic Church was very outspoken against birth control use and *the pill*, Hollywood figured the only people still producing large families had to be Roman Catholics. *(I guess this was to indicate that religion would be the only reason parents would still have a large family).* Films such as *The Sound of Music* (seven Roman Catholic children) and *Yours, Mine, and Ours!* (a blended family of eighteen Roman Catholic children) all positively portrayed large families. Hollywood continued to produce films featuring small nuclear families, such as *Chitty-Chitty Bang*-Bang (two children), *Charlie and the Chocolate Factory,* and *Winnie the Pooh* (one child).

The mid-1960s A nanny instead of MOMMY: The film *Mary Poppins* introduced a new idea to the American Family: a new mommy figure. The idea of another person being the mommy would have seemed odd to families up until the end of the 1960s because moms always stayed home with their children. But in this film, the well-to-do family hired *Mary Poppins*. Nannies had been popular in England for years, but this was a new ideal for Americans. *I remember watching it as a child and thinking how great it would be to have Mary Poppins as my nanny.* This film was very successfully *at brainwashing.* Instead of the mother and father caring for their two children, now the children had a better caretaker, a nanny who could do a more efficient job than either parent. This film must have done an excellent job convincing people that nannies were adequate caregivers because, by the 1980s, it had become quite popular for working mothers to hire a nanny for their children. These parents of the 1980s were the same people who saw the movie Mary Poppins as children. Maybe they dreamed of having someone to play with them as wonderful as Mary Poppins. Look at how one film changed the cultural fabric of a generation!

1960s Televisions Shows continued with the idea that families were now small. T*he Andy Griffith Show, Dick Van Dyke, Flintstones, Bewitched, Dennis the Menace,* and *Hazel* featured families with one child, while

Flipper and Family Affair had two children. Shows like The Andy Griffith Show and My Three Sons got audiences used to families with single parents. In these shows, one of the parents was deceased. Single motherhood emerged on the scene toward the end of the 1960s. Lucille Ball, in the show Lucy portrayed a single mom to two children, and Julia was an African American single mom with one child. In the show Family Affair, the children had a butler act as a nanny. He took the place of the father who had to work. This idea also promoted the theme of another person caring for the children instead of the parent.

1970s films showed us the family as it related historically. Filmmakers did not know what to show us about the family because society was changing rapidly. Hollywood decided to show us historical films or tragedies. The Godfather was about a large Italian family and the dynasty they created. Fiddler on the Roof was the story of a poor Russian Jews with five girls. The parents tackled a changing Russia and its effects on the family. Swiss Family Robinson was a classic that came to life. It featured a loving family with three children who were shipwrecked. Other films such as Earthquake, Towering Inferno, and Jaws portrayed people and their families in tragic circumstances.

1970s TV was the decade of the blended family as Hollywood and TV introduced the theme of the blended family. On TV shows like The Brady Bunch and Eight is Enough. These were large families, but family size was not the result of one mother and father, instead the family size was the result of the death of a previous spouse. TV shows also depicted large families as either impoverished or old-fashioned; The Waltons (a Depression-era poverty-stricken family whose grandparents lived with them) and Little House on the Prairie (the 1800s prairie family whose size grew as the series continued). 1970s TV brought us a new look at single motherhood with shows like One Day at a Time, Alice, The Mary Tyler Moore Show, and The Partridge Family, with themes of single mothers trying to raise their children alone.

1980s Films showed us how societal norms were changing the family. Dad is better than mom was the message of the Academy Award-winning film Kramer vs. Kramer. In ET, a single mom with three children allows ET to join in. Togetherness helps him phone home. In Poltergeist, we see a blended family with three children (the oldest daughter is from a previous marriage). In Sixteen Candles and The Breakfast Club, teens can't relate to their families. The movie Ordinary People tackle teenage suicide. War Games featured working parents who paid no attention to their only child who hacks into federally secure computers. *Risky Business* showed us what could happen when parents leave; their son opens a brothel in their home! *Back to the Future* made fun of the past by making the norms of the past seem odd. *Raising Arizona* is one of the only films of the decade to feature a large family and touch the subject of infertility. An infertile couple steals from a family who used artificial insemination to conceive 5 babies. The infertile couple steals one of the babies figuring, they can't possibly need them all.

1980s TV was the decade of *family groups* living together and *educated mothers*. In the 1980s, TV shows were about small families and divorced families. Shows such as *Kate and Allie, Full House, and One Day at a Time* became the norm on TV. However, in the late 1980s, a TV show that portrayed a very positive pro-family view, *The Cosby Show*, positively portrayed an African American family of working professionals with their five children. Dr. and Mrs. Huxtable were happily married, highly educated, financially successful, and good parents to their five children! This popular program changed the public perception of African American families. During the 1980s, mothers were no longer portrayed as uneducated and working as waitresses. Instead, they were shown as highly educated career moms such as Mrs. Huxtable, a lawyer. On another show called, Family Ties, the mother is an architect.

1990s films showed us families with money. Now that educated mothers could bring in a second income, families were smaller and had more money. We see an upper-middle-class family in *Home Alone*. The family was rich enough to go to Paris for Christmas, but the only problem with all their abundance was that they forgot one of their children! Money certainly made families comfortable, so much so that parents would go to almost any extent to please their children. In *Jingle All the Way*, we saw a father spare no expense to give his only child his Christmas gift. We see a family deal with a challenging issue, such as a deaf son in *Mr. Holland's Opus* and a lying father in *Liar, Liar*. The 1990s were full of parents pushing their children toward higher education. In *Little Man Tate*, Hollywood showed us a single mother whose son was a genius. Family values were portrayed historically in *Sense and Sensibility* but were cut down in films like *Titanic*. Revenge for the pain of divorce was justified in *First Wives Club*.

The 1990s TV was the decade of family dysfunction and group families. Multiple shows portrayed highly dysfunctional families such as in *Roseanne, The Simpsons, Married with Children, and The Osbournes*.

WHAT IS REALLY GOING ON HERE?

Some of the themes these shows tackle were unheard of on TV a decade earlier; children and parents with poor manners, making rude and disgusting remarks, children talking back to their parents and rebelling against their authority, children showing disrespect and using sexual undertones, and children having poor relationships with siblings. These shows convince viewers that all families are dysfunctional, and children cannot be controlled, disciplined, or taught manners. What happened to the wonderful shows from the 1950s and 1960s featuring sweet, stay-at-home moms and polite children who attended church? The trends were very much fueled by what we saw on TV. In the 1960s, working mothers needed new caretakers (introduce the nanny), but by the 1980's better-educated moms were not always the best choice for caring for their children (these families hired a nanny). The downward spiral of working mothers bottomed out in total family dysfunction by the 1990s, so much so, that by the end of the 1990s, trends for women wanting to stay home began as early as 1997. Forty years of television showed us that when mom works, the family doesn't work as well!

The other thing late 1980's/1990's TV continued with is the theme of group homes. The show *Full House* was multiple family members all living under one roof in a sort of group parenting or co-parenting environment. It was a cute show and got the audience used to the idea of children being raised in a non-nuclear home and convinced us that this is ok. The children on the show seemed happy with a lot of laughs. Not sure in real life if this sort of arrangement would be so jolly, and in real life the children might be confused about who is parenting whom. In shows such as the Fresh Prince of Belair, Family Matters, Facts of Life, and the wonder years we started to see life from the child's perspective and parents were now simply props used in the background.

In the first decade of the New Millennium 2000-2010, TV has become the decade of real families. During the 1970s, 1980s 1990s parents were gone from the home. Their children were on *latchkey*, and working parents were so busy juggling career and children they did not have time to be as involved as much as they would like to be. In the mid 1990s, trends show that some parents quit corporate jobs to come home to be with their children, possibly because they were raised with a career mom and did not like it! This led to an increase in parental involvement, not seen in decades and TV shows reflected this change. Reality TV took America by storm and *regular* people and even a few *celebrities* allowed cameras into their living rooms. Families have been portrayed in nearly every way possible. *Wife Swap, Nanny 911, Jon and Kate Plus 8, Duggars: 19 kids and Counting, Table for 12, Kids by the Dozen, Meet the Little People, The Kardashians, Billy the Exterminator,* and *Duck Dynasty*, to name a few. One thing we also see in this new decade are shows where the parents and kids collaborate.

The 2010-2020s

TV exploded between network TV, cable, *Netflix, Prime, Disney Channel* and other networks. Families had a variety of viewing options. The *Disney Channel* introduced quite a few interesting teens, and tween shows where the kids and not the parents seemed to be organizing and running the classroom, the household, etc. *I-Carly, Jessie, KC Undercover, Liv and Maddie*. Parents are somewhat in the background and the shows features the kid's lives and struggles. Some shows have morals while others leave everything up to how the children want it. Swing shifts, working from home, flex schedules, zoom conferences and other options have made being closer to where a parent's children are a better reality.

More reality TV brought us decorating shows, kids baking shows, dating drama, family drama, news shows, travel shows, sports, ethnic shows, LGBT shows and networks, shows with many kinds of families. Shows such as Stranger Things, mysteries and crime scene shows, and even game shows held people's interest. Network TV went out as the cable companies gave people shows they wanted to see.

The 2020s post covid

The family has completely changed. Shows like Full House from the 1990's, gave birth to Modern Family 2000-2010 and now Raven's Home (2017-2023) families have evolved. Due to the covid lockdowns viewers have become addicted to series such as Yellowstone, Heartland, Game of Thrones, Breaking Bad, Suits, West Wing, The Crown, Downton Abby, Mandalorian and so many more.

HOLLYWOOD'S MESSAGES ARE SUBTLE

For almost 50 years, 1950-2000 large families were portrayed as poor in Hollywood movies, TV shows and series, magazine articles, and in the news. This became the stereotypical portrayal of any family with more than three children. Since the 1960s, Hollywood has acted as if large families didn't even exist by completely dismissing their stories from the silver screen. But when they did have to portray them, the larger family was usually impoverished. The subtle brainwashing attitude was that raising a large family is foolish because most large families cannot afford their children. We do not realize that, over time, the media have convinced us how we should think. We think that since we are not seeing things portrayed any other way, this must be the norm for everyone. We are brainwashed by being slowly convinced that all families are small, large families are impoverished, and the parents of many children are irresponsible morons. It is hard even for God's people to realize *this is a mirage* because it is so convincing. After a while, we believe in every circumstance that life is how we see it portrayed on the big screen.

In this new millennium, Hollywood films are portraying large families positively and have added a few movies with happy, involved parents paying attention to their children again. From 1960–2000 Hollywood showed us large families in films who were either poor, religious, uneducated homeschoolers or, somewhat of a trend of the past, by only showing large families in a historical movie. They did not give us any positive portrayals of large families until after 9/11/2001. By 2003 when the country was trying to heal, and the new baby boom was well underway, Hollywood remade the 1950 film *Cheaper by the Dozen*. In the first film version, the father and mother were highly educated industrial engineers, and the story was about a family at the turn of the last century (1910s-1930s). This family could afford a large house with acreage, a vineyard, and several servants. In the 2003 version, the large family was back, but this time money was tight until the father took a new job. The family was not religious, and the children attended public school. The parents were tender and caring, and the film looked positively at large families. *Cheaper By the Dozen, part 2* (2005), showed larger families as the new status symbol, as two large families were featured, one of which was upper middle class. Hollywood also gave us another remake about a large family and remade the 1968 film *Yours, Mine, and Ours*. In the 1968 version, the family was Roman Catholic. In the 2005 version, the family did not have a religious persuasion. This film also showed a large family in a positive financial light. In other words, Hollywood has given the thumbs up to large families if the parents can afford all the children and if the parents have a heart for involvement.

THE BATTLE: GOD'S WORD VS. SECULAR HUMANISM

I began this chapter by emphasizing the battle raging in our culture for quite some time between the ideas of secular humanism and the concrete truths of the Word of God. On one side, secular humanism has changed several generations' ideas about how we view children. Conversely, God has a plan for marriage and family that most of us were not taught, evidenced in our behavior since the 1960s.

Many of God's people do not realize that we do not believe God because if we did, we would not follow the world's agenda. His word says, Enter through the narrow gate.

People are bombarded with secular ideas everywhere we turn. If we stop and compare these opposing sides, we will see how God's Word contrasts the ideas of secular humanism.

1. **God says: Children are His gracious gifts.** The Bible says, every good and perfect gift comes down from the Father of Lights (James 1:17).
2. **Children are what God graciously gives us....** "They are the children God has graciously given your servant." (Genesis 33:5).
3. **Children are a glorious marital gift and the fruit of intimacy.**

Children are a heritage from the LORD, offspring a reward from him (Psalm 127:3).

I will surely bless you and make your descendants as numerous as the stars in the sky... (Genesis 22:17).

...May you increase to thousands upon thousands... (Genesis 24:60).

HUMANISTS do not see children as gracious gifts but rather as financial burdens!

Economists at the United States Department of Agriculture every year come out with a monetary figure of what a child born that year would cost to raise through age 18. In 2000, the figure was $165,630,[17] adjusted to match inflation, but by 2017 this figure was $233,630 and with inflation the 2023 number to raise a child to 18 yrs. age topped $300,000 for the first time, to a whopping $306, 824![18] WOW!

That's a large amount of money! Economists have figured in typical expenses of clothes, food, health and dental care, transportation, childcare, school expenses, etc.; the figure above does not even include college! College is at least another $250,000 for a decent four-year school. It's hard to look at amounts like this and not want to go into a head spin! Believers hear the Department of Agriculture statistics and wonder whether the statistician added in the costs of being a Christian in America, adding in private church school tuition; private Christian college; church camps; and religious books, tapes, and videos.

To provide the best religious environment for their children, believers must have more than $306,824! It's not too hard to weigh the realities of what a couple can afford versus what they might want. After all, parents must think about their future and ask, *"Can I afford to spend my time raising children who will drain that kind of money from me?"*

Money has become the biggest concerns for most parents. A couple often decides to limit their family size to retire with a few dollars in the bank. It is not a sin for a parent to weigh out financial issues, but money should not rule a person's heart and be the only factor dictating their decision. The Bible tells us not to love money or to serve it. We are to be responsible and trust God. Trust in our money can be a testimony to those who do not follow Him. Our lives will reflect the abundant provision of a supernatural God. This idea falls outside the world of secular people who do not live their lives according to a book written long ago. Yet to believers, this kind of trust is what Faith is all about.

4. God says: Children multiply your wealth both spiritually and financially. Scripture says that others will recognize you as blessed if you have children. *Prosperity will be yours (Psalm 128:2).*

...All who see them will acknowledge that they are a people the Lord has blessed (Isaiah 61:9).

I was young and now I am old, yet I have never seen the righteous forsaken or their children begging bread (Psalm 37:25).

5. God promises that our children will grow up to love us and exalt our family as a blessing (Psalm 128).

HUMANISTS do not see children as making a person *RICH* or being a "blessing" but rather children are a burden for working parents and sometimes even an imposition on their mother's career.

In our society, children are pushed into daycare at birth so their mothers can return to their careers. More than 50% of women today work outside the home but don't all have to. Some mothers must work because they do not want to be home dealing with their children. Girls are expected to choose a career path, and the desire for children is often ignored. Feminists tell women it's easy to juggle both. But often, those women who try usually feel guilty the whole time. Now that secular humanism has crept into organized religion, mothers are often presented with the idea that they must contribute to the work of the Lord and *volunteer* in some way. There's nothing wrong with helping at church, but some women do so exhaustively by redirecting their energy away from their homes. Protestant women are constantly being told they must "make their lives count" so they volunteer because they feel pressured and since motherhood has not been viewed as the perfect career for women, it is easy to see how a mother might feel like she is not doing enough for God. At the Catholic Church, motherhood is esteemed, and Catholic mothers do not feel nearly the same pressure to abandon their families to try and do more. Yet due to outside pressures invading the church world, even Catholic mothers are curious whether they are doing enough. Isn't the all-encompassing task of raising children to love God enough?

6. God says: Children are our future! They are our Godly seed to take our place when we die.

Your sons will take the place of your fathers; you will make them princes throughout the land (Psalm 45:16).

7. Children are our heirs (Jeremiah 49:1). They result from following God's scriptural mandate to be fruitful and multiply (Genesis 1:22, 28). God desires that we fill the earth with people to praise His holy name (Psalm 102:18). The more people born; the more people have the opportunity to choose to be His friends.

HUMANISTS care about population growth instead of birthing children to have a future. Even with global population statistics heading downward, humanists still believe our planet will be overcrowded without enough resources for ourselves or our children.

On any given day, we can turn on TV, read USA Today or any other secular newspaper, read in school textbooks, or hear a news report about social problems in our world that come from overpopulation. We hear about people starving in other parts of the world and overcrowding in places like China. Environmentalists show us how we will run out of food and water if we continue to overpopulate the planet with people. These facts are simply untrue and can be scientifically disproven. Our world has plenty of resources; God did not leave us on a planet that cannot satisfy a growing population. However, those who shape our world want us to believe that we have a problem, and if they tell us about it long enough, we will finally believe it. Pastors are not speaking out against the idea that our planet is running out of resources, and most fail to challenge parents with the commandment to be fruitful and multiply. This has led to the attitude in America that the average Christian family should be small. In most churches, when couples choose to have more than three children, people start to ridicule them. Usually, they are labeled as irresponsible, especially if they look like they cannot care for more children in some way.

8. God says: Children are power! They are arrows in the hand of a mighty warrior to mold for God and to aim their lives at overcoming the lying agenda of the evil one.

9. Children can make you powerful when you raise them to become friends of the Lord. *Your children will be mighty in the land (Psalm 112:1-2).* God planned for us to fill the earth with people so that even *children yet to be born* can get to know Him. Believers have failed to realize that our children are our future. They can possess the enemy's gates and take back spiritual land stolen from our family bloodlines. *If you are righteous and walk in God's ways: your descendants will take possession of the cities of their enemies (Genesis 22:17, 24:60).*

HUMANISTS do not view children as people who can know God. Instead, they view each child as someone entitled to life, liberty, and the pursuit of the best of everything his parents can afford to give. We live in this crazy world where a new breed of parents has emerged. These parents act like their child's success directly reflects them, and if their child were to fail at anything, it would mean that the parent is a failure. These parents will fight to the finish to win a ball game, to get their child first in a contest, or in a starring role in the school play. I've been raising children since the early 1980s, and I've never seen anything like the parents of today. They give their children everything they want and far more than they need. Success is everything, and failure is not tolerated. No matter their child's involvement in sports, education, or lessons, their child must be the best! Children are pressured to perform from the time they are born, competing with everyone they meet. It's ridiculous! This new attitude about children seems to come from the idea that since no one wants to raise an unwanted child anymore, the *wanted children* better to be successful at everything they attempt to do.

A child who is *wanted* should lack nothing! Even before birth, the *wanted child* is tended to with special care. Sonograms and tests are administered to ensure that the *wanted child* has all its body parts so that it can keep being wanted. Once assured that all is fine, the parents search for the perfect birth experience, and opportunities abound when the *wanted child* is born. The *wanted child* gets to wear designer baby clothes, take baby gym classes, and learn to use a computer before he is one! Then come the specialty lessons, the expensive private school, the extravagant birthday parties, and so on. Parents in our society believe that *wanted children* deserve these things because they are *wanted*. Much of this behavior could be motivated by guilt. Parents know that they probably could have had a few more children if they had wanted to, but they decided instead to have fewer children and more money to spend. So, they cover their guilt by giving their *wanted child* more of everything. In a sense, the *wanted child* becomes the *worshipped child* with the power to control his parents.

10. God says: Children help us to praise the Lord and take the focus off ourselves. Children help us to be a blessing to others. God's Word says that life is not about what can benefit us but how we can bless others. *Through your offspring, all nations of the earth will be blessed... (Genesis 22:18).*

11. Together with our children, we can bless God by offering praise and worship to His holy name. *Through the praise of children and infants you have established a stronghold against your enemies, to silence the foe and the avenger (Psalm 8:2).*

It is not the dead who praise the Lord, those who go down to silence. It is we who extol the Lord, both now and forevermore (Psalm 115:17-18). Laying down our lives to bring forth the next generation requires servanthood not seen often in society. The focus is not on us but on the goal of raising a Godly generation.

HUMANISTS do not understand what it means to focus our lives on others. They believe everything people do should be to push their agenda forward; everything is for themselves. We are told to *"Go for the gusto because we only go around once!"* Genesis 11:1-9 records the story of the *Tower of Babel*. The people wanted to build a tower to Heaven to *make a name for themselves*. This goal angered God, who came down to see the tower they were building. He did not like what He saw so He confused the people's languages and scattered man to the ends of the earth. "Making a name for oneself' and being successful seems to be a huge goal for many people today. They focus on their careers, retirement, vacations, and financial portfolios—all seeking success and life's pleasures.

12. God says: Children are workers for the harvest.

Then he said to his disciples, "The harvest is plentiful, but the workers are few. Ask the Lord of the harvest, therefore, to send out workers into his harvest field" (Matthew 9:37).

Don't you have a saying, 'It's still four months until harvest'? I tell you, open your eyes and look at the fields! They are ripe for harvest (John 4:35).

One of the most significant purposes for birthing children is so that they can be mighty spiritual workers in God's harvest field. Wherever that harvest field is for them and at whatever point in history they arrive, children can participate and partner with God to help others find the love that the Lord gives. Even when children are small, they can lead their friends in their neighborhoods and schools to God. Yet a child must be conceived before they can ever become a spiritual worker.

HUMANISTS do not believe that children are spiritual workers for God, but rather they are people who will not be fulfilled as adults unless they make a lot of money. Our society places a significant emphasis on educating children so they will grow up to make a large amount of money. Some people worry about getting into a good college from the time their children are born. They feel the child must choose a lucrative career or they will be a failure in life. There is nothing wrong with choosing a financially successful career. Most people go to the secular world to be spiritual lights in darkness to harvest a lost world for the Lord. Making a good salary is a wonderful thing for a believer, but it is not the goal of life. Yet for the humanist, it is imperative because without God they have nothing more to live for than pleasure. These sad pleasure-seekers often feel empty at the end of their lives because they discover, that outside of knowing the Lord, everything else in life is *meaningless!* (Ecclesiastes 1:2).

13. God says: Children are Godly offspring—the fruit of the one-flesh union of marriage.

Has not the one God made you? You belong to him in body and spirit. And what does the one God seek? Godly offspring. So be on your guard, and do not be unfaithful to the wife of your youth (Malachi 2:15).

HUMANISTS say that children are simply what you produce from sex. They are a problem and should be prevented unless wanted. Thus, the reasoning for using birth control is to prevent and keep children from resulting from the pleasurable act of making love.

14. God says: Children are not ours; they are lent to us from God.

Jesus called the children to him and said, "Let the little children come to me, and do not hinder them, for the kingdom of God belongs to such as these" (Luke 18:16).

HUMANISTS do not see children as God's but as something a parent should control and make decisions about. God and His choice are left completely out of the equation.

15. God says: "Be fruitful and multiply and fill the earth with children," then your children can carry the Lord's purposes into future generations, even to those yet to be born!

They will proclaim his righteousness, declaring to a people yet unborn: He has done it! (Psalm 22:31).

Posterity will serve him; future generations will be told about the Lord (Psalm 22:30).

...so, the next generation would know them, even the children yet to be born, and they in turn would tell their children (Psalm 78:6).

Let this be written for a future generation, that a people not yet created may praise the LORD (Psalm 102:18).

16. Children pass the torch from one generation to the next. Parents teach them the ways of God through the generations.

Tell it to your children and let your children tell it to their children and their children to the next generation (Joel 1:3)

Impress them on your children. Talk about them when you sit at home and when you walk along the road, when you lie down and when you get up (Deuteronomy 6:7).

Teach them to your children, talking about them when you sit at home and when you walk along the road, when you lie down and when you get up (Deuteronomy 11:19).

Come, my children, listen to me; I will teach you the fear of the Lord (Psalm 34:11).

things we have heard and known, things our ancestors have told us. We will not hide them from their descendants; we will tell the next generation the praiseworthy deeds of the LORD, his power, and the wonders he has done. He decreed statutes for Jacob and established the law in Israel, which he commanded our ancestors to teach their children (Psalm 78:3-5).

17. Children are our descendants who will receive these promises.

"And afterward, I will pour out my Spirit on all people. Your sons and daughters will prophesy, your old men will dream dreams, your young men will see visions (Joel 2:28).

HUMANISTS do not believe there is a life after this one. They do not believe in eternity; therefore, they are not looking to the future. They believe in living life as if things will be over at death. God has not given some the spiritual eyes to see the blessing children can bring to future generations.

18. God says: Children establish the work of our hands.

May the favor of the Lord our God rest on us; establish the work of our hands for us, yes establish the work of our hands (Psalm 90:17).

God tells us that the next generation should produce even greater things. They should pick up where the last generation left off.

HUMANISTS do not see a child as establishing anything. They see children as burdens, not establishers. Instead, they say, "I will establish the work of my own hands." They see themselves making all their own choices and decisions. They choose everything to satisfy their lives and live for today, not tomorrow.

19. God says: Children keep us from shame.

Blessed is the man whose quiver is full of them. They will not be put to shame when they contend with their opponents in court (Psalm 127:5).

HUMANISTS do not see children as keeping them from shame. They see children as shameful. They do not realize that God is blessing them with children. Instead, humanists focus on the negative aspects of children and how they can shame their parents through poor behaviors, such as drugs, sex, alcohol abuse, suicide, teenage pregnancy, drunk driving, low grades, etc. Children are not seen as a blessing, but a burden.

20. God says: In the spiritual realm, children are our spiritual ammunition to defeat the enemy! Scripture says that one of God's people can chase 1,000 enemies, and two can put 10,000 to flight (Deuteronomy 32:30). When I found this scripture, my excitement was unbearable. God also says that there is power in numbers! When God's people are plentiful, we can come up against society going in the wrong direction, against wicked political systems, against immoral laws, against anti-family legislation and make wicked agenda's back down! I believe this is one of the most significant reasons why the enemy wants us to limit our numbers: Satan knows the power of God's people more than we do!

If one person can put 1,000 of God's enemies to flight, ten family members could scatter 10,000 demons. That is a massive number of demons! When my family is in unity and prays in agreement for the president of the United States' safety or the healing of a deathly ill child, our prayers of unity could put 10,000 demons of the enemy running away from the situation. This is true spiritual power!

Here is a second way that this verse might be interpreted. What if God did the math by tens instead of by simple multiplication? Then this verse would mean that one believer could put 1,000 demons away, two believers could put 10,000 demons away, three family members who are believers could put 100,000 demons away, and four could put 1,000,000 demons away! When praying in unity, a family of my size with 8 children praying, we could put billions of the enemy away! Either way we interpret the numbers, a large Godly family or groups of large Godly families can accomplish much in prayer based on this one factor alone.

This is why Satan so desperately wants us to limit our numbers, he knows the power we have, to fight against him better than we do. If we would only trust the Lord, what greatness we would accomplish for Him! As future generations grasp this idea, the world will see power released like never before! The incredible value our children have in the eyes of God is amazing! The secular humanist fails to see the incredible benefits of this extraordinary gift to humanity.

QUIZ: WHAT ARE MY VIEWS?

Quiz yourself to see if you have subtly adopted any humanistic ideals:

- I believe parents should decide how many children to have so they do not have more children than they want.
- I believe when parents find out their unborn child will be severely handicapped, they should consider not keeping it, it especially if its quality of life would be compromised.
- I believe that parents should not have more children than they can afford.
- I believe politically correct words like pro-choice, vasectomy, tubal ligation, anti-abortion are just keeping up with the times.
- I believe my children should have the best of everything if I can provide it.
- I believe that serving God in some way outside of my family is very important. If I had too many children, I might not be able to give my time to God.
- I believe that being responsible with my time and talents and providing for my family is far more important than family size
- I believe the worst thing that could happen to a woman would be, have a child she does not want.

How did you score? If you answered yes to one or more questions, you have been influenced by the secular humanist ideas that affect our culture and have crept into our churches.

Humanism devalues each of us because it causes us to look to ourselves alone. Have you ever met someone who was incredibly selfish? Did you like that person? Only a life poured out for others will make us truly happy.

Now that you understand what is really going on here, consider this: I have proven with facts and scripture that we all have been hijacked by secular thinking that tells us: "It should be all about ME" or is it, Me first-others last? Thinking it's all about me and or thinking that the world or that God owes us something, all this crazy thinking stems from secular humanism.

I believe the Holy Spirit would like to now cut away these lies from your heart and mind and bring you into a new understanding of the power of putting others first.

Let's start with your family or the future plans you have for your family.

God wants His people to see that children are not expensive burdens but something He will provide for.

He wants His people to know they are the future generation, the royal heirs of God, and valuable participants in His work on earth. They are people made in the image of God to show forth His praises to a dark and depraved world!

Wife's Prayer

Heavenly Father, I had wrong ideas about children, and did not realize it. I've been surrounded by humanism for so long that I had stopped viewing children as *special*, and instead as *burdens*. These were subtle thoughts, but they were there. I think I've been heavily influenced by the Tv shows I've watched, the movies I've seen and the books I've read. But I don't want these humanistic opinions anymore. Please cut the lies away from my heart so I can see children the way you see them. You see *every child as a gift*. Humanism devalues children and puts them in the category of things. Humanism also redefines me as a *worker* and not as a *mother*. Please help me reject all these ideas and see myself as a woman first, with the amazing potential to be a mother, before I see myself as anything else.

Amen

Husband's Prayer

Heavenly Father, I did not realize how much humanism had affected my beliefs. My thoughts on fatherhood have been centered on myself and what I want to have, instead of on what You want to give me. I did not know this option existed. Please change my old way of thinking. I continue to be blown away by these new revelations, but I am also not happy that I've never heard any of this before. I want to learn more about Your ways.

Amen

Christopher's Commentary

Why does it look like the men who use birth control are freer than those who choose to trust God? After all, the men who selectively choose when to have children seem to claim sexual freedom and financial benefits. The men who have their wives on the pill claim to have all the sex they want while ensuring she doesn't give him a child he doesn't want. These men can plan their financial lives and monitor what they want to pay for. They can create enough time to plan and save for one or two educations, and since there aren't a whole lot of children to be paying for, they can send their wives out to work once the children are in school and reap the benefits of a double income. When they are through raising children, they can plan to retire early, and with the ease of a small family, they can spend their early mornings at the gym and their afternoons on the golf course. Sign me up! What more could I want? Less seems like more in so many ways. The Christian man can limit his family size so he can spend his life evangelizing or serving at church because he won't have to worry about providing for the extras a larger family would require. Using birth control for Christian and non-Christian men brings what appears to be *freedom*. I can't argue against these appearances. But I will say that these *freedoms* are a snapshot of the moment instead of a photo album of their entire life.

Why is it that when men are interviewed at the end of their lives, they often say they regret not having more children or spending more time with their wives and children? I guess their sexual and financial *freedoms* did not satisfy. A scene from the 2006 movie, *Click* illustrates my point. The father (Henry Winkler) visits his son at work, but the son (Adam Sandler) is busy working. Now an old man, the father tries to tell his son that he loves him and wants to spend time with him, but his son completely ignores him, not even acknowledging his father's presence in the room! It's a hard scene to watch. You feel for the father, but you realize the son is driven by the same desires his father once had. Similarly, in 1974, Cat Stevens sang about the way of men in his famous song, *Cats in the Cradle*.

My child arrived just the other day, He came to the world in the usual way

But there were planes to catch and bills to pay He learned to walk while I was away

And he was talking before I knew it and as he grew

He said, "I'm going to be like you, Dad, I know I'm going to be like you!"

My son turned ten just the other day

He said, "Thanks for the ball, Dad, come on let's play. Can you teach me to throw?"

I said, "Not today. I got a lot to do,"

He said, "That's ok."

And he walked away but his smile never dimmed

And said, "I'm gonna be like him, yeah, I'm gonna be like him."

Well, he came home from college just the other day, so much like a man I just had to say

"Son, I'm proud of you, can you sit for a while?" He shook his head, and he said with a smile, "What I'd really like Dad is to borrow the car keys. See you later. Can I have them please?"

I've long since retired, my son's moved away I called him up just the other day

I said," I'd like to see you if you don't mind"

He said, "I'd love to Dad if I could find the time

You see my new job's a hassle and the kids have the flu

But it's sure nice talking to you, Dad. It's been sure nice talking to you." And when I hung up the phone, it occurred to me

He'd grown up just like me, my boy was just like me!

The son rejected his father just as he had been rejected! Having a smaller family allowed the father to get away from his annoying child and now his child ignores him! I realize a father could overlook any number of children, but somehow in a larger family, it appears to be a bit harder simply because there are always children around; everywhere you turn.

Often fathers have told me they don't want a large family so they can spend more time with the children they do have. Some men make a reasonable effort, but you are missing the point if you think you are free because you chose small. If you don't have to depend on God as much for finances or trust Him to space your family, I guess life might seem smooth and carefree for a while. You will have some control, and you might like that very much. For a while, you may feel like you are in charge. But how much pleasure do you get from your control? I implore you, if you are a man of God, please realize that using birth control to make sure your family stays small is not about sexual and financial freedom. It is about your heart. Your children will model what you teach them. If you do not teach them to value *family*, you cannot expect them to grow up and place *family* first.

Over the years, I have had countless men look down on me and judge the size of my family, only to turn around years later and remark about how wonderful it must feel to have five daughters to walk down the aisle and or to see eight children married. Business colleagues who once criticized me now tell me how lonely they are. I implore you, if the regrets of old men mean anything to you, their wisdom speaks volumes to me. Your children are not the burdens you think they are. True long-term sexual and financial freedom is about the *family treasures* you end up with. The one with the most children...wins!

Christopher Scott

WHAT IS REALLY GOING ON HERE

Investigate and Questions

- Since the 1950s, TV shows have infiltrated people's homes and have attempted to redefine the family. Read back through the chapter to the list of TV shows that you would have watched growing up, and even are watching now. How do you think these shows have affected your thinking about the family?
- In situational Christianity, the believer's attitude is, *"Whatever I do is OK with God as long as it is the best decision for my life."* How has this attitude affected your views about birth control and family size.
- Describe how the family has changed from how families were 100 years ago. How is cultural society different today from one hundred years ago?
- In the movie *Father of the Bride, part 2*, the mother and daughter give birth at the same time. What are your thoughts about this happening?
- Read Genesis 1:28a, 2:23-24. What was God's first intention for the sexual act; was it for pleasure or to create children?
- What would the world look like if every married Christian couple suddenly stopped using all forms of birth control?
- Read 2 Timothy 3:1-4. In our society, people believe that *if something does not give them great pleasure, they should not have to put up with it.* How does cultural society view an *unplanned child*? Has this view affected the way that you planned your family?
- God's people want to believe the things they are doing with their lives are good. If additional children came into your life today, could you still serve God like you are serving Him now? What would stay the same, and what would change?
- Read James 1:17, Psalms 127:5. Have you ever thought that God may have a different idea than you do about what He wants from your life?
- Did you take the humanistic quiz and the end of the chapter? Are you a humanist? After reading both viewpoints, how has this chapter changed your views on having children?

Impacting Others

Rachel, I wanted to contact you after reading your book and share my thoughts. I have so much to say but have you noticed how the people in your church family always go out of their way to tell you that you are free to stop having children? They try to give you their religious counsel and explain why having children is not Biblical and why they've got it right and why you've got it wrong? They want to make sure that you interpret scripture just like they have, and they want you to stop having any more babies because they stopped, and they want you to know that you aren't bound by scripture to have more children. People think that attending church with you gives them the license to be nosy about your life and comment on things they wouldn't say to others. When they back you into a corner, you try to back up your feelings with what God has spoken to you from His word, about His plan for the family/children/fruitfulness, etc. Then when you kindly and gently give them your answers from scripture, offering them some words of life, they get mad! I think it's conviction, but it tends to make one want to avoid the whole church scene. **Mom to four children in Canada**

Rachel, can I add something about one of my pet peeves? I'm 39 now, and the women in my age group seem to be searching for excuses for ending their childbearing prematurely. They know I want more children, but the excuse they say around me is, "I don't want any more children and can't wait until they grow up because I just want to spend time with my husband!" What does that mean? That I don't want to spend time with mine? By the size of my gang, they can tell I've spent some time with mine already! You know I have another friend, well, not a friend, she's more like an acquaintance, but her husband wanted a fourth child so bad, and he tried and tried to convince her, but she kept saying no. She played in a tennis league, was Vice President of the PTA, and didn't want to be bothered. They had an empty nest with their two children when she was only 45. She said she was so happy. Yet she always seemed so disconnected from her kids. A few years passed after her oldest was off to college, and she had an affair with her tennis instructor. I was reminded how she had always said she wanted to spend time with her husband, and she spent time with a husband, but it wasn't her own. That sounded like nothing more than her excuse. It is unfortunate, but her life fell apart after that. For us, our children help to keep my husband, and I connected. We have realized we don't want to spend all those years alone. We like the noise of the children. We hope and pray that God will send us a new baby when we are 45! **Shawna, Mom to 7 blessings. Clermont, Florida**

Chapter 5

WHO WILL YOU LEAVE BEHIND WHEN YOU DIE?

> *¹⁸ Here am I, and the children the LORD has given me. We are signs and symbols in Israel from the LORD Almighty, who dwells on Mount Zion (Isaiah 8:18).*

My grandfather was a minister for fifty-five years. When I was a child, he and my grandmother heard about a mission family their church wanted to support. My parents also decided to support their mission work as well. One day our family invited this family for dinner when they were in America on break. Even though I was only five or six years old at the time, I remember when they walked in, I knew I was in the presence of people who were very special. They dedicated their lives to the natives in the remote South American jungles. Something else about this family made a lasting impression on me. They were the parents of ten children! In the 1960s, a family this size was unheard of in the Baptist church world and my family had never met anyone with ten children before. The largest family we knew was the Catholic family down the street, and they had six children. My mom was worried about where they would all sit and how we would feed them all at the table. We simply did not know what to think. They visited our home several more times, and their children were always polite and friendly. The entire time I was growing up, this was the only time I was ever exposed to a family as large as theirs.

What these people did was very clever. Besides choosing to serve God as full-time mission workers, by allowing God to bless them with children, they created a spiritual heritage that God still uses today. My family met them nearly sixty years ago. Today, their children are grown and married. Several returned with their spouses to the jungles with their parents until their parent's passed. For several decades the children and grandchildren carried on that work which was started in the 1950s. The size of their family gave them sustaining power. By the grace of God, they replaced themselves with ten children and many more grandchildren. The spiritual mantle of this *family's devotion to God* was supernaturally passed down from father to child.

Tell it to your children and let your children tell it to their children and their children to the next generation (Joel 1:3).

This story is a beautiful example of the amazing spiritual heritage available to every family. A Godly heritage is about passing the fruit of our lives to our children, grandchildren and great-grandchildren.

So, *the next generation would know them, even the children yet to be born, and they in turn would tell their children (Psalm 78:6).*

Passing the fruit of our lives on to our children and then our grandchildren and then onto our great grandchildren is what the Psalmist meant when he asked the Lord to *establish the work of his hands* (Psalm 90:17). He was asking God to give him a personal contribution of eternal value that could be established for generations. We know that no one lives forever as Ecclesiastes 1:4 tells us *generations come and go*, but in every generation, each child born is an eternal creation and each life has a plan and a purpose.

One generation commends your works to another; they tell of your mighty acts (Psalm 145:4).

WHOSE IDEA WAS IT FOR FAMILIES TO GROW LARGE?

It was God's idea from the beginning for parents to create every size of family. This is why the Scriptures are full of genealogies. They are a written picture of the family. God wanted to show us the passing of the generational baton from parent to child to help us see how *each person* is valuable and fits into the bigger picture; the beautiful tapestry God is creating from the families of the earth.

When we look at the issue of what a heritage is about, we see that God put an amazing plan in place for us so that He could give us something of great eternal value; *a large group of offspring* who love the Lord and who can make an impact on this world for Him!

I will perpetuate your memory through all generations: therefore, the nations will praise You forever and ever (Psalm 45:17).

Would you like to make an *investment* in this lifetime that will still produce fruit for many generations? According to Scripture, that investment could very easily be the wonderful children whom God has graciously blessed you with.

When God established His covenant with Abraham, it involved his *offspring*. God told Abraham that his descendants would be more numerous than the stars of the sky and the sand on the seashore (Genesis 22:17). God planned to bless Abraham by giving him a heritage of *people* from his loins. These people would establish Abraham, and they would prove God's validation of his life. God fulfilled His promise and birthed a great nation of people, hoping that these descendants would love Him.

...It is through Isaac that your offspring will be reckoned (Genesis 21:12).

God gave Abraham a *future inheritance*. He desires to provide the same inheritance to each of us through our offspring. Children are God's wealth and symbolize God's approval on a person's life. According to God's word, our children are an investment we make in this lifetime that can produce spiritual fruit forever. The reason why is because children are eternal and so are we. Some day from eternity, we will look back upon our life here on earth and we will be so happy we created these children. Each life has a plan and a purpose. Each life is eternal, and each family is eternal. The goal is for us to all be together someday, living forever together in eternity. Isn't that beautiful!

Let this be written for a future generation that a people not yet created may praise the Lord (Psalm 102:18).

CHILDREN MAKE US RICH

Did you know God considers a person **rich** who is blessed with many children?

May the LORD cause you to flourish, both you and your children (Psalm 115:14).

For a lot of believers, that does not sound right. A *large family* is certainly not part of **the American Dream**. Christians have believed the opposite; children are what will keep them from achieving wealth. People are convinced children are so expensive that if a family has too many, they will not be able to have a home or any money in the bank. Most people believe the only thing children will do is make them poor! Yet, according to God's Word, this is false thinking. God perceives a man with many children as truly rich. A large family is a blessing of the highest magnitude.

I will look on you with favor and make you fruitful and increase your numbers and I will keep my covenant with you (Leviticus 26:9).

The mention of a man as *being rich* was to list his descendants. Men were emulated as the father of a specific tribe or people group, and women were counted worthy for the blessing of the womb which bore the children. Families understood one main principle: large families represent wealth for the family and wealth to society. For civilizations to maintain themselves over long time periods, they must reproduce workers to grow food, men to fill their armies, and families to produce younger workers to replace the aging and dying. *People* are the *wealth* of every society!

Couples today do not seem to understand that their family is wealth. Ministers have failed to teach young couples what it means to create their *heritage* in this way. In ancient times being part of a large family clan often led to family members becoming rulers over entire territories. Throughout history, cities were named after families! Yet today we view each child as adding debt to our credit cards. So instead of having more children, many people in today's world seek their wealth through investments, savings plans, venture capital, and other ways pertaining to money. Money is still the number one "god" of our American culture. Almost everyone in America knows someone focusing their entire life on gaining material wealth.

When a parent gives birth, they worry, "Will we have enough money to raise this child? Can we give our children the things we want them to have?" God's Word asks why we spend our days pursuing the things that will not bring happiness.

Why spend money on what is not bread, and your labor on what does not satisfy? Listen, listen to me, and eat what is good, and you will delight in the richest of fare (Isaiah 55:2).

When we die, we can't take anything with us anyway, and God's goal is that we create families and pursue healthy relationships, but instead many people value the pursuit of money as their insurance plan for happiness.

Accumulating M-O-N-E-Y is not God's idea of true wealth. He spells true wealth as C-H-I-L-D-R-E-N!

Strong societies comprise strong families, but unfortunately, this truth has escaped our modern culture. As I stated in Chapter 2, *Germany, France, Italy, England, Spain, Japan, Russia, Australia, Canada, and the Netherlands and now the USA* are all experiencing a downfall in population, causing society to have more elderly people than youth. There are not enough young workers to pay the taxes! Shockingly, over the next fifty years, there is a real possibility that the people groups, some of these countries were named after, may completely disappear! Can you imagine no more *Italians, Greek, French, German or Japanese people?* Culturally diverse immigrants and interracially blended people will dominate these countries instead. How sad! Unlike modern peoples, the ancients knew the power and importance of building a strong society through reproduction. The pagan *Babylonians, Phoenicians, Egyptians, Greeks, Mayans,* and *Romans* all worshipped goddesses of fertility. Each of these people groups, counted on births for their civilization to move forward. The Ancients encouraged vast world advancement through reproduction.

They desired abundance in children, crops, and cattle. *Human sacrifices to fertility idols* were offered in an attempt for more children. People groups knew events took lives, causing civilizations to fall and people groups to lose their resilience. *Famines, hostile takeovers, wars, infanticide, death by diseases,* and *plagues* were all factors that constantly plagued families and prevented any one family from taking over the earth. There is a great amount of power in reproduction! When those in society do not reproduce after their own kind, those who do reproduce take over by default!

As the result of God's covenant with Abraham, the Children of Israel were blessed even while they were slaves in Egypt:

But the more they were oppressed, the more they multiplied and spread; and the Egyptians came to dread the Israelites (Exodus 1:12).

Why? Because God was fulfilling His promise to Abraham:

I will make you into a great nation and I will bless you. I will make your name great, and you will be a blessing (Genesis 12:2).

Abraham's inheritance (the ancient Hebrews) was taking over Egypt!

Children were seen as a sign of wealth, and a road to royalty, as God's people were encouraged to reproduce and not hinder the blessing of children. Children were valuable commodities, and people *begged* God for them. Both Hannah and Rachel *begged* God in prayer for children, and Rebekah's brothers in Genesis 24:60 prayed over her that her descendants would be many. Then again in Genesis 25:21 her husband Isaac prayed and spoke blessings over her fertility. In Genesis 50:23, Jacob was present at the birth of his grandchildren, and he spoke a blessing over them. In ancient Hebrew homes, this blessing became a tradition to be spoken over every child in the home. Biblical families recognized the value of each new family member to the long-term survival of their family clan. Hebrew families believed God's promise that children made them wealthier, and that each child was a sign that God approved of their family's existence. The more children one had, the more wealth the family could possess and the more successful the family would become!

Many times, large families turned into **royal families.** When a family became large enough to rule over a territory, the family would choose a ruler from one of their own family members.

Our children establish our life's work. Children show that we have been sexually productive. Our efforts will not go unnoticed when we pour our lives into raising mighty warriors for the Lord.

May the favor of the Lord God rest upon us, establish the work of our hands for us—yes, establish the work of our hands (Psalm 90:17).

God considers it noble to be busy caring for and raising our families. *Whatever your hand finds to do, do it with all of your might (Ecclesiastes 9:10a).*

God allows us to give our children both a *physical* and *spiritual* inheritance! Through our children, God allows us to pass along our material possessions, such as our *cars, property, old clothes, family photos,* etc., but do you realize that the blessings received throughout our lives are also transferable? *Spiritual wealth* can be passed over to our children, grandchildren, great-grandchildren, and so on. Future generations will be blessed because of our faithfulness. God says He will bless a thousand generations of those who love Him (Exodus 20:6).

For example, our prayers never die and will transfer to our family. I still benefit from things my grandparents prayed for me sixty years ago. I can still *feel their prayers* years after they prayed them! This scriptural idea of passing ownership of spiritual wealth from parent to child started at the beginning of time and will continue until time passes into eternity!

Someday we each will die, but we hope we will not be forgotten. God's plan certainly takes care of this problem. In God's plan, when we go on to be with Him, our essence lives on through our children who remain on earth. It's almost as if *our voice* is still speaking from the grave. Every new generation reflects the previous generation who lived on earth.

A person's miracle of wealth is seeing their family increase with children, grandchildren, and great-grandchildren. A new family member replaces the previous one, and on and on, it goes down through time. The more ancestors follow in one's footsteps, the more God can multiply the spiritual wealth of that person's life. This is what God considers *true wealth*, which is one reason He is desperately trying to get us to be fruitful and multiply. Whether a child is birthed or adopted, children are wealth to God's people. We must stop blocking Him by using birth control and if we are blessed to be fertile to let Him bless our marriages and families with lots of children!

A VOICE INTO THE FUTURE

A famous family has used the same principle as my missionary friends. In my lifetime, Billy Graham has introduced more people to Christ than probably a multitude of others. God graciously blessed him and his wife with five children, nineteen grandchildren, and numerous great-grandchildren. Several of his children have followed the Graham family's footsteps of serving the Lord. Franklin Graham was a wonderful help to his father. He started Samaritan's Purse, which is an organization that gives to the poor and needy. Anne Graham Lotz, writes books and Bible studies and speaks internationally. Gigi Graham Tchividjian has also written many books, some co-authored with her mother. We can already see the influence Billy Graham and his wife Ruth have had in the lives of their children and grandchildren. With

God's blessing, their influence will continue to be passed down through future grandchildren and great-grandchildren. I wouldn't be surprised if someday we see more amazing things from some of Billy Graham's descendants.

In God's plan, every parent can pass their spiritual gifts on to another generation.

- *So that you, your children, and their children after them may fear the Lord their God... (Deuteronomy 6:2).*
- *Tell it to your children and let your children tell it to their children, and their children to the next generation (Joel 1:3).*
- *We will not hide them from our children, we will tell the next generation the praiseworthy deeds of the LORD, his power and the wonders He has done (Psalm 78:4).*
- *Teach them to your children and to their children after them (Deuteronomy 4:9).*
- *So that it may always go well with you and your children after you... (Deuteronomy 12:28).*
- *So, the next generation will know them, even the children yet to be born, and they in turn will tell their children (Psalm 78:6).*
- *Keep his decrees and commands which I am giving you today so that it may go well with you and your children... (Deuteronomy 4:40).*
- *Parents tell their children about your faithfulness (Isaiah 38:19).*

A GENERATION FORGOTTEN

In the 1960s, the reaction to the ideas of the feminist movement affected women in dramatic ways. Women burned their bras protesting a patriarchal society, they left home and family and set out to take over corporate America. In the 1970s, they got better educated and climbed the corporate ladder to success. By the 1980s and 1990s, women had high-paying jobs and were leaders in virtually every career field. By the 2000's-2020's women have achieved jobs in most every area and have proven they can be leaders in society. But is it this great? There are women in their sixties and seventies who look back at their lives knowing they missed out on family. The success they achieved in their career now holds a distant memory. The accomplishments that once seemed so important do not seem as important now as having some grandbabies. Yes, they play pickle ball, and eat lunch with girlfriends, and then stop by the grocery store and then go home to their cats.

An article updated in 2009 Foreign Policy Magazine called, *The Return of Patriarchy*,[1] Phillip Longman gave us facts which are still true today: *"In the United States, the percentage of women born in the late 1930s who remained childless was nearly 10 percent. By comparison, nearly 20 percent of women born in the late 1950s are reaching the end of their reproductive lives without having had children. The greatly expanded childless segment of contemporary society, whose members are drawn disproportionately from the feminist and countercultural movements of the 1960s and 1970s, will leave no genetic legacy. Nor will their emotional or psychological influence on the next generation compare with that of their parents."*

For whatever reason, in my generation I tried hard to convince people they should consider having another child, but countless friends and colleagues turned a deaf ear to my enthusiasm. Some listened, but more did not. I've met so many people who said, *"I don't want any more children. I'm good with the two I already have, this amount is good enough for me, besides children are so much trouble. I'm done!"* They live for today and do not think that someday they might want some more children but then maybe not. It is ok as this is their choice. Philip Longman's article added this interesting statement, *"We are heading towards a collapse. Countless middle-aged people may regret the life choices they made, that are leading to the extinction of their bloodlines, and yet they have no sons or daughters to share their wisdom."*

Many of the Baby Boomers who did manage to have children are not even becoming grandparents! Infertility has robbed an entire generation out of becoming parents easily. Some of the children of the baby boomers adopt, some spend untold thousands of dollars on fertility treatments, yet some never get to have children. It is so sad! Plus, the thing that stinks most is the children of the baby boomers who do want children are infertile and cannot have them and those who are fertile are desperately trying to keep from having them. It all seems so unfair and odd.

CHILDFREE BY CHOICE: MISS ALL THE FUN!

The September 2013 cover of Time Magazine[2] showed a couple laying on the beach with the caption *"The Childfree Life, when having it all means not having children."* The article goes on to explain why the children of the Baby Boomers and Generation X are *opting out* of parenthood altogether. Quantitively these couples are fertile and could pump out a few children, but they simply don't want to.

To be clear, this movement is not the unfortunate singles, who for whatever reason or life circumstance are prevented from having a child they would especially love to be the parent of, nor are these the unfortunate couples who struggle with infertility. Instead, this movement is full of *fertile people* who call themselves **childfree by choice** and who are purposely choosing to never bring children into this world. They are a far cry from single people who would love children or infertile couples who would have children if their life circumstances were different.

The biggest lie of the childfree by choice movement is that the childfree by choice people claim they "like" children. I can't judge every couple but the reasons for not having children range from *I like them, but I prefer to be their aunt, uncle, schoolteacher or coach* all the way to the other extreme, expressing sheer hatred for children. But instead of parenting children, the childfree by choice couples prefer pets, which they refer to as fur-babies. This is silly. They claim children are a lot of trouble but then why have a pet? Pets are a lot of trouble too, often more trouble than a child! This thinking is sort of an *oxy-moron* and a *cop-out*.

The good part about a baby is that the *infant/toddler time* is very short. Within two years the child is doing many tasks themselves including eating, dressing and toileting. Rather quickly a child can take care for themselves. Fur-babies will always have needs. They can never feed themselves; they can't bath themselves, will always need some grooming plus the biggest negative fur-parents ignore, is that as much as they love their pets, eventually their pet will die. They die long before the adult caring for them passes away and this is a painful reality of investing one's life in pets. Another negative is that a father can never walk his fur-baby down the aisle nor see a grandchild from a fur-baby. *Such folly* these people choose for themselves.

These could-be-parents opt out of a life of building a family because they say it is a lot of time and trouble. How silly they are that they dismiss the hardships pets do bring; kennels when traveling, expensive shots, trips to the emergency vet, proper food, the need to walk the dog, and the tolerating of pet hair everywhere, and putting up with their pet's urine and feces when the pet misses the pad, the cost of pet paraphernalia, etc. Pets are wonderful but pet-parents spent billions of dollars last year on their fur-babies, so they aren't cheap either! All the way around a child is a better deal! They are eternal and are a person's legacy.

When I first found out this *childfree by choice* thing was even a movement, I thought it was a joke. Who in their right mind would not want children especially if they could have them at the perfect time in their lives; once one's career is established and they find the proper life mate, children are usually next on the agenda, especially if you are fertile. But when life is perfect, the childfree still opt out of parenthood. I thought this was the most *off the wall* thing ever! I made a quick video questioning the wisdom of the childfree, trying to understand their position and at least give some wisdom from a mother of 8 children about re-thinking this long-term choice. I then posted it on my Youtube channel.[3] Oh my goodness, the pushback and the anger I got! I couldn't believe the justifying words and the sheer hate they have for children calling them *crotch goblins, parasites and worse than STD's*.

To restate my position, I then wrote a book called **"Childfree by Choice-Is it ALL its' Cracked Up to Be?"** My book can be read on Amazon/Kindle. In the book I examine *12 challenges of the Childfree Lifestyle*[4]. The purpose for my book was to alert the childfree to really think through their decision. I figured someone needed to tell them this choice brings consequences. Of course, I got more pushback from these angry folks, but I do not care, it was the first book that does not *glowingly* support their movement. The childfree people did not like that I wrote a book challenging the voids of their reality.

How dare I point out the obvious? I was cussed out online, called terrible names, referred to in vicious terms. If the movement is so great, then why does one questioning their choices bring such anger and division? I believe it is because *deep inside* the childfree by choice know they might be wrong, and they don't like someone even mentioning there might be consequences for their choices. Even if it is said very nice, they are so filled with angst they don't want to hear it! This movement is sad. People don't realize the window to fertility is open for only a short while and then it closes forever. The choices they make are eternal.

They do not realize they are building a future for themselves that will collapse. They are deceived. The childfree often look down on and make fun of parents, and viciously defend their anti-child, anti-parenthood positions, but parents don't care and realize one day *the shoe will be on the other foot*. We will see who is laughing at the end. From the beginning of time, families have been the building blocks of society, and this will not change. These childfree folks prefer to not contribute to society by raising good citizens and in the end possibly society won't give a care about them. The childfree by choice live strictly for today and dismiss tomorrow. In the end they will be the biggest generational losers of all because they chose to be void of heritage.

THE ONES WITH THE MOST CHILDREN WIN!

God wants us to see children as a great reward in this lifetime; the privilege of birthing, caring for, and loving each child is like winning the grand prize in a big contest!

Elon Musk is the richest man in the world.[5] He has everything money can buy, and he is a hard-working genius, yet he has already found the secret to life in that he realizes having a lot of children is what true happiness is. Elon is the father of 13 children, and I am not 100% in favor of how he got these children, but 12 of these children are here now, and Elon has been quite vocal telling the world they need to be having more children.

In 2023, Elon spoke to the Italian government[6] about economic strategies and he told them if you want to succeed in the future, *"Make more Italians!"* Elon stated the obvious; the rest of Europe and Japan are all dying cultures that could *become extinct* strictly because their young people are not investing their lives in children and family. I love that the richest man in the world has found the secret sauce. He may be an agnostic, but he has figured out *the one with the most children does win* and he is not afraid to speak out about my favorite subject! If Jesus were here, he would be saying the same thing; children are *good for the planet*, and this was why God told us on the first page of our Bible to have children!

I am grateful Elon has the ear to the world, and he is telling the world God's message! I don't know how many people are listening to him, but I applaud his efforts because in the beginning God said, "be fruitful and multiply" for it will be good for the earth to have people. Here we are thousands of years later and the richest man in the world is saying the same thing! I love Elon's frank statements about family, and I would LOVE to meet him to discuss strategies about helping these ideas move forward.

Children are the grand prize of life. According to God's principles, *he who has the most children does win*! It's not really a contest but a person, who raises their children to follow God and have morals, they will be the blessed person. They are and will remain the winners in life. People enter the Publishers Clearing House contest hoping to become the lucky million-dollar winner, and shows like *Who Wants to Be a Millionaire*, *Deal or No Deal*, and Mega-Million State lotteries are popular because people dream of winning the big contest. Yet God says children are your winning ticket! Have as many as you can. Yet our silly and foolish culture frowns on the people with a lot of children. They tell the parents your children are making you poor, but the richest man alive knows they are what makes his life truly rich. *Thanks, Elon, for preaching my message!*

Even when God calls children a prize and a good reward, people say, "No, thank you! We don't want that kind of prize." But God says that *blessed is the man whose quiver [home] is full of children*! (Psalm 127:5.) People do not realize how much they cheat themselves when they limit children from the Lord. It is as if God says, *"I have one hundred billion dollars that I cannot wait to give you,"* and people reply, *"I will be happy with just ten thousand dollars instead. "*By not being open to receiving the one hundred billion, we miss out on the more incredible blessing that God offers. We sin when we dictate to God *what we want* and then control our situation.

God promised Abraham that He would bless him and make him into a mighty nation, over five thousand years ago. God promised him he would create a nation of people from his loins, and God did what he promised. Five thousand years into the future, Abraham's people are still here today! We are no different from Abraham, God wants to give each of us a heritage through our children. He wants to give us a future and a hope, (Jeremiah 29:11). He wants to reward us with a prize far more significant than any prize that humanity could come up with. He wants to provide us with wealth that does not stop in a single lifetime. Family wealth goes on and on and on... down through our generations if we will only allow it!

They will spend their days in prosperity, and their descendants will inherit the land (Psalm 25:13).

And through your offspring all nations on earth will be blessed because you have obeyed me (Genesis 22:18).

SCRIPTURE CALLS CHILDREN THE "FRUIT OF THE WOMB"

I live in central Florida, one of the citrus capitals of the world, and while I've been here, I have grown in my understanding of fruit by watching crops ripen in nearby groves. Years ago, my property was an orange grove, and most of my neighbors still have several fruit trees in their yards. We could pick fruit from our local trees on any given day during harvest time. Citrus stands sold fresh-squeezed juice, and it was cheap and plentiful. Fruit trees lined our roads, and to be perfectly frank, the abundance of citrus was overwhelming at certain times of the year.

Nearly everyone enjoys fruit. Before sugar abuse became so prevalent in our society, fruit was one of the sweetest tastes most people every enjoyed. We like fruit because it tastes good, and it pleases the palate. Scripture talks at great length about fruit. The possibility of eating fruit was what lured Adam and Eve into sin. I find it interesting that God calls our children the *fruit of the womb* and the *fruit of our bodies*. In Luke 1:42 the Scriptures calls Jesus a *fruit, "The angel said to Mary, blessed is the fruit of your womb!"* Children are the *sweet pleasantries* of life brought to earth for our enjoyment.

Webster's Dictionary says *fruit* is the plant's ability to reproduce itself, the reproductive element of a healthy plant. Fruit is something to feast on and enjoy. God calls our children our *fruit* because He wants us to experience His sweetness through children! They are to be a pleasant and sweet fruit dwelling in our household, and they are! They help adults experience the sweet love of our wonderful Heavenly Father. Even on a bad day, the sweetness of a child can make it better. If you know a little child, you know *what sweetness is* because little children are sweetly innocent and pure.

BIRTHING GOD'S MIGHTY WARRIORS

The Scriptures continually tell us that *fruit is a good thing* and something to be desired.

- The Bible says *fruit* is *valuable!* (James 5:7).
- A wife is a *fruitful* vine (Psalm 128:3).
- Be *fruitful* and multiply (Genesis 1:28).
- The *fruit* of your womb will be blessed (Deuteronomy 28:4).
- The *fruit* of the womb is His reward (Psalm 127:3).
- The goal for those who love God is fruitfulness!
- We are to still *bear fruit* even when we are old. It is a blessing to stay young, fresh and green (Psalm 92:14)…Leaves are always green… never fails to *bear fruit*… *(Jeremiah 17:8).*

Fruit represents the productivity level of a plant; it also measures the productivity level of a person's life. When people find out how many children I have, sometimes they say, *"Well, I know what you have been doing!"* They have figured out one thing my husband and I were doing: having a wonderful and *fruitful* sex life. Yes, **God** blessed the fruit of our womb and God blessed our sex life (Deuteronomy 7:13, 28:4). We were both proud to admit this was something that we enjoyed, and our children were the beautiful *fruit* of the joy we shared in the bedroom.

Children are the fruit of the womb (Deuteronomy 7:13).
Children are a heritage (Psalm 127:3).
Children are a treasure (2 Corinthians 4:7).
Children are a sign of strength (Deuteronomy 21:17).
Children are a sign of blessing (Psalm 128:5a, Psalm 37:26).
Children are a sign of wealth (Psalm 128:5b).
Children are God's reward (Psalm 127:3).
Children are a perfect gift from God (James 1:17).
Children are power (Psalm 127:4, 2 Corinthians 4:7).
Children are God's way of saying, "I love you!" (Job 42:12-17, 1 Samuel 2:21.)

DID YOU KNOW THE FRUIT OF SEX IS YOUR CHILDREN?

There is much being said by God's people today about *producing fruit* for the Kingdom of God. People seem *desperate* to produce fruit for the Lord and to make their lives count for eternity. One of the biggest desires amongst believers today is to be productive for God. People who love Jesus are desperately trying to figure out what He wants them to do with their lives.

People want to produce *good fruit* for Him. When Jesus told His disciples to go and *bear fruit* that would last (John 15:16), most New Testament believers have been taught that this means *go convert* new believers and it does. However, it also could mean go find converts in addition to *birthing* new believers. All of God's people back then allowed God to plan their families, so the people to whom Jesus was speaking were already birthing their new converts. It was not until the last century, since birth control infiltrated God's people that believers dismissed the value of birthing new converts and have instead gone out into the world to seek new converts. What an awesome opportunity has been passed by! We should be doing both things, seeking new converts by preaching the gospel to the world and birthing new converts by raising our children in Godly homes.

What is ironic in today's world is that as believers desperately seek to produce good fruit for God, few are telling parents that the greatest ministry calling that God has given them is to birth and train up the next generation of believers in God. The lack of understanding of this role and calling to birth children causes confusion for many believers. They tell others, *"I do not know what God wants me to do with my life."* Yet the answer is right in the Scriptures.

God set things up so we would be *fruit*-bearers. Yet how many times have you heard a sermon about *bearing fruit for Jesus*? I have heard many, but the preacher never mentions that God desires children to be that fruit. Instead, they say God desires souls, or good deeds or prayers or perfecting one of the fruits of the spirit. Sexual intimacy is overlooked, yet it is God's calling on the marriage to bear fruit. When couples are open to God to give them children as the fruit of their marriage, He promised to answer their prayers (John 15:16). Jesus said *my desire is that you go and bear fruit*. When you do, you can have whatever you ask in my Father's name (John 15:16). If this principle is true and if we believe it, then being open to having children leads to answered prayer.

Maybe you never thought about this, but your children represent *you*. If you have two children, then you have two representatives to carry on in your footsteps after you are gone. If you have ten children, you leave ten family members to carry on in your footsteps. When we trust God with our family plan, we will produce the needed heirs to continue for us, but *only God knows that number for each family*.

Children are the fruit that represent reproduction in a person's life. When people say, *"That's my boy!"* or *"He's just like his Daddy,"* or name their child *Junior*, they are acknowledging their child is a reproduction of themselves. People name a son after his father in hopes he will grow up to be *like his father*. This also relates to passing on the family name as a father might say when referring to his son, *"He is my namesake."*

Family names leave a mark on history

Think of the famous families who left their mark on this world. In America, prominent families would be the *Kennedys, the Rockefellers, the Marriotts, The Busch's, the Melons, the Hiltons, the Trumps,* and more. Families pass on their family name and the legacy that represents what their family has accomplished.

In my own Italian family, this was very important. My Italian grandparents had six children, and my father was their namesake; named after his father. My parents decided that when they had children, they would pass on the family name because it was very important to my grandfather. Before I was born, my parents planned to name their first born, Joseph after my father, but when I turned out to be a girl, they picked the name Rachel out of the Bible. Then when they were pregnant with my sister, she was supposed to be named after my father, but she also turned out to be a girl. Finally, nine years later, they had a son, and he got the family name: Joseph Giove, the 3rd. My Italian grandfather died three weeks later happily leaving earth with an heir named after him. Then for years my brother planned to name a son Joseph Giove, the 4th in honor of the family. In 2010, at the birth of his son, he finally did.

This is a picture of legacy. This is what the *childfree by choice* do not understand; the importance of passing a family legacy on to your child. My brother never knew the man he would someday name his son after, but he named him *in honor of this man* who passed on the family name. This is heritage: passing on the traits, dreams, ideas, qualities, ambitions, and love that runs in a family. The Bible's principles fully support legacy, family heritage and passing the baton from one generation to the next to complete the purposes of the calling on a family bloodline. This is also why conceiving children today is so incredibly important. There are children who need to be born *to complete the tasks of their ancestors*, and it is critical they be conceived and allowed to be born. Every generation is living closer to the Lord's return, than the generation that came before, and it is critical in these final generations that we be obedient to the task at hand.

GENERATIONAL WEALTH IS YOURS, ALL YOU HAVE TO DO IS ASK

Many believers do not realize that because of their ancestors, there is *wealth* laid up in *God's Heavenly vaults*, waiting to be released upon the faithful *who will ask for it* (Proverbs 28:10; Proverbs 2:7-8). This is the *generational wealth* that came from passing the baton from father to son and from son to grandson (Psalm 48:13b; Psalm 112:2b).

The *fruit of your family tree* is spiritual wealth, and it may have been put *on hold* for generations, if someone in your family bloodline was disobedient. We see this many times in scripture when God describes one of the kings of Israel. The Scriptures will say *this king did even more evil in the eyes of the Lord, than all that came before him*. The last several generations have not placed a very high value on conceiving children, but instead the emphasis has been on *not conceiving* them. In your family, if your parents or grandparents or even previous ancestors did not value their fertility or did something to *alter God's plan*, then the promised blessing of the generations over the fruit of the womb, may be on "pause".

If you are struggling with infertility and are having trouble conceiving, your infertility could be due to a generational sin. "Repent and turn" is God's formula for restoration. Repent for your fathers or grandfather's vasectomy or your mom's tubal ligation, abortion, being on the pill or preventing children in some other way. Repent for the sins of your ancestors (parents, grandparents etc.), then *reproduction will be restored to you* once again. [See Chapter 11]

God has not taken these reproductive blessings away, they are stored in His Heavenly storage vaults, but they might be waiting to see what you will do. God might want to bless your families with wealth, wisdom, money, property, health, peaceful family relationships, spiritual gifts, etc. These blessings could all be released to which ever family members will obey God with their family planning. These blessings are waiting for a family descendant to claim them. If you want the blessing that God intended for you to receive, repent for the sins of your ancestors and receive God's forgiveness for the past. Through repentance, God will then release the wealth to you. It's as simple as this.

Since God does not forget the righteousness of previous generations, these blessings are still due to this family bloodline (Exodus 20:6).

Unfortunately, there are many believers who do not see the riches of being open to the possibility of a large family. I have heard believers argue that we do not have to have *physical fruit* (children), God can bless us with *spiritual children* birthed through our participation in church related activities. This may be true because God wants us to produce all kinds of eternal fruit. I believe however that our goal should be to be open to producing both physical and spiritual children because this is what God told Abraham to do. God likes both kinds of fruit, both physical children and spiritual children. God's desire is that our physical children become believers, and then they can become our spiritual children as well. If we limit our fruit to only the kind that we want to produce, we will not be following God's system of balance, especially if He wants to give us physical children as part of the fruit of our life's work.

This is why God called *the fruit of the womb* His reward (Psalm 127:3).

GRANDPARENTHOOD: GOD'S ICING ON THE CAKE

If I knew that having grandkids would be this much fun, I would have had them first! This quote, obviously made by a happy grandparent, describes what comes next after parenthood, Grandparenthood! This is part of the wonder of heritage. God planned that as we complete the task of raising our children, God would make us grandparents. The only key is that we had to become a parent first. It is a high honor to be chosen to parent children, and the reward for doing this is to live long enough to see another generation begin.

This was God's blessing to Jacob. Jacob thought he would never see Joseph's face again. But God reunited him with Joseph and gave him the privilege of seeing Joseph's children! Jacob was able to speak a patriarchal blessing over them (Genesis 48:11); a beautiful picture of the love of God!

God's plan is for children to always be in people's lives from the beginning of their marriages until their final days on earth

Grandparenthood captures the essence of aging. It gives people something to look forward to. One of the joys of getting older is the grandchildren. They add a little spark and a lot of fun to the lives of older adults. People find comfort in knowing that in their senior years, their families will take care of them. *Family* gives the older adult a reason to hold on to life. This was God's plan.

God's desire was for people to enjoy family reunions with their children and grandchildren and have happy memories of their children's days in their households. In turn, the role of the elderly is to guide the next generations with the help of the Lord's wisdom.

Children's children are a crown to the aged and parents are the pride of their children (Proverbs 17:6).

The Lord intended for dinner tables (especially during holiday feast times) to be filled with happy families growing together.

Even when I am old and gray, do not forsake me, oh God, until I declare your power to the next generation, your mighty acts to all who are to come! (Psalm 71:18).

By the time people become grandparents, they are seasoned with wisdom. This wisdom was not meant to *fall by the wayside* but to be a blessing to the family members of future generations!

Surprisingly, Hollywood gave a beautiful picture of God's idea for the family in a 1995 movie called *Father of the Bride 2*. This movie embraced a theme that is rarely seen in America anymore, as both the mother and the married daughter were pregnant at the same time. At the movie's end, the father held his new daughter and his new grandson. In that moment while holding two generations in his arms he says, *"Life doesn't get any better than this."* He was right!

The beauty of God was evident in that moment. Life really does not get any better than this because only God could create a miraculous moment such as this. What could give a person a more incredible honor than seeing their child's birth at the same time as their grandchild's?

The old with the new, the experienced with the inexperienced, the elder enjoying this pleasure again.

Birthing one's child at the same time as their grandchild appears odd in our culture, yet this idea is not strange to the Lord or strange to other cultures. It is unfamiliar to Americans and cultures that believe a couple should be wrapping up their childbearing after having two children or by age 35 whichever comes first. But God intended for grandparenthood to overlap parenthood. He created the human body to function so this would naturally occur. If He didn't want couples to still have children when they also became grandparents, He would not have allowed their equipment to continue working! Overlapping the two was always how it was from Biblical days until recent generations.

When people marry young and allow the womb to stay open until menopause, their childbearing years naturally overlap those of their children. It is simple math. It may seem strange because it is no longer seen in our society, yet God created our bodies with lasting fertility so we can have the necessary opportunities to grow our families.

God's perfect plan is that childbearing is to be started when people are young and completed when they are old (Psalm 127:4, Proverbs 5:18, Malachi 2:14, Joel 1:8, Isaiah 54:6). *They will still bear fruit in old age... (Psalm 92:14).*

A HERITAGE COULD GET REALLY BIG!

Another picture of generational heritage is the preservation of the Jewish people. To be a people group that is still somewhat intact, almost five thousand years after God made a covenant with Abraham. God has helped preserve a rich heritage. Millions of Jewish people are the descendants (offspring) of Abraham. Through Judaism, these descendants have been passing on the faith from generation to generation. This is a remarkable thing to observe. It is a living picture of the fulfillment of scripture (Deuteronomy 4:9); *teach God's ways to your children and to their children after them* and this is precisely what the Jews have done. They pass it on to keep the traditions of their faith alive. Whether one agrees with their ceremonies is not important to note here. It is the obedience in passing the information from father to son. This can be seen in their tenacity as a race and as a people group.

I love having a family heritage; it is vital to us. The 2002 movie, *My Big Fat Greek Wedding* reminded me of the riches that come from having parents, brothers, and sisters and the joy that comes from the extended family. The aunts, uncles, and cousins make a heritage so very enjoyable. The family themes from Big Fat Greek Wedding 2 (2016) and Big Fat Greek Wedding 3 (2023) continue to present a picture of family legacy.

I am blessed to have a *Big, Fat, Italian* heritage. As I have aged, I have been more able to appreciate its beauty. My father's parents immigrated to America from Italy in 1927, settling in Washington, D.C., and God blessed them with six children, seventeen grandchildren, twenty-seven great-grandchildren, and quite a few great-great-grandchildren. They are no longer living, but they started a family tradition that we continue. For 48 years on Thanksgiving, it was the tradition for the offspring to get together and celebrate. Every family contributed to the meal in some way. Different aunts would bring their specialties, and many family recipes were cherished over the years. I always enjoyed that day because almost everyone in the extended family was there. Thanksgiving did not seem as special for me unless I got to attend. Most of my cousins are believers, as my grandparents were, and it was always a blessing to see the similarities in our parents and families. I believe the Lord smiled on our family for the 48 years we met as an extended family because on that day our family carried on one of God's traditions; coming together and enjoying the unity of one gigantic family. Most of the aunts and uncles have now all passed, but the family continues ongoing because this is what a family heritage is all about.

I feel richly blessed because both sides of my family have passed along a Godly heritage to me. From what we can trace in our family history, two sets of great-great-grandparents on both sides of the family all knew the Lord, as have their offspring ever since. Our family has experienced many generational blessings and gifts because of this heritage. The torch has been passed on from great-great-grandparent to great-grandchild to grandchild, all the way down to me. I did my best to teach and train my children to love Jesus so that hopefully our heritage will continue beyond me to the grandchildren and great grandchildren. We have had ministers, writers, composers and Godly businesspeople come through our family's bloodline, each dedicated to promoting the purposes of God. We are blessed!

It is a beautiful thing to be living with a heritage of blessings. As a result of Godly predecessors, a rich spiritual inheritance is there. Godly ancestors' actions have brought blessings to my children and me. This fulfills the promise: *I will show love to a thousand generations to those who love me and who keep my commandments (Exodus 20:6).*

If we follow God, He will continue to pass these things on to my grandchildren and great-grandchildren until the Lord returns for us.

- *The righteous stand firm forever (Proverbs 10:25).*
- *The righteous will never be uprooted... (Proverbs 10:30).*
- *the righteous are rewarded with good thing. (Proverbs 13:21).*
- *In the way of righteousness there is life... (Proverbs 12:28).*
- *They will spend their days in prosperity and their descendants will inherit the land (Psalm 25:13).*

When a person is full of Godly ancestry who laid the foundation, those who come later in the family will benefit. When Jesus is the cornerstone of the family (Ephesians 2:20), there will be stability in marriages and in relationships, and the children's morals code and behavior. It is a beautiful blessing coming down upon the kin to anyone who loved God during their lifetime.

YOUR PEOPLE COULD CHANGE THE WORLD!

As we follow in the footsteps of our ancestors, we can change the world if we ask God for this opportunity. Nineteenth-century theologian *Jonathan Edwards* and his wife *Sarah* loved the Lord; God blessed their union with Godly offspring. In 1900 *A. E. Winship* did a study on education and heredity.[7] A summary was published in a booklet on motherhood distributed by **Focus on the Family,** listing the accomplishments of the 1,400 descendants that came from one man and one woman.

The Edwards family produced:

13 college presidents
65 college professors
100 lawyers and a dean of a law school
30 judges

>   66 physicians and a dean of a medical school
>   80 public officials: 3 United States senators, 3 mayors of large cities, 3 state governors
>   1 comptroller of the U. S. Treasury
>   1 vice-president of the United States.

1400 people came from the union of two people who trusted God with their family planning! This is incredible fruit! Their agreement with God fulfilled the verses,

Their descendants will be known among the nations and their offspring among the peoples... (Isaiah 61:9).

The righteous lead blameless lives; blessed are their children after them (Proverbs 20:7).

You, LORD, reign forever; your throne endures from generation to generation (Lamentations 5:19).

The reward of this fruit reflects a blessing on both the male and the female. Throughout scripture and the history of humankind, the women bear the children, but the men claim ownership of the bloodlines.

The family with 1400 descendants started with the sperm of one man and the egg of one woman. Through their pain, the females in this family bloodline can step back in amazement and see what God did through their bodies. It's as if the Lord has given the women their own inheritance. Blessed are the wombs that bore this family's children!

WHOSE BLOODLINE DO YOU BEAR?

Let's say you are reading this message and are a first-generation believer in your family. Birthing or adopting a few children sounds good to you, and this book is starting to change your mind a little about children, but you have not entirely grasped why being a mother is what you are called to do. Let's also assume that having a Godly heritage was never much of a thought to you. It sounds good for some, but you are sure no one else in your bloodline knew God.

I want to challenge you that this may not be the case. I believe that today if a new churchgoer could trace their family roots, they would find other religious ancestors somewhere in their family bloodline. In all actuality, none of us knows who our ancient relatives were. We could be related to famous Biblical people and not even know it! It's cool when you think about it. Only God knows who each person descended from and by what means we have come to know Him. Even if we are not Jewish, somehow, somewhere, someplace, and in some way, we could be related to the Apostle Paul, one of the disciples, King David or Father Abraham, or any other Biblical character or saint of history. They could be a great, great grandpa or grandma of ours! None of us can be completely sure who our ancient relatives were.

HEBREWS 11 – A GENERATIONAL PICTURE

Hebrews 11 is known as The Faith Chapter of the Bible. It is full of stories of God's faithfulness. Many call it the Biblical Hall of Fame. All these people were still living by faith when they died. They did not receive the things promised; they only saw them and welcomed them from a distance... (Hebrews 11:13).

In other words, these precious saints died with a vision of what they were trying to accomplish. God showed them the completed vision, but it was afar off. They died before their complete destiny was fulfilled, but the Scripture says they did not die in vain. Why?

The Scriptures say these saints of old died content. It was because the Lord gave them a revelation about their future inheritance. God showed them that someday, at another time in history, there would come a family member who would fulfill and complete their task!

These were all commended for their faith, yet none of them received what had been promised. Since God had planned something better for us so that only together with us would they be made perfect (Hebrews 11:39-40).

The reason the faithful could not finish their task was not because of their inadequacy or lack of love for the Lord. It was because the generation they were born into was not the appointed time to see the fulfillment of all things!

These saints of old died with the promise of God that He would make sure that everything would be accomplished. Think of the first disciples; they died long before Jesus was planning to return, as did the other saints of history. Each died before the appointed time. Yet here we are 2000 years later, and NOW is the time. Now is the season for the final generations to fulfill these tasks, and what does the enemy do? He works vigorously to get parents to stop producing children and or makes sure the emerging generation is killed!

Children are the key to generational wealth! To eternal wealth, to mansions in glory wealth, to completing tasks started in some of your families at the beginning of time wealth!

Do you want to answer a family member in Heaven and admit you did not want these children?

Think about this for a moment; this is one of the most critical reasons we should be trying to birth God's Mighty Warriors right now instead of trying to prevent them. One of our children may be called to fulfill the task an ancient family relative started back in colonial times or in the Middle Ages or when Jesus walked the earth or when King David was here. We have no idea who we are descended from.

Do we not realize that the blood of many martyrs was shed so that we could get to where we are today?

Hebrews 11:33-38 describes these who were faithful: *who through faith conquered kingdoms, administered justice, and gained what was promised; who shut the mouths of lions, quenched the fury of the flames, and escaped the edge of the sword; whose weakness was turned to strength; and who became powerful in battle and routed foreign armies. Women received back their dead, raised to life again. There were others who were tortured, refusing to be released so that they might gain an even better resurrection. Some faced jeers and flogging, and even chains and imprisonment. They were put to death by stoning; they were sawed in two; they were killed by the sword. They went about in sheepskins and goatskins, destitute, persecuted and mistreated, the world was not worthy of them. They wandered in deserts and mountains, living in caves and in holes in the ground.*

Are we even worthy of our heritage?

We are standing on holy ground and don't even realize it!

Who are we to try to control anything?

Susannah Wesley was the 25th child born in her family. She had 19 children herself! Her 16th child, Charles Wesley wrote over 6000 hymns and poems, and her 15th child, John Wesley, founded the Methodist denomination!

Who are you descended from? How dare we try to keep our children from coming to earth! Our 6th or 9th or 12th, or 17th child might be the one God called to fulfill your ancestor's dream, calling or task. The Bible tells us the generations are each connected when in Matthew 1, it records a complete genealogy from Adam to Jesus Christ. We know the generations continued, past those recorded in the Scriptures, and rest assured that God has continued to track the genealogical heritage and one day it will be revealed. Then all the world will know to whom they were really connected from the beginning to the end! What a glorious revelation that will be for all of us when it is revealed someday in eternity. I don't want my actions to be a contributor in any way that would keep my bloodline from fulfilling our complete destiny!

If you stay open to allowing God to choose your family size, I promise you, the people who need to be here right now will make it because you said "yes" to God's ways. Then one day in eternity, you will stand before the Lord with your completed bloodline all the way back to the beginning of time and you will all say, **here we are Lord, with ALL the children that you graciously blessed us with ... and our descendants**. (Hebrews 2:13). God's way is ALWAYS the best way!

Wife's Prayer

Heavenly Father, I want to have the children that are supposed to come into my family. I want to stand in Heaven with the children that You intend for me to raise. Please help me to be open to receiving these children and open to being pregnant when necessary. I desire to be a part of a great heritage. I repent of my hesitations and look forward to being blessed now and in eternity. Amen

Husband's Prayer

Heavenly Father, I had no idea that you were trying to bless me with a heritage. I have never understood it quite like this before. Now that it is clear, I desire to receive a greater heritage for myself and my family. I repent of my lack of understanding and ask You to help me begin to be open to receiving the children that You've ordained for my bloodline. I want future generations to enjoy the fruit of my Godly actions.

Amen

Christopher's Commentary

Generational wealth is an idea we don't discuss daily, yet it is real, tangible, and scriptural. Several years ago. I became a grandpa. I couldn't believe it. I didn't plan on being one, it just happened one day, and I had a new title. In my mind, that kind of thing happens to old white-haired men with canes, not young men like me! I've repeatedly asked myself how I got to this stage so quickly.

As men, I think we never look very far down the road. Some men do, but for some reason, women seem to plan out certain things more than men. When a father looks at his newborn baby or his two-year-old, he is not thinking about what it will be like when this child is in high school. We might occasionally think about the expenses, but we do not think about our relationship with them. We assume it will be good. In those moments, we are more concerned about what might happen in our job, what bills are due, or where our company might transfer us. Problems down the road in relationships are rarely anticipated or thought much about.

I don't think most men plan their legacies, although it would be an excellent idea. I mean, what is a legacy? I know people remember you by it, but we don't think about it being reflected in others. We usually think it is about what we accomplish ourselves. We also don't think much about death or dying when raising children. That seems very distant down the road. I am sure a few men think about how they will be remembered after they are gone, and these men might be deeply concerned about it, but I think the majority give little thought to this. Instead, we spend our time trying to do a good job with our careers and figure if we do a good job at that, everything else will work itself out.

When one of my guys tells me he is getting the big V (vasectomy), I usually ask, "Why do you want and go do a thing like that?" He usually tells me his fantasy about how much better things will be once it's done and how happy he will be now that his *woman* can't get pregnant. The guy never realizes how much this decision will affect his legacy. He isn't thinking about anything other than the moment, and he wants a short-term solution. He can't see that it has long-term consequences. He is blinded just like I was. He has no idea that the surgeon's cut is a cut to himself and his legacy.

Christopher Scott

Investigate and Questions

- What did God say to you while reading this chapter about heritage?
- Read Hebrews 2:13 What kind of physical or spiritual heritage are you hoping to leave your descendants when you die?
- Read Psalm 78:6 and 102:18. The Psalmist refers to the children yet to be born and the children not yet created. Whose children are these? Are there any factors that might keep these children from being allowed to come to earth? Do you have children yet to be born? Will you allow them to be conceived and born?
- If a person participates in birthing children, and then raises those children to love God, how will this be one of the greatest spiritual investments they could make in their lifetime?
- Read Genesis 21:12 and 22:17. How did Abraham's descendants validate Abraham's life? *(A woman's life can be counted worthy through childbearing)*. How does birthing children establish the life of a woman?
- Read 1 Timothy 2:15. How does birthing children affect a woman spiritually, especially regarding what this verse is communicating?
- Read Hebrews 11:39-40. Have you ever thought about a heritage going on and on, or think about who your ancient ancestors might have been and what actions of your life or of your children's lives might help to fulfill their visions and combine with your dreams?

Impacting Others

When I first read Rachel's book in 2004, I was immediately impressed with the premise that we are birthing God's end-time army. This idea inspired me. I especially liked Chapter 5 because, too often, it's easier to focus on the present and all the pressures of raising a family while forgetting that our decisions in the present will affect the future. When we were engaged, I first said I wanted to have five children, and my husband said he wanted ten which is how many we have now. We both had been raised in families with three children, yet as Bible-believing Christians, we did not immediately question using birth control. That came later in our marriage. At some point along our journey, we began to question if birth control was right to use. It seemed to us that it was taking the reins away from God. Being the parents of ten children is entertaining. My husband is an attorney, and I am also a college grad. Between the two of us, we have five college degrees, and with our ten children, I am sure some look at us and wonder, with all our education, why we have not figured out birth control! We've heard all the jokes and comments from onlookers, but the joys of our family far outweigh the criticisms. We are entering a new phase as our first grandchild was recently born, and we are now grandparents! Even with this joy this past year, our faith was tested when I suffered the loss of three babies to miscarriage. In five months, I suffered the loss. Yet even in this, we would not allow the control to be taken away from God in any way. He is sovereign, and His plan is best even if we do not understand it. Initially, I had planned to buy a copy of Birthing God's Mighty Warriors for each of my children, but Rachel sold out immediately. This book is in a class all by itself. It is full of truths that we've never heard before. One thing I had never heard from anyone was the history of birth control in Egypt. I had always assumed the Egyptians used birth control and the Israelites did not, but I had never seen any information on the subject. Most people think birth control is a recent discovery, which of course, it is not! This book is necessary for everyone who wants to know the truth, even if it is sometimes uncomfortable and challenging. God does not want us to walk blindly through our lives. Throughout her book, Rachel gives ways to defend our position better, see the path before us, and clarify God's end-time goal for the family. I want to add that I have become close to Rachel since we first met online. I have observed her life and her walk. She is a faithful prayer warrior who doesn't shy away when things get ugly. Rachel has had trials like the rest of us, but she stays strong and true. It shows great strength of character to stand steadfast in the midst of life's hardships. **Paula Hands, mother to ten children, and twelve grandchildren, Amarillo, Texas**

Chapter 6

THE DESTINY OF YOUR SEED

Children are arrows in the hand of a mighty warrior. They are like sharp arrows to defend him. Happy and blessed is the man who has a quiver full, for that man will have help when he speaks with his enemies at the gate.
(Psalm 127:4-5 paraphrase)

In Chapter 1, I spoke about how special a woman's role is because when she says yes to motherhood, she flows in her natural God-given calling to give love. In this chapter, I will share with the men the essential value of the contribution of *their seed*.

Twenty-five years ago, as a new millennium dawned, the word *destiny* grew in popularity. Rock groups used the word to name their bands as did schools, towns, businesses, political candidates and the media. Even we felt led to give our daughter the name Destiny because she was born at the turn of the new millennium. This word became one of the defining terms for the newest century on planet Earth. For believers the word destiny invokes the idea of fulfilling our call and or discovering our purpose in God's plan for our lives.

ARROWS IN THE HAND OF A MIGHTY WARRIOR

One of the most important themes of the Scriptures is that believers are in a constant spiritual war against the Prince of Darkness. God wants to make us keenly aware that this fight is for our very souls. One thing I found fascinating as I researched family planning in God's word was that God sees our children as vital instruments of spiritual war. The Scriptures say our children are essential and I believe God wants to communicate with us that our families hold a much deeper purpose in the battle of light vs. darkness than we could ever imagine.

Psalm 127:4 refers to children as man's arrows, and happy will be the man whose quiver is full of them

When God referred to our children as instruments of war, He did not mean that our children would literally be used as *physical ammunition*, and He certainly will not bring harm in any way to their lives. God used this *metaphor of the arrow* because He recognized our need for a great weapon as we fight against the enemy. God could have chosen another symbol to relate this idea, but instead He chose the arrow because of its unique and specific capabilities that separate it from other forms of defense. The arrow is a very efficient and excellent weapon of war.

Without his arrows, a warrior would be a dead man. In ancient days when a warrior was about to go to battle, he would fill his quiver, which was another name for a carrying case. He filled it with as many arrows as it would hold to ensure he had enough ammunition. Each arrow was handcrafted by the warrior and carefully fashioned to achieve the purpose of annihilating the enemy. At the time of battle, the arrow would be skillfully shot toward the enemy, and if done correctly, it would annihilate his opponent every time.

Every arrow counted and was critical to the warrior's survival. Each arrow was precious to the warrior because each one took a long time to make so the warrior was cautious not to waste a single arrow. His goal was for each arrow to hit its target and to be fatal!

An arrow achieves forward motion. Each time, the warrior remained stationary. He did not move off his spot. By aiming his arrow carefully, it was shot out from the warrior's stance, to achieve its purpose.

The goal is for our children to move past us and go out into a future time and place. We each have an estimated lifespan of 120 years (Genesis 6:3). We are each limited by time and space. If one of our children were born today, that child could be alive 120 years from now, well into the next century A.D. 2100. That child's children could go that much further into the future—another 80 to 120 years, potentially well into the next century A.D. 2200 and beyond. Most of us will die before the end of this century (A.D. 2099), but our family could still be contributing to God's work on earth through our children, grandchildren, and great-grandchildren. Think of the opportunity that is available to us and was also available to previous generations. We are a living testament representing our ancestors. Once created, each person in our family can influence the future and the family's purpose will remain into eternity.

If you had been a warrior on past battlefields, how many arrows would you have wanted to help defend you against your enemies? Would it be one, two, five, or ten?

Every time God calls our children *arrows*, this metaphor teaches us a principle of war. Each parent has the *unique opportunity* to raise their children to become victorious mighty warriors on the battlefield of life. Scripture says that our children can stand in victory in areas where we have failed and take back spiritual ground that has been stolen from our families (Genesis 22:17b; 24:60). As conquerors, they can bring new life, they can rule and govern, and they can possess the gates of the enemy.

Our children basically pick up where we leave off. After we die, one of the most unique ways we are blessed will be that our children can continue to bear fruit from our Godly influences. This is a spiritual principle that most people in my generation were never taught and even today a principle few of us have grasped, but Job certainly understood this when all his children were dead. He complained to God. Job knew that his children were his physical and spiritual representatives, and he questioned God (like the rest of us would) while also mourning the deaths of all ten of his children! (Job 21:8). God wants us to grasp this very powerful principle. Our children will live in the future and will replace us! They will be granted opportunities we will never have, go to places we could never go, and accomplish things we could never do.

Children are living proof that their parents once existed on earth. The concept of arrows holds significance to me. When I get to Heaven someday, besides being with Jesus I do want to meet my great- grand parents from both sides of my family. They all died before I was born, but my life was impacted greatly because of their choices. I am especially curious to meet the parents of my grandmother, on my mother's side of the family. Even though I never met them, somehow, I feel I *know* them.

They left five of their *six children* on earth when they died; and I had the wonderful privilege of meeting four of their children because one was my maternal grandmother. There is no way to describe the goodness my grandmother and her siblings possessed. They were all simply exceptional people; sweet, kind, loving, compassionate, gentle, friendly, hospitable, giving and all loved Jesus. Meeting my great-grandparents lovely children indicates what fine people my great grandparents had to be. Their children could not say enough good things about them. My grandmother made a huge contribution to my life. I am so very thankful they raised my grandmother to love Jesus. Their example compels me to want to meet the parents who fashioned these "arrows." They've made me desire to follow in their footsteps of righteousness and I did my best to fashion my children after some of the qualities I leaned from my grandmother.

*Children carry the fruit of the family with them. When people meet our children and grandchildren in the future, a special part of us will remain alive in them. As we pass our legacy on, we can still impact a future generation even when we are in the grave.

HOLY SPERM-THE MIRACLE OF A MANS SEED

In the 1989 movie, *Look Who's Talking,* the movie's first scene featured these cartoon-like *sperm* racing to unite with a sexy female egg. People laughed and the scene was meant to be amusing and comical, but this scene is also a perfect example of how people today view *sperm*. People dismiss its value. They laugh at something that God considers *holy* and *precious*.

We are living in the time of the male vasectomy. This operation has become quite popular. Many women make their husbands go get one, and its widespread acceptance has caused men to think their *sperm* has no value. Most men don't give their *sperm* a second thought and, in our world, *sperm* is viewed simply as a waste product with little importance and something to joke about. Maybe this is why Hollywood made fun of *sperm* at the beginning of their movie.

The significance of a *man's sperm* is not discussed in Bible studies or Sunday school lessons. On a rare occasion, a minister might talk about sperm from the pulpit, but it would only be when he was teaching on seed and might need to refer to a man's seed. *Sperm* is not a matter of discussion. Men also do not go around talking about their sperm unless, on the rare occasion when they find out their wife is pregnant, some might brag about their abilities to be virile. This is perceived as a crude reference. People make jokes about *sperm* because laughter helps to make the reference more comfortable.

However, the Bible is not afraid of discussing a man's sperm and talks about it frequently

God refers to a man's sperm as his *seed* and God considers *seed* to be holy. God considers the sperm of a man to be one of the most *precious commodities* on earth because it houses the ability to *create as God created*.

This holy and precious force inside men's bodies is more significant than every war ever won, every Super Bowl victory, every NBA Championship, or World Series victory, every stock market high, and every accomplishment of material wealth!

Sperm has the ability to change the course of history!

Please realize, your *seed* is precious and powerful and is not to be casually spilled. I already covered the sin of Onan in Genesis 38 in Chapter 3. Onan was the man who used to withdraw himself right before ejaculation and then casually spilled his seed on the ground. God killed him as a result.

Without any fear of God or spiritual repercussions countless men today and even Christian men, place a condom over their penis, ejaculate their sperm into the condom and then flush both the sperm and the condom down the toilet. Men think nothing of it. When a man flushes God's holy and precious gift of life away; his *precious seed is lowered to the value of human excrement*. We've been taught that this is fine with God, but is it ok?

Did you know the *loins* are the part of the body that houses a man's seed? One thing that is fascinating about the loins is that it is the first area that develops in a tiny human. This is not simply a coincidence; I believe God was communicating how precious the reproductive organs are since in the human body they are created first. Our loins are not to be worshipped, but we should value them dearly because God values them. Loins house our reproductive organs, cover and protect the intestines, and are the area of our body where the ability to create life comes from. Throughout the Scriptures, God tells men and women to *gird up their loins* in preparation for engaging the enemy (Exodus 12:11; Luke 12:35; Ephesians 6:14; Proverbs 31:7).

Ezekiel saw God in a vision and God had FIRE emulating from His loins! (Ezekiel 1:27).

Daniel saw God in a vision, and he saw GOLD covering God's loins! (Daniel 10:5).

Isaiah prophesied the Messiah would have RIGHTEOUSNESS over His loins! (Isaiah 11:5).

When we find out from the Scriptures that God has fire and gold covering his loins and Jesus has Righteousness over His loins, isn't this a clue for us that this area of our bodies must be an area of significance?

Especially when the ungodly culture around us is constantly telling us to CUT this area up!

Obviously, God values this area of our body in a far greater way than we have grasped. This area of a man's anatomy is sacred to the Lord because the loins can produce significant people who can change history and become God's mighty warriors.

Ancient cultures placed great value upon their loins. Pagan societies worshipped their reproductive organs and set up altars and phallic obelisks to fertility gods, symbolizing the worship of their genitalia. The ancient Babylonian and Egyptians believed that eternal life was somehow connected to the sexual act. These people groups did not know God, yet they were still able to understand that there was great significance in these reproductive body parts. This was why they worshipped them. Some of these beliefs are still followed by pagans. Eastern Laya yoga, which embraces the New Age idea of energy chakra, refers to this area as the Swadhisthana chakra, from which they believe eternal light emanates.

Loins are very powerful because they contain a person's heritage. Our loins are not to be worshipped, but they are something that we should value dearly because God values them dearly. Our reproductive organs are on each person's physical body, but they are Gods' and should be dedicated to Him. Let me repeat this. Our reproductive organs *should be dedicated to* the Lord. Our entire body is a temple; we are not our own; we have been bought with a price:

Do you not know that your body is a temple of the Holy Spirit, who is in you, whom you have received from God? You are not your own; you were bought with a price. Therefore, honor God with your body (1 Corinthians 6:19-20).

God's desire is that we use our *bodies* for His holy purposes because this will bring us many wonderful blessings, and because our body is not our own this is why it is never a good idea to tamper with or physically alter our reproductive organs especially when they are in good working order. Thus, getting sterilized through a vasectomy or tubal ligation is a sin against one's body.

Therefore, do not let sin reign in your mortal body so that you obey its evil desires. Do not offer up the parts of your body to sin, as instruments of wickedness (Romans 6:12-13a).

Scripture has a lot to say about loins. Throughout scripture, God places a high value upon each man's loins because of their ability to change history through the creation of human beings.

God told Abraham that a son *would be coming from his body* and would be his heir (Genesis 15:4).

God said to Jacob, *...and God said to him, "I am God Almighty; be fruitful and increase in number. A nation and a community of nations will come from you, and kings will be among your descendants (Genesis 35:11).*

All those who went to Egypt with Jacob *and came out of Jacob's loins* were 70 persons (Exodus 1:5).

God told David, *thy son that shall come forth out of thy loins, he shall build the house unto my name (1 Kings 8:19, 2 Chronicles 6:9). If your children keep my commands, they will sit on the throne forever (Psalms 123:12).*

SACRED SEED: THE FRUIT OF THE WOMB IS HIS REWARD

We have already established that children are the fruit of the egg and sperm. In creation before a person can have fruit, they must first have adequate seed. Scripture says God gives seed to the Sower (Isaiah 55:10, 2 Corinthians 9:10).

One of my favorite stories from kindergarten was the story of Johnny Appleseed. I'm sure his story was embellished through folklore, but as the story goes, a college aged kid who loved apples decided to go west from his home in Pennsylvania. Everywhere he went he spread apple seeds on the ground. Not long after he left an area, tiny apple tress grew and eventually, they grew into nurseries and in some places even orchards! He spread these apple seeds from Pennsylvania to West Virginia to Ohio and into Indianna, Illinois, and even Ontario, Canada. The moral of the story is to be a man of good deeds like Johhny Appleseed who with a handful of seeds changed the world. This is a great story to remember when we are talking about the power of seeds.

Seed is power. Farmers have counted on seeds to produce a good food crop throughout history. Seed was considered valuable. If we do not have seeds, we cannot grow new life. In the New Testament, Jesus talked about the parable of the seed, which is mentioned in three of the four gospels! (Matthew 13:3-23; Mark 4:2-20; Luke 8:4-15).

Seed is the essence of life. Webster's Dictionary defines seed as the source, origin, or beginning of anything; the part of a plant that contains the embryo and will develop into a new living organism; sperm; semen; ancestry. Scripture says God gives seed to the Sower as He recognized the need for seed and its purpose of blessing.

Seed is needed to produce children. God put the balance of creation into place at the beginning of time, and without seed, a person cannot reproduce.

Then God said, "Let the land produce vegetation: seed-bearing plants and trees on the land that bear fruit with seed in it, according to their various kinds." And it was so (Genesis 1:11).

God told man to be fruitful and multiply (Genesis 1:28). Then God told Noah to take a male and a female animal to keep SEED alive on the earth (Genesis 7:2-3).

If the seed of the plants and animals was sacred to God, how much more sacred and holy is the seed of humans to God? Onan purposefully spilled his seed on the ground because Onan did not recognize the holiness of his seed. God valued his seed (sperm) more than Onan did. Onan easily discarded it, and God judged him, and he died! (Genesis 38).

Human seed is amazing. Sperm is human seed, and when united with the female's seed (her egg), it produces a family heir. This was why God told Abraham amazing things about his seed:

- Look at the stars; so, shall *your seed* be (Genesis 15:5).
- I will establish my covenant with you and your descendants for generations to come (Genesis 17:7).
- *The promises were spoken to Abraham and to his seed. The scripture does not say, "And to seeds," meaning many people but "and to your seed," meaning one person, who is Christ (Galatians 3:16).*
- *...Until the seed to whom the promise referred had come... (Galatians 3:19).*
- *If you belong to Christ, then you are Abraham's seed, and heirs according to the promise (Galatians 3:29).*

God says that a man's inheritance will come from his sperm, but because so few men realize this power, it has been easy for Satan to disguise his plans to devastate men by successfully clouding the issues.

*Every day, Godly men, who know God's Word, and study the scriptures (but not all the scriptures), these men do not realize what they are doing when they casually submit to the vasectomy operation, severing their precious ability to create with their wife. Satan uses all the tricks.

Men are convinced by rationalizations such as this, *"You've got a couple children. You've done your duty and replenished the earth, so make it easy on yourself and get a vasectomy so you can quit while you are ahead."*

This line of thinking is motivating, sounds logical, and makes sense. The man becomes convinced that God is telling him to get a vasectomy and does not realize his future could change, his desires might change, one of his children could get sick and die. He never thinks. Instead, based on convenience he justifies giving away his future parenting opportunities. This thinking goes against Galatians 6:19-20, which tells men that their bodies are *God's temples*, we are not our own.

Therefore, do not let sin reign in your mortal body so that you obey its evil desires. Do not offer up the parts of your body to sin, as instruments of wickedness... (Romans 6:12-14).

Romans 6 says: **DO NOT offer up your BODY PARTS!** This is exactly what a vasectomy is. It is an **offering up** of a man's *vas deferens body part* as a sacrifice on the altar of convenience! And this is evil, but our ministers have told us for years that the Bible is silent about birth control.... *give me a break!*

CONCEPTION WARS

Every time God does something significant on Earth, Satan works vigorously to destroy the children and steal the blessings they will bring.

During the time of Moses, the Egyptians slaughtered the male babies (trying to kill the deliverer). When Jesus was born, Herod slaughtered the babies trying to kill the Messiah (a would be king of the Jews).

Now as we approach the final events of earth, Satan is working vigorously and on a global scale to prevent the conceptions and births of precious children. He is *pulling out all the stops* utilizing the abortion procedure and abortion pills. Using methodology and social media to convince fertile people to not conceive. He uses environmental toxins, drugs, pollutants and atmospheric changes to get us to epidemic levels of infertility and acceptance of sterilization at our churches, schools, workplaces and everywhere else.

Instead of using a mad dictator to sterilize everyone, in the civilized countries people volunteer! Satan uses people's very *good reasons*. He uses pressure from society, family and friends. He uses the news, print, books, articles and social media to portray subtle messages that two children are the norm for most families.

Unknowingly, a mother or father chooses death to their seed out of convenience. A simple sterilization operation is quick, easy and covered by insurance and they do this even when their children are begging for another family member: *"Mommy and Daddy, can we please have another baby? I want a brother or sister!"* How unfortunate for countless children whose parents have already ensured their little brother or sister will never be born.

What if the first man on earth did what is popular today and altered his fertility? What might have happened to history?

Adam and Eve certainly could have justified their choice. After all, they were alone on Earth. They could have said, *"It is pleasant living here with just the two of us; let us not have any children."* Where would humanity be if they had "opted out" of birthing children? I know this sounds silly, but we opt out today, so what if they did what we do? After giving birth to Cain and Abel, what if Adam or Eve said what so many American parents have said, *"Two children are way more than we can handle. We had better do something quick to ensure this does not happen to us again!"* If Adam or Eve had been casually sterilized after the birth of their first two children, then when their boys were grown and Cain killed Abel, then what would have happened to their seed? God cursed Cain for killing his brother Abel and Cain wandered the earth aimlessly. Poor Eve she lost both of her sons! In God's miraculous mercy, God extended His love toward Eve and allowed her to conceive again, and she birthed Seth. Through Seth's seed, God placed Adam and Eve in the direct blood lineage of Christ! The Bible tells us that Adam gave life to other sons and daughters and lived until he was 930 yr. old (Genesis 5:5). Had Adam or Eve altered their fertility in any way, they would have missed out on additional children.

What about Noah? What if he or his children had already altered their fertility before the Great Flood? After the flood, God repeated His commandment to Noah's family. Again, God said (Genesis 9:1; 9:7), *"Be fruitful and multiply!"* What if Noah's family, who were the sole survivors of the Great Flood, had resisted obeying God's commandment and said, *"Didn't God cause the Great Flood because people were making the earth corrupt? We're not sure we want to start over and create more people. People were the problem! Plus, if we have little ones, they are too much work, and there is so much to do since the flood wiped out civilization. If the eight of us work really hard, we can rebuild and contribute to the good of the earth before we die. If we did birth more children, eventually, our offspring would use up all the earth's resources anyway and might cause global warming, so if we refrain from creating more people, then when we die, the animals can inhabit the earth. It's really for them anyway."*

Can you imagine? The Bible says in the last days, it would be as it was in the days of Noah *before* the flood. Today people can think up many good reasons why they should not birth children, but if Noah and his family had felt the same way as people do today, they would have eliminated humanity from the face of the earth. What if old man Noah or his sons had not desired to obey God's command to get off the ark and make more people? Or what if they had already altered their fertility *before* the flood, then afterwards they could not procreate. Then what would have happened to humankind?

What about Abraham? The great patriarch of the Hebrews started without children. Yet, later scripture refers to Abraham and his wife Sarah as the ones who gave Israel birth (Isaiah 51:2). God didn't speak to Abraham until he was an old man, well along in years. Would God have even considered him if he had altered his fertility? A vasectomy is a modern operation, but ancient men were brutally castrated. This was often a punishment due to warfare or slavery. Abraham's loins were extremely significant to God's plan. God even required *dear, old Abraham* to alter his equipment by getting circumcised! And God required this procedure *before* Abraham could give life to Isaac (Genesis 17:10-14). If Abraham's fertility had been altered in any way, we can be sure that God would have used *someone else* to give *life to the nation* of Israel.

How about the Hebrew slaves of Goshen? Jacob's family arrived in Egypt with 70 people and left Egypt with several million family members! (Exodus 1:12, 17, 20; Jeremiah 29:4-6). If it were not for the obedience of Jacob's seed producing their offspring there never would have been a nation of Israel.

What if other men in scripture had gotten sterilized such as Isaac or Jacob? If Jacob had altered his fertility, he would not have been able to give life to the twelve tribes of Israel. This does not mean there would not have been twelve tribes of Israel; it just means that those tribes would not have come through Jacob's bloodline. If Jacob had been castrated, he would have disqualified himself from seeing his seed used in a powerful way. God would have used someone else instead of Jacob. This would have been sad for the family of Abraham, Isaac and Jacob's bloodline but it illustrates "choice". One man's choice to stop giving his seed, could eliminate the future of multiple descendants. Think of the men today who by their choice are disqualifying themselves from God's plan.

This is not a casual little *snip-snip!* A vasectomy will prevent future heirs from coming through your family!

What about King David? God promised David that from his seed He would produce an eternal king. The Bible says that *"David died and was buried, but he was a prophet and knew that God had promised him on oath,* that he would place one of his descendants on this throne (Acts 2:29-30). In other words, a person in the future would be the king. That heir of King David's seed was JESUS, the greatest arrow ever to add to David's quiver! Jesus said, "I am the root and offspring of David" (Revelation 22:16).

This is one reason why Satan is working hard at convincing Christian men to limit their seed by using birth control or by getting sterilized. Can you imagine the sorrow King David would have felt if he had been castrated before the birth of Solomon? This procedure could have been easily justified since David already had a harem of wives and many children. What if in Heaven, King David learned that because he altered his fertility and never conceived Solomon, David missed out on the privilege of King Jesus, the Son of God, being one of his future descendants? History would have been altered in the same way history IS being altered today by the men. *Wow! This is intense!*

COULD A VASECTOMY PREVENT MY FUTURE HEIRS?

Genesis 14:20 tells us that in honor and obedience, Abraham tithed **one-tenth** of his wealth to Melchizedek, King of Salem. This *truth* is so powerful!

One might even say that Levi, who collects the tenth, paid the tenth through Abraham, because when Melchizedek met Abraham, **Levi was still in the body of his ancestor!** *(Hebrews 7:9-10).*

The Scriptures prove a very powerful principle! In God's eminent glory, He foreknew Levi's conception as Abraham's great-grandson because he was already part of the *seed of Abraham's loins*, but he wouldn't be born until four generations later! *Are we catching this?* Levi's birth would only come from Abraham, Isaac, and Jacob's obedience with their fertility! Levi would not have been conceived if ANY of these men interfered with their fertility!

Place this situation in today's world. Most Christian parents have stopped at two children. Levi, being Jacob's third-born instead of his first-born or second-born, Levi might have easily been prevented if Jacob and Leah had been using birth control!

Fast forward thousands of years to the birth of Jesus whose mother was Mary and from the house of David. Jesus is the seed of David. Essentially this means that Jesus is the distant fruit of Abraham's loins because David and Abraham were distant relatives of the same bloodline. Through *their sperm*, and because of *their obedience*, God connected the generations.

If God foresaw these ancestors coming from Abraham centuries before and if he held Abraham accountable, how much more is God holding men accountable today?

Dear brothers and sisters, do you realize what God's word is saying here? By casually *getting snipped*, you could be preventing the destiny of your entire bloodline!

If we look at these examples of the men from the scriptures, altering their fertility would have been historically and spiritually devastating!

Some of you may be saying to yourselves, *"I see your point, and I agree that those men would have missed out, but they didn't have vasectomies back then, and times have changed, and things on earth are different now. We are modern thinkers; we don't need as many people inhabiting the planet anymore. We are not giving life to new nations, we aren't fighting big wars, we do not need farm hands, and we don't live in tents. Our families do not need as many people, and I have no reason to overpopulate the earth. I can use my gifts, callings, and talents in other capacities."*

I've heard this rationale before and can see the reasoning behind it. It makes sense if you believe the worldview that we are overpopulating the earth instead of repopulating it. However, no matter which view you take, let's consider the above reasoning and how one man's decision to prevent children might affect a person's lineage today.

Suppose your grandfather happened to be the fourth child born to your great-grandparents. Consider what would have happened if, one hundred years ago, your great-grandfather had received a vasectomy after his second child. As a result of your great-grandfather's vasectomy, your grandfather missed being conceived and missed being born. Would that have made a difference to you? If things had happened this way, your grandfather, your father, and you would not be here! Neither would any of your children or your grandchildren! Would your great-grandfather's vasectomy have made any *difference* to you? I think so!

It is incredible how one man's decision can alter the family tree forever and cause multiple generations of family members to miss their destiny!

This is why we must be cautious about how we operate our free will concerning our families. Today's circumstances are no different from past generations. God's people are still *walking through the pages of time*, and God is still doing miracles among us. Times have not changed. The closer God's people get to His return, the more critical our decisions will be to the outcome of the final events of history. This is why we need to cooperate with God's plan. Since the 1960s, God's dear people foolishly chose *what made sense in their situations*, and as a result, we are missing thousands of people who would have been born.

Population analysts projected that the U.S. population would soar to 331,000,000 by 2000. Instead, because of widespread birth control use, sterilization, and abortion, the United States Census Bureau[1] reported that the population in 2000 was 281,421,706, roughly 49,000,000 fewer people than the projected figures! Our rise in 2010 to 313,370,000 due to a high percentage of foreign-born people entering the United States, with our replacement rate falling from 2.1 children to 2.01 less than the replacement rate.

The US birth rate has been falling for years and has fallen every year since 2014 to the lowest rate ever in 2023.[2] America no longer is at the replacement rate of 2.1 children, and it is due to women delaying motherhood until their late thirties and forties, high rates of infertility, lack of one finding a partner to either marry or procreate with, the rise in fertile couples choosing to never become parents and ongoing abortion.

According to a 2023 survey by the Guttmacher Institute, the USA aborts roughly 950,000[3] infants per year. Since the 1973 Roe vs. Wade ruling, America has aborted more than 60,000,000 children. These are people who would have contributed to society. These would have served society in many capacities: doctors, nurses, lawyers, truck drivers, schoolteachers, parents, artists, writers, historians, CEOs and CFOs, computer specialists, internet gurus, scientists, researchers, police officers and firefighters, pro-athletes, bus drivers, inventors, entrepreneurs, musicians, clergy, etc. or some could have harmed society as well, but we will never know.

It has been drummed into the head of Protestants that abortion is so wrong because 60,000,000 children have been killed. It is wrong! And with the reversing of Roe vs. Wade decision in 2022, abortions did not stop but increased. But with all the killing of babies we still never stop to think about the billions of children in the last century whose Christian parents prevented their conceptions!!

Question: Which is worse in God's eyes, aborting children or preventing children? Maybe the answer is both because each go against His plan.

YOUR GREATEST MIGHT NOT BE YOUR FIRSTBORN

We've gotten so used to the modern idea that a family should consist of a mother and father, and a son and a daughter, that we do not realize that many famous people of history were not the first or second-born children in their families. Often the most famous people were born fourth, fifth, sixth, eighth, or tenth. Some were even born eleventh or seventeenth, or twenty-fifth! Six of our American presidents were fifth-born, two were sixth-born, three were seventh-born, and one was eighth-born. At least thirty-one American presidents were from families with at least five children. Both George Washington[4] and Thomas Jefferson were from families with ten children.[5] What if the fathers of these presidents had a vasectomy after their second child? We would have missed out on many outstanding presidents and leaders in our society.

A married couple does not know *who is destined* to come through their bloodline or when they will be born. If God planned to give you four children and you stopped at three, you missed God's blessing of your fourth child. What becomes of that child's destiny? I don't know. Does God hold them back in the Heavenlies to be born in a later generation? I don't know. Are they in the mind of God and are they potentially awaiting conception so they can then later become an influencer on this earth? I don't' know. I don't know exactly how it all works, but I do know that when Abraham tithed a tenth of his money to Melchizedek, the Scriptures tell us that he paid the tithe for his great grandson because the potential for his great grandson Levi to be born four generations later, was still in his loins when he tithed for him. If his father Jacob had not conceived Levi, then the *potential* for Levi to be a future heir was in his great grandfather's loins, but the *choice to conceive* Levi was completely made by his father.

What if your fourth child was destined to become a great leader, to influence business or the intellectual world, to become a U.S. president or a famous writer, a Nobel Prize winner who cured the world of some dreaded disease, or something else amazing? But you chose to not conceive this fourth child because three children are enough. The entire world would be missing out on the gift that your fourth child would have brought, but by your decision that child was never conceived.

In the Scriptures, Jessie, Nunn, Zebedee, Hilkiah, Terran, and Amoz are the fathers of some of the most remarkable men in the Bible. Jessie was the father of David, Nunn was the father of Joshua, Hilkiah was the father of Jeremiah, and Terran was the father of Abraham, and Amoz was the father of Isaiah. Surely these fathers would have loved to have accomplished the same great things their great sons later did.

Do you ever wonder what Zebedee thought when his two sons left his family's fishing business to follow Jesus? Did Zebedee say to himself, *what about me? What about our business? What about us?* The Bible does not tell us that Zebedee had a pity party about why God wasn't using him, nor did he try and run after his sons to persuade them to stay home. Nor did he run up to Jesus and beg Jesus to pick himself instead of his boys.

What about when Samuel anointed David with oil and said David would be the future king? Did David's father Jessie get jealous? Jessie had a Godly response and was grateful.

Out of these *men's loins*, greatness was produced and did not happen accidentally. While these boys sat at their father's table, these men of God shaped the character of our greatest Bible heroes. We may not be as familiar with their fathers' names, but God knows the fathers. God knows the sacrifices and the time and training these men put into their sons' lives. These men's *loins* produced these boys and in eternity each of these fathers will be happy they did not prevent their sons from coming to earth.

DON'T LET GO OF YOUR RUBY SLIPPERS!

In the 1939 movie classic, The *Wizard of Oz*, Dorothy was given precious ruby slippers, but she was ignorant of their value. Dorothy did not know they had the power to bring her home but instead was searching everywhere else for a way to get back home, yet the answer was on her feet! The wicked witch knew the power of those slippers and constantly tried to steal them away from her. Had Dorothy surrendered her precious slippers, she would have been at the mercy of the wicked witch.

Our fertility is akin to Dorothy's ruby slippers. God has given His people the precious ability to create, but most Christians do not realize the value of this power. It must be very great, because Satan wants to take our power away from us the same way the wicked witch tried to take Dorothy's power from her. The enemy already stole our salvation in the Garden of Eden, are we also going to give him our *ability to procreate*? It must be very powerful because the enemy will do *anything* to get it away from us.

With the vasectomy operation the enemy is trying to *steal the ruby slippers* right out from under each husband before he realizes the power he has been given. The enemy has invested much time and energy into trying to halt the spiritual army of God. He especially despises the children being born now. These represent the generations that are here to kick Satan's butt, and he knows it. These are the final mighty warriors. They have a job to do, and they will come here ready to *mess up his plans* and he knows it.

Satan surely does not want the earth filled with the offspring of God's people walking in true unity against him. He is trying extra hard in every way possible to convince Godly people to stop creating these children! Men, you have a choice to make.

A man's material wealth will fade before the next generation is grown, but children are proof their father came to earth. Recognize the value of your sperm and resist the lies coming from the enemy, the culture, other believers, and misinformed people. A casual little *snip-snip* today could prevent thousands of your future heirs from being born. And Satan will love you if you listen to your very good reason and submit to his plan instead of God's.

The greatest events of history are now unfolding, and strategic spiritual people must be conceived and brought to earth. Hebrews 12:1 tells us that we are surrounded by a great cloud of witnesses who are counting on us!

Therefore, since we are surrounded by such a great cloud of witnesses, let us throw off everything that hinders and the sin that so easily entangles and let us run with perseverance the race marked out for us. Fixing our eyes on Christ the author and finished of our faith (Hebrews 12:1-2).

These saints, who watch from above, are counting on you to wake up from your fog and throw off the sin that is trying to entangle you. Fix your eyes on Christ and don't miss the Destiny of your SEED!

Wife's Prayer

Heavenly Father, thank you that I can take part in creating our family heritage. Help me to be a willing participant in your plan. As the one who houses the fertilized ovum, please help me to stay open to my purpose of bringing mighty warriors through our family bloodline. I submit to your will and not my own. I repent for myself and for anyone in my family bloodline who took this for granted. I desire to receive all the children that you want to send me. Please, dear God, help me to be physically capable of bearing children. Please bless my husband and put your hand upon him. Please help him to use wisdom in all our decisions as we seek to be open to your plan.

Amen

Husband's Prayer

Heavenly Father, I need your grace. I had no idea that my seed had such value to you. I repent of taking my seed for granted. I also repent for other men in my family bloodline who did not value our family seed. Please forgive them and remove any curse that might be on our seed. I desire for more mighty warriors to come through our bloodline if this is what you desire. Please give me the heritage that you have for me so that in Heaven and on earth I will not have any regrets. Please give me wisdom in all things and help me hear your voice as I lead my wife in following you in this important area. Amen

Christopher's Commentary

Getting a vasectomy is a trendy idea full of glittering generalities. Usually, men don't stop and think that it can harm them or bring generational destruction. Instead, the world sugarcoats and puts a spin on *getting fixed*. Men who've had vasectomies can recite volumes about their experiences: what clinic they used, how many stitches it took, how many days they were not functioning correctly, how much it cost, and so on. It's etched into their minds, and to these men, a vasectomy was a winning choice. The vasectomy allowed them to continue their sexual pleasures without the fear of getting a woman pregnant. Plus, for the men whose wives are getting older, the vasectomy leaves a door open for possibilities in case they ever want to mess around.

Yes, for the men of our culture, a vasectomy is the answer. What more could we want? On the flip side, giving life is a gift. You can't buy it, but God has entrusted mere men with this treasure. A man's life-giving seed has the power to change the world. Men can't carry a baby, but adding our seed makes conception possible. This might be the most powerful of all the gifts God gives men. You can't put a price tag on it, but we can certainly take it for granted. We can easily waste our seed. Men do it every day. Most don't see it as a waste. We might even laugh at the thought. But if a man's seed is precious to God, shouldn't it also have some meaning to us?

I used to take my seed for granted. I didn't think it was anything special. I figured it was an ongoing commodity that would never run dry. I thought there would always be an abundance, which meant nothing to me. I was disappointed when I realized it could get me into trouble. I could get my wife pregnant, but I didn't want to. Sperm messes men up that way. It causes them to be accountable whether they like it or not.

I didn't realize the power I had, so I didn't think twice about getting a vasectomy. A vasectomy for me was freedom. I was all for it because my sperm caused me nothing but trouble and since the propaganda acts like a vasectomy is no big deal. I thought it was my answer. One $300 cut, a few stitches, a couple days of rest, and I could take care of my *problem*. I can't tell you how many times someone told me I should take care of my problem. It's crazy how casually we treat our sperm and how casually most believers treat vasectomies. Don't we realize that we could lose our legacy for less than the cost of a new set of golf clubs or a new I-PAD!

Christopher Scott

Investigate and Questions

- Read Exodus 1:15. Matthew 2:16. Every time God is about to do something great in the earth, Satan works vigorously to destroy the children. Have you ever wondered about this? What correlations do you see in our times today vs. other strategic times in history?
- Do you believe that part of your destiny involves creating a family, or are you to have a life without children? Why?
- Read Hebrews 7:9-10. How does this verse affect how you view a man's seed/sperm? Do you see your sperm how God sees it? Is it holy? Why or why not?
- The significance of an arrow is that it can go into another time and space. How do children advance God's spiritual cause in another time and place? Have you ever thought about how your children will handle the future? How can you help them be effective for God?
- Read Daniel 10:5, Ezekial 1:27, Isaiah 11:5. Our society treats our reproductive organs very casually; they call male sterilization a little *snip-snip*. How significant do you think this area is to God and how significant is this area of the body to you? What are your thoughts about reproductive organs being powerful weapons to advance God's plans and purposes in the earth. Does that scare you at all? How powerful do you think your loins really are?
- Read Galatians 6:9 and relate it to this statement: "Daily, Godly men who know the Word and study the scriptures submit to severing their ability to create new lives. They do not understand what they are doing to their bodies and future destinies." Do you think it is a sin to mutilate your reproductive organs?
- Genesis 35:11, Deuteronomy 7:13, Leviticus 26:9, Exodus 36:10. What do you suppose God favors? God says that children are his reward. What kind of reward? Are your children your reward, or do they seem to suck the life out of you?

- In this chapter we examine what the consequences might have been if certain men in God's story had gotten sterilized. Meditate a moment on this thought. How would the outcome of history have been different in the men back then had acted the same as the men today and refused to give life to their sons and daughters? Have are vasectomies and tubal ligations altering history today?

Impacting Others

Rachel, you won't believe this, but I read most of this chapter to my husband, who listened halfheartedly (or so I thought). He ho-hummed at a few parts, and I was getting quite discouraged and was wondering why he couldn't understand what you were saying. Yet when I read him the part about the Wizard of Oz and fertility being like the Ruby Slippers, he suddenly got it! I guess he could relate. He would hate to admit that he enjoys The Wizard of Oz with the children because it is his favorite childhood movie. He's not talking about a vasectomy anymore. Pray that we have a third! **Sue Beth, Mom to 3-year-old Tyler and 1-year-old Anthony, Lancaster, PA.**

Rachel, my wife and I got a copy of your book, and she enthusiastically read most of it to me. She is pregnant with our fourth child, and I must work nights right now, and my wife works from home part- time to make ends meet. Our families do not understand, especially my dad! I enjoyed the parts of your book where you shared how your dad also did not understand as well, maybe this is why I am emailing you. My father is a believer, same as yours, but my dad hails from the mindset that two children are plenty. I can tell that the size of my family displeases him, and often we get the "Son, God gave you a brain; why don't you use it?" comment. I've finally came up with a great response. I say, "We are using our brains! We have committed them to the will of God. The Bible tells us repeatedly that children are a gift from God. My BRAIN tells me that I should want the gifts God has for me! I am grateful for your message Rachel. I'm tired of the ridicule I get but not tired of the fight. Keep up the good work of telling others. Hey, can I talk to your husband? **Dan, Dad to three and one on the way, La Vista, Nebraska**

Rachel, I hope you don't think I am unusual to be writing. My wife and I read your book and liked it very much. I am the father of seven children and want to share what I have met with. I am a deacon at my church, and I counsel. Men often tell me that they are planning to get a vasectomy. They know I have seven children and have a conviction, but

they still talk to me. Most often, they say they prayed about it and have peace about it. I don't know why they bring up the subject with me because they know where I stand, but they still tell me for some reason. I always find their answers perplexing because less than a century ago, this question could not have been asked of God. I ask them what do they think men prayed to God before getting a vasectomy was possible? They usually look at me with skepticism. Some of their answers have been very interesting, and some almost comical, but in my simple conversations, I often find they leave the office thinking. I want to share what I have heard because it is thought-provoking. We know that Isaac asked God to open his wife's womb, and God answered. But in turn, what happens when men pray, Lord, please shut my wife's womb? Does this happen? Can God do this? I do not doubt that God might have answered many a prayer like this through the ages, even when God had other children for the couple. Conditions were quite hard, and babies often died, as did the mothers. We forget that birthing babies has not always been easy and is always harder on women than it is on men. My concern about vasectomies being OK is entirely different. With the vasectomy, we think we get to keep enjoying our sexuality, we do not need to make any of the sacrifices, we can continue with marital relations, and we won't have to do any suffering. When men tell me they have peace about their vasectomy, I think to myself, how could God be saying 'yes' to an operation that could have complications and bring a permanent end to sexual relations or live in constant pain? Some men do have complications and marriages do change afterwards. Is God's voice really speaking yes to this man? I question their motives every time a man tells me this.
Thomas, Dad to 7 children in Cary, North Carolina

Chapter 7

A BARREN WOMB IS NEVER SATISFIED!

Every day Godly men and women submit their bodies to the sterilization operation. They love the Lord and are not making a choice to get a vasectomy or tubal ligation because they do not like children or because they are willfully choosing to be disobedient. Many would say they choose to be sterilized because they have a valid reason. Without a solid Biblical foundation, God's people do not realize what they are doing by choosing to become barren.

When my children were small, and people found out I was the mother of eight children, fairly often, people would ask eagerly if they could hold one of my little ones. As they held my babies, they would start sharing their story and telling me how much they longed for another baby in their lives. Some would confess their spouse did not want more children or that they could not have another child for various reasons. Every story was different, but the sorrow was always the same; an unspoken sense of loss, a lingering feeling that something was missing from their lives. I could feel the pain in their words, and each time my heart ached for them. Every encounter, I felt a distinct sadness when meeting people who longed for children they could not have. It always left me feeling sad for them.

Most people in our society envision having children at some point in their lives; it's a dream that few people plan to miss. But sometimes life does not unfold as planned. Couples experience unexpected infertility that robs them of the wonderful experience of parenthood. Infertility brings a unique kind of pain because it's not just circumstances that can be blamed but it's our own bodies that are betraying us! Not being able to gain control over the situation, coupled with the mystery of "why" this is happening, causes the pain to dig in deep. Some people would rather face death than to live their lives without children and they grieve with a longing as profound as the women of ancient times, desperate to hold just one of God's blessings in their arms. For barren women, the dream of having a child is always with them, and the thought of a future without the joyful sounds little ones bring is unbearable. Genesis 30:1 captures the desperation of Rachel's painful statement to her husband Jacob: *"Give me children lest I die!"*

DID THE FEMINIST MOVEMENT SET WOMEN UP FOR REPRODUCTIVE FAILURE?

In the old days, before feminism took hold of women's hearts and society's norms, nearly every girl dreamed of growing up, finding a nice man, getting married and having children. It was the goal and expected path and nearly *every single girl* was on board. This is what women did, but then came feminism. For the first time women were told that their *"little girls' dream"* would not make them happy. Instead, the better option was to reject tradition and go outside of the home with hopes *to get something for "themselves"*. They were to discard the old idea and reach for greater things. It was a lie that all the stay-at-home mothers were unhappy, but the second wave of feminism set the trap, and then the media jumped on board and reinforced the idea and millions of women eventually fell victim.

In the 1960s, I am sure some ladies were desiring to do the same things that were traditionally reserved for men, but these women were far from the majority. Why would a *stay-at-home mother* trade the joy of raising her children at home herself for a life spent away from them? Why would a woman want to deal with the *daily grind* of the workplace, under a boss who does not respect women, while the job drains all her energy? She could be home! Why would a woman want to come home to her children, who she missed all day, to then be so exhausted that she counted the minutes until their bedtime, so she too could collapse into bed herself?

Women were sold a pack of lies! They were told the *workplace was glamorous* and *exciting*. A place where a woman could *meet new people* and *dress up* and the best part was, she could have her *own money!* Some parts of this new dream were true. Women could gain independence if they worked, but why was the goal independence? At the time, a lot of women were raising their children in happy American families and with husbands that came home every night and who loved them. The cost of living was very low, and most couples could get by on one salary. The divorce rate was also very low, but like Satan tricked Eve in the garden, women were *tricked* into thinking there was *something more* they were missing. *Then Wham!* The next wave of feminism hit hard! Women were pushed to try to *do it all* and *have it all*, while trying to find balance between their home life and work life. Eventually the women found they *could not be successful* in both places. There were too many demands. Something or someone was always falling through the cracks. Women fought desperately to keep up. They were expected to mix motherhood with career and millions of women found out this is a very difficult task to achieve, especially when their bodies refused to perform on command.

God outlined a perfect plan for women, but it is only successful when women align with their natural biological timeline. According to God's design, a woman's concentration should be on bringing her family to earth during her prime and very special fertile years when her body is healthiest, and her hormones are at their peak. It is far easier for the woman if she can fully focus on getting pregnant and having babies, rather than try to divide her energy between career ambitions and family.

Feminism completely dismissed God's timeline and robbed women of their most fertile season by promoting a plan that competed with God's design. The feminist movement encouraged women to focus on their careers early during the same years their bodies were most ready for motherhood. By ignoring God's timeline in favor of pursuing success, countless women put off having children, to later find the sadness of infertility. Unknowingly they believed a lie and wasted their most precious fertile years by prioritizing the wrong things.

Their outcome was very sad because women are special creatures. Inside our hearts, God has hidden something incredible. Women have a deep innate need to nurture which distinguishes them from their male counterparts. Women are wonderful because they know how to express love in a way that men miss! When a girl becomes a mother, it is one of the most profound expressions of her heart and the experience of nurturing her child is the purest and most powerful expression of her unique gift of love. I always encourage every woman who hopes to be a mother someday, to try to become one. Motherhood is unlike any other thing a female will ever accomplish for herself, motherhood rocks!

Mommy is the "star" of her child's life!

> Mom is who they long to see,
> Mom is who they come home from war to hug,
> Mom is the one whom they want to see on Christmas morning,
> Mom is the one that they want to share their thoughts with,
> Mom is the one who they worry about when she is old,
> Mom is the one who sustains each child throughout their life!

No one will EVER love a woman more than her children, and nothing is more amazing than the love a mother has for her children in return! Her offspring bring joy to the deepest places in a woman's soul and every day a woman's children light up her heart. I know for me, my children are all adults now, and yet any time I see one of them my heart leaps and my spirit lifts because I am in the presence of someone I love very deeply.

This is why I've always made it my mission to encourage each woman to embrace motherhood regardless of race, religion, background or career. I believe every woman shares a universal sisterhood with all the other women who ever lived, because WE are the people who *mother* the world. Mothers are the "it" people in the eyes of their families, the heart and the glue that holds the love in the family together. When a mother is absent or passes away, there is great heartache because every one's mother is irreplaceable.

Unfortunately, motherhood is the very thing the feminist movement tried to steal from women. As previous generations chose feminism's lie and tossed aside the experience of motherhood, this *social experiment* proved unsuccessful for countless females. This is why today's young women are yearning to reclaim what millions of women lost in second and third wave feminism. These young women want a career, but they also don't want to miss out on family. According to the 2013-2015 National Survey of Family Growth 86%[5] of women aged 15-34 yrs. old expect to have a family someday. Women want to get married and find a partner, but the only problem young women face is that infertility rates are soaring.

Infertility is more common than people realize.

The struggle of infertility causes everyday situations to become painful. Every place the infertile person goes, they see expectant mothers or parents and children. Simple outings to the grocery store or to the park, to the mall or ballgame, or simply when one watches TV, everything can remind an infertile person that they do not have what other people have! It is so sad.

Each new month when the next menstrual cycle comes the woman sees she did not conceive. Her cycle is a constant reminder of what she does not have, questioning why she is not like the others. *"What is wrong with me? Why am I denied this privilege? I just want to be happy!"*

For thousands of years, those who could bear children have been preferred and desired; those who could not were considered **cursed**. At varying times, the infertile have often been severely persecuted. The men were never blamed, but the women bore the pain of infertility. Women have been *blamed* and *put away*, some have been *burned alive*, and others were even *hung!* Even today, with advanced medicine and a deeper understanding of what can cause infertility, women still feel *disgraced* and *humiliated* when dealing with this age-old health condition.

Infertility breaks hearts, postpones plans and causes many a tear, as reasons "why" often go unanswered.

The condition of being unable to conceive children is called *barren* in the Bible. In a previous chapter, I pointed out that *barrenness* is the first disease mentioned in the Bible (Genesis 16:1). The Bible gives us hope with examples of women who had to bear this burden. For these, their *barrenness* meant the family bloodline had no power to remain. The Bible mentions several women who cried, prayed, fasted, gave special offerings, and made vows to conceive. In desperation, these women's only hope was to turn to God. When they plead their case to Him in prayer, the Bible says, *"God remembered"* and blessed them by filling their womb with beautiful babies. Our God is a faithful God!

1 Samuel provides the heart-wrenching story of a barren woman named Hannah. She longed for a child and cried out in agony of spirit as her infertility overwhelmed her. The story has a fantastic ending, as eventually, the Lord opened her womb and gave her a son named Samuel. She then gives him back to the Lord and then later God blesses her with five more children (1 Samuel 1:6).

He settles the childless woman in her home as a happy mother of children. (Psalm 113:9).

Sarah was *barren* and past childbearing years; then she gave birth to Isaac (Genesis 11:30).

Rebekah was *barren*; then she gave birth to Esau and Jacob (Genesis 25:21).

Rachel was *barren*; then she gave birth to Joseph and Benjamin (Genesis 29:31).

Manoah's wife was *barren*; then she gave birth to Samson (Judges 13:2).

Elizabeth was barren and past the age of childbearing and was disgraced. In her old age, God opened her womb, and she gave birth to John the Baptist. When Jesus was in Mary's womb, John the Baptist was the first to react, even while he was still inside his mother's womb (Luke 1:7, 25).

For most of human history, infertility has been considered strictly a female problem, yet today with modern medical diagnosis, doctors are finding that infertility is not specific to females. Malfunctions in the male's reproductive system now cause 30% of the infertility couples suffer. Sometimes it is hard to perceive the difference between infertility in Biblical days and infertility today. We think it was different, but for infertile people modern conveniences have not lessened the impact or severity one feels when they cannot have children.

BEING BARREN IS NEVER SOMETHING GOOD

David's wife, Michael was fertile but then she was cursed with *barrenness* as a punishment for making fun of David dancing before the Lord. The Lord never opened her womb again (2 Samuel 6:23).

The nation of Israel was barren. God also punished the Israelites with *nationwide infertility* more than one time for their disobedience. This punishment was devastating because people in Bible times knew what a loss this curse produced. It prevented their generations from coming through them.

> If you obey these commandments, none will *miscarry* or be *barren* in the land; I will give you a full lifespan (Exodus 23:26).

You will be cursed for disobedience; the *fruit* of your womb *will be cursed* (Deuteronomy 28:18).
I will never again *deprive you* of children (Ezekiel 36:12).
Has Israel no sons, hath she *no heirs*? (Jeremiah 49:1).
If you are disobedient, I will cause you to *eat your children* (Deuteronomy 28:53-57).
In one day, you will be *barren* and *widowed* for your sin (Isaiah 47:9).
No birth, no pregnancy, *no conception* (Hosea 9:11).
Give them *miscarrying wombs* and dry breasts (Hosea 9:14).
Even if they bear children, I will *slay* their cherished *offspring* (Hosea 9:16).

The Bible is clear: *being barren* is not something to desire. Yet even with the Bible spelling it out, American Christians have convinced themselves *being barren* is fine!! Once a couple has the children they desire, an operation to *make them barren forever* is completely acceptable.

Then there is another group who also desires to be barren in every sense of the word. These are fertile people who absolutely despise their gift of fertility. The last thing they ever want to do is become a parent and often resort to sterilization to make sure parenthood never happens! Truly they are deceived, but now those who call themselves, "childfree by choice" want to come into the church and be "accepted" as normal Christian couples. They say *Jesus was not a parent*, but Jesus was a single man. If the Scriptures are to be our guide, then Christians cannot accept the childfree by choice philosophy. To agree with this choice, is going against everything the Bible says about marriage and God's plan for men and women. If a person remains single, then not having children is the acceptable preference, but once married, God is seeking Godly offspring from their union.

There is NO BARRENNESS in God. God is Fertile. God is Reproduction! Only the devil is barren.

Everything God does promotes reproduction. All of creation reinforces reproduction. To side with barrenness means we side with the enemy.

Everything that Satan touches, destroys reproduction.

Devil=barren, God=Reproduction. Whose side are you on?

Choose you this day whom you will serve! (Joshua 24:15).

TWISTED PEOPLE WANT TO BE BARREN!

Throughout my mommy years, I have successfully encouraged couples to have another baby. Sometimes the husband desires another child and his wife does not, while at other times the wife wants more children and her husband does not. Those who listen to the tug on their heart from the Holy Spirit and do have another one always tell me at some point, *"How did you know we needed another? We love this new baby so much!"* Yet I can't take the credit. I am only God's mouthpiece. It is God who allows for the conception and brings the child they desire. More often than not, a new baby awakens our spirits like nothing ever could. New life brings a *special* blessing.

Unfortunately, not everyone wants this blessing nor is ready to receive it. I've discussed throughout this book how there has been enormous resistance in recent decades towards having more than the acceptable number of children. This propaganda has caused people and even God's people, to despise the idea of adding even one more child to their families.

Propaganda against birthing children has been prevalent in the media, education, books, and in churches. I've met with resistance all over the place for even suggesting that someone consider having another child. People act like they need to *convince me* that a baby is not what they need and get downright angry at the mere suggestion of such a thing. I've observed that once people make up their minds, a strong delusion overtakes them, and they shut the idea completely out of their hearts. Once this happens, it is almost impossible to say anything to break through that wall. In their mind, a child is the last thing they want.

"Why don't you have a baby?" "No! That is the last thing I want to do!"

Sometimes when people react negatively to me, I boldly say, *"Then don't have one!"* I am only here to present God's plan as an option; if people reject it, they reject it. I can think about how sad it is that they might miss what God intended for them, but I realize no one should force a person to change their mind. I often ask believers, *"Would you consider praying about it?"* Some people say, *"Sure, I will pray about it, but I am sure I do not want any more children, but I will pray."* While others flat-out said, *"No, I am sure another child is not what I need."* In their heart, it's a *done deal*, and they are convinced they have excellent reasons for feeling this way. It seems sad to me, but I realize sometimes factors in people's lives cause ridiculous amounts of stress, and the children are what must be pushed aside. Only the supernatural power of the Holy Spirit can change their situation. People's negative emotions toward birthing children can only come from one place.

CHOOSING TO BE BARREN...CONFESSIONS OF THE HEART

After we stopped using birth control, it seemed that everywhere we went, someone was commenting on why we were choosing to have a larger family and why they were not! It seems that we live in a very competitive society. The older couples who remain fertile desperately want to get operated on to become sterile, and the infertile younger couples desire to start their families but remain desperately infertile. It's all messed up. One group needs fertility, the other group tosses it to the wind ... and this latter group is the group I want to focus on. I want to share a few situations when my husband and I met someone who told us they felt sterilization was best. To me, these are sad stories about Christian couples who, *by their own choice*, chose what so many people never want to be: *sterile!*

My husband and I were volunteering in the church nursery, and the new church nursery coordinator walked in. She was a pleasant woman in her late thirties. I was in my late thirties as well, and I was holding my newborn while my husband was tending to the toddlers in the room. She commented, *"Oh, you have a new baby. That's so nice."* As we exchanged pleasantries, she told me her youngest child was ten years old, and she missed having a new baby. I said, *"Have you thought about having another?"* She snapped at me, and I was astonished. She said, *"Oh no! I had my tubes tied, and we are so busy, and I work part-time here at church and run another business. Besides, I must work to put our daughter in private school, and we couldn't afford any more children even if I still could get pregnant!"* Her attitude and the tone of her voice changed from sweet to somewhat defensive. I just listened. I had not said anything rude. She was the one who started defending her life and the reason she chose to be sterilized.

As she left the room, my heart went out to her because she admitted she longed for another child, but her decision to make herself barren kept that dream from ever becoming a reality. When those nurturing feelings arose and her heart was tugging, she painfully stuffed down her emotions, trying hard to forget her choice. She may have even resented herself for feeling that way.

Some people would say they believe God could supernaturally allow a woman in this situation to conceive another child. This is possible, and I believe that God can do miracles. Yet until people desire to seek this kind of miracle, the reality is that they will have to live with their choice, and even if they did hope for a miracle, the final decision is still in the Lord's hands. Because we all have our pride, people do not want to admit to themselves or to others that they made a mistake. They tell themselves they cannot have any more children, should not have any more children, and do not want any more children, because they have better things to do, so they move on. Yet occasionally, the truth that they really would have liked to have another child slaps them in the face, but they quickly remind themselves their choice to prevent another child was correct.

I know a family who chose a vasectomy because, in their minds, they had a very good reason. After the birth of their first child, their second child was born at 24 weeks instead of 40 weeks. Usually, an infant born this early either dies or suffers serious complications. Yet God miraculously intervened in their case, and their child became a miracle baby! However, between birth and the miracle, it was not easy. There were many intense moments, and life was upside down for quite a while. They had to go back and forth to the hospital, often crying many tears. They drove many miles to get there and then had to endure watching the baby in incubators and hooked to tubes. Grandparents had to be called in to help with their other child, and friends and relatives had to assist with babysitting and meals. It was a difficult year or so. In the end, everyone survived the ordeal, and today their child is completely normal and healthy, grew up and has children herself. God is faithful!

The doctor told them that they could have more children. It turned out that the prematurity was caused by food poisoning, and the chance of this problem repeating itself was practically nonexistent. Yet this gal's husband was worried about the future and wanted to make sure they had enough money to put both children through private school. The mother wanted to pursue hobbies and church activities. They felt good about their family size; another child might jeopardize things, so they opted for the vasectomy.

We also knew a couple who had their first child, and then the wife had six miscarriages, with several during her second trimester. She was very depressed and finally stopped trying to conceive altogether. People kept coming up to her and saying God told me to pray that you have another baby. Even though she was sorrowful, she would let them pray. After much prayer, she decided to try again, and this time she did not miscarry! It was a miracle! At the baby's birth, she got her tubes tied. She said she never wanted to go through that again.

In another family, the man married at twenty, had a son at twenty-two, and got a vasectomy. He divorced his wife, and years later, he met his second wife. She wanted to start a family. He had his vasectomy reversed, miraculously the operation worked, and he gave her two children. Weeks after the birth of their second child (his third), he got another vasectomy against her wishes. He insisted! When their child was three, she begged him to undo his second vasectomy because she wanted a third child, but he refused. When their children were five and seven, they started begging for a baby brother or sister. She also begged him to undo his vasectomy again, but he refused. Money was not an issue; they were multimillionaires. The wife grew more upset as time passed, and she and the children came to terms with the fact that a third child would never come. Eventually, a wedge grew deep in their relationship, boredom set in, and they separated, each having affairs while separated. Today they are divorced.

In each of these illustrations, the marriage was tested. The couples were exhausted, fearful, sad, and troubled with life and problems. Each made choices because they wanted to move on. Yet I wonder what would have happened in each situation had the couple made a different choice. There is a big difference between God's perspective and our own. When people rely on His strength and power, miracles occur. In three of the four illustrations, miracles had already occurred! In each illustration, different choices could have been made, and their lives could have turned out completely different. Yet we will never know this side of eternity why these things happened the way they did or what God might have had planned after these couples went through these events.

Just suppose that after the couple miscarried six times, the new baby somehow removed the pattern of miscarriage, and God's new plan was for them to have several more children. Yet she got sterilized. *They will never know.* The couple with the premature infant could have enjoyed more children if they had wanted them and possibly, with God's grace, could save money and do all their other activities. *Yet they will never know.* What about the woman who had to work to put her child through private school? If she had stayed open to more children, trusted God, and not gotten sterilized, her finances might have increased due to

God's scriptural promises of provision. The mother might have been able to work by choice instead of having to work because of finances. *She will never know* what could have been. Then there is the dad with three children, two vasectomies, and a sad wife. His refusal drove a wedge into their relationship that was eventually a factor that ended it! God was using his wife and children to get him to wake up. God might have given additional children; but *he will never know*. It won't be until each couple sees the Lord someday and He reviews their lives and shows them how He could have worked within their circumstances. Their lives might have received greater joy if they had only not jumped ahead of God, by taking circumstances into their own hands, but until eternity, *they will never know what could have been*.

There is always hope for a turnaround which is what happened in Danielle's story. At my homeschool co-op, I helped one of the new moms carry some items to her van with her four young boys in tow. Since it was the start of a new year, I had not had a chance to meet Danielle yet. We got to talking and I shared that I had eight children and how having them was the greatest thing I've ever done because our large family has been so much fun! This was when Danielle told me how much she wanted another baby! I said what I always say, *"Why don't you have another baby?"* She then shared that she had these four little ones in a row and her family was already making fun of her and put so much pressure on her that she got her tubes tied. She also shared that her husband was a few years older and had a fantastic income, so money was not the reason, her family simply thought four boys was too overwhelming, so to stop their harassment, she stopped having children. I told her I was sorry. Then I shared a little about our story and how God changed our hearts. I gave her a copy of this book and the rest is history! Within days she read Birthing God's Mighty Warriors cover to cover and called me and said, *"Meeting you was the greatest thing that has ever happened to me and reading your book was confirmation!"* She knew God had more in mind but was not sure God would now bring her more children due to her choice to be sterilized but she wanted to try for a reversal. Within weeks, she scheduled a doctor's appt. and several months later she had a tubal-reversal surgery, and a few months after the operation she was successfully pregnant! (Approximately nine months after meeting me!).

Danielle now has eight children, and they are the *joy of her and her husband's life!* She is the proud Momma of one girl and seven boys! These last four children were in God's plan, but due to her ignorance of God's plan she nearly missed bringing these precious children to earth. Danielle's story is a glorious reminder that children are what bring true joy but sometimes trying to explain to someone, who has made up their mind, that another child will increase their happiness, is very hard. People *want what they want*, and they convince themselves their choice will bring more happiness than another family member. Often it is not until their later years that they realize they could have had more children.

I am the oldest of three children. My parents had my sister and myself one and a half years apart. Then they were done, but nine years later they had a "surprise" child, and we got our baby brother! My sister and I were *over the moon in love* with our little brother and we always asked my parents for another sibling. A few years ago, I had a very insightful discussion with my father who lived to be 91 years old. With dad, it was interesting, we always had these out-of-the-blue conversations when thoughts popped into his head. One day he said, *"You know Rachel when you get older you start to think about how you could have done things differently. After your brother was born, your mother wanted more children, but I told her, "No!" I was worried about the future. I was getting older, and I didn't want to be raising children when I was in my late fifties, but if I could do things over again, I would have let your mother have a few more children. At the time, you girls were in private school, and I thought we wouldn't have enough money for our future expenses, but later we did have the money and you girls grew up and left. Then after your brother grew up, I spent a lot of lonely years without anyone around. I would come home from work and your mom was always working late, and I would have enjoyed a few more people in the house. I used to think you were crazy having all those babies, but you and Chris made the best choice. It's not always about money."* I was blown away by his confession and I said, *"Yeah Dad, and you also enjoy that I gave you so many grandchildren that you always win the man-with-the-most-grandchildren award every year on Father's Day at your church!"* Then, my dad chuckled.

THE BARREN WOMB CRIES OUT FOR SOMETHING TO FILL IT

If one does not invest their time and money into more family members then they will find other ways to spend their time and money. Generally, Americans will buy more things! According to the 2023 U.S. Consumer Spending index[1] Americans spend $136.8 billion on their pets![2] $72.6 billion for weight loss, $36.8 billion on entertainment,

$93.7 billion eating out, $487 billion on computers and electronics, $930 billion on domestic travel, $553.7 billion on sports, which includes sporting events, sport participation and learning new sports.

The American mantra: the busier, the better! Another thing people do is fill their lives with activities. If we stay busy enough, we will not have time to stop and reflect on the deeper issues in our marriages and sex lives. Since the onset of sexual freedom, people have tried many different avenues and adventures, yet they remain empty, dissatisfied, and unfulfilled.

I have heard couples say, *"Our child wants another sibling, but we tell the kids we simply can't afford it."* But by seeing what Americans waste their money on, the reality for most is that the parents don't want to make other choices with their time or their money.

People are looking for answers but since society has de-emphasized that one's family IS the answer, women look for the answer elsewhere and so do the men. Female's high rates of depression prove they are still looking for meaning in a world that has shifted away from family. We've already discussed that in the 1960s, women were continuously being told, *"You can't possibly be happy being a stay-at-home housewife, taking care of your children and volunteering for the PTA, playing tennis or having coffee with your girlfriends. You need involvement! Go out, get yourself a job, throw your children into state run daycare and go find yourself! Stop relying on your husband for support. Go make some money for yourself! You are capable. Be all you can be!"*

This was the message of the 1960s and 1970s so women tried hard to juggle it all but by the late 1990s and into the 2000s women were starting to get *sick of the daily grind*, but the next waves of the feminist movement pushed forward encouraging women to not leave the workforce but to make things work somehow.

After years of women looking for the answer in material things, in workplace success, and in having one's own income, women finally concluded the answer is not here! The true answer is in family. Finally, even some of the Feminist movement's influencers admitted, *"Women can have it all, just not all at the same time,*[3] *meaning maybe, just maybe the answer is NOT in the workforce or one's career. Maybe, just maybe a woman might want to take a break and have children but then return to the workforce as soon as possible."* The feminist's movement had to eat crow and face its own contradictions, but this realization came *too late* for countless marriages and families who fell into the trap feminism set for women.

A popular radio host in the 1980s and 1990s was a psychologist named Dr. Laura. On more than one occasion I heard her say something to the effect of, "*If you were out on a boat with your family and the boat capsized and you could only save your husband or your child, who would you save?*" She would always say, "*You would save your child because your child is a part of you. They are your own flesh and blood. Even if you had the most amazing husband ever, he is still not your flesh and blood.*" Her powerful perspective highlights the deep irreplaceable bond a mother feels for her children.

No amount of career success will ever replace the satisfaction women get from their children. Many generations ago, women knew this! Yet today women have not been taught to follow their heart, so they remain lost and looking for satisfaction elsewhere. Denying that children *just might be the answer* to offset the high rates of female depression. Women still deny their "inner mothering need "and continue to search for a different answer.

THE CHOICE TO BE BARREN IS ALL ABOUT FEAR

When couples are faced with whether to use birth control or get sterilized, they base their decision partly upon *fear factors*. They ask themselves, "*What would we do if we had too many children?*" They are worried that God might cause them to lose control of their lives. Before God does His thing with their fertility, they do their thing by taking control. Maybe this is human nature; we want to control life's circumstances. Yet couples who use birth control to avoid having hardships that might come with a larger number of children do not escape life's casualties. Every couple experiences events that will build their character.

I remember how I felt when I had my first child; I could barely handle him. I was young and still had things I wanted to do. I could easily have severed my childbearing ability in my early twenties because I wasn't sure I liked being a mom. I was not aware of my capabilities, nor did I know how much the future could change me. Only God knew this. As I matured, I found great joy in being a mother—more joy than I thought was there.

Maybe it's human nature to desire to *prevent surprises*. Having had four children in five and a half years myself, I understand what it feels like to feel completely overwhelmed. When you're in it, it's hard to realize these children will someday be older and more manageable. Even when children are older, or maybe because they are older, parents still have days when they wish they could quit being parents or fantasize about running away forever. These are natural feelings for parents but then acting upon those fears is when the devil dangles that *forbidden fruit* in front of us, begging us to take a bite by getting sterilized.

SATAN WANTS YOU BARREN!

I briefly touched on this point in Chapter three but as a review Isaiah 14 tells us that before creation, Satan and one-third of the angels were cast out of Heaven. Scripture tells us Satan is an angel, and as such he is not a human, so he does not have the power to create. Creation alone is reserved for humans because humans are God's offspring. Every new human reflects the creator. While Satan can possess human souls, he operates in a non-creative zone. He does not mate with other demons to produce more demons. He can only manipulate what already exists.

The power to duplicate and re-create ourselves is a gift the human alone possesses! Think of Satan's outrage at the thought of people and their seed outnumbering him! Our ability to create threatens his influence.

Satan is jealous of our fertility, so he is doing everything he can to stop human fertility!

This is why God's people must be very careful with what they do with their gift of fertility. This is not a casual thing. We have the potential to overcome him. Through our seed, we can bring goodness and defeat evil in the earth. Godly people and their children have done so throughout history.

Satan wants *every womb* to be shut down, especially the wombs of those who love Jesus. These couples are the deadliest because their offspring have the most potential to damage Satan's kingdom. When God grants a couple fertility, Satan works vigorously at getting them to say "No," to creating a new life!

Once we start our families, with society and family watching us, it is easy to become overwhelmed. With each new child comes greater responsibility, and it's easy for people to grow weary under the weight of these demands. Lack of support from others and the insistence and pressure to stop making more babies adds to our weariness. It's far easier to use birth control to prevent more children from coming, or to give up altogether and get sterilized. Yet when a fertile couple does do this, I KNOW it grieves the heart of God.

The Old Testament prophets understood what it meant to grieve with God over the sadness of His people's sin. *"Streams of tears flow from my eyes because my people are destroyed"* (Lamentations 3:48). Without support and Biblical understanding people get sterilized having no idea the gravity of the sin they have just committed. It is so sad!

THE CULTURE SAYS: "CHOOSE TO BE BARREN!"

More than once when a man would question our family size, he would tell my husband, *"I got rid of that problem and so can you!"*

People choose to get a vasectomy or tubal-ligation sterilization operation because they believe life *on the other side of fruitfulness* will be much better. People *believe* sterilization guarantees sexual pleasure without pregnancy. Most men figure, "What a great deal!" By getting sterilized, we remove our problem.

People hate the problem! They can't stand that God made it so that sex led to pregnancy!

People despise this; it ruins everything! *"Why couldn't God have created sex without connecting it to birthing babies? It would have been so much better!"* People do think this way, even Christians.

Since the first civilizations, people have been trying to figure out a way to enjoy all the sex they wanted without the commitment of pregnancy. Unfortunately, modern believers could not resist the temptation to do this very thing. They wanted to be like everyone else in our ungodly culture.

Believers thought since modern medicine created more options for controlling the number of children they could have these new options were for them. With neighbors, coworkers, and relatives embracing these new forms of birth control, abortion, and sterilization, and with *their ministers remaining silent on the issue*, it seemed only natural to indulge in these new options.

A BARREN WOMB IS NEVER SATISFIED!

Once medical science figured out a way to remove the threat of pregnancy, Christians jumped on the bandwagon as fast as they could, and their agreement meant, **"We're not doing it God's way anymore! His way stinks—our way is best! Sex for pleasure instead of sex for babies. We win, GOD loses! Yahoo, we defeated God's plan!"** They may not have said this outright, but this is what their actions meant.

The goal was to do away with God's way. Church leaders should have said, "No! we are still going to trust God with our fertility because He knows best." But instead, the opposite occurred.

Everyone craved sexual freedom including churchgoing couples who did not care that *the pill, the vasectomy and the tubal ligation sterilization were created by atheists and eugenicists.* They did not care that these operations had diabolical consequences or whether a person could never experience true sexual pleasure due to how these pills dulled a person's sexual response. Nor did they care that they could hemorrhage and bleed for months or even die from reproductive cancer. People did not care! Their desire for sex without the consequences of pregnancy overshadowed all the risks. People were even willing to die for this or even kill for it.

God's people should have been outraged, resisted, and abstained from the sexual practices of those who do not know the Lord. Yet my research shows, and I've also been a witness to the fact that most believers did not abstain but wholeheartedly wanted to fulfill their sexual fantasies like everyone else.

People loved the pill and sterilization because they both brought freedom to temporarily solve humankind's problem with sex. While using these birth control methods, humanity could achieve *sexual nirvana* in which sex would be completely for pleasure and nothing else; a feat humankind had tried to attain for centuries! They finally got what they wanted! Sex without the possibility of pregnancy, meant that sex would now be fabulous!

Hugh Hefner built his Playboy empire around the idea that a man could have a different sexual partner every night. With the consequence of the act now removed by the freedom of *the pill or the vasectomy*, men everywhere wanted to be Hugh Hefner. Yet the Bible says the wages of sin is death! The road to *sexual utopia* was paved with *venereal disease, affairs, one-night stands, addiction to pornography, perverted intercourse, anal sex, bestiality, sexual paraphernalia, orgies, pedophilia, divorce, and a broken life.* You name it. People tried it all because the pleasure of the act overruled the consequences.

When the pill removed the problem, people were supposed to be much happier, but were they? Did unlimited sex allow couples to finally reach *sexual utopia?* People had a lot more sex. Yet were their sex lives truly more fulfilling? These pills and operations do affect hormones, sexual response, sex drive and physical health, so is sex the greatest ever? When we hold the word of God up against the world's ideals, God's way wins every single time. Sin never turns out as good as people think. God would be a liar if it did, and we know He is not a liar.

If sex was so fulfilling after people started using the pill, then why did marriages rarely end before the pill came out and why did the divorce rate escalate to nearly 50% of marriages after the pill was introduced? It was God who created children to bring lasting happiness from a couple's lovemaking. When people shut the child valve off, they had to find something else to bring them a thrill. Once they were not birthing children, what else was left?

THE SIN OF PREDICTING THE FUTURE

"Mirror, Mirror on the wall, who is fairest of them all?" In the Disney classic *Snow White*, the evil queen turns to sorcery to find answers for her life. In 1 Samuel 28, King Saul visits the *Witch at Endor* to predict the outcome of an upcoming battle. In the story of *The Wizard of Oz*, the wizard looks into his crystal ball, attempting to predict Dorothy's future. In the 1990 movie *Ghost*, a fraudulent psychic, attempts to unmask the future. In the 2006 Harry Potter movie the Goblet of Fire, Harry tries to master the art of crystal gazing. Whether Harry Potter or the psychic in Ghost was serious about contacting the dark side or even jokingly tries this, the fact remains that a person who has the goal of finding out their future has placed their life in serious spiritual jeopardy.

God's word calls predicting the future witchcraft or divination. God warns people not to play with this realm, for it leads to the dark side, far away from His love.

> *The acts of the flesh are obvious: sexual immorality, impurity and debauchery; idolatry and witchcraft; hatred, discord, jealousy, fits of rage, selfish ambition, dissensions, factions and envy; drunkenness, orgies, and the like. I warn you, as I did before, that*

those who live like this will not inherit the kingdom of God (Galatians 5:19-21).

Throughout the Bible, God warns people **not to go to fortune tellers and not to seek knowledge of or speculate about the future.** God wants His people to be holy and set apart and to rely on Him alone to give them this information. Those who walk with the Lord know that God reveals things only on a need-to-know basis. It is not always pleasant, but He does this for our protection. If we knew too much, we would worry about it anyway, and God doesn't want us doing this. Instead, we are to trust that He's got things under control. This way, we do not walk in fear.

When couples begin to analyze their reasons for wanting a vasectomy or tubal ligation, they are in a sense looking into their own crystal ball. They look at how things are today and visualize nothing will ever change in the future. I have asked couples, and they say they are not worried. *"We are positive that neither of us wants another child in our future,"* or *"We cannot afford any more children, and we know that in the future, we will not have enough money to provide the things we want for them."* People think they've got their future all figured out. Or do they?

Things are changing at a rapid pace in our world right now. How can anyone know what they might want in their future? God's Word says that we are not promised tomorrow, yet couples who choose a vasectomy or tubal ligation today take their chance. They are blinded by the false assumption that life situations will stay as they are. God's Word warns us against this kind of thinking when it says,

Do not boast about tomorrow for you do not know what a day may bring (Proverbs 27:1).

Now listen, you who say, "Today or tomorrow we will go to this or that city, spend a year there, carry on business and make money." Why, you do not even know what will happen tomorrow. What is your life? You are a mist that appears for a little while and then vanishes. Instead, you ought to say, "If it is the Lord's will, we will live and do this or that." As it is, you boast in your arrogant schemes. All such boasting is evil (James 4:13-16).

When we say we are positive we will not want another child, we make a massive assumption about our future life circumstances

God's people must be very careful here. Human reasoning takes us into the realms of *witchcraft, divination, idolatry, and fortune telling*. The reasons we use to justify our sterilization mimics how the psychic gets their information. Both must *speculate* upon a future that God says *is His!* Are you catching this? We are playing with spiritual fire! God's people were *warned* about practicing these kinds of evil in the book of Leviticus.

> *...Do not practice divination or seek omens (Leviticus 19:26b).*

> *Do not turn to mediums or seek out spiritists, for you will be defiled by them. I am the Lord your God (Leviticus 19:31).*

> *Let no one be found among you who sacrifices their son or daughter in the fire, who practices divination or sorcery, interprets omens, engages in witchcraft, or casts spells, or who is a medium or spiritist or who consults the dead. Anyone who does these things is detestable to the LORD; because of these same detestable practices the LORD your God will drive out those nations before you. You must be blameless before the LORD your God (Deuteronomy 18:10-13).*

When we speculate about the things the future will bring, we are divining the future, and God says this is witchcraft! Stay away from this realm!

In all actuality, these moments are yet to be lived.

How can a couple be *so positive* about something they have not yet experienced and have no control over? *"We feel certain that we will never change our minds."* How do you know?

I believe that people often act this out with sincerity of heart, but even if their intentions seem innocent, Satan still has a well-laid trap set. It appears that agreeing to be sterilized is one of his most clever deceits in history.

Our speculation causes us to act as if the future is in our hands and that God does not have a part to play. A couple may talk about their decision to near exhaustion, thinking their options out, but in the end, most people *wager their bets* that their future will remain as it is today.

God warns us not to do this! *"The future is mine,"* says the Lord!

In the Bible there was a man named Job. He was one of the wealthiest, most blessed men who ever lived, but he did not own his future. Job was a noble man of high character who had everything, including ten children. In an instant, a tornado killed them all. In a moment, his ten children were gone, and no amount of money could bring them back. The morning it happened Job had no idea he was about to lose his entire family. Considering the brevity of life, anything is possible in the future.

What if all your children were killed in a car accident?
What if all your children died in a healthcare crisis or epidemic?
What if a terrorist killed your children?
What if all your children were taken from you in a war and killed?
What if your boat sank and all your children drowned?
What if someone murdered your children?
What if your spouse died and you wanted another child?
What if your children ask you for another brother or sister?
What if you do change your mind and you want another child?

We never seem to think through uncertain scenarios, but life **can** change. Terrible things can happen. Good things can happen too, but God alone controls our moments not yet lived.

Predicting the future is a sin and using this method to justify the decision to get sterilized is a flawed paradigm. It is a trap set by the enemy for everyone seeking to rationalize their reasons to commit this great sin against their bodies, against their fertility and against their future generations. I plead with you, don't do it!

I know you want a future without the hassles of pregnancy, birth, and little children, but our security is supposed to be in God and not in an operation! The enemy gets us to believe that we have some guarantee, but God's word says, *you do not know what a day might bring forth!* (James 4:13-16).

Sterilization is unlike buying a house or changing careers. This operation physically alters God's original creation in a way that does not bring a long-lasting blessing.

Getting sterilized is a very powerful decision. *It tells God you no longer want to bring little humans to the planet!* If Jesus were here and he knew you were getting sterilized He would say the same words He said at the cross, *"Father forgive them for they know not what they do!"*

Sterilization IS SEVERING the most precious gift God has given you.

Sterilization also has the power to overcome your heart and emotions, causing varying degrees of regret. It also has the power to gnaw at your conscience forever! It can be a tormenting decision, much the same as the emotional letdown one feels after abortion. It is one you will never forget. I plead with you again, don't do it!

I know I can talk until I am blue in the face and still some people will come back with the silliest reasons to justify their decision. By far, the craziest one I've heard repeated is, **"We plan to adopt."**

I am all for adopting children! I believe adoptive parents are some of the greatest people on earth, however a statement about *adopting a child vs. having a physical one* is a thought they might entertain, but a *sterilization operation* is rarely if ever about birthing a child versus adopting one. The truth of the choice is that most parents want convenience, and they do not want additional children in their future, or they would not be doing something permanent to avoid them! Only those deeply serious about wanting another child are willing to mess with the hassle, the joy, the expense and the disappointments of adoption. It is a long, tedious, bothersome, and expensive process. If adoption was truly what a couple felt led to do, most would already be actively pursuing it! The process takes years.

If people do try adoption after sterilization, it is quite rare. The majority might talk a lot about adopting when they are contemplating their sterilization decision, but once *they are clipped*, you never hear much about that again. Instead, I've watched men *buy their wives a dog*, hoping the new pet will distract her. Not that a pet is not a comfort to some, but a pet will never replace a child. Plus, a pet could be more trouble than a child. Pets never grow up, can be very expensive and quite often cause inconveniences when people travel.

CHOOSING TO BE BARREN IS THE OPPOSITE OF HOW YOU WERE MADE

Vasectomies and tubal ligations seek to do one thing: to destroy fertility

In Chapter 3, I told you the history of the sterilization operation. It was not created by Bible-believing medical professionals. It was created by *atheist eugenicists*. These operations cause the body to rebel against the natural flow of the human reproductive system. The doctor must break a perfectly healthy and fully functioning body part, causing that system to operate against its design. Surgeons perform countless surgeries to fix broken bodies, but this operation was designed to do the opposite. To be effective, the body must stop doing what it was created to do.

A BARREN WOMB IS NEVER SATISFIED!

The human body was created to produce offspring. Sterilization is in direct rebellion of the way we are created. The Bible is clear: *rebellion is as the sin of witchcraft*; therefore, God's word is saying, *rebellion is witchcraft* (1 Samuel 15:23).

Is it rebellion to oppose the design of our body? If so, then why have we never heard this before? It is because the truth has been hidden from you!

When you say, *"Dear God, please make our bodies healthy except when we are through with our fertility then we would like that area broken."* The Bible calls this doublemindedness, and the Bible says that double-minded people are unstable in all their ways (James 1:8). Yet, double-minded people can't help it. We can't decide because we *are caught between two opinions*. We've got plans for our lives, and additional children get in the way.

What should we do? Look to God's word for the answer. God always has a way of escape (1 Corinthians 10:13). God's word says that God has the power to close the womb. Ask Him. We beg Him to open the womb when we are ready. If we feel overwhelmed by our current situation, why not ask the Lord to close the womb? We can trust Him, can't we? He has done this for thousands of couples through time, so why not do it for you? Look to Him.

Those around us have no idea God can do this for us. Instead, the world is pulling and tugging on us, trying to entice us with their ungodly answer. The enemy is trying to twist our minds into thinking, *"If I get a sterilization operation, it will give me peace and assurance that the plans God has for me will not be messed up by any children I don't have the time, money, or patience for."* It is not wrong to have other plans. It is not wrong to believe that your family is complete. Yet God's way is to ask Him to do this for you.

For more than 5,000 years, God's people did not have the sterilization option, and believers had to trust the Lord with their sexual organs. It's only in modern times that we somehow pray and feel that we have the right to choose an *unholy operation* created by atheists. If you are truly a believer, then you believe God's word and you trust God. If God's work is complete in your family, ask Him and He will close the womb.

I do not wish to pass judgment on anyone who has made the unfortunate decision of a vasectomy or tubal ligation. I know this operation bites back and brings untold sorrows. It concerns me greatly that Christians rarely, if ever, hear teaching on this subject and have no idea God's word stands against it. I researched through journals and sermon notes to find books on the subject, and I could only uncover a handful of books including mine in the entire Protestant arena and mine speaks out the loudest against this heinous operation.

In the Catholic arena, Catholics are much more fortunate as teachings about the family and the sin of using birth control and getting sterilized is in the catechism and is a subject the Catholic church does teach. However, in liberal Catholic churches (which might in some places be the majority), I've been told the priests may rarely, if ever talk about the subject. After serving the young moms at my local Catholic church for nine years now, I am finding that it is not unusual to meet Catholic youth and young married couples who *know* about the church's teachings but who have never studied what the church teaches on this subject in depth. Overall, a very small percentage of Catholics understand why the church stands against artificial contraceptives. Catholics do have more advantages than Protestant church goers when it comes to this subject. Catholics have Pope Paul VI 1968 Human Vitae encyclical rejecting artificial birth control. They also have Pope John Paul's II *Theology of the Body* encyclicals on human sexuality from the 1980s. These amazing teachings reinforce the Scriptures blessings of motherhood, fatherhood, parenthood and the rejection of artificial contraceptives. Furthermore, Catholics also have Pope Francis regularly making statements about the selfishness of not bearing children. Even still if you asked the average Catholic WHY the church teaches against these things most probably could not tell you. If you asked the average Protestant WHY choosing to use birth control or choosing to be barren is a sin, they would be completely clueless. They might say choosing to not be using birth control is a Catholic thing but would have no idea why they should not be using it themselves or why they should not engage in sterilization.

Silence from the pulpits and lack of teaching is why many dear brothers and sisters in the Lord, both Catholic and Protestant have thought nothing of allowing the medical community to make them infertile. When teaching is absent, people will not know the power of seeking the Lord and trusting Him to close the womb. Unfortunately, those who have taken their fertility into their own hands fall under the *sorrows of the barren womb*, which God's word says, *is never satisfied*, because nothing anyone can do, will fill the void it creates.

What I find to be crazy is when I get someone to simply sit down and talk with me, so I can share what the Scripture says or if I can get them to read this book, every single time *people's eyes are opened*, and their hearts become convicted, and God does miracles.

FOR THE FATHERS...CHOOSING TO BE BARREN WILL AFFECT HER

My husband and I had a very interesting discussion one night about the difference between how men view infertility and how women view infertility and barrenness. We concluded that when a woman is infertile, it feels the same as when a man is impotent. Both problems make the individuals feel somewhat incomplete in their gender roles. A man's ability to relate sexually makes him feel fulfilled. When a woman bears a child, she feels as if she has fulfilled one of her life's purposes. If either one cannot perform their roles, society makes them feel inadequate. When individuals suffer this way, usually their spouses will be very understanding, but all the love and support in the world does not seem to take away the emptiness that people feel when they cannot fulfill their gender role.

So, husbands, please understand that when a woman is infertile, she is suffering because she no longer feels complete as a woman in the same way that a man would suffer if he could not perform sexually. It really hurts! Please be sensitive to the fact that barrenness steals from a woman something that is very special from her role and that this pain can be transferred to a relationship in such a way that it can also deeply affect a man as well.

The vasectomy advertises that a man can have "*All the pleasures of sex without the fear of getting the woman pregnant.*" What man is not going to want this? The number one problem men face with sex: they want to enjoy it, but a child means commitment. One moment of pleasure turns into twenty years of responsibility. The vasectomy takes this problem away forever. Most men figure, why not go for it?

A vasectomy to most men is a no-brainer! —especially after a man has given life to several children and is comfortable with his family size. He figures he's a good dad to the children he already has, so why not accept his *reproductive finale?* With an inexpensive outpatient operation being advertised on gigantic billboards and ads on the internet, it's easy to be convinced that it's time to get clipped and move on. Yet when a man does, he disconnects himself from the power God gave him!

The vasectomy is a very interesting operation in that it shows the struggles of male and female domination. In some marriages, the men want it. They see it to gain pleasure, lose responsibility, and as an open door if he ever wants to mess around, although few men would tell their wife this. They're excited about the possibilities that might arise once they can no longer get a gal pregnant. In other marriages, the women **make** their husbands get it. *"I had the pain of having the babies; now you're going to be the one who gets fixed!"* The men submit and often reluctantly to what she wants. Her dominance and his submission are a statement of her ultimate control *(but her dominance and control are for another book)*. The last group are the *Bravehearts* of the world. They are not letting anyone mess with their equipment. They tell her, *"If you do not want to get pregnant, you will have to figure something out for yourself because no one is touching my MANHOOD!"* You can hear that testosterone roar!

No matter what the motivation for the vasectomy, when the two lovers decide to sever their reproductive ties, it can have deep emotional impacts on each of them. This can affect the couple on multiple levels. After a sterilization operation, life may seem relatively normal at first but over time, the finality of the choice can bring unexpected pain. A husband may feel disconnected from the idea of barrenness because he doesn't have a womb, he may think the emotional impact does not apply to his marriage. Yet in marriage, *her womb* becomes *his womb*, and he may feel the loss because her womb is empty. If she did not want him to have a vasectomy, she might mourn for the babies that will never be, and this could affect how she relates to him. It might create emotional distance between them. Meanwhile the spouse who felt pressure and was made to submit to a vasectomy he did not want, might cope with his sense of loss by withdrawing himself emotionally or even physically from her, immersing himself into new hobbies or projects in an effort to reassure himself that he is still a whole man.

Marriages do change focus after sterilizations. Lovers move on to other things. Some men think *if he can't get her pregnant*, this will make her want him more and want to get together with him sexually more often. Yet the sterilization frequently causes emotional pain, therefore, the *together* part is never quite the same. If she moves on, he will feel her rejection, even if it is subtle, it will be there. He will not understand why she seems so busy, distant, depressed, or disinterested. Their ties have been severed, and the distance can ruin their relationship. This pain can grow into a root for divorce. We don't have any statistics that measure the number of marriages failing after one of the lovers is sterilized, but I'll bet the number is quite high.

Talking about lovers moving on, I've seen this scenario repeated too many times. A couple seems happy with their two children, but the woman decides to get a tubal sterilization declaring, *"We are done!"* Life goes on, the children grow; he works, she works, and one day he realizes he's bored with their routine. His wife has gained a little weight, and their lovemaking is no longer as exciting as it once was, or maybe not even happening anymore. He realizes he's unhappy, bored, discontent and dissatisfied, and longing for something more. Meanwhile she has moved on emotionally, her fertility is barren, but she enjoys nurturing her children who are now older and more independent. She has her girlfriends, her activities, and her own sense of fulfillment. She may be a loving wife, and a dedicated mother and even at times have given him good sex, but still, something is missing. One day a younger, fertile woman enters his life, and she notices him. This excites him in ways he hasn't felt in years. The new connection is thrilling and eventually, he divorces his barren wife for the younger woman, who isn't much older than his daughter! They marry, and because she is fertile, he starts a new family with her. His first wife and family are devastated, but when you see him on the street, he looks happier than he has looked in years. His new wife and family make him feel young again, and he gets a second chance. This man is revived.

I'm not saying I agree with this man's scenario, I am merely making a point. God gave men a fierce innate desire to achieve greatness, motivated by a deep urge to imprint themselves on the world. This hunger for prominence fuels men to leave their mark. This is why they build towering buildings, conquer in business, wage wars, and excel in sports. This is the same force which drives male animals to mark their territory and be willing to fight to the death. This is why getting "fixed" is detrimental for the man. A vasectomy is not just a *little snip-snip*, but it is the severing of a man's gift, of his sacred instinct, of a man's claim to his space. Ultimately whatever drives this man's desire for greatness will find its purest expression in what he does with his sexuality.

FOR THE MOTHERS...A BARREN LIFE HAS CONSEQUENCES

Can you imagine never again holding an angelic infant or watching them sleep and wonder what they must be thinking or witness the moment when they first smile? Far too many women are longing for this blessing just one more time.

A woman has the God-given gift to cuddle, love, and nurture another human being. Women find great pleasure being the caretakers of society. Nurturing is part of a woman's nature which can be seen when little girls play. They hug their dolls and pretend to be the mommy. They enjoy hugging and giving kisses and collecting pretty things to give away. They say *I love you* and express love and nurture right from the start.

God plans that one day every woman's fertility will end, and we call this transition menopause, but when a woman's arms are empty, and another mother's arms are full and this woman's fertility was terminated prematurely, the potential for a woman to suffer regrets runs very high. When a man convinces his wife that because she is exhausted from childbirth, she should have her tubes tied or he should get a vasectomy, she may agree in theory with her husband's reasoning, but she can never turn off the emotional side of her nurturing heart that desires to give love. Women cannot deny what their hearts are telling them. Nurturing is a God-given desire. When a woman realizes what she has done through sterilization or what her husband has convinced her to do, there is a deep grief in her soul. Many women suffer rage and will resent their husband because *he did not defend her right to stay fertile*. Instead, he took from her, and she no longer feels *equal* to the other females around her. The decision to quit being fertile may have seemed correct at first, but later this decision turns to sorrow. *The barren womb is never satisfied (Proverbs 30:16).*

It is common knowledge in the obstetrical/gynecology profession today that the state of women's health in our world is at a critical point. Women are falling apart emotionally and physically. They are depressed, cancerous, infertile and obese. The medical profession cannot seem to stay ahead of hormonal problems. More women are prescribed antidepressants than ever, and the infertility rate is going up faster than the doctors can offer solutions to the problem. If a woman puts off motherhood to pursue a career, she more than likely will not be fertile enough to have children unless she turns towards fertility treatments. Conceiving a child without the use of a fertility treatment after getting off hormonal birth control is harder than ever, taking upwards of a year before fertility returns for 80% of women 35-39 yrs. old, and for 20% these must try to conceive by using fertility treatments and if the woman is 40 years of older fertility declines sharply up to 50% will not conceive naturally. If there are other health factors going on a woman's fruitful years could be over before she gets started. There is a common trend towards sterilization once childbearing is completed as 21.9%, or 1 out of 5 women 30-39 yrs. old and 39% or 2 out of every 5 women 40-45 yrs. old have been sterilized![4] treatments.

How does this affect women? Often women need to be on antidepressants when they cannot conceive or after they have had a tubal ligation. They cannot deny what their hearts are telling them. They feel as if their childbearing years are not complete, and they become depressed. When women feel they no longer have any use they become very unhappy. To no longer be able to have a baby, causes women to no longer feel equal to the other women around them. Feelings of inferiority surface, and eventually, their emotions can get the best of them. A woman may look at her life, as compared to others, and feel inadequate, inferior, or jealous. As a result, some women suffer severe depression with regretful thoughts that haunt them for years. In theory, she may have agreed with the operation, but it is difficult to live with.

A man may think he is getting off easy by not having another child with his wife, but if she does not agree, he will pay in a thousand other ways. When women feel they no longer have any use, they become very unhappy. This is why I named this chapter *"A barren womb is never satisfied"* because choosing to be barren fills a woman with sorrow and most women do not know what to do with these feelings. Women look to fill the *void of her womb* with something. When a woman feels she cannot control the end of her fertility and feels she lost control of her body, this feeling can transpire into other life choices. Even if she enjoys her career, her loss of self may cause her to lack appreciation for her achievements. She is *feeling blue* all the time so she may start whining and complaining to her husband and telling him that she needs a bigger house, a nicer car, new furniture and clothes or she may want to travel to "get away." Even when the couple does not need to buy anything she may still want the temporary satisfaction she gets from shopping. From designer handbags and shoes to shopping online, the "temporary fix" masks the pain she feels in her heart. She is desperately trying to find purpose again.

She is aware things will never be the same as they were before and will always be looking for something to make her pain go away.

Our world needs an answer from God, and I believe that coming back to Him in this area is the answer!

Some people reading this may find it hard to believe that so many women out there are unfulfilled, but it is evident by the actions of countless ladies. Their words reveal what their hearts are feeling. They are mourning their loss because they were cut off by either a husband, by unexpected infertility or by life choices. Countless women never seem to be at peace and are constantly searching for self-improvement.

Have you ever been to a baby shower and listened to the comments of the women? The younger women comment about *how lucky* the pregnant recipient is and how *much they wish* they could have another child, and the mature mothers say they are hoping for grandchildren soon and become teary eyed when the gifts are open as if each gift reminds them of their *baby years*. If an infant is there, the women all want to hold the baby and express their need for a *baby fix*. This may be one reason why most women love baby showers. They are reminders of *the pleasures* of having a baby and reveal the *natural desire* that women desire to show love and nurture.

Women are very special creatures when their nurturing heart is full, but women can also become one gigantic pain-in-the-backside when they feel cheated or robbed of their "nurture-years." Scripture warns men, "It is better to live on the corner of your roof, than it is to live inside your house with a quarreling wife (Proverbs 21:9).

God does have a road to happiness in this area, and if we look to God to find answers, we realize that deep inside the heart of every woman is a need that children are intended to fill. Each woman has a personal desire to nurture, and it varies in degree for each woman. I believe God wants every woman filled to overflowing! Even the woman who is infertile today. God *heals infertile women* and makes the woman *a happy mother of children* (Psalms 113:9). *True contentment* only comes when a woman allows the Lord to fill her nurturing heart!

Woman of God, millions of women regret their decisions or their husband's decisions to get sterilized; do not let yourselves fall into this trap! You have a right to motherhood! Please don't let any person or the enemy steal that gift from you!

A BARREN LIFE HAS CONSEQUENCES...WHAT ABOUT THE MARRIAGE?

The Bible calls marriage holy. It is the state of holy matrimony, meaning the marriage is a sacred covenant between the couple and the Lord. Marriage is also a reflection of the trinity meaning the husband, his wife and God are unified in this sacred state. In a Christian marriage the couple is to recognize that God is to be at the *center* of their relationship and when they recognize God's ongoing presence, they will have a more successful marriage especially when they seek His assistance. When two people say their vows, they each promise God that this holy covenant will be between one man and one woman for life. In marriage, we are to give our lives to each other, and this includes God's gift of sex. Yes, God made the sex act quite pleasurable, but the higher purpose of sex is for the couple to come together to create a child. According to Malachi 2:15, God's goal for marriage for His people is that He is seeking *Godly offspring* from this union.

Therefore, sex is a *holy* act. The *only kind of sex* that makes creating a *new life* possible is sex the way God created it without *protecting oneself* from their lover. Once the couple has two or three children and is still fertile but chooses to stop creating more children, *how does their lovemaking remain holy* for the rest of their fertile years especially when God's part has been removed from the act? Remember pure and holy lovemaking is a picture of the trinity. I believe if Jesus were counseling a Christian couple today who does not want more children, He might pose the question, *"Why have you kicked ME out of your sex life?"* and or, *"Why do you think your sexual intercourse "remains holy" when you have turned the act away from my original plan for your marriage?"* Woah!

Once a couple moves away from God's most important purpose for their lovemaking, which is to create new life together, their only options are to either ask God to shut the woman's womb, completely abstain during her most fertile times or add some form of barrier to their sex act to block God's gift of creation.

Let's look to scripture to see if God gives us answers. Adam and Eve were the first couple to ever be created. Every day God came and walked with them in the beautiful Garden of Eden. The Bible tells us in *Genesis 2:25, "The man and his wife were both naked, but felt no shame."* The day they ate of the forbidden tree, the Bible tells us *Genesis 3:7, "Immediately their eyes were opened, and they knew they were naked, and they sewed fig leaves together to cover themselves."* They were once naked and unafraid but now they were naked and afraid. They were now embarrassed to meet God *unprotected*.

The beauty and holiness of the *unprotected sex act* is that it is so incredibly powerful! There is no other experience that will make a person feel so incredibly loved and unified with another human being. When one lover sees the other and accepts their body and experiences intimacy with them, and then expresses their complete love for who their partner is, in these moments each one feels completely and wholeheartedly loved. The couple is naked and unashamed before their holy God.

Unprotected sex is as *naked* as sex can be. In the unprotected act, the couple is alone with God and there are no barriers between the husband and his wife or between the couple and God.

But in the *protected act*, it is impossible for sex to have the same meaning. Let's look at Adam and Eve again. Before sin entered, Adam and Eve were happily naked in God's presence, but after they introduced sin into their lives, they placed fig leaves over their *genitalia* because they did not want to be in the presence of a holy God unprotected. This was what fear told them to do. They felt vulnerable and were afraid, they ran away because they no longer trusted God. They did not want to be around Him anymore as naked people. Fear entered and trust was gone.

Isn't it interesting that when a couple uses birth control, they cover their *genitalia*, in the attempt to block the purpose of their genitalia? Just like Adam and Eve, they do not trust God. They want to cover themselves because they are threatened by His holiness. When the couple places a *barrier of protection* between the husband and the wife and between the couple and God, their sexual intercourse would no longer be the holy act that God intended their sex to be. Their *protected act* would side-step holiness.

The couple would now suffer the *emotional wounds* that result from placing a wall between each other, and between themselves and God. These emotional wounds might start out small but gradually deepen. If the couple never addresses these wounds, their busy lives might cause them to drift apart from each other and even drift from God! God's plan for them is fruitful and God can't help but want this for their marriage. He is the God of Reproduction, and nothing is barren in the presence of God. But every time they make love, they are in their *protection mode*. Their *protected sex act* communicates a lack of vulnerability. They don't trust God. They don't trust their lovemaking and they don't trust each other. They push away the very thing God wants to bring; closeness and unity, but their protection keeps them from ever getting there. This is something to ponder and pray about.

The *fruit* of any wounds caused by the attempt to protect themselves could lead to relationships that die or marriages that end in divorce. The sad thing is, this outcome is far from what God intended for their marriage. God designed marriage to be a wonderful partnership, a beautiful union between a man and woman who become *one flesh*.

Have you ever read *any* marriage articles or books that talk about the *emotional consequences* of using birth control or getting sterilized? My husband and I never did. Every marriage course we ever took, and every marriage book we ever read, told us to protect ourselves from each other and acted as if *problems* caused by using birth control or sterilization did not exist! We never read *anything* that said that birth control would get in the way of our emotional relationship. Isn't it interesting how this subject of physical and emotional separation, which is exactly an afront to how God created sex, has been *completely ignored* and *left out* of ALL marriage material? You can say you read it here first!

The movement for *zero population growth* in our world filters so much information concerning the consequences of getting sterilized. The *powers that be* do not want us thinking. This may be why we do not have knowledge about these very real marital problems. When a couple chooses to use birth control then later chooses to become barren through a sterilization operation the transition can cause huge amounts of emotional pain! Feelings of rejection will be everywhere. The *freedom* that so many couples seek turns out to not be as wonderful as they thought, because sterilization brings new problems that no one ever talks about.

WHEN ALL MY WALLS ARE DOWN, I AM NAKED, YET UNAFRAID

Problems do arise from birth control and sterilization. Both create walls of rejection. The damage done to relationships IS real and can be severe!

God did not create birth control, man did. He did not bring Eve to Adam and then toss Adam a *box of condoms!* Sex created by God is hot, steamy, and passionate! It is thrilling and beautiful. God's sex is naked, unashamed, and without fear. God dedicated an entire book of His word to show us His idea of how lovers should approach sex. God's version of sex is beautiful and as full of love as it can be, simply read the Song of Solomon.

> Let him kiss me with the kisses of his mouth. ... Oh, how beautiful you are my darling ... Your breasts are like two fawns. ... His left arm is under my head and his right arm embraces me. ... My beloved is mine and I am his. ... Let my beloved come into his garden and taste its choice fruits ... open to me, my sister, my darling ... my breasts are like towers ... My vineyard is mine to give (Song of Solomon 1:2, 2:16, 1:15, 4:5, 2:6, 4:16, 5:2, 8:10, 8:12).

Listen to the lover's passion, the panting, the excitement.

Their love for each other is intoxicating.

During the act the Bible describes God's word does not break for a commercial announcement:

"Her lover pause, momentarily, while he tenderly and gingerly places a condom over his penis so he can protect himself from her fruits OR his lover momentarily leaves his side while she runs to the next room to insert her diaphragm OR she was wonderfully ecstatic and had no fear of reprisal from her lover's fruits, because the pill was her birth control of choice and she trusted that it would keep her lover's sperm from impregnating her."

I guess the Bible forgot to add these modern-day details! Instead, the Song of Solomon gives us a graphic illustration of sex God's way: without fear and without protection!

The lovers are young and hopeful, fully embracing the love the other could give! They do not talk of *needing protection*. They speak as lovesick lovers.

Place me like a seal over your heart... (Song of Solomon 8:6a).

God says, "*Let your lover in!*" Let him embrace every part of you while you embrace every part of him without fear or reservation. This is true intimacy: a complete embrace of your lover's heart, soul, spirit, and body. "*I completely love ALL of you, and you completely love ALL of me, forever. Clinging to each other in sickness and in health, whether we make a large family or a small one, we are together through riches or lack, until death we do part.*"

Yet the passion the Bible describes seems far from the sex lives today's couples experience. Where are the two naked lovers clinging passionately and unashamedly to each other? With up to 50% of marriages ending in divorce once birth control and sterilization became popular, might we consider these probable destroyers of true intimacy?

The Lord glorified the purity of the sexual act and made it a pre-eminent part of His plan. No wonder the enemy attacks so often in the sexual realm! Today the sex act has become so perverted that it makes it hard for us to relate to or understand the purity of God's original plan for sex.

Birth control was invented to protect us from our lovers! *(This doesn't sound very unifying, does it)?*

Its goal is to keep us from experiencing the hardship of birthing the child that could result from our lovemaking. We are told that removing the threat of an unwanted pregnancy will increase our pleasure, but the reality is that using birth control prevents us from achieving true intimacy! When we use contraceptives, pills and gadgets, we miss the thrill of sex "*au naturel*" and this kind of sex is intimate and unprotected. If we desire to be protected from our lover and not allow sex to express itself in procreation, our journey as lovers will always be about *fear!*

Modern relationships start with a struggle: he fears her, and she fears him. "Honey, I love every part of you except the part that causes us to create children together. I need to *protect myself* from this part of you!"

Protection? The very word indicates fear.

When the lovers embrace their need for *protection*, fear creates an emotional wall between them. The Bible doesn't talk about the need for lovers to protect themselves from each other. Perfect love casts out fear (1 John 4:18). Yet society has rejected God's plan and says, "*Sex is for pleasure and not for procreation; therefore, we must protect ourselves from our lovers!*"

Think about Adam and Eve again. They attempted to protect themselves from God because they no longer trusted Him.

"I don't completely trust you!" This is the message the lover is communicating. The first time the lovers express their need *to protect themselves from each other*, they communicate to the other, "I can't completely trust you!" Even if the sex is great and both lovers agree to use birth control, the couple has started building an emotional barrier.

How high it becomes or how vastly it affects their relationship will be up to them. Yet once the idea of *protection* becomes part of their sexual experience, the need for protection in other areas will increase.

Tension outside the bedroom will stem from the need to protect oneself inside the bedroom. Being lovers outside the bedroom will be more challenging because the unspoken need to protect will now be there. All communication will be filtered through this emotional wall.

She will know he is *afraid* of her eggs and *afraid* of her womb and *afraid* of her ability to conceive a child he does not want.

He will know she is *afraid* of his sperm and its power to impregnate her against her will!

Neither one will make the connection, but the expression of protection during sex will speak louder than words!

The sex part might seem fine, but it will be hard to build intimacy because fear will always say in the background, *"I am afraid of you. I'm unsure if I trust you because you only want to protect yourself from me. How can I give you my heart when you are trying to protect yourself?"* This communication of rejection may be subtle, but it will be there!

How can two lovers trust each other when they fear what their partner might do to them?

Proof this is what is going on in male and female communication can be proven by marriage statistics. Lovers who do not use birth control in their marriages have amazing sex lives and a divorce rate between 1 and 3%. Most lovers who use birth control and sterilization are divorcing at more than 40%! Pop culture likes to tell us *"Men are from Mars"* and *"Women are from Venus"* meaning each sex is opposite and cannot relate to each other but might the problem simply be that when the relationship is all about *protecting* the lovers from each other, birth control creates so many emotional woundings, the lovers can no longer communicate because everything in their relationship revolves around fear?

The rejection that birth control and sterilization cause cannot take the entire blame for marital failure. However, it is a serious contributor because *its popularity and use coincide* with the rise of divorce. The emotional barriers and the personal rejection that birth control causes are why few couples today can achieve the intimacy that The Song of Solomon describes.

BABY-MAKING-SEX – A CONTRACEPTIVE HOLIDAY!

The good times roll when the lovers are making babies together. For those who use contraceptives, baby-making-sex is their birth control holiday...and they love it!

Baby-making-sex can be hot and steamy. Without the need for protection, the couple may experience their closest moments. Yet soon after the baby arrives, the joy subsides, and no matter how much they love their new little one, the lovers return to their pattern of *preventing another baby* from conception. They've been taught that this is what people are supposed to do. The pattern of prevention continues until they make a final choice about what to do with their fertility.

Once the *lovers* move away from their most important task of creating a new life together, they find they need to work harder at their marital relationship and commitment.

What is happening to our lovers? He may want sex, and she won't be interested. He is bored, and she is busy with the children. The once-excited bride may notice that her husband does not look at her as he used to. Their years of lovemaking amount to several children who take up all her time. Lovers who protected themselves from each other for the rest of their fertile years are now separating their lives somehow, not by choice but by logistics. He and she are both busy. Yet for some couples they still have a successful relationship, but they do have to work very hard at maintaining the emotional, physical and spiritual progression. For all these couples once the baby making thing is over, using contraceptives is a pain and far too often couples conclude that a tubal ligation or vasectomy is convenient and quick and might even put a little zing back into their sexual relationship.

HE LOVES ME, HE LOVES ME NOT, BUT DID HE EVER REALLY LOVE ME?

God created marriage as a beautiful partnership, but birth control, vasectomies and tubal ligations invite problems.

Has not the Lord made them one? In flesh and spirit, they are His. And why one? Because He was seeking Godly offspring, therefore do not break faith with the wife of your youth (Malachi 2:15, 16).

According to Malachi 2:15-16, when the couple enters into a birth control arrangement, they no longer 100% agree with what God intended. Complete intimacy is what God meant for lovers to experience, and the full expression of that intimacy on a fertile day could result in conceiving offspring. Children are not supposed to be the *fruit* of our *random choices* and *occasional desires*. They were meant to be the fullest expression of our intimate sexual relationship.

When a couple chooses to quit having children and does something to stop their fertility, the freedom that so many seek isn't there. For some, the fruit of the emotional loss could be anger, emotional separation, reading fantasy fiction, boredom in marriage, internet porn, emotional or physical affairs and divorce. Not what God intended for the two lovers who once started out with so much passion and were so much in love.

What God offers lovers is something pure, beautiful, and loving. He desires complete unity; each lover completely accepting every part of their lover. No walls, no protection needed and unconditional acceptance of the other person. This is what God means.

To be *naked* means naked in *mind, body, and spirit*, just like Adam and Eve were in the garden—*naked and unashamed*. When people are naked, they want to be completely loved for who they are.

Lovers who don't use birth control experience total acceptance because everything is out on the table, so to speak. Unprotected sex says," *My lover still loves me, still wants **all** of me and even though my fertility has aged, I know my lover would still want to make babies with me and no one else.*" This is true love! This is Song of Solomon's sex, *"I've always loved you and always will until the end of time because I completely accept you."* A pure expression of love will eliminate fear from the marriage, which is especially important as people age when personal fears arise: *"Does she still want me? Does he still find me attractive? Do I still have value?"* The lover will be at peace. They will *know that they know* where their lover stands because by not using birth control, their lover demonstrated absolute trust.

WHEN THE PRINCE FAILS TO RESCUE HIS MAIDEN

A female lover needs *Prince Charming* to fight for her, conquer her, and take her away.

Take me away with you (Song of Solomon 8:14). Part of lovemaking is the thrill, the chase, the conquering, and then the satisfaction.

When a woman is talked into *getting her tubes tied* and ceasing her ability to give life, she will not feel protected by her lover. Instead, she will feel *unprotected* and *vulnerable* and will hold this against him. Even though she may have had complicated pregnancies and been happy that she could no longer become pregnant, she will retreat emotionally and ask herself, *did he ever really love ME?*

"Where was my prince when I needed him to protect me? Why didn't he defend my right to bear his children? Why didn't he talk me out of this? Why didn't he do something? Why didn't he protect me and my body?"

In her mind, she may feel that **he conquered her, he used her and then threw her away!**

It can be emotionally dangerous when the woman fears her husband no longer wants or needs her. After the couple chooses sterilization, why should a wife get excited about her man anymore? What reason does she have to continue satisfying him? After all, he does not want to have a baby with her. He is through with that part of her, so why should she make love to him when she doesn't feel like it? Women must have a reason for sex. She may now find that sex becomes merely mechanical and lacking in intimacy.

Offspring represented the *fruit* of their union, but if he no longer needs her to create them, she may interpret this as meaning that he no longer needs her. Although they may never discuss it, her feelings of rejection will be there. As her youth begins to fade, she knows he no longer needs her in the same way. If the children need her, she'll be OK, but once they grow and go, she may feel out of sorts and very separated from the intimacy that her marriage once had. Even if she has a career and enjoys stable relationships, she will know that she and her lover aren't the same, and why should he be thrilled with her anymore? What is she to him now that he does not want any more children from her? Could this be a clue why the generation who popularized the pill and birth control all divorced each other? Birth control and sterilization were not part of marriage for thousands of years, and without it the divorce rate was and is practically zero.

(This is one of the most significant points in this entire book)

BARREN FOREVER: FILING FOR A REPRODUCTIVE "DIVORCE"

We've already covered that the lovers who do not use birth control communicate an emotional message of complete acceptance: "I love everything about you. I am committed to you. I am not afraid. I want to be with you and am willing to be ONE with you."

On the other hand, those lovers who use birth control communicate a different emotional message: "I am trying to love you, but I don't completely accept you. I want to say I trust you, but I'm not sure where we are headed." Even though the couple is lovemaking, casual rejection of our lover's body makes a statement. By treating their sex organs as objects of rejection, it makes it easier when the issue of sterilization comes up. The internal mechanism that should stop lovers will not be there!

What difference will it make? Severing their sexual partnership by sterilization will be easy to do, and people casually do it every day. Most would probably deny that it hurt their relationship. Yet when you think about it, this operation marks an event, the same as the day they were married.

There will now be a date and a time when one spouse ultimately rejected their reproductive body part and rejected God's plan to participate with their spouse in the process of creation.

This new date and time will be different from their wedding date. Their wedding was the day they promised to love, honor, and cherish their spouse till death they will part. This new date will represent the physical mutilation that has resulted from the marriage!

Marriage is a vow of love and acceptance, and sterilization is an unspoken vow of rejection of the gift to reproduce with each other.

This is what it looks like:

On this **day**_____ at this **time**_____, you and I choose to no longer be yoked to each other so that we might create a new life together.

From this day forward, I am permanently protected from you, from your seed, and from your baby-making parts. Therefore, our ability to create new lives together has been severed forever.

Signed: your spouse

> **Wow! This *reproductive partnership* has now ended!

> The two lovers are *no longer the same people* they were on their wedding day! The original goals have changed, and God's perfect plan for their intimacy has now been severed. After sterilization, the lovers will never be the same again. It is impossible.

Can a couple still have a good marriage after the physical act of mutilation? Perhaps it is possible, but the lovers must work hard at their communication. The Bible warns us. *Do not break faith with the wife of your youth (Malachi 2:15).*

I believe a **physical reproductive divorce** would fall into this category. There is more to a marriage than creating children, but since the lovers have rejected the goal of *creating offspring together*, personal rejection will always be the filter for love to flow through from this point on. Breaking the faith one has in the other severs the heart. One of the most horrible feelings a person can experience is to feel tossed aside. unwanted or feeling as if they're a thing of the past or less significant. These feelings open people up to fears and temptations.

"It can't be that bad because couples do not stop having sex after one of them gets a sterilization operation." Lovers will still have sex, but people express how their sex lives seem changed afterwards. My husband told me, men have confessed to him after their vasectomies they lost their desire and I've also had girlfriends confess that after they got sterilized, sex became dull and lost its zing!

But think, is this where we are now? By shaking our fist up at God and hating that He connected creation to sex, we now have no other choice but to mutilate ourselves to try and stop Him?

Sterilization makes a mockery of the marriage partnership, and no one ever talks about it or acts as if the problem exists. Without emotional healing, many couples will grow apart over the years; some will have affairs, and some will divorce, but many more will live in a cold marriage filled with emotional separations. They'll stay together because it is too inconvenient to divorce.

*People of God I beg you: **Do not end up with a Reproductive Divorce,** no longer the same person you were on your Wedding Day!

I beg you to Run! **Run away from the atheist doctor's knife who seeks to sever and destroy your precious gift of life!**

I beg you to realize: *Your body is a temple of the Holy Spirit, who is in you, whom you have received from God. You are not your own, you have been bought with a price, therefore honor God with your body (I Corinthians 6:19-20).*

I beg you to offer your body to God: *Therefore, I urge you by the mercies of God to **offer your bodies as a living sacrifice,** holy and pleasing to God- this is your true and proper worship (Romans 12:1).*

I beg you to not be like Adam and Eve: who ran and hid when they should have fallen on their faces in repentance. *The Bible says **return to the Lord and He will return to you**, He has torn us to pieces, but He will heal us; He has injured us, but He will bind up our wounds (Hosea 6:1).*

I beg you, do not be like Adam and Eve who ran and hid when they should have fallen on their faces in repentance. *The Bible says **return to the Lord and He will return to you**, He has torn us to pieces, but He will heal us; He has injured us, but He will bind up our wounds (Hosea 6:1).*

Wife's Prayer

Heavenly Father, please save me from this sorrow! I do not want to suffer the consequences of barrenness. I don't want a reproductive divorce and not be the same person I was when I got married. Thank you for opening my eyes. Please help me to want what You want and not to be afraid. I want to give you everything. Rescue me from myself.

Amen

Husband's Prayer

Heavenly Father, I want to do it Your way! I don't want to spend my life trying to fill the void that comes from barrenness. Forgive me if I have been doing this. Please put me on the proper path. Please give me a vision for my family that will give me peace about the future. Help me to trust You with all my concerns for provision. I repent. Call me back to You.

Amen

Christopher's Commentary

There were two Christophers. The old me was selfish and only thought about himself. Birth control was for me, *"Yeah, baby, use it! I want sex with no consequences. Wow, all for my pleasure!"* I didn't realize that I had made my wife into my sex object, and I didn't care; I just wanted to enjoy sex! I thought we had great sex, as did she, but there were walls of rejection separating us because we were using birth control. We didn't know any different. We didn't realize we were both very afraid of each other. I was afraid that she would get pregnant, and she was afraid that I would make her pregnant. We were both so scared. But then God changed me! He gave me that dream, and I realized I had more to offer my wife and God than I ever thought possible. I could give of myself and my heart. This radically changed new man wants to think of God's plan first and the bigger picture.

Even though I am a new man, I can't help that I was born with a sex drive, and I can't help that in my day, I am surrounded by sexual innuendos everywhere I look. Even with eyes committed to God, there are many sexual distractions, even just going to the grocery store. Maybe this is why I often look away to keep my focus on the Lord where it needs to be. This is when I wonder why God did things the way He did. I was born a man. I can't help how I was made. I was made to struggle.

Yet the new me has been somewhat released because now I view things differently. I still think about sex and procreation but now in a different way. I would be lying to you if I said, *"I don't want sex,"* because I still do. How could you not? But I now realize how much it affects a woman when she is being used. It affects a woman emotionally, spiritually, and physically. As the father of five daughters, I do not want their husbands to see them as instruments and objects of a man's pleasure. I want their husbands to see each of my daughters as a beautiful person God created.

A BARREN WOMB IS NEVER SATISFIED!

The new me does not believe in birth control; it doesn't work! *It allows men and women **to use each other carelessly** yet think it is love, while they are pleasing Satan.* The new me realizes, "Who am I to move into God's position?" Now that I see things in a new way, our sex life, which was always good, is off the charts because we have sex without anything in the way. It is both powerfully enjoyable and sexually and spiritually explosive. I can never go back to how it was before with birth control. After we stopped using it, I began to see my wife as being truly what God made her to be; sexually beautiful and fertile instead of sexually beautiful while despising her fertility. Truly there is a difference once a man changes his attitude about making a child with a woman every time they come together. He must commit his love to her even greater because each time they make love, there is a potential outcome. I can't explain it, but this change in attitude simply deepens love, and makes commitment concrete. I know for me, what Rachel and I and our Heavenly Father had together, is what God intended for marriage to become.

My advice for you is STOP USING BIRTH CONTROL! It separates the two of you from each other. If you think sex is good now when you do use it, wait until you allow yourselves to give to each other completely without the fear you now feel. Once you let go of fear and throw away your birth control, you will come into a deep love for your wife, and the nakedness of your union will be beyond anything that you can put into human words.

Christopher Scott

Investigate and Questions

- Think about the time, effort, and hassle people put into simply trying to prevent a child. Did God give sex so that couples would then need to be afraid of the consequences every time they make love?
- Read Psalm 78:6, 102:18. 2 Corinthians 4:4 *When God's people try to prevent their offspring, Hell cheers!* Have you ever thought about whose agenda is being glorified when a Godly fertile couple prevents conceptions? What are your thoughts?
- This chapter covered stories of couples who chose to be sterilized. After reading their stories, share your thoughts about their choices.
- Read 1 Peter 3:7. Proverbs 21:9. Do you believe that birth control use could cause any issues of emotional separation? Share your thoughts.
- Sterilization is one of the only operations to ever be invented that breaks a working body part which causes an entire system of the body to change and go haywire. What are your thoughts about breaking one's reproductive body parts?
- Read Malachi 2:16. Getting sterilized is a reproductive divorce; no longer the person you were on the day you got married. Have you ever looked at this operation in this way, share your thoughts.
- Do you know if your parents were sterilized? If yes, how do you feel about this? Some people do not discuss this with their children but from the 1960s forward if your family was small and your parents were fertile, they did something to prevent more children from coming? Do you think their marriage was affected by sterilization or using birth control?
- Did you ever ask for another sibling? What did they say?
- Read 1 John 4:18. Ephesians 5:28-30 What do you think about this statement: *I love you, but I do not love your baby-making parts.* Does this thought in any way make you feel rejected or unloved?

- Read Genesis 3:8-10. Why did Adam and Eve cover themselves from God? How is introducing contraceptives any different?
- Song of Solomon 1:2, 2:10, 2:16, 4;16. If contraceptives were to be used, then how come God did not talk about them in His sex book– The Song of Solomon?
- Women who have abortions sometimes think about how their life might have been had they not aborted their child. People who have sterilizations also do the same; sometimes wondering how different their life might have been had they not chosen to become barren. What kind of regrets do you think a sterilized person might have physically and mentally? Could this affect their outlook on their life, marriage or goals?

Impacting Others

Rachel, I loved your book! Thank you for writing it. It answered so many questions that I have had for a long time. I wanted to share why we feel glad we have a large family. We have nine children because we are a blended and quiver full family (long story), but several of our children are now grown. My oldest daughter is a nurse and works in an ICU. A lot of her patients are elderly. She comes home from ICU upset because a lot of them die. It's a hard job for a young gal, but this is where she felt God wanted her to be. I think God is using her job to give her solid convictions about the family He may bless her with one day. She tells me everything and has been sharing that she observes a pattern with her elderly patients. She notices that when one is sick, their spouse usually does not know what to do. They are old! Most are barely getting along, but when they have children who can come, it helps. Some patients don't seem to have anybody, and their children call ICU constantly because they don't live nearby. Often, they must fly in to help. She has noticed that people who do not have many children seem worse off because either no one comes or can stay for long, and when they do arrive, the emotional load of dealing with a sick parent is difficult to cope with. Many times, their other elderly parent is not much better off than the person in an ICU. But my daughter tells me about patients who have more family members or more children, and she says they seem to be better all the way around. Their children and grandchildren show up right away and start asking questions and paying attention to treatment. Larger families seem to keep relatives around for some reason. I think it is because larger families stay together. My daughter says they show up immediately and start sharing the responsibility of the crisis. Often one of their children will keep "hospital watch," and another will shuttle their other parent around. Other family members are there to care for other needs. The situation gets many helping hands, which you need in a crisis. She says it's sad to see people's lives ending all the time. Still, in larger families, the situation seems to become a shared event, with hours spent in the ICU waiting room, children and grandchildren and cousins exchanging stories and catching up on life. If there is a reason to have more children other than for security, it goes a long way in situations like this. I know this testimony is just a sideways observation, but it got me thinking about why being Quiver full is such a blessing. We will always be there for each other. **Mary Alice, Mother to nine Frederick, Md.**

Rachel, we have had eight children in 14 years of marriage, and we live in a part of the country where few people have more than one child. Most people think we are crazy for having this many children, but we know we are a testimony of what God can do. One of the most important things we discovered early on was that we had to keep our relationship as the highest priority. As more children arrived, it was easy for us to get caught up in babies, diapers, and sleeplessness and complain about how our own needs were not being met. Yet we made it a priority to always ask each other if we could do something for the other spouse instead of assuming they knew each other's needs. Marriage is something that people need to work at, and we realized that just because we had more kids than all our friends did not mean that our marriage would be bliss. It took work for it to survive and be a good one! It took effort on our part. We needed time alone and time to be together apart from our children. Alone time for us was not what the world considers as alone time, we did get some alone time, or else we would not be having babies! Yet we made it a point to always try to pray together every day for each child, and we had a weekly date night every week. Since we didn't have family nearby, we found another couple who would swap with us. They had our kids Friday nights, and we had theirs Saturday nights. It worked great until our oldest could sit. When money was good, we would go out to eat. This is one of my husband's favorite things to do, as he is a gourmet connoisseur. Yet when we cannot do that, we go to the bookstore and sip on lattes, take a drive, a walk (when it is not snowing, raining, or freezing), or take our tiny boat to the nearby lake in the summer. I always look forward to date night so I can talk and not be interrupted by a child, the phone, or a crisis. As you can tell, I get wordy... he-he... I also have tried hard to make sure that my husband would not see me worn out. I am his beautiful, sexy wife, and I want him to know that this is who he married. Having many children is not an excuse to let myself go or for him to have to come home to a worn-out wife. Every day I make the children nap in the afternoon, and if they don't want to sleep, they still must stay in their rooms. The house gets quiet for a few moments, and I love this. I am usually nursing and can take a 15 or 20-minute snooze. It gives me physical and emotional energy to get through our evening together. My husband has made it a huge priority every year that we make sure that we go away on our anniversary, often with our newest baby in tow, but we still made it a priority. Often, we had little money set aside, but God provided either through friends or acquaintances; we were given places to stay that gave us a chance to get away and reflect on our marriage. I must say that God has been a faithful God, and someday the kids will be gone, and what will be left will be the marriage and the memories. **Jill, married to John, for 14 years in Massachusetts, parents to 8 children (1.5-13 years old)**

Up to this point, I have been showing you how our choices have affected the physical realm.

There is tangible evidence of pain, sorrow, illness, disease, and divorce resulting from the use of birth control and sterilizations. Now I will switch gears, and in the next several chapters, we will look deeper at how our choices affect the unseen realm which also influences our physical health.

God's word tells us a war is going on in the *spirit world* that surrounds us. There are battalions of unseen forces that hate us and seek to destroy our happiness. Ephesians 6:12 says we struggle not against flesh and blood but against principalities and powers and rulers of darkness in high places and this is why we need the armor of God's love to cover us and protect us.

The road to healing begins when we render the spiritual forces powerless by making correct choices in the physical world. Then the enemy has no more power over us.

We have a choice to make, do we continue to agree with the culture that surrounds us, and the spiritual lies we've been told, or do we start agreeing with what God is revealing? If we choose God, then He will open wide the door to bring us healing- emotionally, physically and spiritually. I must admit I don't always understand exactly how it all works, but if we want freedom, we need to correct the things we have control over, listen carefully to what He reveals in His word, and trust Jesus for the outcome.

Chapter 8

THE IDOL'S ALTAR

> *Break down their altars, smash their sacred stones, cut down their Ashram poles and burn their idols in the fire. For you are a people holy unto the Lord your God. The Lord your God has chosen you out of all the peoples of the earth to be his people, His treasured possession (Deuteronomy 7:5-6).*

From the beginning of time, the devil has been using the same methods to mess up mankind. He may package them differently from generation-to-generation, but his tricks are the same, and over and over people keep falling for them. Century after century the devil ruins lives through his deception and trickery, and the sad thing is, that people who are being deceived do not realize it until it is too late! When we are walking in deception, all we will believe is that our decisions are correct. Later we see that what we thought would be best really was not.

This very thing is what happened to Eve in the Garden of Eden. I do not believe that on the day she committed the first sin, Eve had planned to disobey God. Her day in the garden started like any other. Eve was not thinking, *"Today, I am going to sin."* Eve must have passed that forbidden tree hundreds if not thousands of times, barely noticing it, yet on this day, when she heard a voice calling, she responded and within moments forgot everything she had been told. Eve lost her focus.

The enemy's soothing words caused Eve to turn inward, taking inventory of her wants and desires, which was something she had probably not thought about before. He twisted her mind in such a way

THE IDOL'S ALTAR

that he got Eve to relax her boundaries and look at herself. It was at that moment Eve questioned what she had heard.

God said, "Don't eat!" but never told her *why*. Since she didn't know God's reasoning, the enemy easily persuaded her, *"Did God mean that you could never eat, or did He just want you to wait until you were ready?"* Satan's influence caused Eve to waver between two opinions: God's ideals and her desires. Why couldn't she eat? Did God mean it exactly the way He said? The enemy's motivations caused her to question God's intentions. Eve may have thought that by eating the fruit that she was doing a good thing by choosing to become like God.

The enemy misled Eve to reason out the variables until the enemy got her so confused she didn't know what was true anymore. It was all a big test. God did not repeat His commandment. He said one time, Adam and Eve do not eat from that tree (Genesis 2:16-17). Day by day, the power of His command faded, causing Eve to become vulnerable to reasoning. Since Eve was innocent and knew no sin, she did not recognize the importance of God's motivation to keep her from eating the fruit.

This was Eve's defining moment. *"Why not eat?"*

The enemy convinced Eve that this would be a good thing, and even though Eve never intended to harm her friendship with God, she questioned His goodness. At that moment, she let go of her blessing, and oh, the pain her choice has caused! She and Adam had conversed daily with God, but now they ran and hid because they were afraid of Him. They were now cursed with sin and had to leave that perfect place.

Eve's deception is an excellent example of how the enemy works to bring confusion, and while in every generation, his methods are the same, they are packaged a little bit differently each time.

As I've said throughout this book, for thousands of years, humanity wanted sex without the consequences of pregnancy and when birth control finally advanced to where most in society could partake, our churches went silent. At the tail end of the Baby Boom generation the pill came out. It was released in 1960. That was the year the first Baby Boomer (born 1944) would have turned 16 yrs. old. which means by the time Baby Boomers were old enough to need birth control, the pill was waiting for them on a silver platter, offered to all who would partake.

Does this sound like what Satan said to Eve? *Simply take this little pill and no one will ever know why you don't have a large family of children like your mother, grandmother and great grandmother. This pill will solve that problem and then you can have the life the mothers before you could never have; a life for yourself!* **This was my generation! The people partook, the church partook, we never had a chance to hear God's truth about why the family is so important. My generation was duped.**

Satan knew how to fool us, when to fool us, and who to place around us to cause us to accept everything. Even though God said, *"multiply"* to every generation since the beginning of time, when it was the Baby Boomer's turn, children were optional. We were enlightened to believe that because of the pill every woman should decide what was right for herself. Statements from Baby Boomers who were educators, ministers, colleagues, coworkers, neighbors, friends, the media and everyone around the women echoed the same sentiment. *"Being a mother of more than one or two children is not important in modern societies. It's old fashioned, outdated and ridiculous. Why would anyone want to miss out on all the opportunities available to women and instead throw away their life raising a large family? It's not Biblical anymore to have a large family. It's a grey area and not a commandment we need to obey. Be fruitful and multiply was for another time and was never meant to be followed to the letter of the law."*

My generation was vulnerable like Eve. Because of a lack of teaching on this Biblical truth, we did not understand God's motivation for encouraging us to multiply past having one or two children. We couldn't help that we rejected God's plan. The truth was hidden from us and was replaced with deception about families. We did not know what to believe and our heartfelt desires for personal gain deceived most all the women in my generation. It deceived even me, until God opened my eyes. Ultimately it became about our selfishness. The women in my generation chose to prioritize themselves over their children because starting a family interfered with what they wanted for their lives. Women were forced to choose. Woman would say, *"I don't think God cares if I have one child or ten; besides, I don't like little children, and I don't like being pregnant, and we can't afford a large family. Or We don't want all that responsibility; we want time to be together, besides for us, babies don't fit into our school plans; we both want to get our master's degrees first, and we always said we only wanted two babies anyways. Or God's got to catch up with modern times, my husband wants* to retire young so we can travel, having two children allows us to do that, he doesn't want to be old when he retires. Or I spent a lot of years in school to become an attorney, I don't need a bunch of children, I need to run my practice! Or both of us agreed we would only have one child; we want to get this over with as soon as possible." Eve had her *good* reasons to eat the fruit and because of her *good* reasons she lost her eternal life. The Baby Boom generation had their *good* reasons why not to have children and now so does Generation X and because of all their *good* reasons, we've nearly lost the traditional family.

The Baby Boomers rejected children and now they taught this same reasoning to their children. Unless this twisted idea about family size is stopped by God (thus the reason for this book), the same curse will fall on the Baby Boomer's grandchildren. Many Generation X women accepted the pill and IUD, and they also believe *a child is a parent's choice*. Now Generation Y is up to bat, and we are yet to see what this generation will choose.

It was crazy that for a brief shining moment after 9/11/2001, Americans reflected upon the tragedy of that horrible day by having babies. Children were a reminder of how important family was to Americans. The early 2000s baby boom was short lived, but a few more babies were born who probably would not have been conceived.

AN IDOL? COME ON, THEY'RE NOT REAL ANYMORE!

Being an *idol worshipper* is not a popular teaching of the modern church. People assume idol worship went out in the dark ages and that if they are not bowing down to some pagan deity, there is no reason to worry about Bible verses on idolatry. Even considering that we may have given ourselves to an idol seems ludicrous. But scripture says believers get trapped in idolatry, even those trying to love God and follow His ways.

This is where the modern church has had a huge disconnect; even though we have made great strides in many areas, our culture has led us off a cliff here. In chapter 4, I discussed situational Christian ethics where we justify disobedience to a Christian principle based off our good reasons. We then think we are correct and deny we are committing a sin because the reason is good. God calls this idolatry to self.

What agreement is there between the temple of God and idols? For we are the temple of the living God. As God has said: "I will live with them and walk among them, and I will be their God, and they will be my people (2 Corinthians 6:16).

Idolatry is not just about bowing down to a pagan statue; idolatry is much deeper. It is a choice that affects the heart, because it is an affront to the gospel and to loving God with all our hearts, souls, and minds. Idolatry steals us *away from God* so we can no longer hear Him speaking to us. Considering that we may have given ourselves to an idol is hard for some of us to accept. Most of us do not believe that we could ever become deceived in this way because we love God, and we want to please Him. The Scriptures say that believers do get trapped in idolatry. To understand how we could ever become involved in any way with an idol, we must first figure out what God means by the word idol and see how the enemy uses deception to get our lives intertwined with an unseen entity.

An idol can be anything that robs our heart's attention away from focusing on the Lord. An idol could cause us to *befriend* a thought or idea, or a physical object. In exchange, we feel safe and secure. An excellent example of a modern idol might be a habit, such as smoking, alcohol addiction or playing video games for hours. Scripture has given us guidelines for food and drink, but most believers ignore them, reasoning that we have been granted liberty, so we go ahead and eat anything, drink anything, and do anything we want. Fairly soon, our good meal, our Starbucks habit or our half a glass of wine after dinner, turns into an addiction. The substance that once made us feel good, eventually makes us fat, sick, gives us migraines, or causes us to lose relationships. Our addiction destroys something valuable in our lives and becomes the thing we hold on to. Scripture says this is idolatry and we are to turn away and not pollute our bodies by making an agreement with an idol (Ezekiel 14:6, 20:18, Acts 15:20, 1 John 5:21, 2 Corinthians 6:16).

We might not be bowing down to the TV set, our I-phone, our computer, You-tube, Facebook, or the internet, but we can become addicted to media. There is nothing wrong with occasionally indulging in our favorite media outlet, but if we can't fall asleep without listening to music or watching media, there may be a reason to be concerned. We've given our time and attention to a worthless screen, but this inanimate object, made by human hands, demands our attention and controls us! In other words, idols cause us to become servants to them instead of servants to God. They can rob and steal until we have little time left for God.

You shall not make for yourself an idol in the form of anything in heaven above or on the earth beneath or in the waters below. You shall not bow down to them or worship them (Exodus 20:4).

Recognizing the areas where we have displaced our love for the Lord with both small and large idols is important to our walk with Jesus. Song of Solomon 2:15 warns us that it is the *little foxes that spoil the vine*. What this means is that we may not be sinning in a huge area, but instead maybe we've allowed our time to be stolen by all these littles things (I am preaching to myself!), or we've allowed our body to become addicted by several small habits or we've given our tongue to saying a few not nice things about others. All these little things add up to giving ourselves away to the enemy and we don't even realize it.

Scripture is clear that not only is idol worship a sin, but it also brings a generational curse upon those who are idol worshippers. ...*punishing the children for the sin of the parents to the third and fourth generation of those who hate me (Exodus 20:5).*

But God says *I will bless a thousand generations of those who love Me (Exodus 20:6)* If we turn from these habits, our minds will be able to receive the abundant blessings God intended for us.

The arrogance of man will be brought low, and the pride of men humbled; the Lord alone will be exalted in that day, and the idols will totally disappear (Isaiah 2:17-18).

AS THE ANCIENTS SINNED, SO DO WE TODAY...

As far back as Mesopotamia, Assyria, and Babylon, there were forms of worship that focused on a system of gods and beliefs. These ancient people did not know the living God, so they developed their own religion to answer why things happen the way they do.

They worshipped the sun, the moon, and the stars and thanked the goddess of the earth for its bounty and the celestial beings for spiritual direction and light. We often call their beliefs folklore, mythology or paganism.

Fertility and reproduction were desired, and reproductive organs were worshipped and represented in horrific, disgusting ways. *Oversexed* might be how many of these cultures would be described today. To gain military power and influence, ancient peoples understood the power of numbers. Birthing children and producing crops were considered gifts from the gods. To keep the gods happy, bloodshed was required and because they believed their abundance came from these "gods" they had to use many different witchcraft rituals, ceremonies and sacrifices.

Letting blood through *child sacrifice* (Leviticus 20:3) was one of the many rituals. God called this defilement! (Ezekiel 23:37, 37:23.) He was especially displeased with His people taking part because He had provided leaders who had instructed against such practices, and God's people knew better. Throughout the Scriptures God commanded His people to not do as the people around them. God continually told them to *come out and be separate* from the ways of those you live around (2 Corinthians 6:17). But did the ancient Hebrews listen?

Regardless of God's warnings and punishments, the people of God repeatedly sacrificed their children to Molech, Ashtoreth, and other pagan deities (Leviticus 18:21, Psalm 106:37-38). This was an extreme act of wickedness. The Hebrews knew it was wrong, but they did it anyway. Little by little, they had blended with the people around them because they had forgotten *whose people* they were.

This is exactly what has happened in America to God's people. Countless believers have blended with culture, and we have forgotten whose people we are. Considering food, dress, habit, and lifestyle, it's hard today to tell who a believer is and who isn't. In family planning, nearly everyone uses some form of birth control, abortion, or sterilization. We have the children we want, and we try hard to prevent the children we do not want, but if one slips by us, we can easily sacrifice them at our local abortion mill and then run out for an operation to prevent THAT from ever happening again. Thus, our great sin of idolatry!

In Chapter 4 I gave you a quiz about humanism which most people fail because the culture has done such an excellent job of brainwashing all of us. Now ask yourself, *"What ideas or rationalizations in our culture or at church are against the idea of having a large family or against adding one more child to your family?*

THE IDOL'S ALTAR

We've discussed exhaustively that the birth control pill made the idea that *sex is for pleasure and not for procreation*. Protestant clergy rarely, if ever preach against using it, and Christian couples write books supporting it. We've made birth control our idol. We made sterilization our idol. We made small families our idol. We made personal choice our idol. We hate to admit it, but we can even justify reasons for abortions. Several generations later and twenty-five years after the beginning of a new century, young married church-going couples STILL have no idea that God's word has guidelines for sex, birthing babies, birth control, and sterilization! *Like sheep, we have all been led astray...* (Isaiah 53:6), *and today couples are still being led astray.*

> **Birth control use is an idol, and we have not repented for enshrining it into Protestant church culture.**

SLEEPING WITH THE ENEMY: HOW PEOPLE BECOME CONNECTED TO IDOLS

To understand how people become involved with idols, we must once again think about Eve and realize the devil's number one trick of deception is to lead us by *twisting* our minds. We also need to see from the Word of God that God's people have a history of being led away into idolatry. Idol worship is not something people plan to do but they are led into it *little by little* until it consumes them.

When the enemy desires to deceive us, his goal is to get us involved with something that looks good or sounds good to our human spirit but in the end, as Scriptures says, *leads to the ways of death* (Proverbs 16:25). Without strong Biblical teaching about why God's ways are higher and better and bring goodness, when we hear other people's ideas, because we are human, we can easily be deceived. This is what we read about in the book of Ecclesiastes. This is how the *natural man* understands life.

When we take our eyes off God and consider what *other* people are doing, we often follow this pattern:

1. We *agree* with a new plan or idea no matter what ungodly source brings to us.

2. We find *good* reasons why we should follow and do the same thing.

3. We *participate* with the ungodly and find that we agree with their godless way.

4. We then do what *we* want because it *feels* right.

> God's word says, *my people perish for lack of knowledge*, but for a while *it feels right*, so we have no idea we've taken the wrong path.

In our modern generations, here in America, the devil confused church leadership by using *science* and *convincing arguments* against the traditional large Christian family. They supported a need to be *sensitive* to reducing family size so that couples could have more money. These contemporary ideals sounded good and reasonable but originated with the ungodly progressives at the turn of the previous century! This was even before birth control was available to the masses. In 1930, once the Protestants separated from the Catholics in family planning, they made it seem like the Catholic idea to continue to have large families was now archaic. Protestant pastors started changing the culture themselves by offering personal opinions instead of basing their words on the Word of God.

The Scriptures call this being a *spiritual whore* or a *spiritual prostitute* (Jeremiah 3:1-3, Ezekiel 16:20, Ezekiel 43:9, Hosea 4:12, Hosea 5:3). This means Christians are whoring around with cultural ideas, agreeing with them and doing the same things as everyone else in an ungodly society. Even as modern as we think we are today; we are no different than the Hebrew people in the Bible. God's people repeatedly were attracted to the idols of the cultures that surrounded them and God warned them repeatedly that they were being led away into sin.

Our agreement to ungodly thinking, reasoning, and life choices to choose our way rather than to trust God is akin to *sleeping with the enemy*. But we like it! We get comfort in choosing our own way! It *feels good* to join with those around us rather than trust an *unseen* God. Since the 1960's the Protestants especially:

Agreed that birth control is the answer,

Separated themselves from the old way of trusting God for family size,

Agreed with the new culture, created by atheists,

Rejected the truth that sex is for creating new life,

Adopted the use of birth control, so that sex would be exclusively an act of pleasure,

Received their idol into their bodies, same as a prostitute receives her lover into her body,

They have now suffered as the result of this great sin..." *for the wages of sin is death" (Romans 6:23).*

(Throughout this book, I do need to use some examples to make my points, but when I need to use examples of clergy, I choose to be very careful. The behavior by quite a few ministers, these past sixty-five years, is significant and their position on birth control is important but I will do my best to talk in generalities as my goal is never to point fingers.)

There are Protestant pastors today who have videos on the internet about using birth control. I've watched every one of these videos I can find. One thing that seems a common thread is that these ministers always *give their opinions* about what they believe, but never seem to open their Bibles to wager their opinions against what the Scriptures say. I do believe this might be somewhat innocent. Most come from seminaries where the leaders do not address this subject and unless they had a specific reason, they truly might not have ever studied it in the Bible. I wasn't planning to study it either until God wrecked our life with my husband's dream, so I get their sincere reasoning, even if I believe it is incorrect. I also believe if I could speak with these men, they would at least hear me out. We might not completely agree but if I could at least present scripture, we might find we have some Biblical agreement.

However, there is one well-known minister I'm not so sure about. He goes out of his way to make negative statements about Christians who believe in giving God their family planning. He does not agree this area is an area where God has any say because people encounter life situations where there are no options. He says those who do not agree with his reasoning are *legalistic* believers. I think he only knows one scripture on the subject, which is *be fruitful and multiply*, and he feels following be fruitful and multiply is unbending and unrealistic to our modern thinking. Even though he has a few children himself, he is still a firm believer in supporting the use of artificial contraceptives unless they are a proven abortifacient, but then adds that Protestants are still arguing about which artificial methods are abortifacients, which leads one to believe a couple might still be able to choose whatever they want. From his comments I think at one point he may have met or counseled some crazy folks who have large families, but one wacko family is not the norm for every couple trusting God with their gift of fertility. Nearly all couples, who trust God for each child, end up with beautiful families and are very happy. Yet more than once on his YouTube videos, I have heard this pastor make fun of Catholics who don't use artificial contraceptives and who instead use natural family planning. This minister believes all forms of birth control are subjective and it is up to each person. On one of his videos, he says that if you do not believe like he does and if you would like to show him what the Scriptures say, please email him. Then he says," *And if you do email, he will not read your email and he will have fun deleting it! Seriously?* How immature! He is positive that every interpretation of the Scriptures on this subject is LEGALISTIC. Yet even though I don't agree with him, my heart goes out to this man because his words push back in a way that makes me think he is wounded. He seems to not be able to see the bigger picture, and all he sees is the thick forest full of trees. This is what the message of this book is all about. Seeing through the thick forest of trees that our culture and our ministers have created. We are asking the Lord to show us the path through the thick lies and idols that lurk in the forest.

God's plan is revealed in the Scriptures, but it also must be revealed to each person in their hearts. The church world seems as if they have tangled up all the paths, and has spoon fed us the culture's idolatrous rhetoric of pro-choice and then calls their personal opinions about choice, food from Heaven.

When we disobey what God told us to do, and then disobey how God told us to do it, scripture calls us *sinners*. If we keep it up, *sin becomes our lifestyle.* We don't use birth control only one time. We use it over and over. Each time, we worship and serve *the created thing* rather than *the creator* (Romans 1:25). Each time, we put our faith and trust in our birth control device rather than in God, and for most fertile couples today using birth control is part of their sexual *lifestyle.*

Using birth control has become so completely acceptable in church culture that we do not even realize that we have eliminated our faith in the Lord and replaced it with faith in a pill!

As a person born at the very end of the Baby Boom generation, I come from a generation who was *in-love with the pill* and was so very thankful to the *gods of birth control* that the entire time my generation was fertile, they swore allegiance to the benefits they received from this idol.

This idol called *the birth control pill* kept Baby Boomers from an *inconvenient pregnancy*, and it *made sex easier* by not needing to stop and insert anything or put on anything or use creams or foams. This idol *opened new avenues for premarital sex* so a young person could explore sex without needing marriage. This idol *made having an affair a breeze* because no one got caught by an unwanted pregnancy and if we did not forget to take our daily pill, then our sexual life was carefree and easy. When my generation *put our trust* in this idol, *it blessed us* by keeping us from the conceptions of every one of our unwanted children.

Boomers exchanged their purity and fell passionately in love with the idol of the birth control pill. It became our *habitual lover* and because we have now offered it to our children, the pill is still the lover of countless Millennials, Generation X and even some Generation Y females today.

But mark this: There will be terrible times in the last days. People will be lovers of themselves, lovers of money, boastful, proud, abusive, disobedient to their parents, ungrateful, unholy, without love, unforgiving, slanderous, without self-control, brutal, not lovers of the good, treacherous, rash, conceited, lovers of pleasure more than lovers of God, having a form of godliness but denying its power... (2 Timothy 3:1-5a).

My generation is the one who compromised our inheritance. In one 40-year cycle (1961-2001), while moms and dads were busy limiting their seed, the enemy mounted an end-time battle against reproduction. I believe there is a time coming, even this season is here, when those who want to be birthing children are finding it more difficult to do so. The sins of our ancestors laid the foundation in the earth that is setting up future infertility. Human reproduction has become even harder, and the gift of fertility is now under severe attack on the earth. All forms of reproduction are suffering: our food, our seeds, our health system, our choices, and our lifestyles. OPEN YOUR EYES! See what is happening. Conceptions are not happening like they used too and are becoming more problematic because complacency has allowed evil to take power by enforcing birth control, abortion and finalizing fertility with sterilization.

God is saying repent for these great sins are now over your entire country and over most of the world! Christians in America, throw away your unholy devices and turn from your wicked ways, *if my people who are called by my name will humble themselves and seek my face and turn from their wicked ways, then will I hear from Heaven and forgive their sin and heal their land (2 Chronicles 7:14-16).*

IDOLS LEAD US AWAY INTO FALSE COMFORTS

There is a reason why we get comfort from making wrong decisions. The peace we feel makes us think we are correct, and we do not realize we have been deceived. The *peace* we think we feel is *false peace!* "I prayed about it, and God gave me peace about getting a sterilization operation." Before you go forward with your procedure, please consider these Biblical stories.

Eve had *peace*. She felt good about eating the fruit. She was excited about the possibility of being *like God*. Possibly if Eve would have waited or talked with Adam or talked with God, she might have made a different choice! Yet because Eve had *peace*, she forgot she had options and instead, got caught up in the drama of the moment which led her to commit the first sin.

Nine out of ten of Joseph's brothers *had peace* about selling Joseph into slavery. Their decision caused Joseph to suffer for years in Egypt. Jonah *had peace* when he got on a ship to Tarshish, the opposite direction of Nineveh, but he did it anyways. God punished Jonah by making him live three nasty and horrible days and nights inside a massive fish. In Acts, Ananias and Saphira *had peace* when they sold a piece of property and decided to lie to the Holy Spirit. God punished them with death.

Having a *peaceful feeling* does not necessarily mean we are correct! If our peaceful feeling goes against the Scriptures, then we are in *peaceful deception!* God has provided many scriptures to show us that reproduction was designed to give us great blessings. Sinful humans created sterilization operations, and they will always be against God's plan. **People want to use birth control and to be sterilized because they want convenience.**

Clearly, God warns people, of the deception of sinning against their body. Read these verses as if God was talking to you about using birth control and ending your fertility with sterilization. This verse talks about believers because it says they knew God but took His gifts for granted.

> *For although they knew God they neither glorified Him as God nor gave thanks to Him, but their thinking became futile, and their foolish hearts were darkened (Romans 1:21).*

Again, God is talking about believers, who study the word and know what it says. Yet even with their Biblical knowledge, they exchange the glory of being *fertile* for *infertility*, which is a curse against their own body!

> *Therefore, God gave them over in the sinful desires of their hearts to sexual impurity, for the degrading of their bodies with one another (Romans 1:24).*

What else could God do? People insist on getting sterilized, which degrades the *glory of the man or woman* to *equality with a dog or a cat*, because *we sterilize them* too.

> *They exchanged the truth of God for a lie and worshiped and served created things rather than the Creator, who is forever praised (Romans 1:25).*

These are God's people who exchanged the truth of letting God give them children, for the lie that says it is OK to get an operation or use an artificial device to stop you from creating your children.

WHEN GENERATIONS SACRIFICE THEIR CHILDREN

Throughout time the people groups who sacrificed their children fade away into history. In ancient days people burned their children in the fire and offered them up on altars so that the adults could gain power over the elements. Today, we are killing our children before they can be born. In ancient days these killings were out in public for all to witness. Today the murders are done in the privacy of a doctor's office or at home after taking a pill.

Our altar is the abortion clinic, the gynecologist's table or the toilet. Either the staff disposes of our baby's body, or we flush what is left of our baby, down our commode. The mother walks away and we agree it is simply tissue and agree that nothing has happened. We think we are civilized to kill our offspring this way, but we've taken a child's life and exchanged it for our own. This is how it is done today.

In ancient days direct parental involvement was also required.

They forsook all the commands of the Lord their God and made for themselves two idols in the shape of calves; they worshipped Baal. They sacrificed their sons and daughters. They practiced divination and sought omens and sold themselves to do evil in the eyes of the LORD, arousing His anger (2 Kings 17:16-17).

Parents took their precious baby to the pagan priests who laid their gurgling and kicking baby on an altar. The baby was killed in some brutal way or was thrown alive into a burning furnace. What was the parent's reaction as their child's blood was spilled or their son or daughter was consumed by fire? Were they in disbelief as they are today? Did they convince themselves their child was not real? I would hope they were upset. This sacrifice was meant to cost them something. This was why it was called a *sacrifice*.

How did the ancients justify their behavior when they could see the death of their children as their baby's blood was running off the altar? How cold were these people's hearts? I am sure the bloodshed was commonplace for the priest, as it is today for the abortionist, causing little to no reaction. In the priest or the abortionist's mind, the job is done once the blood has been spilled. But to a parent, this is their own flesh and blood!

In other rituals, the Bible says the parents took their small children and offered them as a burnt offering to Baal, Molech, or other idols (2 Chronicles 28:3, Leviticus 18:21, Leviticus 20:3, 2 Kings 17:17, 2 Kings 21:6, 2 Chronicles 33:6). What a horror to imagine. What would a parent be telling a small child at such a time? *"Be a good little girl or boy and do this for mommy and daddy."* Would their child scream out in pain? *"Mommy, daddy, why are they doing this to me? Help! why are you letting them hurt me?"*

As their children screamed in agony, *"Mommy, daddy, save me!"* What were the parents thinking? I know I couldn't watch! I would have to be hypnotized even to be able to take part. How could a parent's mind become so twisted that they believed sacrificing their precious child's life could be the answer to anything? This behavior deeply grieved God's heart.

Do not give any of your children to be sacrificed to Molech, for you must not profane the name of your God. I am the Lord (Leviticus 18:21).

THE IDOL'S ALTAR

"Say to the Israelites: Any Israelite or alien living in Israel who gives any of his children to Molech must be put to death. The people of the community are to stone him (Leviticus 20:2).

I, Myself, will set My face against him and will cut him off from his people; for by sacrificing his children to Molech, he has defiled My sanctuary and profaned My holy name (Leviticus 20:3).

They sacrificed their sons and daughters in the fire. They practiced divination and sought omens and themselves to do evil in the eyes of the LORD, arousing his anger (2 Kings 17:17).

Today we believe we are *enlightened* people living in modern times who would never allow ourselves to commit such horrors by sacrificing our living children to idols. Yet, if we look at the practices of the abortion industry, we do the same things every day! Christians go to church on Sunday but ignore the practices of a *heinous industry* operating right under their nose. We wonder our other people allow atrocities to take place in their countries (genocidal killings) and yet we are no better. Daily in the abortion clinics of America, we see parallels to these exact same Biblical scenes. The time of history is different, but the babies are still brutally dying. At abortion clinics all over our country, babies are poisoned with saline solutions, burned alive with chemicals, their brains are sucked out while they are still alive, and they are sacrificed daily upon the altars of their mother or father's excuses. These are the reasons we justify murder and are often the same reasons a person uses birth control to prevent conceptions:

I've got better things to do with my life
A baby would ruin my career
I'm pregnant and live with my boyfriend. If he knew, he'd leave
I do not have enough money to raise a child
I am too young to have a baby now
I cannot give up my college education
My dad is a pastor; he would kill me if he found out I am pregnant
We don't need a third child—we already have a boy and a girl
I am too old for another child
This child could have health problems, it's easier to abort

Men and women sacrifice their children every day! *"...They parade their sin like Sodom; they do not hide it. Woe to them! They have brought disaster upon themselves"* (Isaiah 3:9).

By the grace of God, those who have had abortions can be forgiven, healed, and renewed. Also, by the grace of God, many believers have avoided the horrors of abortion. But when we control birth, we are not much better. What future blessing might we sacrifice when we chose not to allow the conception of our next child into our life? We have no idea the greatness of one more precious child that God might have in store for our family!

WHEN DECIEVED BY YOUR IDOL, GOD SAYS, HE WILL "JOIN YOU" IN YOUR IDOLATRY

God's word is very clear. God will allow us to be deceived.

What? Yes, this IS what it says!

Therefore, speak to them and tell them, 'This is what the Sovereign LORD says: When any child of God sets up idols in his heart and puts wicked stumbling blocks before his face and then goes to a prophet, I the LORD will answer them myself in keeping with their great idolatry. I will do this to recapture the hearts of the people of Israel who have all deserted me for their idols (Ezekiel 14:4-5).

The Lord says when your face is turned toward an idol, He will answer you in keeping with your deception. Scary! *Woe to the wicked! Disaster is upon them. They will be paid back for what their hands have done (Isaiah 3:11).*

This is why when a person says, *"God told me that it is O.K. to get a vasectomy,"* please consider the *Yes!* you heard and the *peace* you feel was the *voice* of deception. You may disagree with me but for God to say Yes! it would have to go against everything else He said in His word.

Why do people fall on their faces in repentance when they realize they should have let God plan their families? How come once couples allow the Holy Spirit to convict them about their sterilizations, they go to great lengths to undo these operations? Why do they hear the voice of the Lord after they repent and not before?

Eve should have told Satan, "No! God would never withhold something good from me" and then yelled for help. God would have rescued her.

Instead, the enemy tricked her, and he is tricking everyone else about this subject. No one was there to rescue Eve from her deception, but God has sent me and the message in this book to rescue you from yours!

God has seen the suffering of the last several generations. Many men, women, and children have suffered. He has heard the cries from the babies crying out in the abortion clinics of America. He has heard the cries of divorced people, latchkey kids, daycare babies, and mothers crying out to Him on their way to work. He's listened to the cries of the woman who aborted her first child but who later married but cannot conceive again. He's observed the pain that has already overtaken the past several generations. He is allowing this deception to be exposed in this generation to save millions of couples from the heartaches their parent's generation fell into.

SACRIFICING OUR FERTILITY AT THE IDOL'S ALTAR

It would be impossible for me to name every way the enemy has gotten God's people to side with him over this issue, so to make it easier I've targeted the idols I believe affect birth control and family planning.

Each idol has an altar upon which God's people are making their daily decisions regarding family planning. They live their lives in agreement with ungodly thoughts, excuses, and beliefs that become their *good reasons* for why they should not follow God's plan and do things their way instead. The idol influences each area and causes us to make compromises that lead us away from God's goals for our families. Once this happens, the agreement becomes our argument which *exalts itself up against the knowledge of God!* (2 Corinthians 10:5).

As you read this list, I pray the Holy Spirit will bring His supernatural discernment upon you and convict you of any area where you may be compromising your thoughts or beliefs with one or more of these idols. Scripture says that the Lord is waiting to cleanse us from all unrighteousness (1 John 1:9), and to give us peace of mind. Each idol has its own agenda and however we agree with these idols in our hearts, they keep us from staying open to the possibility of conceiving one more child. These are reasons upon which many of God's people fall away from the Lord.

IDOL #1 The Idol of Human Reasons

On this altar we justify our reasons

Idol #1: Typically, the prevalent attitude is that if God only knew my situation, He would never ask me to multiply. God's miracle-working power, faith, hope, and trust are all dismissed. A couple might be trusting God for a new house or for a new job, but at the same time, will not trust God with their family size. When you are being duped by reasoning, it will cause you to base everything on what you can see from your human perspective. Ultimately, reasoning will cause you to justify excuses until you die. God says please trust me with this area, but you say *"no"* because of every excuse you can come up with. When you are relying on yourself, you may have been deceived by *the Idol of Human Reasoning*, and you need to repent.

IDOL #2 The Idol of Convenience

On this altar, we worship convenience and strive for a life of comfort

Idol #2: There is nothing wrong with wanting to be comfortable, but thousands of couples approach the subject of conceiving a baby from the standpoint of convenience. They don't want to be *put out* with a new baby but would turn right around and get a dog and allow it to inconvenience them. People spoiled by the idol of convenience never want to be inconvenienced by anything, not even God's best plan for their lives. If you are being fooled by this idol you might say, you like things quick and easy, not long and tiresome. In your opinion, too many children are too much inconvenience. You'd rather be working, shopping, or sunbathing by the pool instead of watching your little ones in the pool! For the person who desires conveniences, the height of inconvenience would be a pregnancy! It is not comfortable sharing your body with a baby or having a baby that might be awake at 2 a.m. and need to be fed. It is uncomfortable to nurse the baby and then leak milk all over your clothes. It's not comfortable finding money to raise a child or living on one salary while the other parent stays home, and then arguing about which parent gets to stay home. It is also not comfortable having to start over again with another child. You ask yourself, couldn't we have just had twins and gotten the hassle over with all at once? Parenthood in general, is all too much hassle for Mr.

and Mrs. Spoiled! They grow tired of messing with birth control so it's easier for one of the partners to get snipped. Getting sterilized is all about convenience. If the size of your family is based upon comfort and the need for convenience, you may have been deceived by *the Idol of Convenience* and need to repent of your desires to be selfish and self-seeking.

IDOL #3 The Idol of Materialism

On this altar, we bow down to our possessions and make them more important than our children

Idol #3: It is hard not to have entanglements with this idol if you are an American. We worship our possessions. We want things, we want experiences, and we want to travel and eat in expensive restaurants, and we think we are supposed to have and do all these things! This idol causes people to feel they cannot start their families until they have a certain amount of material possessions: a house, two new cars, a spouse that can afford to not work. Too many children might mean fewer things for our family. On this altar, we dream of a life of new appliances, high-priced vehicles, traveling across the globe, retiring by age fifty-five and unlimited shopping. In our minds, possessions are blessings from God; because He loves us, we deserve these things. When we are being duped by materialism, we believe this! Our allegiance with materialism causes us to want to buy something, anything, just something or go somewhere, anywhere, just go! The only problem is that we've got the idea of blessings in the wrong place, and instead things become what we rely on, count on and worship. God's word says, our prosperity has caused us to forget God (Deuteronomy 8). Instead of using materialism to accomplish great things for God, our self-worth is wrapped up in our zip code. We use our material possessions to bring ourselves comfort and enjoyment. *But the worries of this life, the deceitfulness of wealth and the desires for other things come in and choke the word, making it unfruitful (Mark 4:19).* Are you more in love with things made of plastic, metal, cardboard and fabric instead of being in love with creating a new human being who will last throughout eternity? If you are not conceiving children for fear you can't shop on Amazon, take a trip, or buy a boat, car or RV, or eat out at a nice restaurant then you may have been deceived by *the Idol of Materialism*, and you need to repent.

IDOL #4 The Idol of Money

On this altar, we worship money

Idol #4: In American society, many Christians make family planning decisions based on the fear that children might be too expensive to raise. They often use the excuse that they cannot have too many children because this would mean not being a good steward with their money. They are afraid that God would not provide enough money for their families if they were to have more children than the *socially acceptable* number. Do we consider God's promised supernatural provision for a family? Is it our bank balance we trust in or is it the Lord? Can we trust God to provide for one more child? Often people mask their love for money and their desire for control around Bible verses about stewardship. If you study stewardship, the heart of it is *trust*, not control. Planning is important. *Those who want to get rich fall into temptation and a trap and into many foolish and harmful desires that plunge people into ruin and destruction. For the love of money is a root of all kinds of evil...* (1 Timothy 6:9-10a). If you will not allow God to bring a new family member into your family because you think He will not provide enough money for this child or because you believe it is up to you to decide your financial future, then you may have been deceived by *the Idol of Money* and need to repent.

IDOL #5 The Idol of Medicine and Medical Advice

On this altar we worship doctors' advice, medical advances and medicine

Idol #5: We are blessed in America to have very good medical care, and I believe that God wants us to be thankful for what doctors and modern medicine can offer us. However, most everyone has been taught that if their doctor advises them to do something, it can never be refuted. Doctors admit they don't have all the answers and say *we only "practice" medicine. We have not perfected it yet.* Two doctors can look at the same condition and have opposing opinions, but far too often we trust a doctor's opinion without question. Medical advances promote greater health for all, but just because something is available through modern medicine does not necessarily mean it is suitable for God's people. We have already mentioned that since the medical community made it so that abortion, birth control, and sterilization are all three easily accessible, this does not mean that we should partake. Churchgoers have interpreted *accessibility* as God's endorsement. Yet if your doctor does not know Jesus, his family planning advice might go against God's word. Using a hormone filled pill to prevent conception and or a pill to abort your baby or an operation that takes away your gift of life, might be medically assessable by these doctors, but these things do not line up with what God's word says. These are choices the medical community offers and bids us *to partake* as the serpent also bid Eve to partake of the forbidden fruit.

Please let me reiterate that needing to go to the doctor or listening to a diagnosis does not mean you are deceived or are worshipping the idol of medicine. The sin comes when you entrust the medical establishment with the responsibility to discern right from wrong for your reproductive health. The Word of God gives us a moral code, which must be our guide. God's principles should be measured against every medical procedure to see if they are pure, holy, righteous and for God's people (Philippians 4). If modern medicine overrules what God's word says, then you may have been deceived by *the Idol of Medicine* and need to repent.

IDOL #6 The Idol of Personal Accomplishment or Career Success

On this altar we put our careers, vocation, or ministry callings over our family's priorities

Idol #6: This idol convinces you that *what you need for yourself* is more important than God's plan for your family. We've seen countless people throw away their families for fame in their careers and or fame outside their families. If what you are doing takes all your time, is it the right thing to be doing at this stage in your life? If you decide to not have children or to postpone having children or are not adding children because you are all wrapped up in what *you need to accomplish* for yourself, maybe you need to re-think your priorities, or maybe not. This is something to pray about. This idol gives people *reasons* to either not have a family or to have a limited family so they can do other things they or the culture deems as more important. This is silly. Nearly everything you need to do with your life can be done while raising the greatest blessing of your life, your children. We must recognize that life happens in stages. The career world tells you that if you do not grab success now, after your children are older, you cannot have the same advancements. *Who says?* Do you know how many unhappy female executives there are who did not have families, and are left with career success but have no one to share it with? Proverbs 31 gives us the qualities of the ideal woman. She was a mom but also a very productive person. She was a businesswoman, a nurturer, a counselor, a gifted homemaker, a friend, a servant to others and loved by all. This woman recognized her priority was in her home first, and from the home she excelled. Do you know how many women in the 1990s left corporate America and came home and started home based businesses, that are extremely successful today? Think of the women who started ETSY and PINTREST and other former executives who listened to their hearts, came home to their children, and created businesses that thrived. One of the biggest reasons why ETSY took off, was because it provided a way for home-based businesses to thrive. Some of these ladies' now have such amazing businesses that their grown children are now working with their mothers and will inherit her business someday. This IS accomplishment! Do you know how many episodes of *Shark Tank* are filled with women whose commitment to stay home with their family, sparked a new business idea? Some of these women are both moms and millionaires! If you are making a family planning choice based upon what else you think you need to accomplish, be very careful here. If your chosen vocation is being a mother first, as your most important priority, then that mindset aligns perfectly with what the Word of God says. But if God calls you to do something outside the home, be very careful that this choice does not steal you away from your children's most precious years. No condemnation here, simply weigh out your decision. Women especially don't want more children if that choice means it will be harder to juggle it all. Think about the future. Give God your plan for marriage and family and He will show you how to make it all work. If what you want to do with your career is more important than being open to what He wants to do within your family, you may be deceived by this Idol of Personal Accomplishment and Career Success, and you need to repent.

IDOL #7 The Idol of Age

On this altar, we use age as an excuse

Idol #7: God has made it so that a person's physical body can produce children from as young as eleven years old to at least sixty years old for a female and from twelve years old to over eighty years old for a male. To God, age is not a factor. Yet the worship of our physical *age* persuades people to keep from fulfilling God's family call on their lives. It is not wrong to think about doing certain things at a certain age in your life, however if age is your excuse when God tugs on your heart about having children, then you might be deceived by *the Idol of Age*. When age is used as an excuse in family planning, it is often not a true factor about fertility. Two groups who use age as an extreme factor regarding family planning are the older people and the young people. One group feels they are too young to parent children and have their whole lives, career, and accomplishments ahead of them, so to prevent the children that might interfere they use birth control or get abortions. The other group feels they are too old to parent children. They especially do not want to still be parenting anywhere close to their senior years, so they get sterilized to prevent unwanted children in the later stages of their fertile years. Interestingly, both groups could parent a child if they had to, but since they can use birth control or sterilization, they will not have to. They have created a very logical reason why they should avoid parenting children in this season of their lives. Yet, they will not let age affect their plans about their other life decisions. They will still do every other thing they want to do. I've observed that when age is the excuse, and people say they are too old or too young to birth children, seemingly virile, healthy people suddenly become too immature or too decrepit. They cannot bear the thought of spending their time and efforts parenting and they blame age as the reason. However, maturing people may cease having children because they feel they are too old (and to some, 35 yrs. old, is too old), but they are not planning to spend their lives living in a retirement home anytime soon. With the energy they have left, many have big plans that do not involve the burden of childrearing. The Scriptures do not seem to consider a person's old age as a factor especially when it comes to family planning but if your age is the main reason you use as to why you do not want more children than you might be deceived by *the Idol of Age* and need to repent.

IDOL #8 The Idol of Human Counsel

On this altar, we put faith in human opinions

Idol #8: We may be sincere. Our counselor may be sincere, but all we like sheep, can lead each other astray. When anyone instructs us contrary to the Word of God, then we walk in the counsel of the ungodly and this is sin according to Psalm 1:1. It doesn't matter if the person is a pastor, a doctor, or a counselor, if their advice is unscriptural, it is *tainted* with the worldly ideals of those who do not surrender to God's ways. You need to be very careful and heed God's warning in God's word. Putting your faith in a counselor can be an idol, especially if you pick a counselor who agrees with your reasoning. You can always find someone who agrees with you! *There is a way that seems right to a man, but the end leads to death (Proverbs 16:25).* If you have relied on counsel in family planning and the person does not know God, has no way of knowing the destiny of your family plus did not counsel with lots of scriptures, then you are deceived and are listening to *the Idol of Human Counsel* and you need to repent.

This list is by no means exhaustive, it could go on and on. These are just a few of the idols that have caused millions of couples to miss their opportunity to have the children God wanted to bless them with. It is shamefully sad. These idols trick people, even good people! *The way of the fool seems right in his eyes, but the end leads to death (Proverbs 16:25).*

I know you might be saying to yourself, *"This is far-fetched, there is not really an altar, there are no idols, this is not real, we are not sacrificing anything. This is simply silly."* Oh really? What we do in the spiritual realm is connected to the physical realm.

In the spiritual realm, we make agreements with our idol

WE bow down to birth control and worship a created thing

WE put our faith in what this thing can bring us

In the physical realm we carry out our actions

WE take our idol's pills, patches and shots, we insert its devices, and we kill our seed

THE IDOL'S ALTAR

WE sacrifice our body

WE lay our abilities to reproduce on the surgeon's table (the altar)

WE say, *"Burn it!"* The laser-burns our tubes. The fire consumes our reproductive gift of life!

WE **have sacrificed our body parts** in ultimate allegiance to our idol!

I know what I am talking about, I am from the generation who sacrificed our fertility on the altar of our good reasons!

This is why God warns His people, *"Do not love the world or anything in the world. If anyone loves the world the love of the Father is not in him. For everything in the world, the cravings of the sinful man, the lust of the eyes and the boasting of what he has, does-comes not from the father but from the world"* (I John 2:15-16).

God is clearly speaking to us here: *This is what the LORD says: Stand at the crossroads and look; ask for the ancient paths, ask where the good way is, and walk in it, and you will find rest for your souls. But you said, 'We will not walk in it.' I appointed watchmen over you and said, 'Listen to the sound of the trumpet!' But you said, 'We will not listen!'*

Therefore hear, your nations; you who are witnesses, observe what will happen to them. Hear, you earth: I am bringing disaster on this people, the fruit of their schemes, because they have not listened to My words and have rejected my law (Jeremiah 6:16-19). This IS the Baby Boom Generation's great SIN!

TODAY, GOD SAYS to HIS PEOPLE: REPENT and BIRTH BABIES!

Now is the time! God is speaking to a new generation of young people.

Destroy your agreements with godless idols and decide to follow the Lord in your *sex lives* and marriages to keep you from sacrificing your body parts to an idol. *If you hear His voice, do not harden your heart (Psalm 95:8).*

> **Go back through this chapter and list each place where you see an agreement with a belief, or an attitude motivated by the idols of our culture. If God showed you something about yourself or about your parent's attitudes about family planning, all these lies affect what is happening in your life today.

Follow these steps toward freedom.

*I am going to take you through a prayer. Do not pray these prayers alone, you need someone to pray in agreement with your prayer [minister, priest, church leader, Christian friend, parent, spouse, prayer partner]. *If two on earth agree, it will be done by my Father in Heaven* (Matthew 18:19).

> *He who conceals his sins does not prosper, but whoever confesses and renounces them finds mercy (Proverbs 28:13).*

Pray this prayer to break the agreement with each of the idolatrous lies that govern our culture:

Heavenly Father, Your word says, *we demolish arguments and take captive every thought that sets itself up against the knowledge of God!* Please take captive my thoughts. I now choose to destroy and remove every attitude, every human reason, every allegiance that I have formed with one of these unseen idols, and every agreement I have with these false beliefs. I renounce the false sense of security that I've felt when going along with these lies. I thank you that You grant me Your forgiveness and compassion.

Thankyou Jesus for your sacrifice for me on the cross and for your precious blood which takes away my sins and allows me to ask for Your help. Holy Spirit, thank You for your convicting power and for opening my eyes. You were kind to allow me to see the deception that I have unknowingly participated in, and I thank You for allowing me to see my sin without feeling condemned.

Before your convicting power, I did not feel like I was a person who gravitated towards any idolatrous belief, but after reading this chapter, I now see I am like everyone else who has embraced the lies that surround me. I repent for following my culture. In the Old Testament, the children of Israel did the same thing. Each time when they repented and confessed their sins, and turned from the idols, You gave them a new start, and You restored their lives.

I ask You dear Heavenly Father, to please do the same thing for me. I ask that You forgive me for agreeing with these thoughts (list thoughts God revealed to you) and these attitudes (list any attitude of assumption God revealed to you) that the unseen idol of (name to idol) has led me to. I ask that You forgive me for allowing me to be deceived and for giving my heart's attention away to these false beliefs. I repent for putting myself first, and I repent for trusting in anything other than You. I repent for nearly missing the better part, which is to enjoy the little people You desire to bring into my life. I receive Your blood as my covering over me and my family. I receive it now. Please remove all residue of evil hanging over my life, as the result of my choices, and please fill each area I confess by making me new again. Thank you for Your cleansing power. From this point onward, help me dear God to quickly change these things I have confessed. When wrong thoughts try to come back to me, I ask for the power of Your Holy Spirit to convict me immediately and keep me walking in the correct direction.

I thank You, Jesus, because You do not treat me as my sins deserve or repay me according to my inequities. For as high as the heavens are above the earth, so great is Your love for me, because I fear You. As far as the east is from the west, so far have You removed my transgressions from me. As a father has compassion on his children, so do You, dear Lord Jesus, have compassion on those who fear You; for you know how I was formed, and You remember that I am only dust (Psalm 103:10-14). Thank you, Heavenly Father, for hearing my prayer. I make all these requests in the mighty name of Jesus Christ of Nazareth and by the power of your Holy Spirit. Amen.

> *Who is a God like you, who pardons sin and forgives the transgression of the remnant of his inheritance? You do not stay angry forever but delight to show mercy. You will again have compassion on us; you will tread our sins underfoot and hurl all our iniquities into the depths of the sea*
>
> (Micah 7:18-19).

Christopher's Commentary

According to Wikipedia, "Fear is an emotional response to a perceived threat. It is a basic survival mechanism occurring in response to a specific stimulus, such as pain or the threat of danger."

Listen, guys, the truth is, we are all afraid! So go ahead and admit it. Admitting fear is the key to getting what God has for you. The enemy doesn't want you free. He wants you to live a lie, to be in fear and anxiety over the unknowns in your life, especially in family planning, where fear rules because men are afraid of unwanted pregnancies.

I admit I lived a life of fear before I trusted God with my family size. I could never have told you this before because I didn't see it, but fear was the basis for every decision I made. I used condoms because of fear. I was glad Rachel was on the pill (only for several months), but still, I was glad she was, because of my fears. I was going to get a vasectomy because of the fear of a larger family. Fear ruled me, and I could not get past my fears. Birth control was my idol, although I would have never told you that fear motivated me. I could look to birth control to save me rather than look to the Lord for His ability to prevent pregnancy by not allowing conception.

Once I gave my heart to birth control, I was still not free of fear. Even though I was counting on birth control to keep more children from coming, my concerns were still about how I would pay my mortgage, my children's medical expenses, buy food, travel, etc. My allegiance to birth control did not solve my problem, it kept me from trusting God for the other things in my life.

Because I am the husband, I thought I was supposed to feel *in charge*, but Satan used this against me. He trapped me into thinking I could make it all happen and that it was up to me to balance out the many crises of day-to-day life. True freedom comes with trusting God for everything, but I didn't know I wasn't doing that. I probably trusted Him in some areas, but not completely, and even after God sent me the dream and told me to cancel my vasectomy, I did not automatically trust Him. It was a slow and gradual process. I did not get what God was trying to tell me at first. It took a long time, probably because I was surrounded by men telling me not to trust God because they couldn't do it. These men were not being honest with me. Let's face it, men play games with each other. We want everyone to think we've got it all together. We don't ever want to admit to each other that we are failing too.

Sometimes my wife and I will be on the way home after a random outing of socializing with other couples, and my wife will give me unsolicited information about someone there. Not out of gossip but out of concern, she will tell me, "So and so are not sleeping together." I'm always surprised because the husband usually told me how great things were at home and what a stud, he thought he was. Apparently, one party is unhappy, especially when my wife just prayed with the man's wife about God doing a miracle in their relationship. Things are not what they appear, but a life of fear will do this to people! Fear blinds us and makes us think we have it together, when we don't.

The real reason for this book and my thoughts and insights is that giving your family planning to the Lord is a graduation into what it truly feels like to trust God with your life, because you are giving Him *your bedroom*. This is your domain, the place where you and your wife get real with each other and uncover your true selves and motives.

If fear is shouting at you telling you that you can't trust God, it's a lie, and if you think that your savior is birth control, that is also a lie. Your Heavenly Savior can watch over your life if you will let Him.

> I lift up my eyes to the mountains—where does my help come from? My help comes from the Lord, the maker of heaven and earth. He will not let your foot slip. He who watches over you will not slumber; indeed, he who watches over Israel will neither slumber nor sleep. The LORD watches over you— the LORD is your shade at your right hand; the sun will not harm you by day, nor the moon by night. (Psalm 121:1-4).

He can do his for you. Are you willing? Here's my advice: Be intimate with your wife and trust God for the outcome.

Do not take advantage of each other but fear your God. I am the Lord Your God (Leviticus 25:17)

Christopher Scott

Investigate and Questions

- Read Exodus 20:4, Leviticus 18:21. Do you believe in modern day idols, or do you think this is far-fetched?
- Read Psalms 106:37-38, Isaiah 2:17,18. Do you see a correlation between people's idols and their choices today regarding childbearing?
- Read Romans 1:24-31. How do these verses relate to idolatry and modern people? Do you see how these same verses could be applied to multiple areas in people's sex lives?
- Read Ezekiel 14:6, 20:18, Act 15:20. The Bible says that people who participate in idolatry do so almost as if they were engaging in sexual intercourse with the idol. God calls it defilement. What are your thoughts? Do you think believers today understand God's strong stance against idolatry?
- Ezekiel 14:4,5 the Bible clearly says that God will participate with us. In other words, we will stay in our deception and God will allow it. Knowing this, how does that make you feel?
- In the section where the idols are listed, were there any idols mentioned that you do not think are idols? Which ones and why?
- Which idol on the list clearly stood out to you? Which ones have a hold on our country?
- If you feel comfortable, please discuss or share what the Lord showed you about idols and your own idolatry from this chapter.

Impacting Others

Rachel, thank you so much for writing your book! It has inspired me and given me hope for all the others who may be suffering like I was. I've been giving it out constantly. Can I buy a case from you at a reduced rate? But I didn't write just for that reason; I wanted to share what God has done for me so that my testimony can inspire others to keep trusting Him. Soon we will welcome our 5th child. This pregnancy, like all the others, is a miracle. We started our marriage wanting children very much, yet as the years rolled, I couldn't seem to conceive. I talk now as if it was moments, but Rachel, it was days, weeks, months of horror. At first, I could handle difficult situations, but as my condition stayed, I was always sad. I cried a lot. I couldn't understand why God would put me through this. I love children and work in the medical field, almost exclusively with families and children. My sorrow got so bad I could barely manage to go to work. I thought about having a baby all the time. I couldn't get it off my mind. The first few years, I figured we hadn't conceived because of work schedules and my messed-up cycle, so I didn't go to a specialist. I didn't want to believe there could be a real problem. After two years of not conceiving, we started running tests. At first, they could not figure out my problem but eventually diagnosed me with PCOS. We shared this with our Sunday School class, and people started praying. The hard part was nothing happened for three more years, Rachel three long years! It felt like I could hear my biological clock ticking, and I couldn't believe God had failed me. I wasn't blaming Him, but I married the love of my life, and all I wanted to do was have a baby with him and enjoy a family like everyone else. The pain of being unable to do this affected us and everything else we did together. I was diagnosed with PCOS, so I changed my diet because PCOS can be a hormone-diet-related illness. People kept praying and we kept trying to thank God in all things. I took vitamins and minerals and acupuncture and waited on God. The Bible says in Joel 2:25 that God will give back the years the locust has eaten. One day out of the blue, I must have conceived. I had messed up periods, so I never knew when they would come. So, when I started having nausea, I couldn't believe my eyes when I did my home test. We don't know what made it finally happen except for GOD. One day He allowed what He had not allowed. I couldn't believe it when the doctor confirmed it, except I already knew because of nausea. My son was letting me know that he was there! We were overjoyed and relieved. Now I've had a baby nearly every year since. After this next baby, it will be one baby for every year we were barren. My two specialists say my case is a miracle, the kind they like. I tell them all the time, I thank you for my diagnosis, but God gets the credit on this one, to Him alone be the glory! **Kim, Mother to Zachary, Alex, Mary-Elizabeth, Lauren, and new baby boy in 9 weeks!**

Rachel, I had heard about your book and was so excited to finally get a copy. I finally found a copy at an affordable price through an online dealer. I think it was through one of their used book dealers. It was shipped from somewhere in Europe! I was so grateful to find a copy, though, when I opened it, you had autographed that copy, reading 2 Corinthians 4:8, You are a treasure. I saw your family on a cable show with other large families. My husband and I were beginning to want children, but he had been laid off, and we were afraid about how we might afford a baby. We live in CA, where most of our friends are liberal, and even the Christian couples we know all put children off until they had houses and new cars. Your book planted the seed we needed to seek God's forgiveness for using birth control for so many years and pray for His will in our reproductive life. I've recently been reading it again, as confirmation that I'm doing the right thing, as I struggle through a difficult pregnancy. I've had severe morning sickness since April, losing 35 pounds, and requiring numerous IV fluid treatments. In the past 2 weeks, I've been put on bed rest and medication to stop preterm labor, in hopes of getting me closer to my Feb 2011 due date. Thank you, again, for writing a book about a subject that most people won't touch. It has been such a blessing to my husband Royce and I. God Bless you and your family! **K.N. expectant mommy in California**

A NOTE FROM RACHEL

If you have recently experienced a pregnancy loss, my heart weeps with you and grieves over the child you will never meet on earth. I do love you and want to see this next information in Chapter 9 be a blessing. If you are still grieving, I would prefer that you wait until you feel God has healed your heart before reading it. When you feel *ready*, Chapter 9 will provide answers and prayers for the hope that a future pregnancy will be successful.

Chapter 9

THE DEVIL'S PLAN

Unlocking the Mystery of Miscarriage and Infertility

Congratulations! You are having a baby! The thrill of such words. Perhaps no sweeter thing can be said to you as you enter a time filled with hope and excitement, a time that will change your life forever. With great anticipation, your thoughts arise, "What will my baby look like? I wonder if it is a boy or a girl? Will I be a good parent?" You are delighted at the thought of holding your precious little one in your arms... Then one afternoon, you start to cramp, the pain begins, and then more pain, and then the bleeding starts, and you know your baby is dying. Soon you are sure that your baby is gone. As you do not know the path of the wind, or how the body is formed in a mother's womb, so you cannot understand the work of God, the Maker of all things (Ecclesiastes 11:5).

WHY ARE SO MANY PEOPLE MISCARRYING?

During the twenty-one years I was having my babies, I noticed a tremendous increase in miscarriages. It seemed everywhere I went I would meet couples who had suffered the pain and sorrow of losing a baby. On multiple occasions I had friends who were pregnant and then miscarried and countless times I hugged and cried with a friend who had lost her baby. It's almost as if miscarriages have now become commonplace for a couple to experience at least one, if not multiple miscarriages. For many years, I wondered about what was causing a sharp increase in miscarriages.

A mother's loss is considered a miscarriage if that loss occurs before her twenty-fourth week, however 80%[1] of miscarriages take place before 14 weeks. Early miscarriage often mimics a heavy menstrual cycle, so doctors believe we may not be able to measure the exact rate of miscarriages. Some researchers believe the rate of miscarriage could be as could be as high as 50% of all pregnancies![2]

According to the CDC[3] in 2015 only 65% of pregnancies ended in live births, 18% of pregnancies were aborted and 17% ended in miscarriage.[4] This means only 2/3rd of every pregnancy resulted in a living child who could grow to adulthood. Since 2018, miscarriage rates have been going up 1% a year and now the average rate of measurable miscarriage in 2023, was 17%-31%.[5]

The *average* woman has at least one isolated miscarriage during her fertile years yet increasing numbers of women are having *recurrent miscarriages* which means multiple times they are suffering the loss of their babies. This is very sad for both the woman and her family.

A pregnant woman may unknowingly do something that causes her child to die, such as when the doctor prescribes a drug before he realizes she is pregnant, or a pregnant mother has poor nutrition or suffers from a serious medical condition or has some kind of hormone imbalance. These things do cause miscarriages. A pregnant mother might even have an accident or be exposed to environmental toxins, and these things can cause her pregnancy to end. With proper medical care, some of these causes can be eliminated but what about the other miscarriages?

If simply making a few lifestyle changes was the complete answer, then why do women who live solely on organic foods and in ways that drastically reduce the impact of the environment still experience miscarriages? And why do women who make none of these changes also miscarry? Clearly there must be *another factor* at play, but what is it? All we really know is that the baby dies early in the pregnancy—and the exact cause remains a *mystery*.

In this chapter, I want to take a deeper look at the *mystery of miscarriage* and focus primarily on miscarriages that occur to perfectly healthy women for no apparent reason.

Praise be to the God and Father of our Lord Jesus Christ, the Father of compassion and the God of all comfort who comforts us in all our troubles, so that we can comfort those in any trouble with the comfort we ourselves receive from God (2 Corinthians 1:3-4).

While raising my family, I attended a ladies prayer group that focused on needs in marriages. There were quite a few ladies there and at least a third of the women asked for prayer for either not being able to conceive and for recurrent miscarriages. I looked around the room and wondered, what is going on? What has gone so drastically wrong in my lifetime for this many women to be suffering because they cannot conceive or complete a pregnancy? Could it be possible all these women did something to cause this? If this were true, whatever it was, the believers and those who do not know the Lord, must be doing the same things because both groups of women have been having trouble conceiving and or losing their children to miscarriage for years.

THE SORROW

When women miscarry, it is devastating! There aren't any words. Even when friends and family lend support, there is nothing they can do or say to make it right. The baby is gone, the mother's heart is breaking, and her suffering is catastrophic.

> *So do not fear, for I am with you; do not be dismayed, for I am your God. I will strengthen you and help you; I will uphold you with my righteous right hand (Isaiah 41:10).*

As I've said, over the years I've had several close friends who miscarried. Recently, a young mother I know posted on her blog that she had lost her baby. I read her blog, and I was in tears for her. I know how much she wanted this baby, and her husband and children were devastated. They all wanted this baby so much! Her blog said her daughter had just gone to school and announced how excited she was that her mommy was going to have another baby, but then came home to find out that the baby had died. Why does God allow this? How can a baby be so wanted and yet not allowed to come to earth? Why God? Why does this happen? It seems so unfair!

The process of miscarriage is devastating, and the medical procedures only add to the pain and discomfort. We can only hope and pray during the loss that the mother does not come across a cold-hearted nurse or unsympathetic doctor. Unfortunately, there are a few out there and these heartless meetings only add to the pain the woman is already experiencing.

Answer me when I call to you, my righteous God. Give me relief from my distress; have mercy on me and hear my prayer (Psalm 4:10).

Quite often, mothers are told miscarriage is a *normal part of life*. It's *nature's way* of weeding out a *human* who might have birth defects. We tell mothers to accept that *this is how it is*, or that their miscarriage is *God's will* or that *it's the natural course of nature*. No further explanation is given.

I am worn out from groaning; all night long I flood my bed with weeping and drench my couch with tears. My eyes grow weak with sorrow; they fail because of all my foes. Away from me, all you who do evil, for the Lord has heard my weeping. The Lord has heard my cry for mercy; the Lord accepts my prayer (Psalm 6:6-9).

Accepting this sorrowful situation leaves men and women grieving the loss yet gives no answers and brings no hope. Everyone lives in a deep void with the assumption the grief will eventually fade away, yet the mystery of *Why God, why did my baby die?* destroys their heart and mind.

Have mercy on me, Lord, for I am faint; heal me, for my bones are in agony. My soul is in deep anguish. How long, Lord, how long? Turn, Lord, and deliver me; save me because of your unfailing love (Psalm 6:2-4).

WHAT IS HAPPENING IN MISCARRIAGE

The miracle of birth is an experience of God's love and is *physical proof* that God exists. Through birth, *His love* becomes tangible. We can touch and feel a real child, a beautiful expression of God's love. New life is incredible and demands our attention. It requires us to see and experience the love of God.

The greatest goal of the enemy in miscarriage is to distance a mother from the love of the Father. A female feels love when she connects to the Lord through her womb. The enemy knows that if somehow, he can *steal* this incredible experience from a couple, he can bring discouragement and defeat. If the enemy can stop this connection, he can twist the couple's feelings about God and distance their relationship to Him.

After people miscarry, it is easy to feel separated from God's love because of the intensity of the loss. Our thoughts are trying to find a reason *why this has happened*. Our emotional vulnerability makes it easy to turn away from God's love and align our thoughts with fear. We are vulnerable, upset and feeling let down. We want to *blame someone or something* and we can't help our feelings. Our reality is bleak! Our baby is gone, and the thought that *this could happen again* robs our minds of hope.

Miscarriage is not only painful physically but also very painful emotionally. We're sure we can never go through this again. We want to blame God; He's an easy target. After all, He is God. Why didn't He stop the bleeding and let our baby live? It is easy to believe, it is all *God's fault!* We listen to this mantra in our hearts and then the *mystery* plaques our minds and we don't realize how extremely vulnerable we've become to being bitter against God. *We are missing the child we have never met and are positive that we will never stop wondering about.* Our sorrow becomes an endless cycle. If it happens again and God opens our womb, but then our newly conceived child does not stay in our womb, we do not understand why the enemy is allowed *to steal another baby's life* from our family. More miscarriages mean more sorrow. We grieve and cannot be comforted. We are like...*Rachel weeping for her children and refusing to be comforted, because our children are no more (Jeremiah 31:15, Matthew 2:1).*

We wonder where God is and believe *He cannot possibly love us, or He would not allow us to go through this*. We are afraid to be pregnant for fear of losing another baby. We *feel cursed* and seek to know *why*. Why can't we control our situation? We are mad, sad, hurt, upset, and feel distant from God because we cannot find an answer or a reason to be thankful for our loss.

Trust in the LORD with all your heart and lean not on your own understanding; in all your ways submit to Him, and He will make your paths straight (Proverbs 3:5-6).

Unfortunately, the doctors can't pinpoint the exact problem. They can speculate and offer probable causes, but no one knows *for sure* why a miscarriage occurs or why multiple miscarriages continue to happen.

LORD, IS THERE A SOLUTION?

For many years I did not gain much understanding of the cause of miscarriage. A woman would come into my life, and I would experience her great anticipation only to witness her intense loss. I witnessed the thief coming to *rob, steal and destroy her child's life. Robbing the child of its future* while trying to destroy the parents and planting fear in the mother that her future conceptions might end the same way! It was horrible!

Sometimes I could pray with the mother, and through prayer, a miscarriage was averted. Still, in mothers who had repeated patterns of miscarriage, *something extra* was needed to break the power working against her womb. When a second miscarriage occurred, I'd pray, "What else could we do? Are we not praying often enough or long enough?" I kept petitioning Heaven for answers.

But the Lord is faithful, and He will strengthen and protect you from the evil one. We have confidence in the Lord that you are doing and will continue to do the things we command. May the Lord direct your hearts into God's love and Christ's perseverance (2 Thessalonians 3:3-5).

As I continued to pray, I felt the Lord pointing me to scripture. I had never heard any teaching on miscarriage, but scripture provided a clearer understanding. In every scriptural reference, the Bible referred to *miscarrying wombs* as a punishment for sin, but my immediate reaction was, *this* can't be the cause! These are wonderful people! They are not what I would refer to as *disobedient sinners*. *God also does not bring* guilt and condemnation when people are in pain. This is never God's goal in giving us answers. Romans 8:1 says, *there is no condemnation to those who are in Christ Jesus*, so blaming the victim is not the answer.

As I walked with God over these many years, I have realized that sometimes things happen to us simply because we live in a fallen world. We fall victim to the sins of those around us, the sins of our country, the sins of the medical establishment, the sins of our denomination, sins committed by the leadership at our church, the sins of previous generations, and the sins of our society. Choices by others can affect our lives because of many factors; and maybe this is what is happening in miscarriage.

Who is wise? Let them realize these things. Who is discerning? Let them understand. The ways of the Lord are right; the righteous walk in them, but the rebellious stumble in them (Hosea 14:9).

We are left open and vulnerable when the enemy comes to rob, steal, and destroy. God says, *My people are destroyed from lack of knowledge... (Hosea 4:6).*

I asked the Lord, if your people perish because we lack knowledge, what knowledge are we lacking here? I searched in the Scriptures and the Lord started to give me some answers.

THE ENEMY STEALS BECAUSE HE CAN

You will sow much seed in the field, but you will harvest little because the locusts will devour it (Deuteronomy 28:38).

In miscarriage, the womb is like a vineyard with ripe fruit. The enemy is the thief who comes and steals the fruit of the womb. Why? How do I say this gently? Often it is because he is allowed to. He has been granted *legal, spiritual authority* or *permission* to do so. In the vast unseen world, *permission to take this life* has been granted, and the enemy wastes no time going after our precious seed.

The womb is today's spiritual battlefield. The enemy would rather kill our children at the beginning than mess with them later.

As in the days of Moses and the days of Jesus, this day, this week, this year are the most strategic times in history to be birthing children. The enemy knows that ancient prophecy is being fulfilled every day, and he knows *whose seed these children are connected to*, and he knows the final events of history are coming forth. He seeks to snuff out the life of this emerging end-time generation in every way he can. If the life is ten days, four weeks, 12 weeks past conception or later, it is *open season on children* as far as the enemy is concerned.

Maybe as God's people, we should stop accepting that miscarriage *just happens* and get out our spy glasses to see if there is anything that could be the cause of such suffering. I want an answer, don't you? The Scriptures repeat the theme that when we love the Lord and follow His commands, *we will be blessed*, and if we disobey His commandments, *we will fall under His judgment*. Our choices determine whether we see life or death, blessings or curses in each area. The principle of blessings and curses is repeated throughout the Bible to help unravel the *mystery of hidden sin* and its consequences. *...I have set before you life and death,* *blessings and curses. Now choose life that you and your children may live* (Deuteronomy 30:19).

When people choose life, they choose God; when they choose death, they choose the ways of the evil one. God wants us to *choose life* for the lives of our unborn children so that we can receive all God has for us. He wants us to *avoid death* because *death* always leads us farther away from Him. Since far too many babies are dying, we must find out what is causing this to happen.

Could there be a spiritual reason for this physical misfortune? Miscarriage has always been with us but not at the rate it is today. If we analyze the choices we are making we may see what we are doing that might be causing all the premature deaths to our unborn infants through miscarriage.

Clue #1 THE BABY BOOM GENERATION (born 1944-1961), WAS THE FIRST GENERATION TO SUCCESSFULLY LIMIT THEIR FAMILY SIZE ON A BIG SCALE (fertile 1960-2010)

As I've already covered in much detail in previous chapters, after America won World War 2, those who suffered through the war and the Great Depression were now in their early twenties and celebrated America's victory by getting married and starting a family. America popularized the phrase, *"let the good times roll"* by throwing the hardships of yesteryear behind and reaching for the *good life*. But once these children grew up, they did not want to be like their mothers, who had six children crammed into a three-bedroom home in suburbia. When it was the Baby Boomer's turn, the women believed the *good life* would be even better with fewer mouths to feed. These same women were out to prove something to themselves, and to the men. They wanted *equality* and to achieve this, it meant *less babies* in favor of a career. Baby Boomers ran from everything traditional and reached to redefine themselves. The *good life* was in this generation's grasp, and as one pop song put it, *"Nothing's going to stop us now!"* The desire for success gave birth to the need to control every area of life, and for the women, their reproductive lives were pivotal to their success. Failure meant a woman might not get another opportunity to get what she wanted. Even in Christian circles, the pressure to conform was tremendous!

You are not to do as we do here today, everyone doing as they see fit, since you have not yet reached the resting place and the inheritance that the Lord your God is giving you (Deuteronomy 12:8-9).

Sixty-five years ago, no one considered the effects these actions might have on their future lives or on the lives of their children or grandchildren's generation. Yet *fast forward to today: a* generation later, we see our children are infertile and miscarrying at alarming rates!

In some families, a noted family pattern exists. Every female in the family has some reproductive failure. Either the women have trouble birthing, or have trouble with their periods, or all the females in the family get breast cancer or they all need a premature hysterectomy. Often the problem occurs at or about the same age as the same problem happened to a mother, aunt, or grandmother.

What causes this? Doctors say it is genes because poor health can be passed on at birth. One generation's genes can be affected by the previous generation's actions. If a woman smoked or drank or was a crack mom during her pregnancy, her actions can cause her child to suffer poor health.

How about when the parents of the person struggling with infertility used artificial contraceptives, got sterilized, or had abortions? Could these actions also affect the fertility of the next generation? I started asking God this. Could this be the *mysterious cause* of so many people struggle with infertility and miscarriages? As one generation sows the seed, does the next generation reap the sorrow?

No wonder today's generation is struggling. They are trying to reproduce after the most significant birth control-using generation in history!

Plus, we are still a nation of intense birth control users! People still want *liberty* from birth, *freedom* from sex without consequences, and the *ability* to do *whatever they want* with their fertility and sexuality.

Perhaps you are one of the innocent daughters with an unexpected fertility issue. *You've tried hard to have a baby, and for unknown reasons, you either cannot conceive or you miscarry.* Sweet friend, I do not claim to have all the answers, but I believe the Lord is revealing answers concerning this mystery. Maybe it is not as much of a mystery as we think. Most people my age would say that birth control is nothing more than one of the many choices that needs to be made, and using it is certainly not a sin! We are not likely to see *repentance* from a group that believes birth control is a "right" and believes it is OK with God. The Baby Boomer's generational *desire for control* appears to be one way the enemy gained *legal permission in the spiritual realm to steal* the fruit of their children's wombs. *I will prevent conception* (Hosea 9:11), *punishing the children for the sins of their parents to the third and fourth generation of those who hate Me (Exodus 20:5)*. The Boomer's children would be second generation, and their grandchildren would be third generation, and God says He punishes people till the fourth generation for hating His ways. Wow!

Clue#2 LIVING IN A CULTURE OF DEATH

If we could look at factors that make up most people's circumstances, we might see a *pattern of death* chosen innocently. If you drink the water, it is semi-poisoned. If you go in for a routine gynecological exam, you could leave with a *birth control pill* to regulate your hormones. If you have unusual bleeding, an IUD is inserted. If you had sonograms while in utero, it could have radiated your female eggs. If you eat normal food, it's full of far too many chemicals and artificial hormones, and the increasing need for vaccines and drugs for other health-related issues expose you to toxic metals. All these things can affect your fertility. Everywhere you turn, you can potentially jeopardize your reproductive future.

If you are under 35 yrs. old consider this: the entire time you have been on this planet, you have been raised in a *culture of death*. Abortion was legalized before you were born! Your parents could have legally killed you. Your mother could have prevented your birth by using the *birth control pill, patch, shot, IUD etc*. Your parents probably practiced birth control, and more than likely limited the number of siblings you do have. You may have siblings that were aborted. Even if your parents were believers, they might not have been taught that God cares about this part of their marriage, so they went along with the *pro-choice death culture* accepted by nearly everyone around them.

As a person born at the tail end of the Baby Boomer generation myself, it's clear that my generation messed up. Our fertility choices were incorrect, and we've passed on a world of contamination and *a culture of death* to our children and grandchildren. It's all our fault!

Did Baby Boomers birth control= Gen X and Gen Y miscarriage and infertility?

The Bible tells us the wages of sin is *death in Romans 3:23*. When choice violates God's principles, we suffer loss. We can now see a clear pattern for why so many babies are dying in miscarriage.

Miscarrying wombs are identified in Hosea and in Deuteronomy as the result of God's judgement.

The Baby Boomers set the stage for the *deaths* we are experiencing today. When Baby Boomers embraced the birth control culture and limited their offspring, *life* disappeared from our American culture and *death* took over. In 1960 when *the birth control pill* came out, the mothers said, **"No to birth"** and **"Yes to control."** It was the **mothers** who *led society* away from *producing life* toward embracing *choice*, and *choice* led them to accept *death* to their children. Once our society became trapped in a death culture, many babies died!

What came first: legalized abortion or the birth control pill?

It wasn't until 13 years after the birth control pill was accepted into society and accepted by church-going people. Then the enemy wasted no time to getting abortion legalized and they accepted *death to their infants* in the name of *female freedom of choice!* The women led this revolt, and their daughters who followed are now suffering. Today the *wombs of society* are under the *umbrella of death!* This was granted by the actions of a few but solidified by the silence of the majority.

Years before 1973, the banner over America was life, reproduction, and families. After 1973 the banner over America became choice, control, and reproductive freedom and *it all leads to death*. Even after Roe vs. Wade was turned back over to the states in 2022, the rate of daily abortions did not go down. We are still aborting over 4000 babies per day.[6] In 2023 the country had the highest rate of abortion in ten years!

Birth control users want abortion! They might say they are *pro-life*, but their actions show they are *pro- choice*. Even if they don't like the idea of abortion, they still tolerate it because *when birth control fails* the next choice is *death to the baby* and the only way to get rid of a birth control failure is to kill the precious child by abortion.

The Baby Boom generation is a birth control generation.

THE DEVIL'S PLAN

We allowed abortion to become a legal practice, yoking the American society to a satanic act and the daily shedding of innocent blood! God help us!

> 95% of abortions today are performed as a means of birth control
> 1% abort because of rape and incest
> 1% abort because of fetal abnormalities
> 3% abort due to a mother's health problems
> 25% of mothers choose abortion to postpone childbearing
> 7.9% want no more children, therefore aborting the *surprise baby*
> 21.3% abort because they can't afford a baby
> 10.8% abort because a baby will disrupt their education or job
> 14.1% abort because their partner does not want the child
> 12.2% claim to be too young, and their parent objects
> 3.3% abort for a risk to the baby's health
> 2.1% abort for reasons not mentioned[7]

Once we justify our reasons for why abortion is best for us it far outweighs the reasons to keep our children. If you are *trying to conceive* underneath this *evil umbrella of death* and are unsuccessful, it may be because you are suffering *the fall out* of a culture that once said **yes to life** but now **agrees with death**. This agreement causes innocent people who want children, to suffer loss.

Clue#3 WHEN MINISTERS MAKE FUN OR MAKE NO MENTION

*(*I prayed for a very long time before adding this part. My intention is never to be dishonorable or disrespectful of people in ministry. I would be grieved if this is how this information was perceived. The longer I went over this point in my mind and prayed about it, I felt I would be unjust if I did not state the obvious because these things can be corrected. If I ignore what is staring us in the face, we will not progress as a body of believers. The behavior of Protestant pastors these past sixty-five years is significant, and their position on using birth control is important).*

I've already stated that the idea that *children are a blessing but please do not have too many* is the "unspoken mantra" of the Protestant denominational churches. I've sat in many-a-church-sermon where the pastor joked about being glad that his two children were now grown and out of the house because teens are so much trouble or I've listened to a young pastor with two small children, state that he and his wife were happy to be finished with their family. I've even heard a minister joke about a recent pregnancy scare that prompted him to race down to the vasectomy clinic. People laugh, ha, ha, ha, but it's reinforcing from the church leaders the idea that unplanned children are not acceptable!

I also love hearing wonderful teachings by some of the women speakers, however I *cringe* when I hear a woman start off her teaching by making fun of her fertility. One speaker refers to her choice to end her fertility by saying *"It is finished!"* while making an X gesture over her womb, meaning her fertility is done, it is complete she says. It is over, and never again! The crowd breaks into laughter. I'm not sure if *"it is finished"* means they did something permanent, but since she usually tells the crowd that her third child was an unplanned surprise, she leads us to believe they got sterilized to make it permanent. Another female speaker shares how her husband is from a very large family and jokes about her in-laws not having a TV. She then shares that she and her husband were smart and limited themselves to a very small family, and yes, people do laugh. These two ladies are making what they perceive to be *innocent remarks* to get the crowd going, but when the female influencers are reinforcing the idea that it is *unpleasant* to have more than the acceptable number of children or that an accidental child means fertility is a burden, what are they really saying? The younger women who look to these older leader's wisdom do not stand a chance at hearing the truth about their precious gift of fertility if the speakers communicate the opposite. As our spiritual elders and advisors have increasingly become not *open to life all the time*, their words and statements place a banner in the heavenlies that says, "Anything that gives the parents a choice is practiced here!" If there is a pro-choice agreement that *fertility is not welcomed* here from the men and women who speak to us, it makes it harder to fight against the *outside culture of death* that also wants couples to end their fertility.

Infertility, miscarriages, birth control, vasectomies, and tubal ligations are the Christian world's silent subjects. I've been attending church all my life and I think I could count on one hand the number of times I've ever heard a pastor ask *infertile couples* to please come forward for prayer or ask anyone who has recently suffered a miscarriage to also come forward. Perhaps the ministers believe it would be too embarrassing and maybe it would be, but by ignoring those suffering, ministers fail to point to *Jesus* as the one who can heal these conditions. I've also noticed when speakers do pray for healing, it is always things other than infertility. Why? Surely God wants to heal miscarriages and infertility, yet it is never if ever, a thing we pray for.

I believe we don't see these conditions prayed for because miscarriages and infertility do not affect the majority. Somehow praying for the women in the crowd who would like to have babies gets lost in the shuffle. Thousands are hurting, but male clergy don't know what to do, so they do nothing!

Hurting people need our help, but we cannot get them set free if we don't connect the actions to the effect. Americans have been quietly aborting babies for more than fifty years while justifying the use of birth control and sterilization. What did we think would happen after fifty plus years of *agreeing* with *death*? Our complacency has cost us the fruit of the womb!

Clue #4 FIGURE OUT WHERE YOU STAND BY ASSESSING YOUR CHOICES

Are your choices full of life, or do they err on the side of death? Look carefully because once *death* gains control, *death* will try hard to keep you in its pit! To survive, we must do our best to *agree with life* as much as possible. It is not easy living in a culture that aligns itself with death. In the food we eat, the air we breathe, the music we listen to and the shows we watch, we are constantly absorbing what we read and hear. When death is all around us, we must resist! Again, I want us to be very clear about what we are dealing with. It is two separate realms, one is *physical*, and the other is *spiritual*. Seemingly innocent choices in one realm will automatically affect the other realm.

I've provided a list of potential areas to watch out for. These areas could unknowingly align us with death. Please read through this list and if anything jumps out at you, make a note of it. I've provided prayers of repentance at the end of this chapter. Let the Holy Spirit's voice speak to you. I believe He will show you some new things.

If my people, who are called by My name, will humble themselves and pray and seek My face and turn from their wicked ways, then I will hear from heaven, and I will forgive their sin and will heal their land (2 Chronicles 7:14).

And that you may love the Lord your God, listen to His voice, and hold fast to Him. For the Lord is your life, and He will give you many years in the land (Deuteronomy 30:20a).

POSSIBLE CAUSES OF MISCARRIAGE, DUE TO ALIGNING WITH THE CULTURE OF DEATH

1. Could leaving God's ways and adapting to the ways of society cause a miscarriage? Yes.

Nearly all believers today do not allow God to plan their families. Instead, we have embraced the family planning practices of modern America. God's people use the *same pills*, see the *same doctors*, and have the *same operations* as non-believing counterparts. Why should we expect that just because we are "Christian" that we are favored or have special privileges? According to Scripture, there have been times when women miscarry more often than at other times. Miscarriages were more prevalent at times when God's people turned from God and embraced the customs and cultural practices of the nations around them. Sounds like Christian America right now! The Bible says, *"Come out and be separate!"* But are we separate? We are suffering with the same sorrows as everyone else. Why? It is because we have tied God's hands, and His judgement for these family planning sins follows the **Biblical pattern of history.**

Miscarriage: *I will give them miscarrying wombs and dry breasts (Hosea 9:14).*

Infertility: *I will prevent conception (Hosea 9:11).*

Abortion: *They will bring their children to the slayer (Hosea 9:13).*

*If you do not obey, the **fruit** of your **womb** will be cursed (Deuteronomy 28: 4,18).*

Scripture states that God allows death to infants, and miscarriages are the result of the *sins of God's people*. They are both a *punishment and a warning* to repent and come back to His ways. What that looks like today would be to repent, throw away our gadgets and pills, and return to God's plan. The patterns of miscarriage that we are seeing today are at epidemic proportions, and many people are suffering because they did what they thought was right in their own eyes, instead of obeying God. When God's people live in ignorance of His ways or resist God's plan, they are left *vulnerable and open to the enemy* to take their precious children from them.

THE DEVIL'S PLAN

But if you do not listen and carry out these commands, I will bring upon you sudden terror (fear and phobias), wasting diseases (cancer, aids, auto-immune, etc.) and fever that will destroy your sight (blindness) and drain away your life (sexually transmitted diseases). You will plant seed in vain because your enemy (devil) will eat it (miscarriage) (Leviticus 26:14).

2. Could choosing death over life instead of choosing life over death cause a miscarriage? Yes.

When Moses told the Children of Israel, "Now choose life!" He was telling them that to be blessed by God, that this would have to be a *choice*. God's people must *choose life over death* in their words, or actions if they want to be blessed.

Moses made it clear: When you *choose life*, you choose God and His blessings. When you *choose death*, you choose the devil and his consequences. God wants us to *choose life* not only for our own lives but also for the *lives* of our *unborn children*. He wants us to avoid choosing death, at all costs, because death always leads us to the path of destruction and takes our lives further away from Him.

Who is wise? He will realize these things. Who is discerning? He will understand them. The ways of the Lord are right. The righteous walk in them but the rebellious stumble in them (Hosea 14:9).

Think about the way in which we have been deceived. We can't help that we've been born in an era where many things come to us *instantly*. From information on the internet, to remote controls, to fast food, to instant hot, to microwaves, to copy machines, to on-off switches and so much more. We get impatient when we can't have things immediately. We are so spoiled. We have been conditioned to want everything to serve us and be at our immediate disposal whenever we want.

With our fertility, the medical community offers us instant reproductive control. We take *a pill*, and we control our body's outcome. With a birth control pill, we don't get an unwanted baby. With an abortion pill, we get rid of our baby. We've grown accustomed to treating our reproductive systems the way we treat everything else. Our body is there *to serve us* and what we want.

We want our reproductive bodies to operate sort of how a faucet operates. We get married, but don't want a child from our sex, at least not yet, so we turn our fertility switch *off* by taking a pill. Later, we are ready for a baby, so we go *off the pill*, hoping to switch our baby-making-switch *back on*. If we are incredibly blessed, we get the baby we want. Then, we go back on the pill to switch our baby-making-switch *off* again. This idea of instant fertility blatantly goes against God's design, but we've become conditioned to believe our bodies should behave for us. We expect our reproductive organs to serve our needs because this is what we do in our culture. When our body fights back and bleeds or bloats, miscarries or suffers infertility or God-forbid we suffer cancer of our reproductive glands we cannot figure out why.

In the *world of instant everything*, we find it hard to understand why our bodies don't work as efficiently and carefree as we've been told from the literature, but it doesn't work that way, and the medical community does not tell us the truth. Often, they seem to be working for the other side, *the side of death*. They tell us with a *pill, patch, shot, or operation*, our physical bodies will cooperate with the lifestyle we want and guarantee us our reproductive glands will cooperate. Sometimes after our next round of the pill, patch, IUD or shot, we do get pregnant again but this time we miscarry this baby. Often, we miscarry multiple times! Then we go to our doctor seeking an answer, and instead we get excuses. The doctor tells us maybe you have a hormone imbalance, a compromised fetus, or scar tissue on your uterine wall, etc. but keep trying! We are not given solutions, simply excuses.

I am telling you today, you cannot choose death and expect life! All these *pills and gadgets* either *abort* babies, *prevent* babies, *cause* miscarriages, or *cause* infertility and all of them *promote* death!

When Moses told the Children of Israel, *"Now choose life,"* he was saying to be blessed by God, you must **choose** life! *Choosing life* means always choosing it and being open to its possibilities. It is always in our best health interest to keep things *natural* because this will keep our *baby-making* switch always *on*.

If you've already treated your body unnaturally, throw away your pills, gadgets, substances, etc., these things are bringing death to your door. This is your life and the life of your family we are talking about here!

Come to me, all you who are weary and burdened, and I will give you rest. Take my yoke upon you and learn from me, for I am gentle and humble in heart, and you will find rest for your souls. For my yoke is easy and my burden is light (Matthew 11:28-30).

Also, refrain from speaking casually against your body. Don't say, "I won't get pregnant, I always miscarry." Don't declare over your potential pregnancy, *I don't want to go through this again, I'm not sure I want another child*. The *spirit of death* has wings. Remember, we live in both a physical realm and a spiritual realm. In the spirit realm, your words could be *legal ground* the accuser could use against you to take your baby's life.

3. Could a previous abortion cause a miscarriage? Yes.

The Lord hates... hands that shed innocent blood" (Proverbs 6:16–17).

I will give you over to bloodshed, and it will pursue you (Ezekiel 35:6).

Before I formed you in the womb, I knew you. Before you were born, I set you apart. Do not be afraid, for I am with you, declares the Lord (Jeremiah 1:5,8).

Women who have had abortions are plagued with sorrow that many never seem to get over. As time passes, the mother will think about the day her baby would have been born and can be haunted by this thought. Deep inside she knows she ended a life that was not hers and her emotions cause her to suffer in silence. As a result, she can have severe emotional swings, hormonal disturbances, become depressed, lack creativity and develop a no-care attitude.

And for your lifeblood, I will surely demand an accounting. I will demand an accounting from every animal. And from each human being, too, I will demand an accounting for the life of another human being (Genesis 9:5).

Abortions cause physical scars. A woman's womb, tubes and cervix suffer scar tissue as the result of the abortion plus the abortion procedure brings the *spirit of murder into her life*. The sorrow of abortion can cause *death* to her self-esteem, *death* to her joy for living, *death* to her finances, *death* to her creativity, and *death* in any other area that was previously full of life. *Abortion* breaks the commandment, *thou shalt not murder* (Exodus 20:13) and the Bible says the baby's blood *cries out from the ground* begging for vindication (Genesis 4:10-11).

With abortion, the *ground* would be the mother's womb. *The blood cries out* to appease the baby's death. In the spirit world, since the woman has killed her child, unless she repents, this could be *legal ground* the accuser could use to take the next baby's life. Repentance can bring deliverance of this *death cloud* and restore the woman to wholeness so she can conceive again. If you have not done so already, repent for your abortion, allow the blood of Jesus to wash over you. He will set you free!

Do this so that innocent blood will not be shed in your land, which the Lord your God is giving you as your inheritance, and so that you will not be guilty of bloodshed (Deuteronomy 19:10).

4. Could having sex outside of marriage cause a miscarriage? Yes.

There is a well-known story in 2 Samuel 11 and 12 about how King David lusted after another man's wife and had sex with her outside of marriage. She became pregnant with King David's child and shortly after the baby was born, God caused the newborn to become very ill. Their baby dies as a punishment for having sex outside of marriage, for plotting to get the woman's husband killed, and for committing adultery. This is not a miscarriage, but death to the child did come as a result of their sin.

During the Baby Boomer's sexual revolution, one-night stands were all the rage. *The pill* and *sterilization* brought freedom from pregnancy and nearly every couple slept together on their *very first date!* Keeping one's virginity was rarer in the 1970s and 1980s than it is now, people thought nothing of jumping into bed with the person they just met. It was not until the deadly AIDS epidemic erupted in the late 1980s that this careless behavior slowed down. It was rumored that people who had contracted AIDS were out trying to infect more people. Whether true or an urban legend, finally the thought of getting AIDS scared people enough to think before they had sex with a stranger.

God never meant for people to have sex outside marriage. It brings *death* to their virginity, *death* to intimacy, *death* to trust, and *death* to the *life* of the relationship. Sleeping with or having slept with multiple partners, opens a door in both the physical realm and the spirit realm. Every sexual partner you've ever embraced has left a spiritual mark on your soul. You've take-in their soulish *crud* when you joined your body with theirs. In your involvement with them, you have also embraced everyone and everything your partner received from their other lovers.

If you are a virgin and sleep with one person, if that person had slept with another person before you, you will have been exposed to two other people's souls. If a person sleeps with three people and those three people have also slept with three other people, you expose yourself to twelve people's souls and spirits. This can have profound *spiritual consequences*. Everything they've embraced is now a part of you.

Marriage should be honored by all, and the marriage bed kept pure, for God will judge the adulterer and all the sexually immoral (Hebrews 13:4).

Do you not know that the wicked will not inherit the Kingdom of God? Do not be deceived: neither the sexually immoral nor idolaters nor adulterers...will inherit the kingdom of God (1 Corinthians 6:9-10).

You shall not commit adultery (Exodus 20:14).

If a man commits adultery with another man's wife—with the wife of his neighbor—both the adulterer and the adulteress are to be put to death (Leviticus 20:10).

If you have *committed adultery* at any time in your life, in the physical realm the *fruit of your womb* may be linked to *death*. In the spirit realm, if you broke faith with your partner, this could be *legal ground* the accuser uses against you to take either your fertility or your baby's life. Repent for having premarital sex and seek repentance. The accuser will be silenced, and the blood of Jesus will set you free!

You need to persevere so that when you have done the will of God, you will receive what He has promised (Hebrews 10:36).

5. Could a Generational Curse Cause a Miscarriage? Yes.

Yes, we've already talked about the curse the Baby Boom generation has brought on their offspring. The Bible says the Lord will bless a thousand generations of those who love Him (Exodus 20:6), but the sins of the fathers will be passed down to the children of the fourth generation of those who do not love Him (Exodus 20:5).

God is talking about a real curse. Since we've already talked about this in other parts of this book and in this chapter, we know that when people cannot have children, the *death* in this area may be coming from a previous generation's *unrepentant* sin. God's holiness requires complete repentance to make a person whole again. Remember, the goal of the enemy is *to stop God's people from producing Godly heirs* for the Kingdom of God. The enemy is looking for every opening to squeeze through so he can bring destruction and *take life* away from people, and especially God's people.

Sometimes, it is easy to recognize a curse at work. Two virgins get married, neither have ever had an abortion or done anything conscious against their fertility, yet they cannot conceive or suffer a miscarriage, even when their health is good. They could spend years in sadness wondering why God will not give them children, or recognize they are operating *under a curse.*

Please realize this is not hokey, the Bible tells us *curses are real* and they affect the lives of people who love God every day! When Jesus set us "free from the curse," (Galatians 3:13) it meant through the awesome power of the blood of Jesus, these curses have been broken! But we must repent first and then ask for restoration before our lives can change. *Whatever is bound on earth will be bound in Heaven; whatever is loosed on earth will be loosed in Heaven (Matthew 16:19).*

Another reason why there could be a generational curse at work could be because the previous generations did other evil things besides cutting off one's seed. Psalm 109 is a righteous man's plea to God to ask *Him to judge his unrighteous accusers, who are deceitful and have lying tongues.* He asks God to bring a curse on the children of the unrighteous, which would be the evil man's descendants, and to harm them in these areas:

1. May the unrighteous man's children be wandering beggars and lose their homes [Some families can never keep a home].
2. May a creditor seize their assets [Some families stay in constant debt].
3. May he lose the fruits of his labors [Some men cannot keep a job or get a job].
4. May no one be kind to him or help him [Some people are rarely shown mercy].
5. May his descendants be cut off and not remembered [**miscarriage**, premature death, early adult death].
6. May the parent's sins be remembered before the Lord so that God will *cut off the memory* of them on the earth [Curse over the people to see God wipe out their entire bloodline forever].

What if you or your spouse are one of these cursed people's descendants? You might never know this curse could be affecting your ability to either conceive or keep your child.

We are not responsible for the actions of a previous generation, but their actions could be affecting our lives, as already illustrated by the choices of the Baby Boom generation. If infertility is plaguing you and you see a family pattern of miscarriage, infertility, and reproductive disorders, it may be because of unrepentant sin in your family. If there is a pattern, make note of it and repent for your ancestors, and anything else they might have ignorantly done against their fertility.

Do not be afraid, for I am with you; I will bring your children from the east and gather you from the west (Isaiah 43:5).

6. Can Fear related to Childbearing cause a Miscarriage? Yes.

Fear is a huge problem in many believers' lives. Miscarriages may be the result of fear causing a woman to cast her fruit before its time. (Malachi 3:11). In other words, a woman could be allowing herself to emotionally and physically let go of the fruit of her womb because of her agreement with fear.

Do you have fears related to family planning? Fear can cause more trouble than people can imagine because people are often not in touch with their fear. Fear is a strong enemy that *steals from us* because we give into fear. When we walk in fear we are not walking in the light of God (1 John 1:5). When we give ourselves to shadows and innuendos and what-ifs we can become consumed with fears that control and rob us of God's peace. If we are robbed of God's peace, then the enemy may rob from us in other areas such as stealing the life of our children. In the spirit world, if you are walking in fearful thoughts or making fearful statements this could be *legal ground* the accuser uses against you to take your baby's life. Ask God to reveal fear that you may not even realize you have. Repent and receive *life*.

Fear of the Future:

"What kind of parent will I be? Can I handle another baby?"

"What if my other child rejects this baby? Can we afford this child?"

"What will my family and friends think?"

"Does my husband or my wife want this baby?" In the case of either spouse not wanting the child, emotional or verbal rejection of the seed could cause the female body to desire to empty itself.

Fear of Finances:

"How can we afford another child?" If the man rejects his seed because of fear of the future or fears about providing, it can also cause miscarriage.

Fear of not being able to be Good Parents:

"What if I am not being a good parent?"

"How will I give myself to another child? I am already stressed as it is." We reject the child inside when we speak about what we fear.

Fear of Timing:

"I wish this were happening next year. I am not ready for this baby." Are we giving fear permission by *placing our trust* only in the future that we can see? It is easy to be apprehensive about children and the process of birth, but we must watch our words because death always looks for a door. *I asked the Lord, and He answered me, and He delivered me from all my fears. Those who look to Him are radiant; their faces are never covered with shame (Psalm 34:4-5).*

7. Could the Words a Person Speaks cause a Miscarriage? Possibly, our words can have wings.

The power of life and death are in the tongue (Proverbs 18:21). The words we speak are very powerful and could be the reason your womb is casting its seed before its time. Be careful little mouths what you say...about the future, about being a good parent...about the timing of a new baby.

God *created life* with His words. People can *speak death* or *hold on to life* with their words. None of us realize the awesome power in the words we say, but words do matter! We can live or die based on the things that come out of our mouths. I don't know why certain people can speak anything they like, and it doesn't seem to matter; while others speak something negative, and it comes true. *Why is that?* I don't know, but if miscarriages occur, you must be careful in *every area* where the enemy may seek access. Even the most casual statement could give wings to fear, and if fear is the one who gains legal ground in your life, then fear will waste no time stealing your seed. Your casual words gave it permission. When we walk in *fear*, we are *not* walking in the light of God (1 John 1:5). When we empower *fear*, our words take on new power. The Bible says our body will cast its fruit before its time, emptying itself of our precious seed (Malachi 3:11).

This truth does apply to fertility. Check yourself to see if you are proclaiming a negative destiny over your family. Are you speaking *words of life* and healing words, or are you *speaking death* over yourself?

"I always miscarry."

"My husband is afraid that he might lose me if I get pregnant."

"I have trouble having children."

"I cannot seem to get pregnant."

"I do not know how we could afford another child."

"I do not think I could handle another baby."

These types of words throw negative comments into the spiritual atmosphere. If we keep saying, "*I always miscarry,*" then this will be what we do. There is a good chance that what we speak will come true because we are speaking it into existence and giving the enemy *permission* to carry out our words. When words of *death* are spoken in more significant numbers than words of *life*, repent. Ask God to help you speak *life*.

The Lord is my light and my salvation– whom shall, I fear? The Lord is the stronghold of my life– of whom shall I be afraid? (Psalm 27:1).

8. Could Feelings of Rejection Cause a Miscarriage? Yes.

In Chapter 7, I already discussed how using birth control can bring rejection into a marital relationship. *Rejection* is a powerful force and, in a sense, could be seen as a form of *death* because it is saying to that person: *"I reject you! I do not want you! I do not like you! I wish you were not here! Go away!*

Rejection brings pain and sorrow. The goal of rejection is to rob and steal emotional worth from a person. Many wounded and rejected people feel like it would be best if they had never been born. Everyone desires to be loved and to feel loved and those who feel rejected and wounded often desire to leave the person who is rejecting them, because *love* brings *life* and *rejection* brings *death*. If you have been rejected in the past, you may have *emotional death* hanging over you.

You may also be rejecting others to try to get back at those who harmed you. Without realizing it, you may be sending death out toward others. This could harm your ability to *give life* or to *receive life*.

The goal of rejection is to rob and steal emotional worth from a person. Love brings *life*, but rejecting others is a message of *death*. This could harm your ability to give *life* or to receive *life*. If you have rejection issues, you must ask God to help you forgive those who hurt you. Let go of all bitterness and ask for love.

Be merciful, just as your Father is merciful (James 2:13).

Therefore, confess your sins to each other and pray for each other so that you may be healed... (James 5:16).

And we know that in all things God works for the good of those who love him, who have been called according to his purpose (Romans 8:28).

9. Could Dishonoring a Parent Cause a Miscarriage? Yes.

Our parents are the first people we call *family* and even though we do not get to choose them, God commands us to *"Honor your Father and Mother so that you may live a long and blessed life" (Exodus 20:12)*. Even if your life with them was toxic and they do not deserve respect, God literally says that if you give them honor, God will show you honor. Not everyone has the best parents and a strained relationship with a parent might bring anger, resentment, or a desire to get back at them, but these strong emotions create poor relationships. Since our parents were our *former family*, this could open us up to having problems trying to *create our own family*. Think about it. The one who seeks to destroy is looking for any reason to steal the life of your child through miscarriage. If your relationship with Mom or Dad is strained, ask God for forgiveness and ask to help you be loving toward them. It is ok if you need to set boundaries, but do not cut them off. Your repentance for any hurt feelings can restore your abilities to keep the life of your unborn child and bring great blessing when you turn your parent into a grandparent. *My grace is sufficient for you, for My power is made perfect in weakness (2 Corinthians 12:9).*

10. Could Making Fun of the Things of God cause a Miscarriage or Infertility? Perhaps, it did not help David's wife, Michael.

One female in the Bible made fun of the things of God and was cursed with barrenness for the rest of her life. Saul's daughter Michael, who was married to David, ridiculed him for worshipping the Lord. The scriptures say, *God shut her womb* and never allowed her to conceive again.

In a modern-day setting, it is easy to criticize a pastor, priest or religious teacher. Scripturally we are allowed to disagree, but we must be very careful that we do not judge them. Every church has leaders who mess up, but they are still God's chosen until He removes them.

David understood this. Before he was king, he greatly honored the position and office of the king. He honored King Saul as King of Israel. Even though Saul had become evil and had strayed far from God, David still honored the position Saul held. But years later, Saul's daughter Michael, who married David, did not honor David when he was dancing before the Lord. She despised him and criticized his actions. Her words brought *death* to *her womb* and disqualified her fertility forever.

The enemy is always looking for a way to steal the life of an unborn child and miscarriage is a stolen life. We want to be especially careful whenever we feel the urge to criticize clergy. If our tongue is connected to our womb, keeping our mouths shut is probably a good idea. We don't want to give the enemy any ammunition to use against us. Paul said, *I do not even judge myself. I will wait until the Lord judges me* (1 Corinthians 4:4-5). Someday God will make all the wrongs right. If we want to release *life* over ourselves, we must keep from criticizing things we do not know about or understand. This way, we will not speak *death* through our lack of understanding.

He gives strength to the weary and increases the power of the weak, but those who hope in the Lord will renew their strength. They will soar on wings like eagles; they will run and not grow weary; they will walk and not be faint (Isaiah 40:29, 31).

11. Could Greed in Finances Cause You to Miscarry? Possibly.

Malachi 3:11 talks about our money and our relationship to it. The connection between tithing money and conception seemed to be what unlocked fertility for Abraham. Abraham's 10% tithe to Melchizedek, *preceded* the conception of both Ishmael and Issac (Genesis 14:19, Hebrews 7:4-10, Genesis 21:7).

12. Could Living in a Toxic Environment Cause a Miscarriage? Yes.

It seems every day we are bombarded with new information about the ridiculous amount of environmental toxins we are exposed to. Toxins in our food and water and in pharmaceutical medicines, in vaccines and even in some of our herb formulas. We are exposed to radiation from cell phones, cell towers, toxic lighting, Tv's, computers and microwaves in our cars. Surely being as pure as we can be in our bodies should be our priority. If God leads you to do something specific or to eliminate something, then do it! But the reason I mentioned this last is because we have had miscarriages since the beginning of time when the earth was pure, and the atmosphere was free of current toxins. Since miscarriages have always been with us, we must look to Jesus and God's word to reveal His answers to us.

Now that you have reviewed this exhaustive list, how did you do? Did the Holy Spirit nudge you in a couple of areas? This was only a speculative list of ways our physical and spiritual choices could affect our physical seed. The sins of our culture and the many factors listed might not be why so many babies are miscarried, but these generational actions are certainly contributors. Living in a toxic chemical environment certainly does not help either but when generations sinned in the Bible, it took repentance to break these patterns. This part has never changed. It still takes repentance!

The beauty of the cross is that Jesus shed His blood to bring forgiveness and restoration to us. Scripture is clear that *God's ways are right; the righteous walk in them and find life, and those who choose their own way lose out.*

In my distress I called to the Lord; I cried to my God for help (Psalm 18:6).

Far too often, we've been taught that miscarriages are *nature's way*, and we must accept this as fact. Is this what you want to accept? If yes, then don't read any further but if you would like a different outcome, it's worth a few moments to ask God to help you.

The Bible says *ask and you will receive (Matthew 7:7).* We can't defeat the things we accept. If you want to change, you must turn your fight into prayer. *I can do all things through Him who gives me strength (Philippians 4:13).*

THE DEVIL'S PLAN

The following prayers of forgiveness are worth your time. As you pray the Lord will do His work. *I have set before you life and death, blessings and curses. Now choose life, so that you and your children may live* (Deuteronomy 30:19).

As you read this chapter, I believe the Holy Spirit may have tugged at your heart in a few areas where the accuser may have found *a "hole in your fence"* so to speak and gained *legal access to steal life from your womb and harm your fertility.* Let's kick him out! God is always willing to forgive His children and restore what the enemy has stolen.

I am going to walk you through a series of Repentance Prayers. These are prayers of deep repentance and cleansing. You are taking charge of your life and asking Jesus to make the enemy leave and because of the blood of Jesus, he must go! [Do not pray these prayers alone! As in the previous chapter, wait until you have someone, who can be your partner and support you as you pray. This is a necessity! If you cannot find someone, I advise you not to pray until you do].

**These prayers are a guide. Feel free to read them through first and pray them in your own religious language but if you change any words, do make sure to keep the parts of these prayers that state what you are asking from God.

Prayer of Repentance for Adapting to the Ways of the Ungodly Culture:

Heavenly Father, please forgive me for being too much like *the world*. I did not realize that I had become like the people who surround me in my culture. I want to repent for adopting their ideas and agreeing with their choices about family planning. I desire Your way and to allow You to help me create the family that You desire to send me. Please help me to desire what You want. Please make it seem irresistible and help me to not fear what it might mean to follow You in this area. In the mighty name of Jesus Christ of Nazareth, I ask You to forgive me, cleanse me, and remove any hindrances in my heart and mind that could keep me from obeying Your plan. Please restore a fresh vision for what You can do within my heart and life when I repent of agreement with others in this area. Thank you, Heavenly Father, for hearing my prayer. I make all these requests in the mighty name of Jesus Christ of Nazareth and by the power of your Holy Spirit. Amen.

Prayer of Repentance for choosing Death over Life by seeking to turn your body's reproductive system off and on:

Heavenly Father, I did not realize that I had misunderstood the purpose of what my body was created for. I now realize that my body is not supposed to operate like an appliance with an off-and-on switch but is instead a holy vessel. My wonderful body was created to give life and to bring forth new creations. Without realizing this, I took it for granted that I should be in charge of this process. The cultural ideas I have been influenced by deceived me and I repent of being taken in by this thinking. I realize that human reproduction is a process that cannot be turned off and on. It is a process that You alone should take charge of. You know the rhythms of my body and my spouse's body and what is best for our long-term health. In the mighty name of Jesus Christ of Nazareth, I place back into Your hands what I have taken for granted. I repent and give this back to You, Father God for You alone can forgive me and restore what I have lost. Thank you, Heavenly Father, for hearing my prayer. I make all these requests in the mighty name of Jesus Christ of Nazareth and by the power of your Holy Spirit. Amen.

Prayer of Repentance for using the Pill or IUD:

Heavenly Father, turning to the birth control pill and or inserting an IUD into my womb was an ungodly thing to do but I did not know this at the time. It was quick and easy and made life convenient. But now I do not want to oppose the children You want to give me. I ask for Your forgiveness and plead with You to make my body whole and well again.

If I have murdered any of my children unknowingly, I ask for and receive Your forgiveness. I receive Your cleansing power. If my choice did cause any of my babies to die and if a spirit of *murder*, then attached itself to my life, because of what You did for me on the cross I ask that You make this spirit leave my life now and for this enemy to never be allowed to return. I ask You to break any sadness or sorrow the enemy brought, and I ask that You fill me completely with Your spirit of *love*. Jesus, please renew each area the enemy has robbed me of physically, emotionally, spiritually, and financially. Please hear my prayer and do all this for me by the power of your blood You shed for me at the cross.

Heavenly Father, forgive me for only wanting children when it is convenient for me and for wanting to control my future. I have been proud and arrogant. I depended on my strength and not Your power. If I have made myself and my goals into an idol, I ask that You remove my thoughts from this position, and I ask that You now come and sit in that position in my heart. I am sorry if I have committed the *sin of divination* by trying to control my life or future. Please forgive me. I place the future back into Your hands, and I repent for desiring to ever control in this way. I do not want to be close to the witchcraft realm. I ask that You remove any curse that could come to me because of my ignorance. Please remove any obstacles this enemy has brought into my life and please restore me to completeness. Please bring me to total restoration by Your power.

Heavenly Father, I also ask for healing and forgiveness from depression and depressive condemning thoughts. Please give me a new mind and a new desire. I ask that all darkness and thoughts of sorrow and sadness leave me. I repent for not receiving the children that You intended for me, and I ask that any related thoughts not be able to depress me anymore. I ask you Jesus to please take away any spiritual enemy that brings me depressive thoughts, please make these thoughts leave by the power of Your blood shed for me on the cross. Please bring me Your complete restoration of my heart and mind.

I also ask dear Heavenly Father for forgiveness for using *the pill* and the chemicals it introduced into my body. Please cleanse and heal my system from all the unnecessary hormones that have broken down my body. I ask for forgiveness and ask that You cleanse my body, which is Your temple, and restore me to complete wellness through the power of the blood of Jesus Christ of Nazareth and I receive the peace that comes from Your cleansing power. I now make the active choice to choose *life* that my children and I may live. Thank you, Heavenly Father, for hearing my prayer. I make all these requests in the mighty name of Jesus Christ of Nazareth and by the power of your Holy Spirit. Amen.

Prayer of Repentance for Abortion:

Heavenly Father please forgive me for murdering my innocent baby. I am so sorry. If I could choose again today, I would not have done this. I would have kept my baby. I choose to forgive everyone who was part of my abortion. I choose to forgive my doctor, minister, parent, lover, spouse, friend, or other person who coerced me, encouraged me, falsely counseled me, or had any part in my choice to abort my baby. I choose to consciously forgive each person now and ask for forgiveness through the power of the blood of Jesus Christ of Nazareth.

I repent of this sin of abortion and ask that You forgive me for shedding innocent blood. I want the spirit of *murder* to be removed from my life. I believe that this has caused many complications for me, and I ask that this enemy that represents *murder* to not be allowed to wreak havoc on my life anymore. Because of what Jesus did for me on the cross I ask that the spirit of *murder* and *death* and sorrow to leave me now by the cleansing power of Jesus Christ of Nazareth and I Thank you Jesus for hearing my prayer. Please help me to believe You and to believe that it is possible to accept complete restoration in every area of my life in the physical, spiritual, emotional, financial, and creative realms.

I now choose life and ask that my children and I shall live. If I have become barren since my abortion, I ask dear Heavenly Father, that You have mercy on me and please open my womb. Thank you, Heavenly Father, for hearing my prayer. I make all these requests in the mighty name of Jesus Christ of Nazareth and by the power of your Holy Spirit. Amen.

Prayer of Repentance for Premarital Sex:

Heavenly Father, please forgive me for taking something that is precious and holy to You and misusing it for my own pleasure. I ask forgiveness for not keeping myself pure and I ask that You restore me to purity again so that I may live in holiness before You.

I repent of allowing *death* to come to my life when I misused Your blessing of virginity. Please forgive me. I ask You to please restore me, cleanse me and make me whole. I ask that You restore the love this behavior took away from my heart and mind and please erase all the pain this behavior brought to my emotions. Please help me to receive Your love and restoration. Because of what You did for me on the cross I now ask You to please make any demonic spirit, that has attached itself to my life, to leave right now through the power of the blood You shed for me on the cross, and dear Heavenly Father, please help me to accept a spirit of *life* from You. Please help me believe I can give *life* and receive *life* and believe it is possible to receive my complete and total restoration so that me and my future children may live. Thank you, Heavenly Father, for hearing my prayer. I make all these requests in the mighty name of Jesus Christ of Nazareth and by the power of your Holy Spirit. Amen.

Prayer of Repentance for Generational Curses:

Heavenly Father, please forgive my family bloodline for not desiring Your children. I repent for the sins of my fathers and grandfathers, mothers and grandmothers, and every other ancestor who might not have been open to receiving the wonderful gift of *life* that You wanted to bring to our family tree. I repent of the waste now connected to our family and for the lost people that should have come down through our family bloodline. Please forgive our family for all the sins we committed against our legacy. I ask Jesus that You please remove any demonic spirit that has brought *death* to our family tree or that has attached itself to the generations of our family tree. I renounce a curse of *death* over the female wombs of our family and over the ancestral seed of the men. I ask every spirit of *death* or any curse working against our family members to leave our bloodline through the power of the blood of Jesus Christ of Nazareth. *I renounce the attitude that children are not desired in this family*, and I now receive with joy, a spirit of *life* from the Holy Spirit and ask that all children that have been withheld from our family lineage be restored through the power of Jesus Christ blood shed on the cross for my sins and for the sins of my entire family. Heavenly Father please open the wombs of every woman in this family and allow our family seed to flow again.

I ask that all financial blessings that have been withheld because we did not receive these children, be restored and that the money and wealth of our family bloodline be loosed right now through the power of the blood of Jesus Christ of Nazareth and that every area of *life* be restored to our family, and we receive all these blessings through the power of the Holy Spirit.

I also repent for the evil that my ancestors may have committed. I ask forgiveness for evildoers in my family, poor business practices, cheating, lying, and falsehood. Anywhere death was allowed to attach itself to me by their sins, I ask for new *life* to come now.

Your Word says a curse can be on the generations of those who have faith in idols and an idol is anything that gets between me and my love for You. I repent for my idol worship. I repent for trying to control my destiny, I repent for making decisions without You. Please take away all my sins through the power of the blood of Jesus Christ of

Nazareth, and if a spirit of *death*, has attached itself to me, please make it go by the power of Your blood shed on the cross for my sins. Help me to receive Your cleansing power and Your forgiveness over my finances, over my business practices, and over my family planning decisions. Thank you, Heavenly Father, for hearing my prayer. I make all these requests in the mighty name of Jesus Christ of Nazareth and by the power of your Holy Spirit. Amen.

Prayer of Repentance for Fear:

Heavenly Father, please forgive me for walking in *fear*. At times it seems like I am afraid of everything. Please help me turn my *fears* into trust and help me to pray through my deepest *fears*. I repent for not allowing You to have complete control of my future. It is hard for me to trust You with something I cannot see. Heavenly Father, I am scared about many things and feel so inadequate sometimes with the small things, much less the larger things of life. Please help me trust You more so I can let go of *fear*.

Jesus, I ask your forgiveness for walking in *fear*, and I ask that if a spirit of *fear* has attached itself to my mind that You make it leave through the power of the blood of Jesus Christ of Nazareth. Please help me receive a spirit of *life* from You and please give me new thoughts and a new mind over every part of my life. I ask that the spirit of *life* bring me clarity, a sound mind, and a peace that I have never had before—peace that only Your Spirit can give. I ask that You show me all areas where I have not walked in peace so that *death* may never attach itself to my mind again. I receive Your peace through the power of the blood of Jesus Christ of Nazareth and ask that I never walk in *fear* again. Please help me receive new *life* from Your Holy Spirit so that me and my children will learn how to walk in trust and throw away a walk of *fear*. Thank you, Heavenly Father, for hearing my prayer. I make all these requests in the mighty name of Jesus Christ of Nazareth and by the power of your Holy Spirit. Amen.

Prayer of Repentance for Words I have Spoken:

Heavenly Father, I ask for your cleansing power over the words I speak. I did not realize the incredible power I have to create *life* and to speak *death*. I have spoken repeated negative words over myself, my body, and over the people around me. I repent of speaking ill words about other people and repent because I have used my tongue in gossip and slander to cause others to think poorly about people. I have also used my tongue to speak words that have cursed my health and my physical body. I have also lied by embellishing the truth. I ask that You forgive me for misusing my gift of communication. Please forgive me and cleanse me. Please help me turn my words over to You. I ask that you please forgive me and cleanse me of misusing my tongue to hurt people and to speak words of hate against myself and against others. Jesus, because of what You did for me on the cross I now ask that if any evil spirit has attached itself to my tongue and causes me to lie or to say hateful things, I ask that this spirit leave me and my body right now through the power of the blood of Jesus Christ of Nazareth. I ask Jesus that my tongue line up with the words the Holy Spirit would desire that I speak, and I believe that Your sacrifice for me was so powerful that I can become a person who speaks kindness and not mean words by the power of Your Holy Spirit.

I also ask that if the enemy used my tongue with hateful words that spoke death over a person's reputation, that this evil spirit of *murder* leave my tongue now by the power of the cleansing blood of Jesus Christ of Nazareth. I no longer choose to ruin others' reputations through gossip or slander, and I also choose to no longer tell others that I hate them or myself. Please help me Holy Spirit! I choose *life*, and I ask that You fill me with Your life, Holy Spirit, and renew Your love inside of me so that I may love myself and others. Please heal, cleanse, and forgive me by the power of the blood shed on the cross by Jesus Christ of Nazareth and by the power of Your Holy Spirit. Thank you, Heavenly Father, for hearing my prayer. I make all these requests in the mighty name of Jesus Christ of Nazareth and by the power of your Holy Spirit. Amen.

Prayer of Repentance for Feeling Rejection:

Heavenly Father, I have felt rejected all my life. Sometimes this causes me to live with negative thoughts instead of positive ones. Please forgive me for not believing You. I am afraid to accept that You want to bless me with a child.

I repent of rejecting my seed. I did not realize that this was what I was doing but I now understand because I was thinking negative thoughts, my body was rejecting my seed, instead of receiving it. But I desire to have children and do not want to push them away. Please Jesus, please help me to not reject my child or myself or my spouse or anyone else. In the name of Jesus Christ of Nazareth and by the power of Your Holy

Spirit, please remove the lie of rejection that has invaded my life. I rebuke rejection and send it back to where it came from. No longer will I receive rejection in my life and please help me to never walk in the fear that leads me to reject myself as a parent. I desire to be made complete and whole and happy with myself. Lord, please help me become a positive person and see myself as You see me. Please remove any spirit of *rejection* that has attached itself to my life and please replace it with Your spirit of *life*. Thank you, Heavenly Father, for hearing my prayer. I make all these requests in the mighty name of Jesus Christ of Nazareth and by the power of your Holy Spirit. Amen.

Prayer of Repentance for not Honoring My Parents:

Heavenly Father, please help me to honor my parents, and please help me to never walk in judgement. I desire to obey You in this area, but I need Your supernatural help. Please help me because my parents do things that I disagree with, and this bothers me and upsets me because they make decisions that I do not agree with. I don't know what to do when this happens. Please help me as I struggle to understand them. I am very thankful they contributed to my life in so many wonderful ways and I do not want to disappoint them. Please help me remember they did the best they could and as I give them honor, please help me have my own family. If there is any resentment in me or attitude toward them that may be blocking conception or is causing a miscarriage of their grandchildren, please forgive me and help me to walk in repentance.

Heavenly Father, if a spirit of *death* attached itself to my life because of how I've treated and judged my parents in the past, I ask that it be removed immediately and replaced with a spirit of *life*. Help me to forgive them for things like when I asked them for another sibling and they said, "No." Please forgive them for treating their fertility casually and not honoring your complete purpose for our family. Please forgive them if they resented having children or grandchildren and help them embrace grandparenthood with great joy. Thank you, Lord, for (insert their names). I am thankful that they are mine. I release all my fear, anger, and resentment toward them. I give it to You now. Take it far from me and help me walk in love towards them in all things. Please restore our family. Thank You Heavenly Father, for hearing my prayer. I make all these requests in the mighty name of Jesus Christ of Nazareth and by the power of your Holy Spirit. Amen.

THE DEVIL'S PLAN

Prayer of Repentance for Mocking:

Heavenly Father, please forgive me for passing judgment on Your leaders. You told Job that he spoke of things he did not understand, of things too wonderful for him to know. I have passed judgment because of what I saw on TV or in a leader's life that appeared to be wrong. It may have been wrong, but I put myself in a place of judgment, and I judged Your leaders instead of allowing You to judge them. Please forgive me. Then I used my tongue to gossip about them or to state my own opinion. Help me realize I do not need to comment. If a spirit of *death* has attached itself to my life, due to my actions in this area, I ask that it be removed right now by the power of the blood of Jesus shed for me on the cross and by the power of Your Holy Spirit. If my judgments have caused me to not be able to have children, please remove this curse, and please grant me a spirit of *life* so I can have children once again. Thank you, Heavenly Father, for hearing my prayer. I make all these requests in the mighty name of Jesus Christ of Nazareth and by the power of your Holy Spirit. Amen.

Prayer of Repentance for How I Handle Money:

Heavenly Father, I try to give my money. If I have lacked in this area, please forgive me. I repent, please give me a desire to give more to people and causes that support others. If by not giving, I have caused myself to cast my fruit before its time, please forgive me and help me to hold onto *life*. Because of what Jesus did for me on the cross by shedding His blood and by the power of Your Holy Spirit, I now ask that any curse over my seed, my womb, my life or my finances be removed right now, and if a spirit of *death* has attached itself to my life in this area, I ask that it be removed right now and be replaced by a spirit of *life*. Thank you, Heavenly Father, for hearing my prayer. I make all these requests in the mighty name of Jesus Christ of Nazareth and by the power of your Holy Spirit. Amen.

Prayer of Repentance for What We Do to Our Bodies:

Heavenly Father, there are toxins in my food and toxins in my water and toxins everywhere around me. If I have in any way purposely chosen to ingest foods or additives or chemicals that are harmful to me, I ask that you cleanse my physical body. If anything is aligning my body with a spirit of *death* and is affecting the life of my children, I ask that you supernaturally bring *life* to my body and cease from aligning me with death. Help me walk in the newness of *life*. Thank you, Heavenly

Father, for hearing my prayer. I make all these requests in the mighty name of Jesus Christ of Nazareth and by the power of your Holy Spirit. Amen.

After you repent, it is a good idea to thank God for His great mercy extended toward you!

Most precious Lord,

I want You!

I need You!

I choose You

I now CHOOSE LIFE that my children may live!

I claim Exodus 36:13 over my life and ask that You please never again deprive me of children. I want them all!

Husband and Wife's Prayer of Thanksgiving

Who is a GOD like you, who pardons sin and forgives the transgression of the remnant of His inheritance? You do not stay angry forever but delight to show mercy. You will again have compassion on us; you will tread our sins underfoot and hurl all our iniquities into the depths of the sea (Micah 7:18-19).

Thank You, God, that You do not treat us as our sins deserve or repay us according to our iniquities.

For as high as the heavens are above the earth, so great is His love for those who fear him; as far as the east is from the west, so far has He removed our transgressions from us. As a father has compassion on his children, so the Lord has compassion on those who fear him; for He knows how we are formed, He remembers that we are dust (Psalm 103:11-14).

I thank You, Heavenly Father! I now accept the power of the blood of Jesus Christ my Lord, which He shed for me on the cross. I want this power over my life and over all my sins committed in these areas, past, present, and future. Please remove all residue of *death* hanging over my life from these choices, and please fill each area with Your *life*. Because Your *blood* is now covering me in ALL these places, this means that *death must* pass over. From this moment forward, Satan will never again be allowed to *steal* the *fruit* of my womb. I receive Your forgiveness and ask that You help me to never again fall into judgment for these sins.

Christopher's Commentary

Miscarriage is a subject I hardly want to comment on because Rachel and I have never had a miscarriage. I know this can be a sensitive subject. For any man whose wife has miscarried, it must be hard. For men, I don't think it hits us in the same way that it affects our wives. Men and women grieve separately and differently. I think wives grieve for the loss of the baby and the loss of the event, but men are not emotionally bound because men do not have the baby living inside of us.

The sudden drama of *our baby being gone* is harder to grasp because we were *outside* the experience. We care and can be feeling very sad, but for many fathers, we were just starting to grasp the idea of a new baby coming and then suddenly that baby is gone. We find it harder to express what we are feeling, but for women it seems much easier for them to talk about it. I want to share a comment from one of the men in my prayer group. He was sharing right after his wife miscarried. It sums up what I am trying to say.

"She miscarried the day before yesterday, and I am feeling helpless. It's like I'm watching a video of our life, but I am somehow not in it. I see everything happening, but I am outside of it all. I can't do anything except hold her while she cries. It's weird. I've always been strong, kind of like iron, and I've always been able to help. This time there's nothing I can do to make her better. She's always crying, our baby is not coming back, and I can't fix any of it."

There was a moment of silence after he shared. After that, I think I understood how a husband feels after a miscarriage. We feel helpless, and that's not something we like. The Lord tells us to love our wives, but in this trial, we are unsure what to do or what that love looks like. When in doubt, the best thing is always to tell a woman that she is the most beautiful woman in the world and that you are so glad you chose her. This always improves everything with my wife, no matter what trial we go through. She is *my bride*, and I remind her that she is still *gorgeous*. Her smile always says it all. If this trial is a test, pass it by loving her!

Christopher Scott

Investigate and Questions

- Read Hosea 14:9. What is God saying about the times we are living in? How much do you think the death culture and the overuse of birth control by previous generations is affecting a couple's ability to conceive or keep a pregnancy right now?
- Read Hosea 9:14, Deuteronomy 28:4,18, 38. Do you see any correlation between what God was saying in the Bible days and what is occurring now?
- Read Deuteronomy 30:19. Do you see a connection between the words we speak in the physical world and how they can affect the unseen spiritual world?
- Read Deuteronomy 12:8, 9. God tells us to honor our parents, but often we do not know what that looks like in an environment that does not honor their authority. Have you given them grace in all things? If they did cut off their seed, have you seen a connection to your fertility from the actions of your parents or grandparents? Your thoughts?
- No two people handle grief in the same way. If you ever suffered a miscarriage, did you look for answers or was acceptance the best strategy for you?
- Read Proverbs 18:21. How does this apply to you regarding your fertility? Do you see yourself complaining about the discomforts of pregnancy, breastfeeding, or taking care of little ones? Or have you ever said negative words over your body or your menstrual cycle? Share your thoughts whether you believe there could be a connection between your words and what happens in the physical realm?"
- What did you learn in this chapter that you didn't know before? Are you comfortable with the various correlations between a spirit of death and all the areas that can be used by the enemy to attach to a woman and her womb?

# Impacting Others

Rachel, when you sent out your request for my testimony I wondered if I should share it, but I think I will, because maybe my story will help someone. I have always wanted a family from as far back as I can remember. I knew I wanted to be a mommy. When I got married, I was 22 and ready! After eight months, I was pregnant. I was so excited. I didn't get a pregnancy test at first. I don't know why; I thought it was taboo, so I waited a while. Yet then, one morning, it started. I started cramping and bleeding and feeling achy. "Oh, now I thought I couldn't be miscarrying! No, God, no, I don't want this!" Yet there was nothing I could do to stop it. The bleeding continued. I took off work. We were supposed to go away for our anniversary weekend. We canceled our plans, and I stayed home on pain medicine. On the following Monday, I went in for blood tests. They showed I had been pregnant but had miscarried. My heart sank. How could this have happened? My sweet and hopeful husband told me we should start trying again when allowed. Three months later, I was pregnant again, and I took a home pregnancy test to confirm it. My first miscarriage was in the past; this was a new day. I was so happy this time. It was spring, and the weather was changing. This always puts me in a good mood anyway. I started dreaming of the baby and being a mommy. The baby would be born in the fall, and I started buying little outfits. Yet then it happened again. I started bleeding and had severe pain. I called my doctor, who told me to go to the hospital if the pain got severe; otherwise, she would see me in her office in the morning. The next day I went in for a scan and no baby! My heart grieves just recalling that time. It was a time of sorrow and disappointment. About seven months later, I was pregnant again. I don't remember if I was very excited when the test read positive because now, I was growing fearful of this process. Sadly, I lost that child too. After that loss, I decided I could not handle it if I lost another child. I remember telling my husband that sorrow was overtaking me. What made it worse was that the other women, I interacted with, kept getting pregnant, coworkers, neighbors, my tennis team friends, and women at my church. They all had perfect pregnancies, and I could not handle being around them! I was feeling depressed much of the time. A dear friend noticed my sadness and tried to encourage me. She gave me a sweet card with this verse in it from The Message Bible: "You who serve the Lord your God, He will bless your food and water and will get rid of sickness among you: there won't be any miscarriages nor barren women in your land and will make sure you live complete lives." I didn't have the strength to claim the verse, but I knew in my heart it was for me. I cried out, "God, if you hear me, please heal me!" Shortly after that prayer, I was pregnant again, and somehow this time, I knew that my baby would live. My daughter was born in May 2000. I now have four other children; another daughter who is eight, a son, four, and a new baby girl, five months old. After that prayer, my miscarriages ceased, and the doctors could not figure out what went wrong. Yet I know God healed me, which is as simple as that." **Julie, Seattle, Washington, Mom to four children here and four waiting in Heaven**

Rachel, I have emailed you before. I am struggling now, and I need prayer. I have three girls and a boy. I just had my fourth miscarriage in the past two years. My mother has always been supportive, but not all the way. After the last miscarriage, she said, "Don't you think God might be trying to tell you something?" Her comment hurt. Yet, in her mind, my lack of success is a sign from God that she thinks I am ignoring. I tried to tell her we were committed to God's plan and that He did not promise us that things would always work the way we want, but still, she's been dropping comments about me concentrating on the children I already have. I know she means well and is concerned for my long-term health. So far, I have never agreed to a D and C, nor needed one, for that matter. We always lose the baby real early, and no real hemorrhaging has occurred. Yet I wish the comments wouldn't be said. Until someone can put themselves in my shoes, they can never completely understand the devastation of the loss and the hope that knowing the Lord brings. I must stay positive. **Thank you for your book and for your prayers, Jules**

Rachel, here is my story, I hope it blesses someone. I am the blessed mother of ten amazing children. God has used my children to bless my life, and I feel He has given me far more blessings than I ever deserved! I got pregnant in college and had an abortion, then I got my life straight, returned to my Catholic roots, and married a wonderful man. The other Catholic couples around us were using birth control, but from the beginning, we felt it was an essential element of our faith to let God be in charge. I guess I felt uncomfortable denying someone their life. It seemed as wrong as taking someone's life. In my mind, life is life, and God is in charge. We had our first baby without any complications. Then I got pregnant again and lost the next four! The miscarriages were always before twelve weeks, but still, we were devastated. Then I switched doctors, and he recommended a cervical cerclage. My next two were born at 36 weeks. My fourth was born at 35 weeks and needed to be in the NICU for several weeks. We had four boys at that point, and I was hoping for a girl, but my doctor warned me that my condition was dangerous and that every baby had a chance of being born prematurely. My husband said we should do Natural Family Planning, which only lasted a few months. It was not for us. I then conceived my fifth child, and I was getting tired myself. After he was born, I had a two-and-a-half-year break. We moved when I was pregnant again, and my new doctor did not feel the cerclage surgery was necessary. She examined my cervix and didn't think I needed it. I thought she was crazy, and I still wanted it. My sixth child, a daughter, was born at 38.5 weeks without it. Then I got pregnant again and lost that baby! I didn't know what to think at that point. I was not sure if I should insist on it again or not. I got pregnant with my seventh child, and we decided to do the cerclage, and it popped off at 22 weeks, and they put me on bed rest. She was delivered early at 35 weeks. She only had to stay in the NICU for a week. By then, I was getting older and unsure of what my body was doing. With my eighth, I had an ultrasound, and it was twins. The sonogram showed one of the twins with Down's Syndrome. We asked everyone to pray. We prayed, and we prayed. We begged God for His will to be done and to heal the baby. During that pregnancy, I agreed to the cerclage again, and we had to trust God on a level I never thought possible. Our babies were born early by c-section, and neither had Down's Syndrome! Praise the Lord! However, my doctor warned me never to get pregnant again. By this time, I was 42 yr. old, so it was clear that my childbearing was over anyway. Two and a half years later, I got pregnant again, unsuspectedly, and at 45, I had my tenth child, a little girl. I was on bed rest for 26 weeks, which was very difficult, but I did it. I have no regrets. I am now 53 and never got pregnant again. **Anise, Pittsburg, Penn. mother of ten and five waiting in Heaven**

Chapter 10

TRUTH OR CONSEQUENCES

*What Are We Doing to our Body?
What Happens to our Health when we Interrupt the
Natural Cycles of the Physical Body*

Do not be deceived: God cannot be mocked. A man reaps what he sows *(Galatians 6:7)*. There is a way that appears to be right, but in the end, it leads to death *(Proverbs 14:12)*.

When I was a small child, a popular TV game show was *Truth or Consequences*. The contestants had to perform silly stunts to win prizes, and people loved this show because it was funny. I chose the name for this chapter because one of the themes of scripture is that God's people are to seek truth and follow God's ways, and then they will avoid the consequences of sin.

It is a simple fact; people suffer when they turn from the truth. This is why Hosea, the prophet, mourned, *my people perish for lack of knowledge* (Hosea 4:6). He cried out to God for his people's sorrowful choices, and I've often cried out to God for yours! I want people to know the truth about this subject. This is *the reason* I wrote this book. I want to see people avoid unnecessary pain and suffering.

So far, I've covered the *spiritual* and *emotional consequences* of using birth control and sterilization, but we are yet to explore the *physical consequences* which cause harm to people's health. Unfortunately, many people, mostly women are not properly informed. Marketers use beautiful pictures and wonderful names to promote the pills and devices that will potentially damage men and women's bodies. Women are shown only the solution but never the harm this little pill or device might bring later. The facts are not presented properly.

For reasons unknown to me, there seems to be some sort of *unspoken agreement* between the media, the medical community, and the health industry. They focus only on the pros and never on the cons. If women could get a fair advertisement, it would be an ad showing a beautiful young woman holding her birth control pill at the top and at the bottom show an overweight, worn-out woman in her fifties who tells what years of hormonal imbalance did to her body. Why aren't we told both sides? To be fair, people would need to know this information *before they make decisions* that drastically affect their health. However, this entire industry is not fair, and females are not given all the information they need to make an honest choice.

Finally, after countless females died as the result of the high levels of hormones in the pill, the makers were forced to put warnings[1] on their product inserts, but the small type is rarely read. When *the pill* causes a woman to suffer a heart attack or stroke from a blood clot, they say *she had a heart attack or stroke.* They don't say *the pill* caused her heart attack or stroke. In the thousands of years before these forms of birth control came on the market, it was virtually unheard of for a woman to suffer a heart attack or stroke. Now these rates are epidemic in females, but we don't make the connection. We pay the price for our choices. It seems unfair when women can't be told *the truth* but must be led through *deception*.

POST BIRTH CONTROL SYNDROME

Every day at doctor's offices across the county, teenage women are put on the birth control pill and not for birth control use but for problems with either the young girl's menstrual cycle or for acne regulation. Some of these girls are as young as eleven years of age! *What are we thinking?* When a young woman is placed on *artificial hormones* at this young age, we are creating the possibility that when the day comes and she is ready to have a baby, that either she won't be able to get pregnant with ease or she might never be able to have a baby through the natural process. Doctors admit that long term use of the birth control pill does cause disruption in a female's cycle and some women's reproductive cycles **never** return!

Please tell me the fifteen-year-old teen girl who is thinking about her long-term fertility when she wants her cramps to stop hurting or her pimples to go away? She has no idea that by starting on the pill, the pharmaceutical industry is *setting her up for reproductive failure.*

The goal after going off these artificial hormones is for a woman's cycle to return to normal and for the woman to be fertile so she can have a baby. When this does not happen, women often complain of a myriad of symptoms that arise. Now after years and after numerous females have experienced similar symptoms, doctors have finally labeled these symptoms as post birth control syndrome.

Post birth control syndrome (PBCS)[2] can occur weeks, months and even years after a woman ceases from using her artificial hormonal birth control. These women suffer irregular periods, hormonal imbalances, severe acne or other skin issues, mood swings, anxiety, depression, weight gain, decreased libido, and increased anovulatory cycles because ovulation does not occur. Often due to how these artificial hormones work in female's bodies, permanent damage occurs, and a woman's fertility is gone forever. This is so sad!

Does our country make the birth control advertisers in all those pretty advertisements tell the women that these artificial substances can harm them? NO WAY! Instead, we allow them to show happy and carefree young women all laughing and smiling because they are happily using their birth control product. Sometimes there is information in tiny print at the bottom of the ad, but no one looks at that, or the words of caution mentioned. These warnings are often overlooked, and it is not being made clear that by using these products, women could be seriously damaging their abilities to reproduce. This is a crime against women! The pharmaceutical companies should be fined, and these ads should be illegal. Why should women continue to be their human guinea pigs?

COULD THE PILL CAUSE YOU TO CHOOSE THE WRONG PARTNER?

We already know that using the pill can severely damage fertility and causes females to have heart attacks, blood clots, strokes, high blood pressure, breast and cervical cancer, mental disturbances and more. On top of all these disastrous physical symptoms researchers in the fields of physiology and evolutionary biology now believe they have found a new correlation between artificial hormones and their effect on females. They have found that when women are on *artificial hormones*, they become genetically attracted to men who are genetically less compatible, and they choose a partner they would otherwise not be choosing if they were not using artificial hormones! *This is a fascinating breakthrough.* A study in 1995 by Claus Wedekind suggests that women are naturally attracted to the scent of men with genes that are opposite and stronger than theirs. Then a 2006 study by Lisa DeBruine found that women's preferences in men changed based on their contraceptive use. *Women on the pill* prefer more feminine partners and *women who are not on the pill* prefer the more masculine men. A 2011 follow up study by Dr. Karen L.P.S. found that women who were already on the pill before meeting their partners, reported to be less satisfied with the relationship sexually inside the bedroom and less satisfied psychologically outside the bedroom. When a woman is not on the pill, she would choose a more masculine male due to how her female genes are attracted to his testosterone. If she produces offspring with him the children would be genetically stronger with hardier immune systems. Yet when a woman is on the pill, she prefers a less driven-lower testosterone male and would produce children with genetically weaker immune systems. Isn't this interesting? Given that the world just went through the pandemic, we found there are a lot of weak immune systems out there! Could there be a connection? Researchers have only been conducting studies on this theory since the mid 1990's but evidence continues to increase that artificial hormones do affect a woman's choice in partners, cause weaker immune systems in the offspring and could be the reason why some women continually choose the wrong person.[2a] *One more reason to stay away from artificial hormones!*

WHY HAVE I NOT HEARD THIS INFORMATION BEFORE?

I don't know. Most people are uniformed because they never thought about researching this topic. Nearly everyone believes their doctors and the marketing material. When researching for this chapter, I was amazed at how quickly I came across information. Some might say, *"You can't believe everything you read on the internet!"* Okay, that's a fair comment, but I researched and cross-referenced everything I am sharing in this chapter.

The American medical community has been documenting for years in their medical journals about the physical side effects of *the pill*, the IUD, birth control injections, the patch, sterilizations, birth control vaccines, and so on. These options have been linked to every form of reproductive cancer, ovarian and uterine pains, heavy menstrual bleeding, emotional hysteria, weight gain, headaches, mood swings, autoimmune diseases, heart disease, menopausal difficulties, and blood clots. Complications *are not uncommon* and happen quite frequently across a wide range of users.

There is a growing movement of unhappy women who believe the public is being misinformed. They are speaking out in record numbers through blogs, magazine articles, and other public forums. The internet is filled with websites featuring medical studies, personal testimonies, drug information, and general content with medical professionals leaning more pro and personal sites expressing more con viewpoints. Some women share horrific stories. *Hum, I wonder why?* These complaints are not from religious people or religious organizations but from people from all backgrounds of life and political persuasions. These are the people who *have been damaged* and are now unified by their anger, claiming they were not informed of all the health risks. Most people do not do their own research and hope that others caution them but unless you do your own research and *look before you leap* you will remain uninformed that your birth control choice might leave you with an irreversible health crisis, or even married to a crappy partner.

Medical science does not deny that every 6.4 minutes, over eighty times per day, a woman in the U.S.A. is diagnosed with gynecological cancer.[3] In 2022, 302,980 women were diagnosed with some form of gynecological cancer. 288,000 women will be diagnosed with invasive breast cancer, 43,000 will die of it, 269,000 men will be diagnosed with prostate cancer, and more than 35,000 will die from it. Shockingly the numbers of men and women affected by reproductive cancers are nearly identical![4]

God has given us a *free will* to choose to do whatever we want, but God's word warns us what will happen if we make choices that go in the opposite direction of what God says is best. In Psalm 81:13 God says, '*If My people would but listen to Me."* Why don't we simply heed His words?

TUBAL LIGATION-The Band-Aid Surgery

Are you getting your tubes tied? This has become a cute way of asking a mother if she plans to get this horrific permanent form of birth control.

This surgery was initially marketed to women as the new *"miracle surgery"* and the *"Band-Aid surgery"* by family planning organizations like Planned Parenthood. Women were assured it would miraculously prevent further pregnancies and was such a simple procedure that a band-aid would be all they needed to cover this incision. *No big deal, right?* The first safely performed tubal ligation was in 1930, although doctors had been experimenting with the procedure since 1823. In England, doctors originally aimed to perfect it as a method of population control among the so-called *degenerate poor*.

Approximately 750,000 women in the U.S. each year undergo this operation, about 350,000 will have these operations within 48 hours of giving birth! Tubal ligation is a permanent form of birth control and has been the number one choice of birth control for women over thirty years of age for more than fifty years. In 1994-1996 more than two million sterilizations were performed, for an average of 11.5 sterilizations per 1,000 women.[5] Roughly twenty-five percent of women in the U.S. (up to 140,000,000 to date) have been sterilized.[6]

In 1977, Dr. Reimert Ravenholt,[6] the head of USAID's population office publicly inferred that the agency intended to sterilize 25% of the global population of women, which they have successfully proceeded to do. So far, 33% of women globally have been sterilized. Today it is estimated over *200 million women* are sterilized annually. To reach this goal, the World Health Organization, USAID and other organizations used misinformation, propaganda, and the hands of the women's health care providers. The World Bank has explicitly indicated that population control is more important than reproductive freedom. In developing countries, when women will not cooperate, they use military force. Muslim countries like Egypt and Indonesia will not allow the World Health Organization to sterilize their women. On American soil, methods for depopulation are ongoing but participation remains voluntary.

In this procedure, a female's fallopian tubes are severed using various methods. Years ago, the doctor would cut a woman's fallopian tubes in half and then tie them into a knot. On occasion, the ends of the tubes would grow back together! *"Maybe this was God's way of letting people know He was not favoring their decision!"* The couple then found themselves with a *surprise* baby, and often got abortions when this happened. Later, doctors began perfecting laser techniques to sever the tubes and burn the ends to ensure a female's tube would never grow back. With these laser methods, tubes are burned so completely that afterwards, the chance of a successful reversal is nearly impossible. Supernatural intervention from God would have been the only way a woman could ever naturally have another child.

There are many ways people pay for a tubal ligation but most often it is through their insurance provider. Most insurance plans will pay for the sterilization but will *never pay* for a reversal. Some companies stipulate they will only pay for the operation if the woman has it done right after she gives birth, which is a highly emotional time for a woman and the worst time to make a life altering decision. At birth she is out of sorts, she just delivered a baby, her emotions are high, her hormones are raging, she is exhausted from pregnancy and tired from birth. She is hardly in the *right frame of mind* to make a permanent decision about her reproductive health. To make this a stipulation is a crime against women.

Women are not routinely informed of all the potential health risks of a tubal ligation surgery nor are they told how this operation will change their bodies physically, spiritually, and emotionally. If more women knew the facts, fewer females would allow *such a horrible crime* to be committed against their body. Doctors, the medical community and world population planners have been allowed to *downplay complications* from this operation for years, but the drawbacks have become far too widespread. Finally, doctors were forced to *recognize* post-operation consequences. Doctors now label these symptoms as *Post-Tubal-Ligation Syndrome*.

POST TUBAL LIGATION SYNDROME

Dr. Vicki Huffnagel, a noted feminist, was the first to describe her findings in 1980. She has written numerous reports in medical journals describing her post-tubal observations. She also wrote the first papers demanding a change in the medical consent forms given to women informing them of the risks of this sterilization procedure. You can visit her website for more information: www.tubal.org.[7] There are other nationwide websites trying to inform women on her findings. There is even a national organization focused entirely on this issue and founded by a feminist named Susan Bucher. Her organization is called *The Coalition for Post-Tubal Women* and was established to lend information and support to post-tubal women, often assisting them in getting their health back through reversal surgeries. Susan has co-authored a book with Dr. Vicki Huffnagel called *"What Doctors Don't Tell You About Tubal Ligation and Post Tubal Ligation Syndrome."*[8]

The effects of tubal ligation have ruined so many women's lives that one of the chapters of NOW (National Organization for Women) calls it *"The medical malpractice operation of the century"* and created a resolution against it. This resolution can be read online.[9] NOW desires the medical community inform women of the possible side effects, rather than lead women to think there are zero repercussions.

The National Organization of Women is a very vocal feminist organization that has done much to advance the cause of secular feminism. For this organization to *cry out* for legislation and document this crime against women, reflects the message of this book. Women, we need to return to God's original plan because everything else leads to sorrow and death.

Where are God's people? Are we asleep? God's people are supposed to be the leaders in protecting the rights of people everywhere. We should point the world to the truth about these dreaded tubal ligations. Since God's people have been silent about this and in agreement with these practices, I believe God is using the voice of radical feminists instead. Informing innocent women is what Jesus would do! While the church-going-Christians were all silent and let women continue to be harmed, the radical feminists were willing to take up the fight and speak out to warn women that this operation is a crime against women.

Why would a Godly woman want to get a tubal ligation? Maybe she does not realize that she has come into agreement with society's plan for women, instead of sticking with God's plan, or perhaps she has not thought about the impact this surgery will have on her long-term emotional or physical health. The feminist movement pushes the idea that the pill, abortion and sterilization are the only options for women, offering freedom from unwanted children. However, what they fail to mention is that this so-called "freedom" comes at the cost of a woman's body and health. So, *is she truly free?*

"The tool to reach this goal of sterilizing 25% of women was not done with soldiers but through misinformation, propaganda, and the advance health directives (AHDs) of the women's health care providers and the medical community." Susan J. Belcher (feminist).[10]

Women's rights groups should come after the doctors who pressured women at these vulnerable times to perform this operation without a waiting period. Later, when a woman realizes what she has done to herself, her body, and her future, this can cause irreversible damage to her emotional psyche. Many women become *severely depressed* because they feel robbed of their female body parts and their rights to choose motherhood.

PHYSICAL RISKS OF TUBAL STERILIZATION MOST WOMEN ARE NOT AWARE OF

Women are rarely informed of the complications of the *Band-Aid surgery*, even though these complications are not rare and happen because of the surgery in up to 50% of the women. Symptoms have been reported yet because the media often does not report this information, most women have no idea that other ladies are also suffering these complications.

Doctors have known for thirty-five years that tubal ligations cause adverse symptoms. When women sign consent forms, they are told that the surgery could cause a risk of bowel injury, risk of ectopic pregnancy, and slightly heavier menstrual cycles. Women are routinely not counseled or informed that along with these physical complications, their tubal ligation might cause **heavier periods, hormonal imbalances, ovarian cysts,** or their ovaries could die completely. Instead, women are told they will have a decreased chance of developing ovarian cancer. They are not told this is because the surgery may lead to a hysterectomy and the removal of their ovaries; therefore, there will not be any ovaries to have cancer in! The surgery itself increases the risk of endometrial cancer. The following is a synopsis of the problems arising in thousands of women.

1. **Major complications:** It depends upon which sterilization technique is used, but between 800 and 2,000 women per 100,000 can expect a major complication at the time of the operation, according to the Alan Guttmacher Institute.[11] These complications are infection, injury to the bladder or bleeding of blood vessels, or burning of the bowel. There also can be complications from anesthesia. Laparoscopy can cause bowel perforation and lead to infection in the abdominal cavity, with the risk

of hemorrhaging and infection. Some women have died from cardiac failure.

2. **Post Tubal-Ligation Syndrome symptoms occur in 37% of all women** who have this operation.[12] Women complain of heavy menstrual bleeding (gushing and flooding of blood for days), intense pain in the ovaries, menstrual disturbances requiring hormonal treatment, erosion of the cervix, tumors on the ovaries, and regrowth of the tubes requiring a second operation. Suppose the couple decides to reverse the operation, and the woman gets pregnant. In that case, there is up to a 65% chance that she may have a tubal pregnancy, which results in a failed pregnancy and is life-threatening if not treated in time.

3. Young women usually do not care about the long-term consequences because they are young and do not think this will happen to them. Yet as they age, these factors increasingly work against them and steal their health at a time in their lives when they are trying to enjoy their adult children and grandchildren.

4. **Hormone Replacement Therapy:** The operation can cause a hormone imbalance requiring the woman to go on the pill to try to balance her system. The hormone imbalance causes the blood supply in the veins, arteries, and capillaries to be cut off to the ovaries and uterus, and they begin to atrophy because of lack of use. This can lead to hormone shock and bone loss (possibly one of the causes of osteoporosis in so many women), loss of sex drive, memory loss, confusion, hot flashes, uncontrollable outbursts of anger, and loss of balance in up to 50% of the women![13]

5. **The risk of ovarian and endometrial cancer increases** when a woman does not have additional pregnancies. Pregnancy uses a woman's reproductive body parts and acts as an added protection for a woman's reproductive organs because each pregnancy completes a hormone cycle. The decrease in estrogen due to pregnancy-induced lack of a menstrual cycle, further protects these organs. Risk factors for all reproductive cancers decrease with every pregnancy a woman has. James G. Tappan's study of 489 women after their tubal ligations, found an increase in the rate of cervical cancer to be three and a half times the normal rate.[14]

6. **Tubal ligation can also lead to a future hysterectomy** because the complications can't be controlled, and the woman suffers to the point where removing all reproductive organs is the only solution. This happens in many cases. You hear of a woman getting her tubes tied, and then a few years later, you hear that she needs a total hysterectomy. One study found that hysterectomy was 17% more likely within the first fourteen years after tubal ligation, depending on the woman's symptoms before the tubal. A history of heavier periods, menstrual pain, ovarian cysts, and endometriosis increases the possibility of future hysterectomy.

7. **Increased PMS:** Symptoms intensify following a tubal ligation because progesterone is blocked from the ovaries. This can lead to heavier bleeding and cramping. Furthermore, when a woman is menstruating, it reminds her that she is not pregnant. This sorrow can produce fear and anger. The woman can be difficult to live with. She may feel inadequate and unproductive, worsening her PMS.

    To alleviate symptoms, some women use all-natural progesterone cream. The results vary, but women report this cream helps with mood swings and PMS-type symptoms. Health researchers are not sure if the cream is healthy in the long term because it can affect the endocrine system. The body stores the progesterone in its tissues, which may cause detrimental damage to the balance of organ systems over time. While using this cream, women should be monitored by a doctor to prevent imbalance.

8. After a tubal, weight gain is typical and rarely avoided![15]

9. Intense heart palpitations have been reported in many women.

10. **Depression:** 28% of women[16] who have tubal ligations regret their choices and this often leads to *depression*. Most women who have had their tubes tied need antidepressant drugs to handle difficult situations. Why? The doctors do not know. They prescribe *antidepressants* as part of the treatment because they help with the symptoms. Could emotional sorrow cause depression? Are women feeling sad that they cannot have children anymore? This feeling of being incapable leaves some women feeling empty and depressed.

THERE'S A WHOLE LOT OF BLEEDING GOING ON

I am shocked at the number of women I've met who've shared their reproductive health horror stories with me. Upon further investigation, every story somehow links to their birth control choice. The bleeding is ruining their energy levels and robbing their sex lives. Bleeding and complications are not *rare*, yet complications of these choices appear diminished in medical literature, and I don't know why. Women definitely need to be informed.

One of my close friends had uterine fibroids. The doctor was not sure what caused them. She bled all but three to four days every month! She was bleeding so heavily the rest of the month that she continually wet through her thickest menstrual pads. She was so weak that she had to move from working full time to part-time work hours. She could not have normal sexual relations with her husband because she only had three or four days a month when she was not bleeding. She lost so much blood, that the doctor wanted to remove her uterus to stop the bleeding. She also became anemic from her blood loss.

Another girlfriend had been receiving birth control injections, and after several months developed severe menstrual bleeding, very similar to my other friend. Her doctor could not figure out how to stop the bleeding. It stayed this way for more than six months until she went off the injections. She also could not have regular sexual relations with her husband, and she became weak and anemic from the blood loss. After going off these injections, her periods remained severely abnormal, and it took years before her normal cycles returned. Her periods remained extremely heavy. Basically, the birth control shot ruined her health.

Another friend had a tubal ligation, her periods never returned to normal. For years after her tubal, she was still suffering. She bled heavily for fourteen days of her cycle, and then her cramps were so bad that she had to be in bed or on the couch for seven days straight. At the time this happened, she was a mother under forty, with three small children! She could not have regular sexual relations with her husband because she was either bleeding, cramping, or feeling lousy. She only felt well enough to have sex during ten days of her monthly cycle. By the time she was 45 yrs. old, she had to get a full hysterectomy. This did help to alleviate most of her complications; however, this was many years ago, and after her hysterectomy she did get her energy back but has struggled ever since with weight gain, hair loss from hormone imbalance, and loss of sexual desire among other things. She did not age beautifully.

I look at all these women's lives and how they are suffering, and my heart breaks. It's so unfair! Their lives and health were messed up because they followed the advice of the media, a medical professional, a friend, or family member. They then suffered daily, and for what benefit? A guarantee that each would never have an *unwanted child*. These choices cost them their health. In every case the things the medical community *offered* caused an interruption in their sex lives, their physical health, brought emotional pain and feelings of inferiority, as well as physical pain into their marriages. These stories are not rare. I have a friend who is an OB/GYN nurse who told me that every day, women come into their office with similar problems. All the ladies are stuck in a system that promotes suffering in a *physical way* from choices they made or that someone else persuaded them to make. It's unfair!

I know of several other women, who have not chosen to do as these women have and are not suffering needlessly. In fact, they are not suffering at all. They do not have any problems with their reproductive organs and now into menopause they are aging well and are not suffering from hormone imbalances or suffering with other female complications. None of these ladies were on the pill or used any form of artificial contraceptives or had a tubal ligation. *Their health reflects the blessing of wise choices.* Some people would say, well they are just the lucky ones, not everyone who avoids these things has a smooth transition to menopause. This may be true for a small minority, but are these ladies simply lucky or is their health a picture of what happens when someone does things the natural way that God intended? God's way is always the best way, yet with all the pressure to conform in the media and the things ladies are being told by the medical community, women do not realize they are not doing things the natural way.

God does have a road to blessing, and when God's people come into agreement with how God wants things done, they find those blessings! It seems so simple, yet what we are seeing today is God's plan being rejected. People want sex without the responsibility of children and are willing to do whatever it takes to achieve their goal, even if this means taking a drug, injecting a substance or harming themselves by an operation. And all the while our young girls are left in the dark and are not given proper information, so they follow along like blind sheep. We do not warn them they are becoming trapped in a system that will never give them a choice to be all natural or a choice to protect their health.

All this suffering is so unnecessary. If people would just do things the way God intended, they would not take their lives down this painful path.

After a tubal ligation, some women get depressed, some also bleed heavily, and others suffer ovarian or uterine pain. Some women say they simply *feel horrible* all the time, and others don't have any of these symptoms. The medical community ignores those suffering because these symptoms do not happen to every woman, so they dismiss a female's symptoms stating that this is her body's way of coping.

Tubal ligations are falsely advertised. They try to lead women down a road to *utopia* by envisioning a false paradigm, how about giving women the truth? *After your operation you can have all the sex you want without the fears of another pregnancy*, but you might develop huge health problems that could interrupt the rest of your life... (but we hide this fact from you so we can make money on this operation and on however messed up your health is down the road). Best of luck to you! I wish I could say these were isolated cases, but instead, they are often the norm for the over-forty crowd, many of whom are churchgoers. God's people suffer because they go to doctors who give them the ungodly solution to stop God's plan. God's people take the *same pills*, get the *same IUDs*, same *shots* & birth control *patches*, and have the *same operations*. What do we expect? Can we drink both pure and impure water at the same time? (James 3:11).

The irony of this whole thing is that the desire for increased sexual relations without the risk of pregnancy, is one of the main reasons why husbands want their wives to get their tubes tied. They desire to have *all the sex* they want without the fear of getting her pregnant. Yet when a woman is suffering with the consequences that come from pills and operations, is in constant pain and is bleeding heavily, she is not going to want to have sex! The thought of making love will be the last thing on her mind. A couple's sex life could virtually shut down as the result of these choices and there goes their sex life! It will be shut down, and some men *are convinced they must get it somewhere*. Her complications could cause him to go elsewhere. Let's hope not, but some men do what they want to do, even if it's immoral.

When a woman is suffering, she might not be the most pleasant person to be around, especially if she feels horrible all the time. If she blames her husband, he will not want to live with a woman who is angry at him, unhappy, feels sick, bleeds constantly, and no longer cares about meeting his needs. King Solomon talked about this in Proverbs when he said, it is better *to live on the corner of a roof than share a house with a quarrelsome wife (Proverbs 25:24).*

GOING THROUGH "THE CHANGE"

When a woman watches TV during the day, she will see twenty or thirty commercials describing female health problems. Arthritis formulas, bladder control, drugs for depression, breast cancer, osteoporosis, feminine energy-enhancing drugs, douches, etc., all describe the poor health symptoms of menopause. Young women in our country have become frightened of menopause because they are subtly being convinced that their future involves cancer of some kind, menopausal nightmares, and dramatic declines in health as we age. Instead of being a season that one looks forward to as the time when the body transfers to another role, *menopause* has become something to fear.

Did God intend for this season of a woman's life to be feared? I do not believe that He did. This will probably shock you, but menopausal problems are not mentioned anywhere in the Scriptures and have not been advertised as being an issue down through antiquity. This may sound unusual that God does not address the problem, but it is not because God is ignoring menopausal women but instead it is because menopause problems did not exist in women in past generations. They are a modern paradigm.

For generations, a female's transition to menopause was peaceful, and unnoticeable. Often women did not even realize this was what their bodies were doing because the change was slow and quiet and symptomless. This is why for centuries menopause was called *the silent passage*. Women simply stopped menstruating, and women knew their childbearing season was over. They did not suffer physical symptoms, no hot flashes or hormone swings, no heavy bleeding, no cancer, no cramping, no unusual weight gain, no emotional traumas, no mood swings, or other unusual health problems. *Nothing but peace followed the ladies who did not alter God's plan* and *who used her reproductive organs for the purpose they were created for.* Over the centuries, this would have been nearly every woman because female birth control and sterilization was not available to the masses until the twentieth century.

After eight babies, eight times nursing, zero abortions and not being on *the pill long-term* (except once for three months), I feel very fortunate that I have not suffered these complications. I transitioned into menopause in one month. I didn't even know it happened. I never had a hot flash. I never had any pain and there are quite a few other women out there who, like me, stayed *natural* and had large families and they, also claim to have entered the menopause season of life peacefully. Some might say to me and others like me, "Well, you're just lucky." Possibly, *we should knock on wood!* Please do not think I am bragging; I didn't know when I made my choices that it would even help with my transition to menopause. I am in this experiment as much as the next person, but I do think for my body my multiple pregnancies have helped my overall long term reproductive health. As for the other moms I know who also had multiple pregnancies and *bucked the pregnancy and birth control trends*, so far it appears to have helped. Many of us remain happy and healthy in our pre- and post-menopausal years.

Will we still be healthy long term? Only time will tell, but studies show a decrease in almost every type of reproductive cancer every time a woman goes through a pregnancy and nursing cycle. This process decreases a woman's lifetime number of menstrual cycles and therefore causes a reduced association with endogenous estrogen and progesterone hormones that are produced by the ovaries.

Pregnancy and nursing decrease a woman's risk of multiple hormone cycles, and therefore by *resting the body* during a pregnancy and while also breastfeeding, this assists a female's body in fighting reproductive cancers. Specifically in the breast, where healthy mature cells produce milk. Doctors have confirmed that pregnancy is quite healthy for a woman, and studies have confirmed that women who have at least two children and breastfeed are far less likely to get cancer than women who do not have any children. *"Breastfeeding may have a protective effect that negates the increased risk of breast cancer associated with late pregnancies,"* says Giske Ursin, M.D. Ph.D., associate professor of Preventive Medicine at the University of Southern California.[17] *"As more women choose to delay pregnancy until after 25, it is important to note that breastfeeding provides protection against both estrogen and progesterone receptor positive and negative tumors. Researchers have now hypothesized that these breast cells are more resistant to becoming cancer cells due to the differentiation process.* According to the National Cancer Institute 2011 fact sheet,[18] endometrial and ovarian cancer decrease with each pregnancy. Women who give birth to five or more children have half the risk of developing breast cancer compared to women who do not have any children. Women who breastfeed for at least a year also have a decreased risk of developing breast cancer. Overall, all reproductive cancer rates decrease in women who have had children; and the more children, the more rest from hormone cycles, the better a woman's chances are she will have reduced rates of reproductive cancer.

When artificial birth control for women appeared, so did menopausal complications as well as every other problem affecting the female reproductive organs

What does this tell us? Birth control choices using artificial hormones must be the cause of most menopausal problems and reproductive complications and cancers! God made it so that each pregnancy would increase a woman's chances of having a smoother transition into menopause. Every time that she uses her reproductive organs for what they were intended for, it acts as a *shield of protection* which decreases her chances of experiencing deadly complications in her reproductive health. Even doctors will confirm this is true.[18a] They tell women that when they have at least two children, they are less likely to contract breast cancer than when they do not have any children. If a woman breastfeeds those two children, then her chances for breast cancer decrease even further.

The Bible talks about this cycle of pregnancy, giving birth and breastfeeding and when we research the topic in scripture, we do not hear about any menopause horror stories. Scripture only speaks of menopausal women in a peaceful way. If back then women were experiencing the problems the masses are experiencing today, surely the Bible would have mentioned at least one older lady *having a hot flash!* It does tell us that female gynecological problems were not the norm. In fact, women with feminine complications were so rare that people did not understand these conditions, and suffering ladies became social outcasts.

The story of the woman with the *issue of blood* (Matthew 9:20-22, Mark 5:25-34, Luke 8:43-47), is the only reference to a female health problem in the Bible other than references in Leviticus, telling priests how to handle bodily emissions. None of these Levitical instructions highlighted specific conditions. The Scriptures make few references to older women's illnesses. *Peter's mother-in-law* was healed of a fever. *Naomi* was a grandmother, but there is no mention ever of her being sick. *Grandmother Lois,* who taught Timothy, was also not ill. *Deborah the prophetess,* and *Anna the intercessor,* were both older women, but there is no mention of illness. There is no mention of Eve, Leah, Ruth, Samson's mother or others as having female problems. Sarah and Elizabeth were older women when they gave birth, but neither was sick nor had menopausal problems. Plus, Sarah was described as a post-menopausal beauty! Scripture mentions Rebekah, Rachel and Hannah's infertility, but God restores these women. Rachel dies in childbirth but that was as the result of a curse Jacob spoke over her for hiding her father Laban's idols. Scripture refers to the old as wise, feeble, or slow but not sick with sexual dysfunctions. A few verses compare certain situations to the trauma that a woman experiences while giving birth, but nothing speaks of a *woman's transition into menopause* as being anything *dramatic.* God does not mention menopause anywhere in His Word, which strongly indicates that the complications millions are experiencing are a modern paradigm!

HYSTERECTOMIES

Hysterectomies were invented to save women's lives but at some point, they became oversubscribed, huge money makers for doctors, and millions of women were left with regrets.

Hysterectomy is the second most common surgical procedure performed in the U.S. each year![19]

The word *hysterectomy* comes from ancient Greece where Hippocrates and Plato invented the Greek word *hystera,*[20] which means *womb.* Since women are generally more emotionally excitable than men, the ancients connected *hysteria* or *emotional outbursts* to problems connected with having a womb. The first hysterectomies were in 1824, 1847, and 1878.[21] Eighteenth-century women, on whom doctors attempted these operations, usually died; those who did survive often became *hysterical* with uncontrollable emotions, thus the name *hysterectomy* described the removal of the womb. From 1900 to 1940, a procedure called a subtotal hysterectomy, or a complete hysterectomy was performed on 100% of the women, 100% of the time in the United States. This included removing both the womb and the cervix. The technique lowered the initial mortality rate and caused less blood loss, but during the 1940s-1950s, the rate dropped from 100% subtotal hysterectomy to 29%[22] subtotal, because doctors decided that leaving the cervix intact would give a greater success rate long-term. The cervix helped to keep the woman's sex life alive, so she could still have sexual sensations and feelings. When the cervix was removed, sexual pleasure decreased, however by leaving the cervical stump, some women got cancer.[23]

When medically necessary, a hysterectomy can save a woman's life, stop long term vaginal bleeding and alleviate health conditions that could lead to other health problems. 500,000 women a year have a hysterectomy and 35% of women will have a hysterectomy by age 60![vi] 22,000,000 women have had hysterectomies.[24]

What are the negatives of this operation?

One in ten women will have a serious complication from their surgery and 600-1200 women will die annually from a hysterectomy. 44% of hysterectomies are performed annually due to the pain and bleeding of uterine fibroids and 40-55% of women will suffer complications from the hysterectomy, such as *infections, abnormal bleeding, blood clots, hemorrhage, bowel problems, bladder and kidney infections, and loss of nerves and sensation.* Often these conditions require additional surgeries.[25]

A persistent complaint about hysterectomy is that hysterectomies are not needed as often as women are receiving them! A near 35% surgery rate is high, especially now that doctors admit only 10% of these ladies really needed it.[26] It is now believed that hysterectomies have been oversubscribed. Years ago, when women were completing childbearing, their doctor suggested a *routine* hysterectomy with the reasoning that when her reproductive body parts were removed, her chances of getting cancer in her reproductive organs would decrease. With this reasoning, millions of women agreed to hysterectomies. In 1970-1980 4,342,000 women 15-44 yrs. old agreed to hysterectomies.[27] These were pre-menopausal women! Might I add the doctors and hospitals made a lot of money off these abusive and unnecessary operations. Women started *speaking out* and voicing their anger. The long-term effects of even a partial hysterectomy, caused new problems to develop and did not always solve the old ones. Women's groups began encouraging women to ask questions, to resist being pressured and to only agree to a hysterectomy as a last resort.

How is sex after a hysterectomy? Yes, it damages sex lives! After a hysterectomy, women have complained that they experience sexual dysfunction because removing the uterus and cervix lessens the sensation of orgasm. After a hysterectomy, the vagina becomes narrower and shorter, which makes intercourse quite painful and penetration difficult. The nerves in the vaginal area are often damaged due to the surgery, causing loss of sensation. Sometimes the bladder or intestines are also damaged which causes incontinence. Furthermore, hysterectomies cause hormonal changes, leading to loss of libido, vaginal dryness, and difficulty achieving orgasm. Basically, it ruins sex for the woman.

Are there psychological effects of hysterectomy? Yes, hysterectomy causes a psychological breakdown.[28] After a hysterectomy, some women feel *elated*, some feel *devastated*, others feel *less than a woman* or *feel they let their spouse down* and quite a few feel a *sense of loss* and *deep disappointment*. These emotional gains and losses are draining on women. Researchers have not come up with any concrete evidence that hysterectomies cause harm to a woman's psyche, but they finally admitted that a hysterectomy could cause mild depression. One report said there is increasing evidence that women feel depressed after a hysterectomy due to falling hormone levels, sadness that their childbearing years are over, and psychological feelings of losing their femininity. When researching, I found an article that perfectly describes what thousands of women say they experience after a hysterectomy.

"*No one warned me of the grief that would come from my hysterectomy.*[29] A 41-year-old mother expressed her loss, sorrow, fears and overall fight for mental health. She had no idea that *goodbye uterus* meant *hello grief*. After she wrestled through her decision to get a hysterectomy due to the pain of uterine fibroids, she was unprepared for the *mental anguish* she would suffer. Finally, over time she concluded that her female body parts are not the sum of who she is, and she accepted better health as her new normal. She was only 41 years old and was not headed into middle age yet, and without a uterus, she alleviated her fibroid issue. But only time would tell if the hysterectomy kept her from having further complications and since the bleeding had stopped, she was doing her best to accept her outcome.

Could complications from a tubal ligation sterilization lead to a hysterectomy? Yes! In a study of 374 patients who received tubal ligations, 18.7% returned for a hysterectomy.[30] This number depended on which sterilization method was used. Those with tubes burned instead of tied had a higher return rate for hysterectomy. Another study between 1971 and 1987 analyzed 80,007 women; approximately one-half were sterilized, and the other half were not. The study found that the sterilized women were 10-15% more likely to return for a hysterectomy and were more willing to have the procedure done due to increased complications from their sterilizations.[31] However there are few studies that will directly link the hysterectomy to the tubal ligation procedure even when the female experiences additional symptoms that cause uterine malfunction. Researchers do not all agree it is because the woman had a tubal ligation. They will say it is other factors. Yet if I simply take the ladies I've known over my childbearing lifetime, of those who have gotten tubal ligations and who ended up with a hysterectomy, it would be more like 60-75% of my friends and acquaintances. Overall, tubal ligations increase a female's chances of needing a full hysterectomy. *(I guess I need to get the National Organization for Women to do an independent study to prove this link!).*

People of God, why would you want to drink from the world's reservoir? Unless it is an absolute emergency, don't go down this path! Please refrain from cutting your reproductive organs. Your body is the Lord's, and your body is God's temple.

Do you not know that your bodies are temples of the Holy Spirit, who is in you, whom you have received from God? You are not your own; you were bought at a price. Therefore, honor God with your bodies (1 Corinthians 6:19-20).

We are to offer *our bodies* as a living sacrifice (Romans 12:1). Part of that sacrifice may mean laying down our lives to birth our children. We are to glorify God in our bodies (1 Corinthians 1:20). Know that the Lord is God. It is He who made us and we are His people and the sheep of His pasture (Psalms 100:3).

THE DOCTOR SAYS I SHOULD NOT HAVE ANY MORE CHILDREN

Why did your doctor tell you this? Do you have a serious medical condition? Is your problem so bad that you could die if you got pregnant again? When a woman faces a decision as critical as never being able to birth another child again, it is serious. When a doctor suggests a woman needs to do something to prevent more children, what should she do?

When a woman is faced with this kind of decision, she must be *very careful* to weigh the advice of the professionals against the voice of God and the truths of His word. Since we live in a world of medical malpractice, doctors must look out not only for their patients' desires, but also consider the possibilities of a lawsuit. Doctors can't help this fact. It is what it is. Doctors can be sued, so most err on the side of extreme caution. But every doctor is different. Some are willing to take *a few more risks* than others, and given certain factors, a woman *could* have a successful pregnancy or fail miserably. There is no across the board answer when a woman is faced with health issues.

If you are faced with a condition that might *lead to death* from a pregnancy, please seek several collaborative opinions before making any decisions. Do not think you are letting God down if you must make a choice to cease from childbearing because it truly could take your life away. It is better to be alive to raise your children, than it is to be dead. However, is this *really what you are facing or is there a potential for a lawsuit and this is what the doctors fear*? Overall, this is what you must decide about. If you get several opinions and they are all consistent, then use wisdom!

When selecting a doctor, believers need to investigate the practice in the following areas.

1. Does this doctor practice reproductive medicine according to what God teaches in His Word?

2. Does this doctor have any problem with a woman's desire to have more than the standard number of two or three children? Will that desire be protected?

3. Does this doctor perform c-sections as a routine? *(You can ask the doctor for his c-section percentage and discuss their thoughts about c-sections. You may also find out information by calling the local hospital where the doctor delivers)*. If a doctor has a high C-section rate, a woman is more likely to get a C-section with this doctor. You may find a different doctor who might make a different decision in the same circumstances. Again, we live in a world of potential lawsuits. Doctors want your baby to get here safely and often will cut you. It's safer for

the doctor, but it is also more convenient to schedule a C-section than to be up all-night waiting with a mother in labor. If a woman wants multiple pregnancies, unnecessary C-sections could cause complications as she tries to complete additional pregnancies. *(Be careful and choose your doctor wisely!)*

In 1965 the C-section rate was 4.5%. In recent years large groups of healthy, low-risk women have been opting for C-sections. In 2002 more than 25% of all children born in USA were delivered by C-section, but by 2010 the rate was 32.8% which is one in three births![32] In 2020 the c-section rate slightly dropped to 31.7% but this is still one third of all deliveries ending in a C-section![33]

23 million women have C-sections every year[34] and C-section rates around the globe are reaching epidemic proportions and in many nations the C-section rate is close to 50% of all live births![35] What is going on? The rate has risen sharply in the last decade, the highest level ever reported in the United States. The number of C-sections given to mothers who had no previous C-section jumped seven percent, and the rate of vaginal births after C-section (VBAC) dropped twenty-three percent in 2002. The C-section rate declined from the late 1980s to the mid-1990s but has been on the rise since 1996. In recent years, the VBAC rate has fallen as the C-Section rate has risen, Doctors say that women ask for unnecessary C-sections, even when there is no medical rationale for them. The only benefit is convenience. A C-section can be scheduled around work, or getting grandma into town to watch the children, and for the husband to ask off work. On the flip side, some women are utilizing midwives and at-home births in an attempt to avoid doctors who unnecessarily might cut them. Choose wisely, just because your doctor is nice to talk to, **does not mean they will not cut you** if anything unusual happens. A midwife tends to wait it out, because the midwife cannot perform a C-section and would need to call in her doctor. With midwives the C-section rate is much lower. Remember, this is *your birthing season. Bottom line, it is easier for the doctor to cut you up. Do your research and consider all your options.

Ask if this doctor routinely uses sonograms and are they mandatory? If so, are you okay with this? Please stop and simply Google, *"Are sonograms safe for a developing baby"* and you might be shocked to find a myriad of articles, more negative than positive, about the use and overuse of *routine* sonograms on babies in utero. The Bible describes utero as *the secret place* where the developing baby is with God and formed in the depths of the earth (Psalms 139). A sonogram invades that *secret place*. Doctors admit that a sonogram exam is as loud as a *freight train* coming into a station. If you were a developing baby inside your mother and all you ever knew were quiet echoes and then suddenly you *hear* this *loud near deafening noise*, would *you squirm? Would you want your mommy?* Doctors say the sound does not harm a baby **long term** but how could we ever measure whether it does or not? Most babies squirm and wiggle during their sonograms, so are they experiencing *fright?* Are they terrified? Do they desire comfort? The assumption is that they do hear something. Articles are now claiming babies are not comfortable during sonograms.[36]

Dear mom-to-be if you are reading this, the big question to ask yourself is, "*Will we find out later, after 40 years of performing routine sonograms on the developing child, that they cause cancer, autism, learning disabilities, infertility, asthma, thyroid issues, eye and ear problems or other health conditions?*" I am not sure the medical community would ever admit it. The lawsuits that would follow would break the medical profession. Yet all these conditions, and so many more were not happening routinely to our children until after doctors started performing routine sonograms on every developing baby. This is something to think about and do some research on.

I am not a doctor, and *I do believe in sonograms.* They are a wonderful modern invention, and they *do have a place in obstetrics.* A sonogram is a fantastic diagnostic tool and has saved baby's lives, but is every sonogram necessary? During my birthing years 1983-2004 they became *routine,* and now there is increasing evidence that routine sonograms on a developing baby might be the cause of serious health conditions. Most mothers are not being given any evidence or told to do any research, yet there is increasing concern in the medical community about the harm of sonograms and there are medical reports this. Each mother must make her own decision and there is enough evidence *already* in medical journals to demand more research on sonograms and their effect on the organs, brains, heart, eyes, ears, fertility, body systems, and future health of the developing child.

4. Does this doctor promote easy reproductive choices, including giving abortions, placing IUDs, and putting women on the pill for reasons other than birth control? Does the doctor routinely perform tubal ligations? 50% of sterilizations are done following birth. Many doctors have been accused of pushing this decision on a woman as she

gives birth since it is easier to perform a tubal ligation right after birth and because the insurance company will pay for an after- birth procedure.

5. During labor, will the mother be medicated, will she be allowed to move around, or will she be strapped to a bed? Will she be given the option of laboring on her own? Will this doctor allow the mother to give birth naturally as God intended, or are epidurals encouraged? Speaking of the epidural drug, can it harm a woman? Can it harm her baby? How safe is it long-term. Look it up!

6. Is this doctor a male or a female? A 2002 study examined gender preference in obstetrics from 1978-2001 and found that in 1978, only 9% of residents were women, but by 2001 71.8% were women, and by 2014 it is projected that greater than 50% of all obstetricians and gynecologists will be female. In 2002, 34% of women expressed they preferred a female, while 7% preferred males and 58% expressed no gender preference.[37] Since this profession of birthing babies was nearly 100% an all-female profession down through antiquity, eventually women might demand that obstetrics be returned back to the females.

7. Does this doctor allow God to choose the baby's birthday, or does the doctor control this decision by inducing the mom before her due date? *What woman 38 weeks pregnant, who is tired and uncomfortable will not agree to induction or ask for an induction if she thinks her doctor might cooperate? Is it safe for both mom and baby?* Routine inductions use the drug Pitocin, made from monkeys and horses. Could this drug be harmful to the uterus? If the woman does not progress, could she end up having a C-section, and couldn't this be avoided if she were allowed to wait a bit longer? We've made everything so complicated. For hundreds of years, 2 oz of castor oil was all the women needed to bring on labor *(I'm not saying to try this-it is simply an example)*. Now we use a drug made from animal sources instead.

Take your time to weigh out each factor and be very careful in selecting your doctor. It's easy for a doctor, who sees a woman who has had two c-sections, to tell her she should not have any more children and be content with the children she has. But this advice may not align with her desires. The couple needs to step back and look at all the factors. Women have been known to have up to ten C-sections, and I know this is not for all women, and I am not recommending this, but we live in the greatest age of medicine, and there are many avenues available to us to allow us to proceed when our desires collide with other people's value systems.

God's people must be careful about choosing a doctor because we are all individuals. We each carry our babies differently and labor differently. We each deliver better in different positions based on the curvature of our spine and on the position of our pelvis. If we are not given birthing options, shame on the doctor and shame on us for not investigating our alternatives! If we don't do our research, we will be stuck with the type of birth the doctor chooses for us (good or bad) and we may never know how wonderful another version of birth might have been for us and our baby.

I have had eight children. In my first three births, I was given an epidural drug and was strapped to a delivery table. The last five births were in the hospital using a nurse midwife. I did not use any drugs or painkillers and was allowed to labor on my own by walking around. I was allowed to give birth sitting up because this position is the best for my body, spine, and uterus. Obstetricians have treated me in three separate states over 28 years, and I found that obstetrician practices seem universal in certain routine things. When women get together and discuss their birthing experiences at the average obstetrician and gynecology practice, most of their stories, including mine, will be about the same. For some women, this seems fine, and I believe it is because they do not realize there are other options. Others, especially those who may not have had the kind of birth they had wanted, often gravitate toward midwifery. Some even opt to give birth at home.

For me, being home would not have worked. After giving birth, I need a place to rest for a few days and I need someone to nurture me. With all the noise and children running around at my home, it would not have been my first choice to get some rest. However, I would have opted for home had I not been able to find a wonderful midwife who would let me have the kind of birth I wanted at the hospital.

Birthing centers are also another option and are increasing as well due to rising costs of delivering at the hospital. While the birthing center and home birth options are gaining, and most women love these alternatives, most health professionals advise against these options and consider them risky. Those opposing these choices, have managed to outlaw homebirth in 14 states, but it is now licensed in 24 states and gaining in popularity. However, please take note that being at home or at a birthing center is also not without *risks. One of my girlfriends (thin, healthy, ate only organic food/water, her husband-a chiropractor), nearly bled to death when her routine hospital birth turned to trauma. Her placenta ruptured unexpectedly as she was pushing out her second child. If she had been at a home birth or birthing center, she could have bled out in 13 minutes. Even if the midwife had acted quickly and administered oxytocin, it might not have been enough to stop her intense bleeding, plus she would have had to transfer and wait on an ambulance. If she had been anywhere other than in the hospital she probably would have died. I say all this not to discourage you about alternatives, but to let you know birth is always risky, whether it is at home or at a birthing center or in the hospital. Please do your research, and make sure if you decide to be at home or at a birthing center that you are at least very close to a hospital if an emergency arises and please discuss how emergencies will be handled, and make sure your midwife/doctor has privileges at the nearby hospital.*

Does your doctor agree with your reproductive goals? You have a *spiritual responsibility* to care for and guard your reproductive health. It is your spiritual responsibility to choose a doctor who agrees with what God intended for your reproductive efforts. Otherwise, you may find your childbearing opportunities cut short because of a *routine procedure* performed by a doctor whose goal is to make money off your unfortunate situation.

Remember you only get one chance at having your babies, don't let someone else dictate their path for you. You dictate your path for you. You are the one who will live with your decision forever.

Do not be a blind sheep; research, ask questions, and choose what is best for your health. You will have to live with your choices!! When choosing a doctor, probably only a small percentage of doctors are Spirit-led in this area of medicine and the vast majority are simply practicing medicine the best they know how. A Godly physician will be harder to find, but if you are Catholic, your church may have a list of pro-life physicians in your area, same if you are a reformed Presbyterian, Amish or a Mormon or are attending a church whose pastor agrees with being open to life. If you can't get a recommendation from your church, then you may also find a pro-life practice by contacting a local pro-life pregnancy center. Sometimes these centers know of pro-life doctors in their area and sometimes you can find pro-life doctors on the internet. Orthodox Jews also want doctors who are sensitive to couples desiring larger families. If you are near an Orthodox Jewish synagogue, you may be able to find a recommended physician.

As a believer you do have a *spiritual responsibility* to choose a doctor or midwife whose convictions line up with yours and line up with the principles of God's Word. If the doctor knows the Lord and is pro-life then you can feel confident their advice will be prudent for your situation. Believe it or not there are doctors out there who do practice a *more natural approach* to obstetrics. They are much harder to find, so ask God to lead you.

ONE SIZE DOES NOT FIT ALL!

You only get one chance at having your babies, don't let someone else dictate your path.

Talk show host, Ricki Lake, did a groundbreaking movie exploring the world of medicated hospital births called, *The Business of Being Born*.[38] This movie offers much information and has helped women see how standard maternity care in the United States takes away beautiful birthing experiences and replaces them with a *medical model* of birth.

It reveals how and why the medical community offers a *one-size-fits-all* approach, with every mother getting the same tests, same methods, same procedures and same medicated births. Some tests might not be needed, given a person's healthy history, but because an insurance company will pay for it, these tests are routine, plus most often, sonograms are routine and now for 1 in 3 women a scheduled C-section is the norm.[39]

Possibly watch the movie *The Business of Being Born and* at least consider midwifery. Midwives are mentioned in the scriptures (Genesis 35:17, Exodus 1:17). Contemporary midwives tend toward a more *natural* approach to birth, using herbs and other holistic methods. Some medical nurse midwives even allow epidurals. Midwives usually work under an agreement with a doctor in case a doctor is needed for an emergency. They typically require a mother to meet with their doctor at least once during her care. I have used a midwife for five of my eight births and have been quite comfortable; the midwives delivered me at the hospital. In some states, midwives can deliver at home. Women have served women by attending births since the beginning of time, but at some point, things shifted, and this area of medicine became dominated by men. Maybe it is time we give this area back to the females. Then maybe they will approach birth from a different perspective. Years ago, it was rare to find a female obstetrician, but today the number of female obstetricians is growing, and female preference is changing.

AVOIDING BREAST CANCER

Breast cancer is on the rise. In 2025 319,750 women will be diagnosed with breast cancer. It is the most common cancer diagnosed for women in the USA. About 32% of all newly diagnosed cancers will be breast cancer and breast cancer is the second leading cause of cancer death in women. Women have a 1 in 43 (2.3%) chance of dying from breast cancer and about 42,170 women will die this year from breast cancer. [39a]

Breast cancer has not been at epidemic status at any other time in history except for now in the last sixty-five years since women started ingesting artificial hormones and having a greater number of abortions. The Susan G. Komen[39b] breast cancer foundation admits that breast cancer does increase up to 40% for ladies on the pill, the IUD and other forms of birth control that uses artificial hormones. This truth is unavoidable.

Can breast cancer be avoided? I am not going to get into a huge dialogue here about breast cancer. I believe the chance of getting it can be greatly decreased when we do things God's way. If we don't expose our breasts to the artificial hormones in the pill, the patch, the IUD or other forms of birth control then our risk should decrease with this one decision. Then if we nurse our babies for up to one year, the lower estrogen levels act as a blanket of protection over our breast tissue. If we have multiple pregnancies and breastfeed again, each pregnancy/breastfeeding cycle will decrease the chance of getting breast cancer one more time due to the lower estrogen levels.[39c] Each time a woman completes this pregnancy/breastfeeding cycle, she decreases her chance of getting breast cancer by 4-10%! Of course, there are no guarantees, and other factors could cause breast cancer but by doing things the way God set it up, we certainly can improve our chances of avoiding breast cancer.

Countless women, at the prime of their lives have been diagnosed with breast cancer. I'm trying to help you avoid this consequence. I'll never forget the words of my dear friend. We had been friends for a long time, and I knew she had been on the pill for most of her marriage. I also knew she had a previous abortion. She said to me shortly after her breast cancer diagnosis, *"I can't believe I have to go through this and now this is my life when everything is going so great."* She was 44yrs. old at the time, had two beautiful 10-year-old and 7-year-old daughters, loved her job in PR/advertising, had a beautiful house in a wonderful neighborhood, with plenty of girlfriends and a husband who adored her, and life *was* good. But then she had to undergo chemotherapy, radiation and surgery to remove her breasts, her hair fell out, and she was weak and got super sick, but then she finally recovered. After several years in remission, her cancer came back, and she is no longer with us. Such a sad ending for this beautiful woman and my dear sweet friend. In a chapter named Truth or Consequences, my goal is to not only inform you but to remind you that the choices you make will either bring good health and happiness or bring poor health and unhappiness and possibly even lead to death. Choose wisely.

VASECTOMY

Scientists have been trying for centuries to allow men to still be able to forgo castration yet remain sexually active while relieving their abilities to impregnate their female partner.

The *vas deferens* was named by Berengarius of Carpi (1470-1530).[40] During the dissection of a cadaver, a man named John Hunter came across an occluded *vas deferens*. Once scientists realized there was a special chamber for sperm, they began to try to figure out if there was a way to do something with it. No one knows who first attempted the vasectomy operation on humans, but around the turn of the twentieth century, much experimentation was being forced on criminals and social degenerates.

The vasectomy has become the most common surgical intervention to render a man infertile and over 50,000,000 men have had a vasectomy.[41] It came into vogue in the 1970s when world-population planners vasectomized large groups of men in America and overseas.[42] Today's vasectomy has a one-tenth of one percent failure rate and is considered almost one hundred percent effective in making a man completely sterile. *(The only operation that is one hundred percent effective is castration)*. This is why men choose to have it done. There were approximately 500,000 vasectomies in 2022. The rate of men 18-

64 getting vasectomies in 2007-2009 was up .34% then in 2014 it was .42% and in 2021 that rate was up to .53%, which means 4% of the male population is sterilized.[43] Between 2020 and 2021, there was a 20% increase in childless men under 30 requesting vasectomies. Most vasectomies are performed by urologists in physicians' offices under local anesthesia.

In several places, the Bible warns us about NOT cutting our genitals! It also talks about men, who were forced to be eunuchs; castrated to hinder their sexual performance (2 Kings 9:32, Jeremiah 52:25, Acts 8:27). This was not a good thing or something to be desired. The Bible has spoken. But as far as Protestant church leadership is concerned, Christians can make whatever decision they want. How often does a pastor preach against getting a vasectomy as the topic of his Sunday Morning Sermon? Never! I know I've never heard a sermon from any pulpit preaching against having a vasectomy, but I have heard quite a few jokes from the pulpit about getting one!

Why would a Godly man consider a vasectomy? A Godly man might get a vasectomy if he is uninformed that the Bible speaks against it. Just because a person is a minister don't assume the minister would know this. Since the word vasectomy is not in the Bible, countless believers assume God has nothing to say about their fertility. The number one reason men want one is that they want *convenience.* They still want to have sex but not get their woman pregnant. Even God-fearing men believe that a vasectomy will end the possibility of pregnancy and the bother of condoms or their partner using some form of artificial contraceptives. **It's all about the sex.** If a man thought cutting his genitals could lead to him no longer having sex, a vasectomy would not even be a question! Men wouldn't do it! Few men have any idea there could be complications. Yet, for some, this operation is like lighting a stick of dynamite.

COMPLICATIONS OF VASECTOMY

We already know that a vasectomy is a permanent form of birth control in which a man surrenders his ability to allow his seed to impregnate his partner. Most men do not research the operation at all. They simply ask a few coworkers or friends who got a vasectomy, and if the men they ask had no ill effects, then most decide to go through with it. The clinic routinely tells men the procedure is quick and relatively painless with a little swelling.

Reversals are usually discussed, and men are informed this operation is very hard to reverse successfully because the vas deferens are very tiny. They are about the size of a diaper pin and severing this tiny duct forms scar tissue that hinders effective reversals. Because of these potential complications to reverse this decision, men are advised not to choose vasectomy unless they are positive, they do not wish to father any more children.

Men are not told much about long-term complications from vasectomies. Few know that sometimes vasectomies cause severe pain, now called post-vasectomy pain syndrome.[44] There used to be an online site called dontfixit.com that shared how complications and nonstop pain ruined one man's life after his vasectomy. I believe he has now taken this site down, but the mayo clinic and other medical sites do recognize that some men do suffer post vasectomy syndrome complications. Testicular pain is not very common, only 1-2% of men experience long term pain but when they do, their sex life is severely affected or ruined.

Since the 1970s, medical researchers have suspected that vasectomies may affect men's immune systems and their long-term ability to fight disease. Yet, for now, doctors have declared the operation medically safe. This may be only for the short term because medical researchers have become increasingly curious about the effects that a man's sperm has on his immune system when sperm is forced to be reabsorbed back into his body.

COMMON SENSE

God designed the man's body to *release* his sperm. This is basic anatomy and physiology. After a vasectomy, the man's body still *produces* sperm—about 50,000 spermatozoa each minute, but since it no longer has a way to leave the body, it must be reabsorbed. This *cannot possibly be good* for a man's body. That's like making a man's body reabsorb vomit, excrement, urine or nasal congestion. The body can do it, but the body must *tolerate what* God meant to leave the body.

Doesn't common sense tell us this cannot be good for the body long-term? It seems obvious from a biological viewpoint or from a physiological viewpoint, but men are told every day that it is no big deal. But is it?

If sperm is something to be expelled and is considered a *foe* or an *unfriendly substance* in *the body* what happens over time when the man's body is forced to tolerate, reabsorb and *make friends with the enemy* of his body? Does the man's immune system react in some way?

Does the man's healthy immune system become weak or confused? Are the man's defenses compromised?

When the immune system is unsure whether the sperm is *foreign* or *friendly* the body produces *antigens*, which overtime could cause the immune system to build up an immunity to the man's sperm. This is sort of like an *allergic reaction* to the sperm. Over time it is possible for the man's body to become autoimmune or allergic to itself. When these antigens flood the bloodstream, the body manufactures antibodies to defend itself. One study stated that within two years of having the surgery, these antibodies could be found in 55-75% of men. These antibodies were found to leave the man vulnerable to other forms of disease.

In these non-conclusive studies, researchers found that these diseases develop in men who had enjoyed good health before their vasectomies. Diseases linked to vasectomies included heart disease, hardening of the arteries, prostate and testicular cancer, possibly diabetes, rheumatoid arthritis, Addison's disease-malfunction of the adrenals, lupus, and erythematosus. Nothing was ever conclusive. Men who have been sterilized for twenty or more years showed an increase in non-Hodgkin's lymphoma, multiple myeloma, and kidney stones but it was later debunked.[45]

Sterilizations cause sexual libido to decline[46] in some men and to rise in others. My husband told me that more than once, men complained to him after getting their vasectomies and said they didn't feel the same as they used to, and their sex drive was not like it once was. This could be age, stress at work, or other factors, but what if it's not? What if the operation does affect a man's libido. Is the convenience worth it?

Over the years there have been multiple studies trying to connect vasectomy to various diseases. Most were conducted outside the U.S. and were small studies. Their findings have either been debunked or they only found a very small connection between vasectomy and disease. But when there have *never been any large studies* how are we supposed to know for sure?

One study basically said that within 10 years of a vasectomy, a man will develop a secondary disease due to the long-term harm of daily cannibalizing his sperm. This makes sense. Think about the men in your life, your father, father-in-law or any other very healthy man who was healthy without any other health problems, when he got his vasectomy. Then within ten years, had this man developed any new health problems? Heart disease, immune system dysfunction, had lots of colds and viruses, developed an auto-immune disease, had problems with his skin, experienced some memory loss, cancer or any other disease?

Maybe nothing happened and the man remains healthy, but cannibalizing one's sperm simply cannot be heathy forever because it goes against the design of a man's body. Eventually, by *robbing Peter to pay Paul* it will catch up with him in some way.

Do we need to wait until medical science reveals that vasectomies eventually cause secondary diseases to develop or do we simply listen to what God already told us?

Common sense tells us that God created the man's sperm to leave his body. *Ungodly men* created vasectomies to make sperm be absorbed into the man's body. **The vasectomy was created to interfere and stop a man's healthy reproductive system.** We know that God wants men to be available to create life and this availability allows men's bodies to function as created.

We also know that before this operation became popular, prostate cancer and other reproductive cancers were unheard of in the male and now they are common. We also know the prostate is in the same area of the body as the vas deferens and I am not drawing any medical conclusion, I am simply talking about the anatomy. A man's immune system is the man's defense against all disease and cancer and other illnesses are immune system breakdowns. Cannibalizing one's sperm eventually breaks down the man's immune system. As much as I want to combine two and two to equal four, we must continue to wait for medical science to confirm what God's word already confirms! For now, we can only look at how our body *was meant to function* and whether the vasectomy agrees with natural functions.

Since common sense tells us that a vasectomy can't be healthy, why would a God-fearing husband want to take such a risk? I know it seems so easy now, but if you are a man, you may live a long time. A sterilization operation to prevent more children may ruin your sex life, decrease your libido, decrease sexual pleasure, mess up your immune system, and bring ill health that gets in the way of raising your children. It could even prevent you from meeting your grandchildren!

As I conclude, I've only scratched the surface of the information that is available. I've presented current research and challenged your common sense. Medical studies being what they are, we might have testimonies about others' experiences, yet we still do not have concrete proof about these operations but knowing others have had problems might be enough for some people to at least be cautious.

STERILIZATION REVERSALS

One time I saw an advertisement for a vasectomy, and it said, *"Get the operation that keeps on giving."* And I thought, are they kidding? *"Sterilization is the operation that keeps on hurting!"* In all my interactions with people who have undergone either a tubal ligation or a vasectomy, they boast that they are happy they don't have to worry about that anymore. But then if I follow up and say, *"You mean you really didn't want more children?"* Then the truth comes out and they say, *"Well, my wife didn't want any more pregnancies"* or *"We did but we didn't think we could afford more"*, or a woman might confess, *"My husband didn't want more but I did"*, or other words of regret.

Regrets are the random thoughts that come at Little League when the parents realize this is *their child's last game* and they wish they had another child to enjoy Little League with, or the regret a couple in their early forties feels when they think the wife has *conceived a surprise baby* but then finds out that it's early menopause. Sterilization regrets are those thoughts that catch the sterilized off guard. Once, they were so positive about not wanting another child, yet later their emotions get the best of them, and they regret their decision. For the brave few who can and are willing to take a chance on a reversal, these may become successful enough to undo their sorrowful decision.

Reversal surgery is the surgical attempt to restore an individual's ability to have more children by reconnecting the damaged tubes cut or blocked by surgical procedures. These tubes are the vas deferens in men and the Fallopian tubes in women. Depending on the severity of the original surgery, some people have had a successful reversal. Reversal surgery is considered a major operation and usually requires a hospital stay. The conception of another child determines success rates. Reports have stated that approximately 60% of women and 50% of men become fertile again.[47]

Several factors rule out candidates considering reversal. A patient needs to be in good health and have a fertile partner. A female patient needs to be under forty and still ovulating monthly. A male patient needs to be under fifty. Less than ten years should have passed since their sterilization, and success can occur only if small sections of their tubes were damaged during their sterilization operation. If their tubes were clipped or tied, they have a greater chance of attempting reversal than if tubes were electro-coagulated (burned). The electro-coagulation procedure means the surgeon burns the tube. This is considered very effective and is rarely reversible because the goal of the procedure is to damage a large area of the tube, leaving little for reconnection. The U.S. has used electrocoagulation for years due to its high success rate on both men and women.

The average cost for reversal surgery for women is $5000- $9,000 plus hospital expenses;[48] and the cost for men is $5000-$14,000.[49] Insurance companies rarely cover a reversal, although Medicaid will cover partial expenses in some states. Choosing a doctor to perform this surgery is very important. The surgeon's skill and expertise can affect the surgery's outcome, especially in vasectomies requiring microsurgery.

When researching this subject on the internet, I found that the reversal industry is becoming big business as more people desire to reverse their decisions for all kinds of reasons and doctors offering help are not necessarily religious. There is a doctor in Arkansas who does reversal surgery at a reduced price and other doctors who also offer discounts. Simply google and you will find a list of doctors who specialize in reversals, hopefully you will find one in your state.

A reversal affects all areas of a person's life: *spiritual, physical, and emotional*. Before attempting a reversal, people must understand a few things about their original procedure. Not only is there a physical component to getting sterilized but there is also a spiritual and emotional side of a decision like this. The initial sterilization involved a physical procedure, yet sterilization is a decision of the will and a reflection of the heart. Initially, the man or woman did not want another child. Now their heart and mind have changed, and they do want another child. The attitudes that led to the original decision should be repented for.

Sterilization was an attempt to control fertility. The next chapter includes prayers for sterilization reversals. It would be a good idea to pray those prayers as a couple and to follow the steps listed about healing the emotional wounds that sterilization creates. A couple needs to make sure that the choice to reverse is made with the proper guidance and counsel so that the marriage can be made stronger **no matter what the outcome is.** If a baby is not conceived, the sorrow this could bring is *very hard* for some people. The couple needs to ask forgiveness from each other before their reversal and then be *in agreement* emotionally and spiritually so they can be content with whatever the outcome might be.

ASK GOD TO CLOSE THE WOMB

This entire book is about the story of fertility and what an amazing blessing it is to have children. We see God's plan on the first page of the Bible and on the last page, and then all throughout the Scriptures. We have discussed our idolatrous culture and seen why patterns of infertility have fallen upon seemingly innocent Generation X and Generation Y couples. This chapter, Truth or Consequences, has focused on the evils of going to the outside world and allowing them to cut off God's gift of life. The one thing we have not discussed is that as believers, we often do not realize the spiritual power God has made available to us. We are serving a supernatural God who gave us His supernatural gift of life, yet our body limits the outcome. Even when serving God with everything we have in us, we reach the end of our humanity.

Generally, the number one primary reason a tubal ligation or vasectomy is chosen is because of *convenience* and not because of a health issue. The couple wants convenience. They do not want to be messing with contraceptives anymore. The number two reason these operations are chosen is because of *exhaustion*. The couple feels they have reached their limit and for whatever reason does not want to or cannot use birth control anymore, so they opt for these un-Biblical operations. The number three reason is a *health crisis*. One of the partners is ill or has a risk factor for pregnancy. Out of convenience the couple wants a permanent solution, rather than abstaining during fertile times. The couple doesn't even consider alternatives when there is zero teaching on this subject in all churches except the rare occasion a Protestant minister might mention something about the family or when a visiting Catholic priest might speak against contraceptives. In today's church world-God's people are not hearing what they need to hear. Rather than have an operation, do couples know they have options? Let's look to the Scriptures to see if God gives us any other options.

We see throughout the Scriptures that **wombs were opened**, and **wombs were closed by God**. Scripture is clear: God holds the keys to opening and closing the womb.

I already pointed out that the first disease ever mentioned in the Bible was the disease of being barren and the first barren woman was Abraham's wife. Yet for Abraham there was this great promise of fertility for he and his offspring. At the time, when God had promised numerous offspring, was it *merely a coincidence* that Abraham, his son Issac and his grandson Jacob all experienced infertility in their households? I think it's probably not a coincidence, but was this infertility caused by God or by Satan?

Did God use this infertility to show us a clue about how fertility works? Considering the earth was probably a cleaner place to live than it is today, what would have caused Sarai to suffer barrenness? More than likely her food was organic, without additives or chemicals, her air was clean, without atmospheric radiation or pollution, and she didn't have chemicals affecting her home environment nor artificial birth control affecting her hormones. Why in the world would a woman living in the ancient world experience a closed womb unless God admitted to closing it Himself! Possible God was allowing the barren womb to serve some higher purpose.

As we venture into the Old Testament, God highlights a few situations where **God opens and closes wombs.** After the Scripture tells us that Sarai's womb was closed and had always been closed, we realize *God allowed this* for Sarai, even when being barren would have been seen as a negative for her and Abraham. In this society, a *closed womb* would seem a curse especially when the female was the giver of life and the person whose role was to be the caretaker of the family. Why does God give us these details? What does God want us to see? If you look at the details in each story you will see the Bible does reveal a pattern in these stories. Sometimes, God closed the womb, as in the case of the wombs of Egypt, and when God closed the womb of King David's wife Michael. The Scriptures tell us in these instances *God closed the wombs*, and it was a punishment.

In the case of the Pharoah, the reason was sort of innocent on his behalf. Abraham lied about Sarai being his wife for fear of reprisal, so he told Pharoah she was his sister and technically she was his half-sister. When Pharoah took Sarai into his harem, *God punished* Pharoah and **closed** all Pharoah's wives' wombs! After Pharoah gave Sarai back and after **Abraham prayed**, God **opened** all the *wombs of Pharoah's wives* once again! (Genesis 20:18). In the story of David and his wife Michael, when God punished her and closed her womb, we have no record of King David praying to ask God to open Michaels's womb. She remained barren for the rest of her life as a punishment.

The next pattern we see is that **God visited** Sarah, and she conceives.

Isaac prays and **God allowed** Rebekah to conceive (Genesis 25:21).

Rachel prays and **God remembered,** and she conceives (Genesis 29:31)

Leah was unloved, **God opened** her womb, and she conceives (Genesis 30:17).

Hannah prays and **God remembered,** and she conceives (1 Samuel 1-2).

Elisha promises a baby and the Shunammite *woman* **conceives** (2 Kings 4:13-16)

Manoah was barren, she **became pregnant** (Judges 13:2-3).

He makes the *barren woman* a happy *mother* of children. God is the source of fertility (Psalm 113:9). Shall I cause to bring forth to delivery, yet **shut** the womb? (Isaiah 66:9).

Elizabeth was *barren* and old; **God opens** her womb, and she conceives (Luke 1:7).

All these verses show that God actively opened and closed these ladies' wombs. When they prayed to Him, God remembered them. When prophetic words were spoken about an upcoming baby, God delivers with a pregnancy. God was not sitting up in Heaven ignoring these prayers! He was actively *opening* and *closing* wombs.

Instead of sacrificing your fertility by allowing an unholy operation, look to this pattern of Scripture and consider that when the time comes to be finished with your fertility, pray and *ask God to close* your womb permanently. There are quite a few testimonies today of couples who have asked God to close the wife's womb, and it worked! The wife never conceived again.

We serve a supernatural God. Since scripture makes it clear in all these verses that God can open a woman's womb and does shut a woman's womb, a couple can ask God to do this for them. It is worth asking Him. Isn't it?

God's people must never forget that those who do not know God and who hate His ways created these sterilization operations to take away a person's God-given right to reproduce. The non-believing world offers its lifestyle, and their operations are supported by current medical literature and the media. Yet the issue is, *do God's people partake?* We must remember, God created the womb to give birth and perfectly balanced the hormones; medical science offers this tempting unnatural, artificial substitute. *Do we partake?* God created a way for a man's sperm to leave his body; medical science offers an operation that does not allow it to do so. *Do we partake?* Can we use our *common sense* to see that this is not what God intended for our bodies!

When you choose **God's truth,** you will **avoid the consequences**!

Scripture cautions us *to be on guard and be alert, for the devil is a roaring lion seeking whom he may devour* (1 Peter 5:8). Don't let him devour your health! **The choice is yours!**

Wife's Prayer

Heavenly Father, thank You for this information. I don't want to suffer as so many women have. I desire to be a mommy who is healthy and whole. Help me to make choices that will be correct for my life and that will always bring honor to Your name. Help my husband to do the same. I love You, Lord and I desire to always give You my best.

Amen

Husband's Prayer

Heavenly Father, I thank You for this information. I needed to be informed this way, and this has helped open my eyes. I desire to obey You in all that I do. I never realized just how serious the complications of these operations could become. Help me to make proper decisions as the leader of my home so that I can honor You in all that I do.

Amen

Christopher's Commentary

I told Rachel I liked this chapter because my wife finally talks about the consequences of birth control choices. Men never talk about this or think about it, for that matter. I'm not sure why, except maybe we aren't aware. Few things would cause us to become aware of the negatives. All men see are the positives. Use it, and she doesn't get pregnant.

If you drive anywhere on the highways in the state of Florida, you cannot help but notice the billboards advertising the vasectomy services of Dr. Stein. His signs broadcast over 46,000 vasectomies performed to date, up from 41,000 a few years ago. I'm not sure what kind of person would want to boast about this, but I guess Dr. Stein is quite proud that he has sterilized 46,000 males. His billboards remind men that for *a clinic visit and a small fee*, Dr. Stein can cure what ails them. We've heard Dr. Stein even does vasectomies for a reduced rate for people with low incomes, I guess this is his humanitarian effort, and believe it or not, Dr. Stein also performs reversals. Wow, I can see clearly now. To think I used to agree with all this myself.

Surely Dr. Stein sometimes runs into complications, but those are not on his billboards. His patients are probably not told of any long-term effects when a man's body is forced to absorb his sperm. It's all simple deception, and because men are either unaware or never think anything will happen to them, they want what is offered as a *"snip-snip today, keeps a pregnancy away"*, so they sign up.

All we like sheep are led astray. One of our family friends told Rachel her doctor suggested she get an IUD to solve her ongoing problem with bleeding. The hormones in the IUD were supposed to correct the problem. He did not explain anything else about the IUD except the birth control benefits, so she accepted this option without question because it came from her doctor. This woman is a prayer leader and considers herself *deeply in love with Jesus* and a true believer. Rachel tried to tell her that her IUD is an abortifacient, but she told Rachel, "*When God brings you an answer, there are some things you don't need to pray about.*"

Men never think about any of this, and if their wife is bleeding and her doctor offers a solution so they can get back to having regular sex, men are not going to care about the physical or even the spiritual consequences. If we were less informed and didn't have our convictions about how these things work, back when we were looking for answers, Rachel might have wanted to take the same *quick fix* if we did not have the convictions again. It takes bravery and conviction to turn from the establishment and trust in a higher plan. You know, God never promised us ease, but He did promise blessings when we do things His way.

Christopher Scott

Investigate and Questions

- After reading Proverbs 14:12, would you ever equate reproductive choices with death? Do you realize people have died from their choices? Share your thoughts.
- Read Hosea 4:6, have you considered some birth control options listed: pill, patch, IUD, Depo-Provera, etc.? Was the literature informative? Did they discuss risks and possible side effects? Were you aware of ANY long-term effects on your health? Share your thoughts.
- What do you think about a woman choosing a stronger partner when not on artificial contraceptives and preferring a weaker male when her system is influenced by artificial hormones? And when they have children, their children would be weaker genetically?
- Are you concerned about breast cancer? Does it run in your family? Is breastfeeding an option for you?
- Do you know anyone who regrets being sterilized? If you were sterilized, do you regret it?
- Read 2 Kings 9:32, Jeremiah 52:25, Acts 8:27. Can you list 5 popular reasons men use today when they want to get a vasectomy. How different do you think these same reasons might be if castration were their only option? At other times of history, castrated men were shunned and were outcasts but now getting sterilized is acceptable, how is castration akin to vasectomy?
- Read Genesis 1:27, 1 Kings 9:10, 22:38, Matthew 7:6. Explain the relationship between humans and dogs, between what we do to our dogs and what we do to humans. God views humans as higher beings than animals. Is God de-glorified when humans lower themselves to equality with animals? Share your thoughts.
- How concerned are you that 25% of women over 45 have already been sterilized? On a scale of 1-10 (10 being highest) how much do you think this bothers God? Are you in the age group where those

around you choose vasectomies and tubal ligations? Have you felt any pressure to do this too? If you feel comfortable, please share.
- Read Galatians 6:7. Do you think it applies here? What are your thoughts about getting an operation to break a perfectly working body part? Does it matter to you that this is not what God intended?
- Statistics say that one-half to one-third of all post tubal women suffer from physical problems such as *hot flashes, bleeding, emotional depression, weight gain* and more. Do you know someone who has suffered this way? Have you ever met a woman who got her tubes tied and then needed a total hysterectomy? Are you familiar with the complications she experienced? Please share your thoughts.
- Have you ever heard of vasectomy complications, pain in the groin, lack of libido, etc. Did you ever know a male who experienced any complications? Does it make sense to force sperm to stay in the body? How can this be a good thing?
- Read 1 Peter 5:8. How does this verse apply to this chapter?

Impacting Others

Rachel - thank you for your book! I love it, and started telling all my friends and they've been passing my copy around and now I don't know which one has the book! But I did want to share. When I had my last three babies, I had difficulty fighting off the sonogram police and I love that you put something in here about sonograms! I read reports too and they do not know their effects on babies in utero, so I wanted to decline the sonogram and almost every doctor would not see me! Even if I was willing to sign papers that I would not sue! I even had to go to a midwife group, and they made me sign forms too when I did not want a routine sonogram. If I was bleeding or if the baby appears too large or too small etc. I certainly would get one, but not simply to get a little look-see or a measurement. I always measure large anyway. But I could not believe the amount of pushback I got for simply not wanting to get one, so I agree that you said something in your book. More ladies should do some research. Sonograms are not as good as people think they are. **J.M. Mother to 6 Woodstock, Ga**

Rachel, my husband had a vasectomy. Looking back now, I can see how God was working on our hearts all along. Before the vasectomy, we investigated being foster parents because we figured we would adopt if we changed our minds about more children. But I was telling a dear lady at my church about it (she had nine children herself), and she shared with me the lies and excuses we use to justify a vasectomy. It upset me because this was not what we were doing, but a few days later, I felt convicted when I realized this was what we were doing! When my husband came home, I shared what I was thinking; of course, he thought I was nuts! And I guess I had been obsessing all day, wondering if God would make me like the Duggars. I did not like the idea of having 19 children, especially since I had horrible pregnancies. So, when I talked to him, my husband was relieved we did not have the money for a reversal. I dropped the subject with him, but it kept gnawing at me. Then I talked with another friend who is not at my church, but she homeschools, and she gave me your book. I'm not sure where she got it from, but she said it was the best book she had read on the subject and gave me Nancy Campbell's book "Be Fruitful and Multiply." So, I devoured both and then read them to my husband. That was when we both started to be super convicted and repented. We were finally on the same page. We were both still wrestling with all the normal fears, like "What is God getting us into?" But then, at my Bible study, a mother of three (who wanted lots more children herself) told me to ask God for faith to get the reversal, and then if God provided for that, ask again for faith to have one more child and not to sweat all those what-if fear scenarios. We then agreed that if God could supernaturally provide for the reversal, He could change our hearts. We also realized after going through all the trouble, we might not end up with another baby, and then we might have to deal with that trauma too. Yet somehow, between the fears and the what ifs, we were able to trust Him and were confident God was doing something exceptional with us, and once we agreed, God did provide! Out of the blue, we were given an unexpected financial blessing from a family member, which was just enough to cover the reversal. Now we've had two more children since the reversal. Those pregnancies were also much better than my others. In dealing with my fears, I relaxed and enjoyed being pregnant. The coolest part and biggest blessing for me has been the change in my husband's attitude. Now he says that people who don't want more children are on the same level in their hearts as those who want an abortion. Normally I am the one who is black and white, but when he said this to me, I was amazed at the truth he was sharing. He is a changed man, and I am a changed mother. Now I tell everyone! Thank you, Rachel, so much for the truths in your book. If a changed life is your reward, you have two! **J.D. Mother to 7 children on earth (3 in Heaven), Ohio.**

Chapter 11

SHOULD YOU SEEK A SUPERNATURAL HEALING OF YOUR FAMILY PLANNING ORGANS?

By His stripes we are healed (Isaiah 53:5).

During my many years with the Lord, I have had the incredible privilege of witnessing the power of God healing people of disease. I've witnessed enough healings to know that God can heal anything in our bodies, including infertility. Yes, I do believe God can heal our reproductive organs. When people share that another child is impossible because of endometriosis, or uterine fibroids or low sperm count or prostate problems, or cancers or any other ailment that may be stopping them from reproducing children, I simply say God can heal anything. Skeptical people respond, *"Do you believe that God can heal my womb, ovaries, or my husband's system? Is that kind of thing possible?"* My response is always, *"Why not?"* God heals other body systems, so why not heal the reproductive system! What makes this system any more complicated to heal than any other system? If you suffer from infertility for any reason, God can heal your infertility. Unfortunately, the subject of *healing* is controversial for some people's theology, but *scripture is clear.* In the Bible days God healed ladies of infertility. What makes the times we live in today any different? The Bible says *we have not* because *we ask not* but some people's interpretation of scripture makes them think God only healed people a long time ago. This is simply untrue! God still heals people today, and why wouldn't He? The Bible says God is the *same* yesterday, today and forever and God is the one who wants you to have children.

Throughout this chapter I will examine reasons why we should ask Him to heal us, and I will reveal reasons why your healing could be blocked, and I provide prayers that could release that blockage. I know healing is a *mystery* we can never completely understand but if we want to be healed, I am of the belief that we *ask, seek, knock* and then *stand* on God's promises. If this is a little too *deep* or *charismatic* leaning for you, I am sorry, I cannot apologize for the healing power of God. He is our Lord and if we have a need, we are allowed to ask Him to meet our need. The Lord might not answer with a healing, but we should at least be willing to ask. Luke 18:27 says **the things that are impossible with men are possible with God.**

Healing has been a benefit of following God down through time, so why not now in today's world? The Scriptures remind us in Psalm 103:2,3, "Forget not all His benefits, *He forgives* all your sins and *heals* all your *diseases!* The Bible says the Lord blesses, and the Lord heals. Surely, He can put our physical bodies back together when we are broken.

Now to Him who is able to do exceedingly above all that we ask or imagine, according to His power that is at work within us (Ephesians 3:20).

*I will take away sickness from among you, and none will miscarry or be barren in your land. I will give you a full life spa*n *(Exodus 23:25-26).*

People tell me that they have never heard of God doing miracles or healing people in modern times except maybe through a doctor, yet today, in parts of the world where medical care is scarce, believers are desperate for God to heal them. They have no other option, but God. Missionaries report stories of miraculous healings when desperate people pray. When they cry out to God, He heals them and supplies their need fulfilling Philippians 4:19 that says, "My God will supply all your needs according to His riches in glory by Christ Jesus.

If God can heal a broken body in a foreign country, He certainly can heal a broken body in America.

Is anyone among you sick? Let them call the elders of the church to pray over them and anoint them with oil in the name of the Lord. And the prayer offered in faith will make the sick person well; the Lord will raise them up. If they have sinned, they will be forgiven (James 5:14).

Infertility is on the rise and many couples *want to be parents* but can't seem to conceive. Every month, they remain at a loss. Where are the faithful prayers for these people? I know that God wants to heal the infertile among us but in my sixty-plus years of attending church, I could almost count on my two hands the number of times I have seen faithful ministers, pastors or priests, offer prayer for this kind of healing. *Even though infertility affects nearly 20% of people, asking God to heal infertility vs. healing other things has not been popular.*

The first time I ever heard of a pastor asking God to heal infertility was in 2000 when a girl I met told me she got healed of infertility, after getting prayed for at a local church. She said that it had become a tradition to offer a *special prayer* on *Mother's Day* for *infertile couples* and so she and her husband went and got prayed for. I held her new baby in my arms! I was so amazed, that the next year I visited this church on Mother's Day with my family, so I too could witness this ceremony myself.

The couples who dedicated their children at the Mother's Day Baby Dedication ceremony all came up onto the platform and the pastor prayed over each baby and then at the end of the ceremony, the pastor said to the congregation, *"If you would like to be up here next year dedicating a baby, but you are having trouble conceiving, please stand up. We would like to pray for you."* As couples around the large congregation stood for prayer, groups of believers surrounded them and prayed with them as their pastor said a formal prayer from the pulpit. He didn't say an elaborate prayer but one from the heart that simply said, *Lord please heal these couples and grant them the desires of their heart. Bring them back next year with a baby in their arms*. Every year between nine to twelve months later, babies were born because of these prayers! *(Just thinking about these miracles fills my eyes with tears of joy).*

The year I visited several couples said they were holding a miracle baby and that they could not conceive until the congregation prayed for them. Then the pastor turned to his church members and said, *"See the miracles of the Lord"* and people clapped. Congregants cried, the pastor cried, the parents cried, new grandparents cried as each story touched our hearts. One of the deacons told me that God has never let them down. Since the congregation started praying to heal infertility, every single year couples get healed and come back to share their miracle with the congregation. If the results of this ceremony at First Baptist Church of Orlando when Jim Henry was the pastor, is any indication of what God can do, then what are we waiting for? I know God wants to heal infertility, miscarriages, and complications caused by birth control, abortions, and sterilizations.

Let's STOP the madness and ASK.

> Ask and it will be given to you; seek and you will find; knock and the door will be opened to you (Matthew 7:7).
> Yet ye have not, because ye ask not (James 4:2).
> Let us therefore come boldly unto the throne of grace, that we may obtain mercy, and find grace to help in time of need (Hebrews 4:16).
> The effectual fervent prayer of a righteous man availeth much (James 5:16).
> He has sent me to proclaim freedom for the prisoners and recovery of sight for the blind, to set the oppressed free (Luke 4:18).
> But those who seek the LORD lack no good thing (Psalm 34:10).

If God wants to heal, and if His word says He heals, then why doesn't God heal 100% of the time? I don't know. The Bible says healing is for everyone but not everyone will be healed but most often healings are blocked due to unbelief (Mark 6:5-6). It is also due to the sovereignty of God (Isaiah 55:8-9), yet in Scripture, the Lord instructs us to ask (James 5:14-15). We see in the Scriptures God healed many people. At times He healed everyone in the crowd (Matthew 12:15), and at other times He healed one specific person, such as blind Bartimaeus (Mark 10:46-52). He also healed a group of persons such as in the healing of the ten lepers (Luke 17:11-19).

Scripture does not tell us to dissect why God does what He does. Instead, it tells us to ask! It is still up to the Father whom He chooses to heal so it would be unfortunate to get to Heaven and find out we didn't receive our healing simply because our theology told us we shouldn't ask Him. Even though it has not been popular to ask for a baby or to pray over someone's reproductive organs or to ask God to recreate organs, this does not mean we should accept our broken body as a sign that we are to remain this way. It is a lie. Stop believing the lie and stop accepting that God wants you broken.

God does not promise the outcome when He tells us to pray. Instead, He says pray and see what the Lord can do. This IS what faith looks like. The healing belongs to God, but our part is to ASK and BELIEVE. It is sad when Christians tell each other that they are to accept that their miraculous God is one who fails. Please run from anyone who will not believe with you that this miracle is *possible!* And it might take time to walk out a healing, but this is not a reason to not ask or a reason to back down.

Where does God heal people? We never know the arena in which God will choose to perform His miracles. This is why it is essential to believe that anything could be possible, anytime and anywhere. It is even possible to be healed and conceive as the result of reading this book! By God's grace it has already happened to several of my readers. God is a God of miracles. Healing people glorifies God and brings glory to His name. We never know where God may choose to heal us; out in the open or in our quiet place, this part is completely left up to God. (If you believe God can only heal a person while at a church or when a holy person prays, it is ok. Go ask a minister to pray over you at your local church).

What is the difference between a *healing* and a *miracle*? A *miracle* is an instantaneous event and has immediate evidence; a blind person receives sight, a disabled person walks, a deaf person suddenly hears. Much of the earthly ministry of Jesus was in the realm of instantaneous miracles. A *healing* happens at the exact same time a miracle does, yet *the immediate evidence* will take time to manifest itself completely.

Even when a mother's infertility is instantly healed **when she prays or when a minister prays or when someone else prays, it *will* still *take time* until her next menstrual cycle is missed and at least *nine months* to a year for the miracle healing to become completely *evident*.** This timeline often confuses people. They think that if they do not have instant evidence, God did not heal them, and this is simply not true.

Often after prayer, their body is in the process of being healed, but they don't see it, so they lose hope, and tell others that God did not heal them. But this is not true, instead they simply misunderstand the process.

ASK GOD - Pray

ACTION - Make love

STAND FIRM - Never allow doubt to stop you from believing Jesus!

When you conceive in the next month or even within the next three to six or nine months, do not question God's miraculous intervention! If **you could not conceive** and you **now have conceived,** this pregnancy did not "simply happen." If you are holding a newborn a year or so later, to God be the glory!

Do I have to do anything? Yes, you must believe and receive God's healing. Believe it or not, not everyone believes they can be healed or believes they should be healed. We do not have sound Biblical teaching on healing at a myriad of churches, so people don't understand that God wants to heal them. In fact, some people are so mixed up they believe God wants them to stay this way so they shouldn't pray! Where is the scripture on that? I am not here to debate. We do know across the globe Jesus is healing people on earth every day. I believe we *have not* because we *ask not*, and we should seek, expecting to find, and knock on God's healing door expecting Him to open the door and heal us!

Please keep in mind, trying to be healed is an *emotional* experience. With infertility, I know you lack the ability to conceive and that drains you. I realize you have emotional pain that no one understands. Your body is failing you. You fight comparing yourself to others and you can't help how you feel. You want what others have and you don't understand why you cannot have your own child. I feel for you, and I do understand!

Sometimes healing involves working through emotional issues that you do not realize are there. Maybe you are not conceiving because you had problems in your upbringing and you are afraid to bring a baby into this world, or maybe you are afraid that you might not be a good parent, or maybe you are afraid that pregnancy might make you fat! Your emotions can play tricks on you and prevent you from receiving God's healing power.

Healings must be received. When we pray or when others pray, we must believe God wants this for us so we can then allow ourselves *to be open* to receiving from God. Sadly, not everyone can open their spirit or wants to open up. They might say they *want to be healed or believe they can be healed* but something in their emotions or their psyche stops them from opening their heart and receiving from God. It's weird. I don't know how it works but I've had prayer warriors tell me they prayed over someone for a certain health condition, and they could feel the person *blocking* the prayer. For some reason, their spirit was not open to receive. Again, I do not know exactly how it works but I do know fear can block a healing, lack of forgiveness can block a healing, disbelief can block a healing, and other elements can prevent a person from being open to receive.

Forgiveness is huge. You may have a friend or family member who can get pregnant easily but, in your heart, you resent them, or you are jealous of them. You may say you are happy for them but inside of your soul their pregnancy feels threatening to you or makes you very sad about yourself, but you may not be aware these emotions are there. Ask God to forgive you of any resentment. In the story of infertile Hannah her husband's other wife provoked Hannah and would get in her face and brag how she could have a baby, but Hannah could not. Hannah settled the issue on her knees in prayer and then God gave her a miracle. He gave her Samuel, and five additional children! Everyone has a different set of circumstances, and unforgiveness in a person's heart can be the one factor that separates a wounded heart from receiving the love of God that comes as a healing. These are things I have observed. I do not have all the answers as to why some people get healed and some do not. But I know that God wants your life whole, and if healing is involved, then God wants it to happen for you. Since some people do not know how to ask God for healing, I have written down some steps toward healing for people to pray.

HEALING MUST BE RECEIVED, YOU HAVE TO "WANT IT!"

The gospel gives us two accounts of a story about a female who had a severe health problem, and she sought Jesus for a healing. (Luke 8: 43-43, Mark 5:28-29). The gospel says this woman had been bleeding for twelve years! She had spent her life savings on doctors, and none could stop her vaginal hemorrhaging which no doubt left her weak and anemic. Her *only hope* was to get a touch from Jesus of Nazareth. This woman was fully convinced that one encounter with Jesus would solve her problem. But her dilemma was that Jesus had become very popular and everyone else also wanted a healing touch from Him. Furthermore, this woman had been banned from public as the Jewish laws at the time forbade any woman on her menstrual cycle from being out in the open. The Levitical Laws (Leviticus 15:19-33) called this woman *unclean* for fear drops of her menstrual blood might spill on the ground making the ground *unclean* when stepped in, or if the woman *touched* another person, she might have just been touching her menstrual rags and then that person would be *unclean*. Ritualistic rules made her chances quite impossible as she was not even allowed to be seen in public much less be in close proximity to Jesus. On that fateful day, she defied all rules and broke into the crowd, determined to simply get ahold of even the

SHOULD YOU SEEK A SUPERNATURAL HEALING OF YOUR FAMILY PLANNING ORGANS?

hem of his garment. She believed if she could only *touch Him*, His power might transform her life. Straining she reached through the crowd and grabbed ahold of a piece of his prayer shawl, the long silky tzitzits that hung down from his waist and when she grabbed it, Jesus turned around and said, *"Who touched me? For I felt POWER leave My body!"* The woman came trembling toward Jesus and fell at His feet admitting she was the one who reached out towards Him. Jesus said, *"Daughter be of good cheer your faith has made you well, go home in peace."* And the woman went away rejoicing for she had been made whole and no longer had to live a life of shame. This miracle story is what healing is all about, believing God for your impossible dream!

The first step in asking God for healing is to ask the Lord to change any wrong attitudes that you may received through teachings that dismiss God's ability to heal people today.

Many people of God have been sold a *bill of goods* through incomplete teachings on healing. For years I was told that illness, sickness, and disease were part of God's will and plan for my life. I was told that He brought these things into people's lives to teach them new things. I now believe that these teachings caused me to accept years of lack in many areas of my life because I thought that God wanted me to be poor, sick and lacking. Since I loved God and was trying my best to please Him, I accepted these problems as something that came as part of my Christian Walk. By accepting these beliefs, I was sort of agreeing that my God is a *glass half-empty* sort of God, instead of the *glass full*. (Before you get your *spiritual panties in a wad* and assume I am into prosperity teaching, you would be making an incorrect assumption).

This *glass half empty* assumption is the same thinking that has caused countless believers to *accept* illness as if it always comes from God and to never ask God to do anything about their sickness, and certainly not seek out a healing, not even for a headache. Instead, they don't pray, they take an aspirin. If their child is sick, they go to the pediatrician, and if they can't get pregnant, they go to a fertility specialist, and on and on. These believers never consider that they are *supernatural* believers, serving a *supernatural* God. With God, all things are possible and just as He healed infertile Sarai, without a doctor's help, and He did this, thousands of years ago, He can certainly heal the infertile today!

Those healing skeptics among us might hear stories about God healing other people but tend to believe that either the stories are untrue, or that healing is only possible with a doctor's help or a medical treatment. This limited thinking keeps people where the enemy wants them to be; sick and accepting their sickness and sad that their God cannot help them. Don't get me wrong my message is about having babies and if the only way you can have a baby is by a doctor helping you, a doctor might be the one God uses to help you conceive. If the doctor's methods do not go against scripture, then go for it. But on the flip side, scripture is clear that God is our healer and even if a doctor helps, God ultimately allows your body to conceive.

The Word of God tells us the Lord died for our infirmities (Isaiah 53:4) and that He desires to set us free. Jesus came to bring good news to the poor, and to set the captives free (Isaiah 61:1). Illness, death, and poor health are some of the main things the enemy uses to make people his captives. Too often, God gets blamed for the things the devil is responsible for. Unless God is punishing a person with an illness, which He did do a few times in the Bible, more than likely your infertility or need for a healing is the result of living in a fallen world. Ultimately, God wants people to be well; He wants them to be able to pay their bills; He wants them to be happy; He wants them to go to Heaven. He especially wants to see them enjoying the abundant life on earth (John 10:10).

Does this mean that God never uses illness to punish people? No, because in the Bible God used illness to not only punish people but sometimes to take them out. God punished the children of Israel several times with illness when they complained (Numbers 21:4-9, Exodus 32:35, Numbers 11:33-34). He punished King Uzziah with leprosy for being arrogant (2 Chronicles 26: 16-21), and He punished Moses's sister Miriam with leprosy when she challenged Moses's authority (Numbers 21:1-15). He allowed King David's baby to die after David committed adultery with Bathsheba (2 Samuel 12:15-23), and he punished King Jehoram (2 Chronicles 21:18-19) with an intestinal virus that led to his death. God uses illnesses sometimes as the result of a person's sin, but God also heals illness as the result of His goodness (Psalms 103:2-3). When Jesus died on the cross, He died so that we could be free from sin and one of the results of freeing us from sin is that He freed us from sickness, so that we can be healed. Before Jesus came, people prayed to God to get healed, and He healed them and after Jesus came, they prayed to God and God healed them. All throughout time, God has healed people. It is what He does. Our God is a healer. It is His way.

SHOULD YOU SEEK A SUPERNATURAL HEALING OF YOUR FAMILY PLANNING ORGANS?

Does this mean God's people will always be well, successful, or rich? God's Word promises sustenance. It states that the children of the righteous should never have to beg for bread (Psalm 37:25), so if His word is true and if His people will be obedient, then God's people should be able to at least feel good, and be able to pay their bills, and have enough left over so that they can have something to give to others.

Does God want everyone well? I believe that the answer is yes but not everyone will get well. I do not believe that God *created* sickness. I believe it originated with sin, and the enemy uses illness to bring sorrow into our lives. The Lord may allow us to suffer through an illness, but the flip side is when we cry out for help, often He allows healing and fulfills His promise to rescue us. Sometimes He delays healing to teach us. God did not deem His children to be the sick ones on earth, living dreary lives of nonstop illness while the heathens around them live prosperously. No! No! No! This is such a point of doctrinal confusion for people. Maybe we are not supposed to figure it all out. God offers healing, and we can be healed. It doesn't matter if we cannot prove why everyone isn't healed.

We live in a fallen world, and there are factors that we do not know, but if God wanted us to stay sick, then Isaiah would not have made it clear that *He was wounded for our transgressions and bruised for our infirmities* (Isaiah 53:5), and *by His stripes we are healed.*

Does God allow illness? Yes, I believe He does. He allowed Satan to attack Job, but Job did pray for healing! He did not just *sit there* and take what the enemy gave him. He sought the reasons why and asked to be delivered (Job 30:20). God heard his cry for help and came and set him free, and this is what I am encouraging you to do. The apostle Paul also wrestled with an illness; he called it an instrument of Satan. Paul states he sought the Lord three times for it to be removed and God told him *"No! This illness keeps you humble and brings Me glory."* But do note that Paul did pray fervently, and Paul did ask for healing multiple times. Paul did not give up until he heard from the Lord the verdict about his illness (2 Corinthians 12:7-9). This story clearly illustrates what I am saying. It is an example of a true believer asking, seeking, knocking until Heaven answered. We've already established that the enemy has set a trap here for God's people, but this does not mean God wants His people to stay trapped. He wants us to ask, seek and pursue Him until He answers. It might not be the answer we desire, but God wants to hear from His children so He can give them the desires of their hearts. Often

God does bring healing when His people ask. The problem is it has not been popular to ask.

I do not know if God will recreate a man's vas deferens or reconnect a lady's tubes. In the natural world, we need those things to conceive but can God suspend reality and help someone conceive without all those things intact? I believe He is capable. If He hung the moon and the stars in the sky and created the human body, why can't he override the natural way people conceive? If He does this, we will say it is a miracle. Aren't we in love with a miracle working God? It can't help to ask, seek and knock until God listens and answers us. If our miracle doesn't happen, we can rest in knowing that we did our part by seeking Him.

> *A very important key here is to note that all these characters from our Bible stories did the same thing. After they prayed or after they were prayed for by someone else, the Bible characters did not sit around and do nothing! Instead, every one of them continued to *petition Heaven* for answers and *did not stop* until God answered them.

I believe *persistence* is a huge key to getting what we need from God. To elevate this point, Jesus gave this illustration about prayer in Luke 18:1-18. He tells this story about a widow who repeatedly asks an unjust judge for justice against an adversary. In the beginning, the judge is not willing to help this woman, but she is so persistent and bothers this judge so completely that eventually the judge grants her request because of her persistence. Jesus instructs that God is a much better judge with more compassion and love than the judge in the story and God will answer our prayers when we are persistent.

By the end of this chapter on healing, you will have prayed about the things that might be blocking your healing. If you are not already healed, then *take up your cross* and *take on the assignment* to never stop reminding God that you want this from Him. Do not stop until you get an *answer*. I would love to tell you that you will be healed, but I am not God, I do not know the answer for your life. But I do believe if you persistently petition Heaven, *you will get an answer* one way or another and persistence in prayer is the key. May our Heavenly Father grant your request.

SHOULD YOU SEEK A SUPERNATURAL HEALING OF YOUR FAMILY PLANNING ORGANS?

SUGGESTIONS FOR HOW TO ASK GOD TO HEAL YOU

A common misconception about healing is that a person must be at a church to get healed. You do not necessarily have to be in a church service to ask for healing. God is GOD. He is everywhere and can do anything. He can heal people anywhere, anytime He wants! He did this in scripture all the time. As the Lord was ascending, He told them,

Go into all the world and preach the gospel to every creature...they shall lay hands on the sick and they shall recover (Mark 16:15-18).

If you need God to heal you in the reproductive area, there are two ways to go about it. You can visit your local minister, elder or priest and ask for prayer. *Is anyone sick? Let him call upon the elders of the church, or you can pray for it yourself (James 5:14).* Believers have been given the Holy Spirit. We have the spiritual ability to believe and trust for our healing. If the ministers and elders believe in healing, this may be an excellent place to start, but it is not out of the realm of possibility to ask God to heal you in the privacy of your home as Isaac prayed over Rebecca for God to open her womb and God did (Genesis 25:21) and as God remembered Rachel (Genesis 30:22). Neither of these people were in their synagogues but were instead crying out from the privacy of their homes. Since God is everywhere, He can heal you at home in your living room the same as He could heal you in front of a minister or in a church service. It is the same power.

For the message of the cross is foolishness to those who are perishing, but to us who are being saved it is the power of God (1 Corinthians 1:18).

We must believe that God wants to do this for us and accept His outcome. Some healing may be instant and considered miracles; some may take time to manifest; some may not come because the healing is being blocked; and sometimes, it is not God's timing. Yet, in all situations, it is scriptural to ask God, and He wants us to ask Him. Pray about what God might be leading you to do.

If you would like to pray for healing in the privacy of your home, here are a few suggestions to assist you with the process. Before asking God for healing, most people find that they need to get their hearts in tune with the Lord. This may work best when you can set aside some uninterrupted time. One of the easiest ways to begin to focus on God is to listen to spiritual music. Use whatever music brings your heart into a place of worship and spend some time listening and worshipping Jesus. Some people may want to spend this time alone, while others will want to spend it with their spouse, or prayer partner. During this time, people sing to God; some quote scripture, poems or memorized prayers, simply do whatever brings your heart closer to the Lord. Some people feel more comfortable keeping quiet and reflective while meditating on the words of a song. Some people are comfortable sitting on the floor, others need action and want to walk around and move. You can worship God in whatever way you feel comfortable. But take note of this tip, once you start, it is not uncommon for distracting thoughts to come into your head, so keep a pad nearby to jot your thoughts down.

As you write down business information, grocery lists, what to wear, for work the next day, errands you need to run, etc., you will find that you become less stressed and can more readily focus on God. After a few minutes of acknowledging your distracting thoughts and getting them out of your head and onto a piece of paper, a feeling of peace will come over you as you draw closer to the spirit of God.

> **Note: If you have another place other than your home where you connect to the Lord, then go there. Some people sit in a prayer chapel, some put on their headphones and go for a hike or a walk along the beach, some experience God through His beauty in nature. There is no secret formula. Getting in tune with God is personal, and everyone is different. God's presence is the most wonderful place to be and once you are in His presence you will be ready to make your requests.

Worshipping the Lord and getting quiet makes most people feel wonderful. This is in no way a formula; it is just a suggestion to help establish an atmosphere of comfort that alleviates stress and outside distractions. I believe that once we feel more in tune with the Lord, we may feel ready to concentrate on the next step, which is to acknowledge that you love the Lord.

Wherever you are at home, in nature, in a chapel, etc. once you are in a state of worship, tell Jesus that you love Him, thank Him for His blessings, and for being faithful to you. Name the things you are thankful for. There are no rules. This is your time. Concentrate on the Lord your way and enjoy this time focusing on Him. Once you feel close to God, you are ready to begin praying for healing. When you are ready, you may wish to pray this type of prayer or something similar:

SHOULD YOU SEEK A SUPERNATURAL HEALING OF YOUR FAMILY PLANNING ORGANS?

Heavenly Father, I know that Jesus died so I might be healed. At Calvary, Your blood set me free from the law of sin and death. Through that precious shed blood, I can come to You today and ask for supernatural healing. Please forgive me for not believing Your Word and for not realizing that You do want me to ask for healing. I lay down all the lies and incomplete teachings that have convinced me that You want me to stay this way. I am miserable and I believe that You can and do want to heal me. Please remove the lies I have believed in my heart and mind. Please cleanse my mind of these thought patterns. I receive the mind of Christ (Philippians 2:5) and ask through the power of Your Holy Spirit, for the supernatural ability to believe You for this healing in my body. Please help me to receive from You now. I ask this in the precious name of Your son, Jesus Christ. Amen

CAN I REALLY PRAY FOR MY BODY PARTS TO BE RE-CREATED?

There is a story in the Bible about a man named Ezekiel. He was a prophet during the time when the Hebrew people were exiled in Babylon. God took Ezekiel to a valley full of old dead bones. God said, these bones represent the people of Israel. They have become old dry bones, and all their hope is gone because they believe their nation is finished. But then God said to Ezekiel,

"Prophesy to those bones and say to them: Dry bones, hear the word of the Lord. I will make breathe enter you and you will come to life. I will attach tendons to you and make flesh come upon you and cover you with skin. I will put breath in you, and you will come to life. Then you will know that I am the Lord (Ezekiel 37: 4-6). After Ezekiel says this, the dry bones arise and come together, the bones become covered with flesh and are revived, and then these people form into a large army.

So why am I telling you this story right now? It is because this story illustrates situations where people have become lifeless or hopeless and think things are over, but then comes God, who reaches into their pit of despair, to demonstrate His power to revive.

No matter how broken, empty or lost you feel or how bleak your infertility situation might seem, I am here to tell you that God has the ability to turn things around for you. If God can take a man's words and create an army from *old dry bones*, He certainly can heal your tiny, severed tubes, the size of thin spaghetti, or re-create your womb, which is no larger than an avocado!

PRAYING TO REVERSE A STERILIZATION

Can we pray for this, or do we need a doctor to perform a reversal? This depends on what you believe. If you can find a doctor who can perform your reversal and if you have enough tubes left for the doctor to perform a successful surgery, and if you have the money you need to get it done and if you can travel to this doctor and take time off work, then do this and be blessed of God. I pray you are successful and have more children! But, if any of these factors are not working in your favor, you may have no other choice but to look to God- the author and finisher of your faith.

I believe and will believe with you that God has the supernatural ability to heal you without a doctor, or if you want to ask God to heal you before you seek the assistance of a doctor, then go for it! Ask God to heal your physical body first before trying an alternative route. I'm for anything they can get a couple pregnant!

If you are praying for God to reverse sterilization, one of the most important things is that you must confess that the operation was sin and that it went against God's plan for your life. You need to start with repentance. If you have already prayed and repented of this at another time or somewhere else in this book, and if you desire to repeat the prayer in faith, then ok. It might give you renewed faith to continue to look to God to heal you supernaturally. The following prayer is a prayer of repentance for anyone who willfully got a sterilization operation and who now desires to repent. Please note this prayer is for someone who willfully got sterilized. In the unfortunate circumstances of a female needing a hysterectomy to take out her diseased womb, this is a completely different decision than a person willfully breaking their body so they can have unfruitful sex.

Prayer of Repentance for a Sterilization Operation:

1. *Heavenly Father, I love You. I want You to hear my prayer and heal me today. Thank You that I have received a new mindset and that now I know it is Your will to heal me and set me free from this hardship. Lord, I have made so many mistakes in my life, and sometimes I chose to disobey. Sometimes out of my ignorance of Your plan for my life, I have done things that I didn't even know were wrong. Lord, **I chose to get sterilized**, and this decision has hurt me, my spouse, and my family. I now realize that I was deceived by*

society and its worldly thinking, and I am sorry. Please forgive me Lord, for being ignorant. Your word says Your people perish for lack of knowledge. I allowed this surgery because I did not know it was wrong. Had I known, I would have made a different choice. I repent of my ignorance. Please forgive me.

2. Heavenly Father, I also choose to forgive this day (date of this prayer) **my spouse** for agreeing with this surgery, and for telling me to get it done and or for not stopping me from getting this surgery and or for pressuring me into having this surgery. I choose to forgive my spouse for not wanting any more children, and I ask You, Lord, to forgive me for not wanting any more children. I choose to forgive my spouse for any and all agreements surrounding this surgery. I confess to You this day that I forgive my spouse.

3. Heavenly Father, I choose to forgive this day (date of the prayer), **the doctor** who performed my surgery. I forgive Dr (insert doctor's name). I choose to forgive whether they informed me of my rights or not. I know that this doctor felt they were doing what was best for me. Please forgive me for any resentment I have held in my heart toward this doctor and for allowing myself to submit to this doctor's wisdom and knowledge. At the time, I did not know there was any information in Your Holy Scriptures or that this was a sin.

4. Heavenly Father, I choose to confess and forgive this day (date of the prayer) **myself** for even considering this surgery, and for listening to society and to others who influenced me, for being selfish and for putting my desires for my life above what You may have planned for me. Please forgive me for thinking of myself and not seeking You first, before I had this operation performed. Please help me to forgive myself in all areas. I receive Your forgiveness.

5. Heavenly Father, I choose to forgive this day (date of the prayer) **any family members, friends, or clergy who influenced me.** I forgive anyone whom I have held a grudge against or resented for not stopping me from getting this surgery. I forgive my spouse, my parents, in-laws, grandparents, cousins, aunts, uncles, brothers, sisters, friends, ministers, etc., who I feel did not honor me. I choose to forgive them.

6. *Heavenly Father, I choose to repent of **my anger toward You God,** on this day (date of the prayer). Lord God, I know that You love me, and yet somehow, I wish that You had supernaturally intervened and stopped me. This operation has brought me much pain and sorrow. I choose to let go of my anger towards You. This is anger that I should not have but may have hidden deep inside my heart. I have been angry at You for not stopping me or sending someone to intervene. If I have held any resentment or grudge toward You, Lord, please forgive me and cleanse my heart, mind, and spirit with Your precious and holy blood. Lord, thank You that You hear my prayers and are willing to heal me. Today I would love to be made whole again, and I would love for You to heal me. Healing would mean so much to me Lord and would take away my sorrow. Lord, I thank You that You are the God who heals, saves and delivers. Your Word says that by Your stripes we are healed through Your shed blood on the cross (Isaiah 53:5). I ask that the blood of Jesus cover me, and I ask this in the name of Jesus Christ of Nazareth and by the power of Your Holy Spirit I ask to be healed.*

7. *Heavenly Father **I ask that You heal** (name the body part that needs to be healed, e.g., Lord, please reconnect my tubes or Lord, please reconnect my vas deferens). Lord, **please allow my body to do what it was created for.** Please allow sperm to swim through my tubes again and fertilize my eggs. OR (for the man), please enable sperm to come back through my vas deferens again to fertilize my wife's eggs. Lord, please remove all scar tissue that could block this healing. I desire that my body listen to You, I desire this in the name of Jesus Christ of Nazareth and through the power of Your blood shed on the cross for me. I believe You Lord God, that You can heal me and make me whole. You can make my tubes come open again and reconnect. I agree You can make my tubes grow. I believe in the healing power of Jesus Christ of Nazareth for my eggs and sperm to be youthful and fully functioning, and I ask that my body become reconnected to its purpose once again. Heavenly Father I believe what You said in your word, and I believe what Jesus did for me on the cross makes my request complete. I receive this healing through faith in You. Thank You Heavenly Father, Thank You Jesus, Thank You Holy Spirit, Thank You for my healing! Praise Your holy name!*

FEMALE REPRODUCTIVE COMPLICATIONS

For various reasons, women consent to hysterectomies and later feel this might not have been best for their problem. If you believe God has shown you this, you may want to ask God for a healing. It is not out of the realm of possibility for God to do something supernatural for you. Yet this is a prayer that most would consider *foolish* because many believers today do not believe that God can heal a person in this way. I caution you to seek your heart first before you choose to exercise your faith. If you feel God may want you to seek Him in this way, then continue and ask for this miracle; if you do not believe this type of thing is possible, ask God to lead you in whatever way to move your situation forward. I don't want to give you false hope but on the flip side, I believe God can do anything. Sometimes a person might pray for a long time, asking God to do something and then suddenly, one more prayer is all it takes, and the prayer comes alive and God answers. I don't know where you are in this process, but I fully support you to pray if God gives you the faith for a miracle.

Prayer to ask God to Recreate your Womb after a Hysterectomy:

Heavenly Father, You have given me the faith to ask for something supernatural. In the same way You made Sarah a mother at ninety, and Elizabeth a mother after menopause, I believe You can do something supernatural for me. Your Word says, " With God, all things are possible to those who believe" (Matthew 19:26, Mark 10:27, Luke 18:27), and I am believing and executing my faith to believe that You can do this.

Lord, please give me a new womb because my old womb caused me to have complications. I believe it may have been cursed or made sick due to my choices. Please forgive me if sin was covering my old womb from previous lifestyle choices. I want to repent for anything that could have made it cease functioning. I plead for Your mercy and forgiveness, dear Heavenly Father.

Lord, also, please forgive me for the times I put my faith and trust in the wrong place. In the past, I trusted medical advice and the advice of others who guided me to make decisions that may not been the best thing for me but appeared to be my only option at the time. Maybe it was my best option based on their information, maybe I'll never know for sure. Please forgive me if I was being careless as I forgive those if they have misguided me.

Lord, please remove any residue and scarring from my past. I desire for my body to receive this healing from You, and I agree that my body can be made whole once again. I agree with Your word when the angel Gabriel said to Mary that "Nothing is impossible with God" and when the angel spoke to Sarai and said, "Is anything too hard for the Lord?" Both statements were about future babies who would be born and conceived due to supernatural circumstances. Heavenly Father, since Your word is true, I believe it is possible for my body to be made whole once again through the shed blood of Jesus Christ of Nazareth and by the mighty power of Your Holy Spirit!" Thank You, Jesus! I give You praise!

Lord Jesus because You stand outside of time and space, I am asking you for something everyone else will say is crazy. But because You stand outside of time and space, I believe this is possible. I am asking You dear Heavenly Father that since You are the one who formed me in my mother's womb, that you please recreate my womb once again. You made my womb the first time but due to living in this fallen world, my womb fell victim. Please give me back what the enemy stole from me. Please recreate in me a miraculous new body part. Please rebalance and restore my hormones to complete wellness and please restore other parts of my system that are not completely balanced. Please make me whole in every area again. Please help my hormones and my body to agree with the power of Your Holy Spirit. I release all fear and rejection that could in any way block this healing, and I release love and forgiveness toward myself, toward my body and toward others around me. Thank You Heavenly Father, Thank You Jesus, Thank You Holy Spirit, Thank You for my healing! I believe it is finished. Praise Your holy name!

Prayer to Balance Female Hormonal System:

You may not have felt led to pray for a new womb, but if there is an imbalance in your system due to reproductive complications, you may wish to ask God to heal your imbalance.

Heavenly Father, I want my body to be made whole again. I ask that You balance my system and help my entire body to come back in tune with itself. I agree with Your power to forgive me, and I agree that these body parts, that I desired to shut down, can be healed (name the body parts). I ask that You please forgive me for any time that I rejected the use of my body to participate in reproduction. I am sorry. I did not understand that I was rejecting Your plan. I now desire to obey You and to be made whole again. From now on, I submit my reproductive organs to Your will and not to my interpretations. I ask that my entire system come into agreement with the power of Your Holy Spirit, and I agree with Your will for my life. I believe in the finished work You did for me when You shed Your precious blood for me on the cross. Because You did this for me, by Your sacrifice I can ask to be healed. I ask that you cleanse my physical body and if any other health factors are blocking my desire for healing, I ask You, Heavenly Father, to please heal those areas as well. I believe that I can receive Your supernatural healing power to be as You created me to be. I agree that You are my healer! Thank You Heavenly Father, Thank You Jesus, Thank You Holy Spirit, Thank You for my healing! Praise Your holy name!

MALE REPRODUCTIVE COMPLICATIONS

Prayer for Low Sperm Count or other Male Issues:

Heavenly Father, I want my body to be made whole again because I want to submit to Your will. I believe You can put my body back into rhythm and make me whole. I ask that You renew the health and balance that You intended for my system, and I agree with Your ability to renew my sperm count and to bring it within normal ranges. Through the power of Your Holy Spirit, I know that my body can be healed and made whole so I can get my wife pregnant. I believe in and agree that Your supernatural healing power can renew my body. I also ask that if any other health factors are blocking this healing, that You also heal those areas. I believe everything is possible because You have given me the faith to trust You for this. I don't know how you will do it, Lord, I simply trust in Your almighty power at work through Your Holy Spirit! and I thank You Lord, for doing this for us and I believe that it is truly possible that my body can be restored to youthful wholeness and well-being because of what You did for me Jesus on the cross. I trust in You alone and in your supernatural healing power. Heavenly Father I believe the same power that raised Jesus from the dead can restore my sperm count. You are a faithful God. Thank you, Heavenly Father, for hearing my prayer. Thank You Jesus, Thank You Holy Spirit, Thank You for restoring my health! Praise Your holy name!

BEING HEALED OF BARRENNESS

We have already covered this a bit in previous chapters. We examined how various factors may be why quite a few people are infertile or miscarry. If you have already prayed these prayers, there may be a few more things to look at and to consider bringing in prayer before our Heavenly Father.

Upon examining the lives of individuals in the Bible who found themselves barren, we find that they did things that opened the door for God to release their infertility. Hannah, Rachel, Sarah, Rebecca, and Elizabeth were all barren but then were healed and had babies.

The first family of the covenant, Abraham and Sarai, were barren. The Bible says that God found Abraham to be a righteous and blameless man, yet he and Sarai could not seem to have children until God healed Sarai's barrenness (Genesis 21:1,2,7). Yet Abraham did not sit around waiting. He acted on his faith and moved forward in his relationship with God. The obedience Abraham demonstrated may have aided in the *release* of Sarai's barren womb.

In today's world, most people's infertility is a mystery. No one knows exactly why a person is infertile, but it is not wrong to look at various factors that could affect fertility. Sometimes a person's infertility is a direct result of incorrect choices made with their reproductive health. It might not have been intentional, in fact it might have been innocent, yet it is enough for the enemy to use against this person to keep them from reproducing. When someone asks God for forgiveness, they may be instantly released of the consequences of these mistakes, yet other times there are other factors at work blocking conception, and this keeps God from releasing this person from barrenness.

I believe when trying to break a cycle of infertility, it always helps to start by asking God for forgiveness. This way if the infertility is caused by willfully or by innocently committing a sin, asking for forgiveness will set the person free. Yet in the Bible those who wanted to be released of barrenness often did other things. As you read what Abraham did, the spirit of God may impress upon your heart something else to pray when you are asking God for this healing. This example is in no way a *"formula for forgiveness"*. Jesus set us free from all sin and curses at the cross. We cannot *earn* our healing. I simply included this example so you can see that Abraham continued to walk with God all through his life and continued to trust God and demonstrated his willingness *to do things God's way*.

1. Abraham believed God when things looked the opposite. God made a promise, and it took 25 years to fulfill it! God told Abraham that He would make him into a great nation, and it would be through Sarai, but she was old and had never conceived. But old Abraham did not sit around waiting.
2. He tithed to Melchizedek one-tenth of his money.
3. He entertained angels.

4. He prayed for Sodom and Gomorrah. *(He asked for deliverance and God's mercy).*
5. He lied to Pharoah about Sarai, and when Pharoah took Sarai into his harem, this caused Pharaoh and his household to become barren! Sarai was barren and now Pharoah's household was barren too.

> **This is interesting to note, as **God could have punished Pharoah another way.** Then Pharoah confronts Abraham and rebukes him for lying, and Abraham prays for Pharoah. Pharoah gives Sarai back, and God breaks the curse of barrenness off Pharoah and his household and yet Sarai remains barren. This is interesting to note. We don't know why God did not open Sarai's womb at this point, but we do know Abraham was a man of prayer.

6. Abraham got confused about God's promise and took matters into his own hands and had a son with Hagar, Sarai's handmaiden. He was probably not supposed to do that, but at the time it seemed like a reasonable way to start his family. God redeemed the mistake and told Abraham he would also bless his son, Ishmael and make him into a great nation as well. But still no baby for Sarai.
7. God told Abraham to cut off the skin around the top of his penis. At 99 years old, Abraham circumcised himself *(ouch!)*, along with circumcising the rest of his household, including thirteen-year-old Ishmael. *(Abraham was a brave man!).*

After all these events, finally Sarai gets pregnant—25 years after God first spoke His covenant to Abraham. God changes her name from Sarai to Sarah.

What does God want us to see? There appears to be a correlation between *prayer* that pleads with God, and prayer that *cries out for an answer*, and God then *breaking off* the curse of barrenness. After all the ways that Abraham demonstrated that he believed what God had told him, scripture says that God was *gracious* to Sarah. God's word also says that God *remembered* Rachel and *remembered* Hannah. The word *remembered* indicates that Rachel and Hannah did something to get God's attention. We know they *prayed fervently!* It also says God *allowed* Rebecca to conceive *after Isaac prayed.* Time and again the scriptures are full of verses about how **prayer** gets God's attention.

- Abraham prayed, tithed, was circumcised, and showed hospitality to angels; then God *was gracious* to Sarah (Genesis 14:20, 17:24, 18:2-5, and 21:1-2). Somehow these *actions* got God's attention!
- Rebecca was given a verbal blessing over her fertility, by her family, yet when she wanted to conceive, she was barren. But then Isaac *prayed*, and her barrenness was broken (Genesis 25:21).
- Rachel *prayed*, and God *remembered* her (Genesis 30:22).
- Hannah *prayed*, and God *remembered* her (1 Samuel 1:10-19).
- Notice that in Rachel and Hannah's situation, it was the prayer of the wives and not the husbands, and in Sarah and Rebecca's lives, God used the men. Essentially, there is no definitive answer whether one partner's prayer is any better or more powerful.

Basically, these illustrations reinforce prayer. In the case of Rachel and Hannah, no doubt these women did not simply pray one time and forget about it, I believe they *hounded* God! I believe they prayed so much and so often and were consistent for such a long time that God *finally* gave them what they wanted because they never stopped praying until it happened.

You may want to pray this prayer or something like this and continue praying until God either releases you from the curse of infertility or gives you an answer for why you are struggling with this condition.

Prayer for Conception and Healing Barrenness or Infertility:

Heavenly Father, thank You that I have received a new understanding. I believe it is Your will to heal me and set me free. Lord, I desire to have a baby. I want to birth and raise mighty warriors that will be part of Your end-time spiritual army. I desire to love these children and to raise them to love You. Your Word says that Your favorite way to bless me is to give me a child. I receive in my heart and in my body, this child, and any future children that You want to bring. I believe in Psalm 113 because it says, You make the barren woman a happy mother of children. I want this to be true for myself and my spouse. We want to have children and once we get started, we do not want to limit You in the process.

Lord Jesus, I repent for all things I may have done that could have prevented You from allowing a conception. I repent for my past and present sins that could have blocked Your gift to me. I repent for careless statements that showed my lack of faith or disbelief. Lord, please forgive me for every word I spoke against myself, my spouse, and my future child due to disbelief or ignorance on my part. Please forgive those words, and please remove all curses my words created. Please let every wrong word spoken against me fall to the ground (1 Samuel 3:19) and render them powerless through the power and blood of Jesus Christ of Nazareth. I repent for every statement against my children that my tongue brought forth, and I ask Lord, that today You take over the words of my mouth so that I will not allow any more statements to be said that would speak against my parenthood. Please send an angel to guard my tongue as I continue to believe that You desire to release me from my shortcomings. Thank you, Heavenly Father, I believe You want the best for me. Thank you for hearing my prayer. Thank You Jesus, Thank You Holy Spirit, Thank You for restoring my health! Praise Your holy name!

GENERATIONAL BLOCKAGES

We have also already covered how the decisions of a previous generation could be causing complications in our lives today. We have already prayed prayers of repentance for how their sins could be causing miscarriages, but we did not completely address barrenness. Generational sins could block future conceptions if parents, grandparents, or other direct blood relatives were sterilized. Their action created *an unwritten statement in the Heavenlies* that says this person has severed their seed with intentions to discontinue their family bloodline. Their choice could be what is blocking their descendants from future conceptions. However, this idea does not seem to apply to every family across the board. In one family a parent's sterilization does not appear to affect their children's fertility at all and the children are all fertile, but then in another family, the children's infertility is a mystery. We don't know all the factors at work. There are two families involved and multiple sets of grandparents so other family factors could be affecting fertility, but whatever the case might be with you, it cannot hurt to pray. Once these actions are repented for, if any of the grandparent's choices to be sterilized is what is blocking your ability to conceive then God can remove all barriers and end any conception problems their descendants might be experiencing.

Prayer for the Forgiveness of Ancestral Sins:

Heavenly Father, I ask that You please hear my prayer. I am grieved that I am walking through infertility. It makes me sad every day. I ask that my body be made whole by the power of Jesus's sacrifice on the cross to forgive me of all my sins, including the sins of my ancestors. Today (date), I ask for forgiveness and healing over my family bloodline in the area of birthing and receiving children by the power of Your Holy Spirit, please make the (insert family name) family bloodline whole again.

I agree that this day, (date), is the day our family decided to follow the Lord again in this area. Whether it was out of ignorance on my ancestors' part for why they did not desire children—or if they were simply against children—no matter what their reasoning, I ask for forgiveness for their actions, even actions up to four generations. Lord, wherever my ancestors may have worshiped themselves or worshipped unseen idols, or fell into witchcraft, or chose to control, I ask You to please forgive our family bloodline and stop their actions from robbing my spouse and I from receiving Your blessing of children. I ask that You forgive their ignorance and disbelief and cleanse the (insert family name) family bloodline of this sin so that children may again be restored as a fruit of our family tree. I know how serious this is. Heavenly Father, by the power of Your Holy Spirit, I ask that You do not hold me or my future generations responsible anymore. Please restore our family tree to wholeness through the power of the blood shed on the cross by Jesus Christ of Nazareth. I receive my healing and ask to be restored to complete wholeness. I desire to receive all the children that You want to give me, Lord. Thank You, Heavenly Father, for hearing my prayer. Thank You, Jesus. Thank You, Holy Spirit. Thank You for restoring our family! Praise Your holy name!

REVERSAL OPERATIONS

We have already mentioned that there are doctors who will perform a reversal operation on you or your spouse. If this is the route you take, I pray it is successful but if you do get a reversal and you are still not successful, there are websites dedicated to people who have had a reversal and still cannot get pregnant, and there are also support groups for those who are having trouble conceiving. These can be helpful, and wherever you may be in this decision process, you may find informative answers. Just be careful that you do not spend more time focusing on the negatives, than the positives.

After you have prayed these prayers, every word that comes out of your mouth should be as positive and as hopeful as possible: "*I know I'll be pregnant soon! I know God is going to give me a blessing*"! Try your best to avoid negative and discouraging people. Those who disagree with your faith may tell you that you are crazy to believe that God can restore you. Try to stay away from these skeptics as much as possible. Just quietly agree with God in your heart and continue to ask Him in prayer. Let these words from Hannah bring you the peace you seek, "*For this child I prayed, and the Lord answered my prayer!*" (1 Samuel 1:27). May the Lord grant your request.

EMOTIONAL HEALING

Emotional scarring and rejection may be deep enough to cause barrenness. If you prayed for a reversal or have had a reversal operation and have not yet conceived, is there a possibility you have not repented of the emotional scars the sterilization operation brought into your marriage to begin with? There may be an area of emotional pain that has still not yet been addressed. Events such as barrenness or sterilization often wound people on deep emotional levels and the person may not be in touch with their pain, but this pain could block the couple from receiving God's gift. In chapters seven and nine we talked about how birth control breeds rejection and couples do not realize that by using birth control they harmed their relationship. A couple may want to pray the repentance prayer in the miscarriage chapter. When people feel emotionally rejected, they can *shut down* and *shut out* the other person and I don't want this to happen to you.

Sometimes the best way for a couple to begin to heal emotional wounding is through intimacy. Emotional intimacy starts when each person can share how they are feeling. For some women the pain runs super deep, and they may not even understand the reason behind their sadness, instead they just feel sad. In these moments, a husband's gentle touch can make a huge difference. Some of her wounds could be from another relationship or from abuse. If either partner does not *feel safe* and *loved*, these emotional wounds can affect fertility. Couples have reported that listening to music, reading the Psalms, quoting poetry, or saying prayers to each other has helped the wounded partner open their heart, expressing how these operations or how using birth control made them feel rejected and unloved. When couples can lower their emotional walls and connect on a deep emotional level, then when they do make love, their physical intimacy becomes a powerful expression of unity. Forgiveness, honest confession, vulnerability and the deep unity found in lovemaking are powerful forms of *spiritual warfare* that confront the enemy's influence and can break the cycle of barrenness.

What if nothing happens and these prayers do not work?

These prayers are meant to break off anything in the *unseen* spiritual realm that might be blocking you from receiving a healing from our Heavenly Father. Healings do take time and by petitioning Heaven you are asking and believing God has the power to heal you. Ultimately the outcome is in our Heavenly Father's hands. It is at His option. Sometimes because we live in a fallen world, there are reasons we don't fully understand, and there could still be unknown factors that are hindering your healing. However, it is always better to *take action* and remain persistent in prayer than to do nothing. Far too often we think we are waiting for God, but He is waiting for us to *take up our cross* and walk through this problem with Him. If we do nothing, we lose hope, but by petitioning Heaven, we renew our hope because God eventually answers all our prayers in some way or another.

I am positive that after praying these prayers of forgiveness, you will feel a release of your pain and it will *jump start* the healing process in your heart. These prayers make your requests known to God. They are direct and specific, asking God for the exact things you need. Whenever we confess our sorrow or needs, our confessions bring us closer to God. This is a scriptural principle. If you are sincerely praying, you will feel intimacy with Him and this closeness is worth seeking.

Infertility is a daily struggle, and it might be the thing God has allowed to bring you closer to Him. I don't know why you are suffering with this but sometimes life feels like one gigantic test and your infertility might be one of those challenges that God chooses not to fix the way you expect. Possibly God is trying to teach you how to pray more effectively, and your situation requires persistent prayer before you see complete healing or before God gives you an answer. Sometimes after much prayer, God makes it clear adoption IS His answer.

I wish I could wave a magic wand and heal you instantly, but I do not have that power. What I do know is God loves you and He has a perfect plan for your life. My hope for you is *to be made whole* in whatever way is in God's plan.

SHOULD YOU SEEK A SUPERNATURAL HEALING OF YOUR FAMILY PLANNING ORGANS?

Please let me know your outcome, I am eager to hear your testimony. If you do get to hold a new baby in your arms or if you adopt or if you end up not having a child, please remember you prayed, you asked, and God heard you and His will is now complete. Blessed be the name of the Lord! Amen!

Prayer of Thanksgiving for Both Husband and Wife

Thank You, God for Your cleansing power! Help us to receive all that You are saying in this chapter. We want to be healed and made whole.

Thank You that Your Word says that Your mercies are new every morning. Great is Your faithfulness to us! (Lamentations 3:23.) We claim mercy over our lives and are grateful that You are willing and ready to bring Your healing power. Thank You, Jesus!

Christopher's Commentary

I want to say a few things about healing. I was raised Baptist. We were fundamental and evangelical and convinced that the *front-row seats of Heaven* had our denomination's name on them. I was a mainline Baptist and not some sect, and being an evangelical Baptist, I was convinced *we had the handle on everything Christian*, including healing. How could we not? We believed the Bible cover to cover! At least, that was what I was being told growing up in church, and I did not have enough abilities to question my authorities until I was older. In our denomination, we read all about healing and believed that Jesus healed the sick.

We were told that getting healing was possible, so we should pray and believe, but the doctor was always a big part of the healing. Healing was not talked about without the help of medicine. At our church, we never got to see someone healed right before our eyes as people did in the time of Jesus. We were told getting miraculously healed ended with the apostles, which was why no one raised the dead anymore or did anything like that. It was all disappointing. Powerless and defeated was how I was raised to believe. I knew we could pray, and God answered a few prayers a few times, but often people died. I didn't realize until later in life that I had been given the power to pray for myself or others. Finally, I got my head on straight and realized that if the Lord paid for it on the cross, and He is who He says He is, then healing is for today as much as it was back in Biblical days. Matthew 4:24 says Jesus went to Galilee preaching and teaching and healing every sickness and disease. If Jesus could heal, and He did heal, and since He gave believers the power to pray, I finally concluded that I should at least ask God to heal me, my family, and others. God might not heal as I anticipate, but as a believer, I can ask God and truly believe He will.

I think one of the biggest misunderstandings in the Christian community is the controversy over God's healing touch. You would not think that something as wonderful as getting healed would be controversial, but

SHOULD YOU SEEK A SUPERNATURAL HEALING OF YOUR FAMILY PLANNING ORGANS?

it is. Still, today when you talk about healing, a whole segment of believers shut down. But I don't understand the problem with a group of believers surrounding a church member and praying for their healing, yet certain groups have a problem with this. They don't want it, or they only want their elders to pray instead of allowing all of us to believe and pray.

Other leaders want to teach about it by breaking it down, studying it, analyzing it, and creating courses on it instead of simply allowing it! Sometimes even these same teachers argue about it and quote scripture against it. I don't get it. It's only *healing*. God wants to bless you and me. What kind of God would He be if He deemed a life of sickness void of His healing power? There's no reason to believe in a supernatural God if He can't ever be supernatural. We need to believe in Him and cast aside religious rhetoric.

He loved us and died for us and then left us a piece of Himself to bring restoration to His people and the earth. This is how I see it, and I pray that anyone who opposes God's healing power or is cynical or skeptical will open their eyes and see that the goodness of the Lord remains on earth in the gift of healing for both you and me. As a man, it is even more important that I believe so that my wife and children will see my belief and then believe too.

Christopher Scott

Investigate and Questions

- Read Ephesians 3:20, Luke 1:37, Deuteronomy 7:15, and Psalm 103:2. Does God want everyone to be healed? Why don't we always get the healing we ask for?
- Read Isaiah 61:1. When His word says He brings freedom to the captives, to whom is He referring? Describe how a person is trapped by illness.
- Have you ever wondered why the healing of a mother's womb, prostate cancer, ovarian cysts and or fibroids, endometriosis, or infertility do not seem as popular as healing in other areas? Is there a reason? If more churches prayed for the infertile, would they conceive? Why don't people pray for this more often?
- Read Isaiah 53:4-5. Some argue that these verses do not apply to healing. What are your thoughts?
- Can God heal a person in private the same way He can in public? In the Bible, did people get healed more in public spaces or private places? Does it matter?
- Is there a difference between healing and miracles? Do you understand that difference? Is a pregnancy that occurs nine months to twelve months after prayer, a miracle or a healing, or both?
- Read Mark 11:25 and Isaiah 59:2. Can unforgiveness or anything else we might do block our opportunity to receive a healing touch? If so, how?
- Read Mark 16:15, Luke 9:1, Matthew 10:1, and Matthew 28:18,19. Have those of us who love the Lord been given the power to pray for healing?
- Read 1 Corinthians 15:57. Please share your thoughts.

Impacting Others

Rachel, not sure you realize how much your book has blessed me, but it has. I now have a baby Jonathan Immanuel, born in August 2009! When we got married, we never expected to experience any problems. Our home group prayed for us for over a year while we tried infertility treatments. I suffer from PCOS. My mother had her tubes tied after my brother was born and had so many complications, she had to get a hysterectomy when she was only 42. I never thought it might affect me, and I still am not sure it did, but after I got your book from a friend, it gave me a new perspective on how to pray. My friend Sarah felt burdened to pray for me because she knew how devastated I was not being able to have a baby. She decided to pray several of your prayers every day about cleansing my family lineage and breaking off anything from my mother's hysterectomy. Our dear Lord Jesus mercifully hears our cries because Jonathan came, and I am so happy. I love being a mother. I want more children! Please pray that God will allow me to have more. They say I still have PCOS, but we are believing for more children anyway. **Alissa**

Rachel, I wanted to share my story because your book impacted me so much! Thank you for writing it! My husband Jeremy and I had been trying to conceive for almost two years. We visited several fertility doctors, and they ran all kinds of tests. We had multiple problems with low sperm count, and my cycles were all messed up. During this trial, my Bible study partner located a copy of your book for me after she had read it. Are you going to get it out again? I want to give it to so many people! My girlfriend had told me you had prayers in it for conception. I must admit I agreed with the ideas in your book, but it was painful to think I might not get to have a child, much less several children. I asked God if this would ever be possible because the doctors gave us little hope of conceiving naturally. We had concluded that God's will for our family would be adopting several children, but infertility was breaking our hearts, yet what could we do? I got to the point where I was desperate for a child, if it was mine. I shared our struggles with several Christian friends, and some listened and told us their struggles too. We all prayed for each other, but it never took away the pain of infertility. My heart was breaking every day. The Lord finally brought me to a place where I knew that if this was going to break, we would need others to stand in the gap for us. On one occasion, I broke down in front of my entire mom's group. After that, several women told me they would stand with us. They asked me what to pray, and I gave them your book and told them to pray what God leads. Several times they prayed every prayer in the entire Chapter 9, some from Chapter 10, and all the prayers in Chapter 11 over me! I believe there is something generational, but I don't know much about my grandparents because we didn't get to see them or my cousins much. I don't know. It was just a feeling I had when they prayed those parts. Six months went by after they prayed your prayers, and nothing happened. I cried a lot, trying to believe God would do it. Then one day, I felt nauseous in the morning and couldn't remember my last period. They were still very irregular. I raced to my drawer, where I kept multiple home pregnancy tests, and did one. When the blue line appeared, I screamed! I called Jeremy, and he shouted and then got choked up. Everyone else we told was overjoyed. I don't know exactly which thing we said or did that allowed the Lord to open my womb, but I believe it was a collective effort of ALL the prayers. However, I am writing you because I want you to know that the day my three girlfriends went through the prayers in your book, this powerful feeling came over me. I can still remember that feeling. This is why I am emailing you. I want you to know this. I think people don't understand infertility, but Rachel you seem to get it because the prayers did something. I know it took six months of solid prayer by many people before it completely happened, but no one had specific prayers like your book. Thank you for writing this book! I know it made a difference.* **Tracy, New mommy to Brent, five months old**

Chapter 12

GOD IS CALLING US, BACK TO OUR FUTURE!

> *This day I call Heaven and Earth as witnesses against you that I have set before you life and death, blessings and curses. Now choose LIFE, so that you and your children may live and that you may love the Lord your God and listen to His voice and hold fast to Him for the Lord is your life...*
> *(Deuteronomy 30:19, 20).*

In the 1985 movie *Back to the Future*, the main character, Marty, had the opportunity to *go back in time* to witness the events that led up to his parents dating, courtship, and marriage. Marty quickly realized that if certain events did not occur at the exact same time and in the exact same way, there was a chance that his parents would have never gotten together. If this had happened, he and his siblings would have never been born! Marty also realized their future could be even better if certain events were slightly altered. At the movie's beginning, the audience sees Marty's parents as nerdy and uncool. After he goes back to their past and makes a few slight changes, at the end of the movie the audience witnesses a transformation in Marty's parents from boring nerds to cool adults.

I named this chapter *God Is Calling Us Back to Our Future* because this is what I believe God is doing. God is calling us to follow Scripture's ancient path, but not to bind us. Instead, our obedience will restore us and catapult us forward into our amazing future.

In the film, *Back to the Future*, Marty goes into the past and makes changes that affect his future, which in the world of Hollywood fantasy made for good filmmaking. But in the real world, we cannot return to 1930 and stop the Protestant and Jewish Church leadership who decided to change their birth control doctrine. We also cannot go back and change the 1961 decision by the World Council of Churches that approved the birth control pill for all church going people. We also cannot change that this decision, opened wide the door for global acceptance of the *pro-choice agenda* of abortions, sterilizations and the global goal for Christians, to birth fewer children. If we could go back in time and had been present when either of these decisions were made, we would surely say to church leaders, *"Please seek God longer and harder on this. You don't realize the pain these decisions will cause in the future!"* If only we could return to the past and make changes….

Although going back is impossible, it is possible to go forward and change the future. Now it is time for another generation to make their choice about family planning. If you are young, your generation can take a new path forward and avoid the mistakes of your parents and grandparents. I beg you to do this! As you've read this book, if the Lord impressed upon you to make any changes and to agree with any part of this message, now is your appointed time. The decision to choose a new path of life is yours! Watch what God can do.

A NEW DAY IS DAWNING

Throughout the Scriptures, we see God desiring for His people to *move forward* and the reason why is that God is always moving forward. The Scriptures say, *do not dwell on the former things or remember the things of old, behold I am doing a new thing, now it springs forth, do you get it? I will make a way in the wilderness (Isaiah 43:18,19).* God is always encouraging us to keep a forward focus on Him.

Regarding what God is saying in the message of Birthing God's Mighty Warriors, dwelling in the past would mean *"making the exact same choices for your lives today as the previous generations made when it was their chance."* This also means, staying in the putrid feces those choices produced. If you do the same things, you will get the same outcome and miss what God wants to do in you.

During the destruction of Sodom and Gomorrah, Lot's family was instructed not to watch God's judgment on the city, but Lot's wife disobeyed. She looked back and became a pillar of salt as punishment for her disobedience (Genesis 19:26.) I often wonder why she looked back. I am sure that she had a good reason and didn't want to disobey. Maybe it was noisy, or maybe she heard the cries of the people, or maybe she felt the heat of the burning city against her back. No matter her reason for disobedience, it destroyed her and ended her life! To this day, she is frozen in time and believed to be a disfigured pillar on the side of a road in the Holy Land not far from where Sodom and Gomorrah were believed to be. Lot's wife's disobedience caused her to freeze forever. She could not move forward even if she wanted to. She is a living picture of what will happen when we don't listen! Not only do we stay stagnant, but we miss our future because our future is today.

Lot's wife was unlike her relative Abraham. He received God's vision for his future and was *looking forward* to what God could do. He was not caught up in his wife's present state of barrenness. Instead, he didn't know how God was going to do it, and he didn't know when God would make things happen, but he never let go of the promise that God had given him. He was looking forward in anticipation about what God said. He did not compare himself to God. Instead, he realized the awesomeness of God and His plan. Abraham was projecting his faith forward to the future as other righteous men and women in the Scriptures have also done. In visions, Abraham saw his offspring too numerous to count; Moses saw the Israelites happily living in Canaan; David saw a Savior sitting on his throne; the prophets saw Jesus the Messiah coming to earth; Paul saw the Gentiles receiving Christ; and John saw the events of Revelation unfold. Many missionaries have dreamed of the gospel spreading to their country and throughout the world. This is something that previous generations had visions about and could see but did not have the privilege to attain.

They were all commended for their faith yet none of them received what had been promised (Hebrews 11:39).

These did not receive what had been promised because God had another way. Instead of all these visions being fulfilled while the faithful were here on earth, God chose to continue to fulfill His promises by including as many other faithful people as possible, so that someday we could all share in the rewards of Godly fulfillment.

As each new generation has been met with its challenges, we find ourselves today trying to reverse the sinful patterns of the past so we can link our lives with our righteous ancestors. Every one of these *dreamers in God* knew that one day God would bring a generation here *who could attain* what they were hoping for and *who could reap from their sacrifices*. Oh, how they would have liked to be with us right now. What they would give to have our opportunities today! However, we do need their wisdom, and we must stay focused and not get sidetracked by *all the lies* and *all the reasons why* we cannot birth more children. *Good human reasons* tell us why we should slow down and why we should use birth control. *Good human reasons* also tell us why we should get our tubes tied and why we should not have *any* more children. We must be like the apostle Paul and reach forward to attain what God has promised us. Paul said, *I press forward for the mark of the prize of the high calling of God in Christ Jesus* (Philippians 3:13-14).

The Lord is a warrior, and He loves His Bride, but He is not returning for a Bride who desires to be sterilized or who uses birth control to block His conceptions. No way! His bride will look like Him and He is a God of Reproduction. There is no barrenness in Him, so His bride will be unapologetically fertile, holy and will want to be intimate with Him. She will choose to procreate and have His children! (*and this shall be both in the natural and in the spirit*).

When you birth God's Mighty Warriors in this generation and train them to love the Lord, you will strengthen the spiritual army of God. *They will not contend with the enemies in the gate but will possess the land* (Genesis 22:17-18). If the Lord tarries, our children and grandchildren will build upon the foundations we leave behind! They will keep the momentum going that was started long ago and passed on from father to son and from mother to daughter generation after generation. With each new child born, the wealth of promises will continue to increase as God's people live closer and closer to the time of the Lord's return. Each child born is that much closer to His return and will have even that much greater anointing. Everything is increasing, intensifying, and accelerating toward the pivotal events of history!

Someday in the future, God's people will have a place in that perfect Holy Jerusalem. His people will be His completed Bride, those people who were conceived on earth, and who made themselves ready for Jesus their beloved husband (Revelation 21:2). This is His plan for His people to be one family.

Please understand your family is part of the bigger picture, getting you ready to be a part of the family that God is creating for Himself out of the people-groups of the earth. Every time you faithfully birth a new potential member of God's spiritual army and then train that child to love God, each time you are saying to your beloved bridegroom, *"Come Lord Jesus come. I am doing my best to participate and agree with your vision for the last days."*

AS A PEOPLE READY TO AGREE WITH GOD, LET US SAY, "NO MORE" TO SATAN!

No more, Satan, will we listen to your lies about planning our children.

No more, Satan, will we follow in the footsteps of our humanistic culture.

No more, Satan, will we allow you to deceive us into thinking that additional children are not valuable.

No more, Satan, will we allow others to influence our family planning or listen to their opinions or reasons why they think we shouldn't have more children.

No more, Satan, will we allow you to keep us from intimacy with our Savior that comes from daily trusting Him with our family planning.

No more, Satan, will you keep us from receiving God's favorite gift—children: a heritage, a voice into the future, an arrow to defeat the enemy, and an opportunity to possess the land for generations!

LORD, PLEASE HEAR OUR RIGHTEOUS DECLARATIONS!

We PRAY and DECLARE that we will be a people who will return to Your ways!

We PRAY and DECLARE to call back all the generational blessings that have been held back from our family due to past disobedience with birth control, sterilization, and abortion!

We PRAY and DECLARE that we are your righteous bride, holy and set apart, surrendered to Your plans and purposes!

We PRAY and DECLARE that we will CHOOSE LIFE so that our children, grandchildren, and great-grandchildren will LIVE and by your grace they will possess the gates of Your enemies!!

We ask all this in the Mighty Name of Jesus Christ of Nazareth, the precious son of God- whose salvation grants us new life, through the awesome power of Your Holy Spirit, all for the glory of God the Father. Amen!

Appendix

CONVERSATIONS ON BIRTH CONTROL

Do you think God wants everyone to have a large family? No, I do not. I *do not believe* that every couple is supposed to have five, eight, twelve, or fifteen children. Many couples have trusted God with their family planning throughout their entire marriage and they end up with small families of one, two, or three children. Many Biblical families were not very large unless the man had more than one wife. A few examples of this were:

Noah had three sons but not until he turned 500 years old! Plus, he was married two hundred more years!

Abraham had two sons; one with his wife and one with his concubine, then later he was the father of six more sons with another wife. Abraham was fertile his entire life until he died at 175 years old.

Isaac had two sons.

Jacob had 12 sons and one daughter (but he had two wives and two concubines).

Joseph had two sons.

Moses had one son.

Boaz and Ruth had one son.

Job had 14 sons and six daughters. (His was the largest Biblical family that I could find. He had 20 children from what appears to be one wife—ten children before his hardship and ten children after God restored him.)

CONVERSATIONS ON BIRTH CONTROL

This whole issue is *not the number of children a couple is blessed with* but whether they seek the Lord's will for their lives and trust Him for this decision. When God's people trust Him, they will allow Him to give them the number of children that will make them happy and will make their family feel complete. I am not trying to be anyone's *Holy Spirit* or a *bedroom police officer*. That is not the intention of this book's message. Rather it is a very personal message. When people trust God and place their family planning into His hands, He gives, and they receive. He opens and shuts the womb on a very personal level.

Does every couple who chooses to trust God with their fertility have child after child? I am so afraid to trust God with my womb. Pregnancy is so hard on my body, and I cannot have baby after baby. I can sympathize with your feelings. You are not alone. Many women feel like you and for this reason they struggle with allowing God to plan their families. *Be of good cheer,* when I subscribed to an online forum of homeschool families, women often expressed that once they decided to allow the Lord to *take charge* of their family plan, they were expecting to get pregnant right away, and yet they did not get pregnant right away. Some have waited two years, three years, or even as many as five years. During that time, the Holy Spirit grew a deeper desire for more children in their hearts.

This message I have presented here is one that a person has to be *led by the Holy Spirit* to follow. God must help you see that you and your spouse can trust Him with your sex life. As we give Jesus all the fears that invade our bedroom lives, He will grow a deeper in us a deeper desire to allow Him to have complete control. *You may not be ready yet.* God loves you enough to allow you time to become comfortable trusting Him with your family plan. He is *not trying to force you to obey* in a way that you are not ready for. Just keep seeking Jesus, and *do not allow the enemy to cause you to be afraid to trust your sweet Savior.* As you seek Him, He will lead you to the faith to trust Him with your family planning, body, and with your future.

I want to trust God, but my parents get so upset with me. They think we are being irresponsible by having more children than they think we should have. How do I tell them I am pregnant again; they are going to be mad at me. This is sometimes one of the hardest things to do because we want our *parents* and *in-laws* to be happy for us, yet sometimes some of the rudest comments come from them. Then we wonder, "Don't they want more grandchildren?" After my fourth child and my husband's angel dream, we started to realize that God was telling us to have more children. I knew this would upset my father because he was always worried about the time, education and effort it takes to raise children. One day I told my father, *"We love children, and we feel God wants to give us a few more. If you love me, tell me that you are happy that I am giving you another grandchild. Please do not worry about where we will get the money because we believe God will provide."* Then I said, *"And if you are not happy, tell someone other than me about it, and please just tell me that you are happy for me."* Later when I got pregnant with my fifth child, he said, *"I am happy for you, and I think you are crazy all at the same time!"* Then we have had number six, seven, and eight and he told me that it's OK now because none of his friends have as many grandchildren as he does, and he always wins the Father's Day contest at his church for having the most grandchildren!

Here is a cute way a mother-to-be told her parents she was expecting again. Her parents were also quite concerned about how they could afford all the children that God was blessing them with. She wrote a poem to let them know they were about to be grandparents again.

I bet you never thought when your children left the nest,
They'd give you twenty-three grandkids: that's way above the rest!
No friend of yours could ever boast of having more than you,
Your kids keep multiplying, it's really quite a ZOO!
We are a loving family. Who could ask for anymore?
But come this next December, there will be twenty-four!

The Bible says a quiver full of children is a blessing. Aren't five children a full quiver? Once we had five children, I tied my tubes, and we felt we did the right thing. A quiver in ancient times could come in various sizes and held a varying number of arrows. A quiver was never limited to holding five arrows. A typical warrior's quiver could hold over twenty arrows! Instead of worrying whether you might need a certain number, simply trust God for each child and let Him fill up your family. When you get the "done" feeling then ask Him to close your womb.

Since I have three children, haven't I obeyed the commandment to be fruitful and multiply? Yes, you have but if you are feeling a tug on your heart after reading the message in this book, possibly God might be trying to communicate that for you and your spouse this message is not so much about numbers but instead it's about developing a deeper level of trust. Did you *ask* God about each child, or did you simply choose a number? He may want to increase your wealth by giving you another little person to love.

But to answer your question, please consider this, what if a person shared the gospel with someone two years ago, and then again, this year, and then kept silent for the rest of their life? Would they be fulfilling the Great Commission forever? Most believers would say no, this person should continue to share the gospel because God wants as many people as possible to come to Him. If this is true for the Great Commission then what if a couple decided to have children in 2014, 2018, and 2022 and then got sterilized. Would they be completely fulfilling the commandment to be fruitful and multiply? See Chapter 7. I address this topic under the heading *The Barren Life: What are the consequences for the Marriage?* To stay in a holy position sexually before the Lord, we must be very careful to continue to honor this gift of life.

Fertility is an extraordinary gift you should never take for granted because *you will not always be fertile.* A day will come when your body will no longer create children like it once did. Many a tear has been shed by those who casually raced through this season and stopped in their twenties or early thirties only to realize later their middle-aged lives without children were not as fulfilling as they thought it would be. Parenthood ended all too quickly once their children grew up and their children are into their careers instead of family and are delaying parenthood. They did not realize they would miss them so much. I've met countless people in their 40s and early 50s roaming around middle age *with nothing to do.* Some will admit they wish they had more children but most live in denial. It's easy to see they are trying to figure out the rest of their lives. With no grandchildren coming any time soon, they look to join a pickleball team, hang out at the gym or try cycling and there is nothing wrong with doing these things, but they act bored trying to find something to do. If you are a stressed-out parent with several little children, this might sound wonderful, but I am telling you when I am around these people, all they talk about is where their children are in school or what they are training to become or talk about the latest fad diet or how they hope to get a few grandchildren someday. Do you want this to be you? Because these people do not act as happy as they could be at this season of their life.

It is so easy to get into reasoning whenever we do not like one of God's commands. We rationalize and look for ways to get around what God has spoken. I don't know the number of children God had planned for you. Seek Him in prayer and then ask what to do as you re-read all the scriptures in this book! Do not look to the culture for your answer, do not look anywhere but in the Scriptures and do not listen to anyone but God.

Today can sterilization be an option for Christians if there are valid reasons for it, such as health problems? After reading this book you certainly know a sterilization operation is a sin against your body, a sin against your marriage, a sin against your sex life, and creates a permanent physical separation. It also brings harm on every level: emotionally, spiritually and physically. The Bible also speaks against mutilating one's genitals. Yet whenever a health crisis presents itself, each couple must carefully look to God in prayer. I do not believe sterilization is the best option when there are health complications, especially since there is increasing evidence that sterilization often leads to further medical complications. Would God want you to break one of your healthy body parts to then create a new potential health problem? This kind of reasoning does not agree with the Scriptures so because sterilization is medically available does not mean it is now a healthy long-term option for God's people.

When we look back in history and even today, we can see that sometimes there were *very valid reasons* why people might not have wanted to birth children: health risks to the mother, famines, inadequate living conditions or inadequate medical care, mothers dying during childbirth, having various diseases, but this did not stop people from reproducing. With all these negatives, *women still went to great lengths* to bring children into this world. Each of us alive today has a woman in our past to thank for our existence. Childbirth has always carried its risks and its rewards. Our ancestors had to trust God that their children would be born normal and healthy. Sometimes both the women and their babies died due to complications, yet today we have the finest medical procedures available. Many of the complications met with fifty years ago would result in success today. Few women die from childbirth. Women can be guaranteed almost perfect success.

Even with the most advanced medical techniques in the world, we are led to believe that it is unwise for a woman with *any health risks* to try to bring children into this world. Yet medical personnel will risk a woman's life by giving her an abortion, sterilizing her, or risking her long-term health by putting her on *the pill*. But then when she wants to trust God with birthing a child when the circumstances look risky, the medical community and sometimes her family and other Christians question her foolishness.

If a wife has cancer or another debilitating disease, medical options should be explored with a Godly doctor. There are many wonderful testimonies of people who trusted God when things looked risky, and God came through in miraculous ways. This is what walking in faith is all about. But this is not for the faint of heart. The Lord must carefully lead you to trust Him under these extreme circumstances and *don't feel like a cop-out* if you must decide to stop having children. Sometimes it is wisdom.

There seems to be a long-established pattern in the medical community where Ob/Gyn doctors advise women with health risks *not* to have further children because of the fear of lawsuits. This is a concern for many doctors. The threat to their long-term practice is valid, and because they want to continue practicing medicine, they do caution *at risk* women. They do not want to see a woman have repeated c-sections or make choices that could lead to further complications, so they tend to err on the side of caution and tell the woman not to get pregnant again.

A couple must make wise choices in these circumstances. If they feel God is leading them to have more children, they must find a doctor who supports them. *Is it wisdom to take a risk?* Sometimes it is not. God's people need to consider the doctor's advice and the principles of the Word of God and carefully decide what God is showing them.

A woman should never feel like she has *let the Lord down* if she must make a decision that will protect her health, especially if that decision does not go against God's principles. Women who take such risks should have spent much time in prayer, possibly fasting (if their health allows) and waiting for God to *release their faith to make the wisest decision*. Great things can happen when someone feels God is leading them to trust Him under challenging circumstances. We are people of faith, and it is in these situations that our faith can be strengthened. Walking out our lives as God carefully leads is what it is all about.

What about being over thirty-five years old when you have a baby?
Women over thirty-five have been successfully birthing children for five thousand years and with women delaying motherhood till their mid-late 40's, being thirty-five does not seem old. If God did not want women to bear children over thirty-five, He would not have given their

bodies the ability to do so. Age is relative. God allowed Elizabeth (after menopause) and Sarah (90yr. old) to give birth in their later years; both births were miracles.

Why is it suddenly considered a considerable risk factor for a woman to have a child after thirty-five? A few medical studies have supported an increase in Down's babies for women who give birth over thirty-five. Yet these stats lump every mother in every kind of lifestyle and health situation together and then factor in age to get a standard. Yes, there are genuine risk factors over thirty-five, but these are valid at any age. Pregnancy can be hard on a woman's body. A woman's health and nutrition before she gets pregnant play a considerable role in a successful pregnancy and delivery. If you are a healthy heterosexual who has been eating healthy and has already delivered a healthy child, your chances are good that you can have a healthy pregnancy. The pill has caused many of these complications. During the last forty years, when increased numbers of women chose the pill and delayed childbearing until they were older, we saw an increase in pregnancy problems, especially in those women over thirty-five years old. One reason may be the pill drains a woman's body of nutrients and natural body reserves. If a woman does not concentrate on rebuilding her nutrition before pregnancy, she may suffer physically. Another reason for problems with women over thirty-five could be the American diet. The types of foods that people eat have changed drastically over the last forty years, with increasingly processed food and the depletion of minerals in our soil. People have more x-rays now and eat irradiated food more often, and we also cook with microwaves.

Another thing is that many women go on crash diets while drinking and smoking, which also depletes them of needed nutrients. People are constantly being exposed to chemicals in their food and water. All these things can cause health risks. Last, if the woman has been sexually promiscuous or has had an abortion or several abortions, this too could affect being able to conceive due to contracted disease. Our lifestyle choices affect the success of every potential pregnancy.

By age thirty-five, some women's bodies are so depleted that their abilities to conceive and successfully deliver a healthy newborn are greatly affected. Yet *not every woman over thirty-five is in these risk categories*. Many factors must be examined before a woman over thirty-five decides that she should not have a child. A woman should see her doctor and get a complete health assessment if she feels that she may be too old. Some women use age as their excuse. Women who want to have children have them later and later in life. Last year more women in their fifties gave birth to healthy children than in previous decades.

Not long ago, I met a woman whose spouse told me he wanted another child, but she refused to get pregnant again after their first. She is now forty-seven years old and tells him she is too old. For years this woman did not want another child, so she should have been honest. If a mother wants to have her children after she is thirty-five and is healthy enough, she should. Yet, if women do not want to, they will look for reasons why they cannot. The reasons for not desiring children are usually deeper than their current state of health. Since menopause in a woman (who has not altered her cycle through hormonal birth control) usually occurs in her late forties or early to mid-fifties, I believe that it's clear that God intended for people to birth children until menopause.

Recently I was in a bookstore, and I needed help. The older-looking woman who helped me had a picture of a little girl on her name badge. I asked her who the little girl was, and she said, "That's my daughter. She's three!" "Wow!" I said, "She's cute. Are you going to have more children?" She replied, "Well, I would like to, but I am fifty-one and already have a thirty-year-old and a seventeen-year-old, so we will see. My doctor said I am fertile, so we are trying to decide." I told her that I thought what she was doing was great, and she shared with me how few people reacted the way I did. Most fifty-one-year-old women are not thinking about having more children, but they could be if their bodies would do it. Very few women are open to having a baby when they are this old.

You do not understand. We have prayed about this, and we both feel called to have a certain number of children, and we agree that when these children are born, we will be through. I think this is great! You should have *no problem* trusting God with your family plan. You are saying you agree that when a specific child (the next son or daughter) is born or when a certain number of children are born (such as after number three), you will be complete. If either of these scenarios is the case, then you should easily have no problem with trusting God to then stop sending children without needing a sterilization operation or using permanent birth control to prevent them.

I believe you heard from the Lord, but He does not contradict Himself, so I am unsure what this means for your life. It could mean that after a certain number of children, your womb will be shut, your husband's sperm won't be hardy, or you will receive a permanent rest from childbearing, or God will test you to see if there is a willingness to continue your trust in the bedroom. The enemy created sterilization to permanently steal your ability to give life. Are you *free to get sterilized with God's blessing*? No, the Lord would have to go against His own mandate in Genesis and His other principles of reproduction in scripture. This also goes against the Levitical Laws, which we are free from, but these laws do talk against genital mutilation. I already covered that a permanent operation is a Reproductive Divorce, is unholy and can ruin your sex life! It also disrupts the body's natural abilities. Motivation and a heart attitude are what are important here. God knows your heart. Ask yourself what other believers did before the ungodly sterilization was invented. They trusted God in a way that we are not used to doing.

But we both *agree* to have no more children!

Agreement is a wonderful thing in marriage and is one of the principles of marital harmony. Agreement is an excellent guideline to keep a couple from missing the voice of God. However, just because *you agree* does not mean you are making a correct scriptural decision. You can both agree and not be aware of God's commands and end up missing God's blessings. The Word of God has many examples of this.

1. *Remember Adam and Eve?* (Genesis 3:6). Together, they *agreed* to eat the forbidden fruit in the Garden of Eden, which led them to spiritual death. Their *agreement* put a curse on the entire human race!
2. Scripture commands us to give our money if we want the blessing of the Lord on our finances. A husband and wife may *agree* to withhold money from the church, but their *agreement* could lead them to miss God's blessings in their finances.
3. *Remember Ananias and Sapphira?* (Acts 5:1-10). Together they *agreed* to lie to the Holy Spirit. They sold property and *agreed to lie* about the price so they could keep some of the money for themselves. Then they lied to Peter and the church. Their *agreement* led to their deaths. God *instantly struck them dead*.
4. The crowd who yelled "Crucify Jesus!" unified in *agreement and* said, "Let the curse fall on us and our children" (Matthew 27:25). They all *agreed* because they hated Jesus so much. The curse fell

on them because of their *agreement* and has lasted more than 2,000 years!

If you and your spouse agree on any subject, it is a step in the right direction; however, agreement does not necessarily mean you are correct. We must seek out answers in scripture *before* we decide. If couples would only seek scripture for answers about birth control, sterilization, etc., they would quickly see that God's Word is clear that children are a heritage and meant for blessing. Most couples ask others around them what they think without God's Word to back up their decisions.

You mentioned in chapter one that America has forced people in the past to be sterilized against their will. In the future, do you think that our country could ever force people again to be sterilized for something like global population control? Yes, I do think that anything is possible. I believe that if the body of Christ does not wake up and unify, this will happen. Right now, *America has voluntary sterilization, and many Christians voluntarily submit to it.* If we want our children to be able to have as many children as they want, we must stand up and ask for legislation that will prevent forced sterilization in the future. If we don't do this now, we will suffer the consequences. Just like when abortion became legal while God's people were asleep, we could see a one or two- child limit come upon us. Consider China's 35 year one-child policy that forced sterilizations, abortions and even deaths to children born without a permit. In America, multiple times in multiple states the issue of forcing sterilization has come up due to rising costs of welfare systems. America once forced sterilizations on prisoners, the socially inept and performed them on American Indians all against their will. The only reason people have not been forced to stop reproducing is that birth numbers have fallen worldwide due to infertility and governments know they need workers to bring in revenue to keep the government going so they offer incentives for couples having babies. So, for now I don't think government forced sterilization is on the table but if anything, ever shifted it might be. We've done it in the past but for now, people are probably safe.

What is the number one reason for women choosing to get their tubes tied and or for the husband to get a vasectomy? *I believe people get sterilized for two reasons: what they think will bring convenience and short-term exhaustion.*

After talking with countless people who have chosen sterilization, I believe most make a long-term decision based on circumstance at the exact moment they are living in. They make this decision without considering the long-term effect that sterilization will have on our lives. They don't think the operation through or and don't believe their feelings will change in the future. Often much pressure is put on people to end their fertility. *"Quit while you're ahead!"* Too many decisions are made to end parenthood because parents wonder *what they have gotten themselves into*. From the 1970s though the 1990s, the attitude was, *"Let's just get this thing over with."* When a couple experiences sleepless nights with a colicky baby and doctor bills from sick children, far too often, they've chosen to prevent more children from coming because of that fear. They've gotten themselves into *an endless cycle of hardship*. Without considering their future parental feelings, they decide to get sterilized.

Far too many parents have ended their fertility because they *got lost in the stress* without seeing the long-term joy. *It makes sense at the time*, and since they see others around them making the same decision, they do not consider that their mind could change. They do not realize how fast their children will grow, and don't see how much the *pleasures of parenthood* will increase. Children do become fun and bring endless love and joy! *Often when it's too late, one of them thinks about how pleasant it would have been to have had more children.* They didn't think they would enjoy parenthood as much as they have or think the piano recitals, dance competitions, Little League ball, and school plays would be as much fun as they were. In 2013, my 4th child graduated high school, and I was helping with the Senior Breakfast, and while we waited all the mothers started talking. They were all about my age (mid-forties), and several expressed that they were trying to figure out what they would now do with their lives. One woman said, *"I just never thought it was going to end, but here we are at the end, and I wish I could say, 'Stop the train! I'm not ready to get off yet' but my son is leaving next week for his college football camp, and this truly is the end of life as we've known it."* Thankfully for me, I was just getting started with my last four children! I could not make that statement, *that it was over* until I was 61, and *I enjoyed every minute of raising my last four* even more than my first four children!

A reversal of the operation costs $6000-10,000 and hardly any insurance companies will pay for a reversal surgery and depending on the sterilization method, the surgery might not work! Unless God supernaturally intervenes and heals or provides a way, most couples are stuck and must live with the finality of their decision. They may consider adoption, but many must live with the regrets, sorrow, and the feeling of *what if?* Unfortunately, most couples will end up sad. I believe in a merciful God. I believe He wants to heal couples who have made this decision.

You're making such a big deal about this issue. I am Godly in other areas, and I do not see how getting sterilized will affect me, especially since limiting myself to just a few children will give me more time to serve God. The scriptures say that God would prefer we trust Him with our family plan because He is seeking Godly children from our union. He knows what we all need to be happy, and He stands willing and ready to bless us if we want it. He may stop sending children so that we can do church or charity work, but if we let Him do it, we will be truly trusting God instead of trying to take control of something that is scripturally His, to begin with.

I'm in shock over this whole subject. I have been an *avid pro-lifer* for years and have vigorously fought against abortion. I know you have shown us the evils of birth control and sterilization, but I still think that *abortion is far worse* because it is committing murder and using birth control is *not* the same thing. We've come to believe that abortion is far worse, but I want us to be clear about what has happened. Margaret Sanger used birth control first, and this led to the acceptance of abortion and to the idea of getting sterilized when childbearing was over. *Birth control was the catalyst.* It numbs hearts and brings compromise. Using it makes it easier to accept sterilization and abortion because birth control users are far more likely to consider abortion than those who do not use birth control. These are NOT separate issues. These issues are all intertwined, and here is why; one method kills babies the other prevents babies. It's a conflicting standard. Looking at the two side by side sheds a very interesting light on the evils of both procedures.

1. Abortion *kills* the life of one child.
2. Sterilization *prevents* multiple lives from ever being created.
3. Abortion is murder and *breaks* the commandment: "You shall not murder."
4. Sterilization permanently *breaks the first real commandment and* violates God's first words: "Be fruitful and multiply."
5. 3.Abortion *takes a life* that God has given. Sterilization *prevents life* from being given by God.

6. 4.Abortion *allows hope of new life* again. Sterilization *stops hope of new life again!*

Which do you think is worse now: abortion or sterilization? It is a lot to think about! Abortion is simply another form of birth control. The abortionist kills the unwanted child that could have been prevented if the parents had used a more reliable form of birth control.

Many God-fearing people shout at abortionists and condemn their behaviors but *fail to see their own hypocrisy when they go home and use artificial birth control.* If their birth control method fails, they could find themselves in the same position! If they are using birth control methods that are causing silent abortions, they could already be in the same position and already guilty of murder.

I believe a sterilization is worse than abortion because a mother who has an abortion could conceive another child someday. With a sterilization, it is final! NO MORE BABIES-EVER! Sterilization removes hope, and halts further conceptions. There is no chance for new life because the person permanently blocked God and permanently removed Him from their equation.

Didn't that commandment to be fruitful apply at a specific time when the earth was new and needed people? Today isn't the earth overcrowded? Children have always ensured the blessing of a strong marriage and a stable society. God said *be fruitful and multiply* without restrictions, so as far as the Scriptures are concerned, the earth is not full even with nearly eight billion people. We are in the twenty-first century, and the earth still has many untapped resources to house a growing population. America alone has more than 100 years of coal reserves! Yet greed and governmental strife in some parts of the world cause intense poverty or limit food distribution, but these problems will always be with us (John 12:8) and are not valid reasons to kill our children or to prevent their conceptions. Our lack of producing needed people has created practical problems that are troubling the future of global economies.

The reality is we need more people, and the reality that the global population is plummeting is becoming so clear that even, the richest man in the world, Elon Musk, father of 12 children, is out doing interviews all over the globe, telling people what Jesus would also be telling them! *"Hey people of the world, the planet needs need people!"*

Need I rest my case! When God put His creation into motion, He balanced His world and desired that this balance would continue. What would have happened to creation if the rest of creation acted upon its free will in the same way humans have? What if, long ago, the oak tree had ceased to produce acorns? The oak tree would have become extinct because the lack of acorns would have failed to reproduce additional oak trees. What if birds refused to lay eggs and the sun refused to shine? If every part of God's creation had been given a free will like humankind and then operated according to its own selfish impulses, then today we might not have the grass on the ground, the flowers blooming, the trees changing colors, or certain species of animals still existing, etc. The continued cooperation of God's creation allows our ecosystem to continue.

Today, our world is suffering from the extinction of certain varieties of plants and animals. Through our negligent behavior with pollutants and chemicals these poisons have affected the fertility cycles of certain species and has caused their extinction. Since 1900, over sixty specific animals have become extinct: the African fish frog, the Nubian rhino, the Mexican sidewinder viper, and the oxtail giraffe. Scientists are quite concerned. Environmental imbalances are leading to extreme consequences for plant and animals.

In human reproduction, consequences have become especially evident during the last few generations. Family planning has created an imbalance. In the first half of the twentieth century, we saw generations of women having fewer children and beginning to enter the workforce. In the second half of the twentieth century, huge amounts of women could not conceive. What will things look like fifty years from now if we continue along this path? We will likely see even greater amounts of infertility, more children birthed through surrogates, or if scientifically perfected, the widespread use of artificial wombs. God knew that humans must continue making new people for humanity to survive as a species. Like other forms of creation, humans could become extinct if we keep altering God's plan.

"That sounds ridiculous!" Really? Scientists are starting to think it is not so ridiculous. Globally, we are seeing the degeneration of our species. A 2020 article entitled: *Fertility rate: Jaw-dropping global crash in children being born*[vii] talked about how multiple countries populations will be less than half by 2100. A series of sixty-one studies[viii] were conducted between 1938 and 1991; almost 15,000 semen samples

from fertile men from 23 countries were tested and analyzed. It was concluded that there was a global decline in sperm count. The findings concluded that male sperm count had declined 1% annually since 1930.) Some scientists tried to say later that these findings were inconclusive, but sixty-one studies concluded the same thing!

"Today, the number of infertile men has risen higher than in the last several decades. A 1994 Male Fertility Study, compiled by Norwich Union Healthcare, showed that 2.5 million men or one in ten men have an infertility problem due to low sperm count."[ix] "French scientists discovered in 1994 that 18% of French couples suffered from fertility difficulties. Pierre Jouannet Centre for the Study of Human Eggs and Sperm in Paris examined the sperm levels of Parisian men. He looked at 1,351 sperm donors in Paris who had donated for artificial insemination. In 1973, the average sperm count was 89 million per ml. In 1992 the count had dropped to 60 million per ml, a decline of 33%."[x] In 2017, sperm counts were studied again and have continued to fall in 2023 to the lowest record ever calculated.[xi]

These studies confirm that sperm counts are decreasing, and the probable cause being the widespread use of birth control, chemical pollutants, drug abuse, overuse of pharmaceuticals and vaccines, and a contaminated water supply. The World Health Organization in 2024:[xii] I in 6 people (17%) of couples of childbearing ages will have trouble conceiving. Infertility affects 48-186 million people worldwide.[xiii] 30-40% of the time, it is a female problem, and 10-30% of the time it is exclusively a male problem. The cause of infertility is being debated, but scientists have found a link between industrial pollutants and their effect on the endocrine system. When we add artificial hormones coming primarily from the birth control pill it's easy to see that pollutants are affecting fertility are everywhere.

Economists are concerned but now even people like Elon musk have become concerned that we have not replaced ourselves quick enough. The belief is it will affect our global economy. Previous generations birthed fewer children than their parents and now with sperm counts falling and infertility rising the country cannot catch up. Nations do not have the workers needed to support their social welfare systems and it's getting very serious! People wonder why their leaders relax their immigration policies, but it is because they didn't have enough children and their country needs taxpayers! Presently, Germany, France, Italy, Spain, Poland, Japan, Australia, Israel, Canada, and the Netherlands, these governments are experiencing the problems that come when society with more older people than young. Entire races are approaching extinction, meaning no more Japanese, Italians, French, Irish, Polish, native Spanish, Australians, or Germans!

In December 2023, Elon Musk[xiv] told Italy, the biggest threat to their future economy was not having enough children, and he challenged them to get busy. Along with Italy, countries now pay couples to have children. Presently, those countries with declining birth rates are paying their people to birth children fees up to $36,000 in tax incentives for one child! The money is working because in 2019 Japan, who had previously had the lowest fertility rate in the world started a program to increase revenues to any couple who continued to have children staring at $940 for first child, by the fourth child the couple receives $9400. This program is working, Japan hit its highest fertility rate in 21 years.[xv]

In 2006, Russian leader Vladimir Putin announced that since birth rates in Russia have fallen to the lowest ever, 1.1 child per woman, this is far under the replacement rate for the population. The Russian government is willing to pay $9,200 to any woman who will have a second child. According to Russian State statistics, the average salary in 2005 was less than $300 per month (8,500 rubbles) (New America Foundation for educated workers). Factory workers made about half this: $175-200/month (4,500-5,000 rubbles). To make more money, women often turn toward prostitution, but even top Russian prostitutes didn't make more than $500 per month (15,000 rubbles). So, the incentive of earning $9,200 (250,000 rubles) to birth one child is huge![xvi]

In 2016, China announced it was relaxing its one-child policy and allowed couples to have two children for the first time in 70 years, then in 2021 China relaxed its policy again and is now allowing couples to have up to three children![xvii] Wahoo! By 2050 China will have more than 438 million people older than sixty, with more than 100 million eighty years old or above. China recognizes its need for people to contribute to their tax base.

The ecologists say we cannot allow more people to be born. But the economic leaders say we must birth more people or have an economic collapse. So, whose way is correct? Did God leave us on a planet that cannot sustain future growth, or are the ecologists correct that our planet is about to run out of resources? Those against population growth have done an excellent job convincing us that the world is overcrowded and under-resourced. Yet how can this be? Since the 1970s, statistical economists have been saying that if the population of the entire world stood side by side, they would fill the state of Rhode Island. Others have said the world's population could lay side-by-side and fit into the City of Jacksonville, Florida. Surely trying to live this way would be uncomfortable and sounds ridiculous, but it makes a statement. We are not on a small planet that cannot house all of us! Instead, if their figures are even remotely accurate, they reflect a truth about God. When He created the earth, He created a large enough planet with enough global resources to feed and house its growing population. Surely humanity can take better care of the earth and consider untapped resources. We can sustain the earth for many more generations.

What about single people? Jesus never had children, and I might not get married, so how does this apply to me? Your gift of fertility is a precious gift. If you are single and fertile and can conceive, then once you are married, this book's message will apply to you. But there is no reason to feel pressure that maybe you are outside of God's will if you choose to remain unmarried and never have children. God said *be fruitful and multiply* to couples. Singles have time to be devoted to God. This has great value for God's kingdom. Christian couples who marry but do not want children try to compare themselves to singles living out the vocation of singleness. This is not the same. Jesus never had children, but Jesus was single. Apostle Paul never had children, but Paul was a widower, and his wife died before they had children. Anna in the Temple was single, but a widow. The prophet Jeremiah was commanded to remain single. Childfree by Choice are fertile couples who are in a separate category from those who remain single. They are in rebellion to God's plan to create families that will bless society. If you are single, don't let anyone guilt or condemn you about not bearing a child. This is not what this book's message is about.

I love my Bible study teacher. She is in her mid-sixties and knows the Bible quite well. She says that you have created a doctrine out of a subject that the Bible is silent about, plus she says that abortion is a far greater sin and kills babies while birth control doesn't hurt anyone. She thinks you should be fighting that cause. What can I tell her? For starters, thank her for teaching you the things you have learned. If she is humble and is willing to look at the issue, you can give her a copy of my book (I'll send you a complimentary copy) and ask her to open it to the third chapter. Ask her if she is aware of the history of birth control. Most of the baby boom generation have no idea that birth control has been here since the beginning. Most think it just came in the 1960s. They don't know that it has been considered an unacceptable practice in Christianity. History alone usually gets people to think because they cannot explain away the population explosion of the Jews in Egypt. The Bible clearly says they were multiplying. Since she believes birth control is a subject God is silent about, ask her to explain what God meant when He told His people to marry and have children and do not decrease. What did God mean by using the word decrease? You can also ask her which verse says we can use birth control? I am quite confident that we are on the right track strictly because I used to believe like your teacher, and if it were not for the supernatural intervention of the Holy Spirit, I would still believe as she does. I understand where she comes from and the mentality of the baby boomer generation that stands on these assumptions. Pray for her. I am sure she is a wonderful woman. She has probably never heard a sermon on this subject in her life so she can't really help that she does not know anything about it.

I am a pastor, and I have always taught my people to be responsible. The way you are stating things, it sounds as if you are calling me an instrument of Satan when I tell young couples to be wise and careful to not overwhelm themselves. I am not putting this book out to judge pastors. You have the hardest job ever. This message is not one of condemnation. There is, therefore, now no condemnation (Romans 8:1). Please don't hear this message in that way. I am trying very hard to be cautious with my tone and God knows my heart, but I must point out the truth about where we are. This subject is a touchy subject, but the birth control lobby has so thoroughly propagandized us that we have forgotten what it means to be God's people.

We are to be *a set apart people* in every area including our fertile lives. We serve a fertile God and everything he touches produces life. There is no barrenness in our God! He has placed no limits on our reproduction. Yet the enemy of our souls does not want God's people to reproduce anything and especially not our Godly offspring. My advice is maybe as a pastor the Lord might want to grant you grace to look at this truth in a new light so you can become His voice. Look up all these Scriptures and start teaching your people the truth. None of us can refute that God is into reproducing children and the enemy is into stopping their conceptions and births!

In your opinion, what should a pastor or Christian leader do if they realize that they've sinned in this area by either getting sterilized or trying to control through birth control? The best thing for any person to do when they realize they are convicted is to confess it to the Lord, repent, and become transparent. Honesty and humility can go a long way. Confessing before those you lead could bring great healing to many congregants and release curses of infertility and miscarriage from off the people in your flock.

You mentioned something about people losing out on finances because they are not open to having children. Do you believe that being open to reproduction brings money? Is there a connection between allowing God to plan our family and our wealth? People need finances and resources to raise children. Choosing to allow for more children is not exactly the *key* to financial wealth but when people decide to have more children, the Lord will provide for them. To be blessed, couples must agree with God's financial principles as well and not be irresponsible. Ministries such as Dave Ramsey's Financial Peace University offer great advice about Biblical finances. If God considers each child to be a blessing, then it is His job to release scriptural wealth to those He blesses.

But my God shall supply all your need according to his riches in glory by Christ Jesus (Philippians 4:19)

When couples obey God's principles, there is no reason why they cannot prosper financially. The decision to get sterilized is often financially motivated. People will say, *"We can't afford any more children."* They are saying, *"We don't want to bother with trusting God for the finances involved with more children."* If God's word is true, He will send provision. I believe that when people cut God off from blessing them, they are not guaranteed their finances will be any better. Sterilization allows the enemy an opportunity to steal from them. He will do this in whatever way he can, and with some couples, this will be in finances.

What should I do? I am exhausted from having six babies in a row. I want a rest from childbirth. Am I still trusting God if I want to quit birthing babies for a few years? I believe that too many times, *people* think that a person who trusts God with their fertility is somehow not trusting God if they do not have baby after baby until the mother's health fails. Did God tell us to ignore our health? He allows everything else in His creation a chance to rest. Why not a mother who has just given birth to six babies? A baby is supposed to be a tremendous blessing and not a curse to their mother's long-term health. Running your body *90 to nothing* until your health fails is not God's best.

It sounds like you need a rest. If you look at the patterns of scripture, you can see that God allows rest. God rested after He created the world. Surely after creating six babies, you deserve a rest too. Resting is scriptural. Rest gives us a breather and allows for growth and a new perspective. Rest restores our health.

I believe we must be careful how we interpret what a *season of rest* looks like. You must stay within the boundaries of the Scriptures. For most women, nursing provides the rest their body needs, but this time your body may need something more extensive. Needing a rest, ever so briefly, or taking a rest so that your body can catch up is not a sin, especially when people want more children.

I recommend that you and your husband pray about it and ask God *how He wants you to take your rest.* God looks at the thoughts and intents of the heart and knows our motivation for seeking rest. In our marriage, several times, *God created our abstinence.* After our sixth baby, my husband traveled quite a bit with his job, and it seemed like when we did come together, it was never at times when I was fertile. After months and months, I thought, "God, you are giving me rest!" In his job cycle, every 30 days they had a meeting, which just happened to fall during my fertile time. We felt like God did this for us so that I could rest.

When a mother's health is compromised, God will give her answers. If God convinced you to let Him use your womb, surely, He can give you a solution to a health issue and or heal your body. A mother wrote me once that she had just had her eighth baby, and her uterus was slipping out. She was asking whether she should get pregnant again, ignoring her health, fully knowing that she might need a hysterectomy unless God healed her prolapsed uterus. Don't be silly, make a wise decision and always protect your health the best you can.

As good stewards, we need to be *responsible* for every gift God brings. We feel it necessary to plan our future and understand what we are trying to accomplish. Having a plan is a great idea. Scripture reinforces the need to plan. God is a planner, so it is not wrong for a couple to have a plan. What can be wrong is when the couple decides how many children they should have and do not consult God. They then plan what they want and leave God completely out. He may have other plans. People believe they know what God wants because they do not want children, so they think God must not want to give them. They feel they know what they can handle physically, emotionally, spiritually, and financially and forget that God knows their abilities even better than they do.

One of the reasons I wrote this book was that as I studied this subject in scripture, it became clearer and clearer to me that making this decision for us is not a thought coming from the heart of God but a *human desire*. Our great sin is that we don't even ask God.

The number one thing a couple does not ever pray about is their family size! God has been completely cut out of the conversation! Many are the plans in a man's heart, but it is the Lord's purpose that prevails (Proverbs 19:21). Scripture is clear. God wants this choice. He will allow us to make it ourselves, but we will get what we've chosen...*We will continue with our own plans; we will all follow the stubbornness of our evil hearts (Jeremiah 18:12b).* That is what happens when we don't ask Him.

When I hear Christian teachers start in on the birth control subject from the standpoint of limiting family size so that *we can be responsible*, I want to raise my hand and say, *"Excuse me, can I please throw up now?"* Not that I do not believe in being responsible, it is wisdom to step back and look at your situation before you jump back in but often these *words sound like they are coming straight out of Satan's mouth!* It is so nauseating to listen to one more teaching where God's plan for our lives is limited because it is assumed that we cannot handle things. Don't get me wrong having a plan is Biblical, and we do need one, but teaching that we must *always be careful* not to be *overwhelmed* sounds good if we want to live defeated lives, but it is not *supernatural*. It's human! It's how *humans* view life, not how God views us, or our capabilities! When you get to the end of your life do you want to be satisfied that you achieved the *status quo*, or would you rather know that you *did it all, had it all* and through the miraculous grace of God you did more than YOU could ever ask of imagine for yourself! Live safe but don't live so safe that you miss what God can do through you!

Get alone with God. Be willing to listen for a new plan. Plan your family so you can *leave someone behind you* who you trained to love God so that they can continue to live out the ways of the Lord. Your family is of far greater importance than anything else you could ever accomplish for God!

What about Natural Family Planning? (NFP) Before I answer a question about Natural Family Planning, I want to say I'm not here to pass judgement on anyone who uses the Natural Family Planning Method. I know couples who swear by it. I will try to answer about this method, but I feel God wanted me to highlight what we experienced in this area. I do know faithful couples who seek God monthly and have pure intentions before the Lord and this is why I will not judge the movement, method, *churches, individuals or groups* who use NFP.

As I said before, my husband and I did not start out using NFP. I never heard about watching for signs of fertility. When God moved on our hearts to *fully trust Him* with our gift of life, we gave our complete submission to His plan. Looking back, I probably would not have had four children in 5 ½ years if I had been following NFP. Even with my perfect 28-day cycle, and showing zero signs of infertility, the reality was my biological clock was ticking out very quickly and I didn't know it. If we had practiced NFP we would have slowed down our pace and had less children in 5 ½ years. This would have been OUR plan, but instead when we felt *God open our eyes*, for us this was a moment of deeper surrender. We literally *gave our fertility to Him* and He gave us four more children! I had my 8th child, at 43 years old and was never fertile again. I believe if I had been using NFP and letting some time go by, we might have lost out on having our eighth child for sure, and maybe even our seventh! This would have been sad. I am extremely grateful for my last two children! I'm glad we completely trusted Him with our outcome. For us, this proved to be the perfect thing to do.

What is Natural Family Planning? NFP used to be called the *Calendar Method* or the *Rhythm Method*. It is when a couple abstains from having sexual relations during the wife's most fertile days to avoid a pregnancy. NFP is the only method of birth control the Roman Catholic Church agrees with. This method is also used by people of many backgrounds including naturalists, holistic health practitioners and members of other religions including those of indigenous traditions.

Historically most Catholics do not realize that NFP was only officially permitted by the Church in 1950. Prior to that, Pope Pius XI's 1930 encyclical Casti Connubii reinforced the Catholic Church's theology **opposing all forms of birth control including NFP (Calendar/Rhythm method).** In 1950, following a 20-year outcry from couples facing serious life circumstances and watching their Protestant counterparts using birth control, Pope Pius XII was put under tremendous pressure to change the church's policy. Pope Pius XII allowed for NFP to be used in extreme cases when the couple was going through *intense hardship, financial difficulties, health* issues, or some other *family crisis*. This decision was deemed justified as NFP does not use anything artificial to block "life". While many Catholics welcomed this decision, others saw this *allowance* as a *compromise* and a departure from tradition, but these voices did not raise enough of an outcry to stop the Pope from changing the church's stance.

There are several very important benefits of using NFP. First, it is a 100% *all-natural method*, and it costs nothing to follow. There are no pills, gadgets, shots, creams, patches, foams or inserts. It doesn't *interfere* with the body's natural cycles or cause any negative side effects like with other methods. This alone means neither partner must pay the price of ruining their health. This is a benefit many couples appreciate! One of the most encouraging statistics about NFP is that couples who use it have a divorce rate of practically zero, possibly because of the communication required between the husband and wife and because their emotional and physical connection is deeply rooted in trust.

NFP does present a few challenges. Probably the hardest part is that a couple cannot make love whenever they feel like it. Instead, on the days of the month when a woman's hormones are raging, when she is craving sex and her body is most fertile, the couple must abstain from sexual relations. Opponents of NFP argue that this is a completely *unnatural* because it cheats the woman out of naturally having great sex. Proponents argue that on fertile days, a couple can still enjoy closeness through showing mutual affection by hugging and kissing, and through special moments of intimacy, but still some couples find this not as satisfying and quite difficult to pause their desire for intercourse. *A friend who has 6 children, is using NFP and has a health problem told me that she can't stand that they must wait until she is not fertile because when she is ovulating, she is so hot for her husband, and waiting is torture!"* I don't know what to say here as we did not use NFP, so I didn't have this problem, but if this couple is in mutual agreement and they are avoiding each other until her health gets better than this is their choice. This is certainly better than her husband getting a vasectomy or further complicating her health problems by introducing artificial hormones.

I've heard critiques from naturalists who feel that charting fertility on apps, or taking temperatures makes fertility feel clinical or mechanical and ruins the natural rhythm between a husband and wife. I can respect that perspective, but I tend to believe that knowing one's cycle can empower a woman to achieve pregnancy or not. Even in Biblical times women had to be aware of their cycles so they could follow the strict Levitical laws of cleanliness after childbirth or ritual purity after their monthly menstruation.

In Leviticus 15:19-30, the laws of Niddah instructed women to abstain from sexual relations during her menstruation cycle and for the seven days afterwards, ending with a ceremonial bath called a Mikvah. Then the woman was cleansed and ready for another month of sexual relations. This practice often coincided with a woman's peak of her fertility cycle around day 14. Whether God's people understood the biology or not this process increased the likelihood of the Israelites conceiving male children, which sustained Israel's armies. While a couple *will not suffer eternal condemnation* for having intercourse during the wife's menstruation cycle, (Leviticus 20:18-19), both Scripture and modern medicine caution against it. The bleeding body is more susceptible to infection, urinary tract infections, candida, venereal diseases, it's easier to contact other illnesses and is a risk factor for endometriosis.

A further challenge for couples following NFP is that abstaining during menstruation and abstaining during a female's fertile days leaves limited opportunities for physical intimacy. For some, this will make their marriage stronger demonstrating commitment and sacrifice, but for others, continued abstinence might cause anger and frustration.

Another concern is that some Catholics approach NFP as a Catholic approved birth control with no openness to life. A mom told me; *"I am so grateful we have NFP because it is the church's way to give us birth control without really giving us birth control. My hubby and I do not want a lot of children. I only wanted my two, and the beauty of NFP is that if we use NFP correctly we won't ever have any more children, plus our choice is still blessed by the Pope"*. But Pope John Paul II cautioned against couples having a closed-off mindset, *"The use of natural methods gives a positive proof of mutual respect….it is necessary to guard against a contraceptive mentality…"* (Familiaris Consortio 1981). Pope John Paul II was warning that NFP is not meant to avoid children indefinitely, but to remain open to God's plan. Ultimately this issue truly depends upon where a person's heart is and invites a couple each month to ask the question *are we open to life* or are we abstaining due to _____ , AND are we excited to come together next month during our fertile times? Always praying, always looking to God and watching for those little Holy Spirit nudges that excite us about having another child.

Does scripture permit seasons of abstinence? In *1 Corinthians 7:5*, the Apostle Paul counseled briefly about this when he said *do not deprive yourselves except for a season for prayer and fasting so that you do not fall into temptation.* He was saying, if one partner *wants it* and the other *does not*, then by saying no, this could bring *sexual tension* and *temptation* into the marriage. Therefore, the *only time* it is *scriptural* to deny your spouse *when they want it,* is when you *both agree* to stay away from each other for prayer and fasting. **Then the spouse who wants it, must wait. But when both people don't want sex, there is no scripture that says a couple cannot mutually agree to wait.**

Putting off sex *can happen* due to a myriad of reasons including spouse who travels, sick spouse, sick child, a partner needing to sleep, the wife on her period or whatever. *If you both agree that you both don't want to have sex, then don't have sex!*

There is no place in scripture that commands that you must have sex every day of your married life! Sexual intimacy in marriage has a rhythm, and every couple must find theirs.

Furthermore, abstaining from sex is not a new concept in marriage and abstaining is not always calculated. For 5,000 years couples have had to abstain for various reasons from health-related to times of war. Abstinence was often seen as an *act of love* as in the scene from *Gone with the Wind* where Scarlet O'Hara tells Rhett Butler that Ashley Wilkes abstains due to his wife Melanie's health condition.

Books have been written about the love that grew between a husband and wife while choosing to abstain. These couples claim the periodic season of abstaining, made their hearts grow a richer and a deeper love for when they were able to return to relations whenever they wanted. Couples say learning about each other and not always trying to *"get what you need"* over the *"needs of your spouse"* is what love is all about. But take note, the most successful lovers do try to return to sexual relations during their most fertile times of the month as soon as possible and do not avoid each other indefinitely unless it is for a severe health crisis or another tragic situation. In the 1960s, the widespread use of hormonal birth control changed generational attitudes around the idea of abstinence and emphasized that sex was no longer about any form of self-denial, because with the new pill, sex was *for any time, in any place,* and *to get all that a person could get.* The propaganda from the birth control pill lobby convinced men and women that they no longer had the ability or reason to control their sexual urges, ever! Yet when couples can demonstrate mutual abstinence, they prove that people can have self-control and disprove the idea that people can't abstain when necessary.

OK so those are the benefits and challenges of Natural Family Planning. I'm not here to judge who uses NFP correctly and who does not or if this is a correct method for them or not. As long as couples are seeking God and His best, I pray He blesses their marriage. I know for us, when God opened our eyes, He gave us a desire to trust Him without using any method. We entered His rest when we were able to trust Him in the highest way we could offer our gift of life. We believe other couples also did this same thing down through time. Giving our fertility to God was certainly our greatest test of our faith and strengthened our relationship with the Lord in a very deep way but I cannot condemn couples who do otherwise. All I can do is present God's truths in a clear and concise way, and let my readers choose for themselves.

I do believe for some people who read this book, everything I am saying here will agree with their spirit and be an instant revelation, but for others this will all be so new they will have to feast on these concepts a bit. No judgement here about what you decide. Giving God your bedroom life, body, soul, and spirit is definitely an *all-out adventure with God* and not for the *faint of heart.* If you are willing to trust Him with something so incredibly important as the size of your family and everything else that this decision entails-He will not let you down. In the end, this decision is between you and God and the little Holy Spirit nudges on your heart. It is not up to me to choose what is best for you. I've presented you the truths of God's word. The ball is in your court. If you don't know how much you can trust Him, simply say yes and let Him lead you, this is what we did.

The biggest issue here is that God wants to lead us. We have raised generations of Christian couples who have absolutely no idea that God is the third person in the bedroom, and He wants to be consulted! This IS what this message of Birthing God's Mighty Warriors is all about. *God wants to be asked; He wants to be a voice influencing your family size.* My goodness He loves you enough to give you the gift of fertility and what a great gift! We are not to despise this gift, but to celebrate with God that *He chose our marriage* to be *fruitful* and *fertile* and to *be a blessing!* He wants to give couples the blessings of a happy home filled with sweet children. That is what this message of BGMW is all about- celebrating your gift with God!

Is not using Birth Control a *"religious belief"* and if I stop using it, am I then part of some *crazy sect*? No. Even seculars, naturalists and health practitioners from around the world are helping people move towards a more natural approach because it is heathier. But a few years ago, the media tried to lump all non-birth control couples into a one-dimensional box. In the late 1990's, the media labeled religious couples who had decided to stop using artificial birth control as *Full-Quiver* or *Quiver-full*. This word came from Rick and Jan Hess's 1987 book entitled: *Full Quiver*. In the early 1990s, as one by one the Lord revealed to a handful of Protestant couples that they had been *lied to* by their faithful Protestant denominations. A small minority started re-thinking birth control. It was a small group and an extremely rare group because these were Protestants and stereotypically Protestants use birth control. I guess this book Full Quiver was sold at homeschool conventions in the Midwest because when these Midwestern couples encountered another Protestant family who had more than the 2.0 accepted number of children, sometimes they asked the couple, *"Are you a Full Quiver family?"* meaning *did you read the Full Quiver book too?* This was pre-internet.

After the internet took off, and more couples, both Catholic and Protestant, started to read the book and a few other homeschool books with similar messages such as Mary Pride's book, *The Way Home*, one of these families started an *online chat room* to talk about the messages in these books and discuss how people were living this commitment out in real life. They called it the *Quiver Full Digest*. On the forum, families talked about everything under the sun from homeschooling multiples, to choosing curriculum, to having a home garden, to how to apply for college scholarships and what to do with a colicky baby. Essentially it was a family focused online chat space and since it had been a generation since people had raised more than the 2.0 acceptable number of children, these people needed support for *how to do life* with a few more children than their parents had.

Years later, in the early 2000s, a politically liberal religion reporter named Kathryn Joyce, who is an admitted atheist, was looking for a religious book angle when she stumbled upon what she identified as a ***sect of people*** practicing ***a new religious idea.***

Kathryn spent time researching the topic of Full-Quiver or Quiver Full families. She read the Quiver Full Digest (which had Catholics, Mormons, Amish and Protestant families all in the group's chat space) and labeled these families as a religious "movement." Kathryn only interviewed Quiver Full parents living predominately in the Midwest and interviewed only a limited number of Protestants and I might add these few families were from a limited number of Protestant denominations. In her 2009 book: **Quiver Full: Inside the Christian Patriarchy Movement,** Kathryn painted a very dismal, almost *cult-like* picture of the families she met and labeled this new *movement*. I don't know how many families Kathryn met, but she surmised that *all Quiver Full* families were the same because those she encountered appeared to have similar lifestyles, maybe akin to the TLC show The Duggars of "*19 Kids and Counting.*"

After researching, she placed all large Full Quiver Protestant families into one category based on her checklist which had proved her hypothesis. She only interviewed a handful of families of Protestants- no Catholics, no Mormons, and nearly all these families were from the Midwest, a few from the south but none from other parts of the country. From this *very limited group of families* she then said all the Full Quiver families were following some sort of Quiver Full litmus test: all the moms stayed home, all the girls wore only dresses - none wore jeans, only husbands worked, but at home they were more like dictators. The women had no rights, girls cooked and cleaned, only college for the boys, all lived off-grid, all homeschooled and all were politically conservative. Liberal, atheist Kathryn feared a *religious takeover* if these people ever went mainstream. She feared they might have large families and raise them all to *"Vote Republican!"* She quickly wrote this book *to warn liberals* about Christians birthing militant religious children to take over the culture.

As I said, she interviewed a very small group of homeschoolers who were strictly Protestant, then formed her twisted hypothesis. I will not refute that there are families who have a birth control conviction and who may have similar lifestyles to one another, but to say all families who don't use birth control live a very narrow-minded lifestyle, is simply silly. If this is a movement, then one might say these families have more traditional values than their counterparts but if it truly is a movement then it is not moving very quickly. After thirty years it has still not reached anywhere near becoming something mainstream, especially in Protestant Christianity.

Whenever the media asks me about being full quiver, I try to point out that having children is about having a *conviction*. It is not an all-encompassing lifestyle. I believe this part has been very misrepresented. Many kinds of people allow God to plan their families. *When I was interviewed by Kathryn, I tried to tell her she was being narrowminded. She told me many of my responses to her questions were the opposite of the other families she had interviewed. Unlike the other women she had interviewed, I am a college graduate and was a cheerleader at a major university. I am a former waterski champion. I homeschooled off and on, but all eight children have now graduated from a public high school. My husband was an executive, and I lived in a very exclusive area. The other large families I knew and raised my children around, were not necessarily religious, but were upscale professionals with plenty of money and a belief in higher education. My three older girls were never treated like slaves; each had lives filled with dance, cheerleading, crew team, entrepreneurship, dating and community service. During their teen years, my teens were rarely, if ever home to babysit, but were instead out enjoying their teenage lives. Our family lived in blue jeans and not dresses to the floor. We do live in Florida and my daughters dressed very nice and wore beautiful bathing suits, and I might add, they were not allowed to dress like a "hoochie-mama" on the beach or pose in nearly nude swimsuit photos! I work out most days or ride my bike. My husband was the nicest guy on the planet, and very patient and loving with our children. We traveled. We went on our boat. We vacationed. For a season we practically lived at the theme parks. If we wanted to label ourselves because of our conviction, I would say my husband and my sons are some of the most helpful men in society and it is because they are committed to their jobs and spouses and to the goal of a fun-loving home full of children.*

After Kathryn Joyce's book came out and her media blitz, I combed the internet for people chatting about her book and her findings. Here's what families were saying about the state of being "quiver full", which Joyce claimed was a "new religious movement."

"I don't remember signing up to be Quiver-full, getting a membership card, and a list of rules to follow from some QF organization. After our first two, we realized God was giving us the heartfelt conviction to accept more children as His blessing. I believe that other families have also felt that same moving of the Holy Spirit. Our family is so much fun, and my husband is not a distant, unloving dictator. Our home is filled with joy, and my children love being part of our great big-wonderful family." Mom of 11

"After I read that silly Quiver Full book, I wished Ms. Joyce had interviewed me... I am NOT like any of those things she listed, and yet, I've always had a desire for a large family. I raised my children in Southern California, and I did not homeschool. All my children attended public school. I worked outside the home, and I am highly educated. I speak/read/write two other languages besides English. I have never had a home birth, although, admittedly, I would have liked to have tried. Also, I do not dress like an old hag or a school matron. I love to hang out in my T-shirt and jeans but dress professionally for my business appointments. For the sake of argument, we are not ultra-conservative. We do not live off the grid. My family and I live in a large condo-apartment in the city. We do not home church. I don't know any other large families personally, but one thing I did agree about, I admit I am an exhausted mother. I don't know many moms who aren't, whether they have 2 children or 14, every mom is tired! My husband IS loving, and he is certainly NOT a dictator! If anything, I run the home and pay all the bills, but I do seek his advice before making any major household decisions and I try to do things his way, but he does things my way probably even more. I can't say what's going on in every bedroom where the parents do not use birth control but there is NOTHING being forced with us! We love intimacy but at the end of the day, we're too often exhausted to even think about lovemaking." Mom of 4

"I read that book by that journalist and finished it wondering who she talked to and how she came to the conclusions she did. It was quite strange. For me, this is a matter of obedience to God in family planning. Anything beyond that has nothing to do with anything else. There is no one-size-fits-all large family or couple for that matter. After our first three, God gave us the desire to have more children. Although I would absolutely love to have a little farm in upstate NY, my husband's dream is more like a high-rise in Manhattan, but for now we live comfortably north of New York City. We believe in higher education for all our children, why would we not? My husband would be tickled to see every single one attend the most academically challenging universities and grad schools possible. No large family should feel guilty or a failure because they're urban dwellers, don't garden nor grind their grain, or wear blue jeans, or have any other lifestyle issues. All of that has nothing to do with letting God give you a larger family than others have. Our children are the best choice ever." A loving Mother of 6

"This is fun. I'll try to do Kathryn's little lifestyle checklist that she claims all large Protestant families have in common: Ok, we do homeschool, but we started with our two oldest in public school until God made it clear we were to homeschool them. At first, I was so upset, I homeschooled them kicking and screaming and even now I would not be opposed to putting them back in school at some point, but we are in a homeschool co-op we really like, and it is working out great. While my hubby would be thrilled living in the middle of nowhere, the children and I much prefer our small town with good shopping areas, not far from Atlanta. I had the first nine children in a hospital. #10 was a homebirth because we could not find an OB/GYN that shared our belief that birth should be natural. I wear jeans every day. I've not worn a dress or skirt in years. We do not live off the grid, but we do live conservatively, recycling, catching rainwater, tending to my small herb garden and caring for the environment around us. We do not home church, but instead go to a huge church in our town. None of our friends have ten children, like us, but some wished they did have a larger family. They say we inspire them. For fitness, I am a runner. My children are about 18 months apart, so I am quite busy, but my hubby is very loving towards me and our children. He loves nothing better than to cuddle up in a chair with the kids and read a book or to play video games with them. We have a healthy intimate sex life, I guess we have lots of sex! My hubby is a professional and makes a good living and we would love to see all our children be successful in business, or start their own businesses, but not until after they get their college degree." Mom of 10

"I agree that all families who follow God's plan for the family can't be lumped together in one lifestyle. We do not fit most of that author's categories. I do not homebirth, make food from scratch, wear dresses, or live off grid. I do homeschool, but due to my husband becoming disabled, it looks like I will be going to work soon, and we may end up putting the kids back in school. I have no problem with anyone else doing any of those things, they are simply not for my life and how we want to raise our children. Our conviction is not about fitting into anyone else's preconceived ideas but more about following Jesus and letting Him be Lord. Children are blessings, and sometimes we worry so much about being a perfect specimen of spirituality that we think more about how others see us than following God for ourselves. He only gives us grace for following His will for our lives--not following a particular set of other's expectations. Allowing God to bring new children into our lives is about actual LIFE! The number of children you have doesn't make you holier. It's about where your heart's attitude is. If you have given control of your womb over to God and desire to leave everything up to Him, you are in complete trust with this huge part of your life. It doesn't matter if you have 1, 8, 15, or no children. I know people with more children than us who have decided enough is enough. They are not evil because they feel finished. Just because a couple has a lot of children does not automatically mean they are surrendered. The number of children is irrelevant. It's what God determines for each couple. We are all different. We would love more children. We have seven between us (five I've *given birth to). The two oldest were from my husband's first marriage, and I didn't raise them. They are grown now and don't live with us. I still consider us committed to God's purposes even though the Lord hasn't blessed us with a baby since we came to have this conviction."* Mom of 7

From these comments it is easy to see how Kathryn Joyce's, *Quiverfull: Inside the Christian Patriarchy Movement*, got this "movement" very wrong. Families who choose to go *natural* to plan their families, come in all shapes and sizes and religious beliefs, with every parent deciding how they want to use their gift of life.

In the end, giving God your family planning is not about earning an "A" on some sort of *spiritual* report card. It is simply another area where God asks us to fully trust Him. This trust might look different from couple to couple. It is not the easiest thing in the world to consider, especially in a *spoiled* and *selfish* society where everyone wants everything to serve their wants and desires. Giving God your fertility is the opposite. With this family lifestyle, you will be serving others all the time. It takes conviction, stamina, and commitment to do a good job raising the next generation. And I do know some people who have failed. It doesn't happen very often, but we are human, and things happen to people. In nearly every instance where couples ran into problems, other variables caused the family to have difficulties. Yet it was not the size of the family that caused the problem, problems can happen to any size family! I've only met one actual large-family Quiverfull dropout, and her children were not her problem. There were other factors that affected her life and today she is divorced and an atheist. It is so sad. I'm not sure what happened to her children. This is why I have continued to say *no judgement* here and *no pressure* here. Life can hit anyone hard. All we can do is our best.

If giving God your fertility was a movement and massive amounts of parents ended up *unhappy*, then it would not be a *movement for very long*, nor would its impact have expanded positively across the globe. As God turns this next generation back to trusting Him with all the details of their bedroom life, the best children in history are yet to come. These next generations will take this "family movement" to a new level. It is the most exciting time ever to be Birthing God's Mighty Warriors!

ENDNOTES

CHAPTER 1
(no footnotes)

CHAPTER 2
(no footnotes)

CHAPTER 3

1. Martin Luther quote
2. John Calvin quote
3. https://www.orientalorthodoxy.com/library/texts/quotes/contraception/
4. https://www.orientalorthodoxy.com/library/texts/quotes/contraception/
5. https://www.sefaria.org/topics/rabbi-eliezer-b-hyrcanus?sort=Relevance&tab=notable-sources
6. https://www.jta.org/archive/reform-rabbis-for-intelligent-regulation-of-birth-control
7. https://www.britannica.com/topic/Lambeth-Conference
8. https://indyencyclopedia.org/american-nonconformist-1879-1896/
9. https://www.history.com/this-day-in-history/fda-approves-the-pill
10. https://www.britannica.com/biography/Hugh-Hefner
11. https://www.nbcnews.com/id/wbna19053382
12. https://www.ranker.com/list/pastors-that-fell-from-grace/genevieve-carlton
13. https://theconversation.com/protestants-and-the-pill-how-us-christians-helped-make-birth-control-mainstream-179536
14. https://www.nytimes.com/1961/02/24/archives/national-council-of-churches-backs-artificial-birth-control.html
15. https://www.businessinsider.com/divorce-rate-changes-over-time-2019-1?op=1#at-the-start-of-the-1930s-the-yearly-divorce-rate-briefly-dipped-but-then-climbed-again-to-19-divorces-for-every-1000-people-6
16. https://www.statista.com/statistics/185274/number-of-legal-abortions-in-the-us-since-2000/
17. https://www.mentalfloss.com/article/83685/9-forms-birth-control-used-ancient-world
18. https://www.psychologytoday.com/us/blog/how-we-do-it/201906/the-pope-who-advocated-birth-control
19. https://www.mnnonline.org/news/early-church-conversations-on-politics-abortion-and-faith-still-relevant-today/
20. https://heidelblog.net/2019/01/calvin-on-abortion/
21. https://worldpopulationreview.com/state-rankings/late-term-abortion-laws-by-state
22. https://theweek.com/articles/495327/chinas-looming-woman-shortage-5-possible-consequences
23. https://philosophy.stackexchange.com/questions/95070/why-did-aristotle-and-saint-thomas-aquinas-believe-that-the-fetus-only-receives
24. https://allthatsinteresting.com/silphium
25. https://www.worldhistory.org/article/2024/family-planning-in-greco-roman-antiquity/
26. https://www.desiblitz.com/content/ancient-indian-contraceptives
27. https://rarehistoricalphotos.com/vintage-device-birth-control/
28. https://www.ncesc.com/geographic-pedia/what-did-native-americans-do-for-birth-control/
29. https://www.ancient-origins.net/weird-facts/tutankhamun-condom-0017004
30. https://pubmed.ncbi.nlm.nih.gov/29286023/
31. https://www.historyhit.com/the-history-of-condoms/
32. https://ancientspast.com/history-of-condoms-a-look-at-when-men-started-using-them/
33. https://www.reddit.com/r/Frickin/comments/zoewr5/before_the_invention_of_rubber_condoms_japanese/
34. https://theconversation.com/a-brief-history-of-abortion-from-ancient-egyptian-herbs-to-fighting-stigma-today-213033
35. https://www.historynewsnetwork.org/article/whatever-happened-to-quickening
36. https://www.cbc.ca/news/canada/newfoundland-labrador/nl-history-abortion-1.6694080

ENDNOTES

37. https://heidelblog.net/2016/10/notes-from-the-didache-on-the-early-christian-view-of-abortion/
37a. https://crossexamined.org/christianity-and-abortion-part-2-the-early-churchs-view-of-abortion/
38. https://www.vatican.va/roman_curia/congregations/cfaith/documents/rc_con_cfaith_doc_19741118_declaration-abortion_en.html
38a. https://jwa.org/encyclopedia/article/abortion
39. https://christianity.stackexchange.com/questions/33290/which-denominations-allow-abortions-and-why
40. https://churchandstate.org.uk/2013/03/life-begins-at-conception-wasnt-always-the-churchs-position-a-history-of-abortion/
40a. https://oll.libertyfund.org/titles/malthus-an-essay-on-the-principle-of-population-1798-1st-ed
41. https://christianity.stackexchange.com/questions/33290/which-denominations-allow-abortions-and-why
42. https://christianity.stackexchange.com/questions/33290/which-denominations-allow-abortions-and-why
43. https://christianity.stackexchange.com/questions/33290/which-denominations-allow-abortions-and-why
44. https://brewminate.com/the-four-great-awakenings-in-american-christian-history/
45. https://digitalcommons.wku.edu/theses/910/
46. https://www.history.com/news/comstock-act-1873-obscenity-contraception-mail
47. https://www.britannica.com/biography/Margaret-Sanger
48. https://www.biography.com/scientist/francis-galton
49. https://www.forbes.com/sites/stuartanderson/2022/04/25/the-immigrant-entrepreneur-who-brought-condoms-to-america/
50. https://www.glamour.com/story/the-victorians-did-some-crazy-things-for-birth-control
51. https://bpb-us-e1.wpmucdn.com/blogs.uoregon.edu/dist/7/11428/files/2015/06/Tone-Making-Room-for-Rubbers-2bmghaw.pdf
52. https://www.mentalfloss.com/article/549270/facts-about-margaret-sanger
53. https://www.sethkaller.com/item/1965-21123.99-President-Theodore-Roosevelt-Condemns-Abortion,-Birth-Control,-and-Family-Planning
54. https://www.press.jhu.edu/newsroom/fixing-poor-eugenic-sterilization-and-child-welfare-twentieth-century
55. https://www.usatoday.com/story/opinion/2020/07/23/racism-eugenics-margaret-sanger-deserves-no-honors-column/5480192002/
56. https://www.sanger.hosting.nyu.edu/aboutms/msbio/
57. https://embryo.asu.edu/pages/first-american-birth-control-clinic-brownsville-clinic-1916
58. https://www.wwiisoldier.com/shh-its-a-military-secret-condoms-from-wwi-to-wwii/
59. https://skeptics.stackexchange.com/questions/47885/did-margaret-sanger-say-the-most-merciful-thing-that-a-large-family-does-to-one
60. https://www.britannica.com/topic/American-Birth-Control-League
61. https://www.thecollector.com/the-roaring-twenties-jazz-age/
62. https://www.press.uillinois.edu/wordpress/the-catholic-church-vs-birth-control-the-sanger-papers-features-early-rounds-in-this-epic-battle-by-peter-c-engelman/
63. https://www.encyclopedia.com/religion/encyclopedias-almanacs-transcripts-and-maps/casti-connubii
64. https://artsci.case.edu/dittrick/online-exhibits/history-of-birth-control/contraception-in-america-1900-1950/rhythm-method/
65. https://time.com/archive/6746880/religion-protestant-birth-control/
66. https://books.google.com/books/about/The_Rhythm_of_Sterility_and_Fertility_in.html?id=cOYkAAAAYAAJ
66a. ttps://bpr.studentorg.berkeley.edu/2020/11/04/americas-forgotten-history-of-forced-sterilization/
67. https://socialwelfare.library.vcu.edu/programs/health-nutrition/sanger-margaret/
68. *https://www.salon.com/2013/02/18/mahatma_gandhi_birth_control_is_criminal/*
69. https://allthatsinteresting.com/lysol-birth-control
70. https://www.britannica.com/topic/American-Birth-Control-League
71. *https://www.quotestree.com/2021/03/birth-control-quotes.html*
71a. https://artsci.case.edu/dittrick/online-exhibits/history-of-birth-control/contraception-in-america-1900-1950/rhythm-method/
72. https://www.financialexpress.com/life/india-launched-family-planning-programme-in-1952-1st-

country-to-do-so-mos-health-bharati-pawar-2608275/
https://www.the-scientist.com/birth-of-the-pill-1956-1960-70475
73. https://www.the-scientist.com/birth-of-the-pill-1956-1960-70475
73a. https://artsci.case.edu/dittrick/online-exhibits/history-of-birth-control/contraception-in-america-1900-1950/rhythm-method/
74. https://www.rbf.org/about/our-history/timeline/population-council
75. https://www.nytimes.com/1961/02/24/archives/text-of-birthcontrol-statement-by-church-group.html
76. https://www.britannica.com/event/Griswold-v-State-of-Connecticut
77. https://www.ourbodiesourselves.org
78. https://www.nytimes.com/1966/09/07/archives/margaret-sanger-is-dead-at-82-led-campaign-for-birth-control-mrs.html
79. https://www.boston.com/news/business/2015/08/26/how-boston-university-helped-end-crimes-against-chastity/
80. https://womenandsocialmovements.omeka.net/exhibits/show/feminist-protest-and-the-1970-/pill-hearings
80a. https://www.johnricebooks.com/books-booklets-pamphlets
81. https://time.com/archive/6638346/the-pope-and-birth-control-a-crisis-in-catholic-authority/
81a. https://www.goodreads.com/book/show/80116.The_God_Who_Is_There
81b. https://www.johnricebooks.com/books-booklets-pamphlets
82. https://www.unfpa.org/events/general-assembly-declares-parents-have-exclusive-right-set-family-size
83. https://www.unfpa.org/about-us
84. https://www.cbc.ca/archives/the-birth-control-pill-was-unstoppable-in-the-1960s-1.4856941
85. https://www.usccb.org/issues-and-action/marriage-and-family/natural-family-planning/resources/upload/intl-review-nfp-1983-billings-NFP-yesterday-today-tomorrow.pdf
85a. https://www.theindigenousfoundation.org/articles/a-brief-history-on-the-forced-sterilization-of-indigenous-peoples-in-the-us 65
85b. https://www.beliefnet.com/columnists/pontifications/2008/09/eugenics-lives-louisiana-lawma.html
86. https://www.historynewsnetwork.org/article/a-1970-law-led-to-the-mass-sterilization-of-native
87. https://thehill.com/changing-america/respect/equality/599274-single-women-were-given-the-right-to-birth-control-50-years/
88. https://www.history.com/topics/womens-history/roe-v-wade
89. https://www.amazon.com/Act-Marriage-Tim-LaHaye/dp/0310211778
89a. https://www.heritagebooks.org/products/whatever-happened-to-the-human-race-schaeffer-koop.html
90. https://slate.com/technology/2023/01/today-sponge-hormone-free-birth-control-choice-illusory.html
91. https://lifesciencesintelligence.com/features/exploring-the-5-fda-approved-iuds-types-benefits-and-effectiveness
92. https://www.jognn.org/article/S0884-2175(15)33135-X/abstract
93. https://www.drugs.com/sfx/depo-provera-side-effects.html
94. http://www.cnn.com/HEALTH/9809/02/morning.after.pill.02/
95. https://my.clevelandclinic.org/health/articles/24157-vaginal-ring
96. https://pubmed.ncbi.nlm.nih.gov/11727179/
97. https://americanpregnancy.org/unplanned-pregnancy/birth-control-pills-patches-and-devices/lunelle-monthly-injection/
98. https://www.wired.com/story/missed-period-pills-menstrual-regulation-how-it-works/
99. https://www.ncbi.nlm.nih.gov/pmc/articles/PMC8796292/
100. https://www.drugdangers.com/yaz/
101. https://www.thebusinessof.life/the-business-of-being-born
102. https://www.health.harvard.edu/blog/a-different-nonhormonal-birth-control-option-202108302582
103. https://www.drugwatch.com/yaz/settlements/
103a. https://www.amny.com/entertainment/women-roles-handmaid-s-tale-1-18656550/
103b. https://archokc.org/news/rachels-vineyard-offers-post-abortion-healing
103c. https://thewalrus.ca/why-women-hate-the-pill/
104. https://www.thebusinessof.life/the-business-of-birth-control
105. https://www.npr.org/2022/06/24/1102305878/supreme-court-abortion-roe-v-wade-decision-

ENDNOTES

overturn
106. https://www.economist.com/technology-quarterly/2023/07/17/the-fertility-sector-is-booming
107. https://www.usatoday.com/story/news/politics/elections/2024/06/05/right-to-contraception-act-2024-vote/73983546007/
108. https://www.catholic.com/magazine/print-edition/contraception-and-spiritual-struggle
109. https://blog.adw.org/2014/12/pope-gregory-the-great-advice-to-the-married/
110. https://www.worldhistory.org/Council_of_Trent/
111. https://religiondispatches.org/the-story-behind-the-catholic-churchs-stunning-reversal/
112. https://www.vatican.va/content/pius-xi/en/encyclicals/documents/hf_p-xi_enc_19301231_casti-connubii.html
113. https://religiondispatches.org/the-story-behind-the-catholic-churchs-stunning-reversal/
114. https://www.vatican.va/content/paul-vi/en/encyclicals/documents/hf_p-vi_enc_25071968_humanae-vitae.html
115. https://www.catholiceducation.org/en/marriage-and-family/sexuality/five-key-features-of-the-theology-of-the-body.html
116. https://www.usccb.org/topics/natural-family-planning/natural-family-planning
116a. https://www.beliefnet.com/columnists/christnewstoday/2025/05/pope-leo-xiv-declares-the-family-as-the-stable-union-between-a-man-and-a-woman.html
117. https://books.google.com/books/about/Theology_of_the_Body_Explained.html?id=svA0moWkh30C
118. https://www.npr.org/sections/thetwo-way/2015/02/12/385735269/couples-who-chose-not-to-have-children-are-selfish-pope-says
119. https://www.americamagazine.org/politics-society/2023/05/12/francis-meloni-children-future-italy-245284
120. https://apnews.com/article/italy-vatican-pope-demographics-children-72644b8c2436ad2682e074ac194a068f
121. https://www.guttmacher.org/article/2012/02/guttmacher-statistic-catholic-womens-contraceptive-use
122. https://www.goarch.org/-/for-the-health-of-body-and-soul-an-eastern-orthodox-introduction-to-bioethics
123. https://mormonbeliefs.org/all-about-mormons/do-mormons-believe-in-birth-control/
124. https://www.amjaonline.org/fatwa/en/83665/permissibility-of-these-birth-control-methods
125. https://www.hindu-blog.com/2023/09/hindu-religion-views-on-contraception.html
126. https://www.bbc.co.uk/religion/religions/buddhism/buddhistethics/contraception.shtml
127. https://reformedperspective.ca/children-a-calling-and-a-blessing-a-careful-look-at-the-issue-of-birth-control/
128. https://www.myjewishlearning.com/article/procreation-and-contraception/
129. https://family.adventist.org/resources/real-answers/birth-control-a-seventh-day-adventist-statement-of-consensus/
130. https://www.dmagazine.com/religion/2014/05/the-late-first-baptist-dallas-pastor-w-a-criswell-was-pro-choice/
131. https://www.baptistpress.com/resource-library/news/how-southern-baptists-became-pro-life/
132. https://www.baptistpress.com/resource-library/news/how-southern-baptists-became-pro-life/
133. https://www.galaxie.com/article/jbmw18-1-03
134. https://www.baptistpress.com/resource-library/news/how-southern-baptists-became-pro-life/
135. https://theconversation.com/the-history-of-southern-baptists-shows-they-have-not-always-opposed-abortion-183712
136. https://www.johnstonsarchive.net/baptist/sbcabres.html
137. https://www.sbc.net/resource-library/resolutions/resolution-onabortion-4/
138. https://www.sbc.net/resource-library/resolutions/resolution-on-abortion/
139. https://www.sbc.net/resource-library/resolutions/resolution-on-the-freedom-of-choice-act-hyde-amendment/
140. https://www.sbc.net/resource-library/resolutions/on-anticipation-of-a-historic-moment-in-the-pro-life-movement/
140a. https://people.com/who-is-bill-gothard-the-institute-in-basic-life-principles-founder-7506014
141. https://aboverubies.org
141a. https://www.crossway.org/books/the-way-home-tpb/
142. https://www.goodreads.com/book/show/2450548.A_Full_Quiver_
143. https://www.goodreads.com/book/show/6746297-the-bible-and-birth-control
144. https://christianliferesources.com/2018/05/08/a-scriptural-approach-to-family-planning/

145. https://www.goodreads.com/book/show/165192.Yes_They_re_All_Ours
146. https://www.focusonthefamily.com/family-qa/use-of-contraceptives-in-marriage/
147. https://en.wikipedia.org/wiki/List_of_anti-abortion_organizations_in_the_United_States
148. https://www.goodreads.com/book/show/2814101-be-fruitful-and-multiply
149. https://goodreads.com/book/show/9193699-birthing-god-s-mighty-warriors
150. https://www.goodreads.com/en/book/show/13533082-you-ve-got-to-be-kidding
151. https://www.goodreads.com/book/show/6270778-family-unplanning
152. https://www.newsweek.com/making-babies-quiverfull-way-106691
152a. https://www.clmagazine.org/topic/sexual-morality/blessings-by-the-dozen/
153. https://www.youtube.com/watch?v=sXLy1MCSTys
154. https://www.youtube.com/watch?v=m_CfX2ca8gc
155. https://www.goodreads.com/book/show/562504.Does_the_Birth_Control_Pill_Cause_Abortions_
156. https://en.wikipedia.org/wiki/Kids_by_the_Dozen
157. https://www.goodreads.com/en/book/show/2605331-love-in-the-house
158. https://www.tvinsider.com/show/19-kids-and-counting/
159. https://www.duggarfamily.com/favorite/the-duggars-20-and-counting/
160. https://kathrynjoyce.com/books/quiverfull/
161. https://www.newsweek.com/inside-duggar-familys-conservative-ideology-76547
162. https://www.imdb.com/title/tt1544368/
163. https://www.youtube.com/watch?v=3tIOB74tcds
164. https://www.youtube.com/watch?v=_Is4Yvgp_QA
165. https://www.goodreads.com/book/show/10200031-a-love-that-multiplies
166. https://www.thebirthcontrolmovie.com/the-project-history
167. https://www.thebirthcontrolmovie.com/the-films/is-it-up-to-us
168. https://www.youtube.com/watch?v=RNbn6nnYBqY
169. https://archokc.org/news/rachels-vineyard-offers-post-abortion-healing
170. https://thewalrus.ca/why-women-hate-the-pill/
171. https://baptistnews.com/article/sbc-calls-for-immediate-abolition-of-abortion-
172. https://www.40daysforlife.com/en/
173. https://www.priestsforlife.org
174. https://www.bound4life.com/the-life-band/
175. https://marchforlife.org
176. https://the1916project.com
177. https://www.guttmacher.org/fact-sheet/contraceptive-use-united-states
178. https://www.nytimes.com/1961/02/24/archives/national-council-of-churches-backs-artificial-birth-control.html
179. https://theimaginativeconservative.org/2019/12/birth-control-decline-civilization-steven-kessler.html
180. https://www.cbc.ca/archives/the-birth-control-pill-was-unstoppable-in-the-1960s-1.4856941
181. https://www.nytimes.com/2024/01/23/well/live/birth-control-sex-drive-libido.html
182. https://theconversation.com/theres-convincing-evidence-the-pill-can-cause-depression-and-some-types-are-worse-than-others-184248
183. https://www.mindbodygreen.com/articles/what-birth-control-might-do-to-your-fertility
184. https://usafacts.org/articles/how-have-us-fertility-and-birth-rates-changed-over-time/
185. https://www.upi.com/Archives/1981/04/08/Pope-quotes-Pope-on-birth-control/5966355554000/
186. https://www.disastercenter.com/crime/uscrime.htm
187. https://ualr.edu/socialchange/2018/04/15/reflection-history-sexual-assault-laws-united-states/
188. https://www.businessinsider.com/divorce-rate-changes-over-time-2019-1?op=1#in-the-60s-the-rate-slowly-started-to-climb-again-ending-the-decade-with-a-new-high-32-annual-divorces-for-every-1000-americans-9
189. https://www.cdc.gov/nchs/data/hestat/marriage_rate_2018/marriage_rate_2018.htm
190. https://openlibrary.org/books/OL17004842M/The_decline_of_males
191. https://www.webmd.com/sex/birth-control/birth-control-pill-sex-drive
192. https://www.stlouisfed.org/on-the-economy/2018/july/-/media/project/frbstl/stlouisfed/files/pdfs/community-
193. https://www.daycaresdontcare.org/History/US_daycare_from_1970_to_present.htm
194. https://www.latchkey-kids.com/latchkey-kids-age-limits.htm
195. https://nypost.com/2022/10/29/why-60-years-of-feminism-has-not-made-women-any-happier/
196. development/econmobilitypapers/section2/econmobility_2-1howeelliott_508.pdf

ENDNOTES

197. https://pmc.ncbi.nlm.nih.gov/articles/PMC9255892/
198. https://pdfs.semanticscholar.org/b20f/0e9ee9d299f511e07934d43a55338a542115.pdf
199. https://bioethicsarchive.georgetown.edu/pcbe/reports/cloningreport/fullreport.html
200. https://baptistnews.com/article/new-jersey-governor-signs-cloning-bill/
201. https://www.usccb.org/issues-and-action/human-life-and-dignity/stem-cell-research/farming-humans-for-fun-and-profit
202. https://www.ncregister.com/cna/house-members-highlight-horrific-organ-harvesting-of-aborted-babies
203. https://www.fortunebusinessinsights.com/industry-reports/contraceptive-pills-market-101802

CHAPTER 4

1. https://www.prb.org/resources/the-decline-in-u-s-fertility/
2. https://dictionary.cambridge.org/dictionary/english/humanism
3. https://dictionary.cambridge.org/dictionary/english/hedonism
4. https://dictionary.cambridge.org/dictionary/english/self-worship
5. https://americanhumanist.org
6. https://www.patheos.com/blogs/rogereolson/2018/09/what-is-situation-ethics-what-should-be-a-christians-response/
7. https://www.cdc.gov/mmwr/preview/mmwrhtml/mm5938a2.htm#:~:text=In%202006%20and%202008%2C%20an,Columbia%2C%20and%20two%20U.S.%20territories
8. https://abcnews.go.com/Health/depression-rates-us-adults-reach-new-high-gallup/story?id=99387994
9. https://abcnews.go.com/Health/teen-girls-experiencing-record-high-levels-sadness-violence/story?id=97079978
10. https://www.apa.org/topics/men-boys/depression
11. https://www.focusonthefamily.com/pro-life/abortion/survey-women-go-silently-from-church-to-abortion-clinic/
12. https://www.crossway.org/articles/unpacking-my-body-my-choice/
13. https://www.cdc.gov/nchs/products/databriefs/db388.htm#:~:text=Data%20from%20the%202020%2017%E2%80%932019%20National%20Survey%20of%20Family%20Growth&text=The%20most%20common%20contraceptive%20methods,the%20male%20condom%20(8.4%25)
14. https://www.healthline.com/health-news/why-men-in-us-dont-get-vasectomies
15. https://www.npr.org/2021/06/21/1008656293/the-legacy-of-the-lasting-effects-of-chinas-1-child-policy
16. www.realmendontgetfixed.org
17. https://fnsprod.azureedge.us/sites/default/files/expenditures_on_children_by_families/crc2000.pdf
18. https://www.creditkarma.com/cash-flow/i/how-much-does-it-cost-to-raise-a-child

CHAPTER 5

1. https://foreignpolicy.com/2009/10/20/the-return-of-patriarchy/
2. https://time.com/241/having-it-all-without-having-children/
3. https://www.youtube.com/watch?v=_XU4u3tSsXM
4. https://www.amazon.com/CHILDFREE-CHOICE-all-its-cracked-ebook/dp/B07XWK228M/ref=sr_1_1?crid=2VUYJWPE3O9TK&dib=eyJ2IjoiMSJ9.dCCRZ8kWPYJVadfaNmAiiw.XyPmcD-kif4jQ-KaWy0b1_ornoPuWTam3PGLw4E2xEg&dib_tag=se&keywords=childfree+by+choice+is+it+all+its+cracked+up+to+be+rachel+scott&qid=1724454656&sprefix=childfree+by+choice+is+it+all+its+cracked+up+to+be+rachel+scott%2Caps%2C99&sr=8-1&asin=B07XWK228M&revisionId=9af92e4d&format=1&depth=1
5. https://www.cnn.com/2023/05/31/business/elon-musk-worlds-richest-man-intl-hnk/index.html
6. https://www.businessinsider.nl/elon-musk-tells-italians-to-have-more-children-during-an-appearance-at-a-political-conference-in-rome-make-more-italians/
7. https://www.gutenberg.org/ebooks/15623

CHAPTER 6

1. https://www.census.gov/data/tables/time-series/dec/popchange-data-text.html
2. https://www.cdc.gov/nchs/pressroom/nchs_press_releases/2024/20240525.htm
3. https://www.guttmacher.org/news-release/2024/number-abortions-united-states-likely-be-higher-2023-2020
4. https://www.mountvernon.org/george-washington/family/siblings
5. https://encyclopediavirginia.org/entries/jefferson-thomas-and-his-family/

CHAPTER 7

1. http://www.forbes.com/2006/07/19/spending-income- level_cx_lh_de_0719spending.html
2. https://www.bankrate.com/banking/savings/average-household-budget/#avg-household-expenses
3. https://finance.yahoo.com/news/much-americans-spending-pets-2023-190023470.html
4. https://www.cdc.gov/nchs/data/nhsr/nhsr179.pdf
5. https://www.cdc.gov/nchs/products/databriefs/db260.htm?utm_source=chatgpt.com

CHAPTER 8

1. https://www.youtube.com/watch?v=3Or-Ja2dOvE&t=135s

CHAPTER 9

1. https://time.com/4144897/birth-rate-abortion-miscarriage/
2. https://www.mwhp.com/miscarriage-why-are-rates-skyrocketing/#:~:text=The%20New%20England%20Journal%20of,according%20to%20this%202018%20study.
3. https://www.healthgrades.com/right-care/pregnancy/how-common-is-miscarriage
4. https://www.sciencealert.com/meta-analysis-finds-majority-of-human-pregnancies-end-in-miscarriage-biorxiv
5. https://www.medicalnewstoday.com/articles/322634#miscarriage-rates-by-week
6. https://www.americamagazine.org/faith/2024/03/22/abortion-post-dobbs-guttmacher-institute-study-247561
7. https://www.medicalnewstoday.com/articles/reasons-for-abortions#reasons-for-abortion

CHAPTER 10

1. https://www.accessdata.fda.gov/drugsatfda_docs/label/2005/021690ppi.pdf

2. https://www.healthline.com/health/post-birth-control-syndrom

2a. https://www.unilad.com/news/sex-and-relationships/women-lose- attraction-partner-contraceptive-pill-933074-20250123

3. https://www.mdanderson.org/cancerwise/10-questions-about-gynecologic-cancers-answered.h00-159148401.html
4. https://www.cancer.org/content/dam/cancer-org/research/cancer-facts-and-statistics/annual-cancer-facts-and-figures/2022/2022-cancer-facts-and-figures.pdf
5. https://www.ncbi.nlm.nih.gov/pmc/articles/PMC6203343/
6. https://www.ncbi.nlm.nih.gov/pmc/articles/PMC2492586/
6a. https://www.latimes.com/archives/la-xpm-1994-09-08-me-35791-story.html
7. http://www.tubal.org
8. https://www.amazon.com/Doctors-About-Tubal-Ligation-Syndrome/dp/1411675045
9. https://medium.com/@DrVikki/modernization-act-for-womens-informed-consent-for-tubal-ligation-and-fallopian-tube-devices-for-b0cb7654a70b

ENDNOTES

10. https://www.yesmagazine.org/social-justice/2021/02/08/united-states-forced-sterilization-women
11. https://www.ewtn.com/catholicism/library/tubal-ligation-some-questions-and-answers-11267
12. https://www.nccrm.com/tubal-reversal-surgery/post-tubal-ligation-syndrome/
13. https://www.hotzehwc.com/2022/05/restoring-hormone-balance-counteract-effects-tubal-ligation/
14. https://www.ewtn.com/catholicism/library/tubal-ligation-some-questions-and-answers-11267
15. http://www.tubal.org/symptoms-of-pts.htm
16. https://www.ncbi.nlm.nih.gov/pmc/articles/PMC5267553/
17. https://www.newscientist.com/article/dn11618-breastfeeding-may-protect-older-mothers-from-cancer/
18. https://academic.oup.com/endo/article/163/11/bqac141/6675223?login=false
18a. https://www.healthcentral.com/condition/breast-cancer/does-breastfeeding-prevent-breast-cancer
19. https://www.medicalnewstoday.com/articles/the-controversy-of-female-hysteria
20. http://healthread.net/tubal-ligation.htm
21. https://www.ncbi.nlm.nih.gov/pmc/articles/PMC8723888/
22. https://acsjournals.onlinelibrary.wiley.com/doi/10.1002/cncr.11380
23. https://www.yalemedicine.org/conditions/hysterectomy
24. https://embryo.asu.edu/pages/hysterectomy
25. https://www.hysterectomy.org/get-the-facts/
26. https://www.womenadvancenc.org/2021/12/17/theyre-trying-to-take-our-parts-the-hysterectomy-in-u-s-history-and-today/
27. https://www.cdc.gov/mmwr/preview/mmwrhtml/00001713.htm
28. https://www.medscape.com/s/viewarticle/582384_4?form=fpf
29. https://www.healthline.com/health/hysterectomy-grieve-for-womanhood
30. https://www.prevention.com/health/a34329427/should-you-get-a-hysterectomy/
31. https://www.ewtn.com/catholicism/library/sterilization-questions-and-answers-11233
32. https://pubmed.ncbi.nlm.nih.gov/8213755/
33. https://www.womenadvancenc.org/2021/12/17/theyre-trying-to-take-our-parts-the-hysterectomy-in-u-s-history-and-today/
34. https://www.ariadnelabs.org/resources/articles/study-tracks-long-term-health-risks-to-women-after-having-a-c-section/
35. https://www.cesareanrates.org
36. https://www.newscientist.com/article/dn1639-fetuses-can-hear-ultrasound-examinations/
37. https://www.who.int/news/item/16-06-2021-caesarean-section-rates-continue-to-rise-amid-growing-inequalities-in-access
38. https://en.wikipedia.org/wiki/The_Business_of_Being_Born
39. https://www.contemporaryobgyn.net/view/acog-releases-new-study-obgyn-workforce
39a. https://www.nationalbreastcancer.org/breast-cancer-facts/
39b. https://www.komen.org/breast-cancer/risk-factor/birth-control-pills/
39c. https://www.healthcentral.com/condition/breast-cancer/does-breastfeeding-prevent-breast-cancer
40. https://www.pop.org/problems-side-effects-men-vasectomy/
41. https://www.vasectomy-information.com/what-to-know/history/
42. https://www.urologichistory.museum/the-scope-of-urology-newsletter/issue-11-fall-2022/the-complicated-history-of-the-vasectomy
43. https://medicalxpress.com/news/2023-08-reveal-vasectomies-common.html
44. https://ezvasectomy.com/understanding-post-vasectomy-pain-syndrome-causes-symptoms-and-management/
45. https://www.pop.org/problems-side-effects-men-vasectomy/
46. https://purelyvasectomies.com/blog/does-a-vasectomy-affect-sex-drive/
47. https://my.clevelandclinic.org/health/treatments/17584-tubal-ligation-reversal
48. https://www.tubal-reversal.net/blog/what-is-the-average-tubal-reversal-cost/
49. https://www.goodrx.com/health-topic/mens-health/vasectomy-reversal-cost

CHAPTER 11
(no footnotes)

CHAPTER 12
(no footnotes)

APPENDIX: Conversations on Birth Control Q & A

1. https://www.bbc.com/news/health-53409521
2. www.nytimes.com/1995/02/02/us/study-finds-sperm-counts-are-declining.html
3. https://www.progress.org.uk/uk-men-need-to-think-harder-about-their-fertility/
4. https://time.com/archive/6728727/whats-wrong-with-our-sperm/
5. https://www.ft.com/content/f14ab282-1dd3-46bf-be02-a59aff3a90ed
6. https://www.who.int/news/item/04-04-2023-1-in-6-people-globally-affected-by-infertility
7. https://www.ncbi.nlm.nih.gov/pmc/articles/PMC7863696/
8. https://www.businessinsider.com/elon-musk-warns-developed-world-to-have-more-babies-italy-2023-12?op=1
9. https://money.com/government-pays-have-a-baby-low-birth-rate/
10. https://slate.com/business/2006/05/russia-s-campaign-to-increase-its-birthrate.html
11. https://www.bbc.com/news/world-asia-china-57303592

If you would like to contact
RACHEL SCOTT

For prayer for infertility or if you would like Rachel to speak, counsel, mentor or pray via zoom, you can contact Rachel at

RachelScottSpeaks@gmail.com

To view some of Rachel's National TV Appearances:

Fox News:

pt. 1 http://www.youtube.com/watch?v=sXLy1MCSTys
pt. 2 http://www.youtube.com/watch?v=nX9a6TMAX9E

CNN/HLN The Joy Behar Show:

pt. 1 http://www.youtube.com/watch?v=3tlOB74tcds&feature=related
pt. 2 http://www.youtube.com/watch?v=_ls4Yvgp_QA

CBS/WE TV Documentary:
http://www.youtube.com/watch?v=km9qYJOG60E&feature=related

www.ingramcontent.com/pod-product-compliance
Lightning Source LLC
Chambersburg PA
CBHW072141070526
44585CB00015B/982